EXPLORING
MICROECONOMICS

ROBERT L. SEXTON | 5E

Pepperdine University

SOUTH-WESTERN
CENGAGE Learning

Australia • Brazil • Japan • Korea • Mexico • Singapore • Spain • United Kingdom • United States

SOUTH-WESTERN
CENGAGE Learning™

Exploring Microeconomics, 5e
Robert L. Sexton

Vice President of Editorial, Business:
Jack W. Calhoun

Publisher: Joe Sabatino

Acquisitions Editor: Steven Scoble

Developmental Editor: Daniel Noguera

Associate Marketing Manager: Betty Jung

Marketing Coordinator: Suellen Ruttkay

Content Project Manager:
D. Jean Buttrom

Media Editor: Deepak Kumar

Frontlist Buyer, Manufacturing:
Sandee Milewski

Production Service: S4Carlisle Publishing
Services

Compositor: S4Carlisle Publishing
Services

Senior Art Director: Michelle Kunkler

Cover and Internal Designer: Ke Design

Cover Images:

© Chloe Dulude/veer. com;

© Media Bakery

Photography Manager: Deanna Ettinger

Photo Researcher: Scott Rosen,
Bill Smith Group

For product information and technology assistance, contact us at
Cengage Learning Customer & Sales Support,
1-800-354-9706

For permission to use material from this text or product, submit all requests online at **www.cengage.com/permissions**
Further permissions questions can be emailed to
permissionrequest@cengage.com

Library of Congress Control Number: 2009939190

Student Edition ISBN 13: 978-1-4390-4050-8
Student Edition ISBN 10: 1-4390-4050-8

South-Western Cengage Learning
5191 Natorp Boulevard
Mason, OH 45040
USA

Cengage Learning products are represented in Canada by Nelson Education, Ltd.

For your course and learning solutions, visit **www.cengage.com**

Purchase any of our products at your local college store or at our preferred online store **www.CengageBrain.com**

Printed in the United States of America
2 3 4 5 6 7 13 12 11

To
Elizabeth,
Katherine,
and Tommy

Brief Contents

PART 5   INPUT MARKETS AND MICROECONOMIC POLICY ISSUES

About the Book

Exploring Microeconomics, 5th Edition, was written to not only be a student-friendly textbook, but one that was relevant, one that focused on those few principles and applications that demonstrate the enormous breadth of economics to everyday life. This text is lively, motivating, and exciting, and it helps students relate economics to their world.

The Section-by-Section Approach

Many students are not lacking in ability, but rather are lacking a strategy. Information needs to be moved from short-term memory to long-term memory and then retrieved. Learning theory provides several methods for helping students do this.

Exploring Microeconomics uses a section-by-section approach in its presentation of economic ideas. Information is presented in small, self-contained sections rather than in large blocks of text. Learning theorists call this *chunking*. That is, more information can be stored in the working memory as a result of learning in smaller blocks of information. Also, by using shorter bite-sized pieces, students are not only more likely to read the material but also more likely to reread it, leading to better comprehension and test results. Learning theorists call this *rehearsal*.

Unlike standard textbook construction, this approach is distinctly more compatible with the modern communication style with which most students are familiar and comfortable: short, intense, and exciting bursts of information. Rather than being distracted and discouraged by the seeming enormity of the task before them, students are more likely to work through a short, self-contained section before getting up from their desks. More importantly, instructors benefit from having a student population that has actually read the textbook and prepared for class!

In executing the section-by-section approach in *Exploring Microeconomics,* every effort has been made to take the intimidation out of economics. The idea of sticking to the basics and reinforcing student mastery, concept by concept, has been done with the student in mind. But students aren't the only ones to benefit from this approach. The section-by-section presentation allows instructors greater flexibility in planning their courses.

Exploring Microeconomics was created with flexibility in mind in order to accommodate a variety of teaching styles. Many of the chapters are self-contained, allowing instructors to customize their course. For example, in Part 3, the theory of the firm chapters can be presented in any order. The theory of the firm chapters are introduced in the textbook from the most competitive market structure (perfect competition) to the least competitive market structure (monopoly). After all, almost all firms face a downward-sloping demand curve, not just monopolists. However, instructors who prefer can teach monopoly immediately following perfect competition because each chapter is self-contained.

Each chapter is comprised of approximately six to ten short sections. These sections are self-contained learning units, typically presented in three to six pages that include these helpful learning features:

✷ **Key Questions.** Each section begins with a list of questions that highlight the primary ideas that students should learn from the material. These questions are intended to serve as a preview and to pique interest in the material to come. They also serve as landmarks: if students can answer these questions after reading the material, they have prepared well.

✷ **Section Checks.** It is also important that students learn to self-manage: They should ask themselves: How well am I doing? How does this relate to what I already know? The section-by-section approach provides continual self-testing along every step of the way. Each section ends with four to six short sentences emphasizing the important points in each section. It also includes four to six questions designed to test comprehension of the basic points of the section just covered. Answers are provided at the end of each chapter so students can check their responses. If students can answer these Section Check questions correctly, they can feel confident about proceeding to the next topic.

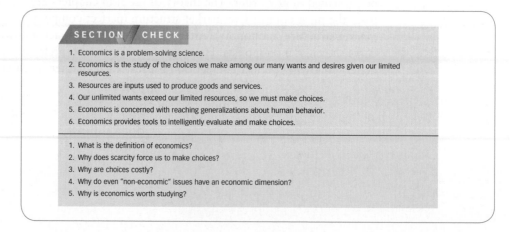

❈ **Integrated Study Guide pages!** These pages, found at the end of each chapter, guide students through various exercises designed to test their comprehension and mastery, including true-false, multiple-choice, and application-type questions. Organized in chronological order to follow the chapter, students can easily refer back to the chapter content for review and support as they proceed through the exercises.

CHAPTER 1 STUDY GUIDE

True or False:

1. When our limited wants exceed our unlimited resources, we face scarcity.
2. Choices are costly because we must give up other opportunities that we value.
3. Living in a world of scarcity involves trade-offs.
4. Self-interest cannot include benevolence.
5. To say that people are rational is to assume that they never make mistakes.
6. Adam Smith described how self-interest can be a force for the common good.
7. According to the National Council of Economic Education, most adults tested in the United States performed well on economic literacy.
8. Rationality could not apply to criminals.
9. Economic theories do not abstract from the particular details of situations so they can better focus on every aspect of the behavior to be explained.
10. Determining whether an economic hypothesis is acceptable is more difficult than in the natural or physical sciences because, unlike a chemist in a chemistry lab, an economist cannot control all the other variables that might influence human behavior.
11. Microeconomics would deal with the analysis of a small individual firm, while macroeconomics would deal with large global firms.
12. A positive statement must be both testable and true.
13. A normative statement is nontestable.
14. The majority of disagreements in economics stem from normative issues.
15. A hypothesis is a normative statement.

Multiple Choice:

1. If a good is scarce,
   a. it only needs to be limited.
   b. it is not possible to produce any more of the good.
   c. our unlimited wants exceed our limited resources.
   d. our limited wants exceed our unlimited resources.

2. Which of the following is true of resources?
   a. Their availability is unlimited.
   b. They are the inputs used to produce goods and services.
   c. Increasing the amount of resources available could eliminate scarcity.
   d. Both b and c.

3. If scarcity were not a fact,
   a. people could have all the goods and services they wanted for free.
   b. it would no longer be necessary to make choices.
   c. poverty, defined as the lack of a minimum level of consumption, would also be eliminated.
   d. all of the above would be true.

4. Economics is concerned with
   a. the choices people must make because resources are scarce.
   b. human decision makers and the factors that influence their choices.
   c. the allocation of limited resources to satisfy unlimited wants.
   d. all of the above.

24

Chapter 4   Supply and Demand   **111**

Interactive Chapter Summary

Fill in the blanks:

1. A(n) _____ is the process of buyers and sellers _____ goods and services.
2. The important point about a market is what it does—it facilitates _____.
3. _____, as a group, determine the demand side of the market. _____, as a group, determine the supply side of the market.
4. A(n) _____ market consists of many buyers and sellers, no single one of whom can influence the market price.
5. According to the law of demand, other things being equal, when the price of a good or service falls, the _____ increases.
6. An individual _____ curve reveals the different amounts of a particular good a person would be willing and able to buy at various possible prices in a particular time interval, other things being equal.
7. The _____ curve for a product is the horizontal summing of the demand curves of the individuals in the market.
8. A change in _____ leads to a change in quantity demanded, illustrated by a(n) _____ demand curve.
9. A change in demand is caused by changes in any of the other factors (besides the good's own price) that would affect how much of the good is purchased: the _____, the _____ of buyers, _____, and _____.
10. An increase in demand is represented by a _____ shift in the demand curve; a decrease in demand is represented by a _____ shift in the demand curve.
11. Two goods are called _____ if an increase in the price of one causes the demand curve for another good to shift to the _____.

12. For normal goods an increase in income leads to a(n) _____ in demand, and a decrease in income leads to a(n) _____ in demand, other things being equal.
13. An increase in the expected future price of a good or an increase in expected future income may _____ current demand.
14. According to the law of supply, the higher the price of the good, the greater the _____, and the lower the price of the good, the smaller the _____.
15. The quantity supplied is positively related to the price because firms supplying goods and services want to increase their _____ and because increasing _____ costs mean that the suppliers will require _____ prices to induce them to increase their output.
16. An individual supply curve is a graphical representation that shows the _____ relationship between the price and the quantity supplied.
17. The market supply curve is a graphical representation of the amount of goods and services that suppliers are _____ and _____ to supply at various prices.
18. Possible supply determinants (factors that determine the position of the supply curve) are _____ prices; _____; _____ of suppliers; and _____, _____, _____, and _____.
19. A fall in input prices will _____ the costs of production, causing the supply curve to shift to the _____.
20. The supply of a good _____ if the price of one of its substitutes in production falls.
21. The supply of a good _____ if the price of one of its substitutes in production rises.

Answers: 1. markets; exchanging 2. trade 3. Buyers; Sellers 4. competitive 5. quantity demanded 6. demand 7. market demand 8. a good's price; movement along 9. prices of related goods; income; tastes; expectations 10. rightward; leftward 11. substitutes; right 12. increase; decrease 13. increase 14. quantity supplied; quantity supplied 15. profits; production; higher 16. positive 17. willing; able 18. input; expectations; number; technology; regulation; taxes and subsidies; weather 19. lower; right 20. increases 21. decreases

Key Terms and Concepts

market 93	market demand curve 95	normal good 100
competitive market 94	change in quantity demanded 97	inferior good 100
law of demand 94	change in demand 98	law of supply 104
individual demand schedule 95	substitutes 99	individual supply curve 105
individual demand curve 95	complements 99	market supply curve 105

Other End-of-Chapter Material Includes:

❈ **Interactive Chapter Summary.** Each chapter ends with an interactive summary of the main ideas in the chapter. Students can fill in the blanks and check their answers against those provided at the end of the summary. It is a useful refresher before class or tests and a good starting point for studying.

❈ **Key Terms and Concepts.** A list of key terms concludes each chapter. If students can define all these terms, they have a good head start on studying.

Visual Learning Features

magery is also important for learning. Visual stimulus helps the learning process. This text uses pictures and visual aids to reinforce valuable concepts and ideas. Information is often stored in visual form; thus, pictures are important in helping students retain important ideas and retrieve them from their long-term memory. Students want a welcoming, magazine-looking text; a brain-friendly environment. The most consistent remark we have received from *Exploring Microeconomics* adopters is that their students are reading their book, and reading the text leads to better test performance.

At every turn this text has been designed with interesting graphics so that visual cues help students learn and remember:

❧ **Photos.** The text contains a number of colorful pictures. They are not, however, mere decoration; rather, these photos are an integral part of the book, for both learning and motivation purposes. The photos are carefully placed where they reinforce important concepts, and they are accompanied with captions designed to encourage students to extend their understanding of particular ideas.

Chapter 11 The Firm: Production and Costs **293**

How many workers could be added to this jackhammer and still be productive (not to mention safe)? If more workers were added, how much output would be derived from each additional worker? Slightly more total output might be realized from the second worker, because the second worker would be using the jackhammer while the first worker was taking a break from "the shakes." However, the fifth or sixth worker would clearly not create any additional output, as workers would just be standing around for their turn. That is, the marginal product (additional output) would eventually fall because of diminishing marginal product.

© BRUCE BURKHARDT/CORBIS

lead to diminishing marginal product. Specifically, as the amount of a variable input is increased, with the amount of other (fixed) inputs held constant, a point will ultimately be reached beyond which marginal product will decline. Beyond this point, output increases but at a decreasing rate. It is the crowding of the fixed input with more and more workers that causes the decline in the marginal product.

The point of this discussion is that production functions conform to the same general pattern as that shown by Moe's Bagel Shop in the third column of Exhibit 1 and illustrated in Exhibit 2(b). In the third column of Exhibit 1, we see that as the number of workers in Moe's Bagel Shop increases, Moe is able to produce more bagels. The first worker is able to produce 10 bagels per hour. When Moe adds a second worker, total bagel output climbs to 24, an increase of 14 bagels per hour. When Moe hires a third worker, bagel output still increases. However, a third worker's marginal production (12 bagels per hour) is less than that of the second worker. In fact, the marginal product continues to drop as more and more workers are added to the bagel shop. This example shows dimin-

---

❧ **Exhibits.** Graphs, tables, and charts are important economic tools. These tools are used throughout *Exploring Microeconomics* to illustrate, clarify, and reinforce economic principles. Text exhibits are designed to be as clear and simple as possible, and they are carefully coordinated with the text material.

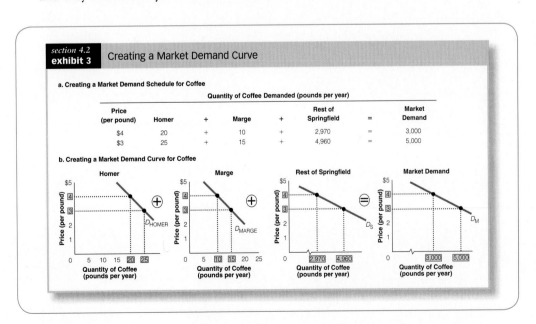

section 4.2 **exhibit 3** Creating a Market Demand Curve

a. Creating a Market Demand Schedule for Coffee

Quantity of Coffee Demanded (pounds per year)

Price (per pound)	Homer	+	Marge	+	Rest of Springfield	=	Market Demand
$4	20	+	10	+	2,970	=	3,000
$3	25	+	15	+	4,960	=	5,000

b. Creating a Market Demand Curve for Coffee

Applications

There are numerous applications to everyday life situations scattered throughout the text. These applications were chosen specifically with students in mind, and they are designed to help them find the connection between economics and their life. With that, economic principles are applied to everyday problems and issues, such as teen smoking, property rights and song swapping, crime, online betting, the NCAA, gift giving, and many others. There are also five special types of boxed applications scattered throughout each chapter:

✢ **In the News.** These applications focus primarily on current news stories that are relevant and thought-provoking. These articles are placed strategically throughout the text to solidify particular concepts. In an effort to emphasize the breadth and diversity of the situations to which economic principles can be applied, these articles have been chosen from a wide range of sources.

in the news The Game Theory of the Bar Scene Problem from *A Beautiful Mind*

The Problem
You and three male friends are at a bar trying to pick up women. Suddenly one blonde and four brunettes enter in a group. What's the individual strategy?

Here are the rules. Each of you wants to talk to the blonde. If more than one of you tries to talk to her, however, she will be put off and talk to no one. At that point it will also be too late to talk to a brunette, as no one likes being second choice. Assume anyone who starts out talking to a brunette will succeed.

The Movie
Nash suggests the group should cooperate. If everyone goes for the blonde, they block each other and no one wins. The brunettes will feel hurt as a second choice and categorically reject advances. Everyone loses.

But what if everyone goes for a brunette? Then each person will succeed, and everyone ends up with a good option.

It's a good thought, except for one question: what about the blonde?

The Equilibrium
The movie is directed so well that it sounds persuasive. But it's sadly incomplete. It misses the essence of noncooperative game theory.

A Nash equilibrium is a state where no one person can improve *given what others are doing*. This means you are picking the best possible action in response to others—the formal term is you are picking a *best response*.

As an example, let's analyze whether everyone going for a brunette is a Nash equilibrium. You are *given* that three of your friends go for brunettes. What is your best response?

You can either go for the brunette or the blonde. With your friends already going for brunettes, you have no competition to go for the blonde. The answer is clear that you would talk to the blonde. That's your best response. Incidentally, this is a Nash equilibrium. You are happy, and your friends cannot

do better. If your friends try to talk to the blonde, they end up with nothing and give up talking to a brunette. So you see, when Nash told his friends to go for the brunettes in the movie, it really does sound like he was leaving the blonde for himself.

The lesson: advice that sounds good for you might really be better for someone else. Be skeptical of the strategic implications.

Now, in practical matters it will be hard to achieve the equilibrium that one person goes for a blonde. There is going to be competition and someone in the group will surely sabotage the mission. So there are two ways you might go about it using strategies outside the game. One is to ignore the current group and wait for another group of blondes (the classic "wait and see" strategy). The second is to let a random group member go for the blonde as the others distract the brunettes (also practiced as "wingman theory").

✢ **Global Watch.** Whether we are concerned with understanding yesterday, today, or tomorrow, and whether we are looking at a small, far-away country or a large next door neighbor, economic principles can strengthen our grasp of many global issues. "Global Watch" articles were chosen to help students understand the magnitude and character of the changes occurring around the world today and to introduce them to some of the economic causes and implications of these changes. To gain a greater perspective on a particular economy or the planet as a whole, it is helpful to compare important economic indicators around the world. For this reason, "Global Watch" applications are sometimes also used to present relevant comparative statistics.

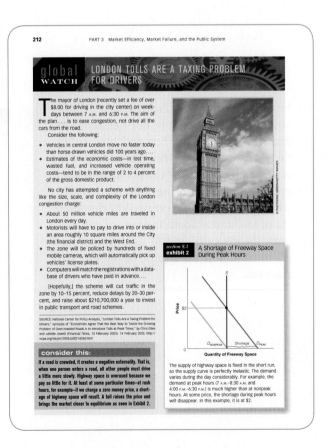

212   PART 3 Market Efficiency, Market Failure, and the Public System

global WATCH LONDON TOLLS ARE A TAXING PROBLEM FOR DRIVERS

The mayor of London [recently set a fee of over $8.00 for driving in the city center] on weekdays between 7 A.M. and 6:30 P.M. The aim of the plan . . . is to ease congestion, not drive all the cars from the road.

Consider the following:

* Vehicles in central London move no faster today than horse-drawn vehicles did 100 years ago. . . .
* Estimates of the economic costs—in lost time, wasted fuel, and increased vehicle operating costs—tend to be in the range of 2 to 4 percent of the gross domestic product.

No city has attempted a scheme with anything like the size, scale, and complexity of the London congestion charge:

* About 50 million vehicle miles are traveled in London every day.
* Motorists will have to pay to drive into or inside an area roughly 10 square miles around the City (the financial district) and the West End.
* The zone will be policed by hundreds of fixed mobile cameras, which will automatically pick up vehicles' license plates.
* Computers will match the registrations with a database of drivers who have paid in advance. . . .

[Hopefully,] the scheme will cut traffic in the zone by 10–15 percent, reduce delays by 20–30 percent, and raise about $210,700,000 a year to invest in public transport and road schemes.

SOURCE: National Center for Policy Analysis, "London Tolls Are a Taxing Problem for Drivers," synopsis of "Economists Agree That the Best Way to Tackle the Growing Problem of Overcrowded Roads is to Introduce Tolls at Peak Times," by Chris Giles and Juliette Jowett (Financial Times, 13 February 2003). 14 February 2003, http://ncpa.org/iss/pri/2003/pi021403d.html

consider this:

If a road is crowded, it creates a negative externality. That is, when one person enters a road, all other people must drive a little more slowly. Highway space is overused because we pay so little for it. At least at some particular times—at rush hours, for example—if we charge a zero money price, a shortage of highway space will result. A toll raises the price and brings the market closer to equilibrium as seen in Exhibit 2.

section 8.1 exhibit 2 A Shortage of Freeway Space During Peak Hours

The supply of highway space is fixed in the short run, so the supply curve is perfectly inelastic. The demand varies during the day considerably. For example, the demand at peak hours (7 A.M.–8:30 A.M. and 4:00 P.M.–6:30 P.M.) is much higher than at nonpeak hours. At some price, the shortage during peak hours will disappear. In this example, it is at $2.

☆ Using What You've Learned. Economic principles aren't just definitions to memorize; they are valuable tools that can help students analyze a whole host of issues and problems in the world around them. Part of learning economics is learning when and how to use new tools. These special boxes are scattered throughout the text as a way of reinforcing and checking students' true comprehension of important or more difficult concepts by assessing their ability to apply what they have learned to a real-world situation. Students can check their work against the answer given in the self-contained box, providing them with immediate feedback and encouragement in the learning process.

☆ Policy Application. These features focus primarily on news stories that involve a government policy decision based upon economic concepts. These applications are scattered throughout the text as a way of reinforcing important or more difficult concepts.

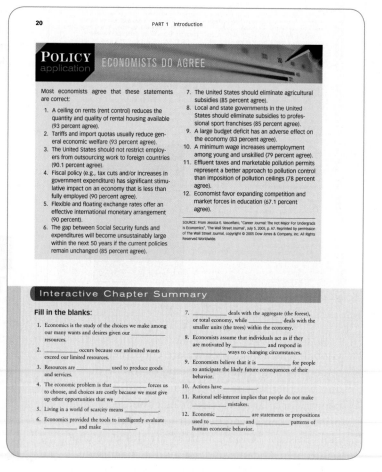

☆ Interactive Summary. Picking up the terminology of economics is not enough; students have to learn when and how to use their new tools. It is this philosophy that serves as the focus for the problem-solving approach in *Exploring Microeconomics,* which is designed to serve two key purposes: (1) to facilitate student mastery of concepts both theoretically and in application, and (2) to communicate a sense of relevancy to students.

The 5th Edition offers an array of instructor resources designed to enhance teaching.

Instructor's Resource CD-ROM

The Instructor's Resource CD-ROM will include electronic versions of the Instructor's Manual, Test Bank, and PowerPoint® slides, as well as ExamView® testing software.

Instructor's Manual

Prepared by Gary Galles (Pepperdine University), the Instructor's Manual, available online and on the Instructor's Resource CD-ROM, follows the textbook's concept-by-concept approach in two parts: chapter outlines and teaching tips. The Teaching Tips section provides analogies, illustrations, and examples to help instructors reinforce each section of the text. Answers to all of the end-of-chapter text questions can also be found in the Instructor's Manual.

Test Bank

Test bank questions, available online and on the Instructor's CD-ROM, have been thoroughly updated. The test bank includes approximately 150 test questions per chapter, consisting of multiple-choice, true-false, and short-answer questions.

ExamView® Testing Software

ExamView®—Computerized Testing Software contains all of the questions in the printed test banks. ExamView is an easy-to-use test creation software compatible with Microsoft Windows. Instructors can add or edit questions, instructions, and answers, and select questions by previewing them on the screen, selecting them randomly, or selecting them by number. Instructors can also create and administer quizzes online over the Internet.

Microsoft PowerPoint® Presentation Slides

✳ **Lecture Presentation in PowerPoint.** This PowerPoint presentation covers all the essential sections presented in each chapter of the book. Graphs, tables, lists, and concepts are animated sequentially to visually engage students. Additional examples and applications are used to reinforce major lessons. The slides are crisp, clear, and colorful. Instructors may adapt or add slides to customize their lectures.

✳ **Exhibits from the Text in PowerPoint.** Every graph and table within the text has been recreated in PowerPoint. These exhibits are available within the lecture presentation, but we have also made them available as a separate batch of slides for those instructors who don't want the lecture slides.

Both the Lecture and Exhibit PowerPoint presentations are available for downloading at the Sexton Companion Web site: **http://www.cengage.com/economics/sexton.**

The 5th Edition offers an array of resources to help students test their understanding of chapter concepts and enhance their overall learning. Found at the student Companion Web site, these interactive resources provide exam preparation and help students get the most from their Principles of Economics course.

Interactive Quizzes

Students can test their understanding of the chapter's concepts with the interactive quiz. Each quiz contains multiple-choice questions, like those found on a typical exam. Questions include detailed feedback for each answer, so that students may know instantly whether they have answered correctly or incorrectly. In addition, they may email the results of the quiz to themselves or their instructor, with a listing of correct and incorrect answers. An Internet connection is required to take the quizzes.

Key Term Glossary and Flashcards

As a study aid, students may use the glossary terms as flashcards to test their knowledge. Students can state the definition of a term, then click on the term to check the correctness of their statement.

Internet Review Quizzes

These exercises are designed to spark students' excitement about researching on the Internet by asking them to access economic data and then answer questions related to the content of the chapter. All Internet exercises are on the Sexton Web site with direct links to the addresses so that students will not have the tedious and error-prone task of entering long Web site addresses.

Economics with Steven Tomlinson Videos

Cengage South-Western is excited to announce its continuous agreement with *Tomlinson Economics Videos*, featuring award-winning teacher and professional communicator, Steven Tomlinson (PhD, Stanford). These Web-based lecture videos—*Economics with Steven Tomlinson, Economic JumpStart®*, and *Economic LearningPath®*—are sure to engage your students, while reinforcing the economic concepts they need to know.

Complete Online Economics Course

Whether using these videos to deliver online lectures for a distance learning class or as the required text for your Principles course, **Economics with Steven Tomlinson** presents and develops the fundamentals of economics. While this video text offers comprehensive coverage of economic principles, with more than 40 hours of video lecture, you can offer your students an exceptional value package and a richer learning experience by pairing the video text with Sexton's 5th Edition. The videos are also available in Microeconomics and Macroeconomics split versions.

Economic JumpStart® Videos

Great resources to accompany any Economics text, these segments are designed to make sure that your students are on a firm foundation before moving on to more advanced topics in the course.

Economic LearningPath® Videos

These segments provide a full resource for students to review what you have covered, reinforce what they have learned, or expand their knowledge of topics that you may not have time to cover in your course.
Visit **www.cengage.com/economics** to learn more.

Global Economic Watch

The global economic downturn, the most important economic event in generations, unfolds day-to-day and hour-to hour. Cengage Learning's Global Economic Watch is a powerful online portal for bringing current events into the classroom.
The Watch includes:

❊ A content-rich blog of breaking news, expert analysis, and commentary
❊ A real-time database of hundreds of relevant and vetted journal, newspaper, and periodical articles, videos, and podcasts—updated four times daily
❊ A thorough overview and timeline of events leading up to the global economic crisis
❊ Discussion and testing content and other teaching/study resources
Visit www.cengage.com/thewatch

EconCentral

Multiple resources for learning and reinforcing principles and concepts are now available in one place!

EconCentral is your one-stop shop for the learning tools and activities to help you succeed. Available for an additional price, EconCentral equips you with a portal to a wealth of resources that help you both study and apply economic concepts. As you read and study the chapters, you can access video tutorials with Ask the Instructor videos. You can also review with Flashcards and the Graphic Workshop, as well as check your understating of the chapter with interactive quizzing.

ECONCENTRAL

Ready to apply chapter concepts to the real world? EconCentral gives you ABC News videos, EconNews articles, Economic debates, Links to economic data, and more. All the study and application resources in EconCentral are organized by chapter to help you get the most from *Exploring Economics*, 5e, and from your lectures.

Visit www.cengage.com/economics/sexton/5e/econcentral to see the study options available!

APLIA™

Created by Paul Romer, one of the nation's leading economists, Aplia enhances teaching and learning by providing online interactive tools and experiments that help economics students become "active learners." This application allows a tight content correlation between Sexton's 5th Edition and Aplia's online tools.

Students Come to Class Prepared

It is a proven fact that students do better in their course work if they come to class prepared. Aplia's activities are engaging and based on discovery learning, requiring students to take an active role in the learning process. When assigned online homework, students are more apt to read the text, come to class better prepared to participate in discussions, and are more able to relate to the economic concepts and theories presented. Learning by doing helps students feel involved, gain confidence in the materials, and see important concepts come to life.

aplia™
Engage. Prepare. Educate.

Assign Homework in an Effective and Efficient Way

Now you can assign homework without increasing your workload! Together, Sexton and Aplia provide the best text and technology resources to give you multiple teaching and learning solutions. Through Aplia, you can assign problem sets and online activities that automatically give feedback and are tracked and graded, all without requiring additional effort. Since Aplia's assignments are closely integrated with Sexton's 5th Edition, your students are applying what they have learned from the text to their homework.

Contact your local Cengage South-Western representative to find out how you can incorporate this exciting technology into your course. For more information, please visit: www.aplia.com.

JoinIn™ *on TurningPoint*®

Made on demand, JoinIn™ on TurningPoint is the only classroom response software tool that gives you true PowerPoint integration. With JoinIn, you are no longer tied to your computer. You can walk about your classroom as you lecture, showing slides while collecting and displaying responses with ease. There is simply no easier or more effective way to turn your lecture hall into a personal, fully interactive experience for your students. If you can use PowerPoint, you can use JoinIn on TurningPoint with Sexton's 5th Edition.

Robert L. Sexton is Distinguished Professor of Economics at Pepperdine University. Professor Sexton has also been a Visiting Professor at the University of California at Los Angeles in the Anderson Graduate School of Management and the Department of Economics. He was also an Assistant Coach in the movie *Benchwarmers* (2006).

Professor Sexton's research ranges across many fields of economics: economics education, labor economics, environmental economics, law and economics, and economic history. He has written several books and has published numerous reference articles, many in top economic journals such as *The American Economic Review, Southern Economic Journal, Economics Letters, Journal of Urban Economics,* and *The Journal of Economic Education.* Professor Sexton has also written more than 100 other articles that have appeared in books, magazines, and newspapers.

Professor Sexton received the Pepperdine Professor of the Year Award in 1991 and he was named a Harriet and Charles Luckman Teaching Fellow in 1994.

Professor Sexton resides in Agoura Hills, California, with his wife, Julie, and their three children, Elizabeth, Katherine, and Tommy.

Acknowledgments

I would like to extend special thanks to the following colleagues for their valuable insight during the manuscript phase of this project. I owe a debt of gratitude to Edward Merkel, Troy University; Doug McNiel and Salvador Contreras, McNeese State University; David McClough, Ohio Northern University; Tim Bettner, University of La Verne; Inge O'Connor, Syracuse University; William Coomber, University of Maryland; Michael Marlow, Cal Poly; Nand Arora, Cleary University; Carlos F. Liard, Central Connecticut State University; Howard Cochran, Belmont University; Abdulhamid Sukar, Cameron University; Harry Karim, Los Angeles Community College; Maria DaCosta, University of Wisconsin-Eau Claire; Kelli Mayes-Denker, Carl Sandburg College; Elnora Farmer, Griffin Technical College; Robert Shoffner, Central Piedmont Community College; Mark Strazicich, Appalachian State University; and Jeffrey Phillips, SUNY Morrisville.

I also wish to thank Gary Galles of Pepperdine University for his help preparing the ancillaries that accompany the 5th Edition, and Mike Ryan of Gainesville State College for providing an invaluable verification of the text and updating the Test Bank.

I am truly indebted to the excellent team of professionals at Cengage Learning. My appreciation goes to Steve Scoble, Senior Acquisitions Editor; Daniel Noguera, Developmental Editor; Jean Buttrom, Content Project Manager; and Michelle Kunkler, Art Director. Also thanks to Joe Sabbatino, Publisher; Betty Jung, Associate Marketing Manager, Bill Hendee, VP/Marketing, Jack Calhoun, VP/Editorial Director, and the Cengage Sales Representatives. I sincerely appreciate your hard work and effort.

In addition, my family deserves special gratitude—my wife, Julie; my daughters, Elizabeth and Katherine; and my son, Tommy. They are an inspiration to my work. Also, special thanks to my brother Bill for all of his work that directly and indirectly helped this project come to fruition.

Thanks to all of my colleagues who reviewed this material for the 5th Edition. From very early on in the revision all the way up to publication, your comments were very important to me.

Robert L. Sexton

PART 1 INTRODUCTION

1

The Role and Method of Economics

As you begin your first course in economics, you may be asking yourself why you're here. What does economics have to do with your life?

Although we can list many good reasons to study economics, perhaps the best reason is that many issues in our lives are at least partly economic in character. A good understanding of economics would allow you to answer such questions as, Why do 10 A.M. classes fill up more quickly than 8 A.M. classes during registration? Why is it so hard to find an apartment in cities such as San Francisco, Berkeley, and New York? Why is teenage unemployment higher than adult unemployment? Why is the price of your prescription drugs so high? How does inflation impact you and your family? Will higher taxes on cigarettes reduce the number of teenagers smoking? If so, by how much? Why do female models make more than male models? Why is it easier for college graduates to find jobs in some years rather than others? Why do U.S. auto producers like tariffs (taxes) on imported cars? Is outsourcing jobs to India a good idea? Is globalization good for the economy? The study of economics improves your understanding of these and many other concerns.

Economics is a unique way of analyzing many areas of human behavior. Indeed, the range of topics to which economic analysis can be applied is broad. Many researchers discover that the economic approach to human behavior sheds light on social problems that have been with us for a long time: discrimination, education, crime, divorce, political favoritism, and more. In fact, your daily newspaper is filled with economics. You can find economics on the domestic page, the international page, the business page, the sports page, the entertainment page, and even the weather page—economics is all around us.

However, before we delve into the details and models of economics, it is important that we present an overview of how economists approach problems—their methodology. How does an economist apply the logic of science to approach a problem? And what are the pitfalls that economists should avoid in economic thinking? We also discuss why economists disagree. ∎

Economics: A Brief Introduction

* What is economics?
* What is scarcity?

Economics—A Word with Many Different Meanings

Some individuals think economics involves the study of the stock market and corporate finance, and it does—in part. Others think that economics is concerned with the wise use of money and other matters of personal finance, and it is—in part. Still others think that economics involves forecasting or predicting what business conditions will be in the future, and again, it does—in part. The word *economics* is, after all, derived from the Greek *Oeconomicus*, which referred to the management of household affairs.

Precisely defined, **economics** is the study of the choices we make among our many wants and desires given our limited resources. What are resources? **Resources** are inputs—land, human effort and skills, and machines and factories, for instance—used to produce goods and services. The problem is that our unlimited wants exceed our limited resources, a fact that we call **scarcity**. Scarcity forces us to decide how best to use our limited resources. This is **the economic problem**: Scarcity forces us to choose, and choices are costly because we must give up other opportunities that we value. Consumers must make choices on what to buy, how much to save, and how much to invest of their limited incomes. Workers must decide what types of jobs they want, when to enter the workforce, where they will work, and number of hours they wish to work. Firms must decide what kinds of products to produce, how much to produce, and how to produce those goods and services at the lowest cost. That is, consumers, workers, and firms all face choices because of scarity.

The economic problem is evident in every aspect of our lives. You may find that the choice between shopping for groceries and browsing at the mall, or between finishing a research paper and going to a movie, is easier to understand when you have a good handle on the "economic way of thinking."

The front pages of our daily newspapers are filled with articles related to economics—either directly or indirectly. News headlines may cover topics such as unemployment, deficits, financial markets, health care, social security, energy issues, war, global warming, and so on.

economics
the study of choices we make among our many wants and desires given our limited resources

resources
inputs used to produce goods and services

scarcity
exists when human wants (material and nonmaterial) exceed available resources

the economic problem
scarcity forces us to choose, and choices are costly because we must give up other opportunities that we value

Economics Is All Around Us

The tools of economics are far reaching. In fact, other social scientists have accused economists of being imperialistic because their tools have been used in so many fields outside the formal area of economics, like crime, education, marriage, divorce, addiction, finance, health, law, politics, and religion.

So while you might think that much of what you desire in life is "non-economic," economics concerns everything an individual might consider worthwhile, including things that you might consider "priceless." For instance, although we may long for love, sexual fulfillment, or spiritual enlightenment, few of us would

in the news **Americans Score Poorly on Economic Literacy**

Average American Grade: F

In 1999, the National Council of Economic Education tested 1,010 adults and 1,085 high school students on their knowledge of basic economic principles. On average, adults got a grade of 57 percent on a test on the basics of economics. Among high school students, the average grade was 48 percent.

✤ Almost two-thirds of those tested did not know that in times of inflation, money does not hold its value.

✤ Only 58 percent of the students understood that when the demand for a product goes up but the supply doesn't, its price is likely to increase.

✤ Half of the adults and about two-thirds of the students didn't know that the stock market brings people who want to buy stocks together with those who want to sell them.

✤ Just over one in three Americans realize that society must make choices about how to use resources.

In 2005, the survey was repeated. As in 1999, virtually all adults (97 percent) and high school students (93 percent) believe it is important for Americans to have a good understanding of economics. Almost all adults (97 percent) believe that economics should be included in high school education. It also showed some good news—students' understanding of economic knowledge increased from a mean score of 51 in 1999 to 62, and the number of students scoring an "A" or "B" nearly doubled.

SOURCE: "What American Teens and Adults Know About Economics," National Council of Economic Education, 1999 and 2005.

---

be able to set a price for them. But even these matters have an economic dimension. Consider spirituality, for example. Concern for spiritual matters has led to the development of institutions such as churches, synagogues, and temples that conduct religious and spiritual services. In economic terms, these services are goods that many people desire. Love and sex likewise have received economists' scrutiny. One product of love, the institution of the family, is an important economic decision-making unit.

Even time has an economic dimension. In fact, in modern culture, time has become perhaps the single most precious resource we have. Everyone has the same limited amount of time per day, and how we divide our time between work and leisure (including study, sleep, exercise, and so on) is a distinctly economic matter. If we choose more work, we must sacrifice leisure. If we choose to study, we must sacrifice time with friends or time spent sleeping or watching TV. Virtually everything we decide to do, then, has an economic dimension.

Living in a world of scarcity involves trade-offs. As you are reading this text, you are giving up other things you value: shopping, spending time

on Facebook or My Space, going to the movies, sleeping, or working out. When we know what the trade-offs are, we can make better choices from the options all around us, every day. George Bernard Shaw stated, "Economy is the art of making the most of life."

Why Study Economics?

Among the many good reasons to study economics, perhaps the best reason is that so many of the things of concern in the world around us are at least partly economic in character. A quick look at newspaper headlines reveals the vast range of problems that are related to economics—global warming, health care, education, and Social Security. The study of economics improves your understanding of these concerns. A student of economics becomes aware that, at a basic level, much of economic life involves choosing among alternative possible courses of action—making choices between our conflicting wants and desires in a world of scarcity. Economics provides some clues as to how to intelligently evaluate these options and determine

in the news How Much Is Your Major Worth?

Another reason you might want to study economics is that starting salaries are high compared to many other majors. According to a recent poll (2008), economics majors can expect an average starting salary of $50,100. Compare this with other majors in terms of starting salaries and mid-career median salaries.

Undergraduate Major	Starting Median Salary	Mid-Career Median Salary
Accounting	$46,000,00	$77,100,00
Agriculture	$42,600,00	$71,900,00
Anthropology	$36,800,00	$61,500,00
Architecture	$41,600,00	$76,800,00
Art History	$35,800,00	$64,900,00
Biology	$38,800,00	$64,800,00
Business Management	$43,000,00	$72,100,00
Chemical Engineering	$63,200,00	$107,000,00
Chemistry	$42,600,00	$79,900,00
Civil Engineering	$53,900,00	$90,500,00
Communications	$38,100,00	$70,000,00
Computer Engineering	$61,400,00	$105,000,00
Computer Science	$55,900,00	$95,500,00
Criminal Justice	$35,000,00	$56,300,00
Drama	$35,900,00	$56,900,00
Economics	**$50,100,00**	**$98,600,00**
Education	$34,900,00	$52,000,00
Electrical Engineering	$60,900,00	$103,000,00

Undergraduate Major	Starting Median Salary	Mid-Career Median Salary
English	$38,000,00	$64,700,00
Film	$37,900,00	$68,500,00
Finance	$47,900,00	$88,300,00
Geography	$41,200,00	$65,500,00
Geology	$43,500,00	$79,500,00
History	$39,200,00	$71,000,00
Information Technology (IT)	$49,100,00	$74,800,00
International Relations	$40,900,00	$80,900,00
Journalism	$35,600,00	$66,700,00
Management Information Systems (MIS)	$49,200,00	$82,300,00
Marketing	$40,800,00	$79,600,00
Math	$45,400,00	$92,400,00
Mechanical Engineering	$57,900,00	$93,600,00
Music	$35,900,00	$55,000,00
Nursing	$54,200,00	$67,000,00
Nutrition	$39,900,00	$55,300,00
Philosophy	$39,900,00	$81,200,00
Physics	$50,300,00	$97,300,00
Political Science	$40,800,00	$78,200,00
Psychology	$35,900,00	$60,400,00
Religion	$34,100,00	$52,000,00
Sociology	$36,500,00	$58,200,00
Spanish	$34,000,00	$53,100,00

SOURCE: Pay Scale Inc.

the most appropriate choices in given situations. But economists learn quickly that there are seldom easy, clear-cut solutions to the problems we face—the easy problems were solved long ago!

Many students take introductory college-level economics courses because they are required to as part of a general education curriculum or breadth requirements. But why do the committees that establish these requirements include economics? In part, economics helps develop a disciplined method of thinking about problems. The problem-solving tools you will develop by studying economics will prove valuable to you both in your personal and professional life, regardless of your career choice. In short, the study of economics provides a systematic, disciplined way of thinking.

Will You Ever Really Use This Stuff?

The basic tools of economics are valuable to people in all walks of life and in all career paths. Newspaper reporters benefit from economics, because the problem-solving perspective it teaches trains them to ask intelligent questions whose answers will better inform their readers. Engineers, architects, and contractors usually have alternative ways to build. Architects learn to combine technical expertise and artistry with the limitations imposed by finite resources. That is, they learn how to evaluate their options from an economic perspective. Clothing designers face similar problems, because costs are a constraint in both creating and marketing new apparel. Will the added cost of a more expensive fabric be outweighed by the added sales revenues that are expected to result? Economists cannot answer such questions in a general sense because the answers depend on the circumstances. Economists can, however, pose these questions and provide criteria that clothing designers can use in evaluating the appropriateness of one fabric as compared to another. The point is that the economic way of thinking causes those in many types of fields to ask the right kind of questions. As John Maynard Keynes once remarked:

> The object of our analysis is not to provide a machine or method of blind manipulation, which will furnish an infallible answer, but to provide ourselves with an organized and orderly method of thinking out particular problems; and, after we have reached a provisional conclusion by

isolating the complicating factors one by one, we then have to go back on ourselves and allow, as well as we can, for the probable interactions of the factors amongst themselves. This is the nature of economic thinking.[1]

Will an Understanding of Economics Make You a Financial Wizard?

Some people think that economics may be a useful course of study, hoping that it will tell them how to become successful in a financial sense. If becoming wealthy is your goal in studying economics, you may be disappointed. Although most economists make a good living, few have become rich from their knowledge of economics. In fact, if economists had some secret for making money in, for example, the stock market, they would likely be using those secrets to their own financial advantage rather than making less money doing things such as teaching. Moreover, if economists did have some secret for making money, they would not be likely to let non-economists in on it, because economic theory suggests (as will be clear later) that disclosure of the secret would reduce or eliminate the possibility of the economists' earning further income from this knowledge. Still, having some knowledge of the workings of market forces is likely to help individuals make more informed and appropriate decisions, including financial decisions. In short, economics won't necessarily make you richer, but it may keep you from making some decisions that would make you poorer.

SECTION CHECK

1. Economics is a problem-solving science.
2. Economics is the study of the choices we make among our many wants and desires given our limited resources.
3. Resources are inputs used to produce goods and services.
4. Our unlimited wants exceed our limited resources, so we must make choices.
5. Economics is concerned with reaching generalizations about human behavior.
6. Economics provides tools to intelligently evaluate and make choices.

1. What is the definition of economics?
2. Why does scarcity force us to make choices?
3. Why are choices costly?
4. Why do even "non-economic" issues have an economic dimension?
5. Why is economics worth studying?

[1] See J. M. Keynes, *General Theory of Employment Interest and Money* (New York: Harcourt Brace, 1936), p. 297.

Economic Behavior

* What is self-interest?
* Why is self-interest not the same as selfishness?
* What is rational behavior?

Self-Interest

Economists assume that individuals act *as if* they are motivated by self-interest and respond in predictable ways to changing circumstances. In other words, self-interest is a good predictor of human behavior in most situations. For example, to a worker, self-interest means pursuing a higher-paying job and/or better working conditions. To a consumer, it means gaining a higher level of satisfaction from limited income and time.

We seldom observe employees asking employers to cut their wages and increase their workload to increase a company's profits. Or how often do you think customers walk into a supermarket demanding to pay more for their

> **rational behavior**
> people do the best they can, based on their values and information, under current and anticipated future circumstances

There was an enormous amount of money and time donated to the victims of Hurricane Katrina. Economists believe that individuals act to promote those items which interest them. Is this self-interested act selfish? Acting in one's own self-interest is only selfish if one's interests are selfish.

REUTERS/DAVID J. PHILLIP/POOL /LANDOV

groceries? In short, a great deal of human behavior can be explained and predicted by assuming people act *as if* they are motivated by their own self-interest.

There is no question that self-interest is a powerful force that motivates people to produce goods and services. But self-interest can include benevolence. Think of the late Mother Teresa, who spent her life caring for others. One could say that her work was in her self-interest, but who would consider her actions selfish? Similarly, workers may be pursuing self-interest when they choose to work harder and longer to increase their charitable giving or saving for their children's education. That is, self-interest to an economist is not a narrow monetary self-interest. The enormous amount of money and time donated to victims of Hurricane Katrina is an example of self-interest too—the self-interest was to help others in need. So don't confuse self-interest with selfishness.

In the United States, people typically give more than $250 billion annually to charities. They also pay more money for environmentally friendly goods. Consumers can derive utility or satisfaction from these choices. It is clearly not selfish—it is in their best interest to care about the environment and those who are less fortunate than themselves.

What Is Rational Behavior?

Economists assume that people, for the most part, engage in rational behavior. And you might think that could not possibly apply to your brother, sister, or roommates. But the key is in the definition. To an economist, **rational behavior** merely means that people do the best they can, based on their values and information, under current and anticipated future circumstances. It is even rational when people make choices they later regret, because they have limited information. Rational behavior applies to the actions people take to pursue their own goals—whatever those goals may be—and they need not be materialistic or widely shared. Therefore, rational behavior applies to criminals and people who dedicate their lives to caring for others. In

Use what you've LEARNED   THE BENEVOLENCE OF SELF-INTEREST

Q How can economists expect to be taken seriously, non-economists are given to complain, when their model of man is so patently inadequate? Mainstream economics assumes that people are driven by the rational pursuit of self-interest. But, as everybody knows, people are not rational and they often act selflessly. Where in this view of man as desiccated calculating-machine is there recognition of the centrality of love, duty, and self-sacrifice in human conduct? What use is a purported science of social behavior that is blind to the necessary conditions for social behavior?

A These questions would be telling if "rational" and "self-interest" meant what these critics take them to mean. But they do not. In mainstream economics, to say that people are rational is not to assume that they never make mistakes, as critics usually suppose. It is merely to say that they do *not* make systematic mistakes; that is, they do not keep making the same mistake over and over again. And when economists talk of self-interest, they are referring not just to satisfaction of material wants, but to a broader idea of "preferences" that can easily encompass, among other things, the welfare of others.

Even when the terms are properly understood, "rational pursuit of self-interest" is a simplifying assumption. But the right question is whether this simplification is fruitful, or so gross that it hides what needs to be examined. Human behavior is far too complicated to be analyzed—to yield patterns and suggest generalizations—without employing some such simplification. And in nearly every branch of economics, rationality has proved a useful one. . . .

Turning from means to ends, what about self-interest? Here the issues are subtler. If economics supposed, at one extreme, that people seek only to maximize their material consumption, then it

would be plain wrong, and that would be that. If, at the other extreme, it assumed that people seek to satisfy their preferences (or some such formula), then it would be true merely by virtue of the meaning of the words—and it would not tell you anything. The assumption built into mainstream economics is much closer to the second of these than the first. . . .

However, the assumption of self-interest is not entirely tautological. Many kinds of apparently selfless behavior may in fact be self-interested in the way economics proposes. . . .

People show consideration for others in the hope or expectation that the favor will be returned. Behavior that establishes a reputation for honesty, or that signals a willingness to enter into commitments, is also, as a rule, self-interested in this sense. That makes it no less conducive to a flourishing society, no less to be praised and encouraged . . . it is self-interest, not love, that holds society together. . . .

When Adam Smith, one of the greatest economic thinkers and author of *The Wealth of Nations* published in 1776, pointed out that if people want dinner, they look not to the benevolence of the butcher, brewer, or baker, but to their regard for their own interest, his aim was not to portray social interaction as mean and narrow. Rather it was to draw attention to the extraordinary and improbable power of self-interest: this stunted, inward-looking trait is transformed, through spontaneous social cooperation, into a force for the common good.

Smith regarded this as almost miraculous. So it is. The main task of economics has been to understand this astonishing process. And by and large, thanks to its simplifying assumptions, it has succeeded. That's not so dismal, is it?

SOURCE: From "The Benevolence of Self-Interest", 'The Economist' (online edition), March 30, 2000. © The Economist Newspaper Limited, London 2000. Reprinted with permission.

GREAT ECONOMIC THINKERS: ADAM SMITH (1723–1790)

Adam Smith was born in a small fishing village just outside of Edinburgh, Scotland, in 1723. At age 4, gypsies (called *tinkers* in Scotland) kidnapped Smith, but he was rescued through the efforts of his uncle. He began studying at Glasgow College when he was just 14 and later continued his studies at Oxford University. He returned to Glasgow at age 28 as a professor of philosophy and logic. (Until the nineteenth century, economics was considered a branch of philosophy, thus Smith never took nor taught a class in economics.) He later resigned that position to become the private tutor to the stepson of Charles Townshend.

Although known for his intelligence, warm hospitality, and charitable spirit, Smith was not without his eccentricities. Notorious for his absent-mindedness, there is a story about Smith taking a trip to a tanning factory and, while engaged in conversation with a friend, walking straight into a large tanning vat. Another tale features Smith walking 15 miles in his sleep, awakening from his sleepwalk to the ringing of church bells, and scurrying back home in his nightgown. Most astonishing and unfortunate, Smith, without explanation, had the majority of his unpublished writings destroyed before his death in 1790.

Adam Smith is considered the founder of economics. He addressed problems of both economic theory and policy in his famous book, *An Inquiry into the Nature and Causes of the Wealth of Nations*, published in 1776. The book was a success from the beginning, with its first edition selling out in just six months, and people have continued to read it for well over two centuries.

Smith believed that the wealth of a nation did not come from the accumulation of gold and silver—the prevailing thought of the day. Smith observed that people tend to pursue their own personal interests and that an "invisible hand" (the market) guides their self-interest, increasing social welfare and general economic well-being. Smith's most powerful and enduring contribution was this idea of an invisible

COURTESY OF ROBERT L. SEXTON

Smith is buried in a small cemetery in Edinburgh, Scotland. The money left on the grave site is usually gone by morning; the homeless prey on the donations to use for food and spirits. Adam Smith is probably smiling somewhere. He had a reputation as a charitable man—"a scale much beyond what might have been expected from his fortunes."

hand of market incentives channeling individuals' efforts and promoting social welfare.

Smith also showed that through division of labor and specialization of tasks, producers could increase their output markedly. While Smith did not invent the market, he demonstrated that free markets, unfettered by monopoly and government regulation, and free trade were at the very foundation of the wealth of a nation. Many of Smith's insights are still central to economics today.

addition, rational behavior does not mean that people do not make mistakes, but it does mean that people learn from past mistakes and that their decisions in the future reflect that information. That is, they do not keep making the same mistake.

In short, rational individuals weigh the benefits and costs of their actions and they only pursue actions if they perceive the benefits to be greater than the costs. We will discuss this concept more thoroughly in the next chapter.

SECTION CHECK

1. Economists assume that people act as if they are motivated by self-interest and respond predictably to changing circumstances.
2. Do not confuse self-interest with selfishness.
3. Rational behavior means that people do the best they can based on their values and information, under current and future anticipated consequences.

---

1. What do economists mean by self-interest?
2. What does rational self-interest involve?
3. How are self-interest and selfishness different?
4. What is rational behavior?

SECTION 1.3

Economic Theory

* What are economic theories?
* What can we expect from theories?
* Why do we need to abstract?
* What is a hypothesis?

* What is empirical analysis?
* What is the *ceteris paribus* assumption?
* What are microeconomics and macroeconomics?

Economic Theories

A theory is an established explanation that accounts for known facts or phenomena. Specifically, economic theories are statements or propositions about patterns of human behavior that occur expectedly under certain circumstances. These theories help us sort out and understand the complexities of economic behavior and guide our analysis. We expect a good theory to explain and predict well. A good economic theory, then, should help us better understand and, ideally, predict human economic behavior.

theory
statement or proposition used to explain and predict behavior in the real world

Abstraction Is Important

Economic theories cannot realistically include every event that has ever occurred. A theory weeds out the irrelevant facts from the relevant ones. We must abstract. A road map of the United States may not include every creek, ridge, and gully between Los Angeles and Chicago; indeed, such an all-inclusive map would be too large and too detailed to be of value. A road map designating major interstate highways will provide enough information to travel by car from Los Angeles to Chicago. Likewise, an economic

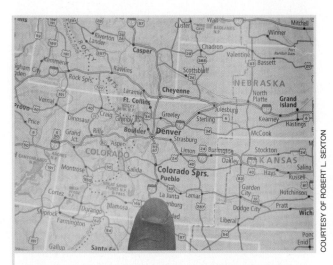

COURTESY OF ROBERT L. SEXTON

How is economic theory like a map? Because of the complexity of human behavior, economists must abstract to focus on the most important components of a particular problem. It is similar to the way that maps highlight the important information (and assume away many minor details) to help people get from here to there.

theory provides a broad view, not a detailed examination, of human economic behavior.

Without abstraction or simplification, the world is too complex to analyze. For the same reason, economists make a number of simplifying *assumptions* in their models. Sometimes economists make very strong assumptions, such as that all people seek self-betterment or all firms attempt to maximize profits. Of course, this may not hold for every single person or firm. Only when we test our models using these assumptions do we find out if they were too simplified or too limiting.

Developing a Testable Proposition

The beginning of any theory is a **hypothesis**, a testable proposition that makes some type of prediction about behavior in response to certain changes in conditions based on our assumptions. In economic theory, a hypothesis is a testable prediction about how people will behave or react to a change in economic circumstances. For example, if we notice an increase in the price of digital video discs (DVDs), we might hypothesize that sales of DVDs will drop, or if the price of DVDs decreases, our hypothesis might be that

hypothesis
a testable proposition

empirical analysis
the use of data to test a hypothesis

DVDs sales will rise. Once we state our hypothesis, we test it by comparing what it predicts will happen to what actually happens.

Using Empirical Analysis

To determine whether our hypothesis is valid, we must engage in **empirical analysis**. That is, we must examine the data to see whether our hypothesis fits well with the facts. If the hypothesis is consistent with real-world observations, we can accept it; if it does not fit well with the facts, we must "go back to the drawing board."

Determining whether a hypothesis is acceptable is more difficult in economics than it is in the natural or physical sciences. Chemists, for example, can observe chemical reactions under laboratory conditions. They can alter the environment to meet the assumptions of the hypothesis and can readily manipulate the variables (chemicals, temperatures, and so on) crucial to the proposed relationship. Such controlled experimentation is seldom possible in economics. The laboratory of economists is usually the real world. Unlike chemists in their labs, economists cannot easily control all the variables that might influence human behavior.

From Hypothesis to Theory

After gathering their data, economic researchers must evaluate the results to determine whether their hypothesis is supported or refuted. If supported, the hypothesis can be tentatively accepted as an economic theory.

Every economic theory is on life-long probation; the hypothesis underlying an economic theory is constantly being tested against empirical findings. Do the observed findings support the prediction? When a hypothesis survives a number of tests, it is accepted until it no longer predicts well.

Science and Stories

Much of scientific discovery is expressed in terms of stories, not unlike the stories told by writers of novels. This similarity is not accidental. The novelist tries to persuade us that a story could almost be true; the scientist tries to persuade us that certain events fall into a certain meaningful pattern. The scientist does not (or is not supposed to) invent the underlying "facts" of the story, whereas the novelist is not so constrained. However, a scientist does select *certain* facts from among many facts that could have been chosen, just as the novelist chooses from an infinite number of possible characters and situations to make the story most persuasive. In both cases, the author "invents" the story. Therefore, we should not be surprised to find order in economic theory any more than we are surprised to find order in a good novel. Scientists would not bother to write about "life" if they were not convinced that they had stories worth telling.

What makes a story "worth telling?" When we look for order in nature, we cannot suppose that the "facts" are a sufficient basis for understanding observed events. The basic problem is that the facts of a complex world simply do not organize themselves. Understanding requires that a *conceptual order* be imposed on these "facts" to counteract the confusion that would otherwise result. For example, objects of different weights falling freely in the air do **not** travel at *precisely* the same rate (largely because of the different effects of air resistance). Yet this piece of information is generally much less significant than the fact that falling bodies do travel at *almost* the same rate (which presumably would be identical in a vacuum). By focusing on the most significant fact—the similarity, not the difference—Galileo was able to impose order on the story of gravity.

> *ceteris paribus*
> holding all other things
> constant

In the same way, to interpret the impact of rising housing prices on the amount of housing desired, economists must separate out the impact of increasing wealth, population, and other contributing factors. Failing to do so would obscure the central insight that people tend to buy less housing at higher prices. Without a story—a theory of causation—scientists could not sort out and understand the complex reality that surrounds us.

The *Ceteris Paribus* Assumption

Virtually all economic theories share a condition usually expressed by the Latin phrase **ceteris paribus**. A rough translation of the phrase is "letting everything else be equal" or "holding everything else constant." When economists try to assess the effect of one variable on another, they must keep the relationship between the two variables isolated from other events that might also influence the situation that the theory tries to explain or predict. A couple of examples will make this concept clearer.

Suppose you develop your own theory describing the relationship between studying and exam performance: If I study harder, I will perform better on the test. That sounds logical, right? Holding other things constant (*ceteris paribus*), your theory is likely to be true. However, what if you studied harder but inadvertently overslept the day of the exam? What if you were so sleepy during the test that you could not think clearly? Or what if you studied the wrong material? Although it might look like additional studying did not improve your performance, the real problem could lie in the impact of other variables, such as sleep deficiency or how you studied.

Why Are Observation and Prediction Harder in the Social Sciences?

Working from observations, scientists try to make generalizations that will enable them to predict certain events. However, observation and prediction are more difficult in the social sciences than in physical sciences such as physics, chemistry, and astronomy. Why? The major reason for the difference is that the social scientists, including economists, are concerned with *human* behavior. And human behavior is more variable and often less readily predictable than the behavior of experiments observed in a laboratory. However, by looking at the actions of a large group of people, economists can still make many reliable predictions about human behavior.

Why Do Economists Predict on a Group Level?

Economists' predictions usually refer to the collective behavior of large groups rather than to that of specific individuals. Why is this? Looking at the behaviors of a large group allows economists to discern general patterns of actions. For example, consider what would happen if the price of air travel from the United States to Europe was reduced drastically, say from $1,000 to $400, because of the invention of a more fuel-efficient jet. What type of predictions could we make about the effect of this price reduction on the buying habits of typical consumers?

What Does Individual Behavior Tell Us?

Let's look first at the responses of individuals. As a result of the price drop, some people will greatly increase their intercontinental travel, taking theater weekends in London or week-long trips to France to indulge in French food. Some people, however, are terribly afraid to fly, and the price reduction will not influence their behavior in the slightest. Others might detest Europe and, despite the lowered airfares, prefer to spend a few days in Aspen, Colorado, instead. A few people might respond to the airfare reduction in precisely the opposite way from ours: At the lower fare, they might make fewer trips to Europe, because they might believe (rightly or wrongly) that the price drop would be accompanied by a reduction in the quality of service, greater crowding, or reduced safety. In short, we cannot predict with any level of certainty how a given individual will respond to this airfare reduction.

What Does Group Behavior Tell Us?

Group behavior is often more predictable than individual behavior. When the weather gets colder, more firewood will be sold. Some individuals may not buy firewood, but we can predict with great accuracy that a group of individuals will establish a pattern of buying more firewood. Similarly, while we cannot say what each individual will do, within a group of persons, we can predict with great accuracy that more flights to Europe from Los Angeles will be sold at lower prices than at higher prices, holding other things such as income and preferences constant. We cannot predict exactly how many more airline tickets will be sold at $400 than

at $1,000, but we can predict the direction of the impact and approximate the extent of the impact. By observing the relationship between the price of goods and services and the quantities people purchase in different places and during different time periods, it is possible to make some reliable generalizations about how much people will react to changes in the prices of goods and services. Economists use this larger picture of the group for most of their theoretical analysis.

The Two Branches of Economics: Microeconomics and Macroeconomics

Conventionally, we distinguish two main branches of economics, microeconomics and macroeconomics. **Microeconomics**, deals with the smaller units within the economy, attempting to understand the decision-making behavior of firms and households and their interaction in markets for particular goods or services. Microeconomic topics include discussions of health care, agricultural subsidies, the price of everyday items such as running shoes, the distribution of income, and the impact of labor unions on wages. **Macroeconomics**, in contrast, deals with the aggregate, or total economy; it looks at economic problems as they influence the whole of society. Topics covered in macroeconomics include discussions of inflation, unemployment, business cycles, and economic growth. To put it simply, microeconomics looks at the trees while macroeconomics looks at the forest.

microeconomics
the study of household and firm behavior and how they interact in the marketplace

macroeconomics
the study of the whole economy, including the topics of inflation, unemployment, and economic growth

aggregate
the total amount—such as the *aggregate level of output*

SECTION CHECK

1. Economic theories are statements used to explain and predict patterns of human behavior.
2. We must abstract and focus on the most important components of a particular problem.
3. A hypothesis makes a prediction about human behavior and is then tested.
4. We use empirical analysis to examine the data and see whether our hypothesis fits well with the facts.
5. In order to isolate the effects of one variable on another, we use the *ceteris paribus* assumption.
6. It is rational for people to act in their own self-interest and try to improve their situation.
7. Microeconomics focuses on smaller units within the economy—firms and households—and how they interact in the marketplace.
8. Macroeconomics deals with the aggregate, or total, economy.

continued

1. What are economic theories?
2. What is the purpose of a theory?
3. Why must economic theories be abstract?
4. What is a hypothesis? How do we determine whether it is tentatively accepted?
5. Why do economists hold other things constant (*ceteris paribus*)?
6. Why are observation and prediction more difficult in the social sciences?
7. Why do economic predictions refer to the behavior of groups of people rather than individuals?
8. Why is the market for running shoes considered a microeconomic topic?
9. Why is inflation considered a macroeconomic topic?

SECTION 1.4

Pitfalls to Avoid in Scientific Thinking

* If two events usually occur together, does it mean one event caused the other to happen?
* What is the fallacy of composition?

In our discussion of economic theory we have not yet mentioned that there are certain pitfalls to avoid that may hinder scientific and logical thinking: confusing correlation and causation, and the fallacy of composition.

Confusing Correlation and Causation

Without a theory of causation, no scientist could sort out and understand the enormous complexity of the real world. But one must always be careful not to confuse correlation with causation. In other words, the fact that two events usually occur together (**correlation**) does not necessarily mean that one caused the other to occur (**causation**). For example, say a groundhog awakes after a long winter of hibernation, climbs out of his hole, and sees his shadow—then six weeks of bad weather ensue. Did the groundhog cause the bad weather? In Europe, the stork population has fallen and so have birth rates. Does this mean that the one event caused the other to occur? It is highly unlikely.

Perhaps the causality runs in the opposite direction. A rooster may always crow before the sun rises, but it does not cause the sunrise; rather, the early light from the sunrise causes the rooster to crow.

correlation
when two events occur together

causation
when one event brings about another event

fallacy of composition
the incorrect view that what is true for the individual is always true for the group

Why Is The Correlation Between Ice Cream Sales and Property Crime Positive?

Did you know that when ice cream sales rise, so do property crime rates? What do you think causes the two events to occur together? The explanation is that property crime peaks in the summer because of warmer weather, more people on vacations (leaving their homes vacant), teenagers out of school, and so on. It just happens that ice cream sales also peak in those months because of the weather. It is the case of a third variable causing both to occur. Or what if there were a positive correlation between sales of cigarette lighters and the incidence of cancer? The suspect might well turn out to be the omitted variable (the so-called "smoking gun"): the cigarette.

The Fallacy of Composition

Economic thinking requires us to be aware of the problems associated with aggregation (adding up all the parts). One of the biggest problems is the **fallacy of composition**. This fallacy states that even if something is true for an individual, it is not necessarily true for many individuals as a group. For example, say you

in the news   Sex on Television and Teenage Pregnancy

When it comes to television programming, sex sells—maybe too well. According to a Rand Corporation study authored by Anita Chandra, there is a link between teenagers' exposure to sexual content on TV and teen pregnancies. Specifically, the study found that teens exposed to high levels of sexual content on television were twice as likely to be involved in a pregnancy in the following three years as teens with limited exposure. The results were published in the November, 2008, edition of the journal *Pediatrics*.

The study's author is quick to point out that the factors leading to teen pregnancies are varied and complex—but warns it is important for parents, teachers, and pediatricians to understand that TV can be one of them.

consider this:

While sex on television may lead to increases in teen pregnancy, isn't it possible the causality runs in the opposite direction—teenagers that are more susceptible to teen pregnancy watch shows with more sexual content? In addition, there are a host of other variables that could be much more statistically significant such as low self-esteem, single-parent households, household income, years of schooling, heavy drug and alcohol use, GPA, child abuse, peer pressure, and so on.

In fact, more women of all ages, not just teenagers, are having children out of wedlock. Actually, the teen birth rate was much higher in 1957 than it is today. The growing concern is over the rise in unwed teenage mothers. However, births to single teens actually account for a smaller percentage of all non-marital births than 20 years ago—so is television to blame? Heed the-author's warning: "the reasons for the rise in teen pregnancies are varied and complex."

---

are at a football game and you decide to stand up to get a better view of the playing field. This works as long as the people seated around you don't stand up. But what happens if everyone stands up at the same time? Then your standing up does nothing to improve your view. Thus, what is true for an individual does not always hold true in the aggregate. The same can be said of getting to school early to get a better parking place—what if everyone arrived early? Or studying harder to get a better grade in a class that is graded on a curve—what if everyone studied harder? These are all examples of the fallacy of composition.

AP IMAGES

Normally, people expect more accidents at higher speeds. This expectation seems reasonable; yet, as shown in the picture, slower driving can be correlated with more accidents. Why the positive correlation? It is a third variable—icy roads—that leads to both lower speeds and increased accidents.

SECTION

1.5

Positive Statements and Normative Statements

* What is a positive statement?
* What is a normative statement?
* Why do economists disagree?

Positive Statement

Most economists view themselves as scientists seeking the truth about the way people behave. They make speculations about economic behavior, and then, ideally, they assess the validity of those predictions based on human experience. Their work emphasizes how people *do* behave, rather than how people *should* behave. In the role of scientist, an economist tries to observe patterns of behavior objectively, without reference to the appropriateness or inappropriateness of that

positive statement
an objective, testable statement that describes what happens and why it happens

behavior. This objective, value-free approach, based on the scientific method, is called positive analysis. In positive analysis, we want to know the impact of variable *A* on variable *B*. We want to be able to test a hypothesis. For example, the following is a **positive statement**: If rent controls are imposed, vacancy rates will fall. This statement is testable. A positive statement does not have to be a true statement, but it does have to be a testable statement.

Keep in mind, however, that it is doubtful that even the most objective scientist can be totally value free in his or her analysis. An economist may well emphasize data or evidence that supports a hypothesis, putting less weight on other evidence that might be contradictory. This tendency, alas, is human nature. But a good economist/scientist strives to be as fair and objective as possible in evaluating evidence and in stating conclusions based on the evidence. In some sense, economists are like engineers; they try to figure out how things work and then describe what would happen if you changed something.

Normative Statement

Economists, like anyone else, have opinions and make value judgments. And when economists, or anyone else for that matter, express opinions about an economic policy or statement, they are indicating in part how they believe things should be, not stating facts about the way things are. In other words, they are performing normative analysis. **Normative statements** involve judgments about what should be or what ought to happen. For example, normative questions might include: Should the government raise the minimum wage? Should the government increase spending in the space program? Should the government give "free" prescription drugs to senior citizens?

normative statements a subjective, contestable statement that attempts to describe what should be done

Positive Versus Normative Analysis

The distinction between positive and normative analysis is important. It is one thing to say that everyone should have universal health care, an untestable normative statement, and quite another to say that universal health care would lead to greater worker productivity, a testable positive statement. It is important to distinguish between positive and normative analysis because many controversies in economics revolve around policy considerations that contain both. For example, what impact would a 3 percent reduction in income taxes across the board have on the economy? This question requires positive analysis. Whether we should have a 3 percent reduction in income taxes requires normative analysis as well. When economists are trying to explain the way the world works, they are scientists. When economists start talking about how the economy should work rather than how it does work, they have entered the normative world of the policymaker. In short, positive statements are attempts to *describe* what happens and why it happens, while normative statements are attempts to *prescribe* what should be done.

Disagreement Is Common in Most Disciplines

Although economists do frequently have opposing views on economic policy questions, they probably disagree less than the media would have you believe. Disagreement is common in most disciplines: Seismologists differ over predictions of earthquakes or volcanic eruption; historians can be at odds over the interpretation of historical events; psychologists disagree on proper ways to rear children; and nutritionists debate the merits of large doses of vitamin C.

The majority of disagreements in economics stem from normative issues; differences in values or policy beliefs result in conflict. For example, a policy might increase efficiency at the expense of a sense of fairness or equity, or it might help a current generation at the expense of a future generation. Because policy decisions involve trade-offs, they will always involve the potential for conflict.

Freedom Versus Fairness

Some economists are concerned about individual freedom and liberty, thinking that any encroachment on individual decision making is bad, other things being equal. People with this philosophic bent are inclined to be skeptical of any increased government involvement in the economy.

On the other hand, some economists are concerned with what they consider an unequal, "unfair," or unfortunate distribution of income, wealth, or power, and view governmental intervention as desirable in righting injustices that they believe exist in a market economy. To these persons, the threat to individual liberty alone is not sufficiently great to reject governmental intervention in the face of perceived economic injustice.

The Validity of an Economic Theory

Aside from philosophic differences, a second reason helps explain why economists may differ on any given policy question. Specifically, they may disagree about the validity of a given economic theory for the policy in question—that is, they disagree over the positive analysis. Why would they disagree over positive analysis? For at least two reasons. One, a particular model may yield mixed results: some empirical evidence supporting it and some not. Two, the information available may be insufficient to make a compelling theory.

A Brighter Day for the Dismal Science— Economics Becomes the Hot Major for Undergrads World-Wide

—BY JESSICA E. VASCELLARO

What's your major? Around the world, college undergraduates' time-honored question is increasingly drawing the same answer: Economics.

U.S. colleges and universities awarded 16,141 degrees to economics majors in the 2003–2004 academic year, up nearly 40 percent from five years earlier. This is according to John. J. Siegfried, an economics professor at Vanderbilt University in Nashville, Tennessee, who tracks 272 colleges and universities around the country for the *Journal of Economic Education*.

Since the mid-1990s, the number of students majoring in economics has been rising, while the number majoring in political science and government has declined and the number majoring in history and sociology has barely grown, according to the U.S. government's National Center for Education Statistics.

"There has been a clear explosion of economics as as major," says Mark Gertler, a professor and chairman of New York University's economics department.

The number of students majoring in economics has been rising even faster at the United States' top colleges. At New York University, for example, the number of economics majors has more than doubled to nearly 800 in the past 10 years. It is now the most popular major.

Economics also is the most popular major at Harvard University, Cambridge, Massachusetts, where 964 students majored in the subject this year. The number of economics majors at Columbia University, New York, has risen 67 percent since 1995. The University of Chicago said that last year 24 percent of its graduating class, or 240 students, departed with economics degrees.

The trend marks a big switch for the so-called dismal science, which experienced large declines in undergraduate enrollments in the early 1990s, as interest in other areas, like sociology, was growing. Behind the turnaround is a clear-eyed reading of supply and demand: In a global economy filled with uncertainty, many students see economics as the best vehicle for landing a job promising good pay and security.

And as its focus broadens, there are even some signs that economics is becoming cool.

In addition to probing the mechanics of inflation and exchange rates, academics now use statistics and an economist's view of how people respond to incentives to study issues such as AIDS research, obesity, and even terrorism. The surprise best seller of the spring, for instance, was *Freakonomics*, co-authored by University of Chicago economist Steven Levitt, that examines issues ranging from corruption among real-estate agents to sumo wrestling.

Pooja Jotwani, a recent graduate of Georgetown University, Washington, says she is certain her economics degree helped her land a job in Lehman Brothers Holdings Inc.'s sales and trading division, where she will earn the industry's standard starting salary of $55,000, or about 45,000 euros, not including bonus. She says the major strengthened her business skills and provided her with something very simple: "financial security."

"People are fascinated with applying the economic mode of reasoning to a wide variety of issues, and these forces are causing them to study economics more and more," says Lawrence Summers, [former] president of Harvard, former U.S. Treasury Secretary, [and head of the Council of Economic Advisors].

Economics and business majors ranked among the five most desirable majors in a 2004 survey of employers by the National Association of Colleges and Employers, along with accounting, electrical engineering, and mechanical engineering. It wasn't just banks and insurance companies that expressed interest in hiring economics majors: Companies in industries such as utilities and retailing did, too . . . .

Roberto Angulo, chief executive of AfterCollege Inc., a San Francisco online recruiting service with

267,000 registered users, says an economics major has practical value on the job. "Students are more employable if they study economics," he says. He graduated from Stanford University in California with an economics degree five years ago.

It isn't just the job calculus that is drawing students to the major: It also is the rapid spread of economic globalization. Many students around the world are wondering what effect global economic trends will have on them.

Foreign students studying in the United States are flocking to the major. Sabrina De Abreu, a student from Argentina about to start her senior year at Harvard, says her country's experiences made her choice easy. "When I grew up in Argentina, my country plunged into a recession," she says. "Understanding economics has become a fundamental part of my life."

Indeed, the rising popularity of the economics major appears to be a global phenomenon. A recent McKinsey Global Institute study found that the share of degrees in economics and business awarded in Poland from 1996 to 2002 more than doubled, to 36 percent from 16 percent; in Russia, the share jumped to 31 percent from 18 percent . . . .

John Sutton, chairman of the economics department at the London School of Economics, says the school's popularity is at an all-time high, in part the result of interest among students from Eastern Europe, where there is a "huge pent-up demand for well-trained professional economists." Dr. Sutton says that as these countries become increasingly open to capitalism, "bright young students are beginning to see economic issues highlighted."

POLICY application   ECONOMISTS DO AGREE

Most economists agree that these statements are correct:

1. A ceiling on rents (rent control) reduces the quantity and quality of rental housing available (93 percent agree).
2. Tariffs and import quotas usually reduce general economic welfare (93 percent agree).
3. The United States should not restrict employers from outsourcing work to foreign countries (90.1 percent agree).
4. Fiscal policy (e.g., tax cuts and/or increases in government expenditure) has significant stimulative impact on an economy that is less than fully employed (90 percent agree).
5. Flexible and floating exchange rates offer an effective international monetary arrangement (90 percent).
6. The gap between Social Security funds and expenditures will become unsustainably large within the next 50 years if the current policies remain unchanged (85 percent agree).
7. The United States should eliminate agricultural subsidies (85 percent agree).
8. Local and state governments in the United States should eliminate subsidies to professional sport franchises (85 percent agree).
9. A large budget deficit has an adverse effect on the economy (83 percent agree).
10. A minimum wage increases unemployment among young and unskilled (79 percent agree).
11. Effluent taxes and marketable pollution permits represent a better approach to pollution control than imposition of pollution ceilings (78 percent agree).
12. Economist favor expanding competition and market forces in education (67.1 percent agree).

Often Economists Do Agree

Although you may not believe it after reading the previous discussion, economists don't always disagree. In fact, according to a survey among members of the American Economic Association, most economists agree on a wide range of issues, including rent control, import tariffs, export restrictions, the use of wage and price controls to curb inflation, and the minimum wage (see Policy Application: Economists Do Agree, in this section).

SECTION CHECK

1. Positive analysis is objective and value-free.
2. Normative analysis involves value judgments and opinions about the desirability of various actions.
3. Disagreement is common in most disciplines.
4. Most disagreement among economists stems from normative issues.

1. What is a positive statement? Must positive statements be testable?
2. What is a normative statement? Is a normative statement testable?
3. Why is the positive/normative distinction important?
4. Why do policy disagreements arise among economists?
5. Is the statement "UFOs land in my backyard at least twice a week" a positive statement? Why or why not?

Interactive Chapter Summary

Fill in the blanks:

1. Economics is the study of the choices we make among our many wants and desires given our _____ resources.

2. _____ occurs because our unlimited wants exceed our limited resources.

3. Resources are _____ used to produce goods and services.

4. The economic problem is that _____ forces us to choose, and choices are costly because we must give up other opportunities that we _____.

5. Living in a world of scarcity means _____.

6. Economics provided the tools to intelligently evaluate _____ and make _____.

7. _____ deals with the aggregate (the forest), or total economy, while _____ deals with the smaller units (the trees) within the economy.

8. Economists assume that individuals act as if they are motivated by _____ and respond in _____ ways to changing circumstances.

9. Economists believe that it is _____ for people to anticipate the likely future consequences of their behavior.

10. Actions have _____.

11. Rational self-interest implies that people do not make _____ mistakes.

12. Economic _____ are statements or propositions used to _____ and _____ patterns of human economic behavior.

13. Because of the complexity of human behavior, economists must _____ to focus on the most important components of a particular problem.

14. A(n) _____ in economic theory is a testable prediction about how people will behave or react to a change in economic circumstances.

15. _____ analysis is the use of data to test a hypothesis.

16. In order to isolate the effects of one variable on another, we use the _____ assumption.

17. When two events usually occur together, it is called _____.

18. When one event brings on another event, it is called _____.

19. The _____ is the incorrect view that what is true for an individual is always true for the group.

20. The objective, value-free approach to economics, based on the scientific method, is called _____ analysis.

21. _____ analysis involves judgments about what should be or what ought to happen.

22. _____ analysis is descriptive; normative analysis is _____.

23. "A tax increase will lead to a lower rate of inflation" is a(n) _____ economic statement.

Answers: 1. limited; unlimited 2. Scarcity 3. inputs 4. scarcity; value 5. trade-offs 6. options; choices 7. Macroeconomics; microeconomics 8. self-interest; predictable 9. rational 10. consequences 11. systematic 12. theories; explain; predict 13. abstract 14. hypothesis 15. Empirical 16. *ceteris paribus* 17. correlation 18. causation 19. fallacy of composition 20. positive 21. Normative 22. Positive; prescriptive 23. positive

Key Terms and Concepts

economics 3
resources 3
scarcity 3
the economic problem 3
rational behavior 7
theory 10

hypothesis 11
empirical analysis 11
ceteris paribus 12
microeconomics 13
macroeconomics 13
aggregate 13

correlation 14
causation 14
fallacy of composition 14
positive statement 16
normative statement 17

Section Check Answers

1.1 Economics: A Brief Introduction

1. What is the definition of economics?
Economics is the study of the choices we make among our many wants and desires given our limited resources.

2. Why does scarcity force us to make choices?
Scarcity—the fact that our wants exceed what our resources can produce—means that we are forced to make choices on how best to use these limited resources.

3. Why are choices costly?
In a world of scarcity, whenever we choose one option, we also choose to do without something else that we also desire. The want that we choose not to satisfy is the opportunity cost of that choice.

4. Why do even "non-economic" issues have an economic dimension?
Even apparently non-economic issues have an economic dimension because economics concerns anything worthwhile to some human being (including love, friendship, charity, etc.) and the choices we make among those things we value.

5. Why is economics worth studying?
Perhaps the best reason to study economics is that so many of the things that concern us are at least partly economic in character. Economics helps us to intelligently evaluate our options and determine the most appropriate choices in many given situations. It helps develop a disciplined method of thinking about problems.

1.2 Economic Behavior

1. What do economists mean by self-interest?
By self-interest, economists simply mean that people try to improve their own situation (as they see it, not necessarily as others see it). Self-interest can also include benevolence.

2. What does rational self-interest involve?
Economists consider individuals to be acting in their rational self-interest if they are striving to do their best

to achieve their goals with their limited income, time, and knowledge, and given their expectations of the likely future consequences (both benefits and costs) of their behavior.

3. How are self-interest and selfishness different?

Self-interest means people are striving to do their best to achieve their goals, which may or may not be selfish. Parents working more hours to give more to their children or a favorite charity can be self-interested but are not selfish.

4. What is rational behavior?

Rational behavior is when people do the best they can based on their values and information, under current and anticipated future consequences. Rational individuals weigh the benefits and costs of their actions and they only pursue actions if they perceive their benefits to be greater than the costs.

1.3 Economic Theory

1. What are economic theories?

A theory is an established explanation that accounts for known facts or phenomena. Economic theories are statements or propositions about patterns of human behavior that are expected to take place under certain circumstances.

2. What is the purpose of a theory?

The purpose of a theory is primarily to explain and predict well. Theories are necessary because the facts of a complex world do not organize themselves.

3. Why must economic theories be abstract?

Economic theories must be abstract because they could not possibly include every possible event, circumstance, or factor that might affect behavior. Like a road map, an economic theory abstracts from some issues to focus more clearly and precisely on the central questions it is designed to understand.

4. What is a hypothesis? How do we determine whether it is tentatively accepted?

A hypothesis is a testable proposal that makes some type of prediction about behavior in response to certain changed conditions. An economic hypothesis is a testable proposal about how people will behave or react to a change in economic circumstances. It is tentatively accepted if its predictions are consistent with what actually happens. In economics, testing involves empirical analysis to see whether the hypothesis is supported by the facts.

5. Why do economists hold other things constant (*ceteris paribus*)?

The hold other things constant, or *ceteris paribus,* assumption is used in economics because in trying to assess the effect of one variable on another, we must isolate their relationship from other important events or variables that might also influence the situation the theory tries to explain or predict.

6. Why are observation and prediction more difficult in the social sciences?

Observation and prediction are more difficult in the social sciences than in physical sciences because social sciences are concerned with human behavior, which is more variable and often less readily predictable than the behavior of experiments observed in a laboratory. Social scientists can seldom run truly "controlled" experiments like those of the biological scientists.

7. Why do economic predictions refer to the behavior of groups of people rather than individuals?

Economists' predictions usually refer to the collective behavior of large groups rather than individuals because looking at the behaviors of a large group of individuals allows economists to discern general patterns of actions and therefore make more reliable generalizations.

8. Why is the market for running shoes considered a microeconomic topic?

Because a single industry is "small" relative to the economy as a whole, the market for running shoes (or the running-shoe industry) is a microeconomic topic.

9. Why is inflation considered a macroeconomic topic?

Inflation—a change in the overall price level—has effects throughout the entire economy, rather than just in certain small areas of the economy, which makes it a macroeconomic topic.

1.4 Pitfalls to Avoid in Scientific Thinking

1. What is the relationship between correlation and causation?

Correlation means that two things are related; causation means that one thing caused the other to occur. Even though causation implies correlation, correlation does not necessarily imply causation.

2. What types of misinterpretation result from confusing correlation and causation?

Confusing correlation between variables with causation can lead to misinterpretation where a person "sees" causation between two variables or events where none exists or where a third variable or event is responsible for causing both of them.

3. What is the fallacy of composition?

The fallacy of composition is the incorrect idea that if something is true for an individual, it must also be true for many individuals as a group.

4. **If you can sometimes get a high grade on an exam without studying, does it mean that additional studying does not lead to higher grades? Explain your answer.**

In some instances a student can get a high grade on an exam without studying. However, because additional studying increases mastery of the material, additional studying would typically increase test performance and grades. That is, even though added studying would not raise grades in some unusual situations, as a generalization, additional studying does lead to higher grades.

1.5 Positive Statements and Normative Statements

1. **What is a positive statements? Must positive statements be testable?**

Positive statements focus on how people actually behave, rather than on how people should behave. They deal with how variable *A* impacts variable *B*. Positive statements must be testable to determine whether their predictions are borne out by the evidence.

2. **What is a normative statement? Is a normative statement testable?**

Normative statements focus on what should be or what ought to happen; They involve opinions about the desirability of various actions or results. Normative statements are not testable, because it is not scientifically possible to establish whether one value judgment is better than another value judgment.

3. **Why is the positive/normative distinction important?**

It is important to distinguish between positive and normative statements because many controversies in economics revolve around policy considerations that contain both. Deciding whether a policy is good requires both positive analysis (what will happen) and normative analysis (is what happens good or bad).

4. **Why do policy disagreements arise among economists?**

As with most disciplines, economists do disagree. However, the majority of those disagreements stem from differences in normative analysis, because the evidence cannot establish whether one set of value judgments is better or more appropriate than other sets of value judgments.

5. **Is the statement "UFOs land in my backyard at least twice a week" a positive statement? Why or why not?**

A positive statement need not be true; it simply needs to be testable to determine whether it is borne out by the evidence.

True or False:

1. When our limited wants exceed our unlimited resources, we face scarcity.

2. Choices are costly because we must give up other opportunities that we value.

3. Living in a world of scarcity involves trade-offs.

4. Self-interest cannot include benevolence.

5. To say that people are rational is to assume that they never make mistakes.

6. Adam Smith described how self-interest can be a force for the common good.

7. According to the National Council of Economic Education, most adults tested in the United States performed well on economic literacy.

8. Rationality could not apply to criminals.

9. Economic theories do not abstract from the particular details of situations so they can better focus on every aspect of the behavior to be explained.

10. Determining whether an economic hypothesis is acceptable is more difficult than in the natural or physical sciences because, unlike a chemist in a chemistry lab, an economist cannot control all the other variables that might influence human behavior.

11. Microeconomics would deal with the analysis of a small individual firm, while macroeconomics would deal with large global firms.

12. A positive statement must be both testable and true.

13. A normative statement is nontestable.

14. The majority of disagreements in economics stem from normative issues.

15. A hypothesis is a normative statement.

Multiple Choice:

1. If a good is scarce,
   a. it only needs to be limited.
   b. it is not possible to produce any more of the good.
   c. our unlimited wants exceed our limited resources.
   d. our limited wants exceed our unlimited resources.

2. Which of the following is true of resources?
   a. Their availability is unlimited.
   b. They are the inputs used to produce goods and services.
   c. Increasing the amount of resources available could eliminate scarcity.
   d. Both b and c.

3. If scarcity were not a fact,
   a. people could have all the goods and services they wanted for free.
   b. it would no longer be necessary to make choices.
   c. poverty, defined as the lack of a minimum level of consumption, would also be eliminated.
   d. all of the above would be true.

4. Economics is concerned with
   a. the choices people must make because resources are scarce.
   b. human decision makers and the factors that influence their choices.
   c. the allocation of limited resources to satisfy unlimited wants.
   d. all of the above.

5. Which of the following would reflect self-interested behavior to an economist?
   a. worker pursuing a higher-paying job and better working conditions
   b. consumer seeking a higher level of satisfaction with her current income
   c. Mother Teresa using her Nobel Prize money to care for the poor
   d. all of the above

6. When economists assume that people act rationally, it means they
   a. always make decisions based on complete and accurate information.
   b. make decisions that will not be regretted later.
   c. do the best they can based on their values and information under current and future circumstances.
   d. make decisions based solely on what is best for society.
   e. commit no errors in judgment.

7. When we look at a particular segment of the economy, such as a given industry, we are studying
   a. macroeconomics.
   b. microeconomics.
   c. normative economics.
   d. positive economics.

8. Which of the following is most likely a topic of discussion in macroeconomics?
   a. an increase in the price of a pizza
   b. a decrease in the production of VCRs by a consumer electronics company
   c. an increase in the wage rate paid to automobile workers
   d. a decrease in the unemployment rate
   e. the entry of new firms into the software industry

9. Economists use theories to
   a. abstract from the complexities of the world.
   b. understand economic behavior.
   c. explain and help predict human behavior.
   d. do all of the above.
   e. do none of the above.

10. The importance of the *ceteris paribus* assumption is that it
    a. allows one to separate normative economic issues from positive economic ones.
    b. allows one to generalize from the whole to the individual.
    c. allows one to analyze the relationship between two variables apart from the influence of other variables.
    d. allows one to hold all variables constant so the economy can be carefully observed in a suspended state.

11. Which of the following statements can explain why correlation between Event A and Event B may not imply causality from A to B?
    a. The observed correlation may be coincidental.
    b. A third variable may be responsible for causing both events.
    c. Causality may run from Event B to Event A instead of in the opposite direction.
    d. All of the above can explain why the correlation may not imply causality.

12. Ten-year-old Tommy observes that people who play football are larger than average and tells his mom that he's going to play football because it will make him big and strong. Tommy is
    a. committing the fallacy of composition.
    b. violating the *ceteris paribus* assumption.
    c. mistaking correlation for causation.
    d. committing the fallacy of decomposition.

13. Which of the following correlations is likely to involve primarily one variable causing the other, rather than a third variable causing them both?
    a. The amount of time a team's third string plays in the game tends to be greater, the larger the team's margin of victory.
    b. Ice cream sales and crime rates both tend to increase at the same time.
    c. A lower price of a particular good and a higher quantity purchased tend to occur at the same time.
    d. The likelihood of rain tends to be greater after you have washed your car.

14. Which of the following is a positive statement?
    a. New tax laws are needed to help the poor.
    b. Teenage unemployment should be reduced.
    c. We should increase Social Security payments to the elderly.
    d. An increase in tax rates will reduce unemployment.
    e. It is only fair that firms protected from competition by government-granted monopolies pay higher corporate taxes.

Problems:

1. In most countries the birth rate has fallen as incomes and the economic opportunities for women have increased. Use economics to explain this pattern.

2. Write your own definition of economics. What are the main elements of the definition?

3. Are the following topics ones that would be covered in microeconomics or macroeconomics?
    a. the effects of an increase in the supply of lumber on the home-building industry
    b. changes in the national unemployment rate
    c. changes in the inflation rate
    d. changes in the country's economic growth rate
    e. the price of concert tickets

4. Identify which of the following headlines represents a microeconomic topic and which represents a macroeconomic topic.
    a. "U.S. Unemployment Rate Reaches Historic Laws"
    b. "General Motors Closes Auto Plant in St. Louis"
    c. "OPEC Action Results in a General Increase in Prices"
    d. "Companies Cut the Cost of Health Care for Employees"
    e. "Lawmakers Worry About the Possibility of a U.S. Recession"
    f. "Colorado Rockies Make Outfielder Highest Paid Ballplayer"

5. The Environmental Protection Agency asks you to help them understand the causes of urban pollution. Air pollution problems are worse the higher the Air Quality Index. You develop the following two hypotheses. Hypothesis I: Air pollution will be a greater problem as the average temperature increases in the urban area. Hypothesis II: Air pollution will be a greater problem as the population increases in the urban area.

   Test each hypothesis with the facts given in the following table. Which hypothesis fits the facts better? Have you developed a theory?

Metropolitan Statistical Area	Days with Polluted Air*	Average Maximum Temperature	Population (thousands)
Cincinnati, OH	30	64.0	1,979
El Paso, TX	13	77.1	680
Milwaukee, WI	12	55.9	1,690
Atlanta, GA	24	72.0	4,112
Philadelphia, PA	33	63.2	5,101
Albany, NY	8	57.6	876
San Diego, CA	20	70.8	2,814
Los Angeles, CA	80	70.6	9,519

*Air Quality Index greater than 100 (2002) **Source:** U.S. Dept. of Commerce, Bureau of Census, 2002 Statistical Abstract of the United States, Tables Nos. 30 and 363; U.S. EPA, Air Trends Report, 2002, EPA.Gov/airtrends/factbook.

6. Do any of the following statements involve fallacies? If so, which ones do they involve?
    a. Because sitting in the back of classrooms is correlated with getting lower grades in the class, students should always sit closer to the front of the classroom.
    b. Historically, the stock market rises in years the NFC team wins the Super Bowl and falls when the AFC wins the Super Bowl; I am rooting for the NFC team to win for the sake of my investment portfolio.
    c. When a basketball team spends more to get better players, it is more successful, which proves that all the teams should spend more to get better players.

d. Gasoline prices were higher last year than in 1970, yet people purchased more gas, which contradicts the law of demand.

e. An increase in the amount of money I have will make me better off, but an increase in the supply of money in the economy will not make Americans as a group better off.

7. In the 1940s, Dr. Melvin Page conducted a national campaign to stop people other than infants from drinking milk. According to Page, milk was a dangerous food and a leading cause of cancer. He pointed to the fact that more people died of cancer in Wisconsin, the nation's leading milk producer, than any other state as proof of his claim. How would you evaluate Dr. Page's claim?

8. Are the following statements normative or positive, or do they contain elements of both normative and positive statements?

a. A higher income-tax rate would generate increased tax revenues. Those extra revenues should be used to give more government aid to the poor.

b. The study of physics is more valuable than the study of sociology, but both should be studied by all college students.

c. An increase in the price of corn will decrease the amount of corn purchased. However, it will increase the amount of wheat purchased.

d. A decrease in the price of butter will increase the amount of butter purchased, but that would be bad because it would increase Americans' cholesterol levels.

e. The birth rate is reduced as economies urbanize, but it also leads to a decreased average age of developing countries' populations.

9. In the debate about clean air standards we have often heard the statement, "A nation as rich as the United States should have no pollution." Why is this a normative statement? Would it help you make a decision on national air quality standards? Describe two positive statements that might be useful in determining the air *quality standards*.

10. Answer the following questions:

a. What is the difference between self-interest and selfishness?

b. Why does inaction have consequences?

c. Why are observation and prediction more difficult in economics than in chemistry?

d. Why do economists look at group behavior rather than individual behavior?

11. Using the map analogy from the chapter, talk about the importance of abstraction. How do you abstract when taking notes in class?

Graphs Are an Important Economic Tool

Sometimes the use of visual aids, such as graphs, greatly enhances our understanding of a theory. It is much the same as finding your way to a friend's house with the aid of a map rather than with detailed verbal or written instructions. Graphs are important tools for economists. They allow us to understand better the workings of the economy. To economists, a graph can be worth a thousand words. This textbook will use graphs throughout to enhance the understanding of important economic relationships. This appendix provides a guide on how to read and create your own graphs.

The most useful graph for our purposes is one that merely connects a vertical line (the *Y*-axis) with a horizontal line (the *X*-axis), as seen in Exhibit 1. The intersection of the two lines occurs at the *origin*, which is where the value of both variables is equal to zero. In Exhibit 1, the graph has

Y-axis
the vertical axis on a graph

X-axis
the horizontal axis on a graph

four quadrants, or boxes. In this textbook, we will be primarily concerned with the shaded box in the upper-right corner. This portion of the graph deals exclusively with positive numbers. Always keep in mind that moving to the right on the horizontal axis and moving up along the vertical axis both lead to higher values.

Using Graphs and Charts

Exhibit 2 presents four common types of graphs. The pie chart in Exhibit 2(a) shows the revenues received from various taxes levied on households and corporations. Each slice in the pie chart represents the percentage of finances that are derived from different sources—for example, personal income taxes account for 43 percent of the federal government's tax revenues. Therefore, pie charts are used to show the relative size of various quantities that add up to 100 percent.

Exhibit 2(b) is a **bar graph** that shows the unemployment rate by age and sex in the United States. The height of the line represents the unemployment rate. Bar graphs are used to show a comparison of quantities.

Exhibit 2(c) is a **time-series graph**. This type of graph shows changes in the value of a variable over time. This visual tool allows us to observe important trends over a certain time period. In Exhibit 2(c) we see a graph that shows trends in the inflation rate over time. The horizontal axis shows us the passage of time, and the vertical axis shows us the inflation rate (annual percent change). From the graph, we can see the trends in the inflation rate from 1961 to 2005.

Exhibit 2(d) is a scatter diagram. Each point on this graph represents a point that corresponds to an actual observation along the *X*-axis and *Y*-axis. It shows the relationship of one variable to another. A linear curve is usually fitted to the scatter of points—it

pie chart
visual display showing the relative size of various quantities that add up to 100 percent

bar graph
visual display showing the comparison of quantities

time-series graph
visual tool to show changes in a variable's value over time

scatter diagram
a graph showing the relationship of one variable to another

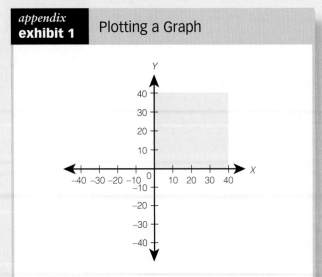

appendix
exhibit 1   Plotting a Graph

In the upper-right corner, we see that the graph includes a positive figure for the *Y*-axis and the *X*-axis. As we move to the right along the horizontal axis, the numerical values increase. As we move up along the vertical axis, the numerical values increase.

appendix
exhibit 2   Pie Chart, Bar Graph, Time-Series Graph, and Scatter Diagram

a. Pie Chart—Tax Revenues—Federal Government

Other Taxes
7%

Social Security Tax
(Payroll Tax)
38%

Personal Income Taxes
44%

Corporate Income Taxes
11%

SOURCE: Economic Report of the President and Bureau
of Economic Analysis, 2009.

b. Bar Graph—U.S. Unemployment, by Sex and Age

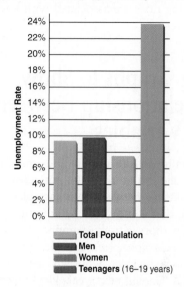

Total Population
Men
Women
Teenagers (16–19 years)

c. Time-Series Graph—Inflation Rate

SOURCE: Bureau of Labor Statistics, August 2009.

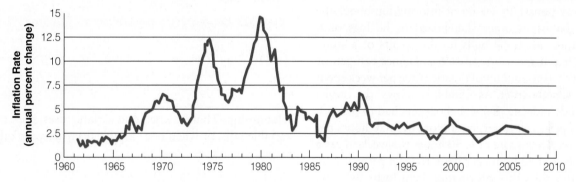

SOURCE: Bureau of Labor Statistics, 2009.

d. Scatter Diagram—Saving Rates and GDP Growth

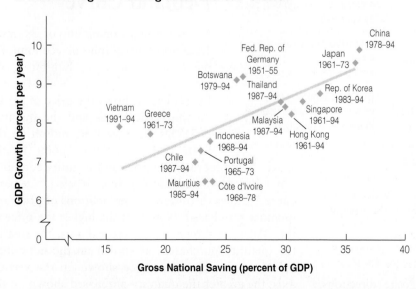

SOURCE: World Bank, World
Development Report, 1996, Oxford
University Press, 1996. Republished
with permission of the World Bank,
from World Bank Development
Report 1996; permission conveyed
through Copyright Clearance
Center, Inc.

represents the best fit for the observations. In this case, the graph shows that rates of economic growth are positively associated with saving rates. Higher saving rates lead to greater economic growth rates, and lower saving rates are associated with lower economic growth rates.

Using Graphs to Show the Relationship Between Two Variables

Even though the graphs and chart in Exhibit 2 are important, they do not allow us to show the relationship between two variables (a **variable** is something that is measured by a number, such as your height). To more closely examine the structures and functions of graphs, let's consider the story of Josh, an avid skateboarder who has aspirations of winning the Z Games next year. He knows that to get there, he'll need to put in many hours of practice. But how many hours? In search of information about the practice habits of other skateboarders, he logs onto the Internet, where he pulls up the results of a study that looked at the score of each Z Games competitor in relation to the amount of practice time per week spent by each skateboarder. As Exhibit 3 shows, the results of the study indicate that skateboarders had to practice 10 hours per week to receive a score of 4, 20 hours per week to receive a score of 6, 30 hours per week to get a score of 8, and 40 hours per week to get a perfect score of 10. How does this information help Josh? By using a graph, he can more clearly understand the relationship between practice time and overall score.

A Positive Relationship

The study on scores and practice times reveals what is called a direct relationship, also called a positive relationship. A positive relationship means that the variables change in the same direction. That is, an increase in one variable (practice time) is accompanied by an increase in the other variable (overall score), or a decrease in one variable (practice time) is accompanied by a decrease in the other variable (overall score). In short, the variables change in the same direction.

A Negative Relationship

When two variables change in opposite directions, they have an inverse relationship, also called a **negative**

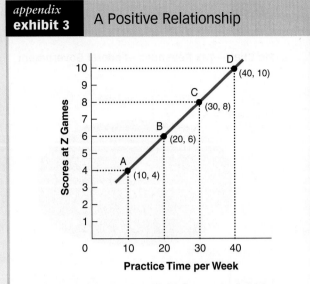

appendix
exhibit 3   A Positive Relationship

The skateboarders' practice times and scores in the competition are plotted on the graph. Each participant is represented by a point. The graph shows that those skateboarders who practiced the most scored the highest, which indicates a positive, or direct, relationship.

variable something that is measured by a number, such as your height

negative relationship when two variables change in opposite directions

positive relationship when two variables change in the same direction

relationship. That is, when one variable rises, the other variable falls, or when one variable decreases, the other variable increases.

The Graph of a Demand Curve

Let's now examine one of the most important graphs in economics—the demand curve. In Exhibit 4, we see Emily's individual demand curve for DVDs. It shows the price of DVDs on the vertical axis and the quantity of DVDs purchased per month on the horizontal axis. Every point in the space shown represents a price and quantity combination. The downward-sloping line, labeled "Demand curve," shows the different combinations of price and quantity purchased. Note that the higher the price of the DVDs, as shown on the vertical axis, the smaller the quantity purchased, as shown on the horizontal axis, and the lower the price shown on the vertical axis, the greater the quantity purchased shown on the horizontal axis.

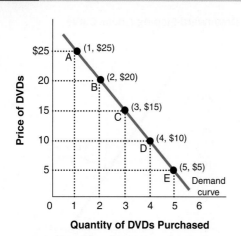

A Negative Relationship

The downward slope of the curve means that price and quantity purchased are inversely, or negatively, related: When one increases, the other decreases. That is, moving down along the demand curve from point A to point E, we see that as the price falls, the quantity purchased increases. Moving up along the demand curve from point E to point A, we see that as the price increases, the quantity purchased falls.

In Exhibit 4, we see that moving up the vertical price axis from the origin, the price of DVDs increases from $5 to $25 in increments of $5. Moving out along the horizontal quantity axis, the quantity purchased increases from zero to five DVDs per month. Point A represents a price of $25 and a quantity of one DVD, point B represents a price of $20 and a quantity of two DVDs, point C a price of $15 and a quantity of three DVDs, and so on. When we connect all the points, we have what economists call a curve. As you can see, curves are sometimes drawn as straight lines for ease of illustration. Moving down along the curve, we see that as the price falls, a greater quantity is demanded; moving up the curve to higher prices, a smaller quantity is demanded. That is, when DVDs become less expensive, Emily buys more DVDs. When DVDs become more expensive, Emily buys fewer DVDs, perhaps choosing to go to the movies or buy a pizza instead.

Using Graphs to Show the Relationship Among Three Variables

Although only two variables are shown on the axes, graphs can be used to show the relationship among three variables. For example, say we add a third variable—income—to our earlier example. Our three variables are now income, price, and quantity purchased. If Emily's income rises—say she gets a raise at work—she is now able and willing to buy more DVDs than before at each possible price. As a result, the whole demand curve shifts outward (to the right) compared with the old curve. That is, the new income gives her more money to use buying more DVDs. This shift is seen in the graph in Exhibit 5(a). On the other hand, if her income falls—say she quits her job to go back to school—she would have less income to buy DVDs. A decrease in this variable causes the whole demand curve to shift inward (to the left) compared with the old curve. This shift is seen in the graph in Exhibit 5(b).

The Difference Between a Movement Along and a Shift in the Curve

It is important to remember the difference between a movement between one point and another along a curve and a shift in the whole curve. A change in one of the variables on the graph, like price or quantity purchased, will cause a movement along the curve, say from point A to point B, as shown in Exhibit 6. A change in one of the variables not shown (held constant in order to show only the relationship between price and quantity), such as income in our example, will cause the whole curve to shift. The change from D_1 to D_2 in Exhibit 6 shows such a shift.

slope
the ratio of rise (change in the *Y* variable) over run (change in the *X* variable)

Slope

In economics, we sometimes refer to the steepness of a line or curve on a graph as the slope. A slope can be either positive (upward sloping) or negative (downward sloping). A curve that is downward sloping represents an inverse, or negative, relationship between the two variables and slants downward from left to right, as seen in Exhibit 7(a). A curve that is upward sloping represents a direct, or positive, relationship between the two variables and slants upward from left to right, as seen in Exhibit 7(b). The numeric value of the slope shows the number of units of change of the *Y*-axis variable for each unit of change in the *X*-axis variable. Slope provides the direction (positive or negative) as well as the magnitude of the relationship between the two variables.

Measuring the Slope of a Linear Curve

A straight-line curve is called a linear curve. The slope of a linear curve between two points measures the

appendix
exhibit 5 Shifting a Curve

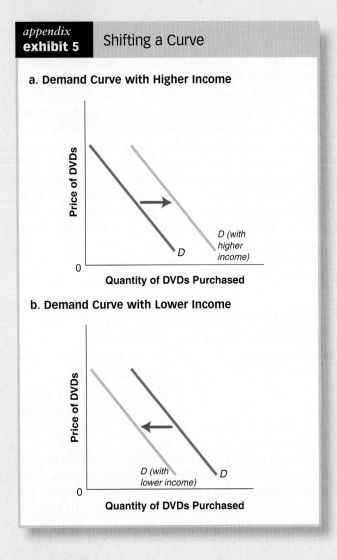

a. Demand Curve with Higher Income

b. Demand Curve with Lower Income

appendix
exhibit 7 Downward- and Upward-Sloping Linear Curve

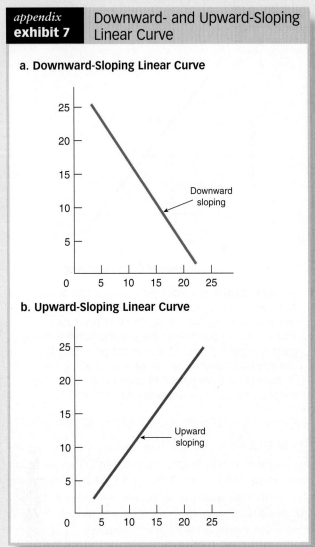

a. Downward-Sloping Linear Curve

b. Upward-Sloping Linear Curve

appendix
exhibit 6 Shifts Versus Movements

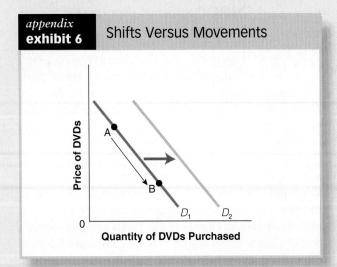

relative rates of change of two variables. Specifically, the slope of a linear curve can be defined as the ratio of the change in the *Y* value to the change in the *X* value. The slope can also be expressed as the ratio of the rise over the run, where the rise is the vertical change and the run is the horizontal change.

Exhibit 8 shows two linear curves, one with a positive slope and one with a negative slope. In Exhibit 8(a), the slope of the positively sloped linear curve from point A to B is 1/2, because the rise is 1 (from 2 to 3) and the run is 2 (from 1 to 3). In Exhibit 8(b), the negatively sloped linear curve has a slope of −4: A rise of −8 (a fall of 8, from 10 to 2) and a run of 2 (from 2 to 4) gives us a slope of −8/2, or −4. Notice the appropriate signs on the slopes: The negatively sloped line carries a minus sign and the positively sloped line, a plus sign.

Finding the Slope of a Nonlinear Curve

In Exhibit 9, we show the slope of a nonlinear curve. A nonlinear curve is a line that actually curves. Here the slope varies from point to point along the curve.

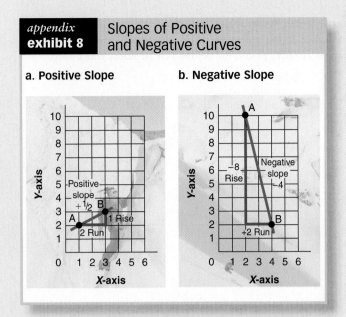

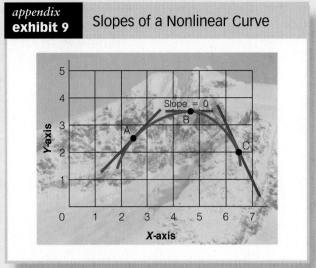

However, we can find the slope of this curve at any given point by drawing a straight line tangent to that point on the curve. A tangency is when a straight line just touches the curve without actually crossing it. At point A, we see that the positively sloped line that is tangent to the curve has a slope of 1: the line rises 1 and runs 1. At point B, the line is horizontal, so it has

zero slope. At point C, we see a slope of –2, because the negatively sloped line has a rise of –2 (a fall of 2) for every run of 1.

Remember, many students have problems with economics simply because they fail to understand graphs, so make sure that you understand this material before going on to Chapter 2.

Key Terms and Concepts

Y-axis 28
X-axis 28
pie chart 28
bar graph 28

time-series graph 28
scatter diagram 28
variable 30
positive relationship 30

negative relationship 30
slope 31

Problems:

1. The following table gives the prices and quantity demanded of oranges (pounds) for the week of December 10–16.

Price ($/lb.)	Quantity Demanded (lbs.)
$0.80	0
0.70	3
0.60	4
0.50	5
0.40	7
0	

a. Plot the data from the table into a graph.
b. Is it a positive or negative relationship? Explain.

Answer

We have created a negatively sloped demand curve. That is, the price and quantity demanded of oranges are inversely related:

$$\uparrow P \Rightarrow \downarrow Q_D \text{ and } \downarrow P \Rightarrow \uparrow Q_D$$

Individual demand curve of a customer for oranges of a certain grade, Week of December 10–16.

The demand curve records the pounds of oranges a consumer desires at various prices in a given week, holding all other factors fixed. Because the individual desires more oranges at lower prices, the demand curve slopes downward.

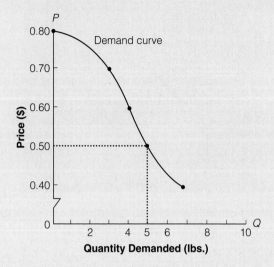

2. Which of the following will lead to a positive relationship? A negative relationship?
   a. Hours studied and grade in a course
   b. The price of ice cream and the amount of ice cream purchased
   c. The amount of seasonal snowfall and the sale of snow shovels

   Answer

   a. positive
   b. negative
   c. positive

3. Below is Emily's demand curve for iTunes. How do we add income, a third variable, to price and quantity purchased on our graph? Using a graph, explain what would happen if Emily had an increase in income. What would happen if Emily has a decrease in income?

   Answer

      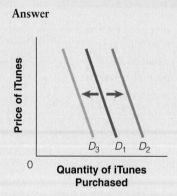

   When income increases, Emily can purchase more at each and every price—a rightward shift from D_1 to D_2. If Emily's income falls, her demand will shift leftward from D_1 to D_3.

4. Use the information in the following table to plot a graph. Is it a positive or negative relationship? What is the slope?

X	Y
1	2
2	4
3	6
4	8
5	10

Answer

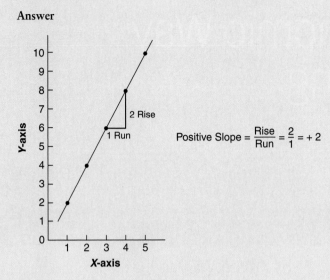

$$\text{Positive Slope} = \frac{\text{Rise}}{\text{Run}} = \frac{2}{1} = +2$$

5. What is a pie chart? Bar graph? Time-series graph? Scatter diagram?

Answer

Pie charts are used to show the relative size of various quantities that add up to 100 percent. Bar graphs are used to show a comparison of quantities of similar items. Time-series graphs allow us to see important trends over a period of time. Scatter diagrams display points of actual observations. Generally, a curve is fitted to the scatter of points to show a trend.

2 The Economic Way of Thinking

Studying economics may teach you how to "think better," because economics helps develop a disciplined method of thinking about problems.

A student of economics becomes aware that, at a basic level, much of economic life involves choosing one course of action rather than another—making choices among our conflicting wants and desires in a world of scarcity. Economics provides insights about how to intelligently evaluate these options and determine the most appropriate choices in given situations. *Most of economics really involves knowing certain principles well and knowing when and how to apply them.*

This chapter presents some important tools that will help you understand the economic way of thinking. The economic way of thinking provides a logical framework for organizing and analyzing your understanding of a broad set of issues, many of which do not even seem directly related to economics as you now know it.

The basic ideas that you learn in this chapter will occur repeatedly throughout the text. If you develop a good understanding of these principles and master the problem-solving skills inherent in them, they will serve you well for the rest of your life. Learning to think like an economist takes time. Like most disciplines, economics has its own specialized vocabulary, including such terms as *elasticity, comparative advantage, supply and demand, deadweight loss,* and *consumer surplus.* Learning economics requires more than picking up this new terminology; however, it also involves using its powerful tools to improve your understanding of a whole host of issues in the world around you. ■

Scarcity

* What are goods and services?
* What are tangible and intangible goods?
* What are economic goods?

Scarcity

Economics is concerned primarily with **scarcity**—how we satisfy our unlimited wants in a world of limited resources. We may want "essential" items such as food, clothing, schooling, and health care. We may want many other items, such as vacations, cars, computers, and concert tickets. We may want more friendship, love, knowledge, and so on. We also may have many goals—perhaps an A in this class, a college education, and a great job. Unfortunately, people are not able to fulfill all their wants and desires, material and nonmaterial. And as long as human wants exceed available resources, scarcity will exist.

Don't confuse scarcity with rarity. Something may be rare, but if it is not desirable, it is not scarce. You won't find many baseball cards of my son (rare)—about 10—but at the same time, few people outside of the immediate family want one. Therefore, the card is rare but not scarce. However, if he becomes a major league star, those cards could become scarce—rare and desirable.

All the things you see here—grass, trees, rocks, animals—are considered land to economists.

COURTESY OF ROBERT L. SEXTON

Scarcity and Resources

The scarce resources used in the production of goods and services can be grouped into four categories: labor, land, capital, and entrepreneurship.

Labor is the total of both physical and mental effort expended by people in the production of goods and services. The services of a teacher, nurse, cosmetic surgeon, professional golfer, and an electrician all fall under the general category of labor.

Land includes the "gifts of nature" or the natural resources used in the production of goods and services. Economists consider land to include trees, animals, water, minerals, and so on, along with the physical space we normally think of as land.

scarcity
exists when human wants (material and nonmaterial) exceed available resources

labor
the physical and human effort used in the production of goods and services

land
the natural resources used in the production of goods and services

capital
the equipment and structures used to produce goods and services

human capital
the productive knowledge and skill people receive from education, on-the-job training, health, and other factors that increase productivity

entrepreneurship
the process of combining labor, land, and capital to produce goods and services

Capital is the equipment and structures used to produce goods and services. Office buildings, tools, machines, and factories are all considered capital goods. When we invest in factories, machines, research and development, or education, we increase the potential to create more goods and services in the future. Capital also includes **human capital**—the productive knowledge and skill people receive from education and on-the-job training.

Entrepreneurship is the process of combining labor, land, and capital to produce goods and services. Entrepreneurs make the tough and risky decisions about what and how to produce goods and services. Entrepreneurs are always looking for new ways to improve production techniques or to create new products. They are lured by the chance of making a profit. It is this opportunity to make a profit that leads entrepreneurs to take risks.

However, not every entrepreneur is a Bill Gates (Microsoft) or a Henry Ford (Ford Motor Company). In some sense, we are all entrepreneurs when we try new products or when we find better ways to manage our households or our study time. Rather than money, then, our profits might take the form of greater enjoyment, additional time for recreation, or better grades.

What Are Goods and Services?

Goods are the items that we value or desire. Goods tend to be **tangible**—objects that can be seen, held, heard, tasted, or smelled. But other goods that we cannot reach out and touch are called intangible goods. **Intangible goods** include fairness for all, friendship, leisure, knowledge, security, prestige, respect, and health.

Services are intangible acts for which people are willing to pay, such as legal counsel, medical care, and education. Services are intangible because they are less overtly visible, but they are certainly no less valuable than goods.

All goods and services, whether tangible or intangible, are produced from scarce resources and can be subjected to economic analysis. Scarce goods created from scarce resources are called **economic goods**. These goods are *desirable but limited* in supply. Without enough economic goods for all of us, we are forced to compete. That is, scarcity ultimately leads to competition for the available goods and services, a subject we will return to often in the text.

What Are Bads?

In contrast to goods, **bads** are those items that we do not desire or want. For most people, garbage, pollution, weeds, and crime are bads. People tend to eliminate or minimize bads, so they will often pay to have bads, like garbage, removed. The elimination of the bad—garbage removal, for example—is a good.

Are Those Who Want More Greedy?

We all want more tangible and intangible goods and services. In economics, we assume that more goods lead to greater satisfaction. However, just

goods
items we value or desire

tangible goods
items we value or desire that we can reach out and touch

intangible goods
goods that we cannot reach out and touch, such as friendship and knowledge

services
intangible items of value provided to consumers, such as education

economic goods
scarce goods created from scarce resources—goods that are desirable but limited in supply

bads
items that we do not desire or want, where less is preferred to more, like terrorism, smog, or poison oak.

because economics assumes that we want more goods does not mean that economics also assumes that we are selfish and greedy. That is, scarcity does not result from people just wanting more for themselves. Many people give much of their income and time to charitable or religious organizations. The ways people allocate their income and time reveal their preferences. The fact that people are willing to give up their money and time for causes that they believe to be important reveals quite conclusively that charitable endeavors are a desirable good. Clearly, then, many desires, such as the desire to build new friendships or help charities, can hardly be defined as selfish; yet they are desires that many people share. In other words, *self-interest* is not the same as *selfishness* or *greed*. Indeed, in a world without scarcity, we would have no use for generosity.

Does Everyone Face Scarcity?

We all face scarcity because we cannot have all the goods and services we desire. However, because we all have different wants and desires,

© STEVE DiPAOLA/REUTERS/CORBIS

Not even millionaire lottery winners can escape scarcity. The problem is that as we get more affluent, we learn of new luxuries to provide us with satisfaction. Even lottery winners may become less content as the excitement wears off and they begin looking for new satisfactions. A 78-year-old man from Michigan just won his second $1 million scratch-off lottery. He says, "I am now going for three."

scarcity affects everyone differently. For example, a child in a developing country may face a scarcity of food and clean drinking water, while a rich man may face a scarcity of garage space for his growing antique car collection. Likewise, a harried middle-class working mother may find time for exercise particularly scarce, while a pharmaceutical company may be concerned with the scarcity of the natural resources it uses in its production process. Its effects may vary, but no one can escape scarcity.

We often hear it said of rich people that "He has everything" or "She can buy anything she wants." Actually, even the richest person must live with scarcity and must, at some point, choose one want or desire over another. And of course, we all have only 24 hours in a day! The problem is that as we get more affluent, we learn of new luxuries to provide us with satisfaction. Wealth, then, creates a new set of wants to be satisfied. No evidence indicates that people would not find a valuable use for additional income, no matter

how rich they became. Even the wealthy individual who decides to donate all her money to charity faces the constraints of scarcity. If she had greater resources, she could do still more for others.

Will Scarcity Ever Be Eradicated?

It is probably clear by now that scarcity never has and never will be eradicated. The same creativity that develops new methods to produce goods and services in greater quantities also reveals new wants. Fashions are always changing. Clothes and shoes that are "in" one year will likely be "out" the next. New wants quickly replace old ones. It is also quite possible that over a period of time, a rising quantity of goods and services will not increase human happiness. Why? Because our wants may grow as fast—if not faster—than our ability to meet those wants.

SECTION CHECK

1. We all have many wants and goals.
2. Scarcity exists when our wants exceed the available resources.
3. Scarce resources can be categorized as: land (all of our natural resources), labor (the physical and mental efforts expended in the production of goods and services), capital (the equipment and structures used to produce goods and services, and the productive knowledge and skill people receive from education and on-the-job training), and entrepreneurship (the process of combining land, labor, and capital into production of goods and services).
4. Goods and services are things that we value.
5. Goods can be tangible (physical) or intangible (love, compassion, and intelligence).
6. Economic goods are goods created from limited resources.
7. We all face scarcity—rich and poor alike.
8. Our wants grow over time, so scarcity will never be eliminated.

---

1. What must be true for something to be an economic good?
2. Does wanting more tangible and intangible goods and services make us selfish?
3. Why does scarcity affect everyone?
4. How and why does scarcity affect each of us differently?
5. Why do you think economists often refer to training that increases the quality of workers' skills as "adding to human capital"?
6. What are some of the ways that students act as entrepreneurs as they seek higher grades?
7. Why might sunshine be scarce in Seattle but not in Tucson?
8. Why can't a country become so technologically advanced that its citizens won't have to choose?

SECTION 2.2   Choices, Costs, and Trade-Offs

* Why do we have to make choices?
* What do we give up when we have to choose?
* Why are "free" lunches not free?

Scarcity Forces Us to Choose

Each of us may want a nice home, two luxury cars, wholesome and good-tasting food, a personal trainer, and a therapist, all enjoyed in a pristine environment with zero pollution. If we had unlimited resources, and thus an ability to produce all the goods and services everyone wants, we would not have to choose among those desires. However, we all face scarcity, and as a consequence, we must make choices. If we did not have to make meaningful economic choices, the study of economics would not be necessary. The essence of economics is to understand fully the implications that scarcity has for wise decision making.

Trade-Offs

In a world of scarcity, we all face trade-offs. If you spend more time at work you might give up an opportunity to go shopping at the mall or watch your favorite TV show. Or when you decide how to spend your income, buying a new car may mean you have to forgo a summer vacation. Businesses have trade-offs too. If a farmer chooses to plant his land in cotton this year, he gives up the opportunity to plant his land in wheat. If a firm decides to produce only cars, it gives up the opportunity to use those resources to produce refrigerators or something else that people value. Society, too, must make trade-offs. For example, the federal government faces trade-offs when it comes to spending tax revenues; additional resources used to enhance the environment may come at the expense of additional resources to provide health, education or national defense.

> **opportunity cost**
> the value of the best forgone alternative that was not chosen

To Choose Is to Lose

Every choice involves a cost. The highest or best forgone opportunity resulting from a decision is called the **opportunity cost**. Another way to put it is that "to choose is to lose" or "an opportunity cost is an opportunity lost." To get more of anything that is desirable, you must accept less of something else that you also value.

For example, time spent exercising costs time that could be spent doing something else that is valuable—perhaps relaxing with friends or studying for an upcoming exam. One of the reasons drivers talk so much on their cell phones is because they have little else to do with their time while driving—a low opportunity cost. However, drivers using cell phones should pay attention; otherwise, they are giving up safety. Trade-offs are everywhere. The famous poet, Robert Frost, understood that to live is to choose. In his poem, "The Road Not Taken," he writes, "two roads diverged in a yellow wood, and sorry I could not travel both."

Bill Gates, Tiger Woods, and Oprah Winfrey all quit college to pursue their dreams. Tiger Woods dropped out of Stanford (an economics major) to join the PGA golf tour. Bill Gates dropped out of Harvard to start a software company. Oprah Winfrey dropped out of Tennessee State to pursue a career in broadcasting. At the early age of 19, she became the co-anchor of the evening news. Staying in school would have cost each of them millions of dollars. We cannot say it would have been the wrong decision to stay in school; but it would have been costly. Their opportunity cost of staying in school was high.

Money Prices and Costs

If you go to the store to buy groceries you have to pay for the items you bought. This amount is called the *money price*. It is an opportunity cost, because you could have used that money to purchase other goods or services. However, additional opportunity costs include the nonprice costs incurred to acquire the groceries—time spent getting to the grocery store, finding a parking place, actual shopping, and waiting in the checkout line. The nonprice costs are measured by assessing the sacrifice involved—the value you place on what you would have done with that time if you had not gone shopping. So the cost of grocery shopping is the price paid for the goods, plus the nonprice costs incurred. Or your concert ticket may have only been $50. But what if you had to wait in line for six hours in the freezing cold? Waiting and enduring the cold are costs too. Seldom are costs just dollars and cents. Shopping at a large discount store may save you on the money price, but cost you time waiting in long checkout lines. Also, buying food in bulk quantities may be less expensive per ounce, but cost inventory space in your pantry, or the food may spoil before it is eaten.

Remember that many costs do not involve money but are still costs. Do I major in economics or engineering? Do I go to Billy Madison University or Tech State University? Should I get an MBA now or work and wait a few years to go back to school?

Policy makers are unavoidably faced with opportunity costs too. Consider airline safety. Both money cost and time costs affect airline safety. New airline safety devices cost money (luggage inspection devices, smoke detectors, fuel tank safeguards, new radar equipment, and so on), and time costs are quite evident with the new security checks. Time waiting in line costs time doing something else that is valuable. New airline safety requirements could also actually cost lives. If the new safety equipment costs are passed on in the form of higher airline ticket prices, people may choose to travel by car, which is far more dangerous per mile traveled than by air. Opportunity costs are everywhere!

How often do people consider the full opportunity of raising a child to age 18? The obvious money costs include food, visits to the doctor, clothes, piano lessons, time spent at soccer practices, and so on. According to the Department of Agriculture, a middle-income family with a child born in 2007 can expect to spend about $270,000 for food, shelter, and other necessities to raise that child through age 17. Other substantial opportunity costs are incurred in rearing a child as well. Consider the opportunity cost of one parent choosing to give up his or her job to stay at home. For a parent who makes that choice, the time spent in child rearing is time that could have been used earning money and pursuing a career.

Is That Really a Free Lunch, a Freeway, or a Free Beach?

The expression "there's no such thing as a free lunch" clarifies the relationship between scarcity and opportunity cost. Suppose the school cafeteria is offering "free" lunches today. Although the lunch is free to you, is it really free from society's perspective?

The Opportunity Cost of Going to College or Having a Child

The average person often does not correctly calculate opportunity costs. For example, the (opportunity) cost of going to college includes not just the direct expenses of tuition and books. Of course, those expenses do involve an opportunity cost because the money used for books and tuition could be used to buy other things that you value. But what about the nonmoney costs? That is, going to college also includes the opportunity cost of your time. Specifically, the time spent going to school is time that could have been spent on a job earning, say, $30,000 over the course of an academic year. What about room and board? That aspect is a little tricky because you would presumably have to pay room and board whether you went to college or not. The relevant question may be how much more it costs you to live at school rather than at home (and living at home may have substantial nonmoney costs). Even if you stayed at home, your parents would sacrifice something; they could rent your room out or use the room for some other purpose such as storage, guest room, home office, a sibling's room, and so on.

COURTESY OF ROBERT L. SEXTON

You may think tuition, room and board are expensive! Now add the opportunity cost of your time—perhaps working during those nine months.

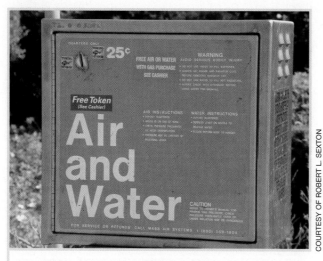

Is air free? How about clean air? Clean air is desirable but limited in cities—that is, it is a scarce good. How about air to a scuba diver? Or how about air to a climbing expedition on Mount Everest? What if you want to fill your tires at this gas station but you didn't buy gas? So in many situations, air is not free; it is scarce.

The answer is no, because some of society's scarce resources will have been used in the preparation of the lunch. The issue is whether the resources that went into creating that lunch could have been used to produce something else of value. Clearly, the scarce resources that went into the production of the lunch—the labor and materials (food-service workers, lettuce, meat, plows, tractors, fertilizer, and so forth)—could have been used in other ways. They had an opportunity cost and thus were not free.

Do not confuse free with a zero monetary price. A number of goods—freeways, free beaches, and free libraries, for instance—do not cost consumers money, but they are still scarce. Few things are free in the sense that they use none of society's scarce resources. So what does a free lunch really mean? It is, technically speaking, a "subsidized" lunch—a lunch using society's scarce resources, but one that the person receiving it does not have to pay for personally.

SECTION CHECK

1. Scarcity means we all have to make choices.
2. When we are forced to choose, we give up the next highest-valued alternative.
3. Opportunity cost is what you give up when you make a choice.

1. Would we have to make choices if we had unlimited resources?
2. What is given up when we make a choice?
3. What do we mean by opportunity cost?
4. Why is there no such thing as a free lunch?
5. Why was the opportunity cost of staying in college higher for Tiger Woods than for most undergraduates?
6. Why is the opportunity cost of time spent getting an MBA typically lower for a 22-year-old straight out of college than for a 45-year-old experienced manager?

SECTION 2.3 Marginal Thinking

* What do we mean by marginal thinking?
* What is the rule of rational choice?
* Why do we use the word *expected* with marginal benefits and costs?

Many Choices We Face Involve Marginal Thinking

Some decisions are "all or nothing," like whether to start a new business or go to work for someone else, or whether to attend graduate school or take a job. But many choices we face involve how *much* of something to do rather than whether to do something. It is not *whether* you eat but *how much* you eat. Or, how many caffe lattes will I buy this week? Or, how often do I change the oil in my car? Or how much of my check do I spend, and how much do I save? Your instructors hope that the question is not *whether* you study this semester but *how much* you study. You might think to yourself, "If I studied a little more, I might be able to improve my grade," or "If I had a little better concentration when I was studying, I could improve my grade." That is, spending more time has an additional expected benefit (a higher grade) and an additional expected cost (giving up time to do something else that is valuable, such as watching TV or sleeping). These examples reflect what economists call **marginal thinking** because the focus is on the additional, or marginal, choices available to you. Or think of marginal as the edge—marginal decisions are made around the edge of what you are currently doing. Marginal choices involve the effects of adding or subtracting from the current situation. In short, they are the small (or large) incremental changes to a plan of action.

Businesses are constantly engaged in marginal thinking. For example, firms have to decide whether the additional (marginal) revenue received from increasing production is greater than the marginal cost of that production.

Always watch out for the difference between average and marginal costs. Suppose an airline had 10 unoccupied seats on a flight from Los Angeles to New York, and the average cost was $400 per seat (the total cost divided by the number of seats—$100,000/250). If 10 people are waiting on standby, each willing to pay $300, should the airline sell them the tickets? Yes! The unoccupied seats earn nothing for the airline. What are the additional (marginal) costs of a few more passengers? The marginal costs are minimal—slight wear and tear on the airplane, handling some extra baggage, and 10 extra in-flight meals. In this case, thinking at the margin can increase total profits, even if it means selling at less than the average cost of production.

Another good example of marginal thinking is an auction. Prices are bid up marginally as the auctioneer calls out one price after another. When bidders view the new price (the marginal cost) to be greater than the value they place on the good (the marginal benefit), they withdraw from further bidding.

In trying to make themselves better off, people alter their behavior if the expected marginal benefits from doing so outweigh the expected marginal costs, which is the **rule of rational choice**. Economic theory is often called marginal analysis because it assumes that people are always weighing the expected marginal benefits against the expected marginal costs. The term *expected* is used with *marginal benefits* and *marginal costs* because the world is uncertain in many important

respects, so the actual result of changing behavior may not always make people better off—but on average it will. However, as a matter of rationality, people are assumed to engage only in behavior that they think ahead of time will make them better off. That is, individuals will only pursue an activity if their expected marginal benefits are greater than their expected marginal costs of pursuing that activity one step further, $E(MB) > E(MC)$.

This fairly unrestrictive and realistic view of individuals seeking self-betterment can be used to analyze a variety of social phenomena.

Suppose that you have to get up for an 8 A.M. class but have been up very late. When the alarm goes off at 7 A.M. you are weighing the marginal benefits and marginal costs of an extra 15 minutes of sleep. If you perceive the marginal benefits of 15 additional minutes of sleep to be greater than the marginal costs of those extra minutes, you may choose to hit the snooze button. Or perhaps you may decide to blow off class completely. But it's unlikely that you will choose that action if it's the day of the final exam—because it is now likely that the **net benefits** (the difference between the expected marginal benefits and the expected marginal costs) of skipping class have changed. When people have opportunities to make themselves better off they usually take them. And they will continue to seek those opportunities as long as they expect a net benefit from doing so.

The rule of rational choice is simply the rule of being sensible, and most economists believe that individuals act *as if* they are sensible and apply the rule of rational choice to their daily lives. It is a rule that can help us understand our decisions to study, walk, shop, exercise, clean house, cook, and perform just about every other action.

It is also a rule that we will continue to use throughout the text. Because whether it is consumers, producers, or policy makers, they all must compare the expected marginal benefits and the expected marginal cost to determine the best level to consume, produce, or provide public programs.

Zero Pollution Would Be Too Costly

Let's use the concept of marginal thinking to evaluate pollution levels. We all know the benefits of a cleaner environment, but what would we have to give up—that is, what marginal costs would we have to incur—to achieve zero pollution? A lot! You could not drive a

marginal thinking
focusing on the additional, or marginal, choices; marginal choices involve the effects of adding or subtracting, from the current situation, the small (or large) incremental changes to a plan of action

rule of rational choice
individuals will pursue an activity if the expected marginal benefits are greater than the expected marginal costs

net benefit
the difference between the expected marginal benefits and the expected marginal costs

POLICY application

ECONOMICS AND FOOTBALL: WEIGHING THE BENEFITS AND COSTS OF GOING FOR IT ON FOURTH DOWN

With just over five minutes to play in yesterday's game against the New York Jets, the Washington Redskins found themselves on their own 23-yard line facing a fourth and one. The team, which was ahead by just three points, elected to do what teams normally do in such situations: They played it safe and punted rather than try to keep the drive alive.

The Jets promptly came back to kick a field goal, tying the game and sending it into overtime. While this particular story had a happy ending for Washington, which won, 23-20, it illustrated the value of an analysis by David Romer, an economist at the University of California, who has concluded that football teams are far too conservative in play calling in fourth-down situations.

You don't have to be particularly interested in sports to find Romer's conclusion intriguing: His hunch about human behavior in general was that although people say they have a certain goal and are willing to do everything they can to achieve it, their actual behavior regularly departs from the optimal path to reach that goal.

In his analysis of football teams, Romer specifically looked at a single question -- whether teams should punt or kick the football on fourth down, or take a chance and run or throw the ball. Romer's calculations don't necessarily tell teams what to do in specific situations such as yesterday's game. But on average, teams that take the risk seem to win more often than lose.

Data from a large number of NFL games show that coaches rarely follow what Romer's calculations predict would give them the best chance of victory. While fans often suggest more aggressive play calling, even fans usually don't go as far as the economist does—his calculations show that teams should regularly be going for it on fourth down, even if it is early in the game, even if the score is tied, and even if the ball is on their own side of the field.

Romer's calculations have been backed up by independent analyses. Coaches have not raised a serious challenge to Romer's analysis, but they have simply ignored his finding.

New England Patriots coach Bill Belichick is among those who has said he agrees with Romer, and Belichick happens to be one of the more successful coaches in the league. Two Sundays ago, as the Patriots were piling up an astronomical score against Washington, Belichick took a chance on a fourth-down play and got his team seven points instead of the three he might have gotten had the team tried a field goal.

When asked by reporters why he took the chance, Belichick's response was the response of someone who really means what he says about maximizing points: "What do you want us to do, kick a field goal?"

Owners and fans have been receptive to Romer's ideas. However, in informal conversations Romer has had with the coaching staffs of various teams, the economist said he has been told to mind his own business in the ivory tower.

Indeed, since Romer wrote his paper a couple of years ago, NFL coaches seem to have gotten even more conservative in their play calling, which the economist attributes to their unwillingness to follow the advice of an academic, however useful it might be. . . .

MIKE BLAKE/REUTERS/LANDOV

POLICY
application

"It used to be that going for it on fourth down was the macho thing to do," Romer said. But after his findings were widely publicized in sports circles, he said: "Now going for it on fourth down is the egghead thing to do. Would you rather be macho or an egghead?"

The interesting question raised by Romer's research applies to a range of settings that have nothing to do with sports. Why do coaches persist in doing something that is less than optimal, when they say their only goal is to win? One theory that Romer has heard is that coaches—like generals, stock fund directors and managers in general—actually have different goals than the people they lead and the people they must answer to. Everyone wants to win, but managers are held to different standards than followers when they lose, especially when they lose after trying something that few others are doing.

consider this:

Coaches must weigh the expected marginal benefits and costs of "going for it" on fourth down. So why don't coaches go for it more often if the data suggests that teams should take more risks? Does Coach Belichick take more risks because he was an economics major in college and has figured it out? Or is it because coaches tend to be more risk averse than their fans and owners because coaches are held to different standards when they lose? So coaches often do what other coaches do and play it safe and punt.

© TIM McGUIRE/CORBIS

Even thrill seekers would likely slow down if fines were higher and/or law enforcement were increased, because such measures would alter the driver's cost-benefit calculation for reckless driving (as would bad brakes, bald tires, and poor visibility). On the other hand, compulsory seat belts and airbags would also alter behavior, because they change the driver's incentives. Seat belts and airbags make accidents less costly, by reducing the chance of serious injury or death; thus they reduce the benefit to safe driving, causing some motorists to drive more recklessly.

car, fly in a plane, or even ride a bicycle, especially if everybody else were riding bikes, too (because congestion is a form of pollution). How would you get to school or work, or go to the movies or the grocery store? Everyone would have to grow their own food because transporting, storing, and producing food uses machinery and equipment that pollute. And even growing your own food would be a problem because many plants emit natural pollutants. We could go on and on. The point is *not* that we shouldn't be concerned about the environment; rather, we have to weigh the expected marginal benefits of a cleaner environment against the expected marginal costs of a cleaner environment. This discussion is not meant to say the environment should not be cleaner, only that zero pollution levels would be far too costly in terms of what we would have to give up.

Optimal (Best) Levels of Safety

Like pollution, crime and safety can have optimal (or best) levels that are greater than zero. Take crime. What would it cost society to have zero crime? It would be prohibitively costly to divert a tremendous amount of our valuable resources toward the complete elimination of crime. In fact, it would be impossible to eliminate crime totally. Even reducing crime significantly would be costly. Because lower crime rates are costly, society must decide how much it is willing to give up. The additional resources for crime prevention can only come from limited resources, which could be used to produce something else the people may value even more.

The same is true for safer products. Nobody wants defective tires on their cars, or cars that are unsafe and roll over at low speeds. However, optimal amounts of safety that are greater than zero are available. The issue is not safe versus unsafe products but rather *how much* safety we want. It is not risk versus no-risk but rather *how much* risk we are willing to take. Additional safety can only come at higher costs. To make all products perfectly safe would be impossible, so we must weigh the benefits and costs

of safer products. In fact, according to one study by Sam Peltzman, a University of Chicago economist, additional safety regulations in cars (mandatory safety belts and padded dashboards) in the late 1960s may have had little impact on highway fatalities. Peltzman found that making cars safer led to more reckless driving and more accidents. The safety regulations did result in fewer deaths per automobile accident, but the total number of deaths remained unchanged because more accidents occurred.

Reckless driving has a benefit in the form of getting somewhere more quickly, but it can also have a cost—an accident or even a fatality. Most people will compare the marginal benefits and marginal costs of safer driving and make the choices that they believe will get them to their destination safely.

SECTION CHECK

1. Economists are usually interested in the effects of additional, or marginal, changes in a given situation.
2. People try to make themselves better off.
3. People make decisions based on what they expect to happen.
4. The rule of rational choice states that individuals will pursue an activity if they expect the marginal benefits to be greater than the marginal costs, or $E(MB) > E(MC)$.
5. The optimal (best) levels of pollution, crime, and safety are greater than zero.

---

1. What are marginal choices? Why does economics focus on them?
2. What is the rule of rational choice?
3. How could the rule of rational choice be expressed in terms of net benefits?
4. Why does rational choice involve expectations?
5. Why do students often stop taking lecture notes when a professor announces that the next few minutes of material will not be on any future test or assignment?
6. If you decide to speed to get to a doctor's appointment and then get in an accident due to speeding, does your decision to speed invalidate the rule of rational choice? Why or why not?
7. If pedestrians felt far safer using crosswalks to cross the street, how could adding crosswalks increase the number of pedestrian accidents?
8. Imagine driving a car with daggers sticking out of the steering wheel—pointing directly at your chest. Would you drive more safely? Why?

SECTION 2.4 Incentives Matter

* Can we predict how people will respond to changes in incentives?
* What are positive incentives?
* What are negative incentives?

People Respond to Changes in Incentives

Because most people are seeking opportunities to make themselves better off, they respond to changes in incentives. That is, they are reacting to changes in expected marginal benefits and expected marginal costs. In fact, much of human behavior can be explained and predicted as a response to incentives.

Positive and Negative Incentives

Almost all of economics can be reduced to incentive [$E(MB)$ versus $E(MC)$] stories, where consumers and producers are driven by incentives that affect expected costs or benefits. Prices, wages, profits, taxes, and subsidies are all examples of economic incentives. Incentives can be classified into two types: positive and negative. **Positive incentives** are those that either increase benefits or reduce costs and thus result in an increased level of the related activity or behavior. **Negative incentives,** on the other hand, either reduce benefits or increase costs, resulting in a decreased level of the related activity or behavior. For example, a tax on cars that emit lots of pollution (an increase in costs) would be a negative incentive that would lead to a reduction in emitted pollution. On the other hand, a subsidy (the opposite of a tax) on hybrid cars—part electric, part internal combustion—would be a positive incentive that would encourage greater production and consumption of hybrid cars. Human behavior is influenced in predictable ways by such changes in economic incentives, and economists use this information to predict what will happen when the benefits and costs of any choice are changed. In short, economists study the incentives and consequences of particular actions.

A subsidy on hybrid electric vehicles would be a positive incentive that would encourage greater production and consumption of these vehicles. A wide variety of incentives are offered at the federal, state, and local levels to encourage the expanded use of alternative-fuel vehicles.

STEPHEN SHAVER/UPI/LANDOV

positive incentive
an incentive that either reduces costs or increases benefits, resulting in an increase in an activity or behavior

negative incentive
an incentive that either increases costs or reduces benefits, resulting in a decrease in the activity or behavior

Because most people seek opportunities that make them better off, we can predict what will happen when incentives are changed. If salaries increase for engineers and decrease for MBAs, we would predict fewer people would go to graduate school in business and more would go into engineering. A permanent change to a much higher price of gasoline would lead us to expect fewer gas guzzlers on the highway. People who work on commission tend to work harder. If the price of downtown parking increased, we would predict that commuters would look for alternative methods to get to work that would save money. If households were taxed to conserve water economists would expect people to use less water and substantially less water than if they were simply asked to conserve water. Incentives matter.

in the news Incentives Matter

Estonia's Total Fertility Rate Increasing in Part Because of Government Program Encouraging Women to Give Birth

Estonia's total fertility rate has increased to an average of 1.5 children per woman from an average of 1.3 children per woman in the late 1990s, which could be the result of a government initiative aimed at sustaining the nation's population by providing women who have children with monthly stipends, the *Wall Street Journal* reports. The initiative, launched in 2004, was pushed after a 2001 world population report by the United Nations showed that Estonia was "one of the fastest-shrinking nations on earth," according to the *Journal*. Under the program, Estonia provides employed women who have children with their monthly salary, up to $1,560 monthly, over a 15-month period and unemployed women with $200 monthly. According to the *Journal*, the average monthly salary in Estonia is $650. The program has helped raise the total fertility rate because many employed women in the country could not afford to take time off from work to have children and because taking time off could have a negative impact on job security, according to the *Journal*. Some other factors that contributed to the lower total fertility rate include advances in birth control and ideas about personal freedom and happiness, the *Journal* reports. Estonia's program could serve as a model for other countries with low total fertility rates, according to the *Journal*. The Estonian government plans to continue formulating strategies—such as expanding preabortion counseling and subsidizing child-care providers and private day care—to help improve the total fertility rate, the *Journal* reports. According to the *Journal*, Estonia needs a total fertility rate of 2.1 children per woman to maintain its current population.

COURTESY OF ROBERT L. SEXTON

consider this:

Estonia is using positive incentives. But what would happen to birth rates if the tax deduction for dependents is removed? Although it would not change everyone's behavior, overall we would expect birth rates to fall if the tax deduction for dependents was eliminated, because it would then be more expensive for couples to raise children. We would also predict that couples would choose to have fewer children if the government imposed a birth tax on couples. Clearly, both of these policy changes would serve as negative incentives to having children, because both increase the costs of having kids. In essence, what either of these policies would do is change the benefit–cost equation, and altering this equation typically leads to predictable results.

SECTION CHECK

1. People respond to incentives in predictable ways.
2. A positive incentive decreases costs or increases benefits, thus encouraging consumption or production.
3. A negative incentive increases costs or reduces benefits, thus discouraging consumption or production.

---

1. What is the difference between positive incentives and negative incentives?
2. According to the rule of rational choice, would you do more or less of something if its expected marginal benefits increased? Why?
3. According to the rule of rational choice, would you do more or less of something if its expected marginal costs increased? Why?
4. How does the rule of rational choice imply that young children are typically more likely to misbehave at a supermarket checkout counter than at home?
5. Why do many parents refuse to let their children have dessert before they eat the rest of their dinner?

SECTION 2.5

Specialization and Trade

* What is the relationship between opportunity cost and specialization?
* What are the advantages of specialization in production?

Why Do People Specialize?

As you look around, you can see that people specialize in what they produce. They tend to dedicate their resources to one primary activity, whether it be child rearing, driving a cab, or making bagels. Why? The answer, short and simple, is opportunity costs. By concentrating their energies on only one, or a few, activities, individuals are **specializing**. This focus allows them to make the best use of (and thus gain the most benefit from) their limited resources. A person, a region, or a country can gain by specializing in the production of the good in which they have a comparative advantage. That is, if they can produce a good or service at a lower opportunity cost than others, we say that they have a **comparative advantage** in the production of that good or service.

> **specializing**
> concentrating in the production of one, or a few, goods
>
> **comparative advantage**
> occurs when a person or country can produce a good or service at a lower opportunity cost than others

We All Specialize

We all specialize to some extent and rely on others to produce most of the goods and services we want. The work that we choose to do reflects our specialization. For example, we may specialize in selling or fixing automobiles. The wages from that work can then be used to buy goods from a farmer who has chosen to specialize in the production of food. Likewise, the farmer can use the money earned from selling his produce to get his tractor fixed by someone who specializes in that activity.

Specialization is evident not only among individuals but among regions and countries as well. In fact, the story of the economic development of the United States and the rest of the world involves specialization. Within the United States, the Midwest with its wheat, the coastal waters of the Northeast with its fishing fleets, and the Northwest with its timber are each examples of regional specialization.

The Advantages of Specialization

In a small business, every employee usually performs a wide variety of tasks—from hiring to word processing to marketing. As the size of the company increases, each employee can perform a more specialized job, with a consequent increase in output per worker. The

SPECIALIZATION, COMPARATIVE ADVANTAGE, AND BASEBALL

Specialization and comparative advantage are important in sports, as they are in other fields. In baseball and softball, teams have resources that they must place in alternative positions to increase the likelihood of a victory. The resource is labor—human effort used to produce something. We can be even more specific, and talk about the particular characteristics or skills of the labor. That is, we have strength of arms, speed, fielding, power hitting, and contact hitting. Where do we play each of these players in the field or place them in the batting line-up to increase our chances to win? The teams that specialize with their varied talent have a better chance of winning. Quicker players are usually positioned in the middle of the field—shortstop, second base, and center field. Slower (less quick) fielders are usually on the corners—third base, first base, left field, and right field. Strength of arm—pitchers, catchers, and right field (it is a long throw from right field to third base). Hitting—speed and contact in the one and two spots, power in the three, four, and five spots, and the relatively poorer contact hitters at the bottom of the line-up.

It is also easy to see the importance of comparative advantage in this example. Suppose there are two players on your softball team, Jessica and Mariah, and you are not sure where they should play in the field. Jessica is good at infield and good at outfield. Mariah is good at infield and bad at outfield, but not as good at Jessica at either. Where should they play Mariah, since Jessica has an absolute advantage over Mariah in the infield and outfield? It would be best to play Mariah in the infield because she is just a little worse than Jessica in the infield and a lot worse than Jessica in the outfield. Remember, comparative advantage is a relative concept.

MCT/LANDOV

Finally, why did hitters put up higher batting averages 100 years ago? Ted Williams was the last player to hit over 400, and that was in 1941. Over 30 hitters exceeded that mark from 1880–1930. Were hitters better back in the old days? Or are pitchers better today? It is probably that pitchers are better today. Part of the reason is training and nutrition for pitchers. But the other reason is specialization. Pitchers rarely throw complete games these days. Often they are only asked to throw five innings of a nine-inning game. It is then up to the middle relievers and the closers to finish up the game. There are also specialty pitchers for different situations—if you need a ground ball you might bring in your sinker ball pitcher. If your computer records suggest that the left-handed batter coming up struggles against left-handed pitching, you might bring in a left-handed reliever. Specialization has changed the game.

primary advantages of specialization are that employees acquire greater skill from repetition, they avoid wasted time in shifting from one task to another, and they do the types of work for which they are best suited—and specialization promotes the use of specialized equipment for specialized tasks.

The advantages of specialization are seen throughout the workplace. For example, in larger firms, specialists conduct personnel relations, and accounting is in the hands of full-time accountants instead of someone with half a dozen other tasks. Owners of small retail stores select the locations for their stores primarily through guesswork, placing them where they believe sales will be high or where empty low-rent buildings are available. In contrast, larger chains have store sites selected by experts who have experience in analyzing the factors that make different locations relatively more desirable, such as traffic patterns, income levels, demographics, and so on.

Use what you've LEARNED — COMPARATIVE ADVANTAGE

Q Should an attorney who types 100 words per minute hire an administrative assistant to type her legal documents, even though he can only type 50 words per minute? If the attorney does the job, she can do it in five hours; if the administrative assistant does the job, it takes him 10 hours. The attorney makes $100 an hour, and the administrative assistant earns $10 an hour. Which one has the comparative advantage (the lowest opportunity cost) in typing documents?

A If the attorney types her own documents, it will cost $500 ($100 per hour x 5 hours). If she has the administrative assistant type her documents, it will cost $100 ($10 per hour x 10 hours). Clearly, then, the lawyer should hire the administrative assistant to type her documents, because the administrative assistant has the comparative advantage (lowest opportunity cost) in this case, despite being half as good in absolute terms.

Specialization and Trade Lead to Greater Wealth and Prosperity

Trade, or voluntary exchange, directly increases wealth by making both parties better off (or they wouldn't trade). It is the prospect of wealth-increasing exchange that leads to productive specialization. That is, trade increases wealth by allowing a person, a region, or a nation to specialize in those products that it produces at a lower opportunity cost and to trade them for products that others produce at a lower opportunity cost. That is, we trade with others because it frees up time and resources to do other things that we do better.

In short, if we divide tasks and produce what we do *relatively* best and trade for the rest, we will be better off than if we were self-sufficient—that is, without trade. Imagine life without trade, where you were completely self-sufficient—growing your own food, making your own clothes, working on your own car, building your own house—do you think you would be better off? For example, say the United States is better at producing wheat than is Brazil, and Brazil is better at producing coffee than is the United States. The United States and Brazil would each benefit if the United States produces wheat and trades some of it to Brazil for coffee. Coffee growers

in the United States could grow coffee in expensive greenhouses, but it would result in higher coffee costs and prices, while leaving fewer resources available for employment in more beneficial jobs, such as wheat production.

This concept is true for individuals as well. Imagine Tom had 10 pounds of tea and Katherine had 10 pounds of coffee. However, Tom preferred coffee to tea and Katherine preferred tea to coffee. So if Tom traded his tea to Katherine for her coffee, both parties would be better off. Trade simply reallocates existing goods, and voluntary exchange increases wealth by making both parties better off—otherwise, they would not agree to trade.

In the words of growth theorist, Paul Romer, "There are huge potential gains from trade. Poor countries can supply their natural and human resources. Rich countries can supply their know-how. When these are combined, everyone can be better off. The challenge is for a country to arrange its laws and institutions so that both sides can profitably engage in trade." Standards of living can be increased through trade and exchange. In fact, the economy as a whole can create more wealth when each person specializes in a task that he or she does best. And through specialization and trade, a country can gain a greater variety of goods and services at a lower cost. So while counties may be competitors inn the global market they are also partners.

SECTION CHECK

1. We all specialize.
2. Specialization is important for individuals, businesses, regions, and nations.
3. Specialization and trade increase wealth.
4. The person, region, or country that can produce a good or service at a lower opportunity cost than other producers has a comparative advantage in the production of that good or service.

(continued)

1. Why do people specialize?

2. What do we mean by comparative advantage?

3. Why does the combination of specialization and trade make us better off?

4. If you can mow your lawn in half the time it takes your spouse or housemate to do it, do you have a comparative advantage in mowing the lawn?

5. If you have a current comparative advantage in doing the dishes, and you then become far more productive than before in completing yard chores, could that eliminate your comparative advantage? Why or why not?

6. Could a student who gets a C in one class but a D or worse in everything else have a comparative advantage over someone who gets a B in that class but an A in everything else? Explain this concept using opportunity cost.

SECTION 2.6   Markets and Improved Efficiency

* How does a market economy allocate scarce resources?
* What are the important signals that market prices communicate?
* What are the effects of price controls?
* What is a market failure?

How Does the Market Work to Allocate Resources?

In a world of scarcity, competition is inescapable, and one method of allocating resources among competing uses is the market economy. The market economy provides a way for millions of producers and consumers to allocate scarce resources. For the most part, markets are efficient. To an economist, **efficiency** is achieved when the economy gets the most out of its scarce resources. In short, efficiency makes the economic pie as large as possible.

Competitive markets are powerful—they can make existing products better and/or less expensive, they can improve production processes, and they can create new products, from video games to life-saving drugs. Buyers and sellers indicate their wants through their action and inaction in the marketplace, and it is this collective "voice" that determines how resources are allocated. But how is this information communicated? Market prices serve as the language of the market system. By understanding what these market prices mean, you can get a better understanding of the vital function that the market economy performs.

Markets may not always lead to your desired tastes and preferences. You may think that markets produce too many pet rocks, chia pets, breast enhancements, and face lifts. Some markets are illegal—the market for

> **efficiency**
> when an economy gets the most out of its scarce resources

cocaine, the market for stolen body parts, the market for child pornography, and the market for indecent radio announcers. Markets do not come with a moral compass; they simply provide what buyers are willing and able to pay for and what sellers are willing and able to produce.

Market Prices Provide Important Information

Market prices communicate important information to both buyers and sellers. These prices communicate information about the relative availability of products to buyers, and they provide sellers with critical information about the relative value that consumers place on those products. In short, buyers look at the price and decide how much they are willing and able to demand and sellers look at the price and decide how much they are able and willing to supply. The market price reflects the value a buyer places on a good and the cost to society of producing that good. Thus, market prices provide a way for both buyers and sellers to communicate about the relative value of resources. To paraphrase Adam Smith, prices adjust like an "invisible hand" to direct buyers and sellers to an outcome that is socially desirable. We will see how this works beginning in Chapter 4.

The basis of a market economy is voluntary exchange and the price system that guides people's choices and produces solutions to the questions of what goods to produce and how to produce and distribute them.

Take something as simple as the production of a pencil. Where did the wood come from? Perhaps the Northwest or Georgia. The graphite may have come from the mines in Michigan and the rubber may be from Malaysia. The paint, the glue, the metal piece that holds the eraser—who knows? The point is that market forces coordinated this production activity among literally thousands of people, some of whom live in different countries and speak different languages. The market brought these people together to make a pencil that sells for 25 cents at your bookstore. It all happened because the market economy provided the incentive for people to pursue activities that benefit others. This same process produces millions of goods and services around the world, from automobiles and computers to pencils and paper clips.

The same is true of the IPod and IPhone. The entrepreneur of Apple have learned how to combine almost 500 generic parts to make something of much greater value. The whole is greater than the sum of the parts.

price controls
government-mandated minimum or maximum prices

market failure
when the economy fails to allocate resources efficiently on its own

What Effect Do Price Controls Have on the Market System?

Government policies called **price controls** sometimes force prices above or below what they would be in a market economy. Unfortunately, these controls often impose harm on the same people they are trying to help, in large part by short-circuiting the market's information-transmission function. That is, price controls effectively strip the market price of its meaning for both buyers and sellers (as we will see in Chapter 5). A sales tax also distorts price signals, leading to a misallocation of resources (as we will see in Chapter 6).

Market Failure

The market mechanism is a simple but effective and efficient general means of allocating resources among alternative uses. When the economy fails to allocate resources efficiently on its own, however, it is known as **market failure**. For example, a steel mill might put soot and other forms of "crud" into the air as a by-product of making steel. When it does,

POLICY application   COUNTRIES THAT DO NOT RELY ON A MARKET SYSTEM

Countries that do not rely on the market system have no clear communication between buyers and sellers. The former Soviet Union, where quality was virtually nonexistent, experienced many shortages of quality goods and surpluses of low-quality goods. For example, thousands of tractors had no spare parts and millions of pairs of shoes were left on shelves because the sizes did not match those of the population. Before the breakup of the Soviet Union, one of President Reagan's favorite stories concerned a man who goes to the Soviet bureau of transportation to order an automobile. He is informed that he will have to put down his money now, but there is a 10-year wait. The man fills out all the various forms, has them processed through the various agencies, and finally he gets to the last agency. He pays them his money and they say, "Come back in 10 years and get your car." He asks, "Morning or afternoon?" The man from the agency says, "We're talking 10 years from now. What is the difference?" He replies, "The plumber is coming in the morning."

AP IMAGES

COURTESY OF ROBERT L. SEXTON

Even though designating these parking spaces for disabled drivers may not be an efficient use of scarce parking spaces (because they are often not used), many believe it is fair to give these drivers a convenient spot. The debate between efficiency and equity is often heated.

it imposes costs on others not connected with using or producing steel from the steel mill. The soot may require homeowners to paint their homes more often, entailing a cost. And studies show that respiratory diseases are greater in areas with more severe air pollution, imposing costs that may even include life itself. In addition, the steel mill might discharge chemicals into a stream, thus killing wildlife and spoiling recreational activities for the local population. In this case, the steel factory does not bear the costs of its polluting actions, and it continues to emit too much pollution. In other words, by transferring the pollution costs onto society, the firm lowers its costs of production and so produces more than the ideal output—which is inefficient because it is an overallocation of resources.

Markets sometimes produce too little of a good—research, for example. Therefore, the government might decide to subsidize promising scientific research that could benefit many people—such as cancer research. When one party prevents other parties from participating in mutually beneficial exchange, it also causes a market failure. This situation occurs in a monopoly, with its single seller of goods. Because the monopolist can raise its end price above the competitive price,

some potential consumers are kept from buying the goods they would have bought at the lower price, and inefficiency occurs. Whether the market economy has produced too little (underallocation) or too much (overallocation), the government can improve society's well-being by intervening. The case of market failure will be taken up in more detail in Chapter 8.

We cannot depend on the market economy to always communicate accurately. Some firms may have market power to distort prices in their favor. For example, the only regional cement company in the area has the ability to charge a higher price and provide lower-quality services than if the company were in a highly competitive market. In this case, the lack of competition can lead to higher prices and reduced product quality. And without adequate information, unscrupulous producers may be able to misrepresent their products to the disadvantage of unwary consumers.

In sum, government *can* help promote efficiency when there is a market failure—making the economic pie larger.

Does the Market Distribute Income Fairly?

Sometimes a painful trade-off exists between how much an economy can produce efficiently and how that output is distributed—the degree of equality. An efficient market rewards those that produce goods and services that others are willing and able to buy. But this does not guarantee a "fair" or equal distribution of income. That is, how the economic pie is divided up. A market economy cannot guarantee everyone adequate amounts of food, shelter, and health care. That is, not only does the market determine what goods are going to be produced and in what quantities, but it also determines the distribution of output among members of society.

As with other aspects of government intervention, the degree-of-equity argument can generate some sharp disagreements. What is "fair" for one person may seem highly "unfair" to someone else. One person may find it terribly unfair for some individuals to earn many times the amount earned by other individuals who work equally hard, and another person may find it highly unfair to ask one group, the relatively rich, to pay a much higher proportion of their income in taxes than another group pays.

Government Is Not Always the Solution

However, just because the government could improve the situation does not mean it will. After all, the political process has its own set of problems, such as special interests, shortsightedness, and imperfect information. For example, government may reduce competition through tariffs and quotas, or it may impose inefficient regulations that restrict entry. That is, there is government failure as well as market failure.

SECTION CHECK

1. Scarcity forces us to allocate our limited resources.
2. Market prices provide important information to buyers and sellers.
3. Price controls distort market signals.
4. A market failure is said to occur when the economy fails to allocate resources efficiently.

---

1. Why must every society choose some manner in which to allocate its scarce resources?
2. How does a market system allocate resources?
3. What do market prices communicate to others in society?
4. How do price controls undermine the market as a communication device?
5. Why can markets sometimes fail to allocate resources efficiently?

Interactive Chapter Summary

Fill in the blanks:

1. As long as human _____ exceed available _____, scarcity will exist.

2. Something may be rare, but if it is not _____it is not scarce.

3. The scarce resources that are used in the production of goods and services can be grouped into four categories: _____, _____, _____, and _____.

4. Capital includes human capital, the _____ people receive from _____.

5. Entrepreneurs are always looking for new ways to improve _____ or _____. They are lured by the chance of making a _____.

6. _____ goods include fairness, friendship, knowledge, security, and health.

7. _____ are intangible items of value, such as education, provided to consumers.

8. Scarce goods created from scarce resources are called _____ goods.

9. Scarcity ultimately leads to _____ for the available goods and services.

10. Because we all have different _____, scarcity affects everyone differently.

11. Economics is the study of the choices we make among our many _____ and _____.

12. In a world of scarcity, we all face _____.

13. The highest or best forgone alternative resulting from a decision is called the _____.

14. The cost of grocery shopping is the _____ paid for the goods plus the _____ costs incurred.

15. Many choices involve _____ of something to do rather than whether to do something.

16. Economists emphasize _____ thinking because the focus is on additional, or _____, choices, which involve the effects of _____ or _____ the current situation.

17. The rule of rational choice is that in trying to make themselves better off, people alter their behavior if the _____ to them from doing so outweigh the _____ they will bear.

18. In acting rationally, people respond to _____.

19. If the benefits of some activity _____ and/or if the costs _____, economists expect the amount of that activity to rise. Economists call these _____ incentives. Likewise, if the benefits of some activity _____ and/or if the costs _____, economists expect the amount of that activity to fall. Economists call these _____ incentives.

20. Because most people seek opportunities that make them better off, we can _____ what will happen when incentives are _____.

21. People _____ by concentrating their energies on the activity to which they are best suited because

individuals incur _____ opportunity costs as a result.

22. If a person, a region, or a country can produce a good or service at a lower opportunity cost than others can, we say that they have a(n) _____ in the production of that good or service.

23. The primary advantages of specialization are that employees acquire greater _____ from repetition, they avoid _____ time in shifting from one task to another, and they do the types of work for which they are _____ suited.

24. We trade with others because it frees up time and resources to do other things we do _____.

25. Produce what we do _____ best and _____ for the _____.

26. Market prices serve as the _____ of the market system. They communicate information about the _____ to buyers, and they provide sellers with critical information about the _____ that buyers place on those products. This communication results in a shifting of resources from those uses that are _____ valued to those that are _____ valued.

27. The basis of a market economy is _____ exchange and the _____ system that guides people's choices regarding what goods to produce and how to produce those goods and distribute them.

28. _____ can lead the economy to fail to allocate resources efficiently, as in the cases of pollution and scientific research.

29. Sometimes a painful trade-off exists between how much an economy can produce _____ and how that output is _____.

30. In the case of market _____, appropriate government policies could improve on market outcomes.

Answers: 1. wants; resources 2. desirable 3. land; labor; capital; entrepreneurship 4. knowledge and skill; education and on-the-job training 5. production techniques; products; profit 6. Intangible 7. Services 8. economic 9. competition 10. wants and desires 11. wants; desires 12. trade-offs 13. opportunity cost 14. price; nonprice 15. how much 16. marginal; marginal; adding to; subtracting from 17. expected marginal benefits; expected marginal costs 18. incentives 19. rise; fall; positive; fall; rise; negative 20. predict; changed 21. specialize; lower 22. comparative advantage 23. skill; wasted; best 24. better; rest 25. relatively; trade; language; relative availability of products; relative value; less; more 27. voluntary; price 28. Market failure 29. efficiently; distributed 30. failure

Key Terms and Concepts

scarcity 37
labor 37
land 37
capital 37
human capital 37
entrepreneurship 37
goods 38
tangible goods 38

intangible goods 38
services 38
economic goods 38
bads 38
opportunity cost 40
marginal thinking 43
rule of rational choice 43
net benefit 43

positive incentive 47
negative incentive 47
specializing 49
comparative advantage 49
efficiency 52
price controls 53
market failure 53

Section Check Answers

2.1 Scarcity

1. What must be true for something to be an economic good?

An economic good, tangible or intangible, is any good or service that we value or desire. This definition includes the reduction of things we don't want—bads—as a good.

2. Does wanting more tangible and intangible goods and services make us selfish?

No. Among the goods many of us want more of are helping others (charity), so to say we all want more goods and services does not imply that we are selfish.

3. Why does scarcity affect everyone?

Because no one can have all the goods and services that he or she desires, we all face scarcity as a fact of life.

4. **How and why does scarcity affect each of us differently?**

   Because our desires and the extent of the resources we have available to meet those desires vary, scarcity affects each of us differently.

5. **Why do you think economists often refer to training that increases the quality of workers' skills as "adding to human capital"?**

   Training increases a worker's ability to produce further goods, just as capital goods increase an economy's ability to produce further goods. Because of this similarity in their effects on productive abilities, training is often referred to as adding to workers' human capital.

6. **What are some of the ways that students act as entrepreneurs as they seek higher grades?**

   Students act as entrepreneurs in seeking higher grades in a wide variety of ways. They sometimes form study groups, often assigning different material to different members. They often share notes. They study harder for those questions they believe will be more likely to be tested. Sometimes they try to get hold of old tests or to cheat. All of these activities and more are part of different students' efforts to discover the lowest-cost way for them to get higher grades.

7. **Why might sunshine be scarce in Seattle but not in Tucson?**

   For a good to be scarce means we want more of it than we are able to have. Residents of Tucson typically have all the sunshine they wish, while rain may be something that is scarce relative to residents' desires. For residents of Seattle, where the sun shines much less and it rains much more, the opposite might well be true.

8. **Why can't a country become so technologically advanced that its citizens won't have to choose?**

   No matter how productive a country becomes, citizens' desires will continue to outstrip their ability to satisfy them. As we get more productive, and incomes grow, we discover new wants that we would like to satisfy, so our ability to produce never catches up with our wants.

2.2 Choices, Costs, and Trade-Offs

1. **Would we have to make choices if we had unlimited resources?**

   We would not have to make choices if we had unlimited resources, because we would then be able to produce all the goods and services anyone wanted, and having more of one thing would not require having less of other goods or services.

2. **What is given up when we make a choice?**

   What is given up when we make a choice is the opportunity to pursue other valued alternatives with the same time or resources.

3. **What do we mean by opportunity cost?**

   The opportunity cost of a choice is the highest valued forgone opportunity resulting from a decision. It can usefully be thought of as the value of the opportunity a person would have chosen if his most preferred option was taken away from him.

4. **Why is there no such thing as a free lunch?**

   There is no such thing as a free lunch because the production of any good uses up some of society's resources, which are therefore no longer available to produce other goods we want.

5. **Why was the opportunity cost of staying in college higher for Tiger Woods than for most undergraduates?**

   The forgone alternative to Tiger Woods of staying in school—starting a highly paid professional golf career sooner than he could otherwise—was far more lucrative than the alternatives facing most undergraduates. Because his forgone alternative was more valuable for Tiger Woods, his opportunity cost of staying in school was higher than for most.

6. **Why is the opportunity cost of time spent getting an MBA typically lower for a 22-year-old straight out of college than for a 45-year-old experienced manager?**

   The opportunity cost of time for a 45-year-old experienced manager—the earnings he would have to give up to spend a given period getting an MBA—is higher than that of a 22-year-old straight out of college, whose income earning alternatives are far less.

2.3 Marginal Thinking

1. **What are marginal choices? Why does economics focus on them?**

   Marginal choices are choices of how much of something to do, rather than whether to do something. Economics focuses on marginal choices because those are the sorts of choices we usually face: Should I do a little more of this or a little less of that?

2. **What is the rule of rational choice?**

   The rule of rational choice is that in trying to make themselves better off, people alter their behavior if the expected marginal benefits from doing so outweigh the expected marginal costs they will bear. If the expected marginal benefits of an action exceed the expected marginal costs, a person will do more of that action; if the expected marginal benefits of an action are less than the expected marginal costs, a person will do less of that action.

3. **How could the rule of rational choice be expressed in terms of net benefits?**

   Because net benefits are expected to be positive when expected marginal benefits exceed expected marginal cost to the decision maker, the rule of rational choice could be restated as: People will make choices for which net benefits are expected to be positive.

4. Why does rational choice involve expectations?

Because the world is uncertain in many important respects, we can seldom know for certain whether the marginal benefits of an action will in fact exceed the marginal costs. Therefore, the rule of rational choice deals with expectations decision makers hold at the time they make their decisions, recognizing that mistakes can be made.

5. Why do students often stop taking lecture notes when a professor announces that the next few minutes of material will not be on any future test or assignment?

The benefit, in terms of grades, from taking notes in class falls when the material discussed will not be tested or "rewarded," and when the benefits of lecture note taking are smaller in this situation, students do less of it.

6. If you decide to speed to get to a doctor's appointment and then get in an accident due to speeding, does your decision to speed invalidate the rule of rational choice? Why or why not?

No. Remember, the rule of rational choice deals with expectations at the time decisions were made. If you thought you would get in an accident due to speeding in this situation, you would not have decided to speed. The fact that you got in an accident doesn't invalidate the rule of rational choice; it only means your expectations at the time you decided to speed were incorrect.

7. If pedestrians felt far safer using crosswalks to cross the street, how could adding crosswalks increase the number of pedestrian accidents?

Just like safer cars can lead people to drive less safely, if pedestrians felt safer in crosswalks, they might cross less safely, such as taking less care to look both ways. The result of pedestrians taking less care may well be an increase in the number of pedestrian accidents.

8. Imagine driving a car with daggers sticking out of the steering wheel—pointing directly at your chest. Would you drive more safely? Why?

Because the cost to you of an accident would be so much higher in this case, you would drive far more safely as a result.

2.4 Incentives Matter

1. What is the difference between positive incentives and negative incentives?

Positive incentives are those that either increase benefits or decrease costs of an action, encouraging the action; negative incentives are those that either decrease benefits or increase costs of an action, discouraging the action.

2. According to the rule of rational choice, would you do more or less of something if its expected marginal benefits increased? Why?

You would do more of something if its expected marginal benefits increased, because then the marginal expected benefits would exceed the marginal expected costs for more "units" of the relevant action.

3. According to the rule of rational choice, would you do more or less of something if its expected marginal costs increased? Why?

You would do less of something if its expected marginal costs increased, because then the marginal expected benefits would exceed the marginal expected costs for fewer "units" of the relevant action.

4. How does the rule of rational choice imply that young children are typically more likely to misbehave at a supermarket checkout counter than at home?

When a young child is at a supermarket checkout counter, the benefit of misbehaving—the potential payoff to pestering Mom or Dad for candy—is greater. Also, because his parents are less likely to punish him, or to punish him as severely, in public as in private when he pesters them, the costs are lower as well. The benefits of misbehavior are higher and the costs are lower at a supermarket checkout counter, so more child misbehavior is to be expected there.

5. Why do many parents refuse to let their children have dessert before they eat the rest of their dinner?

Children often find that the costs of eating many foods at dinner exceed the benefits (e.g., "If it's green, it must be disgusting."), but that is seldom so of dessert. If parents let their children eat dessert first, they would often not eat the food that was "good for them." But by adding the benefit of getting dessert to the choice of eating their other food, parents can often get their children to eat the rest of their dinner, too.

2.5 Specialization and Trade

1. Why do people specialize?

People specialize because by concentrating their energies on the activities to which they are best suited, individuals incur lower opportunity costs. That is, they specialize in doing those things they can do at lower opportunity costs than others, and let others who can do other things at lower opportunity costs than they can specialize in doing them.

2. What do we mean by comparative advantage?

A person, region, or country has a comparative advantage in producing a good or service when it can produce it at a lower opportunity cost than other persons, regions, or countries.

3. **Why does the combination of specialization and trade make us better off?**

   Trade increases wealth by allowing a person, region, or a nation to specialize in those products that it produces relatively better than others and to trade for those products that others produce relatively better than they do. Exploiting our comparative advantages, and then trading, allows us to produce, and therefore consume, more than we could otherwise from our scarce resources.

4. **If you can mow your lawn in half the time it takes your spouse or housemate to do it, do you have a comparative advantage in mowing the lawn?**

   Your faster speed at mowing the lawn does not establish that you have a comparative advantage in mowing. That can only be established relative to other tasks. The person with a comparative advantage in mowing lawns is the one with the lowest opportunity cost, and that could be your spouse or housemate in this case. For instance, if you could earn $12 an hour, mowing the lawn in half an hour implies an opportunity cost of $6 of forgone output elsewhere. If they could only earn $5 per hour (because they were less than half as productive doing other things compared to you), the opportunity cost of them mowing the lawn in an hour is $5. In this case, your spouse or housemate has a comparative advantage in mowing the lawn.

5. **If you have a current comparative advantage in doing the dishes, and you then become far more productive than before in completing yard chores, could that eliminate your comparative advantage? Why or why not?**

   The opportunity cost of you doing the dishes is the value of other chores you must give up to do the dishes. Therefore, an increase in your productivity doing yard chores would increase the opportunity cost of doing the dishes, and could well eliminate your current comparative advantage in doing the dishes compared to other members of your family.

6. **Could a student who gets a C in one class but a D or worse in everything else have a comparative advantage over someone who gets a B in that class but an A in everything else? Explain this concept using opportunity cost.**

   A student who gets a C in a class is less good, in an absolute sense, at that class than a student who gets a B in it. But if the C student gets Ds in other classes, he is relatively, or comparatively, better at the C class, while if the B student gets As in other classes, she is relatively, or comparatively, worse at that class.

2.6 Markets and Improved Efficiency

1. **Why must every society choose some manner in which to allocate its scarce resources?**

   Every society must choose some manner in which to allocate its scarce resources because the collective wants of its members always far outweigh what the scarce resources nature has provided can produce.

2. **How does a market system allocate resources?**

   A market system allows individuals, both as producers and consumers, to indicate their wants and desires through their actions—how much they are willing to buy or sell at various prices. The market then acts to bring about that level of prices that allows buyers and sellers to coordinate their plans.

3. **What do market prices communicate to others in society?**

   The prices charged by suppliers communicate the relative availability of products to consumers; the prices consumers are willing to pay communicate the relative value consumers place on products to producers. That is, market prices provide a way for both consumers and suppliers to communicate about the relative value of resources.

4. **How do price controls undermine the market as a communication device?**

   Price controls—both price floors and price ceilings—prevent the market from communicating relevant information between consumers and suppliers. A price floor set above the market price prevents suppliers from communicating their willingness to sell for less to consumers. A price ceiling set below the market price prevents consumers from indicating their willingness to pay more to suppliers.

5. **Why can markets sometimes fail to allocate resources efficiently?**

   Markets can sometimes fail to allocate resources efficiently. Such situations, called market failures, represent situations such as externalities, where costs can be imposed on some individuals without their consent (e.g., from dumping "crud" in their air or water), where information in the market may not be communicated honestly and accurately, and where firms may have market power to distort prices in their favor (against consumers' interests).

True or False:

1. In economics, labor includes physical and mental effort, and land includes natural resources.

2. Entrepreneurship is the process of combining labor, land, and capital together to produce goods and services.

3. Even intangible goods can be subjected to economic analysis.

4. Even the wealthy individual who decides to donate all of her money to charity faces the constraints of scarcity.

5. Increases in production could enable us to eliminate scarcity.

6. If we had unlimited resources, we would not have to choose among our desires.

7. Scarcity implies that "there's no such thing as a free lunch."

8. The actual result of changing behavior following the rule of rational choice will always make people better off.

9. In terms of the rule of rational choice, zero levels of pollution, crime, and safety would be far too costly in terms of what we would have to give up to achieve them.

10. Most choices in economics are all or nothing.

11. Good economic thinking requires thinking about average amounts rather than marginal amounts.

12. Positive incentives are those that either increase benefits or reduce costs, resulting in an increase in the level of the related activity or behavior; negative incentives either reduce benefits or increase costs, resulting in a decrease in the level of the related activity or behavior.

13. The safety issue is generally not whether a product is safe, but rather how much safety consumers want.

14. People can gain by specializing in the production of the good in which they have a comparative advantage.

15. Without the ability to trade, people would not tend to specialize in those areas where they have a comparative advantage.

16. Voluntary trade directly increases wealth by making both parties better off, and it is the prospect of wealth-increasing exchange that leads to productive specialization.

17. Government price controls can short-circuit the market's information transmission function.

18. When the economy produces too little or too much of something, the government can potentially improve society's well-being by intervening.

19. Not only does the market determine what goods are going to be produced and in what quantities, but it also determines the distribution of output among members of society.

Multiple Choice:

1. Which of the following is part of the economic way of thinking?
   a. When an option becomes less costly, individuals will become more likely to choose it.
   b. Costs are incurred whenever scarce resources are used to produce goods or services.
   c. The value of a good is determined by its cost of production.
   d. Both a and b are part of the economic way of thinking.

2. Ted has decided to buy a burger and fries at a restaurant but is considering whether to buy a drink as well. If the price of a burger is $2.00, fries are $1.00, drinks are $1.00, and a value meal with all three costs $3.40, the marginal cost to Ted of the drink is
   a. $1.00.
   b. $0.40.
   c. $1.40.
   d. $3.40.
   e. impossible to determine from the information given.

3. If a country wants to maximize the value of its output, each job should be carried out by the person who
   a. has the highest opportunity cost.
   b. has a comparative advantage in that activity.
   c. can complete the particular job most rapidly.
   d. enjoys that job the least.

4. Who would be most likely to drop out of college before graduation?
   a. an economics major who wishes to go to graduate school
   b. a math major with a B+ average
   c. a chemistry major who has just been reading about the terrific jobs available for those with chemistry degrees
   d. a star baseball player who has just received a multimillion-dollar major league contract offer after his junior year

5. "If I hadn't been set up on this blind date tonight, I would have saved $50 and spent the evening watching TV." The opportunity cost of the date is
   a. $50.
   b. $50, plus the cost to you of giving up a night of TV.
   c. smaller, the more you enjoy the date.
   d. higher, the more you like that night's TV shows.
   e. described by both b and d.

6. Say you had an 8 A.M. economics class, but you would still come to campus at the same time even if you skipped your economics class. The cost of coming to the economics class would include
   a. the value of the time it took to drive to campus.
   b. the cost of the gasoline it took to get to campus.
   c. the cost of insuring the car for that day.
   d. both a and b.
   e. none of the above.

7. Which of the following would be likely to raise your opportunity cost of attending a big basketball game this Sunday night?
   a. A friend calls you up and offers you free tickets to a concert by one of your favorite bands on Sunday night.
   b. Your employer offers you double your usual wage to work this Sunday night.
   c. Late Friday afternoon, your physics professor makes a surprise announcement that there will be a major exam on Monday morning.
   d. All of the above.

8. Which of the following demonstrates marginal thinking?
   a. deciding to never eat meat
   b. deciding to spend one more hour studying economics tonight because you think the improvement on your next test will be large enough to make it worthwhile to you
   c. working out an extra hour per week
   d. both b and c

9. If resources and goods are free to move across states, and if Florida producers choose to specialize in growing grapefruit and Georgia producers choose to specialize in growing peaches, then we could reasonably conclude that
   a. Georgia has a comparative advantage in producing peaches.
   b. Florida has a comparative advantage in producing peaches.
   c. the opportunity cost of growing peaches is lower in Georgia than in Florida.
   d. the opportunity cost of growing grapefruit is lower in Florida than in Georgia.
   e. all of the above except b are true.

10. If a driver who had no change and whose cell phone battery was dead got stranded near a pay phone and chose to buy a quarter and a dime from a passerby for a dollar bill,
    a. the passerby was made better off and the driver was made worse off by the transaction.
    b. both the passerby and the driver were made better off by the transaction.
    c. the transaction made the driver worse off by 65 cents.
    d. both a and c are true.

11. Which of the following is *not* true?
    a. Voluntary exchange is expected to be advantageous to both parties to the exchange.
    b. What one trader gains from a trade, the other must lose.
    c. If one party to a potential voluntary trade decides it does not advance his interests, he can veto the potential trade.
    d. The expectation of gain motivates people to engage in trade.

12. Which of the following is true?
    a. Scarcity and poverty are basically the same thing.
    b. The absence of scarcity means that a minimal level of income is provided to all individuals.
    c. Goods are scarce because of greed.
    d. Even in the wealthiest of countries, the desire for material goods is greater than productive capabilities.

13. An example of a capital resource is
    a. stock in a computer software company.
    b. the funds in a CD account at a bank.
    c. a bond issued by a company selling electric generators.
    d. a dump truck.
    e. an employee of a moving company.

14. Which of the following statements is true?
    a. The opportunity cost of a decision is always expressed in monetary terms.
    b. The opportunity cost of a decision is the value of the best forgone alternative.
    c. Some economic decisions have zero opportunity cost.
    d. The opportunity cost of attending college is the same for all students at the same university but may differ among students at different universities.
    e. None of the above statements is true.

15. The opportunity cost of attending college is likely to include all except which of the following?
    a. the cost of required textbooks
    b. tuition fees
    c. the income you forgo in order to attend classes
    d. the cost of haircuts received during the school term
    e. the cost of paper and pencils needed to take notes

16. The opportunity cost of an airplane flight
    a. differs across passengers only to the extent that each traveler pays a different airfare.
    b. is identical for all passengers and equal to the number of hours a particular flight takes.
    c. differs across passengers to the extent that both the airfare paid and the highest valued use of travel time vary.
    d. is equal to the cost of a bus ticket, the next best form of alternative transportation to flying.

17. Lance's boss offers him twice his usual wage rate to work tonight instead of taking his girlfriend on a romantic date. This offer will likely
    a. not affect the opportunity cost of going on the date.
    b. reduce the opportunity cost of going on the date because giving up the additional work dollars will make his girlfriend feel even more appreciated.
    c. increase the opportunity cost of going on the date.
    d. not be taken into consideration by Lance when deciding what to do tonight.

18. Which of the following best defines rational behavior?
    a. analyzing the total costs of a decision
    b. analyzing the total benefits of a decision
    c. undertaking an activity as long as the total benefit of all activities exceeds the total cost of all activities
    d. undertaking activities whenever the marginal benefit exceeds the marginal cost
    e. undertaking activities as long as the marginal benefit exceeds zero

19. Gallons of milk at a local grocery store are priced at one for $4 or two for $6. The marginal cost of buying a second gallon of milk equals
    a. $6.
    b. $4.
    c. $3.
    d. $2.
    e. $0.

20. Which of the following statements is most consistent with the rule of rational choice?
    a. The Environmental Protection Agency should strive to eliminate virtually all air and water pollution.
    b. When evaluating new prescription drugs, the Food and Drug Administration should weigh each drug's potential health benefits against the potential health risks posed by known side effects.
    c. Police forces should be enlarged until virtually all crime is eliminated.
    d. Manufacturers of automobiles should seek to make cars safer, no matter the costs involved.

21. Kelly is an attorney and also an excellent typist. She can type 120 words per minute, but she is pressed for time because she has all the legal work she can handle at $75.00 per hour. Kelly's friend Todd works as a waiter and would like some typing work (provided that he can make at least his wage as a waiter, which is $25.00 per hour). Todd can type only 60 words per minute.
    a. Kelly should do all the typing because she is faster.
    b. Todd should do the typing as long as his earnings are more than $25.00 and less than $37.50 per hour.
    c. Unless Todd can match Kelly's typing speed, he should remain a waiter.
    d. Todd should do the typing, and Kelly should pay him $20.00 per hour.
    e. Both a and c are correct.

Problems:

1. Which of the following goods are scarce?
    a. garbage
    b. salt water in the ocean
    c. clothes
    d. clean air in a big city
    e. dirty air in a big city
    f. a public library

2. Explain the difference between poverty and scarcity.

3. The automotive revolution after World War II reduced the time involved for travel and shipping goods. This innovation allowed the U.S. economy to produce more goods and services since it freed resources involved in transportation for other uses. The transportation revolution also increased wants. Identify two ways the car and truck revealed new wants.

4. The price of a one-way bus trip from Los Angeles to New York City is $150.00. Sarah, a school teacher, pays the same price in February (during the school year) as in July (during her vacation), so the cost is the same in February as in July. Do you agree?

5. McDonald's once ran a promotion that whenever St. Louis Cardinal's slugger Mark McGwire hit a home run into the upper deck at Busch Stadium, McDonald's gave anyone with a ticket to that day's game a free Big Mac. If holders of ticket stubs have to stand in line for 10 minutes, is the Big Mac really "free"?

6. List some things that you need. Then ask yourself if you would still want some of those things if the price were five times higher. Would you still want them if the price were 10 times higher?

7. List the opportunity costs of the following:
    a. going to college
    b. missing a lecture
    c. withdrawing and spending $100 from your savings account, which earns 5 percent interest annually
    d. going snowboarding on the weekend before final examinations

8. Which of the following activities require marginal thinking, and why?
   a. studying
   b. eating
   c. driving
   d. shopping
   e. getting ready for a night out

9. Should you go to the movies this Friday? List the factors that affect the possible benefits and costs of this decision. Explain where uncertainty affects the benefits and costs.

10. Explain why following the rule of rational choice makes a person better off.

11. Which of the following are positive incentives? Negative incentives? Why?
    a. a fine for not cleaning up after your dog defecates in the park
    b. a trip to Hawaii paid for by your parents or significant other for earning an A in your economics course
    c. a higher tax on cigarettes and alcohol
    d. a subsidy for installing solar panels on your house

12. Modern medicine has made organ transplants a common occurrence, yet the number of organs that people want far exceeds the available supply. According to CNN, 10 people die each day because of a lack of transplantable organs like kidneys and livers. Some economists have recommended that an organ market be established through which doctors and others could pay people for the right to use their organs when they die. The law currently forbids the sale of organs. What do you think of such a proposal? What kind of incentives would an organ market provide for people to allow others to use their organs? What would happen to the supply of organs if, instead of relying on donated kidneys, livers, and retinas, doctors and hospitals could bid for them? What drawbacks would a free market in organs have? Have you made arrangements to leave your organs to your local organ bank? Would you do so if you could receive $50,000 for them?

13. Throughout history, many countries have chosen the path of autarky, choosing to not trade with other countries. Explain why this path would make a country poorer.

14. Farmer Fran can grow soybeans and corn. She can grow 50 bushels of soybeans or 100 bushels of corn on an acre of her land for the same cost. The price of soybeans is $1.50 per bushel and the price of corn is $0.60 per bushel. Show the benefits to Fran of specialization. What should she specialize in?

15. Which region has a comparative advantage in the following goods:
    a. wheat: Colombia or the United States?
    b. coffee: Colombia or the United States?
    c. timber: Iowa or Washington?
    d. corn: Iowa or Washington?

16. Why is it important that the country or region with the lower opportunity cost produce the good? How would you use the concept of comparative advantage to argue for reducing restrictions on trade between countries?

17. People communicate with each other in the market through the effect their decisions to buy or sell have on prices. Indicate how each of the following would affect prices by putting a check in the appropriate space.
    a. People who see an energetic and lovable Jack Russell Terrier in a popular TV series want Jack Russell Terriers as pets. The price of Jack Russell Terriers _____ Rises _____ Falls
    b. Aging retirees flock to Tampa, Florida, to live. The price of housing in Tampa _____ Rises _____ Falls
    c. Weather-related crop failures in Colombia and Costa Rica reduce coffee supplies. The price of coffee _____ Rises _____ Falls
    d. Sugar cane fields in Hawaii and Louisiana are replaced with housing. The price of sugar _____ Rises _____ Falls
    e. More and more students graduate from U.S. medical schools. The wages of U.S. doctors _____ Rises _____ Falls
    f. Americans are driving more and they are driving bigger, gas-guzzling cars like sports utility vehicles. The price of gasoline _____ Rises _____ Falls

18. Prices communicate information about the relative value of resources. Which of the following would cause the relative value and, hence, the price of potatoes to rise?
    a. Fungus infestation wipes out half the Idaho potato crop.
    b. The price of potato chips rises.
    c. Scientists find that eating potato chips makes you better looking.
    d. The prices of wheat, rice, and other potato substitutes fall dramatically.

19. Imagine that you are trying to decide whether to cross a street without using the designated crosswalk at the traffic signal. What are the expected marginal benefits of crossing? The expected marginal costs? How would the following conditions change your benefit–cost equation?
    a. The street was busy.
    b. The street was empty and it was 3 A.M.
    c. You were in a huge hurry.
    d. A police officer was standing 100 feet away.
    e. The closest crosswalk was a mile away.
    f. The closest crosswalk was 10 feet away.

3

Scarcity, Trade-Offs, and Production Possibilities

This chapter builds on the foundations of the preceding chapters. We have learned that we have unlimited wants and limited resources— that is, we all face scarcity. And scarcity forces us to choose.

To get one thing we like, we usually have to give up something else we want—that is, people face trade-offs. Recognizing these trade-offs will allow us to make better decisions.

Every economy must transform the resources that nature provides into goods and services. Economics is the study of that process. This chapter begins with a discussion of how every economy must respond to three fundamental questions: What goods and services will be produced? How will the goods and services be produced? Who will get the goods and services?

In this chapter, we introduce our first economic models: the circular flow model and the production possibilities curve. In the circular flow model, we show how decisions made by households and firms interact with each other. Our second model, the production possibilities curve, employs many of the most important concepts in economics: scarcity, trade-offs, increasing opportunity costs, efficiency, investment in capital goods, and economic growth. ■

SECTION
3.1
The Three Economic Questions Every Society Faces

* What goods and services will be produced?
* How will the goods and services be produced?
* Who will get the goods and services?

Scarcity and the Allocation of Resources

Collectively, our wants far exceed what can be produced from nature's scarce resources. So how should we allocate those scarce resources? Some methods of resource allocation might seem bad and counterproductive—for example, the "survival of the fittest" competition that takes place on the floor of the jungle. Physical violence has been used since the beginning of time, as people, regions, and countries attacked one another to gain control over resources. We could argue that government should allocate scarce resources on the basis of equal shares or according to need. However, this approach poses problems because of diverse individual preferences, the difficulty of ascertaining needs, and the negative work and investment incentives involved. In reality, society is made up of many approaches to resource allocation. For now, we will focus on one form of allocating goods and services found in most countries—the market economy.

Because of scarcity, certain economic questions must be answered, regardless of the level of affluence of the society or its political structure. We will consider three fundamental questions that every society inevitably faces: (1) What goods and services will be produced? (2) How will the goods and services be produced? (3) Who will get the goods and services produced? These questions are unavoidable in a world of scarcity.

How do we decide which colors and options to include with these cars?

consumer sovereignty
consumers vote with their dollars in a market economy; this accounts for what is produced

What Goods and Services Will Be Produced?

How do individuals control production decisions in market-oriented economies? Questions arise such as should society produce more baseball stadiums or more schools? Should Apple produce more iPhones or laptops? The government has a limited budget, too,

and must make choices on how much to spend on defense, health care, highways, and education. In short, consumers, firms, and government must all make choices about what goods and services will be produced and each one of those decisions has an opportunity cost— the highest valued alternative forgone. In the marketplace, the answer to these and other similar questions is that people "vote" in economic affairs with their dollars (or pounds or yen). This concept is called **consumer sovereignty.** Consumer sovereignty explains how individual consumers in market economies determine what is to be produced.

Televisions, DVD players, cell phones, ipods, camcorders, and computers, for example, became part of our lives because consumers "voted" hundreds of dollars apiece on these goods. As they bought more color TVs, consumers "voted" fewer dollars on regular color

TVs and more on high definition TVs. Similarly, vinyl record albums gave way to tapes, CDs to downloadable music as consumers voted for these items with their dollars. If consumers vote for more fuel efficient cars and healthier foods, then firms that wish to remain profitable must listen and respond.

How Different Types of Economic Systems Answer the Question "What Goods and Services Will Be Produced?"

Economies are organized in different ways to answer the question of what is to be produced. The dispute over the best way to answer this question has inflamed passions for centuries. Should a central planning board make the decisions, as in North Korea and Cuba? Sometimes this highly centralized economic system is referred to as a **command economy**. Under this type of regime, decisions about how many tractors or automobiles to produce are largely determined by a government official or committee associated with the central planning organization. That same group decides on the number and size of school buildings, refrigerators, shoes, and so on. Other countries, including the United States, much of Europe, and, increasingly, Asia and elsewhere have largely adopted a decentralized decision-making process where literally millions of individual producers and consumers of goods and services determine what goods, and how many of them, will be produced. A country that uses such a decentralized decision-making process is often said to have a **market economy**. Actually, no nation has a pure market economy. The United States, along with most countries, is said to have a **mixed economy**. In such an economy, the government and the private sector together determine the allocation of resources.

command economy
economy in which the government uses central planning to coordinate most economic activities

market economy
an economy that allocates goods and services through the private decisions of consumers, input suppliers, and firms

mixed economy
an economy where government and the private sector determine the allocation of resources

labor intensive
production that uses a large amount of labor

capital intensive
production that uses a large amount of capital

machines or more workers. For example, a company might decide to move their production to a plant in another country that uses more workers and fewer machines.

A ditch can be dug by many workers using their hands, by a few workers with shovels, or by one person with a backhoe. Someone must decide which method is most appropriate. From this example, you might be tempted to conclude that it is desirable to use the biggest, most elaborate form of capital. But would you really want to plant your spring flowers with huge earthmoving machinery? That is, the most capital-intensive method of production may not always be the best. The best method is the least-cost method.

What Is the Best Form of Production?

The best or "optimal" form of production will usually vary from one economy to the next. For example, earthmoving machinery is used in digging large ditches in the United States and Europe, while in developing countries, shovels are often used. Why do these optimal forms of production vary? Compared with capital, labor is relatively cheap and plentiful in developing countries but relatively scarce and expensive in the United States. In contrast, capital (machines and tools, mainly) is comparatively plentiful and cheap in the United States but scarcer and more costly in developing countries. That is, in developing countries, production tends to be more **labor intensive**, or labor driven. In the United States, production tends to be more **capital intensive**, or capital driven. Each nation tends to use the production processes that conserve its relatively scarce (and thus relatively more expensive) resources and use more of its relatively abundant resources.

How Will the Goods and Services Be Produced?

All economies, regardless of their political structure, must decide how to produce the goods and services that they want—because of scarcity. Goods and services can generally be produced in several ways. Firms may face a trade-off between using more

Who Will Get the Goods and Services Produced?

In every society, some mechanism must exist to determine how goods and services are to be distributed among the population. Who gets what? Why do some people get to consume or use far more goods and services than others? This question of distribution is so important that wars and revolutions have been fought over it. Both the French and Russian revolutions were concerned fundamentally with the distribution of goods and services. Even in societies where political questions are usually settled peacefully, the question of the distribution of income is an issue that always arouses strong emotional responses. As we will see, in a market economy with private ownership and control of the means of production, the amounts of goods and services an individual can obtain depend on her or his income. Income, in turn, will depend on the quantity and quality of the scarce resources the individual controls. Income is also determined by the price others are willing and able to pay for what you have to sell. If you are a medical doctor and make $300,000 a year, that is income you will have available to buy goods and services. If you also own a condominium you rent out in Aspen, Colorado, you will have an even greater amount of income to spend on goods and services. For instance, markets reward education, hard work, and training. Education (years of schooling) and earnings are highly (positively) correlated. For example, Oprah Winfrey makes a lot of money because she has unique and marketable skills as a talk show host. This basis for distribution may or may not be viewed as "fair," an issue we will look at in detail later in this book.

Castaway and Resource Allocation

In the movie *Castaway*, Chuck Noland's (played by Tom Hanks) plane crashes and he finds himself on a

Actor Kurt Russell gets paid a lot of money because he controls scarce resources: his talent and his name recognition. As we will see in Chapter 5, people's talents and other goods and services in limited supply relative to demand will command high prices. He also has good taste in his reading material!

Use what you've LEARNED   MARKET SIGNALS

Q Adam was a college graduate with a major in art. A few years ago, Adam decided that he wanted to pursue a vocation that utilized his talent. In response, he shut himself up in his studio and created a watercolor collection. With high hopes, Adam put his collection on display for buyers. After several years of displaying his art, however, the only one interested in the collection was his 18-year-old sister, who wanted the picture frames for her room. Recognizing that Adam was having trouble pursuing his chosen occupation, Adam's friend Karl told him that the market had failed. In the meantime, Adam

turned to house painting (interior and exterior) and business was booming. Adam hired five workers and would often be painting all day and into the evenings and weekends. Do you think the market has failed?

A No. Markets provide important signals, and the signal being sent in this situation is that Adam should look for some other means of support—something that society values. Remember the function of consumer sovereignty in the marketplace. Clearly, consumers were not voting for Adam's art. The market seems to be telling Adam: less painting on canvas and more painting on walls, doors, and trim.

Chuck Noland (Tom Hanks) had to make the best use of his scarce resources to survive on the island.

deserted island, and he has to find a way to survive. On the island, he must find answers to the *what, how,* and *for whom* questions. The *for whom* question is pretty easy: He is the only one on the island—he gets what is produced. The *what* question is pretty easy, too: He is trying to survive, so he is looking to produce food, shelter, and clothing. The *how* question is where this scene becomes interesting. Noland salvages several boxes from the plane crash. After a failed attempt to leave the island, he decides to open the boxes to see whether they contain anything useful. He first finds a pair of ice skates. He uses the blades of the ice skates as a knife to open coconuts, to cut a dress to convert into a fishing net, and to sharpen a stick to use as a spear for catching fish. He uses the laces from the skate and the bubble wrap in the package to dress an injury. He uses the raft as a lean-to for his shelter. He builds a fire and even "makes" a friend out of a volleyball. In short, Noland must use his entrepreneurial talents to make the best use of the scarce resources to survive on the island.

SECTION CHECK

1. Every economy has to decide what goods and services to produce.
2. In a decentralized market economy, millions of buyers and sellers determine what and how much to produce.
3. In a mixed economy, the government and the private sector determine the allocation of resources.
4. The best form of production is the one that conserves the relatively scarce (more costly) resources and uses more of the abundant (less costly) resources.
5. When capital is relatively scarce and labor plentiful, production tends to be labor intensive.
6. When capital is relatively abundant and labor relatively scarce, production tends to be capital intensive.
7. In a market economy, the amount of goods and services one is able to obtain depends on one's income.
8. The amount of an individual's income depends on the quantity and quality of the scarce resources that he or she controls.

1. Why does scarcity force us to decide what to produce?
2. How is a command economy different from a market economy?
3. How does consumer sovereignty determine production decisions in a market economy?
4. Do you think that what and how much an economy produces depends on who will get the goods and services produced in that economy? Why or why not?
5. Why do consumers have to "vote" for a product with their dollars for it to be a success?
6. Why must we choose among multiple ways of producing the goods and services we want?
7. Why might production be labor intensive in one economy but be capital intensive in another?
8. If a tourist from the United States on an overseas trip notices that other countries don't produce crops "like they do back home," would he be right to conclude that farmers in the other countries produce crops less efficiently than U.S. farmers?
9. In what way does scarcity determine income?
10. What are the most important functions of the market system?

The Circular Flow Model

* What are product markets?
* What are factor markets?
* What is the circular flow model?

How do we explain how the millions of people in an economy interact when it comes to buying, selling, producing, working, hiring, and so on? A continuous flow of goods and services is bought and sold between the producers of goods and services (which we call firms) and the buyers of goods and services (which we call households). A continuous flow of income also moves from firms to households as firms buy inputs to produce the goods and services they sell. In our simple economy, these exchanges take place in product markets and factor markets.

Product Markets

Product markets are the markets for consumer goods and services. In the product market, households are buyers and firms are sellers. Households buy the goods and services that firms produce and sell. The payments from the households to the firms, for the purchases of goods and services, flow to the firms at the same time as goods and services flow to the households.

Factor Markets

Factor or input markets are where households sell the use of their inputs (capital, land, labor, and entrepreneurship) to firms. In the factor market, households are the sellers and firms are the buyers. Households receive money payments from firms as compensation for the labor, land, capital, and entrepreneurship needed to produce goods and services. These

product markets
markets where households are buyers and firms are sellers of goods and services

factor (or input) markets
markets where households sell the use of their inputs (capital, land, labor, and entrepreneurship) to firms

simple circular flow model
an illustration of the continuous flow of goods, services, inputs, and payments between firms and households

payments take the form of wages (salaries), rent, interest payments, and profit.

The Simple Circular Flow Model

The **simple circular flow model** is illustrated in Exhibit 1. In the top half of the exhibit, the product markets, households purchase goods and services that firms have produced. In the lower half of the exhibit, the factor (or input) markets, households sell the inputs that firms use to produce goods and services. Households receive income (wages, rent, interest, and profit) from firms for the inputs used in production (capital, land, labor, and entrepreneurship).

Let's take a simple example to see how the circular flow model works. Suppose a teacher's supply of labor generates personal income in the form of wages (the factor market), which she can use to buy automobiles, vacations, food, and other goods (the product market). Suppose she buys an automobile (product market); the automobile dealer now has revenue to pay for his inputs (factor market)—wages to workers, purchase of new cars to replenish his inventory, rent for his building, and so on. So we see that in the simple circular flow model, income flows from firms to households (factor markets), and spending flows from households to firms (product markets). The simple circular flow model shows how households and firms interact in product markets and factor markets and how the two markets are interrelated.

section 3.2
exhibit 1   The Circular Flow Diagram

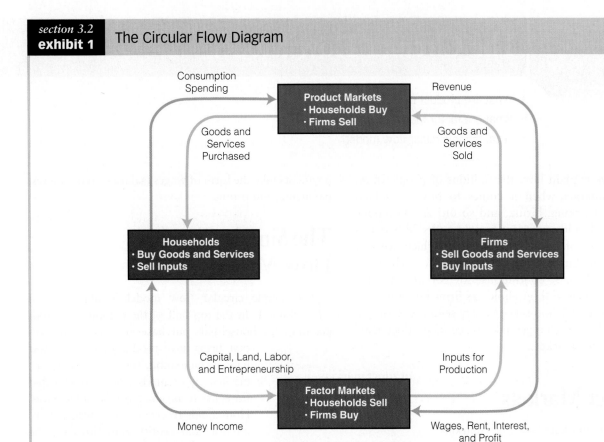

The circular flow diagram is a visual model of the economy. Households and firms interact with each other in product markets (where households buy and firms sell) and factor markets (where households sell and firms buy). For example, households receive income from firms in exchange for working and providing other inputs. Households then recycle that income to firms in exchange for goods and services. Dollars flow clockwise, and goods and services flow counterclockwise.

SECTION ✓ CHECK

1. In the product market, households are buyers and firms are sellers.
2. In the factor market, households are sellers and firms are buyers.
3. Wages, rent, interest, and profits are the payments for the labor, land, capital, and entrepreneurship needed to produce goods and services. These transactions are carried out in factor, or input, markets.
4. The circular flow model illustrates the flow of goods, services, and payments among firms and households.

1. Why does the circular flow of money move in the opposite direction from the flow of goods and services?
2. What is bought and sold in factor markets?
3. What is bought and sold in product markets?

The Production Possibilities Curve

* What is a production possibilities curve?
* What are unemployed resources?
* What are underemployed resources?
* What is efficiency?
* What is the law of increasing opportunity costs?

The Production Possibilities Curve

The economic concepts of scarcity, choice, and trade-offs can be illustrated visually by means of a simple graph called a production possibilities curve. The production possibilities curve represents the potential total output combinations of any two goods for an economy, given the inputs and technology available to the economy. That is, it illustrates an economy's potential for allocating its limited resources in producing various combinations of goods, in a given time period.

> **production possibilities curve**
> the potential total output combinations of any two goods for an economy

your expected grade in history (on the horizontal axis). Suppose you have a part-time restaurant job, so you choose to study 10 hours a week. You like both courses and are equally adept at studying for both.

We see in Exhibit 1 that the production possibilities curve is a straight line. For example, if you spend the full 10 hours studying economics, your expected grade in economics is 95 percent (an A), and your expected grade in history is 55 percent (an F). Of course, this outcome assumes you can study zero

The Production Possibilities Curve for Grades in Economics and History

What would the production possibilities curve look like if you were "producing" grades in two of your classes—say, economics and history? Exhibit 1 shows a hypothetical production possibilities curve for your expected grade in economics (on the vertical axis), and

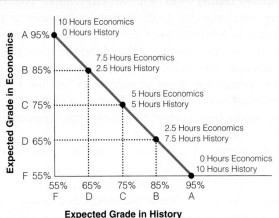

Because Tia and Tamera only have so many hours a week to study, studying more for economics and less for history might hurt their grade in history, *ceteris paribus*. Life is full of trade-offs.

COURTESY OF ROBERT L. SEXTON

**section 3.3
exhibit 1** Production Possibilities Curve: "Producing" Grades in Economics and History

Expected Grade in Economics (vertical axis)

- A 95% 10 Hours Economics / 0 Hours History
- B 85% 7.5 Hours Economics / 2.5 Hours History
- C 75% 5 Hours Economics / 5 Hours History
- D 65% 2.5 Hours Economics / 7.5 Hours History
- F 55% 0 Hours Economics / 10 Hours History

Expected Grade in History (horizontal axis): 55% F, 65% D, 75% C, 85% B, 95% A

The production possibilities curve highlights the concept of trade-offs. Assuming you choose to study a total of 10 hours a week, moving down the production possibilities curve shows that if you use your time to study history instead of economics, you can raise your expected grade in history but only at the expense of lowering your expected grade in economics. That is, with a straight-line production possibilities curve, the opportunity costs are constant.

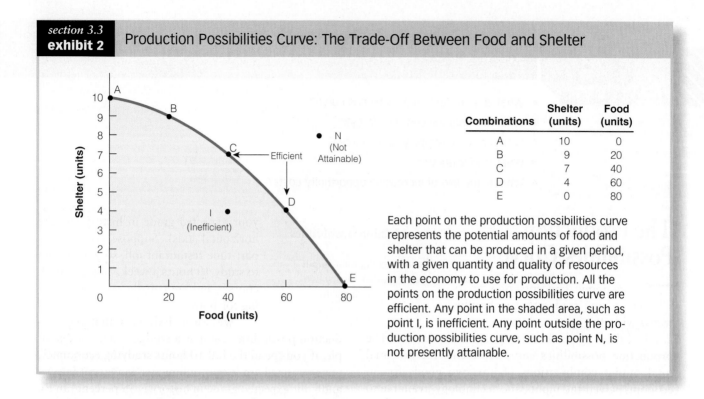

Combinations	Shelter (units)	Food (units)
A	10	0
B	9	20
C	7	40
D	4	60
E	0	80

Each point on the production possibilities curve represents the potential amounts of food and shelter that can be produced in a given period, with a given quantity and quality of resources in the economy to use for production. All the points on the production possibilities curve are efficient. Any point in the shaded area, such as point I, is inefficient. Any point outside the production possibilities curve, such as point N, is not presently attainable.

hours a week and still get a 55 percent average or study the full 10 hours a week and get a 95 percent average. Moving down the production possibilities curve, we see that as you spend more of your time studying history and less on economics, you can raise your expected grade in history but only at the expense of lowering your expected grade in economics. Specifically, moving down along the straight-line production possibilities curve, the trade-off is one lower percentage point in economics for one higher percentage point in history. That is, with a straight-line production possibilities curve, the opportunity costs are constant.

Of course, if you were to increase your overall study time, you would expect higher grades in both courses. But that would be on a different production possibilities curve. Along the production possibilities curve shown in Exhibit 1, we assume that technology and the number of study hours are given.

The Production Possibilities Curve for Food and Shelter

To illustrate the production possibilities curve more clearly, imagine living in an economy that produces just two goods, food and shelter. The fact that we have many goods in the real world makes actual decision making more complicated, but it does not alter the

basic principles being illustrated. Each point on the production possibilities curve shown in Exhibit 2 represents the potential amounts of food and shelter that we can produce in a given period, with a given quantity and quality of resources in the economy available for production.

Notice in Exhibit 2 that if we devote all our resources to making shelters, we can produce 10 units of shelter but no food (point A). If, on the other hand, we choose to devote all our resources to producing food, we end up with 80 units of food but no shelters (point E).

In reality, nations rarely opt for production possibility A or E, preferring instead to produce a mixture of goods. For example, our fictional economy might produce 9 units of shelter and 20 units of food (point B) or perhaps 7 units of shelter and 40 units of food (point C). Still other combinations along the curve, such as point D, are possible.

Off the Production Possibilities Curve

The economy cannot operate at point N (not attainable) during the given period because not enough resources are currently available to produce that level of output. However, it is possible the economy can operate inside the production possibilities curve, at point I (inefficient). If the economy is operating at point I, or any other point inside the production possibilities curve, it is not at full capacity and is operating inefficiently. In short, the economy is not using all its scarce resources efficiently; as a result, actual output is less than potential output.

Using Resources Efficiently

Most modern economies have resources that are idle, at least some of the time—during periods of high unemployment, for instance. If those resources were not idle, people would have more scarce goods and services available for their use. Unemployed resources create a serious problem. For example, consider an unemployed coal miner who is unable to find work at a "reasonable" wage, or those unemployed in depressed times when factories are already operating below capacity. Clearly, the resources of these individuals are not being used efficiently.

The fact that factories can operate below capacity suggests that it is not just labor resources that should be most effectively used. Rather, all resources entering into production should be used effectively. However,

---

Use what you've LEARNED — THE PRODUCTION POSSIBILITIES CURVE

Q Imagine that you are the overseer on a small island that only produces two goods, cattle and wheat. About a quarter of the land is not fertile enough for growing wheat, so cattle graze on it. What would happen if you tried to produce more and more wheat, extending your planting even to the less fertile soil?

A Under the law of increasing opportunity cost, as you plant more and more of your acreage in wheat, you would move into some of the rocky, less fertile land, and, consequently, wheat yields on the additional acreage would fall. If you try to plant the entire island with wheat, you would find that some of the rocky, less fertile acreage would yield virtually no extra wheat. It would, however, have been great for cattle grazing—a large loss. Thus, the opportunity cost of using that marginal land for wheat rather than cattle grazing would be high. The law of increasing opportunity cost occurs because resources are not

homogeneous (identical) and are not equally adaptable for producing cattle and wheat; some acres are more suitable for cattle grazing, while others are more suitable for wheat growing. This relationship is shown in Exhibit 3, where the vertical lines represent the opportunity cost of growing 10 more bushels of wheat in terms of cattle production sacrificed. You can see that as wheat production increases, the opportunity cost in terms of lost cattle production rises.

section 3.3 exhibit 3   Opportunity Costs for Cattle and Wheat

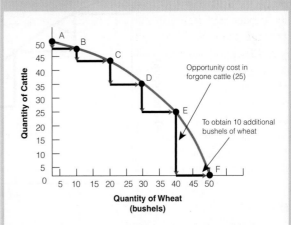

The opportunity cost of each 10 bushels of wheat in terms of forgone cattle is measured by the vertical distances. Moving from point A to point F, the opportunity cost of wheat in terms of forgone cattle rises.

social concern focuses on labor, for several reasons. A primary reason is that labor costs are the largest share of production costs. Another major reason is that unemployed or underemployed laborers (whose resources are not being used to their full potential) may have mouths to feed at home, while an unemployed machine does not (although the owner of the unemployed machine may).

Inefficiency and Efficiency

Suppose for some reason employment is widespread or resources are not being put to their best uses. The economy would then be operating at a point inside the production possibilities curve, such as I in Exhibit 2, where the economy is operating inefficiently. At point I, 4 units of shelter and 40 units of food are being produced. By putting unemployed resources to work or by putting already employed resources to better uses, we could expand the output of shelter by 3 units (moving to point C) without giving up any units of food. Alternatively, we could boost food output by 20 units (moving to point D) without reducing shelter output. We could even get more of both food and shelter by moving to a point on the curve between C and D.

Increasing or improving the utilization of resources, then, can lead to greater output of all goods. You may recall from Chapter 2, an efficient use of our resources means that more of everything we want can be available for our use. Thus, *efficiency* requires society to use its resources to the fullest extent—getting the most from our scarce resources and wasting none. If resources are being used efficiently—that is, at some point along a production possibilities curve—then more of one good or service requires the sacrifice of another good or service. Efficiency does not tell us which point along the production possibilities curve is *best*, but it does tell us that points inside the curve cannot be best, because some resources are wasted.

The Law of Increasing Opportunity Cost

As in Exhibit 2, the production possibilities curve in Exhibit 4 is not a straight line like that in Exhibit 1. It is concave from below (that is, bowed outward from the origin). Looking at Exhibit 4, you can see that at low food output, an increase in the amount of food produced will lead to only a small reduction in the

---

section 3.3
exhibit 4   Increasing Opportunity Cost and the Production Possibilities Curve

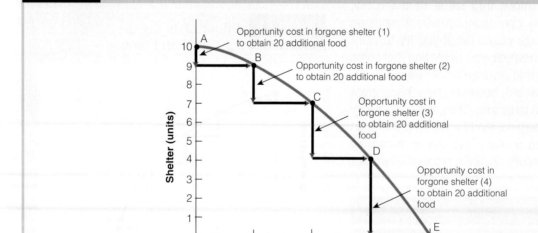

The production possibilities curve also illustrates the opportunity cost of producing more of a given product. For example, if we are to increase food output from 40 units to 60 units (moving from point C to point D), we must produce 3 fewer units of shelter. The opportunity cost of those 20 additional units of food is the 3 units of shelter we must forgo. We can see that, moving down the curve from A to E, each additional 20 units of food costs society more and more shelter—the law of increasing opportunity cost.

number of units of shelter produced. For example, increasing food output from 0 to 20 (moving from point A to point B on the curve) requires the use of resources capable of producing 1 unit of shelter. In other words, for the first 20 units of food, 1 unit of shelter must be given up. When food output is higher, however, more units of shelter must be given up when switching additional resources from the production of shelter to food. Moving from point D to point E, for example, an increase in food output of 20 (from 60 to 80) reduces the production of shelters from 4 to 0. At this point, then, the cost of those 20 additional units of food is 4 units of shelter, considerably more than the 1 unit of shelter required in the earlier scenario. This difference shows us that opportunity costs do not remain constant but rise because more units of food and fewer units of shelter are produced. It is this **increasing opportunity cost**, then, that is represented by the bowed production possibilities curve.

increasing opportunity cost
the opportunity cost of producing additional units of a good rises as society produces more of that good

What Is the Reason for the Law of Increasing Opportunity Cost?

The basic reason for the increasing opportunity cost is that some resources and skills cannot be easily adapted from their current uses to alternative uses. And, the more you produce of one good, the more you are forced to employ inputs that are relatively more suitable for producing other goods. For example, at low levels of food output, additional increases in food output can be obtained easily by switching relatively low skilled carpenters from making shelters to producing food. However, to get even more food output, workers who are less well suited or appropriate for producing food (i.e., they are better adapted to making shelters) must be released from shelter making to increase food output. For example, a skilled carpenter may be an expert at making shelters but a very bad farmer because he lacks the training and skills necessary in that occupation. So using the skilled carpenter to farm results in a relatively greater opportunity cost than using the unskilled carpenter to farm. The production of additional units of food becomes increasingly costly as progressively lower-skilled farmers (but good carpenters) convert to farming.

In short, resources tend to be specialized. As a result, we lose some of their productivity when we transfer those resources from producing what they are relatively good at to producing something they are relatively bad at.

SECTION CHECK

1. The production possibilities curve represents the potential total output combinations of two goods available to a society given its resources and existing technology.

2. If the economy is operating within the production possibilities curve, the economy is operating inefficiently; actual output is less than potential output. A point outside the production possibilities curve is currently unattainable.

3. Efficiency requires society to use its resources to the fullest extent—no wasted resources.

4. A bowed production possibilities curve means that the opportunity costs of producing additional units of a good rise as society produces more of that good (the law of increasing opportunity costs).

---

1. What does a production possibilities curve illustrate?

2. How are opportunity costs shown by the production possibilities curve?

3. Why do the opportunity costs of added production increase with output?

4. How does the production possibilities curve illustrate increasing opportunity costs?

5. Why are we concerned with widespread amounts of unemployed or underemployed resources in a society?

6. What do we mean by *efficiency,* and how is it related to underemployment of resources?

7. How are efficiency and inefficiency illustrated by a production possibilities curve?

8. Will a country that makes being unemployed illegal be more productive than one that does not? Why or why not?

9. If a 68-year-old worker in the United States chooses not to work at all, does that mean that the United States is functioning inside its production possibilities curve? Why or why not?

Economic Growth and the Production Possibilities Curve

* How much should we sacrifice today to get more in the future?
* How do we show economic growth on the production possibilities curve?

Generating Economic Growth

How have some nations been able to rapidly expand their outputs of goods and services over time, while others have been unable to increase their standards of living at all?

The economy can only grow with qualitative or quantitative changes in the factors of production—land, labor, capital, and entrepreneurship. Advancement in technology, improvements in labor productivity, or new sources of natural resources (such as previously undiscovered oil) could lead to outward shifts of the production possibilities curve.

In terms of the production possibilities curve, an outward shift in the possible combinations of goods and services produced leads to economic growth, as seen in Exhibit 1. With growth comes the possibility of having more of both goods than was previously available. Suppose we were producing at point C (7 units of shelter, 40 units of food) on our original production possibilities curve. Additional resources and/or new methods of using them (technological progress) can lead to new production possibilities, creating the potential for more of all goods (or more of some with no less of others). These increases will push the production possibilities curve outward. For example, if we invest in human capital by training the workers making the shelters, it will increase the productivity of those workers. As a result, they will produce more units of shelter. Ultimately, then, we will use fewer resources to make shelters, freeing them to be used for farming, which will result in more units of food. Notice that at point F (future) on the new curve, we can produce 9 units of shelter and 70 units of food, more of both goods than we previously could produce, at point C.

Growth Does Not Eliminate Scarcity

With all of this discussion of growth, it is important to remember that growth, or increases in a society's output, does not make scarcity disappear.

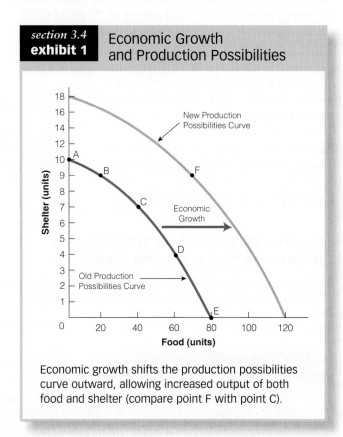

section 3.4 exhibit 1 Economic Growth and Production Possibilities

Economic growth shifts the production possibilities curve outward, allowing increased output of both food and shelter (compare point F with point C).

When output grows more rapidly than population, people are better off. But they still face trade-offs; at any point along the production possibilities curve, to get more of one thing, you must give up something else. There are no free lunches on the production possibilities curve.

Capital Goods Versus Consumption Goods

Economies that choose to invest more of their resources for the future will grow faster than those that don't. To generate economic growth, a society must produce fewer consumer goods—video games, DVD players, cell phones, cars, vacations, and so on—in the present and produce more capital goods—machines, factories, tools, education, and the like. The society that devotes a larger share of its productive capacity to capital

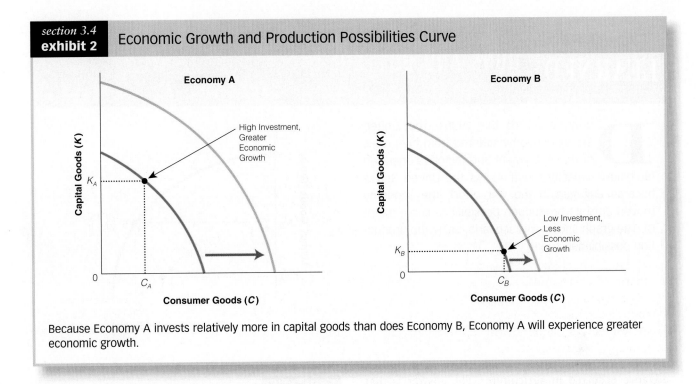

section 3.4
exhibit 2   Economic Growth and Production Possibilities Curve

Because Economy A invests relatively more in capital goods than does Economy B, Economy A will experience greater economic growth.

goods than to consumer goods will experience greater economic growth. It must sacrifice some present consumption of consumer goods and services to experience growth in the future. Why? Investing in capital goods, such as computers and other new technological equipment, as well as upgrading skills and knowledge, expands the ability to produce in the future. It shifts the economy's production possibilities curve outward, increasing the future production capacity of the economy. That is, the economy that invests more now (consumes less now) will be able to produce, and therefore consume, more in the future. In Exhibit 2, we see that Economy A invests more in capital goods than Economy B. Consequently, Economy A's production possibilities curve shifts outward further than does Economy B's over time.

The Effects of a Technological Change on the Production Possibilities Curve

In Exhibit 3, we see that a technological advance does not have to impact all sectors of the economy equally. There is a technological advance in food production but not in housing production. The technological advance in agriculture causes the production possibilities curve to extend out further on the horizontal axis which measures food production. We can move to any point on the new production

possibilities curve. For example, we could move from point A on the original production possibilities curve to point B on the new production possibilities curve. This would lead to 150 more units of food and the same amount of housing—200 units. Or, we could move from point A to point C, which would allow us to produce more units of both food and housing. How do we produce more housing, when the technological

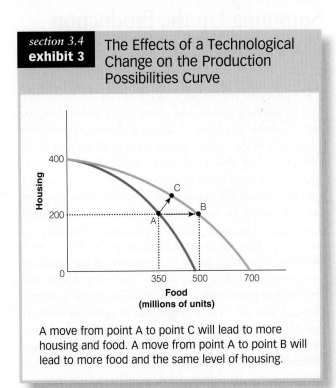

section 3.4
exhibit 3   The Effects of a Technological Change on the Production Possibilities Curve

A move from point A to point C will lead to more housing and food. A move from point A to point B will lead to more food and the same level of housing.

During most of the 1930s, the United States economy suffered from high rates of unemployment and factories operated far below capacity (point A). As the United States became engaged in the war effort, the economy moved onto its production possibilities curve (point B). The graph shows this scenario, using the production possibilities curve.

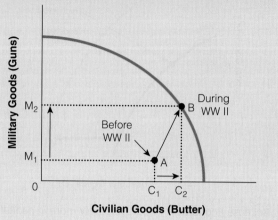

advance occurred in agriculture? The answer is that the technological advance in agriculture allows us to produce more from a given quantity of resources. That is, it allows us to shift some of our resources out of agriculture into housing. This is actually an ongoing story in U.S. economic history. In colonial days, about 90 percent of the population made a living in agriculture. Today it is less than 3 percent.

Summing Up the Production Possibilities Curve

The production possibilities curve shown in Exhibit 4 illustrates the choices faced by an economy that makes military goods and consumer goods. How are the economic concepts of scarcity, choice, opportunity costs, efficiency, and economic growth illustrated in the framework of this production possibilities curve? In Exhibit 4, we can show scarcity because resource combinations outside the initial production possibilities curve, such as point D, are unattainable without economic growth. If the economy is operating efficiently, we are somewhere on that production possibilities curve, perhaps point B or point C. However, if the economy is operating inefficiently, we are operating inside that production possibilities curve, at point A, for example. We can also see in this graph that to get more military goods, you must give up consumer goods, which represents the opportunity cost. The trade-offs between military goods and consumer goods are very real. When North Korea's leaders decided to build up their military,

section 3.4
exhibit 4   Production Possibilities Curve

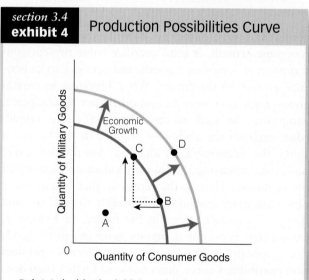

Point A, inside the initial production possibilities curve, represents inefficiency. Points B and C, on the curve, are efficient points and represent two possible output combinations. Point D can only be attained with economic growth, illustrated by the outward shift in the production possibilities curve.

it came at the expense of consumer goods. North Korea experienced a devastating famine in the 1990s and was again on the brink of famine in 2008. The 1990s famine was estimated to have killed roughly 4 percent of their population. Finally, we see that over time, with economic growth, the whole production possibilities curve can shift outward, making point D attainable.

SECTION CHECK

1. Economies must decide how much current consumption they are willing to sacrifice for greater growth in the future.
2. Economic growth is represented by an outward shift of the production possibilities curve.
3. Economic growth increases the possibility of producing more of all goods.
4. Despite economic growth, scarcity inevitably remains a fact of life.

1. What is the essential question behind issues of economic growth?
2. What is the connection between sacrifices and economic growth?
3. How is economic growth shown in terms of production possibilities curves?
4. Why doesn't economic growth eliminate scarcity?
5. What would happen to the production possibilities curve in an economy where a new innovation greatly increased its ability to produce shelter but did not change its ability to produce food?
6. If people reduced their saving (thus reducing the funds available for investment), what would that change do to society's production possibilities curve over time?

Interactive Chapter Summary

Fill in the blanks:

1. Because of scarcity, certain economic questions must be answered regardless of the level of affluence of the society or its political structure. Three fundamental questions that inevitably must be faced in a world of scarcity are (1) _____ will be produced? (2) _____ the goods and services be produced? (3) _____ the goods and services produced?

2. Market economies largely rely on a(n) _____ decision-making process, where literally millions of individual producers and consumers of goods and services determine what will be produced.

3. Most countries, including the United States, have _____ economies, in which the government and private sector determine the allocation of resources.

4. The _____-cost method is the most appropriate method for producing a given product.

5. Methods of production used where capital is relatively scarce will be _____, and methods of production used where labor is relatively scarce will be _____.

6. In a market economy, the amount of goods and services one is able to obtain depends on one's _____, which depends on the quality and quantity of the scarce _____ he or she controls.

7. The markets where households are buyers and firms are sellers of goods and services are called _____ markets.

8. The markets where households sell the use of their _____ (capital, land, labor, and entrepreneurship) to _____ are called _____ or _____ markets.

9. The simple _____ model shows the continuous flow of goods, services, inputs, and payments through the _____ and _____ markets among households and _____.

10. A(n) _____ curve represents the potential total output combinations of any two goods for an economy.

11. On a production possibilities curve, we assume that the economy has a given quantity and quality of _____ and _____ available to use for production.

12. On a straight-line production possibilities curve, the _____ are constant.

13. If an economy is operating _____ its production possibilities curve, it is not at full capacity and is operating _____. Such an economy's actual output is less than _____ output.

14. By putting _____ resources to work or by putting already employed resources to _____ uses, we could expand output.

15. _____ requires society to use its resources to the fullest extent—getting the _____ we can out of our scarce resources.

16. If the production possibilities curve is concave from below (that is, bowed outward from the origin), it reflects _____ opportunity costs of producing additional amounts of a good.

17. On a bowed production possibilities curve (concave to the origin), the opportunity costs of producing additional units of a good rises as society produces more of that good. This relationship is called the law of _____.

18. Resources tend to be specialized, so we lose some of their productivity when we transfer those resources from producing what they are relatively _____ at to producing something they are relatively _____ at.

19. To generate economic growth, a society must produce _____ consumer goods and _____ capital goods in the present.

20. Advancements in _____, improvements in _____, or new _____ could all lead to outward shifts of the production possibilities curve.

21. Increases in a society's output do not make _____ disappear. Even when output has grown more rapidly than population so that people are made better off, they still face _____.

22. The production possibilities curve can be used to illustrate the economic concepts of _____ (resource combinations outside the production possibilities curve are unattainable), _____ (selecting among the alternative bundles available along the production possibilities curve), _____ (how much of one good you give up to get another unit of the second good as you move along the production possibilities curve), _____ (being on the production possibilities curve rather than inside it), and _____ (shifting the production possibilities curve outward).

Answers: 1. what goods and services; how will; who will get 2. decentralized 3. mixed 4. least 5. labor intensive; capital intensive 6. income; resources 7. product 8. inputs; firms; factor; input 9. circular flow; product; factor; firms 10. production possibilities 11. resources; technology 12. opportunity costs 13. inside; inefficiently; potential 14. unemployed; better 15. Efficiency; most 16. increasing 17. increasing opportunity costs 18. good; bad 19. fewer; more 20. technology; labor productivity; natural resource finds 21. scarcity; trade-offs 22. scarcity; choice; opportunity costs; efficiency; economic growth

Key Terms and Concepts

consumer sovereignty 67
command economy 68
market economy 68
mixed economy 68

labor intensive 68
capital intensive 68
product markets 71
factor (or input) markets 71

simple circular flow model 71
production possibilities curve 73
increasing opportunity cost 77

Section Check Answers

3.1 The Three Economic Questions Every Society Faces

1. Why does scarcity force us to decide what to produce?

Because our wants exceed the amount of goods and services that can be produced from our limited resources, it must be decided which wants should have priority over others.

2. How is a command economy different from a market economy?

A command economy makes decisions about what and how much to produce centrally by members of a planning board or organization. A market economy makes those decisions as the result of decentralized decision making by individual producers and consumers, coordinated by their offers to buy and sell on markets.

3. How does consumer sovereignty determine production decisions in a market economy?

Consumer sovereignty determines production decisions in a market economy because producers make what they believe consumers will "vote" for by being willing to pay for them.

4. Do you think that what and how much an economy produces depends on who will get the goods and services produced in that economy? Why or why not?

Who will get the goods produced in an economy affects the incentives of the producers. The less a producer will benefit from increased production, the smaller are incentives to increase production, and the smaller will be total output in an economy.

5. **Why do consumers have to "vote" for a product with their dollars for it to be a success?**

   In the market sector, products can be profitable only if they attract dollar votes from consumers.

6. **Why must we choose among multiple ways of producing the goods and services we want?**

   We must choose among multiple ways of producing the goods and services we want because goods can generally be produced in several ways, using different combinations of resources.

7. **Why might production be labor intensive in one economy but be capital intensive in another?**

   Production will tend to be labor intensive where labor is relatively plentiful, and therefore relatively less expensive; it will tend to be capital intensive where capital is relatively plentiful, and therefore relatively less expensive. When the manner of production is different in different situations because factors of production have different relative prices, each of those methods will be more efficient where they are used.

8. **If a tourist from the United States on an overseas trip notices that other countries don't produce crops "like they do back home," would he be right to conclude that farmers in the other countries produce crops less efficiently than U.S. farmers?**

   No. The different ways of farming in different areas reflect the different relative scarcities of land, labor, and capital they face. Factors of production that are relatively scarce in an economy are also relatively costly there as a result. Producers there economize on the use of those more costly resources by using more of relatively less scarce, and less costly, resources instead. For example, where land is scarce, it is intensively cultivated with relatively cheaper (less scarce) labor and capital, but where capital is scarce, relatively cheaper (less scarce) land and labor are substituted for capital.

9. **In what way does scarcity determine income?**

   Relative scarcity determines the market values of the scarce resources people offer to others in exchange for income.

10. **What are the most important functions of the market system?**

    They transmit information through price signals, they provide incentives, and they distribute income.

3.2 The Circular Flow Model

1. **Why does the circular flow of money move in the opposite direction from the flow of goods and services?**

   The circular flow of money moves in the opposite direction from the flow of goods and services because the money flows are the payments made in exchange for the goods and services.

2. **What is bought and sold in factor markets?**

   The factors of production—capital, land, labor, and entrepreneurship—are sold in factor, or input, markets.

3. **What is bought and sold in product markets?**

   Consumer and investment goods and services are sold in product markets.

3.3 The Production Possibilities Curve

1. **What does a production possibilities curve illustrate?**

   The production possibilities curve illustrates the potential output combinations of two goods in an economy operating at full capacity, given the inputs and technology available to the economy.

2. **How are opportunity costs shown by the production possibilities curve?**

   Opportunity cost—the forgone output of one good necessary to increase output of another good—is illustrated by the slope, or trade-off, between the two goods at a given point on the production possibilities curve.

3. **Why do the opportunity costs of added production increase with output?**

   Opportunity costs of added production increase with output because some resources cannot be easily adapted from their current uses to alternative uses. At first, easily adaptable resources can be switched to producing more of a good. But once those easily adapted resources have been switched, producing further output requires the use of resources less well adapted to expanding that output, raising the opportunity cost of output.

4. **How does the production possibilities curve illustrate increasing opportunity costs?**

   Increasing opportunity costs are illustrated by a bowed (concave from below) production possibilities curve. It shows that initial units of one good can be produced by giving up little of another good, but progressive increases in output will require greater and greater sacrifices of the other good.

5. **Why are we concerned with widespread amounts of unemployed or underemployed resources in a society?**

   We are concerned with widespread amounts of unemployed or underemployed resources in a society because, if we could reduce the extent of unemployed or underemployed resources, people could have more scarce goods and services available for their use.

6. **What do we mean by *efficiency,* and how is it related to underemployment of resources?**

Efficiency means getting the most we can out of our scarce resources. Underemployment of resources means a society is not getting the most it can out of these resources, either because they are not fully employed or because they are not matched to the uses best suited to them.

7. **How are efficiency and inefficiency illustrated by a production possibilities curve?**

Efficient combinations of outputs are illustrated by points on the production possibilities curve, along which more of one good can be produced only if less of some other good is also produced. Inefficient combinations of outputs are illustrated by points inside the production possibilities curve, because more of both goods could then be produced with the resources available to the economy.

8. **Will a country that makes being unemployed illegal be more productive than one that does not? Why or why not?**

A more productive economy is one that makes the best use of those who wish to work. Making unemployment illegal (as was true in the old USSR) does not eliminate underemployment, nor does it guarantee that people and other resources are employed where they are most productive (especially because it is more difficult to search for a better job when you are working than when you are not working).

9. **If a 68-year-old worker in the United States chooses not to work at all, does that mean that the United States is functioning inside its production possibilities curve? Why or why not?**

Individuals who choose retirement rather than work must consider themselves better off not working, when all the relevant considerations are taken into account. They are therefore as fully employed, given their circumstances, as they would like to be, and so the choice does not imply that the United States would be inside its production possibilities curve as a result. However, if such workers became more willing to work, that would shift the United States' production possibilities curve outward.

3.4 Economic Growth and the Production Possibilities Curve

1. **What is the essential question behind issues of economic growth?**

The essential question behind issues of economic growth is: How much are we willing to give up today to get more in the future?

2. **What is the connection between sacrifices and economic growth?**

The more current consumption is sacrificed in an economy, the larger the fraction of its current resources it can devote to producing investment goods, which will increase its rate of economic growth.

3. **How is economic growth shown in terms of production possibilities curves?**

Economic growth—the expansion of what an economy can produce—is shown as an outward shift in the production possibilities curve, with formerly unattainable output combinations now made possible.

4. **Why doesn't economic growth eliminate scarcity?**

Economic growth doesn't eliminate scarcity because people's wants still exceed what they are capable of producing, so that trade-offs among scarce goods must still be made.

5. **What would happen to the production possibilities curve in an economy where a new innovation greatly increased its ability to produce shelter but did not change its ability to produce food?**

This innovation would increase the amount of shelter the economy could produce, shifting out the production possibilities curve's intercept on the shelter axis, but not changing its intercept on the food axis. If shelter is on the vertical axis and food is on the horizontal axis of the production possibilities curve, such a technological change would leave the vertical intercept unchanged, but make it less steep (reflecting the reduced opportunity cost of producing additional food), shifting out the curve's intercept with the horizontal axis.

6. **If people reduced their saving (thus reducing the funds available for investment), what would that change do to society's production possibilities curve over time?**

The less people save, the slower the capital stock of the economy will grow through new investment (because saving is the source of the funds for investment), and so the slower the production possibilities curve would shift out over time.

True or False:

1. Consumer sovereignty describes how individual consumers in market economies determine what is to be produced.

2. Command economies rely on central planning, where decisions about what and how many are largely determined by a government official associated with the central planning organization.

3. All economies, regardless of political structure, must decide how, from several possible ways, to produce the goods and services that they want.

4. In any economy, it would always be less efficient to dig ditches by having many workers use their hands than to use workers with shovels or a backhoe.

5. Each nation tends to use the production processes that conserve its relatively scarce (and thus relatively more expensive) resources and use more of its relatively abundant resources.

6. In a market economy, with private ownership and control of the means of production, the amount of output one is able to obtain depends on the quantity and quality of the scarce resources that the individual controls.

7. The market where households sell the use of their inputs to firms is called the product market.

8. The circular flow model illustrates the continuous flow of goods, services, inputs, and payments between firms and households.

9. With a straight-line production possibilities curve, the opportunity cost of producing another unit of a good increases with its output.

10. The economy cannot produce beyond the levels indicated by the production possibilities curve during a given time period, but it is possible to operate inside the production possibilities curve.

11. Underutilized resources or those not being put to their best uses are illustrated by output combinations along the production possibilities curve.

12. We all have an interest in the efficient use of all of society's resources because more of everything we care about can be available for our use as a result.

13. If resources are being used efficiently, at a point along a production possibilities curve, more of one good or service requires the sacrifice of another good or service as a cost.

14. The basic reason for increasing opportunity cost is that some resources and skills cannot be easily adapted from their current uses to alternative uses.

15. Investing in capital goods will increase the future production capacity of an economy, so an economy that invests more now (consumes less now) will be able to produce, and therefore consume, more in the future.

16. An economy can grow despite a lack of qualitative and quantitative improvements in the factors of production.

17. Economic growth means a movement along an economy's production possibilities curve in the direction of producing more consumer goods.

18. From a point inside the production possibilities curve, in order to get more of one thing, an economy must give up something else.

Multiple Choice:

1. Which of the following is not a question that all societies must answer?
   a. How can scarcity be eliminated?
   b. What goods and services will be produced?
   c. Who will get the goods and services?
   d. How will the goods and services be produced?
   e. All of the above are questions that all societies must answer.

2. Economic disputes over the distribution of income are generally associated with which economic question?
   a. Who should produce the goods?
   b. What goods and services will be produced?
   c. Who will get the goods and services?
   d. How will the goods and services be produced?

3. Three economic questions must be determined in all societies. What are they?
   a. How much will be produced? When will it be produced? How much will it cost?
   b. What will the price of each good be? Who will produce each good? Who will consume each good?
   c. What is the opportunity cost of production? Does the society have a comparative advantage in production? Will consumers desire the goods being produced?
   d. What goods and services will be produced? How will the goods and services be produced? Who will get the goods and services?

4. The private ownership of property and the use of the market system to direct and coordinate economic activity are most characteristic of
   a. a command economy.
   b. a mixed economy.
   c. a market economy.
   d. a traditional economy.

5. The degree of government involvement in the economy is greatest in
   a. a command economy.
   b. a mixed economy.
   c. a market economy.
   d. a traditional economy.

6. When a command economy is utilized to resolve economic questions regarding the allocation of resources, then
   a. everyone will receive an equal share of the output produced.
   b. the preferences of individuals are of no importance.
   c. economic efficiency will be assured.
   d. the role of markets will be replaced by political decision making.

7. In a circular flow diagram,
   a. goods and services flow in a clockwise direction.
   b. goods and services flow in a counterclockwise direction.
   c. product markets appear at the top of the diagram.
   d. factor markets appear at the left of the diagram.
   e. both b and c are true.

8. Which of the following is true?
   a. In the product markets, firms are buyers and households are sellers.
   b. In the factor markets, firms are sellers and households are buyers.
   c. Firms receive money payments from households for capital, land, labor, and entrepreneurship.
   d. All of the above are true.
   e. None of the above are true.

9. In the circular flow model,
   a. firms supply both products and resources.
   b. firms demand both products and resources.
   c. firms demand resources and supply products.
   d. firms supply resources and demand products.

10. A point beyond the boundary of an economy's production possibilities curve is
    a. efficient.
    b. inefficient.
    c. attainable.
    d. unattainable.
    e. both attainable and efficient.

Use the diagram to answer questions 11 through 14.

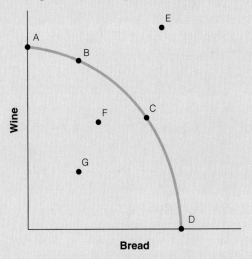

Bread

11. Currently, it is not possible to produce at
    a. point A.
    b. point B.
    c. point E.
    d. point G.
    e. either point E or point G.

12. An economy is operating at full employment, and then workers in the bread industry are laid off. This change is portrayed in the movement from
    a. A to B.
    b. B to E.
    c. C to F.
    d. G to F.
    e. None of the above are correct.

13. Along the production possibilities curve, the most efficient point of production depicted is
    a. point B.
    b. point C.
    c. point D.
    d. point G.
    e. All points on the production possibilities curve are equally efficient.

14. The opportunity cost of one more unit of bread is greater at point _____ than at point _____.
    a. G; B
    b. C; A
    c. A; C
    d. None of the above. The opportunity cost of a good is constant everywhere along the production possibilities curve.

15. Which of the following is consistent with the implications of the production possibilities curve?
    a. If the resources in an economy are being used efficiently, scarcity will not be a problem.
    b. If the resources in an economy are being used efficiently, more of one good can be produced only if less of another good is produced.
    c. Producing more of any one good will require smaller and smaller sacrifices of other goods as more of that good is being produced in an economy.
    d. An economy will automatically attain that level of output at which all of its resources are fully employed.
    e. Both b and c are consistent with the implications of the production possibilities curve.

16. Consider a production possibilities curve for an economy producing bicycles and video game players. It is possible to increase the production of bicycles without sacrificing video game players if
    a. the production possibilities curve shifts outward due to technological progress.
    b. the production possibilities curve shifts outward due to increased immigration (which enlarges the labor force).
    c. the economy moves from a point inside the production possibilities curve to a point on the curve.
    d. any of the above occurs.
    e. either a or b, but not c, occurs.

17. What determines the position and shape of a society's production possibilities curve?
    a. the physical resources of that society
    b. the skills of the workforce
    c. the level of technology of the society
    d. the number of factories available to the society
    e. all of the above

18. Which of the following is the most accurate statement about a production possibilities curve?
    a. An economy can produce at any point inside or outside its production possibilities curve.
    b. An economy can produce only on its production possibilities curve.
    c. An economy can produce at any point on or inside its production possibilities curve, but not outside the curve.
    d. An economy can produce at any point inside its production possibilities curve, but not on or outside the curve.

19. Which of the following is most likely to shift the production possibilities curve outward?
    a. an increase in unemployment
    b. a decrease in the stock of physical or human capital
    c. a decrease in the labor force
    d. a technological advance

20. Which of the following is least likely to shift the production possibilities curve outward?
    a. a change in preferences away from one of the goods and toward the other
    b. an invention that reduces the amount of natural resources necessary for producing a good
    c. the discovery of new natural resources
    d. a reduction in people's preferences for leisure

21. Inefficiency is best illustrated by which of the following?
    a. forgoing civilian goods in order to produce more military goods
    b. limiting economic growth by reducing capital spending
    c. having high levels of unemployment of labor and other resources that could be productively employed
    d. producing outside the production possibilities frontier
    e. all of the above

22. Suppose Country A produces few consumption goods and many investment goods while Country B produces few investment goods and many consumption goods. Other things being equal, you would expect
    a. per capita income to grow more rapidly in Country B.
    b. population to grow faster in Country B.
    c. the production possibilities curve for Country A to shift out more rapidly than that of Country B.
    d. that if both countries started with identical production possibilities curves, in 20 years, people in Country B will be able to produce more consumer goods than people in Country A.
    e. that both c and d are true.

23. A virulent disease spreads throughout the population of an economy, causing death and disability. This event can be portrayed as
    a. a movement from a point on the production possibilities curve to a point inside the curve.
    b. a movement from a point on the production possibilities curve to the northeast.
    c. a movement along the production possibilities curve to the southeast.
    d. an outward shift of the production possibilities curve.
    e. an inward shift of the production possibilities curve.

24. Say that a technological change doubles an economy's ability to produce good X and triples the economy's ability to produce good Y. As a result,
    a. the economy will tend to produce less X and more Y than before.
    b. the opportunity cost of producing units of Y in terms of X forgone will tend to fall.

c. the production possibilities curve will shift out further along the X-axis than along the Y-axis.

d. both b and c would be true.

Problems:

1. What are the three basic economic questions? How are decisions made differently in a market economy than in planned economies?

2. Recently the American Film Institute selected *Citizen Kane* as the best movie of all time. *Citizen Kane* is a fictional psychological biography of one of the most powerful newspaper publishers in history, William Randolph Hearst. *Titanic,* an epic romance about the sinking of the *Titanic,* has made the most money of any film in history. Unlike *Titanic, Citizen Kane* was not a box office success. Do you think Hollywood will make more movies like *Titanic* or like *Citizen Kane?* Why?

3. As women's wages and employment opportunities have expanded over the past 50 years, Americans have purchased more and more labor-saving home appliances like automatic washers and dryers, dishwashers, and microwave ovens. Do you think these phenomena are related? Could higher wages and better job opportunities lead to a more capital-intensive way of performing household chores? Explain.

4. Identify where the appropriate entries go in the circular flow diagram.

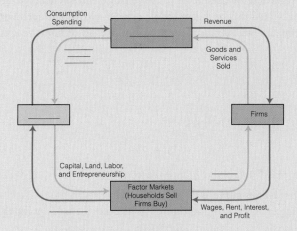

5. Identify whether each of the following transactions takes place in the factor market or the product market.
   a. Billy buys a sofa from Home Time Furniture for his new home.
   b. Home Time Furniture pays its manager her weekly salary.
   c. The manager buys dinner at Billy's Café.
   d. After he pays all of his employees their wages and pays his other bills, the owner of Billy's Café takes his profit.

6. Given the following production possibilities curve:

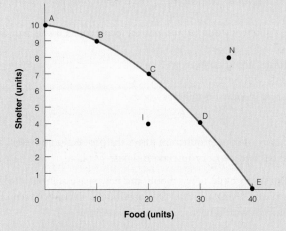

   a. Does this production possibilities curve show increasing opportunity costs? Explain.
   b. What is the opportunity cost of moving from point I to point D? Explain.

c. What is the opportunity cost of moving from point C to point B?

d. Which of points A–E is the most efficient? Explain.

7. During wartime, countries shift production from civilian goods, like automobiles and clothing, to military goods, like tanks and military uniforms. When the United States entered World War I in April 1917, for example, the federal government created the War Industries Board and charged it with determining production priorities and converting plants to meet war needs. In the following year, automobile production fell 43 percent as output of military vehicles soared. When the war ended, 19 months later, in November 1918, the government cancelled $2.5 billion in military contracts and the nation resumed normal production. Assuming that in 1917 the United States was at point A on the production possibilities curves shown, show what happened between April 1917 and November 1918. Show what happened once the war ended.

8. How would the following events be shown using a production possibilities curve for shelter and food?

a. The economy is experiencing double-digit unemployment.

b. Economic growth is increasing at more than 5 percent per year.

c. Society decides it wants less shelter and more food.

d. Society decides it wants more shelter and less food.

9. In *A Bend in the River,* Nobel Prize winner V. S. Naipaul describes an underdeveloped country in which the government's constantly changing tax policies and vague laws regarding ownership of property cause entrepreneurs to become demoralized and unresponsive to economic opportunities. Could this be a case of idle or unemployed entrepreneurs? How can tax laws and rules governing property affect entrepreneurs' willingness to start new businesses or improve existing enterprises?

10. Using the following table, answer the questions:

	Combinations				
	A	B	C	D	E
Guns	1	2	3	4	5
Butter	20	18	14	8	0

a. What are the assumptions for a given production possibilities curve?

b. What is the opportunity cost of one gun when moving from point B to point C? When moving from point D to point E?

c. Do these combinations demonstrate constant or increasing opportunity costs?

11. Economy A produces more capital goods and fewer consumer goods than Economy B. Which economy will grow more rapidly? Draw two production possibilities curves, one for Economy A and one for Economy B. Demonstrate graphically how one economy can grow more rapidly than the other.

12. Why one nation experiences economic growth and another doesn't is a question that has intrigued economists since Adam Smith wrote *An Inquiry into the Nature and Causes of the Wealth of Nations* in 1776. Explain why each of the following would limit economic growth.

a. The politically connected elite secure a large share of a country's output and put the proceeds in Swiss banks.

b. A country has a very low output per person.

c. The national philosophy is live for the moment and forget about tomorrow.

d. The government closes all of the schools so more people will be available for work.

e. The country fears military invasion and spends half of its income on military goods.

13. How does education add to a nation's capital stock?

14. How does a technological advance that increases the efficiency of shoe production affect the production possibilities curve between shoes and pizza? Is it possible to produce more shoes and pizza or just more shoes? Explain.

15. A politician running for president of the United States promises to build new schools and new space stations during the next four years without sacrificing any other goods and services. Using a production possibilities curve between schools and space stations, explain under what conditions the politician would be able to keep his promise.

PART 2 SUPPLY AND DEMAND

4 Supply and Demand

According to Thomas Carlyle, a nineteenth-century philosopher, "Teach a parrot the term 'supply and demand' and you've got an economist." Unfortunately, economics is more complicated than that.

However, if Carlyle was hinting at the importance of supply and demand, he was right on target. Supply and demand is without a doubt the most powerful tool in the economist's toolbox. It can help explain much of what goes on in the world and help predict what will happen tomorrow. In this chapter, we begin with an introduction to markets. Every market has a demand side and a supply side. Buyers represent the demand side of the market and sellers represent the supply side. In this chapter, we will learn about the law of demand and the law of supply and the factors that can change supply and demand. In the following chapter, we will put it together to show markets in motion. ■

Markets

* What is a market?
* Why is it so difficult to define a market?

Defining a Market

Although we usually think of a market as a place where some sort of exchange occurs, a market is not really a place at all. A **market** is the process of buyers and sellers exchanging goods and services. Supermarkets, the New York Stock Exchange, drug stores, roadside stands, garage sales, Internet stores, and restaurants are all markets.

> **market**
> the process of buyers and sellers exchanging goods and services

Every market is different. That is, the conditions under which the exchange between buyers and sellers takes place can vary. These differences make it difficult to precisely define a market. After all, an incredible variety of exchange arrangements exist in the real world—organized securities markets, wholesale auction markets, foreign exchange markets, real estate markets, labor markets, and so forth.

Goods being priced and traded in various ways at various locations by various kinds of buyers and sellers further compound the problem of defining a market.

PETER FOLEY/REUTERS/LANDOV

The stock market involves many buyers and sellers; and profit statements and stock prices are readily available. New information is quickly understood by buyers and sellers and is incorporated into the price of the stock. When people expect a company to do better in the future, the price of the stock rises; when people expect the company to do poorly in the future, the price of the stock falls.

AP IMAGES

eBay is an Internet auction company that brings together millions of buyers and sellers from all over the world. The gains from these mutually beneficial exchanges are large. Craigslist also uses the power of the internet to connect many buyers and sellers in local markets.

For some goods, such as housing, markets are numerous but limited to a geographic area. Homes in Santa Barbara, California, for example (about 100 miles from downtown Los Angeles), do not compete directly with homes in Los Angeles. Why? Because people who work in Los Angeles will generally look for homes within commuting distance. Even within cities, separate markets for homes are differentiated by amenities such as more living space, newer construction, larger lots, and better schools.

In a similar manner, markets are numerous but geographically limited for a good such as cement. Because transportation costs are so high relative to the selling price, the good is not shipped any substantial distance, and buyers are usually in contact only with local producers. Price and output are thus determined in a number of small markets. In other markets, such as those for gold or automobiles, markets are global. The important point is not what a market looks like, but what it does—it facilitates trade.

Buyers and Sellers

The roles of buyers and sellers in markets are important. Buyers, as a group, determine the demand side of the market. Buyers include the consumers who purchase the goods and services and the firms that buy inputs—labor, capital, and raw materials. Sellers, as a group, determine the supply side of the market. Sellers include the firms that produce and sell goods and services and the resource owners who sell their inputs to firms—workers who "sell" their labor and resource owners who sell raw materials and capital. The interaction of buyers and sellers determines market prices and output—through the forces of supply and demand.

In the next few chapters, we focus on how supply and demand work in a competitive market. A

> **competitive market**
> a market where the many buyers and sellers have little market power—each buyer's or seller's effect on market price is negligible

competitive market is one in which a number of buyers and sellers are offering similar products, and no single buyer or seller can influence the market price. That is, buyers and sellers have little market power. Because many markets contain a large degree of competitiveness, the lessons of supply and demand can be applied to many different types of problems.

The supply and demand model is particularly useful in markets like agriculture, finance, labor, construction, services, wholesale, and retail.

In short, a model is only as good as it explains and predicts. The model of supply and demand is very good at predicting changes in prices and quantities in many markets large and small.

SECTION CHECK

1. Markets consist of buyers and sellers exchanging goods and services with one another.
2. Markets can be regional, national, or global.
3. Buyers determine the demand side of the market and sellers determine the supply side of the market.

---

1. Why is it difficult to define a market precisely?
2. Why do you get your produce at a supermarket rather than directly from farmers?
3. Why do the prices people pay for similar items at garage sales vary more than for similar items in a department store?

SECTION 4.2 # Demand

* What is the law of demand?
* What is an individual demand curve?
* What is a market demand curve?

The Law of Demand

Sometimes observed behavior is so pervasive it is called a law—the law of demand, for example. According to the law of demand, the quantity of a good or service demanded varies inversely (negatively) with its price, *ceteris paribus*. More directly, the law

> **law of demand**
> the quantity of a good or service demanded varies inversely (negatively) with its price, *ceteris paribus*

of demand says that, other things being equal, when the price (P) of a good or service falls, the quantity demanded (Q_D) increases. Conversely, if the price of a good or service rises, the quantity demanded decreases.

$$P \uparrow \Rightarrow Q_D \downarrow \quad \text{and} \quad P \downarrow \Rightarrow Q_D \uparrow$$

Individual Demand

An Individual Demand Schedule

The individual demand schedule shows the relationship between the price of the good and the quantity demanded. For example, suppose Elizabeth enjoys drinking coffee. How many pounds of coffee would Elizabeth be willing and able to buy at various prices during the year? At a price of $3 a pound, Elizabeth buys 15 pounds of coffee over the course of a year. If the price is higher, at $4 per pound, she might buy only 10 pounds; if it is lower, say $1 per pound, she might buy 25 pounds of coffee during the year. Elizabeth's demand for coffee for the year is summarized in the demand schedule in Exhibit 1. Elizabeth might not be consciously aware of the amounts that she would purchase at prices other than the prevailing one, but that does not alter the fact that she has a schedule in the sense that she would have bought various other amounts had other prices prevailed. It must be emphasized that the schedule is a list of alternative possibilities. At any one time, only one of the prices will prevail, and thus a certain quantity will be purchased.

individual demand schedule
a schedule that shows the relationship between price and quantity demanded

individual demand curve
a graphical representation that shows the inverse relationship between price and quantity demanded

market demand curve
the horizontal summation of individual demand curves

An Individual Demand Curve

By plotting the different prices and corresponding quantities demanded in Elizabeth's demand schedule in Exhibit 1 and then connecting them, we can create the individual demand curve for Elizabeth shown in Exhibit 2. From the curve, we can see that when the price is higher, the quantity demanded is lower, and when the price is lower, the quantity demanded is higher. The demand curve shows how the quantity demanded of the good changes as its price varies.

What Is a Market Demand Curve?

Although we introduced the concept of the demand curve in terms of the individual, economists usually speak of the demand curve in terms of large groups of people—a whole nation, a community, or a trading area. That is, to analyze how the market works, we will need to use market demand. As you know, every individual has his or her demand curve for every product. The horizontal summing of the demand curves of many individuals is called the market demand curve.

Suppose the consumer group is composed of Homer, Marge, and the rest of their small community, Springfield, and that the product is still coffee. The effect of price on the quantity of coffee demanded by Marge, Homer, and the rest of Springfield is given in the demand schedule and demand curves shown in Exhibit 3. At $4 per pound, Homer would be willing and able to buy 20 pounds of coffee per year, Marge would be willing and able to buy 10 pounds, and the rest of Springfield would be willing and able to buy 2,970 pounds. At $3 per pound, Homer would be

---

section 4.2 **exhibit 2**	Elizabeth's Demand Curve for Coffee

The dots represent various quantities of coffee that Elizabeth would be willing and able to buy at different prices in a given period. The demand curve shows how the quantity demanded varies inversely with the price of the good when we hold everything else constant—*ceteris paribus*. Because of this inverse relationship between price and quantity demanded, the demand curve is downward sloping.

---

section 4.2 **exhibit 1**	Elizabeth's Demand Schedule for Coffee

Price of Coffee (per pound)	Quantity of Coffee Demanded (pounds per year)
$5	5
4	10
3	15
2	20
1	25

section 4.2
exhibit 3   Creating a Market Demand Curve

a. Creating a Market Demand Schedule for Coffee

	Quantity of Coffee Demanded (pounds per year)							
Price (per pound)	Homer	+	Marge	+	Rest of Springfield	=	Market Demand
$4	20	+	10	+	2,970	=	3,000
$3	25	+	15	+	4,960	=	5,000

b. Creating a Market Demand Curve for Coffee

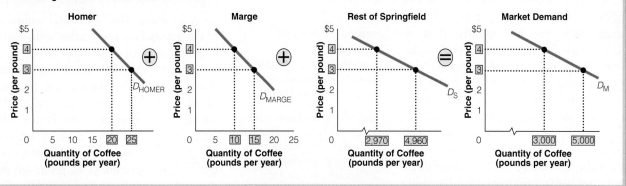

section 4.2
exhibit 4   A Market Demand Curve

a. Market Demand Schedule for Coffee

Price (per pound)	Quantity Demanded (pounds per year)
$5	1,000
4	3,000
3	5,000
2	8,000
1	12,000

b. Market Demand Curve for Coffee

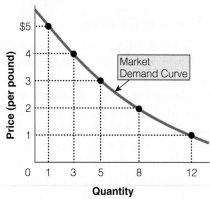

The market demand curve shows the amounts that all the buyers in the market would be willing and able to buy at various prices. We find the market demand curve by adding horizontally the individual demand curves. For example, when the price of coffee is $2 per pound, consumers in the market collectively would be willing and able to buy 8,000 pounds per year. At $1 per pound, the amount collectively demanded would be 12,000 pounds per year.

willing and able to buy 25 pounds of coffee per year, Marge would be willing and able to buy 15 pounds, and the rest of Springfield would be willing and able to buy 4,960 pounds. The market demand curve is simply the (horizontal) sum of the quantities Homer, Marge, and the rest of Springfield demand at each price. That is, at

$4, the quantity demanded in the market would be 3,000 pounds of coffee (20 + 10 + 2,970 = 3,000), and at $3, the quantity demanded in the market would be 5,000 pounds of coffee (25 + 15 + 4,960 = 5,000).

In Exhibit 4, we offer a more complete set of prices and quantities from the market demand for coffee during the year. Remember, the market demand curve shows the amounts that all the buyers in the market would be willing and able to buy at various prices. For example, when the price of coffee is $2 per pound, consumers in the market collectively would be willing and able to buy 8,000 pounds per year. At $1 per pound, the amount collectively demanded would

be 12,000 pounds per year. The market demand curve is the negative (inverse) relationship between price and the total quantity demanded, while holding all other factors that affect how much consumers are able and willing to pay constant, *ceteris paribus*. For the most part, we are interested in how the market works, so we will primarily use market demand curves.

SECTION CHECK

1. The law of demand states that when the price of a good falls (rises), the quantity demanded rises (falls), *ceteris paribus*.

2. An individual demand curve is a graphical representation of the relationship between the price and the quantity demanded.

3. The market demand curve shows the amount of a good that all buyers in the market would be willing and able to buy at various prices.

---

1. What is an inverse relationship?
2. How do lower prices change buyers' incentives?
3. How do higher prices change buyers' incentives?
4. What is an individual demand schedule?
5. What is the difference between an individual demand curve and a market demand curve?
6. Why does the amount of dating on campus tend to decline just before and during final exams?

SECTION 4.3

Shifts in the Demand Curve

* What is the difference between a change in demand and a change in quantity demanded?
* What are the determinants of demand?
* What are substitutes and complements?
* What are normal and inferior goods?
* How does the number of buyers affect the demand curve?
* How do changes in taste affect the demand curve?
* How do changing expectations affect the demand curve?

A Change in Demand Versus a Change in Quantity Demanded

Consumers are influenced by the prices of goods when they make their purchasing decisions. At lower prices, people prefer to buy more of a good than they do at higher prices, holding other factors constant. Why? Primarily, it is because many goods are substitutes

change in quantity demanded
a change in a good's own price leads to a change in quantity demanded, a move along a given demand curve

for one another. For example, an increase in the price of coffee might tempt some buyers to switch from buying coffee to buying tea or soft drinks.

Understanding this relationship between price and quantity demanded is so important that economists make a clear distinction between it and the various other factors that can influence consumer behavior. A change in a good's own price is said to lead to a **change in quantity demanded.** That is, it "moves you along" a given demand curve. The demand curve is drawn under the assumption that all other things are held constant, except the price of the good. However, economists know that price is not the only thing that affects the quantity of a good that people buy. The other factors that influence the demand curve are called *determinants of demand*, and a change in these other factors *shifts the entire demand curve*. These determinants of demand are called demand shifters and they lead to changes in demand.

change in demand
the prices of related goods, income, number of buyers, tastes, and expectations can change the demand for a good; that is, a change in one of these factors shifts the entire demand curve

possible demand shifters are the prices of related goods, income, number of buyers, tastes, and expectations. We will now look more closely at each of these variables.

The Prices of Related Goods

In deciding how much of a good or service to buy, consumers are influenced by the price of that good or service, a relationship summarized in the law of demand. However, sometimes consumers are also influenced by the prices of *related* goods and services—substitutes and complements.

Substitutes

Substitutes are generally goods for which one could be used in place of the other. To many, substitutes would include butter and margarine, domestic and foreign cars, movie tickets and video rentals, jackets and sweaters, Exxon and Shell gasoline, and Nikes and Reeboks.

Suppose you go into a store to buy a couple of six packs of Coca-Cola and you see that Pepsi is on sale for half its usual price. Is it possible that you might decide to buy Pepsi instead of Coca-Cola? Economists argue that many people would. Empirical tests have confirmed that consumers are responsive to both the price of the good in question and the prices of related goods. When goods are substitutes, the more people buy of one good, the less they will buy of the other. Suppose there is a fall in the price of Pepsi; this would cause an increase in the quantity demanded for Pepsi (a movement down along the demand

Shifts in Demand

An increase in demand shifts the demand curve to the right; a decrease in demand shifts the demand curve to the left, as shown in Exhibit 1. Some

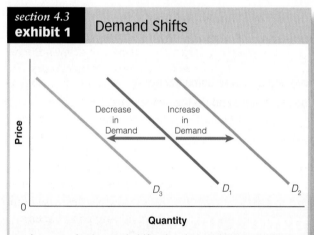

section 4.3
exhibit 1   Demand Shifts

An increase in demand shifts the demand curve to the right. A decrease in demand shifts the demand curve to the left.

Use what you've LEARNED   SUBSTITUTE GOODS

Q Can you describe the change we would expect to see in the demand curve for Sprite if the relative price for 7-Up increased significantly?

A If the price of one good increases and, as a result, an individual buys more of another good, the two related goods are substitutes. That is, buying more

of one reduces purchases of the other. In Exhibit 2(a), we see that as the price of 7-Up increases—a movement up along the demand curve for 7-Up, from point A to point B. The price increase for 7-Up causes a reduction in the quantity demanded of 7-Up. If the two goods are substitutes, the higher price for 7-Up will cause an increase in the demand for Sprite (a rightward shift), as seen in Exhibit 2 (b).

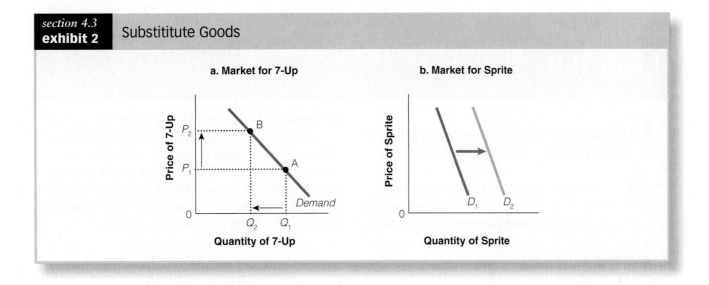

section 4.3
exhibit 2   Substitite Goods

a. Market for 7-Up

Price of 7-Up

P_2 ⋯⋯ B

P_1 ⋯⋯⋯⋯ A

Demand

0   Q_2 Q_1

Quantity of 7-Up

b. Market for Sprite

Price of Sprite

0   D_1 D_2

Quantity of Sprite

curve). Many Coke drinkers may switch to the new relatively lower priced Pepsi—causing a reduction in demand for Coca-Cola; shifting the demand curve for Coca-Cola to the left. Alternatively, if there is an increase in the price of Pepsi, this causes a decrease in the quantity demanded of Pepsi (a movement up along the demand curve). At the new higher price for Pepsi, many Pepsi drinkers will switch to the relatively lower priced Coca-Cola—shifting the demand curve for Coca-Cola to the right. In this example, Pepsi and Coca-Cola are said to be substitutes.

Two goods are **substitutes** if an increase (a decrease) in the price of one good causes the demand curve for another good to shift to the right (left)—a direct (or positive) relationship.

substitutes
an increase (decrease) in the price of one good causes the demand curve for another good to shift to the right (left)

complements
an increase (decrease) in the price of one good shifts the demand curve for another good to the left (right)

rise—a movement down along the demand curve for motorcycles. As more people buy motorcycles, they will demand more motorcycle helmets—the demand curve for motorcycle helmets shifts to the right. In short, when goods are **complements,** the more people buy of one good, the more they will buy of the other. That is, if a decrease in the price of good A leads to an increase in the demand for good B, the two goods are complements. Alternatively, if an increase in the price of good A leads to a decrease in the demand for good B, the two goods are complements.

Complements

$$P_{\text{GOOD A}} \uparrow \Rightarrow \downarrow D_{\text{GOOD B}}$$
$$P_{\text{GOOD A}} \downarrow \Rightarrow \uparrow D_{\text{GOOD B}}$$

Income

Economists have observed that generally the consumption of goods and services is positively related to the income available to consumers. Empirical studies support the notion that as individuals receive more income, they tend to increase their purchases of most goods and services. Other things held equal, rising income usually leads to an increase in the demand for goods (a rightward shift of the demand curve), and decreasing income usually leads to a decrease in the demand for goods (a leftward shift of the demand curve).

Substitutes

$$P_{\text{GOOD A}} \uparrow \Rightarrow \uparrow D_{\text{GOOD B}}$$
$$P_{\text{GOOD A}} \downarrow \Rightarrow \downarrow D_{\text{GOOD B}}$$

Complements

Complements are goods that "go together," often consumed and used simultaneously, such as skis and bindings, peanut butter and jelly, hot dogs and buns, digital music players and downloadable music, and printers and ink cartridges. For example, if the price of motorcycles falls, the quantity of motorcycles demanded will

Use what you've LEARNED   COMPLEMENTARY GOODS

Q If the price of computers fell markedly, what do you think would happen to the demand for printers?

A If computers and printers are complements, the decrease in the price of computers will lead to more computers purchased (a movement down along the demand curve from point A to point B) and an increase in the demand for printers (a rightward shift). Of course, the opposite is true too—an increase in the price of computers will lead to fewer people purchasing computers (a movement up along the demand curve for computers from point B to point A) and a lower demand for printers (a leftward shift).

section 4.3
exhibit 3   Complementary Goods

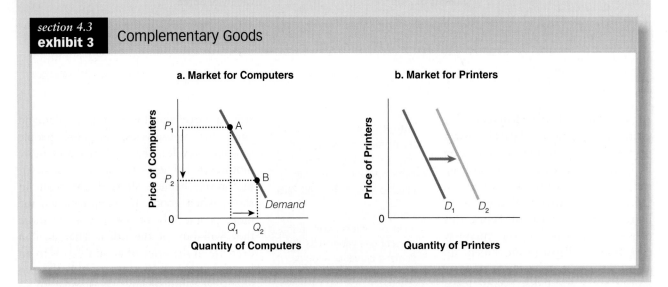

a. Market for Computers

b. Market for Printers

Normal and Inferior Goods

If demand for a good increases when incomes rise and decreases when incomes fall, the good is called a **normal good**. Most goods are normal goods. Consumers will typically buy more CDs, clothes, pizzas, and trips to the movies as their incomes rise. However, if demand for a good decreases when incomes rise or if demand increases when incomes fall, the good is called an **inferior good**. These goods include inexpensive cuts of meat, second-hand clothing, or retread tires, which customers generally buy only because they cannot afford more expensive substitutes. As incomes rise, buyers shift to preferred substitutes and decrease their demand for the inferior goods. Suppose most individuals prefer hamburger to beans, but low-income families buy beans because they are less

normal good
if income increases, the demand for a good increases; if income decreases, the demand for a good decreases

inferior good
if income increases, the demand for a good decreases; if income decreases, the demand for a good increases

expensive. As incomes rise, many consumers may switch from buying beans to buying hamburgers. Hamburgers may be inferior too; as incomes rise still further, consumers may substitute steak or chicken for hamburger. The term *inferior* in this sense does not refer to the quality of the good in question but shows that demand decreases when income increases and demand increases when income decreases. So beans are inferior not because they are low quality, but because you buy less of them as income increases.

Or, if people's incomes rise and they increase their demand for movie tickets, we say that movie tickets are a normal good. But if people's incomes fall and they increase their demand for bus rides, we say bus rides are an inferior good. Whether goods are normal or inferior, the point here is that income influences demand—usually positively, but sometimes negatively.

Normal Good

Income ↑ ⇒ Demand ↑

Income ↓ ⇒ Demand ↓

Inferior Good

Income ↑ ⇒ Demand ↓

Income ↓ ⇒ Demand ↑

Number of Buyers

The demand for a good or service will vary with the size of the potential consumer population. The demand for wheat, for example, rises as population increases, because the added population wants to consume wheat products, such as bread or cereal. Marketing experts, who closely follow the patterns of consumer behavior regarding a particular good or service, are usually vitally concerned with the *demographics* of the product—the vital statistics of the potential consumer population, including size, race, income, and age characteristics. For example, market researchers for baby food companies keep a close watch on the birth rate.

Consumer's Preferences and Information

The demand for a good or service may increase or decrease suddenly with changes in people's tastes or preferences. Changes in taste may be triggered by advertising or promotion, by a news story, by the behavior of some popular public figure, and so on. Changes in taste are particularly noticeable in apparel. Skirt lengths, coat lapels, shoe styles, and tie sizes change frequently.

Changes in preferences naturally lead to changes in demand. A person may grow tired of one type of recreation or food and try another type. People may decide they want more organic food; consequently, we will see more stores and restaurants catering to this change in taste. Changes in occupation, number of dependents, state of health, and age also tend to alter preferences. The birth of a baby might cause a family to spend less on recreation and more on food and clothing. Illness increases the demand for medicine and lessens purchases of other goods. A cold winter increases the demand for heating oil. Changes in customs and traditions also affect preferences, and the development of new products draws consumer preferences away from other goods. Compact discs replaced record albums, just as DVD players replaced VCRs. A change in information can also impact consumers' demand. For example, a breakout of *E. coli*

or new information about a defective and/or dangerous product, such as a baby's crib, can reduce demand.

Expectations

Sometimes the demand for a good or service in a given period will dramatically increase or decrease because consumers expect the good to change in price or availability at some future date. If people expect the future price to be higher, they will purchase more of the good now before the price increase. If people expect the future price to be lower, they will purchase less of the good now and wait for the price decrease. For example, if you expect the price of computers to fall soon, you may be less willing to buy one today. Or, if you expect to earn additional income next month, you may be more willing to dip into your current savings to buy something this month.

© MIKE PANIC ISTOCKPHOTO.COM

Body piercing and tattoos have risen in popularity in recent years. The demand for these services has been pushed to the right. According to the Pew Research Center thirty-six percent of 18-25 year olds have at least one tattoo.

NORMAL AND INFERIOR GOODS

Q Chester Field owns a high-quality furniture shop. If a boom in the economy occurs (higher average income per person and fewer people unemployed), can Chester expect to sell more high-quality furniture?

A Yes. Furniture is generally considered a normal good, so a rise in income will increase the demand for high-quality furniture, as shown in (a). However, if Chester sells unfinished, used, or low-quality furniture, the demand for his products might fall, as higher incomes allow customers to buy furniture that is finished, new, or of higher quality. Chester's furniture would then be an inferior good, as shown in Exhibit 4(b).

section 4.3
exhibit 4   Normal and Inferior Goods

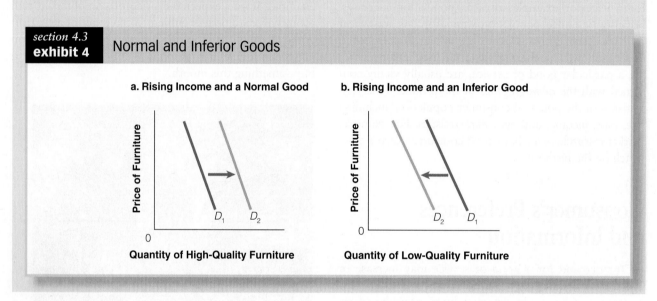

a. Rising Income and a Normal Good

Price of Furniture

D_1 D_2

0

Quantity of High-Quality Furniture

b. Rising Income and an Inferior Good

Price of Furniture

D_2 D_1

0

Quantity of Low-Quality Furniture

Changes in Demand Versus Changes in Quantity Demanded—Revisited

Economists put particular emphasis on the impact on consumer behavior of a change in the price of a good. We are interested in distinguishing between consumer behavior related to the price of a good itself (movement *along* a demand curve) and behavior related to changes in other factors (shifts of the demand curve).

As indicated earlier, if the price of a good changes, it causes a *change in quantity demanded*. If one of the other factors (determinants) influencing consumer behavior changes, it results in a *change in demand*. The effects of some of the determinants that cause changes in demand (shifters) are reviewed in Exhibit 5. For example, there are two different ways to curb teenage smoking: raise the price of cigarettes (a reduction in the quantity of cigarettes demanded) or decrease the demand for cigarettes (a leftward shift in the demand curve for cigarettes). Both would reduce the amount of smoking. Specifically, to increase the price of cigarettes, the government could impose a higher tax on manufacturers. Most of this would be passed on to consumers in the form of higher prices (more on this in Chapter 6). Or to shift the demand curve leftward, the government could adopt policies to discourage smoking, such as advertising bans and increasing consumer awareness of the harmful side effects of smoking—disease and death.

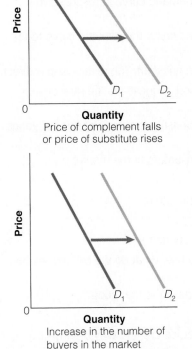

Quantity
Price of complement falls
or price of substitute rises

Quantity
Income increases (normal good)

Quantity
Income increases (inferior good)

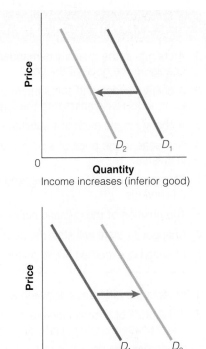

Quantity
Increase in the number of
buyers in the market

Quantity
Taste change in favor of the good

Quantity
Future price increase expected

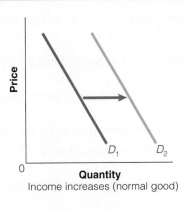

Use what you've LEARNED

CHANGES IN DEMAND VERSUS CHANGES IN QUANTITY DEMANDED

Q How would you use a graph to demonstrate the two following scenarios? (1) Someone buys more DVDs because the price of DVDs has fallen; and (2) a student buys more DVDs because she just got a 20 percent raise at work giving her additional income.

A In Exhibit 6, the movement from A to B is called an increase in quantity demanded; the movement from B to A is called a decrease in quantity demanded. Economists use the phrase "increase or decrease in quantity demanded" to describe movements along a given demand curve. However, the change from A to C is called an increase in demand, and the change from C to A is called a decrease in demand. The phrase "increase or decrease in demand" is reserved for a shift in the whole curve. So if an individual buys more DVDs because the price fell, we call it an increase in quantity demanded. However, if she buys more DVDs even at the current price, say $15, we say it is an increase

in demand. In this case, the increase in income was responsible for the increase in demand, because she chose to spend some of her new income on DVDs.

section 4.3
exhibit 6 Change in Demand Versus Change in Quantity Demanded

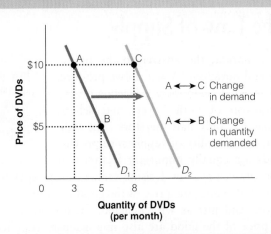

A ←→ C Change in demand

A ←→ B Change in quantity demanded

Quantity of DVDs (per month)

SECTION ✓ CHECK

1. A change in the quantity demanded describes a movement along a given demand curve in response to a change in the price of the good.

2. A change in demand shifts the entire demand curve. An increase in demand shifts the demand curve to the right; a decrease shifts it to the left.

3. A change in the price of a substitute shifts the demand curve for the good in question. The relationship is direct.

4. A change in the price of a complement shifts the demand curve for the good in question. The relationship is inverse.

5. Changes in income cause demand curve shifts. For normal goods the relationship is direct; for inferior goods it is inverse.

6. The position of the demand curve will vary according to the number of consumers in the market.

7. Changes in taste will shift the demand curve.

8. Changes in expected future prices and income can shift the current demand curve.

---

1. What is the difference between a change in demand and a change in quantity demanded?

2. If the price of zucchini increases, causing the demand for yellow squash to rise, what do we call the relationship between zucchini and yellow squash?

3. If incomes rise and, as a result, demand for jet skis increases, how do we describe that good?

4. How do expectations about the future influence the demand curve?

5. Would a change in the price of ice cream cause a change in the demand for ice cream? Why or why not?

6. Would a change in the price of ice cream likely cause a change in the demand for frozen yogurt, a substitute?

7. If plane travel is a normal good and bus travel is an inferior good, what will happen to the demand curves for plane and bus travel if people's incomes increase?

SECTION 4.4

Supply

* What is the law of supply?
* What is an individual supply curve?
* What is a market supply curve?

The Law of Supply

In a market, the answer to the fundamental question, "What do we produce, and in what quantities?" depends on the interaction of both buyers and sellers. Demand is only half the story. The willingness and ability of suppliers to provide goods are equally important factors that must be weighed by decision makers in all societies. As with demand, the price of the good is an important factor. And just as with demand, factors other than the price of the good are also important to suppliers,

> **law of supply**
> the higher (lower) the price of the good, the greater (smaller) the quantity supplied

such as the cost of inputs or advances in technology. While behavior will vary among individual suppliers, economists expect that, other things being equal, the quantity supplied will vary directly with the price of the good, a relationship called the **law of supply.** According to the law of supply, the higher the price of the good (P), the greater the quantity supplied (Q_s), and the lower the price of the good, the smaller the quantity supplied.

$$P \uparrow \Rightarrow Q_s \uparrow \quad \text{and} \quad P \downarrow \Rightarrow Q_s \downarrow$$

The relationship described by the law of supply is a direct, or positive, relationship, because the variables move in the same direction.

A Positive Relationship Between Price and Quantity Supplied

Firms supplying goods and services want to increase their profits, and the higher the price per unit, the greater the profitability generated by supplying more of that good. For example, if you were a coffee grower, wouldn't you much rather be paid $5 a pound than $1 a pound, *ceteris paribus?*

When the price of coffee is low, the coffee business is less profitable and less coffee will be produced. Some suppliers may even shut down, reducing their quantity supplied to zero.

An Individual Supply Curve

To illustrate the concept of an individual supply curve, consider the amount of coffee that an individual supplier, Juan Valdes, is willing and able to supply in one year. The law of supply can be illustrated, like the law of demand, by a table or graph. Juan's supply schedule for coffee is shown in Exhibit 1(a). The combinations of price and quantity supplied were then plotted and joined to create the individual supply curve shown in Exhibit 1(b). Note that the individual supply curve is upward sloping as you move from left to right. At higher prices, it will be more attractive to increase production. Existing firms or growers will produce more at higher prices than at lower prices.

The Market Supply Curve

The market supply curve may be thought of as the horizontal summation of the supply curves for individual firms. The market supply curve shows how the total quantity supplied varies positively with the price of a good, while holding constant all other factors that affect how much producers are able and willing to supply. The market supply schedule, which reflects the total quantity supplied at each price by all of the coffee producers, is shown in Exhibit 2(a). Exhibit 2(b) illustrates the resulting market supply curve for this group of coffee producers.

individual supply curve
a graphical representation that shows the positive relationship between the price and quantity supplied

market supply curve
a graphical representation of the amount of goods and services that suppliers are willing and able to supply at various prices

---

section 4.4
exhibit 1 An Individual Supply Curve

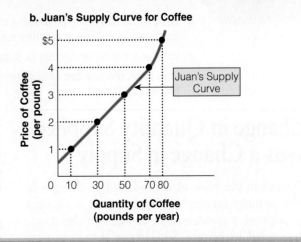

a. Juan's Supply Schedule for Coffee

Price (per pound)	Quantity Supplied (pounds per year)
$5	80
4	70
3	50
2	30
1	10

Other things being equal, the quantity supplied will vary directly with the price of the good. As the price rises (falls), the quantity supplied increases (decreases).

b. Juan's Supply Curve for Coffee

Juan's Supply Curve

section 4.4 exhibit 2	A Market Supply Curve

a. Market Supply Schedule for Coffee

	Quantity Supplied (pounds per year)				
Price (per pound)	Juan	+	Other Producers	=	Market Supply
$5	80	+	7,920	=	8,000
4	70	+	6,930	=	7,000
3	50	+	4,950	=	5,000
2	30	+	2,970	=	3,000
1	10	+	990	=	1,000

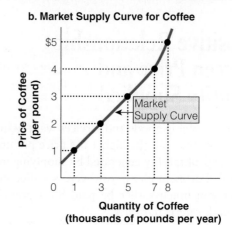

b. Market Supply Curve for Coffee

The dots on this graph indicate different quantities of coffee that producers would be willing and able to supply at various prices. The line connecting those combinations is the market supply curve.

SECTION CHECK

1. The law of supply states that the higher (lower) the price of a good, the greater (smaller) the quantity supplied.

2. The relationship between price and quantity supplied is positive because profit opportunities are greater at higher prices and because the higher production costs of increased output mean that suppliers will require higher prices.

3. The market supply curve is a graphical representation of the amount of goods and services that suppliers are willing and able to supply at various prices.

---

1. What are the two reasons why a supply curve is positively sloped?

2. What is the difference between an individual supply curve and a market supply curve?

SECTION 4.5
Shifts in the Supply Curve

* What is the difference between a change in supply and a change in quantity supplied?

* What are the determinants of supply?

* How does the number of suppliers affect the supply curve?

* How does technology affect the supply curve?

* How do taxes affect the supply curve?

A Change in Quantity Supplied Versus a Change in Supply

Changes in the price of a good lead to changes in the quantity supplied by suppliers, just as changes in the price of a good lead to changes in the quantity demanded by buyers. Similarly, a change in supply, whether an increase or a decrease, can occur for reasons other than changes in the price of the product itself, just as changes in demand may be due to factors (determinants) other than the price of the good. In other words, a change in the price of the good in question is shown as a movement along a given supply curve, leading to a change in quantity supplied. A change in any other factor that can affect supplier behavior (input prices, the prices of related products, expectations, number of suppliers, technology, regulation, taxes and subsidies, and weather) results in *a shift in the entire supply curve*, leading to a change in supply.

Shifts in Supply

An increase in supply shifts the supply curve to the right; a decrease in supply shifts the supply curve to the left, as shown in Exhibit 1. Anything that affects the costs of production will influence supply and the position of the supply curve. We will now look at some of the possible determinants of supply—factors that determine the position of the supply curve—in greater depth.

Input Prices

Suppliers are strongly influenced by the costs of inputs used in the production process, such as steel used for automobiles or microchips used in computers. For example, higher labor, materials, energy, or other input costs increase the costs of production, causing the supply curve to shift to the left at each and every price. If input prices fall, the costs of production decrease, causing the supply curve to shift to the right—more will be supplied at each and every price.

Prices of Related Goods

The supply of a good increases if the price of one of its substitutes in production falls; and the supply of a good decreases if the price of one of its substitutes in production rises. Suppose you own your own farm, on which you plant cotton and wheat. One year, the price of wheat falls, and farmers reduce the quantity of wheat supplied, as shown in Exhibit 2(a). What effect does the lower price of wheat have on your cotton production? It increases the supply of cotton. You want to produce relatively less of the crop that has fallen in price (wheat) and relatively more of the now more attractive other crop (cotton). Cotton and wheat are *substitutes in production* because both goods can be produced using the same resources. Producers tend to substitute the production of

more profitable products for that of less profitable products. So the decrease in the price in the wheat market has caused an increase in supply (a rightward shift) in the cotton market, as seen in Exhibit 2(b).

If the price of wheat, a substitute in production, increases, then that crop becomes more profitable. This leads to an increase in the quantity supplied of wheat. Consequently, farmers will shift their resources out of the relatively lower-priced crop (cotton); the result is a decrease in supply of cotton.

Other examples of substitutes in production include automobile producers that have to decide between producing sedans and pick-ups or construction companies that have to choose between building single residential houses or commercial buildings.

Some goods are *complements in production*. Producing one good does not prevent the production of the other, but actually enables production of the other. For example, leather and beef are complements in production. Suppose the price of a beef rises and as a result cattle ranchers increase the quantity supplied of beef, moving up the supply curve for beef, as seen in Exhibit 2(c). When cattle ranchers produce more beef they automatically produce more leather. Thus, when the price of beef increases, the supply of the related good, leather, shifts to the right, as seen in Exhibit 2(d). Suppose the price of beef falls, and as a result, the quantity supplied of beef falls; this leads to a decrease (a leftward shift) in the supply of leather.

Other examples of complements in production where goods are produced simultaneously from the same resource include: a lumber mill that produces lumber and sawdust or an oil refinery that can produce gasoline or heating oil from the same resource—crude oil.

Expectations

Another factor shifting supply is suppliers' expectations. If producers expect a higher price in the future, they will supply less now than they otherwise would have, preferring to wait and sell when their goods will be more valuable. For example, if a cotton producer expected the future price of cotton to be higher next year, he might decide to store some of his current production of cotton for next year when the price will be higher. Similarly, if producers expect now that the price will be lower later, they will supply more now. Oil refiners will often store some of their spring supply of gasoline for summer because gasoline prices typically peak in summer. In addition, some of the heating oil for the fall is stored to supply it in the winter when heating oil prices peak.

Number of Suppliers

We are normally interested in market demand and supply (because together they determine prices and quantities) rather than in the behavior of individual consumers and firms. As we discussed earlier in the chapter, the supply

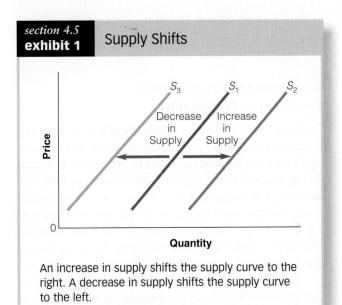

section 4.5
exhibit 1   Supply Shifts

An increase in supply shifts the supply curve to the right. A decrease in supply shifts the supply curve to the left.

section 4.5
exhibit 2   Substitutes and Complements in Production

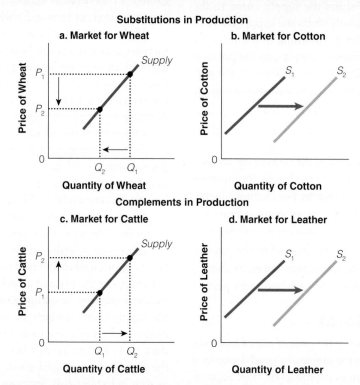

Substitutions in Production

a. Market for Wheat

b. Market for Cotton

Complements in Production

c. Market for Cattle

d. Market for Leather

If land can be used for either wheat or cotton, a decrease in the price of wheat causes a decease in the quantity supplied; a movement down along the supply curve in Exhibit 2(a). This may cause some farmers to shift out of the production of wheat and into the substitute in production—cotton—shifting the cotton supply curve to the right in Exhibit 2(b). If the price of the complement in production increases (cattle), it becomes more profitable and and as a result cattle ranchers increase the quantity supplied of beef, moving up the supply curve for beef, as seen in Exhibit 2 (c). When cattle ranchers produce more beef they also produce more leather. Thus, when the price of beef increases, the supply of the related good, leather, shifts to the right, as seen in Exhibit 2(d).

curves of individual suppliers can be summed horizontally to create a market supply curve. An increase in the number of suppliers leads to an increase in supply, denoted by a rightward shift in the supply curve. For example, think of the number of gourmet coffee shops that have sprung up over the last 15 to 20 years, shifting the supply curve of gourmet coffee to the right. An exodus of suppliers has the opposite impact, a decrease in supply, which is indicated by a leftward shift in the supply curve.

Technology

Technological change can lower the firm's costs of production through productivity advances. These changes allow the firm to spend less on inputs and produce the same level of output. Human creativity works to find new ways to produce goods and services using fewer or less costly inputs of labor, natural resources, or capital. Because the

firm can now produce the good at a lower cost it will supply more of the good at each and every price—the supply curve shifts to the right.

Government (Regulation, Taxes, and Subsidies)

Supply may also change because of changes in the legal and regulatory environment in which firms operate. Government regulations can influence the costs of production to a firm, leading to cost-induced supply changes similar to those just discussed. For example, if new safety or clean air requirements increase labor and capital costs, the increased cost will result, other things being equal, in a decrease in supply, shifting the supply curve to the left, or up. However, deregulation can shift the supply curve to the right.

Certain types of taxes can also alter the costs of production borne by the supplier, causing the supply curve to shift to the left at each price. A subsidy, the opposite of a tax, can lower a firm's costs and shift the supply curve to the right. For example, the government sometimes provides farmers with subsidies to encourage the production of certain agricultural products.

Weather

In addition, weather can sometimes dramatically affect the supply of certain commodities, particularly agricultural products and transportation services. A drought or freezing temperatures will almost certainly cause the supply curves for many crops to shift to the left, while exceptionally good weather can shift a supply curve to the right. For example, unusually cold weather in California during the winter of 2006 destroyed billions of dollars worth of citrus fruit. Hurricane Rita disrupted oil and refining processes. Both events shifted the supply curve for those products to the left.

Change in Supply Versus Change in Quantity Supplied—Revisited

If the price of a good changes, it leads to a change in the quantity supplied. If one of the other factors influences sellers' behavior, we say it results in a change in supply.

For example, if production costs rise because of a wage increase or higher fuel costs, other things remaining constant, we would expect a decrease in supply—that is, a leftward shift in the supply curve. Alternatively, if some variable, such as lower input prices, causes the costs of production to fall, the supply curve will shift to the right. Exhibit 3 illustrates the effects of some of the determinants that cause shifts in the supply curve.

A major disaster such as a flood or hurricane can reduce the supply of crops and livestock. Occasionally, floods have spilled over the banks of the Mississippi River—bursting through levees and destroying crops and animals.

section 4.5
exhibit 3   Possible Supply Shifts

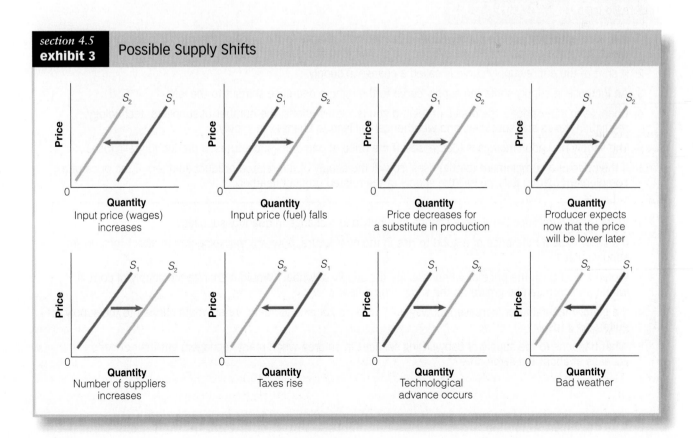

Use what you've LEARNED
CHANGE IN SUPPLY VERSUS CHANGE IN QUANTITY SUPPLIED

Q How would you graph the following two scenarios: (1) the price of cotton rises; and (2) good weather causes an unusually abundant cotton harvest?

A In the first scenario, the price of cotton increases, so the quantity supplied changes (i.e., a movement along the supply curve). In the second scenario, the good weather causes the supply curve for cotton to shift to the right, which is called a change in supply (not quantity supplied). A shift in the whole supply curve is caused by one of the other variables, not by a change in the price of the good in question.

As shown in Exhibit 4, the movement from A to B is called an increase in quantity supplied, and the movement from B to A is called a decrease in quantity supplied. However, the change from B to C is

called an increase in supply, and the movement from C to B is called a decrease in supply.

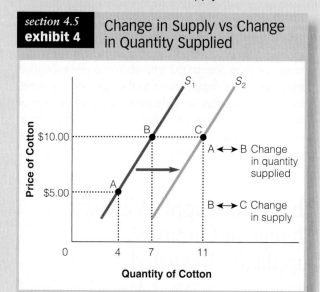

section 4.5
exhibit 4   Change in Supply vs Change in Quantity Supplied

SECTION CHECK

1. A movement along a given supply curve is caused by a change in the price of the good in question. As we move along the supply curve, we experience a change in the quantity supplied.

2. A shift of the entire supply curve is called a change in supply.

3. An increase in supply shifts the supply curve to the right; a decrease shifts it to the left.

4. Changes in Input prices, the prices of related goods, expectations, the number of suppliers, technology, regulation, taxes and subsidies, and weather can all lead to changes in supply.

5. The supply of a good increases (decreases) if the price of one of its substitutes in production falls (rises).

6. If the price of a complement (cattle) rises, so will the supply of the related product (leather). If the price of a complement (cattle) falls, so will the supply of the related product (leather).

---

1. What is the difference between a change in supply and a change in quantity supplied?

2. If a seller expects the price of a good to rise in the near future, how will that expectation affect the current supply curve?

3. Would a change in the price of wheat change the supply of wheat? Would it change the supply of corn, if wheat and corn can be grown on the same type of land?

4. If a guitar manufacturer increased its wages in order to keep its workers, what would happen to the supply of guitars as a result?

5. What happens to the supply of baby-sitting services in an area when many teenagers get their driver's licenses at about the same time?

Interactive Chapter Summary

Fill in the blanks:

1. A(n) _____ is the process of buyers and sellers _____ goods and services.

2. The important point about a market is what it does—it facilitates _____.

3. _____, as a group, determine the demand side of the market. _____, as a group, determine the supply side of the market.

4. A(n) _____ market consists of many buyers and sellers, no single one of whom can influence the market price.

5. According to the law of demand, other things being equal, when the price of a good or service falls, the _____ increases.

6. An individual _____ curve reveals the different amounts of a particular good a person would be willing and able to buy at various possible prices in a particular time interval, other things being equal.

7. The _____ curve for a product is the horizontal summing of the demand curves of the individuals in the market.

8. A change in _____ leads to a change in quantity demanded, illustrated by a(n) _____ demand curve.

9. A change in demand is caused by changes in any of the other factors (besides the good's own price) that would affect how much of the good is purchased: the _____, _____, the _____ of buyers, _____, and _____.

10. An increase in demand is represented by a _____ shift in the demand curve; a decrease in demand is represented by a _____ shift in the demand curve.

11. Two goods are called _____ if an increase in the price of one causes the demand curve for another good to shift to the _____.

12. For normal goods an increase in income leads to a(n) _____ in demand, and a decrease in income leads to a(n) _____ in demand, other things being equal.

13. An increase in the expected future price of a good or an increase in expected future income may _____ current demand.

14. According to the law of supply, the higher the price of the good, the greater the _____, and the lower the price of the good, the smaller the _____.

15. The quantity supplied is positively related to the price because firms supplying goods and services want to increase their _____ and because increasing _____ costs mean that the suppliers will require _____ prices to induce them to increase their output.

16. An individual supply curve is a graphical representation that shows the _____ relationship between the price and the quantity supplied.

17. The market supply curve is a graphical representation of the amount of goods and services that suppliers are _____ and _____ to supply at various prices.

18. Possible supply determinants (factors that determine the position of the supply curve) are _____ prices; _____; _____ of suppliers; and _____, _____, _____, and _____.

19. A fall in input prices will _____ the costs of production, causing the supply curve to shift to the _____.

20. The supply of a good _____ if the price of one of its substitutes in production falls.

21. The supply of a good _____ if the price of one of its substitutes in production rises.

Answers: 1. market; exchanging 2. trade 3. Buyers; Sellers 4. competitive 5. quantity demanded 6. demand 7. market demand 8. a good's price; movement along 9. prices of related goods; income; tastes; expectations; number 10. rightward; leftward 11. substitutes; right 12. increase; decrease 13. increase 14. quantity supplied; quantity supplied 15. profits; production; higher 16. positive 17. willing; able 18. input; expectations; number; technology; regulation; taxes and subsidies; weather 19. lower; right 20. increases 21. decreases

Key Terms and Concepts

market 93
competitive market 94
law of demand 94
individual demand schedule 95
individual demand curve 95

market demand curve 95
change in quantity demanded 97
change in demand 98
substitutes 99
complements 99

normal good 100
inferior good 100
law of supply 104
individual supply curve 105
market supply curve 105

Section Check Answers

4.1 Markets

1. Why is it difficult to define a market precisely?
Every market is different. An incredible variety of exchange arrangements arise for different types of products, different degrees of organization, different geographical extents, and so on.

2. Why do you get your produce at a supermarket rather than directly from farmers?
Supermarkets act as middlepersons between growers of produce and consumers of produce. You hire them to do this task for you when you buy produce from them, rather than directly from growers, because they conduct those transactions at lower costs than you could (if you could do it more cheaply than supermarkets, you would buy directly rather than from supermarkets).

3. Why do the prices people pay for similar items at garage sales vary more than for similar items in a department store?
Items for sale at department stores are more standardized, easier to compare, and more heavily advertised, which makes consumers more aware of the prices at which they could get a particular good elsewhere, reducing the differences in price that can persist among department stores. Garage sale items are nonstandardized, costly to compare, and not advertised, which means people are often quite unaware of how much a given item could be purchased for elsewhere, so that price differences for similar items at different garage sales can be substantial.

4.2 Demand

1. What is an inverse relationship?
An inverse, or negative, relationship is one where one variable changes in the opposite direction from the other—if one increases, the other decreases.

2. How do lower prices change buyers' incentives?
A lower price for a good means that the opportunity cost to buyers of purchasing it is lower than before, and self-interest leads buyers to buy more of it as a result.

3. How do higher prices change buyers' incentives?
A higher price for a good means that the opportunity cost to buyers of purchasing it is higher than before, and self-interest leads buyers to buy less of it as a result.

4. What is an individual demand schedule?
An individual demand schedule reveals the different amounts of a good or service a person would be willing to buy at various possible prices in a particular time interval.

5. What is the difference between an individual demand curve and a market demand curve?
The market demand curve shows the total amounts of a good or service all the buyers as a group are willing to buy at various possible prices in a particular time interval. The market quantity demanded at a given price is just the sum of the quantities demanded by each individual buyer at that price.

6. Why does the amount of dating on campus tend to decline just before and during final exams?
The opportunity cost of dating—in this case, the value to students of the studying time forgone—is higher just before and during final exams than during most of the rest of an academic term. Because the cost is higher, students do less of it.

4.3 Shifts in the Demand Curve

1. What is the difference between a change in demand and a change in quantity demanded?
A change in demand shifts the entire demand curve, while a change in quantity demanded refers to a movement along a given demand curve, caused by a change in the good's price.

2. If the price of zucchini increases, causing the demand for yellow squash to rise, what do we call the relationship between zucchini and yellow squash?
Whenever an increased price of one good increases the demand for another, they are substitutes. The fact that some people consider zucchini an alternative to yellow squash explains in part why zucchini becomes more costly. Therefore, some people substitute into buying relatively cheaper yellow squash now instead.

3. If incomes rise and, as a result, demand for jet skis increases, how do we describe that good?
If income rises and, as a result, demand for jet skis increases, we call jet skis a normal good, because for most (or normal) goods, we would rather have more of them than less, so an increase in income would lead to an increase in demand for such goods.

4. How do expectations about the future influence the demand curve?
Expectations about the future influence the demand curve because buying a good in the future is an alternative to buying it now. Therefore, the higher

future prices are expected to be compared to the present, the less attractive future purchases become, and the greater the current demand for that good, as people buy more now when it is expected to be cheaper, rather than later, when it is expected to be more costly.

5. **Would a change in the price of ice cream cause a change in the demand for ice cream? Why or why not?**

No. The demand for ice cream represents the different quantities of ice cream that would be purchased at different prices. In other words, it represents the relationship between the price of ice cream and the quantity of ice cream demanded. Changing the price of ice cream does not change this relationship, so it does not change demand.

6. **Would a change in the price of ice cream likely cause a change in the demand for frozen yogurt, a substitute?**

Yes. Changing the price of ice cream, a substitute for frozen yogurt, would change the quantity of frozen yogurt demanded at a given price. This change in price means that the whole relationship between the price and quantity of frozen yogurt demanded has changed, which means the demand for frozen yogurt has changed.

7. **If plane travel is a normal good and bus travel is an inferior good, what will happen to the demand curves for plane and bus travel if people's incomes increase?**

The demand for plane travel and all other normal goods will increase if incomes increase, while the demand for bus travel and all other inferior goods will decrease if incomes increase.

4.4 Supply

1. **What are the two reasons why a supply curve is positively sloped?**

A supply curve is positively sloped because (1) the benefits to sellers from selling increase as the price they receive increases, and (2) the opportunity costs of supplying additional output rise with output (the law of increasing opportunity costs), so it takes a higher price to make increasing output in the self-interest of sellers.

2. **What is the difference between an individual supply curve and a market supply curve?**

The market supply curve shows the total amounts of a good all the sellers as a group are willing to sell at various prices in a particular time period. The market quantity supplied at a given price is just the sum of the quantities supplied by each individual seller at that price.

4.5 Shifts in the Supply Curve

1. **What is the difference between a change in supply and a change in quantity supplied?**

A change in supply shifts the entire supply curve, while a change in quantity supplied refers to a movement along a given supply curve.

2. **If a seller expects the price of a good to rise in the near future, how will that expectation affect the current supply curve?**

Selling a good in the future is an alternative to selling it now. Therefore, the higher the expected future price relative to the current price, the more attractive future sales become, and the less attractive current sales become. This will lead sellers to reduce (shift left) the current supply of that good, as they want to sell later, when the good is expected to be more valuable, rather than now.

3. **Would a change in the price of wheat change the supply of wheat? Would it change the supply of corn, if wheat and corn can be grown on the same type of land?**

The supply of wheat represents the different quantities of wheat that would be offered for sale at different prices. In other words, it represents the relationship between the price of wheat and the quantity of wheat supplied. Changing the price of wheat does not change this relationship, so it does not change the supply of wheat. However, a change in the price of wheat changes the relative attractiveness of raising wheat instead of corn, which changes the supply of corn.

4. **If a guitar manufacturer increased its wages in order to keep its workers, what would happen to the supply of guitars as a result?**

An increase in wages, or any other input price, would decrease (shift left) the supply of guitars, making fewer guitars available for sale at any given price, by raising the opportunity cost of producing guitars.

5. **What happens to the supply of baby-sitting services in an area when many teenagers get their driver's licenses at about the same time?**

When teenagers get their driver's licenses, their increased mobility expands their alternatives to baby-sitting substantially, raising the opportunity cost of baby-sitting. This change decreases (shifts left) the supply of baby-sitting services.

True or False:

1. Differences in the conditions under which the exchange between buyers and sellers occurs make it difficult to precisely define a market.

2. All markets are effectively global in scope.

3. The relationship between price and quantity demanded is inverse or negative.

4. The market demand curve is the vertical summation of individual demand curves.

5. A change in a good's price does not change its demand.

6. A change in demand is illustrated by a shift in the entire demand curve.

7. Because personal tastes differ, substitutes for one person may not be substitutes for another person.

8. Two goods are complements if an increase in the price of one causes an increase in the demand for the other.

9. Those goods for which falling income leads to decreased demand are called inferior goods.

10. Either an increase in the number of buyers or an increase in tastes or preferences for a good or service will increase the market demand for a good or service.

11. A decrease in the price of ice cream would cause an increase in the demand for frozen yogurt, a substitute.

12. The law of supply states that, other things being equal, the quantity supplied will vary directly (a positive relationship) with the price of the good.

13. The market supply curve for a product is the vertical summation of the supply curves for individual firms.

14. A change in the price of a good leads to a change in the quantity supplied, but not to a change in its supply.

15. An increase in supply leads to a movement up along the supply curve.

16. A decrease in supply shifts the supply curve to the left.

17. Just as demanders will demand more now if the price of a good is expected to rise in the near future, sellers will supply more now if the price of a good is expected to rise in the near future.

18. Both technological progress and cost-increasing regulations will increase supply.

Multiple Choice:

1. Which of the following is a market?
   a. a garage sale
   b. a restaurant
   c. the New York Stock Exchange
   d. an eBay auction
   e. all of the above

2. In a competitive market,
   a. there are a number of buyers and sellers.
   b. no single buyer or seller can appreciably affect the market price.
   c. sellers offer similar products.
   d. all of the above are true.

3. If the demand for milk is downward sloping, then an increase in the price of milk will result in a(n)
   a. increase in the demand for milk.
   b. decrease in the demand for milk.
   c. increase in the quantity of milk demanded.
   d. decrease in the quantity of milk demanded.
   e. decrease in the supply of milk.

4. Which of the following would be most likely to increase the demand for jelly?
   a. an increase in the price of peanut butter, which is often used with jelly
   b. an increase in income; jelly is a normal good
   c. a decrease in the price of jelly
   d. medical research that finds that daily consumption of jelly makes people live 10 years *less*, on average

5. Which of the following would *not* cause a change in the demand for cheese?
   a. an increase in the price of crackers, which are consumed with cheese
   b. an increase in the income of cheese consumers
   c. an increase in the population of cheese lovers
   d. an increase in the price of cheese

6. *Ceteris paribus*, an increase in the price of DVD players would tend to
   a. decrease the demand for DVD players.
   b. increase the price of televisions, a complement to DVD players.
   c. increase the demand for DVD players.
   d. decrease the demand for DVDs.

7. Whenever the price of Good A decreases, the demand for Good B increases. Goods A and B appear to be
   a. complements.
   b. substitutes.
   c. inferior goods.
   d. normal goods.
   e. inverse goods.

8. Whenever the price of Good A increases, the demand for Good B increases as well. Goods A and B appear to be
   a. complements.
   b. substitutes.
   c. inferior goods.
   d. normal goods.
   e. inverse goods.

9. The difference between a change in quantity demanded and a change in demand is that a change in
   a. quantity demanded is caused by a change in a good's own price, while a change in demand is caused by a change in some other variable, such as income, tastes, or expectations.
   b. demand is caused by a change in a good's own price, while a change in quantity demanded is caused by a change in some other variable, such as income, tastes, or expectations.
   c. quantity demanded is a change in the amount people actually buy, while a change in demand is a change in the amount they want to buy.
   d. This is a trick question. A change in demand and a change in quantity demanded are the same thing.

10. Suppose CNN announces that bad weather in Central America has greatly reduced the number of cocoa bean plants and for this reason the price of chocolate is expected to rise soon. As a result,
    a. the current market demand for chocolate will decrease.
    b. the current market demand for chocolate will increase.
    c. the current quantity demanded for chocolate will decrease.
    d. no change will occur in the current market for chocolate.

11. An upward-sloping supply curve shows that
    a. buyers are willing to pay more for particularly scarce products.
    b. suppliers expand production as the product price falls.
    c. suppliers are willing to increase production of their goods if they receive higher prices for them.
    d. buyers are willing to buy more as the product price falls.

12. Along a supply curve,
    a. supply changes as price changes.
    b. quantity supplied changes as price changes.
    c. supply changes as technology changes.
    d. quantity supplied changes as technology changes.

13. All of the following factors will affect the supply of shoes except one. Which will *not* affect the supply of shoes?
    a. higher wages for shoe factory workers
    b. higher prices for leather
    c. a technological improvement that reduces waste of leather and other raw materials in shoe production
    d. an increase in consumer income

14. The difference between a change in quantity supplied and a change in supply is that a change in
    a. quantity supplied is caused by a change in a good's own price, while a change in supply is caused by a change in some other variable, such as input prices, prices of related goods, expectations, or taxes.
    b. supply is caused by a change in a good's own price, while a change in the quantity supplied is caused by a change in some other variable, such as input prices, prices of related goods, expectations, or taxes.
    c. quantity supplied is a change in the amount people want to sell, while a change in supply is a change in the amount they actually sell.
    d. supply and a change in the quantity supplied are the same thing.

15. Antonio's makes the greatest pizza and delivers it hot to all the dorms around campus. Last week Antonio's supplier of pepperoni informed him of a 25 percent increase in price. Which variable determining the position of the supply curve has changed, and what effect does it have on supply?
    a. future expectations; supply decreases
    b. future expectations; supply increases
    c. input prices; supply decreases
    d. input prices; supply increases
    e. technology; supply increases

16. Which of the following is *not* a determinant of supply?
    a. input prices
    b. technology
    c. tastes
    d. expectations
    e. the prices of related goods

17. If incomes are rising, in the market for an inferior good,
    a. demand will rise.
    b. demand will fall.
    c. supply will rise.
    d. supply will fall.

18. If a farmer were choosing between growing wheat on his own land and growing soybeans on his own land,
    a. an increase in the price of soybeans would increase his supply of soybeans.
    b. an increase in the price of soybeans would increase his supply of wheat.
    c. an increase in the price of soybeans would decrease his supply of soybeans.
    d. an increase in the price of soybeans would decrease his supply of wheat.
    e. an increase in the price of soybeans would not change his supply of either wheat or soybeans.

19. A supply curve illustrates a(n) _____ relationship between _____ and _____.
    a. direct; price; supply
    b. direct; price; quantity demanded
    c. direct; price; quantity supplied
    d. introverted; price; quantity demanded
    e. inverse; price; quantity supplied

20. A leftward shift in supply could be caused by
    a. an improvement in productive technology.
    b. a decrease in income.
    c. some firms leaving the industry.
    d. a fall in the price of inputs to the industry.

Problems:

1. Is the market for laptop computers local, national, or global?

2. Sid moves from New York City, where he lived in a small condominium, to rural Minnesota, where he buys a big house on five acres of land. Using the law of demand, what do you think is true of land prices in New York City relative to those in rural Minnesota?

3. The following table shows Hillary's demand schedule for Cherry Blossom Makeup. Graph Hillary's demand curve.

Price (dollars per ounce)	Quantity Demanded (ounces per week)
$15	5 oz.
12	10
9	15
6	20
3	25

4. The following table shows Cherry Blossom Makeup demand schedules for Hillary's friends, Barbara and Nancy. If Hillary, Barbara, and Nancy constitute the whole market for Cherry Blossom Makeup, complete the market demand schedule and graph the market demand curve.

Price (dollars per ounce)	Quantity Demanded (ounces per week)			
	Hillary	Barbara	Nancy	Market
$15	5	0	15	
12	10	5	20	
9	15	10	25	
6	20	15	30	
3	25	20	35	

5. What would be the effects of each of the following on the demand for hamburger in Hilo, Hawaii? In each case, identify the responsible determinant of demand.
   a. The price of chicken falls.
   b. The price of hamburger buns doubles.
   c. Scientists find that eating hamburger prolongs life.
   d. The population of Hilo doubles.

6. What would be the effect of each of the following on the demand for Chevrolets in the United States? In each case, identify the responsible determinant of demand.
   a. The price of Fords plummets.
   b. Consumers believe that the price of Chevrolets will rise next year.
   c. The incomes of Americans rise.
   d. The price of gasoline falls dramatically.

7. The following graph shows three market demand curves for cantaloupe. Starting at point A,
    a. which point represents an increase in quantity demanded?
    b. which point represents an increase in demand?
    c. which point represents a decrease in demand?
    d. which point represents a decrease in quantity demanded?

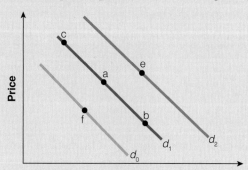

Quantity of Cantaloupes per Year

8. Using the demand curve, show the effect of the following events on the market for beef:
    a. Consumer income increases.
    b. The price of beef increases.
    c. An outbreak of "mad cow" disease occurs.
    d. The price of chicken (a substitute) increases.
    e. The price of barbecue grills (a complement) increases.

9. Draw the demand curves for the following goods. If the price of the first good listed rises, what will happen to the demand for the second good, and why?
    a. hamburger and ketchup
    b. Coca-Cola and Pepsi
    c. camera and film
    d. golf clubs and golf balls
    e. skateboard and razor scooter

10. If the price of ice cream increased,
    a. what would be the effect on the demand for ice cream?
    b. what would be the effect on the demand for frozen yogurt?

11. Using the graph below, answer the following questions:
    a. What is the shift from D_1 to D_2 called?
    b. What is the movement from b to a called?
    c. What is the movement from a to b called?
    d. What is the shift from D_2 to D_1 called?

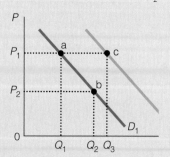

12. Felix is a wheat farmer who has two fields he can use to grow wheat. The first field is right next to his house and the topsoil is rich and thick. The second field is 10 miles away in the mountains and the soil is rocky. At current wheat prices, Felix just produces from the field next to his house because the market price for wheat is just high enough to cover his costs of production including a reasonable profit. What would have to happen to the market price of wheat for Felix to have the incentive to produce from the second field?

13. Show the impact of each of the following events on the oil market.
    a. OPEC becomes more effective in limiting the supply of oil.
    b. OPEC becomes less effective in limiting the supply of oil.
    c. The price for natural gas (a substitute for heating oil) rises.
    d. New oil discoveries occur in Alaska.
    e. Electric and hybrid cars become subsidized and their prices fall.

14. The following table shows the supply schedule for Rolling Rock Oil Co. Plot Rolling Rock's supply curve on a graph.

Price (dollars per barrel)	Quantity Supplied (barrels per month)
$5	10,000
10	15,000
15	20,000
20	25,000
25	30,000

15. The following table shows the supply schedules for Rolling Rock and two other petroleum companies. Armadillo Oil and Pecos Petroleum. Assuming these three companies make up the entire supply side of the oil market, complete the market supply schedule and draw the market supply curve on a graph.

Price (dollars per barrel)	Quantity Supplied (barrels per month)			
	Rolling Rock	Armadillo Oil	Pecos Petroleum	Market
$5	10,000	8,000	2,000	_____
10	15,000	10,000	5,000	_____
15	20,000	12,000	8,000	_____
20	25,000	14,000	11,000	_____
25	30,000	16,000	14,000	_____

16. If the price of corn rose,
    a. what would be the effect on the supply of corn?
    b. what would be the effect on the supply of wheat?

17. Using the graph below, answer the following questions:
    a. What is the shift from S_1 to S_2 called?
    b. What is the movement from a to b called?
    c. What is the movement from b to a called?
    d. What is the shift from S_2 to S_1 called?

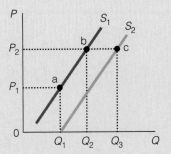

18. What would be the effect of each of the following on the supply of salsa in the United States? In each case, identify the responsible determinant of supply.
    a. Tomato prices skyrocket
    b. Congress places a 26 percent tax on salsa.
    c. Ed Scissorhands introduces a new, faster vegetable chopper.
    d. J. Lo, Beyonce, and Adam Sandler each introduce a new brand of salsa.

19. What would be the effects of each of the following on the supply of coffee worldwide? In each case, identify the responsible determinant of supply.
    a. Freezing temperatures wipe out half of Brazil's coffee crop.
    b. Wages of coffee workers in Latin America rise as unionization efforts succeed.
    c. Indonesia offers big subsidies to its coffee producers.
    d. Genetic engineering produces a super coffee bean that grows faster and needs less care.
    e. Coffee suppliers expect prices to be higher in the future.

20. The following graph shows three market supply curves for cantaloupe. Compared to point A, which point represents
    a. an increase in quantity supplied?
    b. an increase in supply?
    c. a decrease in quantity supplied?
    d. a decrease in supply?

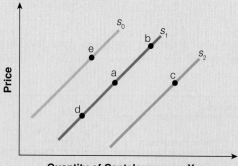

Bringing Supply and Demand Together

5

In the words of the great economist Alfred Marshall, "Like scissors that function by the interaction of two distinct blades, supply and demand interact to determine the price and quantity exchanged."

In this chapter, we bring the market supply and demand curves together. It is market demand and supply that determine the quantity of each good that is produced and the price at which it is sold. In this chapter, we learn how markets with many buyers and sellers adjust to temporary shortages and surpluses, as prices move back to equilibrium. In addition, we will study the impact of a change in one or more of the determinants of supply and demand and see how it impacts the market price and quantity exchanged. That is, if you want to know how an event or policy may affect the economy, you must know supply and demand. We will then explore the impact of price controls, which are government mandates to set a price above or below the equilibrium price. We will also see that policies can have unintended effects—adverse effects that the policymakers did not anticipate. ■

Market Equilibrium Price and Quantity

* What is the equilibrium price?
* What is the equilibrium quantity?

* What is a shortage?
* What is a surplus?

Enough has been said for now about supply and demand separately. We now bring the market supply and demand together.

market equilibrium
the point at which the market supply and market demand curves intersect

equilibrium price
the price at the intersection of the market supply and demand curves; at this price, the quantity demanded equals the quantity supplied

equilibrium quantity
the quantity at the intersection of the market supply and demand curves; at the equilibrium quantity, the quantity demanded equals the quantity supplied

Equilibrium Price and Quantity

The market equilibrium is found at the point at which the market supply and market demand curves intersect. The price at the intersection of the market supply curve and the market demand curve is called the equilibrium price, and the quantity is called the equilibrium quantity. At the equilibrium price, the amount that buyers are willing and able to buy is exactly equal to the amount that sellers are willing and

able to produce. The equilibrium market solution is best understood with the help of a simple graph. Let's return to the coffee example we used in our earlier discussions of supply and demand. Exhibit 1 combines the market demand curve for coffee with the market supply curve. At $3 per pound, buyers are willing to buy 5,000 pounds of coffee and sellers are willing to supply 5,000 pounds of coffee. Neither may be "happy" about the price; the buyers would probably like a lower price and the sellers would probably like a higher price. But both buyers and sellers are able to carry out their purchase and sales plans at the $3 price. At any other price, either suppliers or demanders would be unable to trade as much as they would like.

Equilibrium is not some mythical notion. It is very real. Every morning fishermen bring in their fresh catch. Along the pier, they negotiate with fish brokers—sellers find buyers and buyers find sellers. Equilibrium is reached when the quantity demanded equals the quantity supplied.

section 5.1
exhibit 1   Market Equilibrium

The equilibrium is found at the intersection of the market supply and demand curves. The equilibrium price is $3 per pound, and the equilibrium quantity is 5,000 pounds of coffee. At the equilibrium quantity, the quantity demanded equals the quantity supplied.

Shortages and Surpluses

What happens when the market price is not equal to the equilibrium price? Suppose the market price is above the equilibrium price, as seen in Exhibit 2(a). At $4 per pound, the quantity of coffee demanded would be 3,000 pounds, but the quantity supplied would be 7,000 pounds. At this price, a **surplus**, or excess quantity supplied, would exist. That is, at this price, growers would be willing to sell more coffee than demanders would be willing to buy. To get rid of the unwanted surplus, frustrated suppliers would cut their price and cut back on production. And as price falls, consumers would buy more, ultimately eliminating the unsold surplus and returning the market to the equilibrium level.

What would happen if the market price of coffee were below the equilibrium price? As seen in Exhibit 2(b), at $2 per pound, the yearly quantity demanded of 8,000 pounds would be greater than the 3,000 pounds

> **surplus**
> a situation where quantity supplied exceeds quantity demanded
>
> **shortage**
> a situation where quantity demanded exceeds quantity supplied

that producers would be willing to supply at that low price. So at $2 per pound, a **shortage** or excess quantity demanded of 5,000 pounds would exist. Because of the coffee shortage, frustrated buyers would be forced to compete for the existing supply, bidding up the price. The rising price would have two effects: (1) Producers would be willing to increase the quantity supplied, and (2) the higher price would decrease the quantity demanded. Together, these two effects would ultimately eliminate the shortage, returning the market to equilibrium.

Scarcity and Shortages

People often confuse scarcity with shortages. Remember most goods are scarce—desirable but limited. A shortage occurs when the quantity demanded is greater than the quantity supplied at the current price. We can eliminate shortages by increasing the price but we cannot eliminate scarcity.

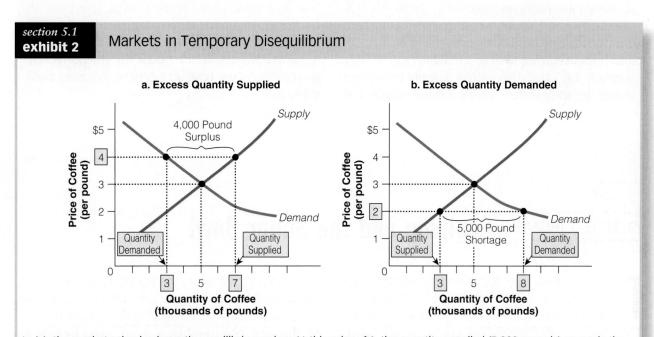

section 5.1
exhibit 2 Markets in Temporary Disequilibrium

In (a), the market price is above the equilibrium price. At this price, $4, the quantity supplied (7,000 pounds) exceeds the quantity demanded (3,000 pounds), resulting in a surplus of 4,000 pounds. To get rid of the unwanted surplus, suppliers cut their prices. As prices fall, consumers buy more, eliminating the surplus and moving the market back to equilibrium. In (b), the market price is below the equilibrium price. At this price, $2, the quantity demanded (8,000 pounds) exceeds the quantity supplied (3,000 pounds), and a shortage of 5,000 pounds is the result. The many frustrated buyers compete for the existing supply, offering to buy more and driving the price up toward the equilibrium level. Therefore, with both shortages and surpluses, market prices tend to pull the market back to the equilibrium level.

Q Imagine that you own a butcher shop. Recently, you have noticed that at about noon, you run out of your daily supply of chicken. Puzzling over your predicament, you hypothesize that you are charging less than the equilibrium price for your chicken. Should you raise the price of your chicken? Explain using a simple graph.

A If the price you are charging is below the equilibrium price (P_E), you can draw a horizontal line from that price straight across Exhibit 3 and see where it intersects the supply and demand curves. The point where this horizontal line intersects the demand curve indicates how much chicken consumers are willing to buy at the below-equilibrium price (P_1). Likewise, the intersection of this horizontal line with the supply curve indicates how much chicken producers are willing to supply at P_1. From this, it is clear that a shortage (or excess quantity demanded) exists, because consumers want more chicken (Q_D) than producers are willing to supply (Q_S) at this relatively low price. This excess quantity demanded results in competition among buyers, which will

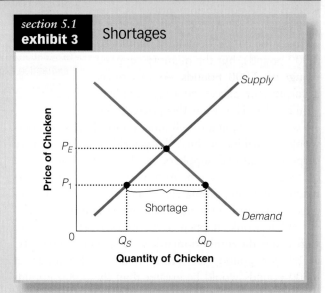

section 5.1
exhibit 3   Shortages

push prices up and reduce or eliminate the shortage. That is, it would make sense to raise your price on chicken. As the price moves up toward the equilibrium price, consumers will be willing to purchase less (some will substitute fish, steak, or ground round), and producers will have an incentive to supply more chicken.

in the news Scalping and the Super Bowl

The Super Bowl is a high demand, limited supply sports event. The face value on most Super Bowl tickets is in the $700 to $900 range. Many of the recipients of the tickets are corporate sponsors or are affiliated with the teams playing in the game. There are also some tickets that are allocated through a lottery. However, at the face value for the tickets at P_1, the quantity demanded far exceeds the quantity supplied as seen in Exhibit 4. In other words, the National Football League (NFL) has not priced their tickets equal to what the market will bear. Consequently, some fans are willing to pay much more, sometimes $6,000 to $7,000, for these tickets

from scalpers, who buy the tickets at face value and try to sell them for a higher price. While ticket scalping is illegal in many states, scalpers will still descend on the host city to make a profit, even though the probability of arrest and conviction are substantial.

But is ticket scalping for athletic events and concerts really so objectionable? Could scalpers be transferring tickets into the hands of those who value them the most? The buyer must value attending the event more than the scalped price of the ticket or he would not buy the ticket. The seller would not sell her ticket unless she valued the money from the ticket more than attending the event. That is, the scalper has helped transfer tickets from those placing lower values on them to those placing higher values on them. The sponsors of the event are the losers, in the form of lost profits, for failing to charge the higher equilibrium market price. Why would the NFL not charge the higher price? Perhaps it sends a sign of goodwill to NFL fans, even if they have no appreciable chance of getting a ticket. That is, maybe the NFL is willing to take a hit on short-run profits to make sure they keep their base of fans (long-run profits).

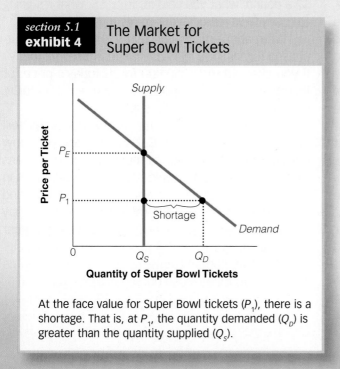

section 5.1
exhibit 4   The Market for Super Bowl Tickets

At the face value for Super Bowl tickets (P_1), there is a shortage. That is, at P_1, the quantity demanded (Q_D) is greater than the quantity supplied (Q_S).

in the news   The Role of Prices in the Aftermath of Hurricane Katrina

The fallout from Hurricane Katrina has featured a lot of ignorance and demagoguery about prices. Let's look at some of it. One undeniable fact is that the hurricane disaster changed scarcity conditions. There are fewer stores, fewer units of housing, less gasoline and a shortage of many other goods and services used on a daily basis. Rising prices are not only a manifestation of these changed scarcity conditions, they help us cope, adjust and get us on the road to recovery.

Here's a which-is-better question for you. Suppose a hotel room rented for $79 a night prior to Hurricane Katrina's devastation. Based on that price, an evacuating family of four might rent two adjoining rooms. When they arrive at the hotel, they find the rooms rent for $200; they decide to make do with one room. In my book, that's wonderful. The family voluntarily opted to make a room available for another family who had to evacuate or whose home was

(continued)

in the news | The Role of Prices in the Aftermath of Hurricane Katrina (cont.)

destroyed. Demagogues will call this price-gouging, but I ask you, which is preferable: a room available at $200 or a room unavailable at $79? Rising prices get people to voluntarily economize on goods and services rendered scarcer by the disaster.

After Hurricane Katrina struck, gasoline prices shot up almost a dollar nearly overnight. Some people have been quick to call this price-gouging, particularly since wholesalers and retailers were charging the higher price for gasoline already purchased and in their tanks prior to the hurricane. The fact of business is that what a seller paid for something doesn't necessarily determine its selling price. Put in a bit more sophisticated way: Historical costs have nothing to do with selling price. For example, suppose you maintained a 10-pound inventory of coffee in your cupboard. When I ran out, you'd occasionally sell me a pound for $2. Suppose there's a freeze in Brazil destroying much of the coffee crop, driving coffee prices to $5 a pound. Then I come around to purchase coffee. Are you going to charge me $2 a pound, what you paid for it, or $5, what it's going to cost you to restock your coffee inventory?

What about the house that you might have purchased for $50,000 in 1970 that you're selling today? If you charged me $250,000 for it, today's price for its replacement, as opposed to what you paid for it, are you guilty of price-gouging?

Recovering from Katrina means resources will have to be moved to the Gulf Coast. I ask you, how does one get electricians, plumbers and other artisans to give up their comfortable homes and livelihoods in Virginia and Pennsylvania and travel to Mobile and New Orleans to help in the recovery? If you said pay them higher prices, go to the head of the class. Higher prices, along with windfall profits, are economic signals of unmet human wants. As such, they encourage producers to meet those human wants....

– BY WALTER E. WILLIAMS
SEPTEMBER 14, 2005, TOWNHALL.COM

SECTION CHECK

1. The intersection of the supply and demand curves shows the equilibrium price and equilibrium quantity in a market.
2. A surplus is a situation where quantity supplied exceeds quantity demanded.
3. A shortage is a situation where quantity demanded exceeds quantity supplied.
4. Shortages and surpluses set in motion actions by many buyers and sellers that will move the market toward the equilibrium price and quantity unless otherwise prevented.

---

1. How does the intersection of supply and demand indicate the equilibrium price and quantity in a market?
2. What can cause a change in the supply and demand equilibrium?
3. What must be true about the price charged for a shortage to occur?
4. What must be true about the price charged for a surplus to occur?
5. Why do market forces tend to eliminate both shortages and surpluses?
6. If tea prices were above their equilibrium level, what force would tend to push tea prices down? If tea prices were below their equilibrium level, what force would tend to push tea prices up?

Changes in Equilibrium Price and Quantity

✳ What happens to equilibrium price and quantity when the demand curve shifts?

✳ What happens to equilibrium price and quantity when the supply curve shifts?

✳ What happens when both supply and demand shift in the same time period?

✳ What is an indeterminate solution?

When one of the many determinants of demand or supply (input prices, prices of related products, number of suppliers, expectations, technology, and so on) changes, the demand and/or supply curves will shift, leading to changes in the equilibrium price and equilibrium quantity. We first consider a change in demand.

had significant health benefits. We would expect an increase in the demand for coffee. An increase in demand, *ceteris paribus*, will lead to a higher equilibrium price and a higher equilibrium quantity, as shown in Exhibit 1. The rightward shift of the demand curve results in an increase in both equilibrium price and quantity, *ceteris paribus*.

A Change in Demand

A shift in the demand curve—caused by a change in the price of a related good (substitutes or complements), income, the number of buyers, tastes, or expectations—results in a change in both equilibrium price and equilibrium quantity, assuming the supply curve has not changed. But how and why does this relationship happen? The answer can be most clearly explained by means of an example. Suppose a new study claimed that two cups of coffee per day

A Change in Supply

Like a shift in demand, a shift in the supply curve will also influence both equilibrium price and equilibrium quantity, assuming that demand for the product has not changed. For example, what impact would unfavorable weather conditions have in coffee-producing countries? Such conditions could cause a reduction in the supply of coffee. A decrease in supply, *ceteris paribus*, will lead to a higher equilibrium price and a lower equilibrium quantity, as shown in Exhibit 2.

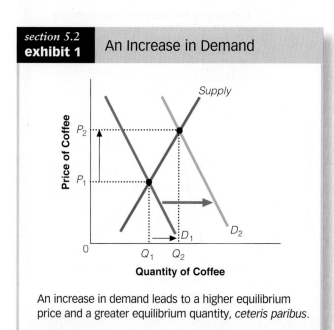

section 5.2 **exhibit 1**   An Increase in Demand

An increase in demand leads to a higher equilibrium price and a greater equilibrium quantity, *ceteris paribus*.

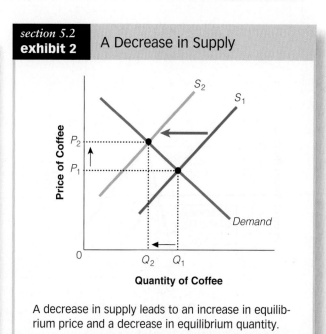

section 5.2 **exhibit 2**   A Decrease in Supply

A decrease in supply leads to an increase in equilibrium price and a decrease in equilibrium quantity.

Use what you've LEARNED

CHANGE IN DEMAND

Q In ski resorts such as Aspen and Sun Valley, hotel prices are higher in February (in-season when more skiers want to ski) than in May (off-season when fewer skiers want to ski). If the May hotel prices were charged in February, what problem would arise? What if we charged February's price in May?

A In the (likely) event that supply is not altered significantly, demand is chiefly responsible for the higher prices in the prime skiing months. In Exhibit 3(a), if prices were maintained at the off-season rates (P_{May}) all year long, a shortage would exist—the difference between points A and B in Exhibit 3(a). This excess demand at the off-peak prices causes prime-season rates to be higher. After all, why would a self-interested resort owner rent you a room for less than its opportunity cost (what someone else would be willing to pay)? For example, at the Hotel Jerome in Aspen, the price per night of a Deluxe King room is almost 6 times higher in late December (in-season) than it is in mid-May (off- season). In Exhibit 3(b), we see that if hotels

What would happen if the Hotel Jerome, pictured above, charged the lower out-of-season rate for resort rentals during peak ski season?

were to charge the in-season price (P_{Feb}) during the off-season (May), a surplus would result—the difference between points C and D. Now, it would be this excess supply during the off-season (at in-season prices) that would cause the price to fall. Who needs all the empty rooms?

section 5.2
exhibit 3   The Market for Aspen Rentals

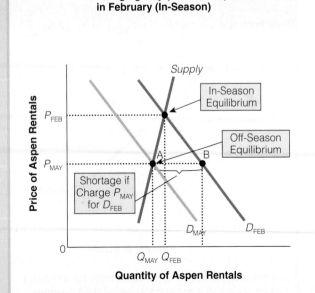

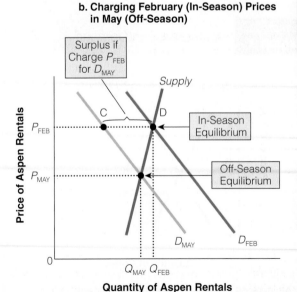

a. Charging May (Off-Season) Prices in February (In-Season)

b. Charging February (In-Season) Prices in May (Off-Season)

Changes in Both Supply and Demand

We have discussed that, as part of the continual process of adjustment that occurs in the marketplace, supply and demand can each shift in response to many different factors, with the market then adjusting toward the new equilibrium. We have, so far, only considered what happens when just one such change occurs at a time. In these cases, we learned that the results of the adjustments in supply and demand on the equilibrium price and quantity are predictable. However, both supply and demand will often shift in the same time period. Can we predict what will happen to equilibrium prices and equilibrium quantities in these situations?

As you will see, when supply and demand move at the same time, we can predict the change in one variable (price or quantity), but we are unable to predict the direction of the effect on the other variable with any certainty. The change in the second variable,

then, is said to be *indeterminate*, because it cannot be determined without additional information about the size of the relative shifts in supply and demand. This concept will become clearer to you as we work through the following example.

An Increase in Supply and a Decrease in Demand

In Exhibits 4(a) and 4(b), we have an increase in supply and a decrease in demand. These changes will clearly result in a decrease in the equilibrium price, because both the increase in supply and the decrease in demand work to push this price down. This drop in equilibrium price (from P_1 to P_2) is shown in the movement from E_1 to E_2 in Exhibits 4(a) and 4(b).

The effect of these changes on equilibrium price is clear, but how does the equilibrium quantity change? The impact on equilibrium quantity is indeterminate because the increase in supply increases the equilibrium quantity and the decrease in demand decreases it. In this scenario, the change in the equilibrium quantity

---

section 5.2 **exhibit 4**	Shifts in Supply and Demand

a. A Small Increase in Supply and a Large Decrease in Demand

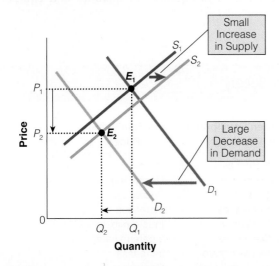

If the decrease in demand (leftward shift) is greater than the increase in supply (rightward shift), the equilibrium price and equilibrium quantity will fall.

b. A Large Increase in Supply and a Small Decrease in Demand

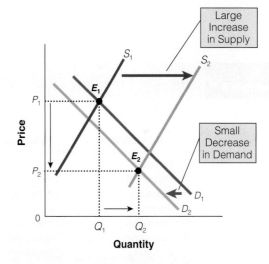

If the increase in supply (rightward shift) is greater than the decrease in demand (leftward shift), the equilibrium price will fall and the equilibrium quantity will rise.

will vary depending on the relative changes in supply and demand. If, as shown in Exhibit 4(a), the decrease in demand is greater than the increase in supply, the equilibrium quantity will decrease. If, however, as shown in Exhibit 4(b), the increase in supply is greater than the decrease in demand, the equilibrium quantity will increase.

An Increase in Demand and Supply

It is also possible that both supply and demand will increase (or decrease). This situation, for example, has happened with flat screen televisions (and with DVDs, laptops, cell phones, high definition (HD) televisions, digital cameras, and other electronic equipment, too). As a result of technological breakthroughs and new factories manufacturing HD televisions, the supply curve for HD televisions shifted to the right. That is, at any given price, more HD televisions were offered than before. But with rising income and an increasing number of buyers in the market, the demand for HD televisions increased as well. As shown in Exhibit 5, both the increased demand and the increased supply caused an increase in the equilibrium quantity—more HD televisions were sold. The equilibrium price could have gone either up (because of increased demand) or down (because of increased supply), depending on the relative sizes of the demand and supply shifts. In this case, price is the indeterminate variable. However, in the case of HD televisions, we know that the supply curve shifted more than the demand curve, so that the effect of increased supply pushing prices down outweighed the effect of increased demand pushing prices up. As a result, the equilibrium price of HD televisions has fallen (from P_1 to P_2) over time.

The Combinations of Supply and Demand Shifts

The eight possible changes in demand and/or supply are presented in Exhibit 6, along with the resulting changes in equilibrium quantity and equilibrium

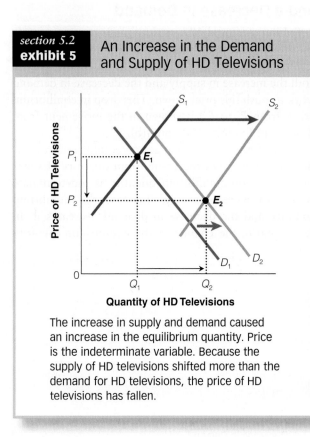

section 5.2
exhibit 5 An Increase in the Demand and Supply of HD Televisions

The increase in supply and demand caused an increase in the equilibrium quantity. Price is the indeterminate variable. Because the supply of HD televisions shifted more than the demand for HD televisions, the price of HD televisions has fallen.

section 5.2
exhibit 6 The Effect of Changing Demand and/or Supply

If Demand	and Supply	Then Equilibrium Quantity	and Equilibrium Price
1. Increases	Stays unchanged	Increases	Increases
2. Decreases	Stays unchanged	Decreases	Decreases
3. Stays unchanged	Increases	Increases	Decreases
4. Stays unchanged	Decreases	Decreases	Increases
5. Increases	Increases	Increases	Indeterminate*
6. Decreases	Decreases	Decreases	Indeterminate*
7. Increases	Decreases	Indeterminate*	Increases
8. Decreases	Increases	Indeterminate*	Decreases

*May increase, decrease, or remain the same, depending on the size of the change in demand relative to the change in supply.

price. Even though you could memorize the impact of the various possible changes in demand and supply, it would be more profitable to draw a graph, as shown in Exhibit 7, whenever a situation of changing demand and/or supply arises. Remember that an increase in either demand or supply means a rightward shift in the

curve, while a decrease in either means a leftward shift. Also, when both demand and supply change, one of the two equilibrium values, price or quantity, will change in an indeterminate manner (increase or decrease), depending on the relative magnitude of the changes in supply and demand.

section 5.2
exhibit 7   The Combination of Supply and Demand Shifts

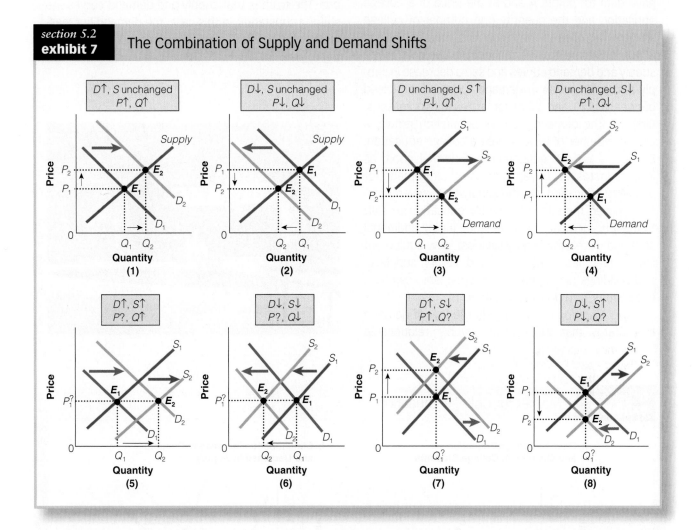

COLLEGE ENROLLMENT AND THE PRICE OF GOING TO COLLEGE

Use what you've LEARNED

Q How is it possible that the price of a college education has increased significantly over the past 37 years, yet many more students are attending college? Does this relationship defy the law of demand?

A If we know the price of a college education (adjusted for inflation) and the number of students enrolled in college for the two years 1970 and 2010, we can tell a plausible story using the analysis of
(continued)

Use what you've LEARNED

COLLEGE ENROLLMENT AND THE
PRICE OF GOING TO COLLEGE (cont.)

supply and demand. In Exhibit 8(a), suppose that we have data for points A and B; the price of a college education and the quantity (the number of college students enrolled in the respective years, 1970 and 2010). In Exhibit 8(b), we connect the two points with supply and demand curves and see a decrease in supply and an increase in demand. Demand increased between 1970 and 2010 for at least two reasons. First, on the demand side, as population grows, a greater number of buyers want a college education. Second, a college education is a normal good; as income increases, buyers increase their demand for a college education. On the supply side, several factors caused the supply curve for education to shift to the left: the cost of maintenance (hiring additional staff and increasing faculty salaries), new equipment (computers, lab equipment, and library supplies), and buildings (additional classrooms, labs, cafeteria expansions, and dormitory space).

This situation does not defy the law of demand that states that there is an inverse relationship between price and quantity demanded, *ceteris paribus*. The truth is that supply and demand curves are shifting constantly. In this case, the demand (increasing) and supply (decreasing) caused price and quantity to rise.

COURTESY OF ROBERT L. SEXTON

section 5.2
exhibit 8   Market for College Education

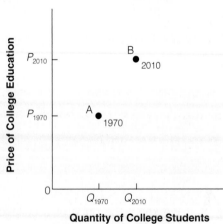

a. Price of College Education and Quantity of College Students

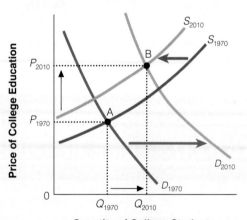

b. Simultaneous Increase in Demand and Decrease in Supply

Q During the second half of the twentieth century, demand for chicken increased because of rising income and the purported health benefits. However, as the demand for chicken increased, the price fell. Why? (*Hint:* Remember it is supply and demand.)

A Even though the demand for chicken did increase (a small rightward shift), the supply of chicken increased even more—technological advances in the poultry industry and many new suppliers caused the supply curve to shift rightward. In order for the price to fall, the supply must have shifted further to the right than the demand curve. The result is more chickens consumed at a lower price.

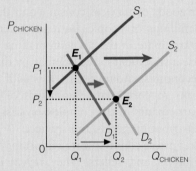

Q Suppose the demand of gasoline increases because of world economic growth and higher incomes. At the same time, supply decreases because of hostilities in the Middle East and refinery problems. What can we predict would happen to the price and quantity of gasoline?

A The increase in demand (rightward shift) and the decrease in supply (leftward shift) would lead to an increase in price. We are not sure about the quantity of gasoline consumed—it depends on the magnitude of the shifts in the demand and supply curves. That is, quantity is indeterminate.

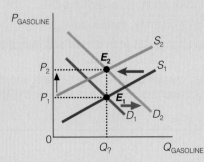

Q Suppose the demand for air travel decreases because of air safety concerns. At the same time, the price of jet fuel increases. What do you think will happen to the price and quantity of air travel?

A The decrease in demand (leftward shift) for air travel and the decrease in supply (leftward shift) result from the higher input cost of jet fuel. These factors reduce the quantity of air travel. The price change will depend on the magnitude of the shifts in the demand and supply curves. That is, price is indeterminate.

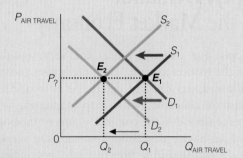

Q Hypothetically, suppose a new study reveals that sugar can have "huge" negative health consequences, causing a large decrease in demand. In addition, a slight reduction in the sugar yield occurs because of bad weather in sugar-producing areas. What do you think will happen to the price and quantity of sugar?

A A large decrease in demand (leftward shift) for sugar and a small decrease in supply (leftward shift) because of bad weather lead to a reduction in price and a large reduction in quantity.

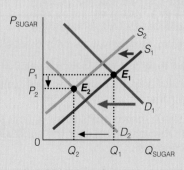

(continued)

Q As the price of oil rises, many may switch to burning natural gas to save money. Can buyers of natural gas expect any surprises?

A If oil and natural gas are substitutes, then the higher price for oil will cause an increase in demand for natural gas (rightward shift). As a result, the price and quantity of natural gas will rise.

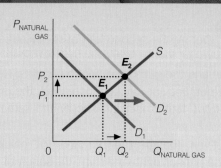

Supply, Demand, and the Market Economy

Supply and demand are at the very foundation of the market system. They determine the prices of goods and services and determine how our scarce resources are allocated. What is truly amazing is how producers respond to the complex wants of the population without having tremendous shortages or surpluses, despite the fact that in a "free market," no single individual or agency makes decisions about what to produce. The market system provides a way for millions of producers and consumers to allocate scarce resources. Buyers and sellers indicate their wants through their actions and inactions in the marketplace, and this collective "voice" determines how resources are allocated. But how is this information communicated? Market prices serve as the language of the market system.

We often say the decision is made by "the market" or "market forces," but this is of little help in pinpointing the name and the place of the decision maker. In fact, no single person makes decisions about the quantity and quality of television, cars, beds, or any other goods or services consumed in the economy. Literally millions of people, both producers and consumers, participate in the decision-making process. To paraphrase a statement made popular by the first great modern economist, Adam Smith, it is as if an invisible hand works to coordinate the efforts of millions of diverse participants in the complex process of producing and distributing goods and services.

Market prices communicate important information to both buyers and sellers. They reveal information about the relative availability of products to buyers and they provide sellers with critical information about the relative value that consumers place on those products. In effect, market prices provide a way for both buyers and sellers to communicate about the relative value of resources. This communication results in a shifting of resources from those uses that are less valued to those that are more valued.

1. Does an increase in demand create a shortage or surplus at the original price?

2. What happens to the equilibrium price and quantity as a result of a demand increase?

3. Does an increase in supply create a shortage or surplus at the original price?

4. Assuming the market is already at equilibrium, what happens to the equilibrium price and quantity as a result of a supply increase?

5. Why do heating oil prices tend to be higher in the winter?

6. Why are evening and weekend long-distance calls cheaper than weekday long-distance calls?

7. What would have to be true for both supply and demand to shift in the same time period?

8. When both supply and demand shift, what added information do we need to know in order to determine in which direction the indeterminate variable changes?

9. If both buyers and sellers of grapes expect grape prices to rise in the near future, what will happen to grape prices and sales today?

10. If demand for peanut butter increases and supply decreases, what will happen to equilibrium price and quantity?

SECTION 5.3

Price Controls

* What are price controls?
* What are price ceilings?
* What are price floors?

* What is the law of unintended consequences?

Price Controls

Although nonequilibrium prices can occur naturally in the private sector, reflecting uncertainty, they seldom last for long. Governments, however, may impose nonequilibrium prices for significant periods. Price controls involve the use of the power of the state to establish prices different from the equilibrium prices that would otherwise prevail. The motivations for price controls vary with the market under consideration. For example, a **price ceiling**, a legal maximum price, is often set for goods deemed important to low-income households, such as housing. Or a **price floor**, a legal minimum price, may be set on wages because wages are the primary source of income for most people.

Price controls are not always implemented by the federal government. Local governments (and more rarely, private companies) can and do impose local price controls. One fairly well-known example is rent control. The inflation of the late 1970s meant rapidly rising rents; and some communities, such as Santa Monica, California, decided to do something about it. In response, they limited how much landlords could charge for rental housing.

> **price ceiling**
> a legally established maximum price
>
> **price floor**
> a legally established minimum price

Price Ceilings: Rent Controls

Rent control experiences can be found in many cities across the country. San Francisco, Berkeley, and New York City all have had some form of rent control. Although the rules may vary from city to city and over time, generally the price (or rent) of an apartment remains fixed over the tenure of an occupant, except for allowable annual increases tied to the cost of living or some other price index. When an occupant moves out, the owners can usually, but not always, raise the rent to a near-market level for the next occupant. The controlled rents for existing occupants, however, are generally well below market rental rates.

Results of Rent Controls

Most people living in rent-controlled apartments are getting a good deal, one that they would lose by moving as their family circumstances or income changes. Tenants thus are reluctant to give up their governmentally granted right to a below-market-rent apartment. In addition, because the rents received by landlords are constrained and below market levels, the

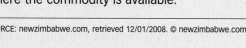

ZIMBABWE PRICE CONTROLS SPARK FOOD SHORTAGES

—BY MACDONALD DZIRUTWE

ZIMBABWE'S government and the country's businesses have clashed over prices of basic commodities, now blamed for widespread shortages days after disputed polls won by President Robert Mugabe's ruling party.

Prices shot up by as much as 100 percent after the March 31 parliamentary elections in which Mugabe's ZANU-PF government defeated the opposition Movement for Democratic Change (MDC), but the government swiftly moved in, ordering businesses to reverse the increases.

"Increases were actually delayed to avoid harsh criticism of the government ahead of the elections but now the government is saying you can not increase prices without consulting us . . . that's not what we agreed," a spokesman for the Confederation of Zimbabwe Industries told Reuters.

The staple maize-meal, sugar and cooking oil have disappeared from most shops in Harare's city centre and suburbs while most pumps at fuel stations have run dry, forcing motorists to brace for long queues.

Maize-meal supplies were already erratic in the country in recent months with supermarkets out of stocks for days on end and long queues quickly form where the commodity is available.

SOURCE: newzimbabwe.com, retrieved 12/01/2008. © newzimbabwe.com.

AP PHOTO/KAREL PRINSLOO

consider this:

In July of 2007, Zimbabwe's government threatened to seize any business that did not roll their prices back. But many shop-keepers and manufacturers threatened to shut down and lay off workers rather than produce at a loss. Gasoline was disappearing from the pumps and many workers were forced to walk to work. Shoppers were told to queue (wait in line) for whatever products were left on the shelf. Police were sent in to enforce the price controls which resulted in hundreds of shop owners being arrested for not lowering prices enough. In short, price controls and the resulting shortages can turn into social unrest. This is not the first time Zimbabwe has tried price controls; they are usually short-lived and poorly enforced. In 2009, the finance minister Patrick Chinamasa announced the government is abandoning price controls. Mr. Chinamasa told parliament "that price controls would be abandoned because they had "unintentionally" harmed businesses and added to Zimbabwe's hyperinflation."

rate of return (roughly, the profit) on housing investments falls compared with that on other forms of real estate not subject to rent controls, such as office rents or mortgage payments on condominiums. Hence, the incentive to construct new housing is reduced.

Further, when landlords are limited in the rents they can charge, they have little incentive to improve or upgrade apartments—by putting in new kitchen appliances or new carpeting, for instance. In fact, rent controls give landlords some incentive to avoid routine maintenance, thereby lowering the cost of apartment ownership to a figure approximating the controlled rental price, although the quality of the housing stock will deteriorate over time.

Another impact of rent controls is that they promote housing discrimination. Where rent controls do not exist, prejudiced landlords might willingly rent to people they believe are undesirable simply because the undesirables are the only ones willing to pay the requested rents (and the landlords are not willing to lower their rents substantially to get desirable renters because of the possible loss of thousands of dollars in income). With rent controls, each rent-controlled apartment is likely to attract many possible renters, some desirable and some undesirable as judged by the landlord, simply because the rent is at a below-equilibrium price. Landlords can indulge in their "taste" for discrimination without any additional financial loss beyond that required by the controls. Consequently, they will be more likely to choose to rent to desirable people, perhaps a family without children or pets, rather than to undesirable ones, perhaps a family with lower income and so a greater risk of nonpayment.

Exhibit 1 shows the impact of rent controls. If the price ceiling (P_{RC}) is set below the equilibrium price (P_E), consumers are willing to buy Q_D, but producers are only willing to supply Q_S. The rent control policy will therefore create a persistent shortage, the difference between Q_D and Q_S.

Price Floors: The Minimum Wage

The argument for a minimum wage is simple: Existing wages for workers in some types of labor markets do not allow for a very high standard of living, and a minimum wage allows those workers to live better than before. Ever since 1938, when the first minimum wage was established (at 25 cents per hour), the federal government has, by legislation, made it illegal to pay most workers an amount below the current legislated minimum wage. As of July of 2009, the federal minimum wage was set at $7.25. A number of states also have minimum wage laws. In cases where an employee is subject to both state and federal minimum wage laws, the employee is entitled to the higher minimum wage.

Let's examine graphically the impact of a minimum wage on low-skilled workers. In Exhibit 2, suppose the government sets the minimum wage, W_{MIN}, above the market equilibrium wage, W_E. In Exhibit 2, we see that the price floor is binding. That is, there is a surplus of low-skilled workers at W_{MIN}, because the quantity of labor supplied is greater than the quantity of labor demanded. The reason for the surplus of low-skilled workers (unemployment) at W_{MIN} is that more people are willing to work than employers are willing and able to hire.

---

section 5.3 exhibit 1   Rent Controls

The impact of a rent ceiling set below the equilibrium price is a persistent shortage.

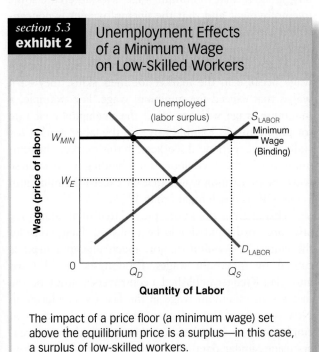

section 5.3 exhibit 2   Unemployment Effects of a Minimum Wage on Low-Skilled Workers

The impact of a price floor (a minimum wage) set above the equilibrium price is a surplus—in this case, a surplus of low-skilled workers.

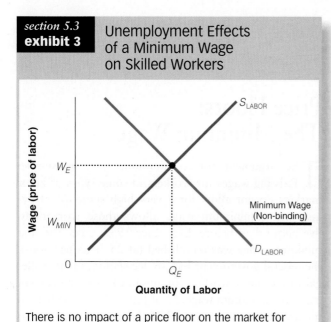

section 5.3
exhibit 3

Unemployment Effects
of a Minimum Wage
on Skilled Workers

There is no impact of a price floor on the market for skilled workers. In this market, the price floor (the minimum wage) is not binding.

In 1974, the government imposed price ceilings on gasoline. The result was shortages. In some cities, such as Chicago, Portland, and New York, drivers waited over an hour to fill up their tanks. As you know, the value of your time has an opportunity cost.

Notice that not everyone loses from a minimum wage. Workers who continue to hold jobs have higher incomes—those between 0 and Q_D in Exhibit 2. However, many low-skilled workers suffer from a minimum wage—those between Q_D and Q_S in Exhibit 2—because they either lose their jobs or are unable to get them in the first place. Although studies disagree somewhat on the precise magnitudes, they largely agree that minimum wage laws do create some unemployment and that the unemployment is concentrated among teenagers—the least-experienced and least-skilled members of the labor force.

Most U.S. workers are not affected by the minimum wage because in the market for their skills, they earn wages that exceed the minimum wage. For example, a minimum wage will not affect the unemployment rate for physicians. In Exhibit 3, we see the labor market for skilled and experienced workers. In this market, the minimum wage (the price floor) is not binding because these workers are earning wages that far exceed the minimum wage—W_E is much higher than W_{MIN}.

This analysis does not "prove" that minimum wage laws are "bad" and should be abolished. First, consider the empirical question of how much unemployment is caused by minimum wages. Economists David Card and Alan Kreuger published a controversial study on the increase in minimum wage in the fast food industry in New Jersey and Pennsylvania. They found the effect on employment to be quite small. However, other researchers using similar data have found the effect on employment to be much larger. In fact, most empirical studies indicate that a 10 percent increase in the minimum wage

would reduce employment of teenagers between 1 and 3 percent. Second, some might believe that the cost of unemployment resulting from a minimum wage is a reasonable price to pay for ensuring that those with jobs get a "decent" wage. However, opponents of minimum wage argue that it might induce teenagers to drop out of school. Less than one-third of minimum wage earners are from families with incomes below the poverty line. In fact, many recipients of the minimum wage are part-time teenage workers from middle income families. More efficient methods transfer income to low-wage workers; perhaps a wage subsidy like a earned income tax credit. This is a government program that supplements low wage-workers. Of course, there are no free lunches so subsidies in the form of wages, income, or rent ultimately cost taxpayers. We will revisit this topic in upcoming chapters.

However, the analysis does point out there is a cost to having a minimum wage: The burden of the minimum wage falls not only on low-skilled workers and employers but also on consumers of products made more costly by the minimum wage.

Price Ceilings: Price Controls on Gasoline

Another example of price ceilings leading to shortages is the price controls imposed on gasoline in 1974. In 1973, the Organization of Petroleum Exporting Nations (OPEC) reduced the supply of oil. Because crude oil is the most important input in the production of gasoline, this reduction in the supply of oil caused a shift in the supply curve for gasoline leftward from S_1 to S_2 in Exhibit 4. In an effort to prevent sharply rising prices, the government

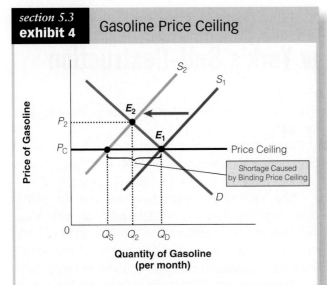

section 5.3
exhibit 4   Gasoline Price Ceiling

The higher price of crude oil (a major input for gasoline) caused the supply curve to shift leftward from S_1 to S_2. Without price controls, the price would have risen to P_2. However, with the binding price ceiling consumers were able and willing to buy Q_D but producers were able and willing to sell Q_S. Therefore, a shortage of $Q_D - Q_S$ occurred at P_C.

What do you think would happen to the number of teenagers getting jobs if we raised the minimum wage to $50 an hour?

DOUG MENUEZ/PHOTODISC/GETTY IMAGES

imposed price controls on gasoline in 1974. The government told gasoline stations they could not charge more than P_C for gasoline. But people wanted to buy more gasoline than was available at the controlled price, P_C. That is, a shortage developed at P_C, as you can see in Exhibit 4. Some customers were lucky enough to get their gasoline at P_C (0 to Q_S), but others were left wanting (Q_S to Q_D). The price ceiling was binding. Consequently, people wasted hours waiting in line for gasoline. Some gas stations sold their gas on a first-come, first-served basis. Some states implemented an even/odd license plate system. If your license plate ended in an odd number, you could buy gas on only odd numbered days. In addition, quantity restrictions meant that some stations would only allow you to buy a few gallons a day; when they ran out of gas, they closed for the day. Many gas stations were closed in the evenings and on weekends.

A number of government officials wanted to put the blame on OPEC, but if prices were allowed to rise to their equilibrium at E_2, shortages would have been avoided. Instead, it would have meant higher prices at P_2 and a greater quantity sold, Q_2 rather than Q_S. Of course, not everybody was unhappy with the price ceiling. Recall our discussion of opportunity cost in Chapter 2. People place different values on their time. People with a low opportunity cost of time but who cannot as easily afford the higher price per gallon (e.g., poor retired senior citizens) would be

unintended consequences
the secondary effects of an action that may occur after the initial effects

more likely to favor the controls. Surgeons, lawyers, and others who have high hourly wages and salaries would view the controls less favorably, because the time spent waiting in line may be worth more to them than paying the higher price for gasoline.

Unintended Consequences

When markets are altered for policy reasons, it is wise to remember that actions do not always have the results that were initially intended—in other words, actions can have **unintended consequences**. As economists, we must always look for the secondary effects of an action, which may occur along with the initial effects. For example, the government is often well intentioned when it adopts price controls to help low-skilled workers or tenants in search of affordable housing; however, such policies may also cause unintended consequences that could completely undermine the intended effects. For example, rent controls may have the immediate effect of lowering rents, but secondary effects may well include low vacancy rates, discrimination against low-income and large families, deterioration of the quality of rental units, and black markets. Similarly, a sizable increase in the minimum wage may help many low-skilled workers or apprentices but may also result in higher unemployment and/or a reduction in fringe benefits, such as vacations and discounts to employees. Society has to make tough decisions, and if the government subsidizes some programs or groups of people in one area, then something must always be given up somewhere else. The "law of scarcity" cannot be repealed!

in the news   Rent Control: New York's Self-Destruction

"**[R]**ent control appears to be the most efficient technique presently known to destroy a city—except for bombing," Swedish economist Assar Lindbeck observed in a 1972 book. Rent control is a big cause of New York City's chronic financial mess, a huge cause of its notorious housing scarcity and a neat illustration of its political unreality. Ending it would be a big step toward unleashing a construction boom and boosting its economy to offset destructive tax increases.

New York has maintained price controls on rent since World War II....William Tucker, the writer who has studied the costs most closely, estimates the direct costs of rent control at $2 billion a year, exclusive of the effect of shrinking the property tax base.

Rent control . . . has inhibited construction in the city. During the recession of 1990–91, the city actually lost more housing units than it gained. . . .

The Manhattan Institute chartered an elaborate study by Henry O. Pollakowski, an MIT housing expert. He concluded, "tenants in low- and moderate-income areas receive little or no benefit from rent stabilization, while tenants in more affluent locations are effectively subsidized for a substantial portion of their rent."

SOURCE: Robert L. Bartley, "Rent Control: New York's Self-Destruction," *Wall Street Journal*, May 19, 2003, p. A17.

Use what you've LEARNED   BINDING PRICE CONTROLS

Q If binding price controls are imposed by the government at levels that are either above or below the equilibrium price, is the quantity of goods bought (and sold) less than the equilibrium quantity?

A If a price ceiling (a legally established maximum price) is set below the equilibrium price, quantity demanded will be greater than quantity supplied, resulting in a shortage at that price. Because producers will only increase the quantity supplied at higher prices, *ceteris paribus*, only Q_1 will be bought and sold. Alternatively, if a price floor (a legally established minimum price) is set above the equilibrium price, quantity supplied will be greater than quantity demanded, causing a surplus at that price. Because consumers will only increase their quantity demanded, *ceteris paribus*, at lower prices, only Q_1 will be bought and sold.

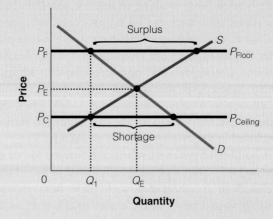

SECTION CHECK

1. Price controls involve government mandates to keep prices above or below the market-determined equilibrium price.
2. Price ceilings are government-imposed maximum prices.
3. If price ceilings are set below the equilibrium price, shortages will result.
4. Price floors are government-imposed minimum prices.
5. If price floors are set above the equilibrium price, surpluses will result.
6. The law of unintended consequences states that the results of certain actions may not always be as clear as they initially appear.

---

1. How is rent control an example of a price ceiling?
2. What predictable effects result from price ceilings such as rent control?
3. How is the minimum wage law an example of a price floor?
4. What predictable effects result from price floors such as the minimum wage?
5. What may happen to the amount of discrimination against groups such as families with children, pet owners, smokers, or students when rent control is imposed?
6. Why does rent control often lead to condominium conversions?
7. What is the law of unintended consequences?
8. Why is the law of unintended consequences so important in making public policy?

Interactive Chapter Summary

Fill in the blanks:

1. The price at the intersection of the market demand curve and the market supply curve is called the _____ price, and the quantity is called the _____ quantity.

2. A situation where quantity supplied is greater than quantity demanded is called a(n) _____.

3. A situation where quantity demanded is greater than quantity supplied is called a(n) _____.

4. At a price greater than the equilibrium price, a(n) _____, or excess quantity supplied, would exist. Sellers would be willing to sell _____ than demanders would be willing to buy. Frustrated suppliers would _____ their price and _____ on production, and consumers would buy _____, returning the market to equilibrium.

5. An increase in demand results in a(n) _____ equilibrium price and a(n) _____ equilibrium quantity.

6. A decrease in supply results in a(n) _____ equilibrium price and a(n) _____ equilibrium quantity.

7. If demand decreases and supply increases, but the decrease in demand is greater than the increase in supply, the equilibrium quantity will _____.

8. If supply decreases and demand increases, the equilibrium price will _____ and the equilibrium quantity will be _____.

9. A price _____ is a legally established maximum price; a price _____ is a legally established minimum price.

10. Rent controls distort market signals and lead to _____ of rent-controlled apartments.

11. The quality of rent-controlled apartments would tend to _____ over time.

12. An increase in the minimum wage would tend to create _____ unemployment for low-skilled workers.

13. The secondary effects of an action that may occur after the initial effects are called _____.

Answers: 1. equilibrium; equilibrium 2. surplus 3. shortage 4. surplus; more; lower; cut back; more 5. greater; greater 6. higher; lower 7. decrease 8. increase; indeterminate 9. ceiling; floor 10. shortages 11. decline 12. additional 13. unintended consequences

Key Terms and Concepts

market equilibrium 122
equilibrium price 122
equilibrium quantity 122

surplus 123
shortage 123
price ceiling 135

price floor 135
unintended consequences 139

Section Check Answers

5.1 Market Equilibrium Price and Quantity

1. How does the intersection of supply and demand indicate the equilibrium price and quantity in a market?

The intersection of supply and demand indicates the equilibrium price and quantity in a market because at higher prices, sellers would be frustrated by their inability to sell all they would like, leading sellers to compete by lowering the price they charge; at lower prices, buyers would be frustrated by their inability to buy all they would like, leading buyers to compete by increasing the price they offer to pay.

2. What can cause a change in the supply and demand equilibrium?

Changes in any of the demand curve shifters or the supply curve shifters will change the supply and demand equilibrium.

3. What must be true about the price charged for a shortage to occur?

The price charged must be less than the equilibrium price, with the result that buyers would like to buy more at that price than sellers are willing to sell.

4. What must be true about the price charged for a surplus to occur?

The price charged must be greater than the equilibrium price, with the result that sellers would like to sell more at that price than buyers are willing to buy.

5. Why do market forces tend to eliminate both shortages and surpluses?

Market forces tend to eliminate both shortages and surpluses because of the self-interest of the market participants. A seller is better off successfully selling at a lower equilibrium price than not being able to sell at a higher price (the surplus situation) and a buyer is better off successfully buying at a higher equilibrium price than not being able to buy at a lower price (the shortage situation). Therefore, we expect market forces to eliminate both shortages and surpluses.

6. If tea prices were above their equilibrium level, what force would tend to push tea prices down? If tea prices were below their equilibrium level, what force would tend to push tea prices up?

If tea prices were above their equilibrium level, sellers frustrated by their inability to sell as much tea as they would like at those prices would compete the price of tea down, as they tried to make more attractive offers to tea buyers. If tea prices were below their equilibrium level, buyers frustrated by their inability to buy as much tea as they would like at those prices would compete the price of tea up, as they tried to make more attractive offers to tea sellers.

5.2 Changes in Equilibrium Price and Quantity

1. Does an increase in demand create a shortage or surplus at the original price?

An increase in demand increases the quantity demanded at the original equilibrium price, but it does not change the quantity supplied at that price, meaning that it would create a shortage at the original equilibrium price.

2. What happens to the equilibrium price and quantity as a result of a demand increase?

Frustrated buyers unable to buy all they would like at the original equilibrium price will compete the market price higher, and that higher price will induce suppliers to increase their quantity supplied. The result is a higher market price and a larger market output.

3. Does an increase in supply create a shortage or surplus at the original price?

An increase in supply increases the quantity supplied at the original equilibrium price, but it does not change the quantity demanded at that price, meaning that it would create a surplus at the original equilibrium price.

4. Assuming the market is already at equilibrium, what happens to the equilibrium price and quantity as a result of a supply increase?

Frustrated sellers unable to sell all they would like at the original equilibrium price will compete the market price lower, and that lower price will induce demanders to increase their quantity demanded. The result is a lower market price and a larger market output.

5. Why do heating oil prices tend to be higher in the winter?

The demand for heating oil is higher in cold weather winter months. The result of this higher winter heating oil demand, for a given supply curve, is higher prices for heating oil in the winter.

6. Why are evening and weekend long-distance calls cheaper than weekday long-distance calls?

The demand for long-distance calls is greatest during weekday business hours, but far lower during other hours. Because the demand for "off-peak" long-distance calls is lower, for a given supply curve, prices during those hours are lower.

7. What would have to be true for both supply and demand to shift in the same time period?

For both supply and demand to shift in the same time period, one or more of both the supply curve shifters and the demand curve shifters would have to change in that same time period.

8. When both supply and demand shift, what added information do we need to know in order to determine in which direction the indeterminate variable changes?

When both supply and demand shift, we need to know which of the shifts is of greater magnitude, so we can know which of the opposing effects in the indeterminate variable is larger; whichever effect is larger will determine the direction of the net effect on the indeterminate variable.

9. If both buyers and sellers of grapes expect grape prices to rise in the near future, what will happen to grape prices and sales today?

If grape buyers expect grape prices to rise in the near future, it will increase their current demand to buy grapes, which would tend to increase current prices and increase the current quantity of grapes sold. If grape sellers expect grape prices to rise in the near future, it will decrease their current supply of grapes for sale, which would tend to increase current prices and decrease the current quantity of grapes sold. Because both these effects tend to increase the current price of grapes, grape prices will rise. However, the supply and demand curve shifts tend to change current sales in opposing directions, so without knowing which of these shifts was of a greater magnitude, we do not know what will happen to current grape sales. They could go up, go down, or even stay the same.

10. If demand for peanut butter increases and supply decreases, what will happen to equilibrium price and quantity?

An increase in the demand for peanut butter increases the equilibrium price and quantity of peanut butter sold. A decrease in the supply of peanut butter increases the equilibrium price and decreases the quantity of peanut butter sold. The result is an increase in peanut butter prices and an indeterminate effect on the quantity of peanut butter sold.

5.3 Price Controls

1. How is rent control an example of a price ceiling?

A price ceiling is a maximum price set below the equilibrium price by the government. Rent control is an example because the controlled rents are held below the market equilibrium rent level.

2. What predictable effects result from price ceilings such as rent control?

The predictable effects resulting from price ceilings include shortages, reduced amounts of the controlled good being made available by suppliers, reductions in the quality of the controlled good, and increased discrimination among potential buyers of the good.

3. How is the minimum wage law an example of a price floor?

A price floor is a minimum price set above the equilibrium price by the government. The minimum wage law is an example because the minimum is set above the market equilibrium wage level for some low-skill workers.

4. What predictable effects result from price floors such as the minimum wage?

The predictable effects resulting from price floors include surpluses, reduced amounts of the controlled good being purchased by demanders, increases in the quality of the controlled good, and increased discrimination among potential sellers of the good.

5. What may happen to the amount of discrimination against groups such as families with children, pet owners, smokers, or students when rent control is imposed?

Rent control laws prevent prospective renters from compensating landlords through higher rents for any characteristic landlords find less attractive, whether it is bothersome noise from children or pets, odors from smokers, increased numbers of renters per unit, risks of nonpayment by lower income tenants such as students, and so on. As a result, it lowers the cost of discriminating against anyone with what landlords consider unattractive characteristics, because other prospective renters without those characteristics are willing to pay the same controlled rent.

6. Why does rent control often lead to condominium conversions?

Rent control applies to rental apartments, but not to apartments owned by their occupants. Therefore, one way to get around rent control restrictions on apartment owners' ability to receive the market value of their apartments is to convert those apartments to condominiums by selling them to tenants instead (what was once a controlled rent becomes part of an uncontrolled mortgage payment).

7. What is the law of unintended consequences?

The law of unintended consequences is the term used to remind us that the results of actions are not always as clear as they appear, because the secondary effects of an action may cause its results to include many consequences that were not part of what was intended.

8. Why is the law of unintended consequences so important in making public policy?

It is impossible to change just one incentive to achieve a particular result through a government policy. A policy will change the incentives facing multiple individuals making multiple decisions, and changes in all those affected choices will result. Sometimes, the unintended consequences can be so substantial that they completely undermine the intended effects of a policy.

True or False:

1. If the quantity demanded does not equal the quantity supplied, a shortage will always occur.

2. At the equilibrium price, the quantity demanded equals the quantity supplied.

3. A decrease in demand results in a lower equilibrium price and a higher equilibrium quantity.

4. An increase in supply results in a lower equilibrium price and a higher equilibrium quantity.

5. An increase in supply, combined with a decrease in demand, will decrease the equilibrium price but result in an indeterminate change in the equilibrium quantity.

6. If supply increases and demand decreases, but the increase in supply is greater than the decrease in demand, the equilibrium quantity will decrease.

7. An increase in both demand and supply increases the equilibrium quantity.

8. Neither a price ceiling at the equilibrium price nor a price floor at the equilibrium price would have any effect on the market price or quantity exchanged.

9. A price ceiling decreases the quantity of a good exchanged, but a price floor increases the quantity of a good exchanged.

10. A minimum wage (price floor) is likely to be binding in the market for experienced and skilled workers.

Multiple Choice:

1. A market will experience a _____ in a situation where quantity supplied exceeds quantity demanded and a _____ in a situation where quantity demanded exceeds quantity supplied.
   a. shortage; shortage
   b. surplus; surplus
   c. shortage; surplus
   d. surplus; shortage

2. The price of a good will tend to rise when
   a. a temporary shortage at the current price occurs (assuming no price controls are imposed).
   b. a temporary surplus at the current price occurs (assuming no price controls are imposed).
   c. demand decreases.
   d. supply increases.

3. Other things equal, a decrease in consumer income would
   a. increase the price and increase the quantity of autos exchanged.
   b. increase the price and decrease the quantity of autos exchanged.
   c. decrease the price and increase the quantity of autos exchanged.
   d. decrease the price and decrease the quantity of autos exchanged.

4. An increase in the expected future price of a good by consumers would, other things equal,
   a. increase the current price and increase the current quantity exchanged.
   b. increase the current price and decrease the current quantity exchanged.
   c. decrease the current price and increase the current quantity exchanged.
   d. decrease the current price and decrease the current quantity exchanged.

5. Assume that airline travel is a normal good and intercity bus travel is an inferior good. Higher incomes would
   a. increase both the price and the quantity of airline travel.
   b. decrease both the price and quantity of airline travel.
   c. increase the price and decrease the quantity of intercity bus travel.
   d. decrease the price and increase the quantity of intercity bus travel.

6. If you observed the price of a good increasing and the quantity exchanged decreasing, it would be most likely caused by
   a. an increase in demand.
   b. a decrease in demand.
   c. an increase in supply.
   d. a decrease in supply.

7. If you observed the price of a good increasing and the quantity exchanged increasing, it would be most likely caused by
   a. an increase in demand.
   b. a decrease in demand.
   c. an increase in supply.
   d. a decrease in supply.

8. If you observed the price of a good decreasing and the quantity exchanged increasing, it would be most likely caused by
   a. an increase in demand.
   b. a decrease in demand.
   c. an increase in supply.
   d. a decrease in supply.

9. If you observed the price of a good decreasing and the quantity exchanged decreasing, it would be most likely caused by
   a. an increase in demand.
   b. a decrease in demand.
   c. an increase in supply.
   d. a decrease in supply.

10. If many cooks consider butter and margarine to be substitutes, and the price of butter rises, then in the market for margarine
    a. the equilibrium price will rise, while the change to equilibrium quantity is indeterminate.
    b. the equilibrium price will rise, and the equilibrium quantity will fall.
    c. both the equilibrium price and equilibrium quantity will rise.
    d. both the equilibrium price and equilibrium quantity will fall.
    e. the equilibrium price will fall, and the equilibrium quantity will rise.

11. If you observed that the market price of a good rose while the quantity exchanged fell, which of the following could have caused the change?
    a. an increase in supply
    b. a decrease in supply
    c. an increase in demand
    d. a decrease in demand
    e. none of the above

12. If both supply and demand decreased, but supply decreased more than demand, the result would be
    a. a higher price and a lower equilibrium quantity.
    b. a lower price and a lower equilibrium quantity.
    c. no change in the price and a lower equilibrium quantity.
    d. a higher price and a greater equilibrium quantity.
    e. a lower price and a greater equilibrium quantity.

13. If the equilibrium price of wheat is $3 per bushel and then a price floor of $2.50 per bushel is imposed by the government,
    a. there will be no effect on the wheat market.
    b. there will be a shortage of wheat.
    c. there will be a surplus of wheat.
    d. the price of wheat will decrease.

14. If both supply and demand for a good shifted the same amount to the right, then we would expect that
    a. both the price and quantity exchanged would increase.
    b. price would not change and quantity exchanged would increase.
    c. the price would increase and quantity exchanged would not change.
    d. neither the price nor the quantity exchanged would change.

15. If, in a given market, the price of inputs increases and income increases (assuming it is a normal good), then
    a. price would increase but the change in quantity exchanged would be indeterminate.
    b. price would decrease but the change in quantity exchanged would be indeterminate.
    c. quantity exchanged would increase but the change in price would be indeterminate.
    d. quantity exchanged would decrease but the change in price would be indeterminate.

16. Which of the following is true?
    a. A price ceiling reduces the quantity exchanged in the market, but a price floor increases the quantity exchanged in the market.
    b. A price ceiling increases the quantity exchanged in the market, but a price floor decreases the quantity exchanged in the market.
    c. Both price floors and price ceilings reduce the quantity exchanged in the market.
    d. Both price floors and price ceilings increase the quantity exchanged in the market.

17. If a price floor was set at the current equilibrium price, which of the following would cause a surplus as a result?
    a. an increase in demand
    b. a decrease in demand
    c. an increase in supply
    d. a decrease in supply
    e. either b or c

18. The quantity exchanged on a market tends to
    a. increase for both price floors and price ceilings.
    b. decrease for both price floors and price ceilings.
    c. increase for price floors and decrease for price ceilings.
    d. decrease for price floors and increase for price ceilings.

19. A current shortage is due to a price ceiling. If the price ceiling is removed,
    a. price would increase, quantity supplied would increase, and quantity demanded would decrease.
    b. price would increase, quantity supplied would decrease, and quantity demanded would increase.
    c. price would decrease, quantity supplied would increase, and quantity demanded would decrease.
    d. price would decrease, quantity supplied would decrease, and quantity demanded would increase.

20. A current surplus is due to a price floor. If the price floor is removed,
    a. price would increase, quantity demanded would increase, and quantity supplied would increase.
    b. price would increase, quantity demanded would decrease, and quantity supplied would decrease.
    c. price would decrease, quantity demanded would increase, and quantity supplied would decrease.
    d. price would decrease, quantity demanded would decrease, and quantity supplied would increase.

21. Which of the following will most likely occur with a 20 percent increase in the minimum wage?
    a. higher unemployment rates among experienced and skilled workers
    b. higher unemployment rates among young and low-skilled workers
    c. lower unemployment rates for young and low-skilled workers
    d. the price floor (minimum wage) will be binding in the young and low-skilled labor market but not in the experienced and skilled labor market
    e. both b and d

Problems:

1. The following table shows the hypothetical monthly demand and supply schedules for cans of macadamia nuts in Hawaii.

Price	Quantity Demanded (cans)	Quantity Supplied (cans)
$6	700	100
7	600	200
8	500	300
9	400	400
10	300	500

   a. What is the equilibrium price of macadamia nuts in Hawaii?
   b. At a price of $7 per can, is there equilibrium, a surplus, or a shortage? If it is a surplus or shortage, how large is it?
   c. At a price of $10, is there equilibrium, a surplus, or a shortage? If it is a surplus or shortage, how large is it?

2. When asked about the reason for a lifeguard shortage that threatened to keep one-third of the city's beaches closed for the summer, the Deputy Parks Commissioner of New York responded that "Kids seem to want to do work that's more in tune with a career. Maybe they prefer carpal tunnel syndrome to sunburn." What do you think is causing the shortage? What would you advise the Deputy Parks Commissioner to do in order to alleviate the shortage?

3. Using supply and demand curves, show the effect of each of the following events on the market for wheat.
   a. The midwestern United States (a major wheat-producing area) suffers a flood.
   b. The price of corn decreases (assume that many farmers can grow either corn or wheat).
   c. The Midwest has great weather.
   d. The price of fertilizer declines.
   e. More individuals start growing wheat.

4. If a price is above the equilibrium price, explain the forces that bring the market back to the equilibrium price and quantity. If a price is below the equilibrium price, explain the forces that bring the market back to the equilibrium price and quantity.

5. Beginning from an initial equilibrium, draw the effects of the changes in the following list in terms of the relevant supply and demand curves.
   a. an increase in the price of hot dogs on the hamburger market
   b. a decrease in the number of taxicab companies in New York City on cab trips
   c. effect of El Niño rain storms destroying the broccoli crop in two California counties

6. Use supply and demand curves to show:
   a. simultaneous increases in supply and demand, with a large increase in supply and a small increase in demand.
   b. simultaneous increases in supply and demand, with a small increase in supply and a large increase in demand.
   c. simultaneous decreases in supply and demand, with a large decrease in supply and a small decrease in demand.
   d. simultaneous decrease in supply and demand, with a small decrease in supply and a large decrease in demand.

7. The market for baseball tickets at your college stadium, which seats 2,000, is the following:

Price	Quantity Demanded	Quantity Supplied
$2	4,000	2,000
4	2,000	2,000
6	1,000	2,000
8	500	2,000

   a. What is the equilibrium price?
   b. What is unusual about the supply curve?
   c. At what prices would a shortage occur?
   d. At what prices would a surplus occur?
   e. Suppose that the addition of new students (all big baseball fans) next year will add 1,000 to the quantity demanded at each price. What will this increase do to next year's demand curve? What is the new equilibrium price?

8. What would be the impact of a rental price ceiling set above the equilibrium rental price for apartments? Below the equilibrium rental price?

9. What would be the impact of a price floor set above the equilibrium price for dairy products? Below the equilibrium price?

10. Giving in to pressure from voters who charge that local theater owners are gouging their customers with ticket prices as high as $10 per movie, the city council of a Midwestern city imposes a price ceiling of $2 on all movies. What effect is this likely to have on the market for movies in this particular city? What will happen to the quantity of tickets demanded? What will happen to the quantity supplied? Who gains? Who loses?

11. Why do price floors and price ceilings both reduce the quantity of goods traded in those markets?

12. Why do 10 A.M. classes fill up before 8 A.M. classes during class registration? Use supply and demand curves to help explain your answer.

13. What would happen to the equilibrium price and quantity exchanged in the following cases?
    a. an increase in income and a decreasing price of a complement, for a normal good
    b. a technological advance and lower input prices
    c. an increase in the price of a substitute and an increase in income, for an inferior good
    d. producers' expectations that prices will soon fall, and increasingly costly government regulations

14. Assume the following information for the demand and supply curves for good Z.

Demand		Supply	
Price	Quantity Demanded	Price	Quantity Supplied
$10	10	$1	10
9	20	2	15
8	30	3	20
7	40	4	25
6	50	5	30
5	60	6	35
4	70	7	40
3	80	8	45
2	90	9	50
1	100	10	55

    a. Draw the corresponding supply and demand curves.
    b. What are the equilibrium price and quantity traded?
    c. Would a price of $9 result in a shortage or a surplus? How large?
    d. Would a price of $3 result in a shortage or a surplus? How large?
    e. If the demand for Z increased by 15 units at every price, what would the new equilibrium price and quantity traded be?
    f. Given the original demand for Z, if the supply of Z were increased by 15 units at every price, what would the new equilibrium price and quantity traded be?

15. Refer to the following supply and demand curve diagram.

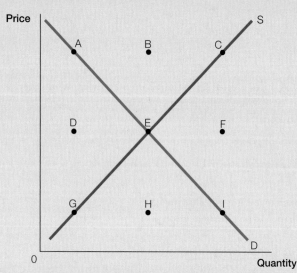

a. Starting from an initial equilibrium at E, what shift or shifts in supply and/or demand could move the equilibrium price and quantity to each of points A through I?
b. Starting from an initial equilibrium at E, what would happen if both a decrease in the price of a substitute in production and an increase in income occurred, if it is a normal good?
c. Starting from an initial equilibrium at E, what would happen if both an increase in the price of an input and an advance in technology occurred?
d. If a price floor is imposed above the equilibrium price, which of A through I would tend to be the quantity supplied, and which would tend to be the quantity demanded? Which would be the new quantity exchanged?
e. If a price ceiling is imposed below the equilibrium price, which of A through I would tend to be the quantity supplied, and which would tend to be the quantity demanded? Which would be the new quantity exchanged?

Elasticities

If a rock group increases the price it charges for concert tickets, what impact would that have on ticket sales? More precisely, would ticket sales fall a little or a lot?

Will the group make more money by lowering the price or by raising the price? This chapter will allow you to answer these types of questions and more.

Some of the results in this chapter may surprise you. A huge flood in the Midwest that destroyed much of this year's wheat crop would leave some wheat farmers better off. Ideal weather that led to a bountiful crop of wheat everywhere might leave most wheat farmers worse off. As you will soon find out, these issues hinge importantly on the tools of elasticity.

In this chapter, we will also see the importance of elasticity in determining the effects of taxes. If a tax is levied on the seller, will the seller pay all of the taxes? If the tax were levied on the buyer—who pays the larger share of taxes? We will see that elasticity is critical in the determination of tax burden. Elasticities will also help us to more fully understand many policy issues—from illegal drugs to luxury taxes. If Congress were to impose a large tax on yachts, what do you think would happen to yacht sales? What would happen to employment in the boat industry? ∎

Price Elasticity of Demand

* What is price elasticity of demand?
* How do we measure consumers' responses to price changes?
* What determines the price elasticity of demand?

In learning and applying the law of demand, we have established the basic fact that quantity demanded changes inversely with change in price, *ceteris paribus*. But how much does quantity demanded change? The extent to which a change in price affects quantity demanded may vary considerably from product to product and over the various price ranges for the same product. The **price elasticity of demand** measures the responsiveness of quantity demanded to a change in price. Specifically, price elasticity is defined as the percentage change in quantity demanded divided by the percentage change in price, or

$$\text{Price elasticity of demand}(E_D) = \frac{\text{Percentage change in quantity demanded}}{\text{Percentage change in price}}$$

Note that, following the law of demand, price and quantity demanded show an inverse relationship. For this reason, the price elasticity of demand is, in theory, always negative. But in practice and for simplicity, this quantity is always expressed in absolute value terms—that is, as a positive number.

Is the Demand Curve Elastic or Inelastic?

It is important to understand the basic intuition behind elasticities, which requires a focus on the percentage changes in quantity demanded and price.

Think of elasticity as an elastic rubber band. If the quantity demanded is responsive to even a small change in price, we call it elastic. On the other hand, if even a huge change in price results in only a small change in quantity demanded, then the demand is said to be inelastic. For example, if a 10 percent increase in the price leads to a 50 percent reduction in the quantity demanded, we say that demand is elastic because the quantity demanded is sensitive to the price change.

$$E_D = \frac{\%\Delta Q_D}{\%\Delta P} = \frac{50\%}{10\%} = 5$$

Demand is elastic in this case because a 10 percent change in price led to a larger (50 percent) change in quantity demanded.

Alternatively, if a 10 percent increase in the price leads to a 1 percent reduction in quantity demanded, we say that demand is *inelastic* because the quantity demanded did not respond much to the price reduction.

$$E_D = \frac{\%\Delta Q_D}{\%\Delta P} = \frac{1\%}{10\%} = 0.10$$

Demand is inelastic in this case because a 10 percent change in price led to a smaller (1 percent) change in quantity demanded.

Types of Demand Curves

Economists refer to a variety of demand curves based on the magnitude of their elasticity. A demand curve, or a portion of a demand curve, can be elastic, inelastic, or unit elastic.

Demand is **elastic** when the elasticity is greater than 1 ($E_D > 1$)—the quantity demanded changes proportionally more than the price changes. In this case, a given percentage increase in price, say 10 percent, leads to a larger percentage change in quantity demanded, say 20 percent, as seen in Exhibit 1(a). If the curve is *perfectly elastic,* the demand curve is horizontal. The elasticity coefficient is infinity because even the slightest change in price will lead to a huge change in quantity demanded—for example, a tiny increase in price will cause the quantity demanded to fall to zero. In Exhibit 1(b), a *perfectly elastic* demand curve (horizontal) is illustrated.

Demand is **inelastic** when the elasticity is less than 1; the quantity demanded changes proportionally less than the price changes. In this case, a given percentage (for example, 10 percent) change in price is accompanied by a smaller (for example, 5 percent) reduction in quantity demanded, as seen in Exhibit 2(a). If

price elasticity of demand
the measure of the responsiveness of quantity demanded to a change in price

elastic
when the quantity demanded is greater than the percentage change in price ($E_D > 1$)

inelastic
when the quantity demanded is less than the percentage change in price ($E_D < 1$)

---

section 6.1
exhibit 1   Elastic Demand

a. Elastic Demand ($E_D > 1$)

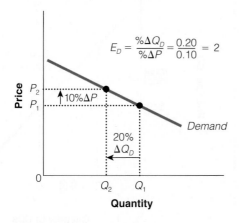

$$E_D = \frac{\%\Delta Q_D}{\%\Delta P} = \frac{0.20}{0.10} = 2$$

A small percentage change in price leads to a larger percentage change in quantity demanded.

b. Perfectly Elastic Demand ($E_D = \infty$)

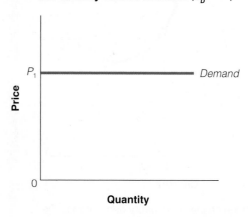

A small percentage change in price will change quantity demanded by an infinite amount.

---

section 6.1
exhibit 2   Inelastic Demand

a. Inelastic Demand ($E_D < 1$)

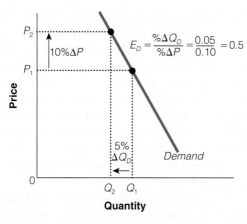

$$E_D = \frac{\%\Delta Q_D}{\%\Delta P} = \frac{0.05}{0.10} = 0.5$$

A change in price leads to a smaller percentage change in quantity demanded.

b. Perfectly Inelastic Demand ($E_D = 0$)

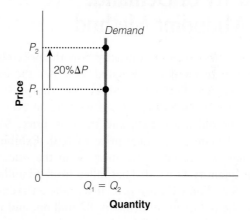

The quantity demanded does not change regardless of the percentage change in price.

---

the demand curve is *perfectly inelastic,* the quantity demanded is the same regardless of the price. The elasticity coefficient is zero because the quantity demanded does not respond to a change in price. This relationship is illustrated in Exhibit 2(b).

Goods for which E_D equals one ($E_D = 1$) are said to have **unit elastic demand.** In this case, the quantity demanded changes proportionately to price

changes. For example, a 10 percent increase in price will lead to a 10 percent reduction in quantity demanded. This relationship is illustrated in Exhibit 3.

The price elasticity of demand is closely related to the slope of the demand curve. Generally speaking, the flatter the demand curve passing through a given point, the more elastic the demand. The steeper the demand curve passing through a given point, the less elastic the demand.

unit elastic demand
demand with a price elasticity of 1; the percentage change in quantity demanded is equal to the percentage change in price

section 6.1
exhibit 3 Unit Elastic Demand

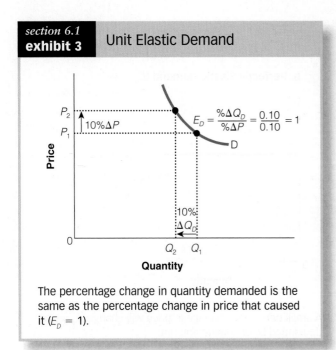

The percentage change in quantity demanded is the same as the percentage change in price that caused it ($E_D = 1$).

section 6.1
exhibit 4   Calculating the Price Elasticity of Demand

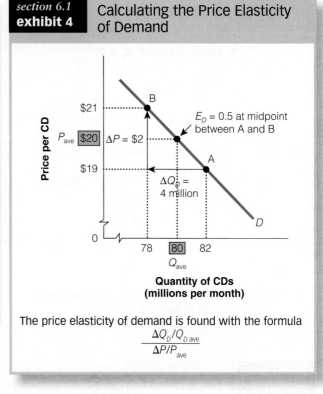

The price elasticity of demand is found with the formula

$$\frac{\Delta Q_D / Q_{D\,ave}}{\Delta P / P_{ave}}$$

Calculating the Price Elasticity of Demand: The Midpoint Method

To get a clear picture of exactly how the price elasticity of demand is calculated, consider the case for the compact disc (CD) market. Say the price of CDs increases from $19 to $21. If we take an average between the old price, $19, and the new price, $21, we can calculate an average price of $20. Exhibit 4 shows that as a result of the increase in the price of CDs, the quantity demanded has fallen from 82 million CDs to 78 million CDs per year. If we take an average between the old quantity demand, 82 million, and the new quantity demanded, 78 million, we have an average quantity demanded of 80 million CDs per year. That is, the $2 increase in the price of CDs has led to a 4-million-CD reduction in quantity demanded. How can we figure out the price elasticity of demand?

You might ask why we are using the average price and average quantity. The answer is that if we did not use the average amounts, we would come up with different values for the elasticity of demand depending on whether we moved up or down the demand curve. When the change in price and quantity are of significant magnitude, the exact meaning of the term *percentage change* requires clarification, and the terms *price* and *quantity* must be defined more precisely. The issue thus is, should the percentage change be figured on the basis of price and quantity before or after the change has occurred? For example, a price rise from $10 to $15 constitutes a 50 percent change if the original price ($10) is used in figuring the percentage ($5/$10), or a 33 percent change if the price after the change ($15) is used ($5/$15). For small changes, the distinction is not important, but for large changes, it is. To avoid this confusion, economists often use this average technique. Specifically, we are actually calculating the elasticity at a midpoint between the old and new prices and quantities.

Now to figure out the price elasticity of demand, we must first calculate the percentage change in price. To find the percentage change in price, we take the change in price (ΔP) and divide it by the average price (P_{ave}). (Note: The Greek letter delta, Δ, means "change in.")

Percentage change in price $= \Delta P / P_{ave}$

In our CD example, the original price was $19, and the new price is $21. The change in price (ΔP) is $2, and the average price (P_{ave}) is $20. The percentage change in price can then be calculated as

Percentage change in price $= \$2/\$20$
$= 1/10 = 0.10 = 10 \text{ percent}$

Next, we must calculate the percentage change in quantity demanded. To find the percentage change in quantity demanded, we take the change in quantity demanded (ΔQ_D) and divide it by the average quantity demanded ($Q_{D\,ave}$).

Percentage change in quantity demanded
$$= \Delta Q_D / Q_{D\,ave}$$

In our CD example, the original quantity demanded was 82 million, and the new quantity demanded is 78 million. The change in quantity demanded (ΔQ_D) is 4 million, and the average quantity demanded ($Q_{D\,ave}$) is 80 million. The percentage change in quantity demanded can then be calculated as

Percentage change in quantity demanded = 4 million/80 million = 1/20 = 0.05 = 5 percent

Because the price elasticity of demand is equal to the percentage change in quantity demanded divided by the percentage change in price, the price elasticity of demand for CDs between point A and point B can be shown as

$$E_D = \frac{\text{Percentage change in quantity demanded}}{\text{Percentage change in price}}$$
$$= \frac{\Delta Q_D / Q_{D\,ave}}{\Delta P / P_{ave}} = \frac{4 \text{ million}/80 \text{ million}}{\$2/\$20}$$
$$= \frac{1/20}{1/10} = \frac{5\%}{10\%} = 0.5$$

If bus fares increase, will ridership fall a little or a lot? It all depends on the price elasticity of demand. If the price elasticity of demand is elastic, a 50-cent price increase will lead to a relatively large reduction in bus travel as riders find viable substitutes. If the price elasticity of demand is inelastic, a 50-cent price increase will lead to a relatively small reduction in bus ridership as riders are not able to find good alternatives to bus transportation.

KEITH BROFSKY/PHOTODISC/GETTY IMAGES

The Determinants of the Price Elasticity of Demand

As you have learned, the elasticity of demand for a specific good refers to movements along its demand curve as its price changes. A lower price will increase quantity demanded, and a higher price will reduce quantity demanded. But what factors will influence the magnitude of the change in quantity demanded in response to a price change? That is, what will make the demand curve relatively more elastic (where Q_D is responsive to price changes), and what will make the demand curve relatively less elastic (where Q_D is less responsive to price changes)?

For the most part, the price elasticity of demand depends on three factors: (1) the availability of close substitutes, (2) the proportion of income spent on the good, and (3) the amount of time that has elapsed since the price change.

Availability of Close Substitutes

Goods *with* close substitutes tend to have more elastic demands. Why? Because if the price of such a good increases, consumers can easily switch to other now relatively lower priced substitutes. In many examples, such as one brand of root beer as opposed to another, or different brands of gasoline, the ease of substitution will make demand quite elastic for most individuals.

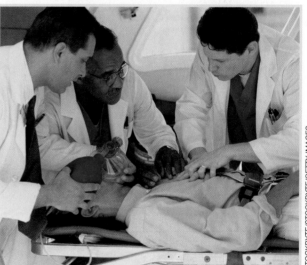

Unlike most tangible items (such as specific types of food or cars), there are few substitutes for a physician and medical care when you have an emergency. Because the number of available substitutes is limited, the demand for emergency medical care is relatively inelastic.

STOCKBYTE/STOCKBYTE/GETTY IMAGES

Goods *without* close substitutes, such as insulin for diabetics, cigarettes for chain smokers, heroin for addicts, or emergency medical care for those with appendicitis or broken legs, tend to have inelastic demands. The demand for an antivenom shot after a rattle snake bite is another example. Once bitten, that demand curve becomes extremely inelastic.

The degree of substitutability can also depend on whether the good is a necessity or a luxury. Goods that are necessities, such as food, have no ready substitutes and thus tend to have lower elasticities than do luxury items, such as jewelry.

When the good is broadly defined, it tends to be less elastic than when it is narrowly defined. For example, the elasticity of demand for food, a broad category, tends to be inelastic because few substitutes are available for food. But for a certain type of food, such as pizza, a narrowly defined good, it is much easier to find a substitute—perhaps tacos, burgers, salads, burritos, or chili fries. That is, the demand for a particular type of food is more elastic because more and better substitutes are available than for food as an entire category.

Proportion of Income Spent on the Good

The smaller the proportion of income spent on a good, the lower its elasticity of demand. If the amount spent on a good relative to income is small, then the impact of a change in its price on one's budget will also be small. As a result, consumers will respond less to price changes for small-ticket items than for similar percentage changes in large-ticket items, where a price change could potentially have a large impact on the consumer's budget. For example, a 50 percent increase in the price of salt will have a much smaller impact on consumers' behavior than a similar percentage increase in the price of a new automobile. Similarly, a 50 percent increase in the cost of private university tuition will have a greater impact on students' (and sometimes parents') budgets than a 50 percent increase in textbook prices.

Time

For many goods, the more time that people have to adapt to a new price change, the greater the elasticity of demand. Immediately after a price change, consumers may be unable to locate good alternatives or easily change their consumption patterns. But as time passes, consumers have more time to find or develop suitable substitutes and to plan and implement changes in their patterns of consumption. For example, drivers may not respond immediately to an increase in gas prices, perhaps believing it to be temporary. However, if the price persists over a longer period, we would expect people to drive less, buy more fuel-efficient cars, move closer to work, carpool, take the bus, or even bike to work. So for many goods, especially nondurable goods

Some studies show that a 10 percent increase in the price of cigarettes will lead to a 7 percent reduction in the quantity demanded of youth smoking. In this price range, however, demand is still inelastic at −0.7. Of course, proponents of higher taxes to discourage underage smoking would like to see a more elastic demand, where a 10 percent increase in the price of cigarettes would lead to a reduction in quantity demanded of more than 10 percent.

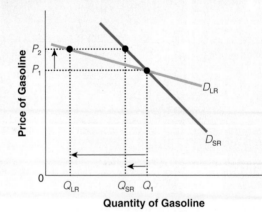

section 6.1
exhibit 5   Short-Run and Long-Run Demand Curves

For many goods, such as gasoline, price is much more elastic in the long run than in the short run because buyers have more time to find suitable substitutes or change their consumption patterns. In the short run, the increase in price from P_1 to P_2 has only a small effect on the quantity demanded for gasoline. In the long run, the effect of the price increase will be much larger.

(goods that do not last a long time), the short-run demand curve is generally less elastic than the long-run demand curve, as illustrated in Exhibit 5.

Estimated Price Elasticities of Demand

Because of shifts in supply and demand curves, researchers have a difficult task when trying to estimate empirically the price elasticity of demand for a particular good or service. Despite this difficulty, Exhibit 6 presents some estimates for the price elasticity of demand for certain goods. As you would expect, certain goods like medical care, air travel and gasoline are all relatively price inelastic in the short run because buyers have fewer substitutes. On the other hand, air travel in the long run is much more sensitive to price (elastic) because the available substitutes are much more plentiful. Exhibit 6 shows that the price elasticity of demand for air travel is 2.4, which means that a 1 percent increase in price will lead to a 2.4 percent reduction in quantity demanded. Notice, in each case where the data are available, the estimates of the long-run price elasticities of demand are greater than the short-run price elasticities of demand. In short, the price elasticity of demand is greater when the price change persists over a longer time periods.

section 6.1
exhibit 6   Price Elasticities of Demand for Selected Goods

Good	Short Run	Long Run
Salt	—	0.1
Air travel	0.1	2.4
Gasoline	0.2	0.7
Medical care and hospitalization	0.3	0.9
Jewelry and watches	0.4	0.7
Physician services	0.6	—
Alcohol	0.9	3.6
Movies	0.9	3.7
China, glassware	1.5	2.6
Automobiles	1.9	2.2
Chevrolets	—	4.0

SOURCES: Adapted from Robert Archibald and Robert Gillingham, "An Analysis of the Short-Run Consumer Demand for Gasoline Using Household Survey Data," *Review of Economics and Statistics* 62 (November 1980): 622–628; Hendrik S. Houthakker and Lester D. Taylor, Consumer Demand in the United States: Analyses and Projections (Cambridge, Mass.: Harvard University Press, 1970), pp. 56–149; Richard Voith, "The Long-Run Elasticity of Demand for Commuter Rail Transportation," *Journal of Urban Economics* 30 (November 1991): 360–372.

SECTION CHECK

1. Price elasticity of demand measures the percentage change in quantity demanded divided by the percentage change in price that caused it, moving along a demand curve.
2. The elasticity of demand is calculated using the midpoint formula $= \dfrac{\Delta Q_D/Q_{D\,ave}}{\Delta P/P_{ave}}$.
3. If the demand for a good is price elastic in the relevant range, quantity demanded is very responsive D *ave* to a price change. If the demand for a good is relatively price inelastic, quantity demanded is not very responsive to a price change.
4. The price elasticity of demand depends on: (1) the availability of close substitutes, (2) the proportion of income spent on the good, and (3) the amount of time that buyers have to respond to a price change.

1. What question is the price elasticity of demand designed to answer?
2. How is the price elasticity of demand calculated?
3. What is the difference between a relatively price elastic demand curve and a relatively price inelastic demand curve?
4. What is the relationship between the price elasticity of demand and the slope at a given point on a demand curve?
5. What factors tend to make demand curves more price elastic?
6. Why would a tax on a particular brand of cigarettes be less effective at reducing smoking than a tax on all brands of cigarettes?
7. Why is the price elasticity of demand for products at a 24-hour convenience store likely to be lower at 2 A.M. than at 2 P.M.?
8. Why is the price elasticity of demand for turkeys likely to be lower, but the price elasticity of demand for turkeys at a particular store likely to be greater, at Thanksgiving than at other times of the year?

Total Revenue and the Price Elasticity of Demand

* What is total revenue?
* What is the relationship between total revenue and the price elasticity of demand?
* Does the price elasticity of demand vary along a linear demand curve?

How Does the Price Elasticity of Demand Impact Total Revenue?

The price elasticity of demand for a good also has implications for total revenue. Total revenue (TR) is the amount sellers receive for a good or service. Total revenue is simply the price of the good (P) times the quantity of the good sold (Q): $TR = P \times Q$. The elasticity of demand will help to predict how changes in the price will impact total revenue earned by the producer for selling the good. Let's see how this works.

In Exhibit 1, we see that when the demand is price elastic ($E_D > 1$), total revenues will rise as the price declines, because the percentage increase in the quantity demanded is greater than the percentage reduction in price. For example, if the price of a good is cut in half (say from $10 to $5) and the quantity demanded more than doubles (say from 40 to 100), total revenue will rise from $400 ($10 × 40 = $400) to $500 ($5 × 100 = $500). Equivalently, if the price rises from $5 to $10 and the quantity demanded falls from 100 to 40 units, then total revenue will fall from $500 to $400. As this example illustrates, if the demand curve is relatively elastic, total revenue will vary inversely with a price change.

You can see from the following what happens to total revenue when demand is price elastic. (*Note:* The size of the price and quantity arrows represents the size of the percentage changes.)

When Demand Is Price Elastic

$$\downarrow TR = \uparrow P \times \downarrow Q$$

or

$$\uparrow TR = \downarrow P \times \uparrow Q$$

On the other hand, if demand for a good is relatively inelastic ($E_D < 1$), the total revenue will be lower at lower prices than at higher prices because a given

total revenue (TR)
the amount sellers receive for a good or service, calculated as the product price times the quantity sold

price reduction will be accompanied by a proportionately smaller increase in quantity demanded. For example, as shown in Exhibit 2, if the price of a good is cut (say from $10 to $5) and the quantity demanded less than doubles (say it increases from 30 to 40), then total revenue will fall from $300 ($10 × 30 = $300) to $200 ($5 × 40 = $200). Equivalently, if the price increases from $5 to $10 and the quantity demanded falls from 40 to 30, total revenue will increase from $200 to $300. To summarize, then: If the demand curve is inelastic, total revenue will vary directly with a price change.

When Demand Is Price Inelastic

$$\downarrow TR = \uparrow P \times \downarrow Q$$

or

$$\uparrow TR = \downarrow P \times \uparrow Q$$

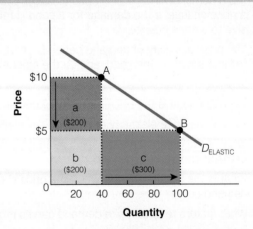

section 6.2
exhibit 1
Elastic Demand and Total Revenue

At point A, total revenue is $400 ($10 × 40 × $400), or area a + b. If the price falls to $5 at point B, the total revenue is $500 ($5 × 100 = $500), or area b + c. Total revenue increased by $100. We can also see in the graph that total revenue increased, because the area b + c is greater than area a + b, or c > a.

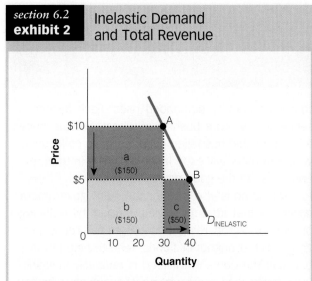

section 6.2
exhibit 2
Inelastic Demand and Total Revenue

At point A, total revenue is $300 ($10 × 30 = $300), or area a + b. If the price falls to $5 at point B, the total revenue is $200 ($5 × 40 = $200), or area b + c. Total revenue falls by $100. We can also see in the graph that total revenue decreases, because area a + b is greater than area b + c, or a > c.

In this case, the "net" effect on total revenue is reversed but easy to see. (Again, the size of the price and quantity arrows represents the size of the percentage changes.)

Price Elasticity Changes Along a Linear Demand Curve

As already shown (Section 6.1, Exhibit 1), the slopes of demand curves can be used to estimate their *relative* elasticities of demand: The steeper one demand curve is relative to another, the more inelastic it is relative to the other. However, except for the extreme cases of perfectly elastic and perfectly inelastic curves, great care must be taken when trying to estimate the degree of elasticity of one demand curve from its slope. In fact, as we will soon see, a straight-line demand curve with a constant slope will change elasticity continuously as you move up or down it. It is because the slope is the ratio of changes in the two variables (price and quantity) while the elasticity is the ratio of percentage changes in the two variables.

We can easily demonstrate that the elasticity of demand varies along a linear demand curve by using what we already know about the interrelationship between price and total revenue. Exhibit 4 shows a linear (constant slope) demand curve. In Exhibit 4(a), we see that when the price falls on the upper half of the demand curve from P_1 to P_2, and quantity demanded increases from Q_1 to Q_2, total revenue increases. That is, the new area of total revenue (area b + c) is larger than the old area of total revenue (area a + b). It is

Use what you've LEARNED — ELASTICITIES AND TOTAL REVENUE

Q Is a poor wheat harvest bad for all farmers and is a great wheat harvest good for all farmers? (Hint: Assume that demand for wheat is inelastic—the demand for food is generally inelastic.)

A Without a simultaneous reduction in demand, a reduction in supply from a poor harvest results in higher prices. With that, if demand for the wheat is inelastic over the pertinent portion of the demand curve, the price increase will cause farmers' total revenues to rise. As shown in Exhibit 3(a), if demand for the crop is inelastic, an increase in price will cause farmers to lose the revenue indicated by area c. They will, however, experience an increase in revenue equal to area a, resulting in an overall increase

in total revenue equal to area a−c. Clearly, if some farmers lose their entire crop because of, say, bad weather, they will be worse off; but collectively,

(continued)

Use what you've LEARNED   ELASTICITIES AND TOTAL REVENUE (cont.)

farmers can profit from events that reduce crop size—and they do, because the demand for most agricultural products is inelastic. Interestingly, if all farmers were hurt equally, say losing one-third of their crop, each farmer would be better off. Of course, consumers would be worse off, because the price of agricultural products would be higher. Alternatively, what if phenomenal weather led to record wheat harvests or a technological advance led to more productive wheat farmers? Either event would increase the supply from S_1 to S_2 in Exhibit 3(b). The increase in supply leads to a decrease in price, from P_1 to P_2. Because the demand for wheat is inelastic, the quantity sold of wheat rises less than proportionately to the fall in the price. That is, in percentage terms, the price falls more

than the quantity demanded rises. Each farmer is selling a few more bushels of wheat, but the price of each bushel has fallen even more, so collectively wheat farmers will experience a decline in total revenue despite the good news.

The same is also true for the many government programs that attempt to help farmers by reducing production—crop restriction programs. These programs, like droughts or floods, tend to help farmers because the demand for food is relatively inelastic. But it hurts consumers who now have to pay a higher price for less food. Farm technology may be good for consumers because it shifts the supply curve to the right and lowers prices. However it may be bad for some small farmers because it could put them out of business. See Exhibit 3(b).

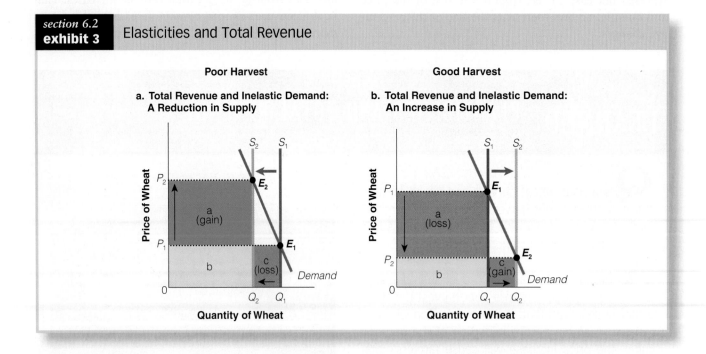

Poor Harvest

**a. Total Revenue and Inelastic Demand:
A Reduction in Supply**

Good Harvest

**b. Total Revenue and Inelastic Demand:
An Increase in Supply**

also true that if price increased in this region (from P_2 to P_1), total revenue would fall, because b + c is greater than a + b. In this region of the demand curve, then, there is a negative relationship between price and

total revenue. As we discussed earlier, this is characteristic of an elastic demand curve ($E_D > 1$).

Exhibit 4(b) illustrates what happens to total revenue on the lower half of the same demand curve. When

Price Elasticity Along a Linear Demand Curve

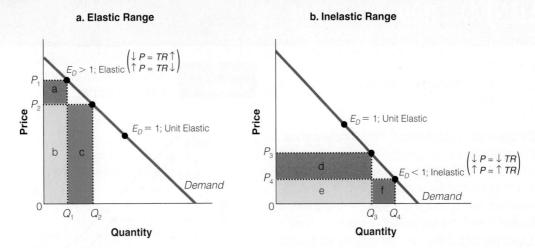

a. Elastic Range

$E_D > 1$; Elastic $\left(\begin{array}{l}\downarrow P = TR \uparrow \\ \uparrow P = TR \downarrow\end{array}\right)$

P_1

a

P_2

$E_D = 1$; Unit Elastic

b   c

Demand

Price

0   Q_1 Q_2

Quantity

b. Inelastic Range

$E_D = 1$; Unit Elastic

P_3

d

P_4

$E_D < 1$; Inelastic $\left(\begin{array}{l}\downarrow P = \downarrow TR \\ \uparrow P = \uparrow TR\end{array}\right)$

e   f

Demand

Price

0   Q_3 Q_4

Quantity

The slope is constant along a linear demand curve, but the elasticity varies. Moving down along the demand curve, the elasticity is elastic at higher prices and inelastic at lower prices. It is unit elastic between the inelastic and elastic ranges.

the price falls from P_3 to P_4 and the quantity demanded increases from Q_3 to Q_4, total revenue actually decreases, because the new area of total revenue (area e + f) is less than the old area of total revenue (area d + e). Likewise, it is clear that an increase in price from P_4 to P_3 would increase total revenue. In this case, there is a positive relationship between price and total revenue, which, as we discussed, is characteristic of an inelastic demand curve ($E_D < 1$). Together, parts (a) and (b) of Exhibit 4 illustrate that, although the slope remains constant, the elasticity of a linear demand curve changes along the length of the curve—from relatively elastic at higher price ranges to relatively inelastic at lower price ranges.

SECTION CHECK

1. Total revenue is the price of the good times the quantity sold ($TR = P \times Q$).
2. If demand is price elastic ($E_D > 1$), total revenue will vary inversely with a change in price.
3. If demand is price inelastic ($E_D < 1$), total revenue will vary in the same direction as a change in price.
4. A linear demand curve is more price elastic at higher price ranges and more price inelastic at lower price ranges, and it is unit elastic at the midpoint: $E_D = 1$.

1. Why does total revenue vary inversely with price if demand is relatively price elastic?
2. Why does total revenue vary directly with price if demand is relatively price inelastic?
3. Why is a linear demand curve more price elastic at higher price ranges and more price inelastic at lower price ranges?
4. If demand for some good was perfectly price inelastic, how would total revenue from its sales change as its price changed?
5. Assume that both you and Art, your partner in a picture-framing business, want to increase your firm's total revenue. You argue that in order to achieve this goal, you should lower your prices; Art, on the other hand, thinks that you should raise your prices. What assumptions are each of you making about your firm's price elasticity of demand?

Use what you've LEARNED
ELASTICITY VARIES ALONG A LINEAR DEMAND CURVE

Q Why do economists emphasize elasticity at the current price?

A Because for most demand (and supply) curves, the price elasticity varies along the curve. Thus, for most goods we usually refer to a particular point or a section of the demand (or supply) curves. In Exhibit 5, we see that the upper half of the straight-line demand curve is elastic and the lower half is inelastic. Notice on the lower half of the demand curve, a higher (lower) price increases (decreases) total revenue—that is, in this lower region, demand is inelastic. However, on the top half of the demand curve, a lower (higher) price increases (decreases) total revenue—that is, in this region demand is elastic.

For example, when the price increases from $2 to $3, the total revenue increases from $32 to $42—an increase in price increases total revenue, so demand is inelastic in this portion of the demand curve. But when the price increases from $8 to $9, the total revenue falls from $32 to $18—an increase in price lowers total revenue, so demand is elastic in this portion of the demand curve.

Specifically, when the price is high and the quantity demanded is low, this portion of the demand curve is elastic. Why? It is because a $1 reduction in price is a smaller percentage change when the price is high than when it is low. Similarly, an increase in 2 units of output is a larger percentage change when quantity demanded is lower. So we have a relatively small change in price leading to a proportionately greater change in quantity demanded—that is, demand is elastic on this portion of the demand curve. Of course, the opposite is true when the price is low and the quantity demanded is high. Why? It is because a $1 change in price is a larger percentage

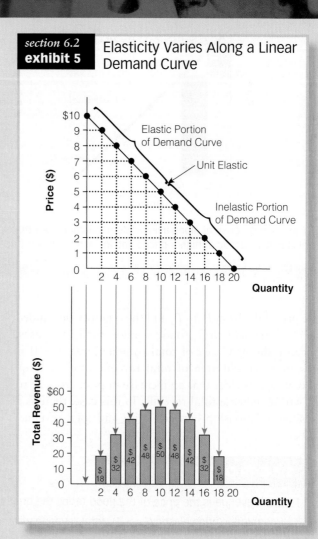

section 6.2 **exhibit 5** Elasticity Varies Along a Linear Demand Curve

change when the price is low and an increase in 2 units of output is a smaller percentage change when the quantity demanded is larger. That is, a relatively larger percentage change in price will lead to a relatively smaller change in quantity demanded—demand is relatively inelastic on this portion of the demand curve.

Other Types of Demand Elasticities

* What is the cross-price elasticity of demand?
* What is the income elasticity of demand?

The Cross-Price Elasticity of Demand

The price of a good is not the only factor that affects the quantity consumers will purchase. Sometimes the quantity of one good demanded is affected by the price of a related good. For example, if the price of potato chips falls, what is the impact, if any, on the demand for soda (a complement)? Or if the price of soda increases, to what degree will the demand for iced tea (a substitute) be affected? The cross-price elasticity of demand measures both the direction and magnitude of the impact that a price change for one good will have on the demand for another good. Specifically, the **cross-price elasticity of demand** is defined as the percentage change in the demand of one good (good A) divided by the percentage change in price of another good (good B), or

> **cross-price elasticity of demand**
> the measure of the impact that a price change of one good will have on the demand of another good.

$$\text{Cross-price elasticity demand} = \frac{\text{\% change in the demand for Good A}}{\text{\% change in the price for Good B}}$$

The cross-price elasticity of demand indicates not only the degree of the connection between the two variables but also whether the goods in question are substitutes or complements for one another.

Calculating the Cross-Price Elasticity of Demand

Let's calculate the cross-price elasticity of demand between soda and iced tea, where a 10 percent increase in the price of soda results in a 20 percent increase in the demand for iced tea. In this case, the cross-price elasticity of demand would be +2 (+20 percent ÷ +10 percent = +2).

Consumers responded to the soda price increase by buying less soda (moving along the demand curve for soda) and increasing the demand for iced tea (shifting the demand curve for iced tea). In general, if the cross-price elasticity is positive, we can conclude that the two goods are substitutes because the price of one good and the demand for the other move in the same direction.

As another example, let's calculate the cross-price elasticity of demand between potato chips and soda, where a 10 percent decrease in the price of potato chips results in a 30 percent increase in the demand for soda. In this case, the cross-price elasticity of demand is −3 (+30 percent ÷ −10 percent = −3). The demand for chips increases as a result of the price decrease, as consumers then purchase additional soda to wash down those extra bags of salty chips. Potato chips and soda, then, are complements. In general, if the cross-price elasticity is negative, we can conclude that the two goods are complements because the price of one good and the demand for the other move in opposite directions.

Cross-Price Elasticity and Sodas

According to economist Jean-Pierre Dube, Coca-Cola is a good substitute for Pepsi—the cross-price elasticity is a 0.34. In other words, a 10 percent increase in the price of a Pepsi 12 pack will lead to an increase in the sales of Coca-Cola 12 packs by 3.4 percent. But six packs of Coca-Cola and Diet Coke are even a better substitute with a cross-price elasticity of 1.15; a 10 percent increase in the price of a six pack of Diet Coke will lead to a 15 percent increase in the sales of six packs of Coca-Cola. And a 10 percent increase in the price of a 12 pack of Mountain Dew will lead to a 7.7 percent increase in the sales of 12 packs of Pepsi.

The Income Elasticity of Demand

Sometimes it is useful to measure how responsive demand is to a change in income. The income elasticity of demand is a measure of the relationship between a relative change in income and the consequent relative change in demand, *ceteris paribus*. The income elasticity of demand coefficient not only expresses the degree of the connection between the two variables, but it also indicates whether the *good in* question is normal or inferior. Specifically, the **income elasticity of demand** is defined as the percentage change in the demand divided by the percentage change in income, or

Income elasticity of demand

$$= \frac{\% \, \Delta \text{ in demand}}{\% \, \Delta \text{ in income}}$$

Calculating the Income Elasticity of Demand

Let's calculate the income elasticity of demand for lobster, where a 10 percent increase in income

income elasticity of demand
the percentage change in demand divided by the percentage change in consumer's income

results in a 15 percent increase in the demand for lobster. In this case, the income elasticity of demand is +1.5 (+15 percent ÷ +10 percent = +1.5). Lobster, then, is a normal good because an increase in income results in an increase in demand. In general, if the income elasticity is positive, then the good in question is a normal good because income and demand move in the same direction.

global WATCH — ENDANGERED SPECIES GET A LIFT FROM VIAGRA

—BY KATE MELVILLE

Much to the dismay of Western conservationists, traditional Chinese medicine has often relied on a bizarre mix of animal parts to cure ailments ranging from gout to erectile dysfunction. But that may be changing, and the beneficiaries are a wide range of animal species that have traditionally been sought for their virility-enhancing properties. A study, in the journal *Environmental Conservation*, suggests that Chinese men are switching from traditional Chinese medicine remedies to the drug Viagra to treat erectile dysfunction.

The researchers, from the University of New South Wales (UNSW) and the University of Alaska, say they predicted the trend at the advent of Viagra's release in 1998, but at the time were pooh-poohed by conservationists. "When we proposed that Viagra might make inroads into traditional Chinese medicine treatments for impotence, conservationists told us we were naïve and that consumers were unwilling to use a product outside their own medical tradition," said UNSW researcher Bill von Hippel.

The study was based on data from men attending a large traditional Chinese medicine clinic in Hong Kong. They were questioned about their use of traditional and Western treatments of arthritis, indigestion, gout, and impotence. The findings were unambiguous, said von Hippel. "First, significantly more men had formerly used a traditional Chinese medicine treatment for impotence than were current users. Second, they were significantly more likely to be using a Western treatment for impotence than a traditional treatment. Finally, among men who formerly used either Western or traditional treatments

DUSAN002/SHUTTERSTOCK.COM

for impotence, they were more likely to switch from a traditional treatment to Western drug than vice versa. In fact, nobody had switched from a Western drug to a traditional treatment for impotence."

"The fact is that prior to the commercial availability of Viagra in 1998, no product in any medical tradition had been proven to be an effective and non-intrusive treatment of erectile dysfunction. So despite their history of using traditional medicines and their alleged suspicions of Western medicine, the men we interviewed chose the product that works best," von Hippel added. . .

consider this:

It looks like the cross-price elasticity between Viagra and traditional Chinese medicine from a mix of animal parts is positive. This may be very good news for endangered species.

In comparison, let's calculate the income elasticity of demand for beans, where a 10 percent increase in income results in a 15 percent decrease in the demand for beans. In this case, the income elasticity of demand is −1.5 (−15 percent ÷ +10 percent = −1.5). In this example, then, beans are an inferior good because an increase in income results in a decrease in the demand for beans. If the income elasticity is negative, then the good in question is an inferior good because the change in income and the change in demand move in opposite directions.

SECTION CHECK

1. The cross-price elasticity of demand is the percentage change in the demand of one good divided by the percentage change in the price of another related good.

2. If the sign on the cross-price elasticity is positive, the two goods are substitutes; if it is negative, the two goods are complements.

3. The income elasticity of demand is the percentage change in demand divided by the percentage change in income.

4. If the income elasticity is positive, then the good is a normal good; if it is negative, the good is an inferior good.

---

1. How does the cross-price elasticity of demand tell you whether two goods are substitutes? Complements?

2. How does the income elasticity of demand tell you whether a good is normal? Inferior?

3. If the cross-price elasticity of demand between potato chips and popcorn was positive and large, would popcorn makers benefit from a tax imposed on potato chips?

4. As people's incomes rise, why will they spend an increasing portion of their incomes on goods with income elasticities greater than 1 (DVDs) and a decreasing portion of their incomes on goods with income elasticities less than 1 (food)?

5. If people spent three times as much on restaurant meals and four times as much on DVDs as their incomes doubled, would restaurant meals or DVDs have a greater income elasticity of demand?

SECTION 6.4
Price Elasticity of Supply

* What is the price elasticity of supply?
* How does time affect the supply elasticity?
* How does the relative elasticity of supply and demand determine the tax burden?

What Is the Price Elasticity of Supply?

According to the law of supply, there is a positive relationship between price and quantity supplied, *ceteris paribus*. But by how much does quantity supplied change as price changes? It is often helpful to know the degree to which a change in price changes the quantity supplied.

price elasticity of supply
the measure of the sensitivity of the quantity supplied to changes in price of a good

The price elasticity of supply measures how responsive the quantity sellers are willing and able to sell is to changes in price. In other words, it measures the relative change in the quantity supplied that results from a change in price. Specifically, the price elasticity of supply (E_s) is defined as the percentage change in the quantity supplied divided by the percentage change in price, or

$$E_s = \frac{\%\ \Delta\ in\ the\ quantity\ supplied}{\%\ \Delta\ in\ price}$$

Calculating the Price Elasticity of Supply

The price elasticity of supply is calculated in much the same manner as the price elasticity of demand. Consider, for example, the case in which it is determined that a 10 percent increase in the price of artichokes results in a 25 percent increase in the quantity of artichokes supplied after, say, a few harvest seasons. In this case, the price elasticity is +2.5 (+25 percent ÷ +10 percent = +2.5). This coefficient indicates that each 1 percent increase in the price of artichokes induces a 2.5 percent increase in the quantity of artichokes supplied.

Types of Supply Curves

As with the elasticity of demand, the ranges of the price elasticity of supply center on whether the elasticity coefficient is greater than or less than 1. Goods with a supply elasticity that is greater than 1 ($E_S > 1$) are said to be relatively elastic in supply. With that, a 1 percent change in price will result in a greater than 1 percent change in quantity supplied. In our example, artichokes were elastic in supply because a 1 percent price increase resulted in a 2.5 percent increase in quantity supplied. An example of an *elastic supply curve* is shown in Exhibit 1(a).

Goods with a supply elasticity that is less than 1 ($E_S < 1$) are said to be inelastic in supply. In other words, a 1 percent change in the price of these goods will induce a proportionately smaller change in the quantity supplied. An example of an *inelastic supply curve* is shown in Exhibit 1(b).

Finally, two extreme cases of price elasticity of supply are perfectly inelastic supply and perfectly elastic supply. In a condition of *perfectly inelastic supply,* an increase in price will not change the quantity supplied. In this case the elasticity of supply is zero. For example, in a sports arena in the short run (that is, in a period too brief to adjust the structure), the number of seats available will be almost fixed, say at 20,000 seats. Additional portable seats might be available, but for the most part, even if a higher price is charged, only 20,000 seats will be available. We say that the elasticity of supply is zero, which describes a perfectly inelastic supply curve. Famous paintings, such as Van Gogh's *Starry Night,* provide another example: Only one original exists; therefore, only one can be supplied, regardless of price. An example of this condition is shown in Exhibit 1(c).

At the other extreme is a perfectly elastic supply curve, where the elasticity equals infinity, as shown in Exhibit 1(d). In a condition of *perfectly elastic supply,* the price does not change at all. It is the same regardless of the quantity supplied, and the elasticity of supply is infinite.

Firms would supply as much as the market wants at the market price (P_1) or above. However, firms would supply nothing below the market price because they would not be able to cover their costs of production. Most cases fall somewhere between the two extremes of perfectly elastic and perfectly inelastic.

How Does Time Affect Supply Elasticities?

Time is usually critical in supply elasticities (as well as in demand elasticities), because it is more costly for sellers to bring forth and release products in a shorter period. For example, higher wheat prices may cause farmers to grow more wheat, but big changes cannot occur until the next growing season. That is, immediately after harvest season, the supply of wheat is relatively inelastic, but over a longer time extending over the next growing period, the supply curve becomes much more elastic. Thus, supply tends to be more elastic in the long run than in the short run, as shown in Exhibit 2.

Another example of a good whose supply is completely inelastic in the short run is rental units in most urban areas without rent controls. There is generally only a fixed amount of rental units available in the short run. Thus, in the short run, an increase in demand will only lead to higher prices (rents). However, in the long run, the higher prices (rents) provide an incentive to renovate and build new rental units.

In the short run, firms can increase output by using their existing facilities to a greater capacity, paying workers to work overtime, and hiring additional workers. However, firms will be able to change output much more in the long run when firms can build new factories or close existing ones. In addition, some firms can enter as others exit. In other words, the quantity supplied will be much more elastic in the long run than in the short run.

Elasticities and Taxes: Combining Supply and Demand Elasticities

Who pays the tax? Someone may be legally required to send the check to the government but that is not necessarily the party that bears the burden of the tax.

The relative elasticity of supply and demand determines the distribution of the tax burden for a good.

section 6.4
exhibit 1
section 6.4
exhibit 1   The Price Elasticity of Supply

a. Elastic Supply ($E_s > 1$)

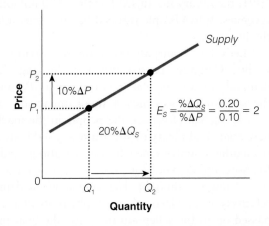

A change in price leads to a larger percentage change in quantity supplied.

b. Inelastic Supply ($E_s < 1$)

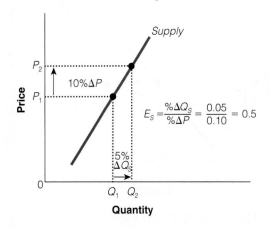

A change in price leads to a smaller percentage change in quantity supplied.

c. Perfectly Inelastic Supply ($E_s = 0$)

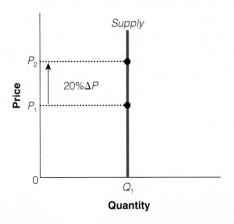

The quantity supplied does not change regardless of the change in price.

d. Perfectly Elastic Supply ($E_s = \infty$)

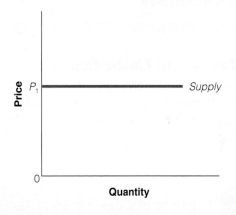

Even a small percentage change in price will change quantity supplied by an infinite amount.

As we will see, if demand is relatively less elastic than supply in the relevant tax region, the largest portion of the tax is paid by the consumer. However, if demand is relatively more elastic than supply in the relevant tax region, the largest portion of the tax is paid by the producer.

In Exhibit 3(a), the pre-tax equilibrium price is $1.00 and the pre-tax equilibrium quantity is Q_{BT}—the quantity before tax. If the government imposes a $0.50 tax on the seller, the supply curve shifts vertically by the amount of the tax (just as if an input price rose $0.50).

When demand is relatively less elastic than supply in the relevant region, the consumer bears more of the burden of the tax. For example, in Exhibit 3(a), the demand curve is relatively less elastic than the supply curve. In response to the tax, the consumer pays $1.40 per unit, $0.40 more than the consumer paid before the tax increase. The producer, however, receives $0.90 per unit, which is $0.10 less than the producer received before the tax.

In Exhibit 3(b), demand is relatively more elastic than the supply in the relevant region. Here we see that the greater burden of the same $0.50 tax falls on the producer. That is, the producer is now responsible for $0.40 of the tax, while the consumer only pays $0.10. In general, then, the tax burden falls on the side of the market that is relatively less elastic.

section 6.4
exhibit 2

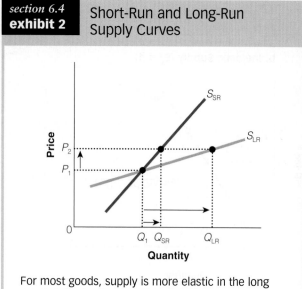

section 6.4
exhibit 2 Short-Run and Long-Run Supply Curves

For most goods, supply is more elastic in the long run than in the short run. For example, if the price of a certain good increases, firms have an incentive to produce more but are constrained by the size of their plants. In the long run, they can increase their capacity and produce more.

Yachts, Taxes, and Elasticities

In 1991, Congress levied a 10 percent luxury tax. The tax applied to the "first retail sale" of luxury goods with sales prices above the following thresholds: automobiles

$30,000; boats, $100,000; private planes, $250,000; and furs and jewelry, $10,000. The Congressional Budget Office forecasted that the luxury tax would raise about $1.5 billion over five years. However, in 1991, the luxury tax raised less than $30 million in tax revenues. Why? People stopped buying items subject to the luxury tax.

Let's focus our attention on the luxury tax on yachts. Congress passed this tax thinking that the demand for yachts was relatively inelastic and that the tax would have only a small impact on the sale of new yachts. However, the people in the market for new boats had plenty of substitutes—used boats, boats from other countries, new houses, vacations, and so on. In short, the demand for new yachts was more elastic than Congress thought. Remember, when demand is relatively more elastic than supply, most of the tax is passed on to the seller—in this case, the boat industry (workers and retailers). And supply was relatively inelastic because boat factories are not easy to change in the short run. So sellers received a lower price for their boats, and sales fell. In the first year after the tax, yacht retailers reported a 77 percent drop in sales, and approximately 25,000 workers were laid off. The point is that incorrectly predicting elasticities can lead to huge social, political, and economic problems. After intense lobbying by industry groups, Congress repealed the luxury tax on boats in 1993, and on January 1, 2003, the tax on cars finally expired.

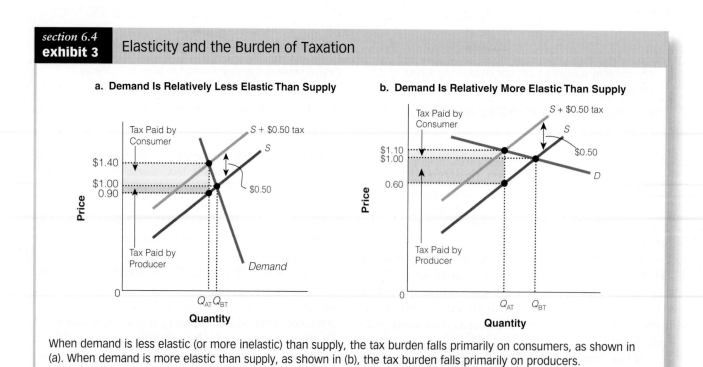

section 6.4
exhibit 3 Elasticity and the Burden of Taxation

When demand is less elastic (or more inelastic) than supply, the tax burden falls primarily on consumers, as shown in (a). When demand is more elastic than supply, as shown in (b), the tax burden falls primarily on producers.

Use what you've LEARNED

FARM PRICES FALL OVER THE LAST HALF-CENTURY

Q In the last half-century, farm prices experienced a steady decline—roughly 2 percent per year. Why?

A The demand for farm products grew more slowly than supply. Productivity advances in agriculture caused large increases in supply. And because of the inelastic demand for farm products, farmers' incomes fell considerably. That is, the total revenues ($P \times Q$) that farmers collected at the higher price, P_1, was much greater, area $0P_1E_1Q_1$, than the total revenue collected by farmers now when prices are lower, P_2, at area $0P_2E_2Q_2$.

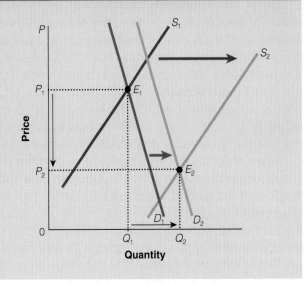

in the news   Drugs Across the Border

T he United States spends billions of dollars a year to halt the importation of illegal drugs across the border. Although these efforts are clearly targeted at suppliers, who really pays the higher enforcement and evasion costs? The government crackdown has increased the probability of apprehension and conviction for drug smugglers. That increase in risk for suppliers increases their cost of doing business, raising the cost of importing and distributing illegal drugs. This would shift the supply curve for illegal drugs to the left, from S_1 to S_2, as seen in Exhibit 4. For most drug users—addicts, in particular—the price of drugs such as cocaine and heroin lies in the highly inelastic region of the demand curve. Because the demand for drugs is

section 6.4 exhibit 4 Government Effort to Reduce the Supply of Illegal Drugs

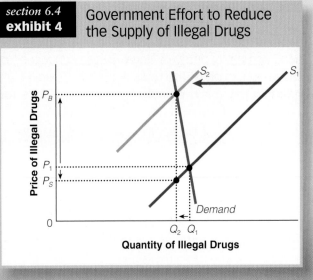

(continued)

Drugs Across the Border (cont.)

relatively inelastic in this region, the seller would be able to shift most of this cost onto the consumer (think of it as similar to the tax shift just discussed). The buyer now has to pay a much higher price, P_B, and the seller receives a slightly lower price, P_S. That is, enforcement efforts increase the price of illegal drugs, but only a small reduction in quantity demanded results from this price increase. Increased enforcement efforts may have unintended consequences due to the fact that buyers bear the majority of the burden of this price increase. Tighter smuggling controls may, in fact, result in higher levels of burglary, muggings, and white-collar crime, as more cash-strapped buyers search for alternative ways of funding their increasingly expensive habit. In addition, with the huge financial rewards in the drug trade, tougher enforcement and higher illegal drug prices could lead to even greater corruption in law enforcement and the judicial system.

These possible reactions do not mean we should abandon our efforts against illegal drugs. Illegal drugs can impose huge personal and social costs—billions of dollars of lost productivity and immeasurable personal tragedy. However, solely targeting the supply side can have unintended consequences. Policy makers may get their best results by focusing on a reduction in demand—changing user preferences. For example, if drug education leads to a reduction in the demand for drugs, the demand curve will shift to the left—reducing the price and the quantity of illegal drugs exchanged, as shown in Exhibit 5. The remaining drug users, at Q_2, will now pay a lower price, P_2. This lower price for

drugs will lead to fewer drug-related crimes, *ceteris paribus*.

It is also possible that the elasticity of demand for illegal drugs may be more elastic in the long run than the short run. In the short run, as the price rises, the quantity demanded falls less than proportionately because of the addictive nature of illegal drugs (this relationship is also true for goods such as tobacco and alcohol). However, in the long run, the demand for illegal drugs may be more elastic; that is, the higher price may deter many younger, and poorer, people from experimenting with illegal drugs.

section 6.4
exhibit 5   Drug Education Reduces Demand

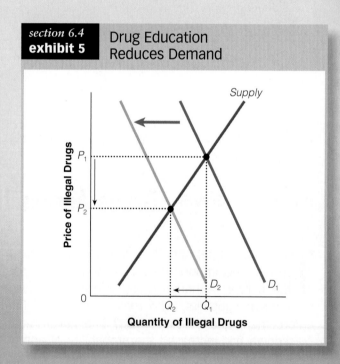

Use what you've LEARNED   OIL PRICES

One reason that small changes in supply (or demand) lead to large changes in oil prices and small changes in quantity is because of the inelasticity of demand (and supply) in the short run. Because bringing the production of oil to market takes a long time, the elasticity of supply is relatively low— supply is inelastic. Few substitutes for oil products (e.g., gasoline) are available in the short run as seen in (a).

However, in the long run, demand and supply are more elastic. At higher prices, consumers will replace gas guzzlers with more fuel-efficient cars, and non-OPEC oil producers will expand exploration and production. Thus, in the long run, when supply and demand are much more elastic, a reduction in supply will have a smaller impact on price, as seen in (b).

section 6.4
exhibit 6

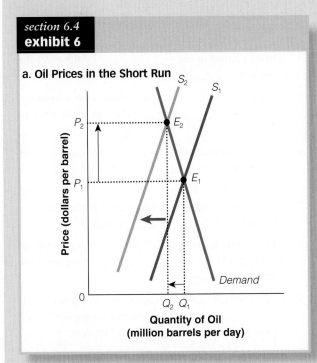

a. Oil Prices in the Short Run

section 6.4
exhibit 7

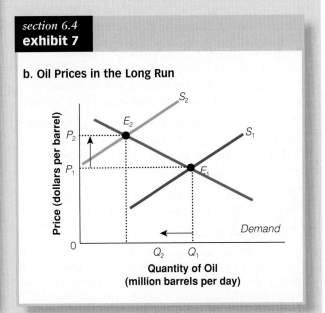

b. Oil Prices in the Long Run

SECTION CHECK

1. The price elasticity of supply measures the relative change in the quantity supplied that results from a change in price.
2. If the supply price elasticity is greater than 1, it is elastic; if it is less than 1, it is inelastic.
3. Supply tends to be more elastic in the long run than in the short run.
4. The relative elasticity of supply and demand determines the distribution of the tax burden for a good. If demand is more elastic than supply, producers bear the greater burden of the tax; if the supply is more elastic than the demand, consumers bear the greater burden.

1. What does it mean to say the elasticity of supply for one good is greater than that for another?
2. Why does supply tend to be more elastic in the long run than in the short run?
3. How do the relative elasticities of supply and demand determine who bears the greater burden of a tax?

Interactive Chapter Summary

Fill in the blanks:

1. The price elasticity of demand measures the responsiveness of quantity _____ to a change in price.

2. The price elasticity of demand is defined as the percentage change in _____ divided by the percentage change in _____.

3. If the price elasticity of demand is elastic, it means the quantity demanded changes by a relatively _____ amount than the price change.

4. If the price elasticity of demand is inelastic, it means the quantity demanded changes by a relatively _____ amount than the price change.

5. A demand curve or a portion of a demand curve can be relatively _____, _____, or relatively _____.

6. For the most part, the price elasticity of demand depends on the availability of _____, the _____ spent on the good, and the amount of _____ people have to adapt to a price change.

7. The elasticity of demand for a Ford automobile would likely be _____ elastic than the demand for automobiles, because there are more and better substitutes for a certain type of car than for a car itself.

8. The smaller the proportion of income spent on a good, the _____ its elasticity of demand.

9. The more time that people have to adapt to a new price change, the _____ the elasticity of demand. The more time that passes, the more time consumers have to find or develop suitable _____ and to plan and implement changes in their patterns of consumption.

10. When demand is price elastic, total revenues will _____ as the price declines because the percentage increase in the _____ is greater than the percentage reduction in price.

11. When demand is price inelastic, total revenues will _____ as the price declines because the percentage increase in the _____ is less than the percentage reduction in price.

12. When the price falls on the _____ half of a straight-line demand curve, demand is relatively _____. When the price falls on the lower half of a straight-line demand curve, demand is relatively _____.

13. The cross-price elasticity of demand is defined as the percentage change in the _____ _____ of good A divided by the percentage change in _____ of good B.

14. The income elasticity of demand is defined as the percentage change in the _____ by the percentage change in _____.

15. The price elasticity of supply measures the sensitivity of the quantity _____ to changes in the price of the good.

16. The price elasticity of supply is defined as the percentage change in the _____ divided by the percentage change in _____.

17. Goods with a supply elasticity that is greater than 1 are called relatively _____ in supply.

18. When supply is inelastic, a 1 percent change in the price of a good will induce a _____ 1 percent change in the quantity supplied.

19. Time is usually critical in supply elasticities because it is _____ costly for sellers to bring forth and release products in a shorter period of time.

20. The relative _____ determines the distribution of the tax burden for a good.

21. If demand is relatively _____ elastic than supply in the relevant region, the largest portion of a tax is paid by the producer.

Answers: 1. demanded 2. quantity demanded; price 3. larger 4. smaller 5. elastic, unit elastic, inelastic 6. close substitutes; proportion of income; time 7. more 8. lower 9. greater; substitutes 10. rise; quantity demanded 11. fall; quantity supplied 12. upper; elastic; inelastic 13. demand; price 14. demand; income 15. supplied 16. quantity supplied; price 17. elastic 18. less than 19. more 20. elasticity of supply and demand 21. more.

Key Terms and Concepts

price elasticity of demand 152
elastic 152
inelastic 152

unit elastic demand 153
total revenue (TR) 158
cross-price elasticity of demand 163

income elasticity of demand 164
price elasticity of supply 165

Section Check Answers

6.1 Price Elasticity of Demand

1. What question is the price elasticity of demand designed to answer?

The price elasticity of demand is designed to answer the question: How responsive is quantity demanded to changes in the price of a good?

2. How is the price elasticity of demand calculated?

The price elasticity of demand is calculated as the percentage change in quantity demanded, divided by the percentage change in the price that caused the change in quantity demanded.

3. What is the difference between a relatively price elastic demand curve and a relatively price inelastic demand curve?

Quantity demanded changes relatively more than price along a relatively price elastic segment of a demand curve, while quantity demanded changes relatively less than price along a relatively price inelastic segment of a demand curve.

4. What is the relationship between the price elasticity of demand and the slope at a given point on a demand curve?

At a given point on a demand curve, the flatter the demand curve, the more quantity demanded changes for a given change in price, so the greater is the elasticity of demand.

5. What factors tend to make demand curves more price elastic?

Demand curves tend to become more elastic, the larger the number of close substitutes available for the good, the larger proportion of income spent on the good, and the greater the amount of time that buyers have to respond to a change in the good's price.

6. Why would a tax on a particular brand of cigarettes be less effective at reducing smoking than a tax on all brands of cigarettes?

A tax on one brand of cigarettes would allow smokers to avoid the tax by switching brands rather than by smoking less, but a tax on all brands would raise the cost of smoking any cigarettes. A tax on all brands of cigarettes would therefore be more effective in reducing smoking.

7. Why is the price elasticity of demand for products at a 24-hour convenience store likely to be lower at 2 A.M. than at 2 P.M.?

Fewer alternative stores are open at 2 A.M. than at 2 P.M., and with fewer good substitutes, the price elasticity of demand for products at 24-hour convenience stores is greater at 2 P.M.

8. Why is the price elasticity of demand for turkeys likely to be lower, but the price elasticity of demand for turkeys at a particular store likely to be greater, at Thanksgiving than at other times of the year?

For many people, far fewer good substitutes are acceptable for turkey at Thanksgiving than at other times, so that the demand for turkeys is more inelastic at Thanksgiving. But grocery stores looking to attract customers for their entire large Thanksgiving shopping trip also often offer and heavily advertise turkeys at far better prices than normally, which means shoppers have available more good substitutes and a more price elastic demand curve for buying a turkey at a particular store than normally.

6.2 Total Revenue and the Price Elasticity of Demand

1. Why does total revenue vary inversely with price if demand is relatively price elastic?

Total revenue varies inversely with price if demand is relatively price elastic, because the quantity demanded (which equals the quantity sold) changes relatively more than price along a relatively elastic demand curve. Therefore, total revenue, which equals price times quantity demanded (sold) at that price, will change in the same direction as quantity demanded and in the opposite direction from the change in price.

2. Why does total revenue vary directly with price, if demand is relatively price inelastic?

Total revenue varies in the same direction as price, if demand is relatively price inelastic, because the quantity demanded (which equals the quantity sold) changes relatively less than price along a relatively inelastic demand curve. Therefore, total revenue, which equals price times quantity demanded (and sold) at that price, will change in the same direction as price and in the opposite direction from the change in quantity demanded.

3. Why is a linear demand curve more price elastic at higher price ranges and more price inelastic at lower price ranges?

Along the upper half of a linear (constant slope) demand curve, total revenue increases as the price falls, indicating that demand is relatively price elastic. Along the lower half of a linear (constant slope) demand curve, total revenue decreases as the price falls, indicating that demand is relatively price inelastic.

4. **If demand for some good was perfectly price inelastic, how would total revenue from its sales change as its price changed?**

   A perfectly price inelastic demand curve would be one where the quantity sold did not vary with the price. In such an (imaginary) case, total revenue would increase proportionately with price—a 10 percent increase in price with the same quantity sold would result in a 10 percent increase in total revenue.

5. **Assume that both you and Art, your partner in a picture-framing business, want to increase your firm's total revenue. You argue that in order to achieve this goal, you should lower your prices; Art, on the other hand, thinks that you should raise your prices. What assumptions are each of you making about your firm's price elasticity of demand?**

   You are assuming that a lower price will increase total revenue, which implies you think the demand for your picture frames is relatively price elastic. Art is assuming that an increase in your price will increase your total revenue, which implies he thinks the demand for your picture frames is relatively price inelastic.

6.3 Other Types of Demand Elasticities

1. **How does the cross-price elasticity of demand tell you whether two goods are substitutes? Complements?**

   Two goods are substitutes when an increase (decrease) in the price of one good causes an increase (decrease) in the demand for another good. Substitutes have a positive cross-price elasticity. Two goods are complements when an increase (decrease) in the price of one good decreases (increases) the demand for another food. Compliments have a negative cross-price elasticity.

2. **How does the income elasticity of demand tell you whether a good is normal? Inferior?**

   If demand for a good increases (decreases) when income rises (falls), it is a normal good and has a positive income elasticity. If demand for a good decreases (increases) when income rises (falls), it is an inferior good and has a negative income elasticity.

3. **If the cross-price elasticity of demand between potato chips and popcorn was positive and large, would popcorn makers benefit from a tax imposed on potato chips?**

   A large positive cross-price elasticity of demand between potato chips and popcorn indicates that they are close substitutes. A tax on potato chips, which would raise the price of potato chips as a result, would also substantially increase the demand for popcorn, increasing the price of popcorn and the quantity of popcorn sold, increasing the profits of popcorn makers.

4. **As people's incomes rise, why will they spend an increasing portion of their incomes on goods with income elasticities greater than 1 (DVDs) and a decreasing portion of their incomes on goods with income elasticities less than 1 (food)?**

   An income elasticity of 1 would mean people spent the same fraction or share of their income on a particular good as their incomes increase. An income elasticity greater than 1 would mean people spent an increasing fraction or share of their income on a particular good as their incomes increase, and an income elasticity less than 1 would mean people spent a decreasing fraction or share of their income on a particular good as their incomes increase.

5. **If people spent three times as much on restaurant meals and four times as much on DVDs as their incomes doubled, would restaurant meals or DVDs have a greater income elasticity of demand?**

   DVDs would have a higher income elasticity of demand (4) in this case than restaurant meals (3).

6.4 Price Elasticity of Supply

1. **What does it mean to say the elasticity of supply for one good is greater than that for another?**

   For the elasticity of supply for one good to be greater than for another, the percentage increase in quantity supplied that results from a given percentage change in price will be greater for the first good than for the second.

2. **Why does supply tend to be more elastic in the long run than in the short run?**

   Just as the cost of buyers changing their behavior is lower, the longer they have to adapt, leading to long-run demand curves being more elastic than short-run demand curves, the same is true of suppliers. The cost of producers changing their behavior is lower, the longer they have to adapt, leading to long-run supply curves being more elastic than short-run supply curves.

3. **How do the relative elasticities of supply and demand determine who bears the greater burden of a tax?**

   When demand is more elastic than supply, the tax burden falls mainly on producers; when supply is more elastic than demand, the tax burden falls mainly on consumers.

True or False:

1. If a small change in quantity demanded results from a huge change in price, then demand is said to be elastic.

2. A segment of a demand curve has an elasticity less than 1 if the percentage change in quantity demanded is less than the percentage change in price that caused it.

3. A perfectly elastic demand curve would be horizontal, but a perfectly inelastic demand curve would be vertical.

4. Using the formula, the same elasticity results whether going from a higher (lower) price to a lower (higher) price.

5. Along a segment of a demand curve that is unit elastic, quantity demanded would change by 10 percent as a result of a 10 percent change in the price.

6. Goods with close substitutes tend to have more elastic demands, while goods without close substitutes tend to have less elastic demands.

7. We would expect that the elasticity of demand for Ford automobiles would be greater than the demand for insulin by diabetics.

8. Based on the percentage of a person's budget devoted to a particular item, you would expect that the elasticity of demand for salt would be greater than the elasticity of demand for attending a university.

9. The short-run demand curve is generally more elastic than the long-run demand curve.

10. Along a demand curve, if the price rises and total revenue falls as a result, then demand must be relatively elastic along that range of the demand curve.

11. If demand is inelastic, the price and total revenue will move in opposite directions along the demand curve.

12. A straight-line demand curve will have a constant elasticity of demand along its length.

13. The price elasticity of supply measures the relative change in the quantity supplied that results from a change in price.

14. When supply is relatively elastic, a 10 percent change in price will result in a greater than 10 percent change in quantity supplied.

15. A perfectly elastic supply curve would be vertical, but a perfectly inelastic supply curve would be horizontal.

16. Goods with a supply elasticity that is less than 1 are called relatively inelastic in supply.

17. Unlike demand, supply tends to be more elastic in the long run than in the short run.

18. If demand has a lower elasticity than supply in the relevant region, the largest portion of a tax is paid by the producer.

19. Who bears the burden of a tax has nothing to do with who actually pays the tax at the time of the purchase.

Multiple Choice:

1. Price elasticity of demand is defined as the _____ change in quantity demanded divided by the _____ change in price.
   a. total; percentage
   b. percentage; marginal
   c. marginal; percentage
   d. percentage; percentage
   e. total; total

2. Demand is said to be _____ when the quantity demanded is not very responsive to changes in price.
   a. independent
   b. inelastic
   c. unit elastic
   d. elastic

3. For a given decrease in price, the greater the elasticity of demand, the greater the resulting
   a. increase in quantity demanded.
   b. increase in demand.
   c. decrease in quantity demanded.
   d. decrease in demand.

4. When demand is inelastic,
   a. price elasticity of demand is less than 1.
   b. consumers are not very responsive to changes in price.
   c. the percentage change in quantity demanded resulting from a price change is less than the percentage change in price.
   d. all of the above are correct.

5. Using the midpoint formula for the elasticity of demand, if a price increase from $57 to $63 reduces quantity demanded from 66 units to 54 units, the elasticity of demand
   a. equals 0.5.
   b. equals 1.
   c. equals 2.
   d. cannot be determined from the information given.

6. Which of the following will not tend to increase the elasticity of demand for a good?
   a. an increase in the availability of close substitutes
   b. an increase in the amount of time people have to adjust to a change in the price
   c. an increase in the proportion of income spent on the good
   d. all of the above will increase the elasticity of demand for a good

7. Which of the following would tend to have the most elastic demand curve?
   a. automobiles
   b. Chevrolet automobiles
   c. a and b would be the same
   d. none of the above

8. Iron Mike's steel mill finds that a 10 percent increase in its price leads to a 14 percent decrease in the quantity it is able to sell. The demand curve for the mill's output is
   a. elastic.
   b. inelastic.
   c. unit elastic.
   d. perfectly elastic.

9. Price elasticity of demand is said to be greater
   a. the shorter the period of time consumers have to adjust to price changes.
   b. the longer the period of time consumers have to adjust to price changes.
   c. when there are fewer available substitutes.
   d. when the elasticity of supply is greater.

10. If recent sharp increases in the price of insulin have had only a small effect on the amount of insulin purchased, then the demand for insulin is
    a. elastic.
    b. inelastic.
    c. unit elastic.
    d. perfectly elastic.

11. The price-elasticity-of-demand coefficient for herbal tea is estimated to be equal to 0.5. It is expected, therefore, that a 10 percent decrease in price would lead to _____ in the quantity of herbal tea demanded.
    a. a 5 percent decrease
    b. a 5 percent increase
    c. a 10 percent decrease
    d. a 10 percent increase
    e. a 0.5 percent increase

12. The long-run demand curve for gasoline is likely to be
    a. more elastic than the short-run demand curve for gasoline.
    b. more inelastic than the short-run demand curve for gasoline.
    c. the same as the short-run demand curve for gasoline.
    d. more inelastic than the short-run supply of gasoline.

13. Demand curves for goods tend to become more inelastic
    a. when more good substitutes for the good are available.
    b. when the good makes up a larger portion of a person's income.
    c. when people have less time to adapt to a given price change.
    d. when any of the above is true.
    e. in none of the above situations.

14. When the local symphony recently raised the ticket price for its summer concerts in the park, the symphony was surprised to see that its total revenue had actually decreased. The reason was that the elasticity of demand for tickets was
    a. unit elastic.
    b. unit inelastic.
    c. inelastic.
    d. elastic.

15. For a given increase in price, the greater the elasticity of supply, the greater the resulting
    a. decrease in quantity supplied.
    b. decrease in supply.
    c. increase in quantity supplied.
    d. increase in supply.

16. If the demand for gasoline is highly inelastic and the supply is highly elastic, and then a tax is imposed on gasoline, it will be paid
    a. largely by the sellers of gasoline.
    b. largely by the buyers of gasoline.
    c. equally by the sellers and buyers of gasoline.
    d. by the government.

17. An increase in demand will increase the price but not the quantity sold in a market if
    a. supply is perfectly elastic.
    b. supply is perfectly inelastic.
    c. supply is relatively elastic.
    d. supply is relatively inelastic.

18. A straight-line demand curve would
    a. have the same elasticity along its entire length.
    b. have a higher elasticity of demand near its top than near its bottom.
    c. have a lower elasticity of demand near its bottom than near its top.
    d. be relatively inelastic at high prices, but relatively elastic at low prices.

19. The longer the time horizon, a permanent increase in demand will tend to increase the quantity traded _____, and increases the price _____.
    a. more; more
    b. more; less
    c. less; more
    d. less; less

20. If you observed that price increased 20 percent when the quantity traded increased by 10 percent, then
    a. the elasticity of demand is 2.0.
    b. the elasticity of demand is 0.5.
    c. the elasticity of supply is 2.0.
    d. the elasticity of supply is 0.5.

21. If the cross-price elasticity of demand between two goods is negative, we know that
    a. they are substitutes.
    b. they are complements.
    c. they are both inferior goods.
    d. they are both normal goods.

22. If the income elasticity of demand for good A is 0.5 and the income elasticity of demand for good B is 1.5, then
    a. both A and B are normal goods.
    b. both A and B are inferior goods.
    c. A is a normal good, but B is an inferior good.
    d. A is an inferior good, but B is a normal good.

23. If good X has a negative cross-price elasticity of demand with good Y and good X also has a negative income elasticity of demand, then
    a. X is a substitute for Y, and X is a normal good.
    b. X is a substitute for Y, and X is an inferior good.
    c. X is a complement for Y, and X is a normal good.
    d. X is a complement for Y, and X is an inferior good.

Problems:

1. In each of the following cases, indicate which good you think has a relatively *more* price elastic demand and identify the most likely reason, in terms of the determinants of the elasticity of demand (more substitutes, greater share of budget, or more time to adjust).
    a. cars or Chevrolets
    b. salt or housing
    c. going to a New York Mets game or a Cleveland Indians game
    d. natural gas this month or over the course of a year

2. How might your elasticity of demand for copying and binding services vary if your work presentation is next week versus in two hours?

3. The San Francisco Giants want to boost revenues from ticket sales next season. You are hired as an economic consultant and asked to advise the Giants whether to raise or lower ticket prices next year. If the elasticity of demand for Giants game tickets is estimated to be −1.6, what would you advise? If the elasticity of demand equals −0.4?

4. For each of the following pairs, identify which one is likely to exhibit more elastic demand:
    a. shampoo; Paul Mitchell Shampoo
    b. air travel prompted by an illness in the family; vacation air travel
    c. paper clips; an apartment rental
    d. prescription heart medication; generic aspirin

5. Using the midpoint formula for calculating the elasticity of demand, if the price of a good fell from $42 to $38, what would be the elasticity of demand if the quantity demanded changed from:
    a. $19 to $21?
    b. $27 to $33?
    c. $195 to $205?

6. Explain why using the midpoint formula for calculating the elasticity of demand gives the same result whether price increases or decreases, but using the initial price and quantity instead of the average does not.

7. Why is a more narrowly defined good (pizza) likely to have a greater elasticity of demand than a more broadly defined good (food)?

8. If the elasticity of demand for hamburgers equals −1.5 and the quantity demanded equals 40,000, predict what will happen to the quantity demanded of hamburgers when the price increases by 10 percent. If the price falls by 5 percent, what will happen?

9. Evaluate the following statement: "Along a downward-sloping linear demand curve, the slope and therefore the elasticity of demand are both 'constant.'"

10. If the midpoint on a straight-line demand curve is at a price of $7, what can we say about the elasticity of demand for a price change from $12 to $10? What about from $6 to $4?

11. Assume the following weekly demand schedule for Sunshine DVD Rentals in Cloverdale.

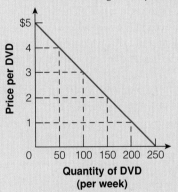

   a. When Sunshine DVD Rentals lowers their rental price from $4 to $3, what happens to its total revenue?
   b. Between a price of $4 and a price of $3, is the demand for Sunshine DVD Rentals in Cloverdale elastic or inelastic?
   c. Between a price of $2 and a price of $1, is the demand for Sunshine DVD Rentals in Cloverdale elastic or inelastic?

12. The Cowtown Hotel is the only first-class hotel in Fort Worth. The hotel owners hired economics advisors for advice about improving the hotel's profitability. They suggested the hotel could increase this year's revenue by raising prices. The owners asked, "Won't raising prices reduce the quantity of hotel rooms demanded and increase vacancies?" What do you think the advisors replied? Why would they suggest increasing prices?

13. A movie production company faces a linear demand curve for its film, and it seeks to maximize total revenue from the film's distribution. At what level should the price be set? Where is demand elastic, inelastic, or unit elastic? Explain.

14. Isabella always spends $50 on red roses each month and simply adjusts the quantity she purchases as the price changes. What can you say about Isabella's elasticity of demand for roses?

15. If taxi fares in a city rise, what will happen to the total revenue received by taxi operators? If the fares charged for subway rides, a substitute for taxi rides, do not change, what will happen to the total revenue earned by the subway as a result?

16. Mayor George Henry has a problem. He doesn't want to anger voters by taxing them because he wants to be reelected, but the town of Gapville needs more revenue for its schools. He has a choice between taxing tickets to professional basketball games or taxing food. If the demand for food is relatively inelastic while the supply is relatively elastic, and if the demand for professional basketball games is relatively elastic while the supply is relatively inelastic, in which case would the tax burden fall primarily on consumers? In which case would the tax burden fall primarily on producers?

17. Indicate whether a pair of products are substitutes, complements, or neither based upon the following estimates for the cross-price elasticity of demand:
   a. 0.5
   b. −0.5

18. Using the midpoint formula for calculating the elasticity of supply, if the price of a good rose from $95 to $105, what would be the elasticity of supply if the quantity supplied changed from:
   a. 38 to 42?
   b. 78 to 82?
   c. 54 to 66?

19. Why is an increase in price more likely to decrease the total revenue of a seller in the long run than in the short run?

20. If both supply curves and demand curves are more elastic in the long run than in the short run, how does the incidence of a tax change from the short run to the long run as a result? What happens to the revenue raised from a given tax over time, *ceteris paribus*?

21. Assume you had the following observations on U.S. intercity rail travel: Between 1990 and 1993 rail travel increased from 17.5 passenger miles per person to 19 passenger miles per person. At the same time neither per-mile railroad price or incomes changed but the per-mile price of intercity airline travel increased by 7.5 percent. Between 1995 and 1998 per capita incomes rose by approximately 13 percent while the price of travel by rail and plane stayed constant. Intercity rail travel was 20 passenger miles per person in 1995 and 19.5 in 1998. Assuming the demand for travel didn't change between these periods:
   a. calculate the income elasticity of demand for intercity rail travel.
   b. calculate the cross-price elasticity of demand for intercity rail travel.
   c. are air travel and rail travel substitutes or complements? Is intercity rail travel a normal or an inferior good?

7

Market Efficiency and Welfare

In earlier chapters, we saw how the market forces of supply and demand allocate society's scarce resources. However, we did not discuss whether this outcome was desirable or to whom.

Are the price and output that result from the equilibrium of supply and demand right from society's standpoint?

Using the tools of consumer and producer surplus, we can demonstrate the *efficiency* of a competitive market. In other words, we can show that the equilibrium price and quantity in a competitive market maximize the economic welfare of consumers and producers. Maximizing total surplus (the sum of consumer and producer surplus) leads to an efficient allocation of resources. Efficiency makes the size of the economic pie as large as possible. How we distribute that economic pie (equity) is the subject of future chapters. Efficiency can be measured on objective, positive grounds while equity involves normative analysis.

We can also use the tools of consumer and producer surplus to study the *welfare effects* of

government policy—rent controls, taxes, and agricultural support prices. To economists, *welfare* does not mean a government payment to the poor; rather, it is a way that we measure the impact of a policy on a particular group, such as consumers or producers. By calculating the changes in producer and consumer surplus that result from government intervention, we can measure the impact of such policies on buyers and sellers. For example, economists and policymakers may want to know how much a consumer or producer might benefit or be harmed by a tax or subsidy that alters the equilibrium price and quantity.

Let's begin by presenting the most widely used tool for measuring consumer and producer welfare. ■

Consumer Surplus and Producer Surplus

* What is consumer surplus?
* What is producer surplus?
* How do we measure the total gains from trade?

Consumer Surplus

In a competitive market, consumers and producers buy and sell at the market equilibrium price. However, some consumers will be willing and able to pay more for the good than they have to. But they would never knowingly buy something that is worth less to them. That is, what a consumer actually pays for a unit of a good is usually less than the amount she is *willing* to pay. For example, you would be willing and able to pay far more than the market price for a rope ladder to get out of a burning building. You would be willing to pay more than the market price for a tank of gasoline if you had run out of gas on a desolate highway in the desert. **Consumer surplus** is the monetary difference between the amount a consumer is willing and able to pay for an additional unit of a good and what the consumer actually pays—the market price. Consumer surplus for the whole market is the sum of all the individual consumer surpluses for those consumers who have purchased the good.

Imagine it is 115 degrees in the shade. Do you think you would get more consumer surplus from your first glass of iced tea than you would from a fifth glass?

Marginal Willingness to Pay Falls as More Is Consumed

consumer surplus
the difference between the price a consumer is willing and able to pay for an additional unit of a good and the price the consumer actually pays; for the whole market, it is the sum of all the individual consumer surpluses

Suppose it is a hot day and iced tea is going for $1 per glass, but Julie is willing to pay $4 for the first glass (point a), $2 for the second glass (point b), and $0.50 for the third glass (point c), reflecting the law of demand. How much consumer surplus will Julie receive? First, it is important to note the general fact that if the consumer is a buyer of several units of a good, the earlier units will have greater marginal value and therefore create more consumer surplus, because *marginal willingness to pay* falls as greater quantities are consumed in any period. In fact, you can think of the demand curve as a marginal benefit curve—the additional benefit derived from consuming one more unit. Notice in Exhibit 1 that Julie's demand curve for iced tea has a step-like shape. This is demonstrated by Julie's willingness to pay $4 and $2 successively for the first two glasses of iced tea. Thus, Julie will receive $3 of consumer surplus for the first glass ($4 − $1) and $1 of consumer surplus for the second glass ($2 − $1), for a total consumer surplus of $4, as seen in Exhibit 1. Julie will not be willing to purchase the third glass, because her willingness to pay is less than its price ($0.50 versus $1.00).

In Exhibit 2, we can easily measure the consumer surplus in the market by using a market demand curve rather than an individual demand curve. In short, the market consumer surplus is the area under the market demand curve and above the market price (the shaded area in Exhibit 2). The market for chocolate contains millions of potential buyers, so we will get a smooth demand curve. Because the demand curve represents the *marginal benefits* consumers receive from consuming an additional unit, we can conclude that all buyers of chocolate receive at least some consumer surplus in the market because the marginal benefit is greater than the market price—the shaded area in Exhibit 2.

section 7.1
exhibit 1
Julie's Consumer Surplus for Iced Tea

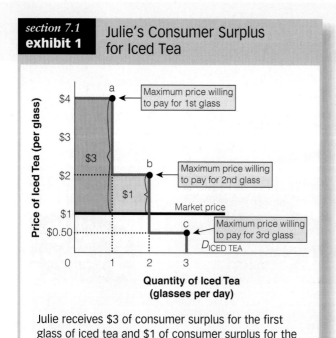

Julie receives $3 of consumer surplus for the first glass of iced tea and $1 of consumer surplus for the second glass. Her total consumer surplus is $4.

section 7.1
exhibit 3
Impact of an Increase in Supply on Consumer Surplus

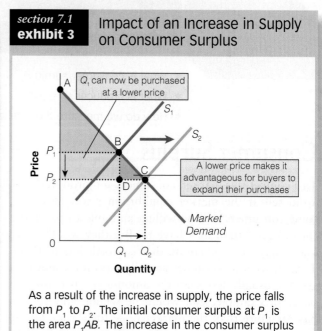

As a result of the increase in supply, the price falls from P_1 to P_2. The initial consumer surplus at P_1 is the area P_1AB. The increase in the consumer surplus from the fall in price is from P_1 to P_2.

section 7.1
exhibit 2
Consumer Surplus

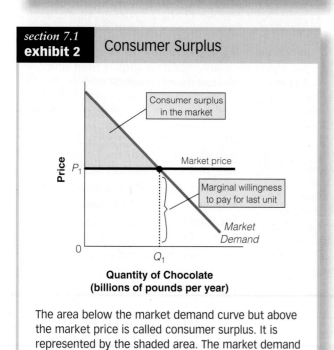

The area below the market demand curve but above the market price is called consumer surplus. It is represented by the shaded area. The market demand curve is smooth because many buyers purchase chocolate each year.

increase your consumer surplus for each unit you were already consuming and will also increase your consumer surplus from additional purchases at the lower price. Conversely, a decrease in supply and increase in price will lower your consumer surplus.

Exhibit 3 shows the gain in consumer surplus associated with, say, a technological advance that shifts the supply curve to the right. As a result, equilibrium price falls (from P_1 to P_2) and quantity rises (from Q_1 to Q_2). Consumer surplus then increases from area P_1AB to area P_2AC, or a gain in consumer surplus of P_1BCP_2. The increase in consumer surplus has two parts. First, there is an increase in consumer surplus, because Q_1 can now be purchased at a lower price; this amount of additional consumer surplus is illustrated by area P_1BDP_2 in Exhibit 3. Second, the lower price makes it advantageous for buyers to expand their purchases from Q_1 to Q_2. The net benefit to buyers from expanding their consumption from Q_1 to Q_2 is illustrated by area BCD.

Price Changes and Changes in Consumer Surplus

Imagine that the price of your favorite beverage fell because of an increase in supply. Wouldn't you feel better off? An increase in supply and a lower price will

Producer Surplus

As we have just seen, the difference between what a consumer would be willing and able to pay for a given quantity of a good and what a consumer actually has to pay is called consumer surplus. The parallel concept for producers is called producer surplus. **Producer surplus** is the difference between what a producer is paid for a good and the cost of producing one unit of that good. Producers would never knowingly sell a good that is worth more to them than the asking price. Imagine selling coffee for half of what it cost to produce—you won't be in business very long with that pricing strategy. The supply curve shows the minimum amount that sellers must receive to be willing to supply any given quantity; that is, the supply curve reflects the marginal cost to sellers. The **marginal cost** is the cost of producing one more unit of a good. In other words, the supply curve is the marginal cost curve, just like the demand curve is the marginal benefit curve. Because some units can be produced at a cost that is lower than the market price, the seller receives a surplus, or a net benefit, from producing those units. For example, in Exhibit 4, the market price is $5. Say the firm's marginal cost is $2 for the first unit, $3 for the second unit, $4 for the third unit, and $5 for the fourth unit. Because producer surplus for a particular unit is the difference between the market price and the seller's cost of producing that unit, producer surplus would be as follows: The first unit would yield $3; the second unit would yield $2; the third unit would yield $1; and the fourth unit would add no more to producer surplus, because the market price equals the seller's cost.

> **producer surplus**
> the difference between what a producer is paid for a good and the cost of producing that unit of the good; for the market, it is the sum of all the individual sellers' producer surpluses—the area above the market supply curve and below the market price
>
> **marginal cost**
> the cost of producing one more unit of a good

When there are a lot of producers, the supply curve is more or less smooth, like in Exhibit 5. Total producer surplus for the market is obtained by summing all the producer surpluses of all the sellers—the area above the market supply curve and below the market price up to the quantity actually produced—the shaded area in Exhibit 5. Producer surplus is a measurement of how much sellers gain from trading in the market.

Suppose an increase in market demand causes the market price to rise, say from P_1 to P_2; the seller now receives a higher price per unit, so additional producer surplus is generated. In Exhibit 6, we see the additions to producer surplus. Part of the added surplus (area P_2DBP_1) is due to a higher price for the quantity already being produced (up to Q_1) and part (area DCB) is due to the expansion of output made profitable by the higher price (from Q_1 to Q_2).

Market Efficiency and Producer and Consumer Surplus

With the tools of consumer and producer surplus, we can better analyze the total gains from exchange. The demand curve represents a collection of maximum prices that consumers are willing and able to pay for

---

section 7.1 exhibit 4   A Firm's Producer Surplus

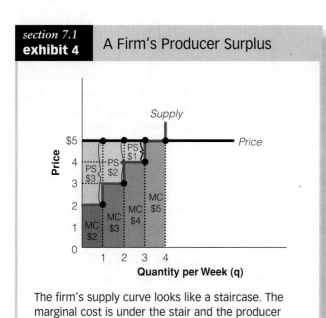

The firm's supply curve looks like a staircase. The marginal cost is under the stair and the producer surplus is above the red stair and below the market price for each unit.

---

section 7.1 exhibit 5   Market Producer Surplus

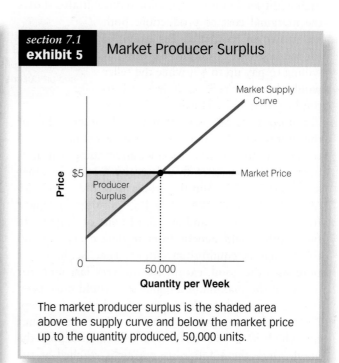

The market producer surplus is the shaded area above the supply curve and below the market price up to the quantity produced, 50,000 units.

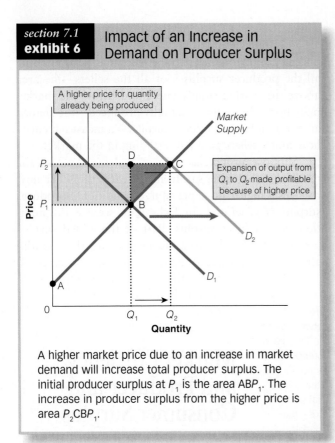

A higher market price due to an increase in market demand will increase total producer surplus. The initial producer surplus at P_1 is the area ABP_1. The increase in producer surplus from the higher price is area P_2CBP_1.

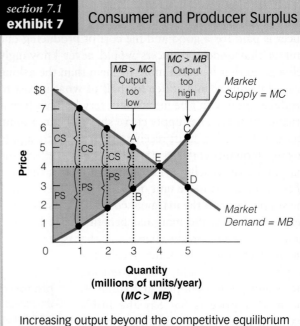

Increasing output beyond the competitive equilibrium output, 4 million units, decreases welfare, because the cost of producing this extra output exceeds the value the buyer places on it ($MC > MB$)—producing 5 million units rather than 4 million units leads to a deadweight loss of area ECD. Reducing output below the competitive equilibrium output level, 4 million units, reduces total welfare, because the buyer values the extra output by more than it costs to produce that output—producing 3 million units rather than 4 million units leads to a deadweight loss of area EAB, $MB > MC$, only at equillibrium, E, is $MB = MC$.

additional quantities of a good or service. It also shows the marginal benefits derived by consumers. The supply curve represents a collection of minimum prices that suppliers require to be willing and able to supply each additional unit of a good or service. It also shows the marginal cost of production. Both are shown in Exhibit 7. For example, for the first unit of output, the buyer is willing to pay up to $7, while the seller would have to receive at least $1 to produce that unit. However, the equilibrium price is $4, as indicated by the intersection of the supply and demand curves. It is clear that the two would gain from getting together and trading that unit, because the consumer would receive $3 of consumer surplus ($7 − $4), and the producer would receive $3 of producer surplus ($4 − $1). Both would also benefit from trading the second and third units of output—in fact, both would benefit from trading every unit up to the market equilibrium output. That is, the buyer purchases the good, except for the very last unit, for less than the maximum amount she would have been willing to pay; the seller receives for the good, except for the last unit, more than the minimum amount for which he would have been willing to supply the good. Once the equilibrium output is reached at the

> **total welfare gains**
> the sum of consumer
> and producer surpluses

equilibrium price, all the mutually beneficial trade opportunities between the demander and supplier will have taken place, and the sum of consumer surplus and producer surplus is maximized. This is where the marginal benefit to buyers is equal to the marginal cost to producers. Both buyer and seller are better off from each of the units traded than they would have been if they had not exchanged them.

It is important to recognize that, in this case, the **total welfare gains** to the economy from trade in this good is the sum of the consumer and producer surpluses created. That is, consumers benefit from additional amounts of consumer surplus, and producers benefit from additional amounts of producer surplus. Improvements in welfare come from additions to both consumer and producer surpluses. In competitive markets with large numbers of buyers and sellers, at the market equilibrium price and quantity, the net gains to society are as large as possible.

in the news   Is Santa a Deadweight Loss?

In America, retailers make 25% of their yearly sales and 60% of their profits between Thanksgiving and Christmas. Even so, economists find something to worry about in the nature of the purchase being made.

Much of the holiday spending is on gifts for others. At the simplest level, giving gifts involves the giver thinking of something that the recipient would like—he tries to guess her preferences, as economists say—and then buying the gift and delivering it. Yet this guessing of preferences is no mean feat; indeed, it is often done badly. Every year, ties go unworn and books unread. And even if a gift is enjoyed, it may not be what the recipient would have bought had she spent the money herself.

Intrigued by this mismatch between wants and gifts, in 1993 Joel Waldfogel, then an economist at Yale University, sought to establish the disparity in dollar terms. In a paper that has proved seminal in the literature on the issue, he asked students two questions at the end of the holiday season: first, estimate the total amount paid (by givers) for all holiday gifts you received; second, apart from sentimental value of the items, if you did not have them, how much would you be willing to pay to get them? His results were gloomy: on average, a gift was valued by the recipient well below the price paid by the giver.

The most conservative estimate put the average receiver's valuation at 90% of the buying price. The missing 10% is what economists call a deadweight loss: a waste of resources that could be averted without making anyone worse off. In other words, if the giver gave the cash value of the purchase instead of the gift itself, the recipient could then buy what she really wants, and be better off for no extra cost.

Perhaps not surprisingly, the most effective gifts (those with the smallest deadweight loss) were those from close friends and relations, while non-cash gifts from extended family were the least efficient. As the age difference between giver and recipient grew, so did the inefficiency. All of which suggests what many grandparents know: when buying gifts for someone with largely unknown preferences, the

COURTESY OF ROBERT L. SEXTON

best present is one that is totally flexible (cash) or very flexible (gift vouchers).

If the results are generalized, a waste of one dollar in ten represents a huge aggregate loss to society. It suggests that in America, where givers spend $40 billion on Christmas gifts, $4 billion is being lost annually in the process of gift giving. Add in birthdays, weddings, and non-Christian occasions and the figure would balloon. So should economists advocate an end to gift giving, or at least press for money to become the gift of choice?

Sentimental Value

There are a number of reasons to think not. First, recipients may not know their own preferences very well. Some of the best gifts, after all, are the unexpected items that you would never have thought of buying but turn out to be especially well picked. And preferences can change. So by giving a jazz CD, for example, the giver may be encouraging the recipient to enjoy something that was shunned before. This, and a desire to build skills, is presumably the hope held by the many parents who ignore their children's pleas for video games and give them books instead.

(continued)

Second, the giver may have access to items—because of travel or an employee discount, for example—that the recipient does not know existed, cannot buy, or can only buy at a higher price. Finally, there are items that a recipient would like to receive but not purchase. If someone else buys them, however, they can be enjoyed guilt-free. This might explain the high volume of chocolate that changes hands over the holidays.

But there is a more powerful argument for gift giving, deliberately ignored by most surveys. Gift giving, some economists think, is a process that adds value to an item over and above what it would otherwise be worth to the recipient. Intuition backs this up, of course. A gift's worth is not only a function of its price but also of the giver and the circumstances in which it is given.

Hence, a wedding ring is more valuable to its owner than to a jeweler, and the imprint of a child's hand on dried clay is priceless to a loving grandparent. Moreover, not only can gift giving add value for the recipient, but it can be fun for the giver, too. It is good, in other words, to give as well as to receive.

The lesson then, for gift givers? Try hard to guess the preferences of each person on your list and then choose a gift that will have high sentimental value. As economists have studied hard to tell you, it's the thought that counts.

SOURCE: From "Economics Focus: Is Santa a Deadweight Loss?", 'The Economist', December 20, 2001. © The Economist Newspaper Limited, London 2001. Reprinted with permission.

Why would it be inefficient to produce only 3 million units? The demand curve in Exhibit 7 indicates that the buyer is willing to pay $5 for the 3 millionth unit. The supply curve shows that it only costs the seller $3 to produce that unit. That is, as long as the buyer values the extra output by more than it costs to produce that unit, total welfare would increase by expanding output. In fact, if output is expanded from 3 million units to 4 million units, total welfare (the sum of consumer and producer surpluses) will increase by area AEB in Exhibit 7.

What if 5 million units are produced? The demand curve shows that the buyer is only willing to pay $3 for the 5 millionth unit. However, the supply curve shows that it would cost about $5.50 to produce that 5 millionth unit. Thus, increasing output beyond equilibrium decreases total welfare, because the cost of producing this extra output is greater than the value the buyer places on it. If output is reduced from 5 million units to 4 million units, total welfare will increase by area ECD in Exhibit 7.

deadweight loss
net loss of total surplus that results from an action that alters a market equilibrium

Not producing the efficient level of output, in this case 4 million units, leads to what economists call a **deadweight loss**. A deadweight loss is the reduction in both consumer and producer surpluses—it is the net loss of total surplus that results from the misallocation of resources.

In a competitive equilibrium, supply equals demand at the equilibrium. This means that the buyers value the last unit of output consumed by exactly the same amount that it cost to produce. If consumers valued the last unit by more than it cost to produce, welfare could be increased by expanding output. If consumers valued the last unit by less than it cost to produce, then welfare could be increased by producing less output.

In sum, *market efficiency* occurs when we have maximized the sum of consumer and producer surplus, when the margin of benefits of the last unit consumed is equal to the marginal cost of productivity, $MB = MC$.

GREAT ECONOMIC THINKERS   ALFRED MARSHALL (1842–1924)

Alfred Marshall was born outside of London in 1842. His father, a domineering man who was a cashier for the Bank of England, wanted nothing more than for Alfred to become a minister. But the young Marshall enjoyed math and chess, both of which were forbidden by his authoritarian father. When he was older, Marshall turned down a theological scholarship to Oxford to study at Cambridge, with the financial support of a wealthy uncle. Here he earned academic honors in mathematics. Upon graduating, Marshall set upon a period of self-discovery. He traveled to Germany to study metaphysics, later adopting the philosophy of agnosticism, and moved on to studying ethics. He found within himself a deep sorrow and disgust over the condition of society. He resolved to use his skills to lessen poverty and human suffering, and, in wanting to use his mathematics in this broader capacity, Marshall soon developed a fascination with economics.

Marshall became a fellow and lecturer in political economy at Cambridge. He had been teaching for nine years when, in 1877, he married a former student, Mary Paley. Because of the university's celibacy rules, Marshall had to give up his position at Cambridge. He moved on to teach at University College at Bristol and at Oxford. But in 1885, the rules were relaxed and Marshall returned to Cambridge as the Chair in Political Economy, a position that he held until 1908, when he resigned to devote more time to writing.

Before this point in time, economics was grouped with philosophy and the "moral sciences." Marshall fought all of his life for economics to be set apart as a field all its own. In 1903, Marshall finally succeeded in persuading Cambridge to establish a separate economics course, paving the way for the discipline as it exists today. As this event clearly demonstrates, Marshall exerted a great deal of influence on the development of economic thought in his time. Marshall popularized the heavy use of illustration, real-world examples, and current events in teaching, as well as the modern diagrammatic approach to economics. Relatively early in his career, it was being said that Marshall's former students occupied half of the economic chairs in the United Kingdom. His most famous student was John Maynard Keynes.

Marshall is most famous for refining the marginal approach. He was intrigued by the self-adjusting and self-correcting nature of economic markets, and he was also interested in time—how long did it take for markets to adjust? Marshall coined the analogy that compares the tools of supply and demand to the blades on a pair of scissors—that is, it is fruitless to talk about whether it was supply or demand that determined the market price; rather, one should consider both in unison. After all, the upper blade is not of more importance than the lower when using a pair of scissors to cut a piece of paper. Marshall was also responsible for refining some of the most important tools in economics—elasticity and consumer and producer surplus. Marshall's book *Principles of Economics* was published in 1890; immensely popular, the book went into eight editions. Much of the content in *Principles* is still at the core of microeconomics texts today.

SECTION CHECK

1. The difference between how much a consumer is willing and able to pay and how much a consumer has to pay for a unit of a good is called consumer surplus.

2. An increase in supply will lead to a lower price and an increase in consumer surplus; a decrease in supply will lead to a higher price and a decrease in consumer surplus.

3. Producer surplus is the difference between what a producer is paid for a good and the cost of producing that good.

4. An increase in demand will lead to a higher market price and an increase in producer surplus; a decrease in demand will lead to a lower market price and a decrease in producer surplus.

(continued)

5. We can think of the demand curve as a marginal benefit curve and the supply curve as a marginal cost curve.

6. Total welfare gains from trade to the economy can be measured by the sum of consumer and producer surpluses.

---

1. What is consumer surplus?

2. Why do the earlier units consumed at a given price add more consumer surplus than the later units consumed?

3. Why does a decrease in a good's price increase the consumer surplus from consumption of that good?

4. Why might the consumer surplus from purchases of diamond rings be less than the consumer surplus from purchases of far less expensive stones?

5. What is producer surplus?

6. Why do the earlier units produced at a given price add more producer surplus than the later units produced?

7. Why does an increase in a good's price increase the producer surplus from production of that good?

8. Why might the producer surplus from sales of diamond rings, which are expensive, be less than the producer surplus from sales of far less expensive stones?

9. Why is the efficient level of output in an industry defined as the output where the sum of consumer and producer surplus is maximized?

10. Why does a reduction in output below the efficient level create a deadweight loss?

11. Why does an expansion in output beyond the efficient level create a deadweight loss?

SECTION 7.2
The Welfare Effects of Taxes, Subsidies, and Price Controls

* What are the welfare effects of a tax?
* What is the relationship between a deadweight loss and price elasticities?

* What are the welfare effects of subsidies?
* What are the welfare effects of price controls?

In the previous section we used the tools of consumer and producer surplus to measure the efficiency of a competitive market—that is, how the equilibrium price and quantity in a competitive market lead to the maximization of aggregate welfare (for both buyers and sellers). Now we can use the same tools, consumer and producer surplus, to measure the welfare effects of various government programs—taxes and price controls. When economists refer to the **welfare effects** of a government policy, they are referring to the gains and losses associated with government intervention. This use of the term should not be confused with the more common reference to a welfare recipient who is getting aid from the government.

welfare effects
the gains and losses associated with government intervention in markets

Using Consumer and Producer Surplus to Find the Welfare Effects of a Tax

To simplify the explanation of elasticity and the tax incidence, we will not complicate the illustration by shifting the supply curve (tax levied on sellers) or demand curve (tax levied on buyers) as we did in Section 6.4. We will simply show the result a tax must cause. The tax is illustrated by the vertical distance between the supply and demand curves at the new after-tax output—shown as the bold vertical line in

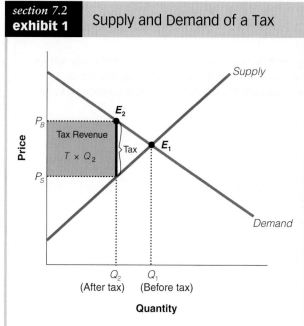

section 7.2
exhibit 1   Supply and Demand of a Tax

After the tax, the buyers pay a higher price, P_B, and the sellers receive a lower price, P_S; and the equilibrium quantity of the good (both bought and sold) falls from Q_1 to Q_2. The tax revenue collected is measured by multiplying the amount of the tax times that quantity of the good sold after the tax is imposed ($T \times Q_2$).

Exhibit 1. After the tax, the buyers pay a higher price, P_B, and the sellers receive a lower price, P_S; and the equilibrium quantity of the good (both bought and sold) falls from Q_1 to Q_2. The tax revenue collected is measured by multiplying the amount of the tax times the quantity of the good sold after the tax is imposed ($T \times Q_2$).

In Exhibit 2, we can now use consumer and producer surpluses to measure the amount of welfare loss associated with a tax. First, consider the amounts of consumer and producer surplus before the tax. Before

the tax is imposed, the price is P_1 and the quantity is Q_1; at that price and output, the amount of consumer surplus is area a + b + c, and the amount of producer surplus is area d + e + f. To get the total surplus, or total welfare, we add consumer and producer surpluses, area a + b + c + d + e + f. Without a tax, tax revenues are zero.

After the tax, the price the buyer pays is P_B, the price the seller receives is P_S, and the output falls to Q_2. As a result of the higher price and lower output from the tax, consumer surplus is smaller—area a. After the tax, sellers receive a lower price, so producer surplus is smaller—area f. However, some of the loss in consumer and producer surpluses is transferred in the form of tax revenues to the government, which can be used to reduce other taxes, fund public projects, or be redistributed to others in society. This transfer of society's resources is not a loss from society's perspective. The net loss to society can be found by measuring the difference between the loss in consumer surplus (area b + c) plus the loss in producer surplus (area d + e) and the gain in tax revenue (area b + d). The reduction in total surplus is area c + e, or the shaded area in Exhibit 2. This deadweight loss from the tax is the reduction in producer and consumer surpluses minus the tax revenue transferred to the government.

Deadweight loss occurs because the tax reduces the quantity exchanged below the original output level, Q_1, reducing the size of the total surplus realized from trade. The problem is that the tax distorts market incentives: The price to buyers is higher than before the tax, so they consume less; and the price to sellers is lower than before the tax, so they produce less. These effects lead to deadweight loss, or market inefficiencies—the waste associated with not producing the efficient level of output. That is, the tax causes a deadweight loss because it prevents some mutual beneficial trade between buyers and sellers.

Use what you've LEARNED   SHOULD WE USE TAXES TO REDUCE DEPENDENCY ON FOREIGN OIL?

Q What if we placed a $0.50 tax on gasoline to reduce dependence on foreign oil and to raise the tax revenue?

A If the demand and supply curves are both equally elastic, as in Exhibit 2, both consumers and

producers will share the burden equally. The tax collected would be b + d, but total loss in consumer surplus (b + c) and producer surplus (d + e) would be greater than the gains in tax revenue. Not surprisingly, both consumers and producers fight such a tax every time it is proposed.

The net loss to society due to a tax can be found by measuring the difference between the loss in consumer surplus (area b + c) plus the loss in producer surplus (area d + e) and the gain in tax revenue (area b + d). The deadweight loss from the tax is the reduction in the consumer and producer surpluses minus the tax revenue transferred to the government, area c + e.

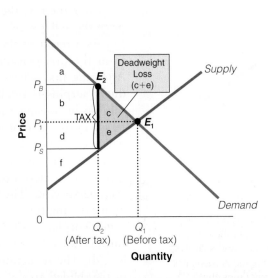

	Before Tax	After Tax	Change
Consumer Surplus	a + b + c	a	−b − c
Producer Surplus	d + e + f	f	−d − e
Tax Revenue ($T \times Q_2$)	zero	b + d	b + d
Total Welfare	a + b + c + d + e + f	a + b + d + f	−c − e

All taxes lead to deadweight loss. The deadweight loss is important because if the people are to benefit from the tax, then more than $1 of benefit must be produced from $1 of government expenditure. For example, if a gasoline tax leads to $100 million in tax revenues and $20 million in deadweight loss, then the government needs to provide a benefit to the public of more than $120 million with the $100 million revenues.

Elasticity and the Size of the Deadweight Loss

The size of the deadweight loss from a tax, as well as how the burdens are shared between buyers and sellers, depends on the price elasticities of supply and demand. In Exhibit 3(a) we can see that, other things being equal, the less elastic the demand curve, the smaller the deadweight loss. Similarly, the less elastic the supply curve, other things being equal, the smaller the deadweight loss, as shown in Exhibit 3(b). However,

when the supply and/or demand curves become more elastic, the deadweight loss becomes larger, because a given tax reduces the quantity exchanged by a greater amount, as seen in Exhibit 3(c). Recall that elasticities measure how responsive buyers and sellers are to price changes. That is, the more elastic the curves are, the greater the change in output and the larger the deadweight loss.

Elasticity differences can help us understand tax policy. Goods that are heavily taxed, such as alcohol, cigarettes, and gasoline, often have a relatively inelastic demand curve in the short run, so the tax burden falls primarily on the buyer. It also means that the deadweight loss to society is smaller for the tax revenue raised than if the demand curve were more elastic. In other words, because consumers cannot find many close substitutes in the short run, they reduce their consumption only slightly at the higher after-tax price. Even though the deadweight loss is smaller, it is still positive, because the reduced after-tax price received by sellers and the increased after-tax price paid by buyers reduces the quantity exchanged below the previous market equilibrium level.

section 7.2
exhibit 3   Elasticity and Deadweight Loss

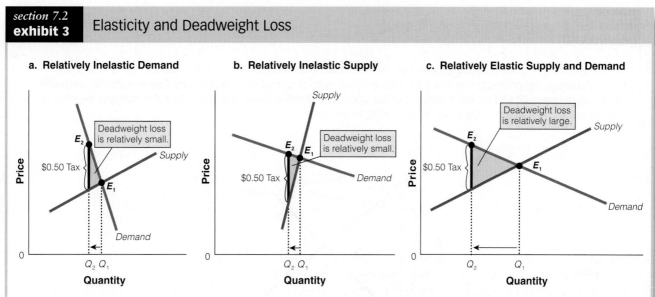

In (a) and (b), we see that when one of the two curves is relatively price inelastic, the deadweight loss from the tax is relatively small. However, when the supply and/or demand curves become more elastic, the deadweight loss becomes larger, because a given tax reduces the quantity exchanged by a greater amount, as seen in (c). The more elastic the curves are, the greater the change in output and the larger the deadweight loss.

The Welfare Effects of Subsidies

If taxes cause deadweight or welfare losses, do subsidies create welfare gains? For example, what if a government subsidy (paid by taxpayers) was provided in a particular market? Think of a subsidy as a negative tax. Before the subsidy, say the equilibrium price was P_1 and the equilibrium quantity was Q_1, as shown in Exhibit 4. The consumer surplus is area a + b, and the producer surplus is area c + d. The sum of producer and consumer surpluses is maximized (a + b + c + d), with no deadweight loss.

In Exhibit 4, we see that the subsidy lowers the price to the buyer to P_B and increases the quantity exchanged to Q_2. The subsidy results in an increase in consumer surplus from area a + b to area a + b + c + g, a gain of c + g. And producer surplus increases from area c + d to area c + d + b + e, a gain of b + e. With gains in both consumer and producer surpluses, it looks like a gain in welfare, right? Not quite. Remember that the government is paying for this subsidy, and the cost to government (taxpayers) of the subsidy is area b + e + f + c + g (the subsidy per unit times the number of units subsidized). That is, the cost to government (taxpayers), area b + e + f + c + g, is greater than the gains to consumers, c + g, and the gains to producers, b + e, by area f. Area f is the deadweight or welfare loss to society from the subsidy because it results in the production of more than the competitive market equilibrium, and the market value of that expansion to

buyers is less than the marginal cost of producing that expansion to sellers. In short, the market overproduces relative to the efficient level of output, Q_1.

Price Ceilings and Welfare Effects

As we saw in Chapter 5, price controls involve the use of the power of the government to establish prices different from the equilibrium market price that would otherwise prevail. The motivations for price controls vary with the markets under consideration. A maximum, or ceiling, is often set for goods deemed important, such as housing. A minimum price, or floor, may be set on wages because wages are the primary source of income for most people, or on agricultural products, in order to guarantee that producers will get a certain minimum price for their products.

If a price ceiling (that is, a legally established maximum price) is binding and set below the equilibrium price at P_{MAX}, the quantity demanded will be greater than the quantity supplied at that price, and a shortage will occur. At this price, buyers will compete for the limited supply, Q_2.

We can see the welfare effects of a price ceiling by observing the change in consumer and producer surpluses from the implementation of the price ceiling in Exhibit 5. Before the price ceiling, the buyer receives area a + b + c of consumer surplus at price P_1 and

With a subsidy, the price producers receive (P_S) is the price consumers pay (P_B) plus the subsidy ($\$S$). Because the subsidy leads to the production of more than the efficient level of output Q_1, a deadweight loss results. For each unit produced between Q_1 and Q_2, the supply curve lies above the demand curve, indicating that the marginal benefits to consumers are less than society's cost of producing those units.

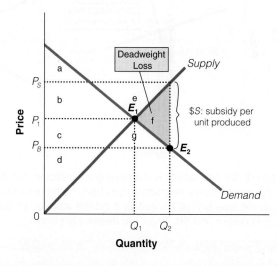

	Before Tax Subsidy	After Tax Subsidy	Change
Consumer Surplus	a + b	a + b + c + g	c + g
Producer Surplus	c + d	c + d + b + e	b + e
Government (Taxpayers)	zero	−b − e − f − c − g	−b − e − f − c − g
Total Welfare (CS + PS − G)	a + b + c + d	a + b + c + d − f	−f

quantity Q_1. However, after the price ceiling is implemented at P_{MAX}, consumers can buy the good at a lower price but cannot buy as much as before (they can only buy Q_2 instead of Q_1). Because consumers can now buy Q_2 at a lower price, they gain area d of consumer surplus after the price ceiling. However, they lose area c of consumer surplus because they can only purchase Q_2 rather than Q_1 of output. Thus, the change in consumer surplus is d − c. In this case, area d is larger than area e and area c and the consumer gains from the price ceiling.

The price the seller receives for Q_2 is P_{MAX} (the ceiling price), so producer surplus falls from area d + e + f before the price ceiling to area f after the price ceiling, for a loss of area d + e. That is, any possible gain to consumers will be more than offset by the losses to producers. The price ceiling has caused a deadweight loss of area c + e.

There is a deadweight loss because less is sold at Q_2 than at Q_1; and consumers value those units between Q_2 and Q_1 by more than it cost to produce them. For example, at Q_2, consumers will value the unit at P_2,

which is much higher than it cost to produce it—the point on the supply curve at Q_2.

Applications of Consumer and Producer Surplus

Rent Controls

If consumers use no additional resources, search costs, or side payments for a rent controlled unit, the consumer surplus is equal to a + b + d in Exhibit 5. If landlords were able to extract P_2 from renters, consumer surplus would be reduced to area a. Landlords are able to collect higher "rent" using a variety of methods. They might have the tenant slip them a couple hundred dollars each month; they might charge a high rate for parking in the garage; they might rent used furniture at a high rate; or they might charge an exorbitant key price—the price for changing the locks for a new tenant. These types of arrangements take place in so-called

exhibit 5   Welfare Effects of a Price Ceiling

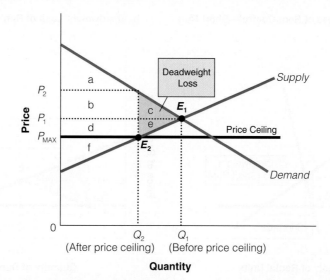

	Before Price Ceiling	After Price Ceiling	Change
Consumer Surplus	a + b + c	a + b + d	d − c
Producer Surplus	d + e + f	f	−d − e
Total Welfare (CS + PS)	a + b + c + d + e + f	a + b + d + f	−c − e

If area d is larger than area c, consumers in the aggregate would be better off from the price ceiling. However, any possible gain to consumers will be more than offset by the losses to producers, area d + e. Price ceiling causes a deadweight loss of c + e.

black markets—markets where goods are transacted outside the boundaries of the law. One problem is that law-abiding citizens will be among those least likely to find a rental unit. Other problems include black market prices that are likely to be higher than the price would be if restrictions were lifted and the inability to use legal means to enforce contracts and resolve disputes.

If the landlord is able to charge P_2, then the area b + d of consumer surplus will be lost by consumers and gained by the landlord. This redistribution from the buyer to the seller does not change the size of the deadweight loss; it remains area c + e.

The measure of the deadweight loss in the price ceiling case may underestimate the true cost to consumers. At least two inefficiencies are not measured. One, consumers may spend a lot of time looking for rental units because vacancy rates will be very low—only Q_2 is available and consumers are willing to pay as much as P_2 for Q_2 units. Two, someone may have been lucky to find a rental unit at the ceiling price, P_{MAX}, but someone who values it more, say at P_2, may not be able to find a rental unit.

It is important to distinguish between deadweight loss, which measures the overall efficiency loss, and the

distribution of the gains and losses from a particular policy. For example, as a rent control tenant, you may be pleased with the outcome—a lower price than you would ordinarily pay (a transfer from landlord to tenant) providing that you can find a vacant rent-controlled unit.

Rent Controls—Short Run Versus Long Run

In the absence of rent control (a price ceiling), the equilibrium price is P_1 and the equilibrium quantity is Q_1, with no deadweight loss. However, a price ceiling leads to a deadweight loss, but the size of the deadweight loss depends on elasticity: The deadweight loss is greater in the short run (less elastic supply) than the long run (more elastic supply). Why? A city that enacts a rent control program will not lose many rental units in the next week. That is, even at lowered legal prices, roughly the same number of units will be available this week as last week; thus, in the short run the supply of rental units is virtually fixed—relatively inelastic, as seen in Exhibit 6(a). In the long run, however, the supply of rental units is much more elastic; landlords respond to the lower rental prices by allowing rental

section 7.2
exhibit 6   Deadweight Loss of Rent Control: Short Run vs. Long Run

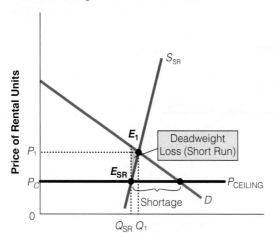

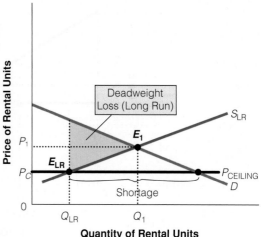

a. Deadweight Loss of Rent Control—Short Run

b. Deadweight Loss of Rent Control—Long Run

The reduction in rental units in response to the rent ceiling price P_c is much smaller in the short run (Q_1 to Q_{SR}) than in the long run (Q_1 to Q_{LR}). The deadweight loss is also much greater in the long run than in the short run, as indicated by the shaded areas in the two graphs. In addition, the size of the shortage is much greater in the long run than in the short run.

units to deteriorate and building fewer new rental units. In the long run, then, the supply curve is much more elastic, as seen in Exhibit 6(b). It is also true that demand becomes more elastic over time as buyers respond to the lower prices by looking for their own apartment (rather than sharing one) or moving to the city to try to rent an apartment below the equilibrium rental price. What economic implications do these varying elasticities have on rent control policies?

In Exhibit 6(a), only a small reduction in rental unit availability occurs in the short term as a result of the newly imposed rent control price—a move from Q_1 to Q_{SR}. The corresponding deadweight loss is small, indicated by the shaded area in Exhibit 6(a). However, the long-run response to the rent ceiling price is much larger: The quantity of rental units falls from Q_1 to Q_{LR}, and the size of the deadweight loss and the shortage are both larger, as seen in Exhibit 6(b). Hence, rent controls are much more harmful in the long run than the short run, from an efficiency standpoint.

Price Floors

Since the Great Depression, several agricultural programs have been promoted as assisting small-scale farmers. Such a price-support system guarantees a minimum price—promising a dairy farmer a price of

$4 per pound for cheese, for example. The reasoning is that the equilibrium price of $3 is too low and would not provide enough revenue for small-volume farmers to maintain a "decent" standard of living. A price floor sets a minimum price that is the lowest price a consumer can legally pay for a good.

The Welfare Effects of a Price Floor When the Government Buys the Surplus

Who gains and who loses under price-support programs when the government buys the surplus? In Exhibit 7, the equilibrium price and quantity without the price floor are at P_1 and Q_1, respectively. Without the price floor, consumer surplus is area a + b + c, and producer surplus is area e + f, for a total surplus of area a + b + c + e + f.

After the price floor is in effect, price rises to P_2; output falls to Q_2; consumer surplus falls from area a + b + c to area a, a loss of b + c; and producer surplus increases from area e + f to area b + c + d + e + f, a gain of area b + c + d. If those changes were the end of the story, we would say that producers gained (area b + c + d) more than consumers lost (area b + c), and, on net, society would benefit

QUANTIFYING CONSUMER AND PRODUCER SURPLUSES

You may recall from your geometry class that the area of a triangle is ½ base × height. Suppose the government imposes a price ceiling on wheat at $2 per bushel. Use the graph to answer the following questions: What would be the change in consumer surplus? In producer surplus? In the deadweight loss?

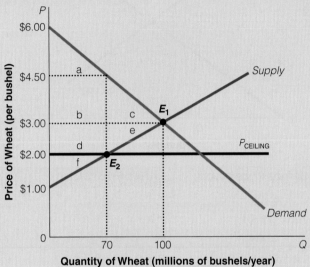

	No Ceiling	Ceiling	Change ($ millions)
Consumer Surplus	a + b + c	a + b + d	d − c = $47.50 ($70 − $22.50)
Producer Surplus	d + e + f	f	− d − e = − $85 (−$70 − $15)
Total Welfare (CS + PS)	a + b + c + d + e + f	a + b + d + f	− c − e = −$32.50

Suppose the government imposes a $0.50 per gallon gasoline tax. Use the graph to answer the following questions: How much is the annual revenue from the tax? How much is the loss to consumers and producers? How much is the deadweight loss?

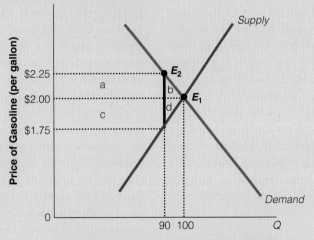

The total revenue from the tax is $45 billion ($0.50 × 90 billion gallons). This amount is also a cost to consumers and producers of $45 billion in tax revenues. The total loss to producers and consumers is larger than the revenues raised because consumers lose (a + b) and producers lose (c + d) and the government gains (a + c), so society is out the deadweight loss, or $2.5 billion per year [(½)($0.50) × 10 billion gallons per year].

section 7.2
exhibit 7 **Welfare Effects of a Price Floor When Government Buys the Surplus**

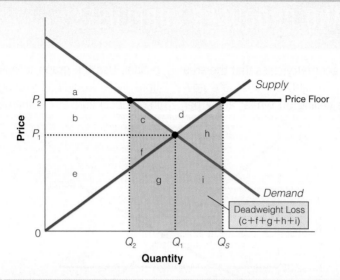

	Before Price Floor	**After Price Floor**	**Change**
Consumer Surplus	a + b + c	a	−b − c
Producer Surplus	e + f	b + c + d + e + f	b + c + d
Government (Taxpayers)	zero	−c − d − f − g − h − i	−c − d − f − g − h − i
Total Welfare	a + b + c + e + f	a + b + e −g − h − i	−c − f − g − h − i

After the price floor is implemented, the price rises to P_2 and output falls to Q_2; the result is a loss in consumer surplus of area b + c but a gain in producer surplus of area b + c + d. However, these changes are not the end of the story, because the cost to the government (taxpayers), area c + d + f + g + h + i, is greater than the gain to producers, area d, so the deadweight loss is area c + f + g + h + i.

by area d from the implementation of the price floor. However, those changes are *not* the end of the story. The government (taxpayers) must pay for the surplus it buys, area c + d + f + g + h + i. That is, the cost to government, area c + d + f + g + h + i, is greater than the gain to producers, area d. Assuming no alternative use of the surplus the government purchases, the result is a deadweight loss from the price floor of area c + f + g + h + i. Why? Consumers are consuming less than the previous market equilibrium output, eliminating mutually beneficial exchanges, while sellers are producing more than is being consumed, with the excess production stored, destroyed, or exported.

Deficiency Payment Program

Another possibility is the deficiency payment program. In Exhibit 8, if the government sets the target price at P_2, producers will supply Q_2 and sell all they can at the market price, P_M. The government then pays the producers a deficiency payment (DP)—the vertical distance between the price the producers receive, P_M, and the price they were guaranteed, P_2. Producer surplus increases from area c + d to area c + d + b + e, which is a gain of area b + e, because producers can sell a greater quantity at a higher price. Consumer surplus increases from area a + b to area a + b +c + g, which is a gain of area c + g, because consumers can buy a greater quantity at a lower price. The cost to government ($Q_2 \times$ DP), area b + e + f + c + g, is greater than the gains in producer and consumer surpluses (area b + e + c + g), and the deadweight loss is area f. The deadweight loss occurs because the program increases the output beyond the efficient level of output, Q_1. From Q_1 to Q_2, the marginal cost to sellers for producing the good (the height of the supply curve) is greater than the marginal benefit to consumers (the height of the demand curve).

Compare area f in Exhibit 8 with the much larger deadweight loss for price supports in Exhibit 7. The deficiency payment program does not lead to the production of crops that will not be consumed, or to the storage problem we saw with the previous price-support program in Exhibit 8.

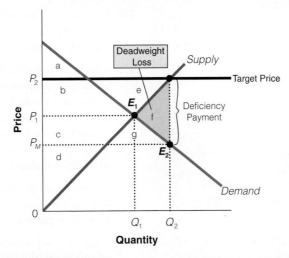

| section 7.2 exhibit 8 | Welfare Effects of a Deficiency Payment Plan |

	Before Plan	**After Plan**	**Change**
Consumer Surplus	a + b	a + b + c + g	c + g
Producer Surplus	c + d	c + d + b + e	b + e
Government (Taxpayers)	zero	−b − e − f − c − g	−b − e − f − c − g
Total Welfare (CS + PS − G)	a + b + c + d	a + b + c + d − f	−f

The cost to government (taxpayers), area b + e + f + c + g, is greater than the gains to producer and consumer surplus, area b + e + c + g. The deficiency payment program increases the output level beyond the efficient output level of Q_1. From Q_1 to Q_2, the marginal cost of producing the good (the height of the supply curve) is greater than the marginal benefit to the consumer (the height of the demand curve)—area f.

SECTION CHECK

1. Taxes distort market incentives—the price to buyers is higher than before the tax, so they are able to consume less and the price to sellers is lower than before the tax, so they produce less. This situation leads to deadweight loss, or market inefficiencies—the waste associated with not producing the efficient output.

2. The size of the deadweight loss from a tax, as well as how the burdens are shared between buyers and sellers, depends on the elasticities of supply and demand.

3. A price ceiling causes a deadweight loss because the efficient level of output is not produced.

4. A price floor causes a deadweight loss because consumers are consuming less than the efficient output, eliminating mutually beneficial exchanges, and sellers are producing more than is being consumed.

1. Could a tax be imposed without a welfare cost?

2. How does the elasticity of demand represent the ability of buyers to "dodge" a tax?

3. If both supply and demand were highly elastic, how large would the effect be on the quantity exchanged, the tax revenue, and the welfare costs of a tax?

4. What impact would a larger tax have on trade in the market? What will happen to the size of the deadweight loss?

5. What would be the effect of a price ceiling?

6. What would be the effect of a price floor if the government does not buy up the surplus?

7. What causes the welfare cost of subsidies?

8. Why does a deficiency payment program have the same welfare cost analysis as a subsidy?

Interactive Chapter Summary

Fill in the blanks:

1. The monetary difference between the price a consumer is willing and able to pay for an additional unit of a good and the price the consumer actually pays is called _____.

2. We can think of the demand curve as a _____ curve.

3. Consumer surplus for the whole market is shown graphically as the area under the market _____ (willingness to pay for the units consumed) and above the _____ (what must be paid for those units).

4. A lower market price due to an increase in supply will _____ consumer surplus.

5. A _____ is the difference between what a producer is paid for a good and the cost of producing that unit of the good.

6. We can think of the supply curve as a _____ curve.

7. Part of the added producer surplus when the price rises as a result of an increase in demand is due to a higher price for the quantity _____ being produced, and part is due to the expansion of _____ made profitable by the higher price.

8. The demand curve represents a collection of _____ prices that consumers are willing and able to pay for additional quantities of a good or service, while the supply curve represents a collection of _____ prices that suppliers require to be willing to supply additional quantities of that good or service.

9. The total welfare gain to the economy from trade in a good is the sum of the _____ and _____ created.

10. In competitive markets, with large numbers of buyers and sellers at the market equilibrium price and quantity, the net gains to society are _____ as possible.

11. After a tax is imposed, consumers pay a(n) _____ price and lose the corresponding amount of consumer surplus as a result. Producers receive a _____ price after tax and lose the corresponding amount of producer surplus as a result. The government _____ the amount of the tax revenue generated, which is transferred to others in society.

12. The size of the deadweight loss from a tax, as well as how the burdens are shared between buyers and sellers, depends on the relative _____.

13. When there is a subsidy, the market _____ relative to the efficient level of output.

14. Because the _____ leads to the production of more than the efficient level of output, a _____ results.

15. With a _____, any possible gain to consumers will be more than offset by the losses to producers.

16. With a price floor where the government buys up the surplus, the cost to the government is _____ than the gain to _____.

17. With no alternative use of the government purchases from a price floor, a _____ will result because consumers are consuming _____ than the previous market equilibrium output and sellers are producing _____ than is being consumed.

18. With a deficiency payment program, the deadweight loss is _____ than with an agricultural price support program when the government buys the surplus.

Answers: 1. consumer surplus 2. marginal benefit 3. demand curve; market price 4. increase 5. producer surplus 6. marginal cost 7. already; output 8. maximum; minimum 9. consumer surplus; producer surplus 10. as large 11. higher; lower; gains 12. elasticities of supply and demand 13. overproduces 14. subsidy; deadweight loss 15. price ceiling 16. greater; producers 17. deadweight loss; less; more 18. smaller

Key Terms and Concepts

consumer surplus 183

producer surplus 185

marginal cost 185

total welfare gains 186

deadweight loss 188

welfare effects 190

Section Check Answers

7.1 Consumer Surplus and Producer Surplus

1. What is consumer surplus?

Consumer surplus is defined as the monetary difference between what a consumer is willing to pay for a good and what the consumer is required to pay for it.

2. Why do the earlier units consumed at a given price add more consumer surplus than the later units consumed?

Because what a consumer is willing to pay for a good declines as more of that good is consumed, the difference between what he is willing to pay and the price he must pay also declines for later units.

3. Why does a decrease in a good's price increase the consumer surplus from consumption of that good?

A decrease in a good's price increases the consumer surplus from consumption of that good by lowering the price for those goods that were bought at the higher price and by increasing consumer surplus from increased purchases at the lower price.

4. Why might the consumer surplus from purchases of diamond rings be less than the consumer surplus from purchases of far less expensive stones?

Consumer surplus is the difference between what people would have been willing to pay for the amount of the good consumed and what they must pay. Even though the marginal value of less expensive stones is lower than the marginal value of a diamond ring to buyers, the difference between the total value of the far larger number of less expensive stones purchased and what consumers had to pay may well be larger than that difference for diamond rings.

5. What is producer surplus?

Producer surplus is defined as the monetary difference between what a producer is paid for a good and the producer's cost.

6. Why do the earlier units produced at a given price add more producer surplus than the later units produced?

Because the earlier (lowest cost) units can be produced at a cost that is lower than the market price, but the cost of producing additional units rises, the earlier units produced at a given price add more producer surplus than the later units produced.

7. Why does an increase in a good's price increase the producer surplus from production of that good?

An increase in a good's price increases the producer surplus from production of that good because it results in a higher price for the quantity already being produced and because the expansion in output in response to the higher price also increases profits.

8. Why might the producer surplus from sales of diamond rings, which are expensive, be less than the producer surplus from sales of far less expensive stones?

Producer surplus is the difference between what a producer is paid for a good and the producer's cost. Even though the price, or marginal value, of a less expensive stone is lower than the price, or marginal value of a diamond ring to buyers, the difference between the total that sellers receive for those stones in revenue and the producer's cost of the far larger number of less expensive stones produced may well be larger than that difference for diamond rings.

9. Why is the efficient level of output in an industry defined as the output where the sum of consumer and producer surplus is maximized?

The sum of consumer surplus plus producer surplus measures the total welfare gains from trade in an industry, and the most efficient level of output is the one that maximizes the total welfare gains.

10. Why does a reduction in output below the efficient level create a deadweight loss?

A reduction in output below the efficient level eliminates trades whose benefits would have exceeded their costs; the resulting loss in consumer surplus and producer surplus is a deadweight loss.

11. Why does an expansion in output beyond the efficient level create a deadweight loss?

An expansion in output beyond the efficient level involves trades whose benefits are less than their costs; the resulting loss in consumer surplus and producer surplus is a deadweight loss.

7.2 The Welfare Effects of Taxes, Subsidies, and Price Controls

1. Could a tax be imposed without a welfare cost?

A tax would not impose a welfare cost only if the quantity exchanged did not change as a result—only when supply was perfectly inelastic or in the nonexistent case where the demand curve was perfectly inelastic. In all other cases, a tax would create a welfare cost by eliminating some mutually beneficial trades (and the wealth they would have created) that would otherwise have taken place.

2. **How does the elasticity of demand represent the ability of buyers to "dodge" a tax?**

The elasticity of demand represents the ability of buyers to "dodge" a tax, because it represents how easily buyers could shift their purchases into other goods. If it is relatively low cost to consumers to shift out of buying a particular good when a tax is imposed on it—that is, demand is relatively elastic—they can dodge much of the burden of the tax by shifting their purchases to other goods. If it is relatively high cost to consumers to shift out of buying a particular good when a tax is imposed on it—that is, demand is relatively inelastic—they cannot dodge much of the burden of the tax by shifting their purchases to other goods.

3. **If both supply and demand were highly elastic, how large would the effect be on the quantity exchanged, the tax revenue, and the welfare costs of a tax?**

The more elastic are supply and/or demand, the larger the change in the quantity exchanged that would result from a given tax. Given that tax revenue equals the tax per unit times the number of units traded after the imposition of a tax, the smaller after-tax quantity traded would reduce the tax revenue raised, other things equal. Because the greater change in the quantity traded wipes out more mutually beneficial trades than if demand and/or supply was more inelastic, the welfare cost in such a case would also be greater, other things equal.

4. **What impact would a larger tax have on trade in the market? What will happen to the size of the deadweight loss?**

A larger tax creates a larger wedge between the price including tax paid by consumers and the price net of tax received by producers, resulting in a greater increase in prices paid by consumers and a greater decrease in price received by producers, and the laws of supply and demand imply that the quantity exchanged falls more as a result. The number of mutually beneficial trades eliminated will be greater and the consequent welfare cost will be greater as a result.

5. **What would be the effect of a price ceiling?**

A price ceiling reduces the quantity exchanged, because the lower regulated price reduces the quantity sellers are willing to sell. This lower quantity causes a welfare cost equal to the net gains from those exchanges that no longer take place. However, that price ceiling would also redistribute income, harming sellers, increasing the well-being of those who remain able to buy successfully at the lower price, and decreasing the well-being of those who can no longer buy successfully at the lower price.

6. **What would be the effect of a price floor if the government does not buy up the surplus?**

Just as in the case of a tax, a price floor where the government does not buy up the surplus reduces the quantity exchanged, thus causing a welfare cost equal to the net gains from the exchanges that no longer take place. However, that price floor would also redistribute income, harming buyers, increasing the incomes of those who remain able to sell successfully at the higher price, and decreasing the incomes of those who can no longer sell successfully at the higher price.

7. **What causes the welfare cost of subsidies?**

Subsidies cause people to produce units of output whose benefits (without the subsidy) are less than the costs, reducing the total gains from trade.

8. **Why does a deficiency payment program have the same welfare cost analysis as a subsidy?**

Both tend to increase output beyond the efficient level, so that units whose benefits (without the subsidy) are less than the costs, reducing the total gains from trade in the same way; further, the dollar cost of the deficiency payments are equal to the dollar amount of taxes necessary to finance the subsidy, in the case where each increases production the same amount.

True or False:

1. A lower price will increase your consumer surplus for each of the units you were already consuming and will also increase your consumer surplus from increased purchases at the lower price.

2. Because some units can be produced at a cost that is lower than the market price, the seller receives a surplus, or net benefit, from producing those units.

3. Producer surplus is shown graphically as the area under the demand curve and above the supply curve.

4. If the market price of a good falls as a result of a decrease in demand, additional producer surplus is generated.

5. At the market equilibrium, both consumers and producers benefit from trading every unit up to the market equilibrium output.

6. Once the equilibrium output is reached at the equilibrium price, all of the mutually beneficial trade opportunities between the suppliers and the demanders will have taken place, and the sum of consumer and producer surplus is maximized.

7. The deadweight loss of a tax is the difference between the lost consumer and producer surpluses and the tax revenue generated.

8. The deadweight loss of a tax occurs because the tax reduces the quantity exchanged below the original output level, reducing the size of the total surplus realized from trade.

9. Other things being equal, the more elastic the demand curve or the more elastic the supply curve, the smaller the deadweight loss of a tax.

10. If either the supply or demand curve becomes more inelastic, a given tax will reduce the quantity exchanged by a greater amount.

11. Those goods that are heavily taxed often have a relatively inelastic demand curve in the short run, so the burden falls mainly on the buyer, and the deadweight loss to society is smaller than if the demand curve were more elastic.

12. Consumers never benefit from a binding price ceiling.

13. Any possible gains to consumers are more than offset by losses to producers when a binding price ceiling is in place.

14. With an agricultural price-support program where the government buys up the surplus, a net benefit is realized because the benefits to producers are greater than the cost to consumers.

15. The deadweight loss is greater in an agricultural price-support program than in a deficiency payment plan.

Multiple Choice:

1. In a supply and demand graph, the triangular area under the demand curve but above the market price is
   a. the consumer surplus.
   b. the producer surplus.
   c. the marginal cost.
   d. the deadweight loss.
   e. the net gain to society from trading that good.

   Use the following demand schedule to answer questions 2 and 3.
   Fred's demand schedule for DVDs is as follows: At $30 each, he would buy 1; at $25, he would buy 2; at $15, he would buy 3; and at $10, he would buy 4.

2. If the price of DVDs is $20, the consumer surplus Fred receives from purchasing two DVDs would be
   a. $10.
   b. $15.
   c. $20.
   d. $55.
   e. $90.

3. If the price of DVDs is $25, the consumer surplus Fred receives from purchasing one DVD would be
   a. $0.
   b. $5.
   c. $25.
   d. $55.
   e. $70.

4. Which of the following is not true about consumer surplus?
   a. Consumer surplus is the difference between what consumers are willing to pay and what they actually pay.
   b. Consumer surplus is shown graphically as the area under the demand curve but above the market price.
   c. An increase in the market price due to a decrease in supply will increase consumer surplus.
   d. A decrease in market price due to an increase in supply will increase consumer surplus.

5. Which of the following is not true about producer surplus?
   a. Producer surplus is the difference between what sellers are paid and their cost of producing those units.
   b. Producer surplus is shown graphically as the area under the market price but above the supply curve.
   c. An increase in the market price due to an increase in demand will increase producer surplus.
   d. All of the above are true about producer surplus.

6. At the market equilibrium price and quantity, the total welfare gains from trade are measured by
   a. the total consumer surplus captured by consumers.
   b. the total producer surplus captured by producers.
   c. the sum of consumer surplus and producer surplus.
   d. the consumer surplus minus the producer surplus.

7. In a supply and demand graph, the triangular area under the demand curve but above the supply curve is
   a. the consumer surplus.
   b. the producer surplus.
   c. the marginal cost.
   d. the deadweight loss.
   e. the net gain to society from trading that good.

8. In a supply and demand graph, the triangular area between the demand curve and the supply curve lost because of the imposition of a tax, price ceiling, or price floor is
   a. the consumer surplus.
   b. the producer surplus.
   c. the marginal cost.
   d. the deadweight loss.
   e. the net gain to society from trading that good.

9. Taxes on goods with _____ demand curves will tend to raise more tax revenue for the government than taxes on goods with _____ demand curves.
   a. elastic; unit elastic
   b. elastic; inelastic
   c. inelastic; elastic
   d. unit elastic; inelastic

10. After the imposition of a tax,
    a. consumers pay a higher price, including the tax.
    b. consumers lose consumer surplus.
    c. producers receive a lower price after taxes.
    d. producers lose producer surplus.
    e. all of the above occur.

11. Other things being equal, for a given tax, if the demand curve is less elastic,
    a. the greater the tax revenue raised and the greater the deadweight cost of the tax.
    b. the greater the tax revenue raised and the smaller the deadweight cost of the tax.
    c. the less the tax revenue raised and the greater the deadweight cost of the tax.
    d. the less the tax revenue raised and the smaller the deadweight cost of the tax.

12. An increase in a subsidy will increase
    a. consumer surplus.
    b. producer surplus.
    c. the deadweight loss.
    d. all of the above.

13. With a subsidy,
    a. the price producers receive is the price consumers pay plus the subsidy.
    b. the subsidy leads to the production of more than the efficient level of output.
    c. there is a deadweight loss.
    d. all of the above are true.

14. The longer the time people have to adjust to a tax, the _____ revenue it will raise and the _____ quantity traded will fall.
    a. more; more
    b. more; less
    c. less; more
    d. less; less

15. A permanent increase in price would tend to decrease the consumer surplus by _____ or increase the producer surplus by _____ in the long run than in the short run.
    a. more; more
    b. more; less
    c. less; more
    d. less; less

16. In the case of a price floor, if the government buys up the surplus,
    a. consumer surplus decreases.
    b. producer surplus increases.
    c. a greater deadweight loss occurs than with a deficiency payment system.
    d. all of the above are true.

17. The longer a price ceiling is left below the equilibrium price in a market, the _____ is the reduction in the quantity exchanged and the _____ is the resulting deadweight loss.
    a. greater; greater
    b. greater; smaller
    c. smaller; greater
    d. smaller; smaller

18. With a deficiency payment program,
    a. the government sets the target price at the equilibrium price.
    b. producer and consumer surplus falls.
    c. there is a deadweight loss because the program increases the output beyond the efficient level of output.
    d. all of the above are true.

Problems:

1. Refer to the following exhibit.

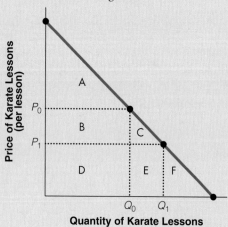

Quantity of Karate Lessons

a. If the price of each karate lesson is P_0, the consumer surplus is equal to what area?
b. If the price falls from P_0 to P_1, the change in consumer surplus is equal to what area?

2. Steve loves potato chips. His weekly demand curve is shown in the following exhibit.

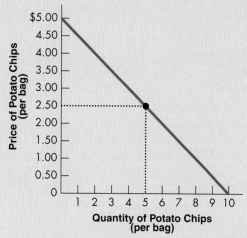

Quantity of Potato Chips (per bag)

a. How much is Steve willing to pay for one bag of potato chips?
b. How much is Steve willing to pay for a second bag of potato chips?
c. If the actual market price of potato chips is $2.50, and Steve buys five bags as shown, what is the value of his consumer surplus?
d. What is Steve's total willingness to pay for five bags?

3. If a freeze ruined this year's lettuce crop, show what would happen to consumer surplus.

4. If demand for apples increased as a result of a news story that highlighted the health benefits of two apples a day, what would happen to producer surplus?

5. How is total surplus (the sum of consumer and producer surpluses) related to the efficient level of output? Using a supply and demand curve, demonstrate that producing less than the equilibrium output will lead to an inefficient allocation of resources—a deadweight loss.

6. If the government's goal is to raise tax revenue, which of the following are good markets to tax?
   a. luxury yachts
   b. alcohol
   c. movies
   d. gasoline
   e. grapefruit juice

7. Which of the following do you think are good markets for the government to tax if the goal is to boost tax revenue? Which will lead to the least amount of deadweight loss? Why?
   a. luxury yachts
   b. alcohol
   c. motor homes
   d. cigarettes
   e. gasoline
   f. pizza

8. Elasticity of demand in the market for one-bedroom apartments is 2.0, elasticity of supply is 0.5, the current market price is $1,000, and the equilibrium number of one-bedroom apartments is 10,000. If the government imposes a price ceiling of $800 on this market, predict the size of the resulting apartment shortage.

9. Use the diagram to answer the following questions (a–d).

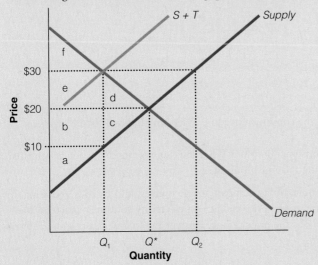

   a. At the equilibrium price before the tax is imposed, what area represents consumer surplus? What area represents producer surplus?
   b. Say that a tax of $T per unit is imposed in the industry. What area now represents consumer surplus? What area represents producer surplus?
   c. What area represents the deadweight cost of the tax?
   d. What area represents how much tax revenue is raised by the tax?

10. Use consumer and producer surplus to show the deadweight loss from a subsidy (producing more than the equilibrium output). (*Hint:* Remember that taxpayers will have to pay for the subsidy.)

11. Use the diagram to answer the following questions (a–c).

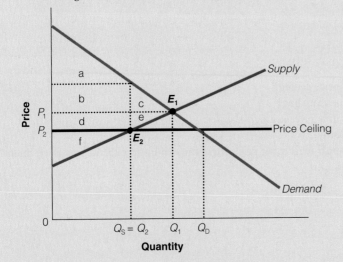

a. At the initial equilibrium price, what area represents consumer surplus? What area represents producer surplus?

b. After the price ceiling is imposed, what area represents consumer surplus? What area represents producer surplus?

c. What area represents the deadweight loss cost of the price ceiling?

12. Use the diagram to answer the following questions (a–c).

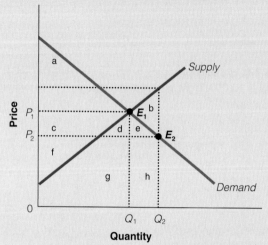

a. At the competitive output, Q_1, what area represents the consumer surplus? What area represents the producer surplus?

b. At the larger output, Q_2, what area represents the consumer surplus? What area represents the producer surplus?

c. What area represents the deadweight loss of producing too much output?

13. The 2000–2001 California energy crisis produced brownouts, utility company bankruptcies, and worries about high prices. The California electric power regulatory program imposed price ceilings on electricity sold to consumers. The following exhibit describes the California situation with P_S as the price ceiling. Answer the following questions referring to this exhibit.

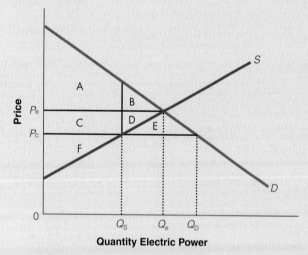

a. What was the loss imposed on consumers by this price ceiling?

b. What was the loss imposed on producers by this price ceiling?

c. What was the total loss imposed on California by this price ceiling?

d. Using this exhibit, explain the brownouts in California.

e. What would have to be true for consumers to support market set prices? Use the exhibit to explain why there might not be support among consumers for raising prices.

Market Failure

In the last several chapters, we concluded that markets are efficient. But we made some assumptions about how markets work. If these assumptions do not hold, our conclusion about efficiency may be flawed.

What are the assumptions?

First, in our model of supply and demand, we assumed that markets are perfectly competitive—many buyers and sellers exchanging similar goods in an environment where buyers and sellers can easily enter and exit the market. This is not always true. In some markets, few firms may have control over the market price. When firms can control the market price, we say that they have market power. This market power can cause inefficiency because it will lead to higher prices and lower quantities than the competitive solution.

Sometimes the market system fails to produce efficient outcomes because of side effects economists call *externalities*. With *positive externalities*, the private market supplies too little of the good in question (such as education). In the case of *negative externalities* (such as pollution), the market supplies too much.

Another possible source of market failure is that competitive markets provide less than the efficient quantity of public goods. A public good is a good or service that someone can consume simultaneously with everyone else even if he or she doesn't pay for it. For example, everyone enjoys the benefits of national defense and yet it would be difficult to exclude anyone from receiving these benefits. The problem is that if consumers know it is too difficult to exclude them, then they could avoid paying their share of the public good (take a free ride), and producers would find it unprofitable to provide the good. Therefore, the government provides important public goods such as national defense.

Many economists believe that asymmetric information can cause market failures. *Asymmetric information* is a situation where some people know what other people don't know. This can lead to adverse selection where an informed party benefits in an exchange by taking advantage of knowing more than the other party. ■

Externalities

* What is a negative externality?
* How are negative externalities internalized?

* What is a positive externality?
* How are positive externalities internalized?

Even if the economy is competitive, it is still possible that the market system fails to produce the efficient level of output because of side effects economists call **externalities**. With **positive externalities**, the private market supplies too little of the good in question (such as education). In the case of **negative externalities** (such as pollution), the market supplies too much. Both types of externalities are caused by economic agents—producers and consumers—receiving the wrong signals. That is, the free market works well in providing most goods but does less well without regulations, taxes, and subsidies in providing others.

> **externality**
> a benefit or cost from consumption or production that spills over onto those who are not consuming or producing the good
>
> **positive externality**
> occurs when benefits spill over to an outside party who is not involved in producing or consuming the good
>
> **negative externality**
> occurs when costs spill over to an outside party who is not involved in producing or consuming the good

Negative Externalities in Production

The classic example of a negative externality in production is air pollution from a factory, such as a steel mill. If the firm uses clean air in production and returns dirty air to the atmosphere, it creates a negative externality. The polluted air "spills over" to outside parties. Now people in the neighboring communities may experience higher incidences of disease, dirtier houses, and other property damage. Such damages are real costs; but because no one owns the air, the firm does not have to pay for its use, unlike the other resources the firm uses in production. A steel mill pays for labor, capital, energy, and raw materials because it must compensate the owners of those inputs for their use. If a firm can avoid paying the costs it imposes on others—the external costs—it has lowered its own costs of production, but not the true costs to society.

Examples of negative externalities are numerous: the roommate who plays his stereo too loud at 2:00 A.M., the neighbor's dog that barks all night long or leaves "messages" on your front lawn, or the gardener

who runs her leaf blower on full power at 7:00 A.M. on a Saturday. Driving our cars may be another area in which people don't bear the full costs of their choices. We pay the price to purchase cars, as well as to maintain, insure, and fuel them—those are the private costs. But do we pay for all of our external costs such as emissions, congestion, wear and tear on our highways, and the possible harm to those driving in cars smaller than ours?

Graphing Negative External Costs in Production

Let's take a look at the steel industry. In Exhibit 1, we see the market for steel. Notice that at each level of output, the first supply curve, S_{PRIVATE}, is lower than the second, S_{SOCIAL}. The reason is simple: S_{PRIVATE} only includes the private costs to the firm—the capital, entrepreneurship, land, and labor for which it must pay. However, S_{SOCIAL} includes all of these costs, plus the external costs that production imposes on others. If the firm could somehow be required to compensate society for the damage it causes, the cost of production for the firm would increase and would shift the supply curve to the left. That is, the true social cost of producing steel is represented by S_{SOCIAL} in Exhibit 1. The equilibrium at P_2 and Q_2 is efficient. The market equilibrium is not efficient because the true supply curve is above the demand curve at Q_1. At Q_1 the marginal benefits (point a) are less than the marginal cost (point b) and society would be better off if the firm produced less steel. The deadweight loss from overproduction is measured by the shaded area in Exhibit 1. From society's standpoint, Q_2 is the efficient level of output because it represents all the costs (private plus external costs) associated with the production of this good. If the suppliers of steel are not aware of or not responsible for the external costs, they will tend to produce too much, Q_1 from society's standpoint and efficiency would be improved if less were produced.

section 8.1 exhibit 1
Negative Externalities in Production

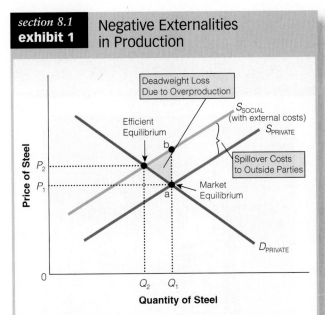

When a negative externality in production is present, firms do not bear the full cost of their actions, and they will produce more than the efficient level of output: Q_1 rather than Q_2. $S_{PRIVATE}$ reflects the private cost of the firm. S_{SOCIAL} reflects the private costs plus the external (or spillover) costs that the steel production imposes on others. If the supply curve is $S_{PRIVATE}$, the market equilibrium is at P_1 and Q_1. This level is not efficient and leads to a deadweight loss—the shaded area. However, when the supply curve is S_{SOCIAL}, then the equilibrium occurs at P_2 and Q_2, which is the efficient equilibrium.

In the United States, people deposit large amounts of solid waste as litter on beaches, campgrounds, highways, and vacant lots. Some of this litter is removed by government agencies, and some of it biodegrades over many years. Several solutions are possible for the litter problem. Stiffer fines and penalties and more aggressive monitoring could be employed. Alternatively, through education and civic pride, individuals and groups could be encouraged to pick up trash.

What Can the Government Do to Correct for Negative Externalities?

The government can intervene in market decisions in an attempt to take account of these negative externalities. It may do this by estimating the amount of those external costs and then taxing the manufacturer by that amount, forcing the manufacturer to internalize (bear) the costs.

Pollution Taxes

Pollution taxes are designed to internalize negative externalities. If government could impose a pollution tax equal to the exact size of the external cost, then the firm would produce the efficient level of output, Q_2. That is, the tax would shift the supply curve for steel leftward to S_{SOCIAL} and would provide an incentive for the firm to produce at the socially optimum level of output. Additionally, tax revenues would be generated that could be used to compensate those who had suffered damage from the pollution or in some other productive way.

Regulation

Alternatively, the government could use regulation. The government might simply prohibit certain types of activities that cause pollution or force firms to adopt a specific technology to reduce their emissions. However, regulators, would have to know the best available technology for each and every industry. The purchase and use of new pollution-control devices will increase the cost of production and shift the supply curve to the left, from $S_{PRIVATE}$ to S_{SOCIAL}.

Which Is Better—Pollution Tax or Regulation?

Most economists agree that a pollution tax, or a corrective tax, is more efficient than regulation. The pollution tax is good because it gets rid of the externality and moves society closer to the efficient level of output. The tax also gives firms an incentive to find and apply new technology to further reduce pollution levels in their plant and consequently lower the tax they would have to pay. Under regulation, a firm has little incentive to further reduce emissions once it reaches the predetermined level set by the regulated standard.

For example, a gas tax is a form of pollution tax: It helps reduce the externalities of pollution and congestion. The higher the tax, the fewer the vehicles on the road, the fewer miles driven, and the more fuel efficient

global WATCH
LONDON TOLLS ARE A TAXING PROBLEM FOR DRIVERS

The mayor of London [recently set a fee of over $8.00 for driving in the city center] on weekdays between 7 A.M. and 6:30 P.M. The aim of the plan. . . is to ease congestion, not drive all the cars from the road.

Consider the following:

✻ Vehicles in central London move no faster today than horse-drawn vehicles did 100 years ago. . . .

✻ Estimates of the economic costs—in lost time, wasted fuel, and increased vehicle operating costs—tend to be in the range of 2 to 4 percent of the gross domestic product.

No city has attempted a scheme with anything like the size, scale, and complexity of the London congestion charge:

✻ About 50 million vehicle miles are traveled in London every day.

✻ Motorists will have to pay to drive into or inside an area roughly 10 square miles around the City (the financial district) and the West End.

✻ The zone will be policed by hundreds of fixed mobile cameras, which will automatically pick up vehicles' license plates.

✻ Computers will match the registrations with a database of drivers who have paid in advance. . . .

[Hopefully,] the scheme will cut traffic in the zone by 10–15 percent, reduce delays by 20–30 percent, and raise about $210,700,000 a year to invest in public transport and road schemes.

SOURCE: National Center for Policy Analysis, "London Tolls Are a Taxing Problem for Drivers," synopsis of "Economists Agree That the Best Way to Tackle the Growing Problem of Overcrowded Roads Is to Introduce Tolls at Peak Times," by Chris Giles and Juliette Joweit (*Financial Times,* 13 February 2003). 14 February 2003; http://ncpa.org/iss/pri/2003/pd021403d.html

PHOTODISC

consider this:

If a road is crowded, it creates a negative externality. That is, when one person enters a road, all other people must drive a little more slowly. Highway space is overused because we pay so little for it. At least at some particular times—at rush hours, for example—if we charge a zero money price, a shortage of highway space will result. A toll raises the price and brings the market closer to equilibrium as seen in Exhibit 2.

---

section 8.1
exhibit 2   A Shortage of Freeway Space During Peak Hours

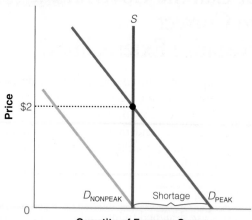

Quantity of Freeway Space

The supply of highway space is fixed in the short run, so the supply curve is perfectly inelastic. The demand varies during the day considerably. For example, the demand at peak hours (7 A.M.–8:30 A.M. and 4:00 P.M.–6:30 P.M.) is much higher than at nonpeak hours. At some price, the shortage during peak hours will disappear. In this example, it is at $2.

vehicles purchased, each of which leads to less congestion and pollution. Therefore, the pollution tax, unlike other taxes, can enhance economic efficiency while generating revenue for the government.

Positive Externalities in Consumption

Unlike negative externalities, positive externalities benefit others. For some goods, the individual consumer receives all the benefits. If you buy a hamburger, for example, you get all its benefits. On the other hand, consider education. This is a positive externality in consumption whose benefits extend beyond the individual consumer of education. Certainly, when you "buy" an education, you receive many of its benefits: greater future income, more choice of future occupations, and the consumption value of knowing more about life as a result of classroom (and extracurricular) learning. However, these benefits, great as they may be, are not all the benefits associated with your education. You may be less likely to be unemployed or commit crimes; you may end up curing cancer or solving some other social problem. These nontrivial benefits are the positive external benefits of education.

Many economists like the gas tax because it is easy to collect, difficult for users to avoid, and encourages fuel economy. It puts the tax on highway users. But completely internalizing the externality may cost an additional $2 a gallon; the national average gas tax is $0.50. In England, the gas tax is over $3 per gallon. It is much more efficient to pay for transportation improvements by using a gas tax than a sales tax because it associates the tax with those who are creating the externality.

The government frequently subsidizes education. Why? Presumably because the private market does not provide enough. It is argued that the education of a person benefits not only that person but all society, because a more informed citizenry can make more intelligent collective decisions, which benefits everyone. Public health departments sometimes offer "free" inoculations against certain communicable diseases, such as influenza, because by protecting one group of citizens, everyone gets some protection; if one citizen is prevented from getting the disease, that person cannot pass it on to others. Many governmental efforts in the field of health and education are justified on the basis of positive externalities. Of course, because positive externalities are often difficult to measure, it is hard to demonstrate empirically whether many governmental education and health programs achieve their intended purposes.

In short, the presence of positive externalities interferes with reaching economic efficiency because of the tendency for the market to underallocate (produce too little) of this good.

Graphing Positive External Benefits of Consumption

Let's take the case of a new vaccine against the common cold. The market for the vaccine is shown in Exhibit 3. The demand curve, $D_{PRIVATE}$, represents the prices and quantities that buyers would be willing to pay in the private market to reduce their probability of catching the common cold. The supply curve shows the amounts that suppliers would offer for sale at different prices. However, at the equilibrium market output, Q_1, the output of vaccinations falls far short of the efficient level, Q_2. Why? Many people benefit from the vaccines, including those who do not have to pay for them; they are now less likely to be infected because others took the vaccine. If we could add the benefits derived by nonpaying consumers, the demand curve would shift to the right, from $D_{PRIVATE}$ to D_{SOCIAL}. The greater level of output, Q_2, that would result if D_{SOCIAL} were the observed demand reflects the efficient output level.

The market equilibrium at P_1 and Q_1 is not efficient because D_{SOCIAL} is above $D_{PRIVATE}$ for all levels of output between Q_1 and Q_2. That is, at Q_1 the marginal benefits (D_{SOCIAL}) at point b are greater than the marginal cost (S_{SOCIAL}) at point a. Consequently, a deadweight loss is associated with the underproduction. In short, too little of the good is produced. Because producers are unable to collect payments from all those who benefit

section 8.1 exhibit 3   Positive Externalities in Consumption

The private demand curve plus external benefits is presented as the demand curve D_{SOCIAL}. This demand curve is to the right of the private demand curve, $D_{PRIVATE}$. At Q_1 the marginal benefits (point b) are greater than the marginal cost (point a) leading to a deadweight loss—the shaded area. The market equilibrium output, Q_1, falls short of the efficient level of output, Q_2. The market produces too little of the good or service.

from the good or service, the market has a tendency to underproduce. In this case, the market is not producing enough vaccinations from society's standpoint and an *underallocation* of resources occurs.

What Can the Government Do to Correct for Positive Externalities?

How could society correct for this market failure? Two particular methods of achieving the higher preferred output are subsidies and regulation.

Subsidies

Government could provide a subsidy—either give refunds to individuals who receive an inoculation or provide an incentive for businesses to give their employees "free" inoculations at the office. If the subsidy was exactly equal to the external benefit of inoculation, the demand curve would shift from $D_{PRIVATE}$ to D_{SOCIAL}, resulting in an efficient level of output, Q_2.

Regulation

The government could also pass a regulation requiring each person to get an inoculation. This approach would also shift the demand curve rightward toward the efficient level of output.

In summary, with positive externalities, the private market supplies too little of the good in question (such as education or inoculations for communicable diseases). In the case of negative externalities, the market supplies too much. In either case, buyers and sellers are receiving the wrong signals. The producers and consumers are not doing what they do because they are evil; rather, whether well-intentioned or ill-intentioned, they are behaving according to the incentives they face. The free market, then, works fine in providing most goods, but it functions less well without regulations, taxes, and subsidies in providing others.

Nongovernmental Solutions to Externalities

Sometimes the externality problems can be handled by individuals without the intervention of government, and people may decide to take steps on their own

These types of systems use a hidden radio transmitter to help owners retrieve their stolen cars. If the devices also help law enforcement break up rings of car thieves, they will have spillover benefits (positive externalities) for car owners who do not own the devices, because they will reduce the probability of their cars being stolen.

Sometimes it is difficult to enforce statutes that are designed to reduce negative externalities such as drunk driving. In this case, police officers are soliciting the public's help. However, the sign is a bit confusing. Perhaps the sign should say "To Report a Drunk Driver—Call 911."

in the news   Outlawing Text Messaging While Driving— Legislators in Several States Respond to Safety Concerns

—BY BRET SCHULTE

Suddenly, those drivers talking on their cellphones seem relatively harmless, at least when compared to drivers who are staring at their cellphones, texting. An estimated 20 percent of drivers are sending or receiving text messages while behind the wheel, according to a Nationwide Insurance study. And, according to another poll, that number skyrockets to 66 percent when drivers 18 to 24 are isolated. The practice, especially popular among young people, is exacting a deadly toll.

No one knows how many vehicular crashes are related to drivers distracted by text messaging, but anecdotal evidence is mounting. A fiery crash made headlines in June when five female friends died in a collision with a tractor trailer just a week after graduating from their suburban Rochester, N.Y., high school. Police discovered the teenage driver had been texting moments before the crash. Similar accidents are happening with increasingly regularity nationwide.

Now, at least 16 states are considering legislation that would outlaw or restrict the practice. "Certainly, texting is the issue du jour this year in the legislatures," says Matt Sundeen of the National Conference of State Legislatures. That means another fight over the role of National Conference of State Legislatures. That means another fight over the role of government in regulating cellphone use, but it's one that proponents of new laws expect to win. Indeed, a Harris Interactive Poll from August shows 9 out of 10 American adults believe that sending text messages or E-mails while driving is "distracting, dangerous, and should be outlawed."

Only two states expressly prohibit texting while driving. Washington banned the practice last May, and New Jersey followed suit in November. Similar bills are now in the works in Delaware, Florida, Hawaii, Iowa, Kansas, Kentucky, Maryland, Massachusetts, Michigan, New Hampshire, New York, Ohio, Rhode Island, Tennessee, Virginia, and West Virginia.

Sundeen cites two reasons for the proposed legislation: the growing sophistication of cellphones that are increasingly catered to texting and, perhaps more important, the growing number of "high-profile accidents—and those always tend to translate into legislation."

In Iowa, Democratic Rep. McKinley Bailey proposed a texting ban that would target only beginning drivers, ages 16 and 17. He wrote the bill because of several text-related accidents after the last legislative session ended. Not everyone was for it. The ACLU called it discriminatory against young people, and Bailey received some phone calls from people who saw the ban as "an erosion of freedom," he says. Some Republicans are also trying to muster opposition. But, he notes, "overall, the response was positive." In fact, party leaders liked it so well that they're rewriting the bill to include a texting ban on drivers of all ages.

Experts say anti-texting laws are following on the heels of a wave of more general bans on the use of cellphones while driving. Five states already prohibit all drivers from using hand-held phones, and 24 more have considered similar legislation. Several states have such restrictions for younger drivers.

consider this:

Many would consider that texting while driving creates a negative externality—distracting and dangerous for other drivers. The dangers of multitasking behind the wheel are well documented. Of course, if you pull over to the side of the road and use your cell phone to report a crime or an accident, the use of the phone may provide a positive externality.

to minimize negative externalities. Moral and social codes may prevent some people from littering, driving gas-guzzling cars, or using gas-powered mowers and log-burning fireplaces. The same self-regulation also applies to positive externalities. Philanthropists, for example, frequently donate money to public and private schools. In part, this must be because they view the positive externalities from education as a good buy for their charitable dollars.

SECTION CHECK

1. When the action of one party poses a cost on another party, it is called a negative externality.
2. The government can use taxes or other forms of regulation to correct the overallocation problem associated with negative externalities.
3. When the action of one party benefits another party, it is called a positive externality.
4. The government can provide subsidies or other forms of regulation to correct the underallocation problem associated with positive externalities.

---

1. Why are externalities also called spillover effects?
2. How do external costs affect the price and output of a polluting activity?
3. How can the government intervene to force producers to internalize external costs?
4. How do external benefits affect the output of an activity that causes them?
5. How can the government intervene to force external benefits to be internalized?
6. Why do most cities have more stringent noise laws for the early morning and late evening hours than for during the day?

SECTION 8.2 Public Goods

* What is a public good?
* What is the free-rider problem?
* Why does the government provide public goods?

* What is a common resource good?
* What is the tragedy of the commons?

Private Goods Versus Public Goods

Externalities are not the only culprit behind resource misallocation. A public good is another source of market failure. As used by economists, this term refers not to how these particular goods are purchased—by a government agency rather than some private economic agent—but to the properties that characterize them. In this section, we learn the difference between private goods, public goods, and common resources.

public good
a good that is nonrivalrous in consumption and nonexcludable

private good
a good with rivalrous consumption and excludability

Private Goods

A private good such as a cheeseburger has two critical properties in this context; it is rival and excludable. First, a cheeseburger is rival in consumption because if one person eats a particular cheeseburger, nobody else can eat the same cheeseburger. Second, a cheeseburger is excludable. It is easy to keep someone from eating your cheeseburger by not giving it to him. Most goods in the economy like food, clothing, cars, and houses are private goods that are rival and excludable.

Public Goods

The consumption of public goods, unlike private goods, is neither rival nor excludable. A public good is not rival because everyone can consume the good simultaneously; that is, one person's use of it does not diminish another's ability to use it. A public good is likewise *not excludable* because once the good is produced, it is prohibitively costly to exclude anyone from consuming the good. Consider national defense. Everyone enjoys the benefits of national defense (not rival) and it would be too costly to exclude anyone from those benefits (not excludable). That is, once the military has its defense in place, everyone is protected simultaneously (not rival) and it would be prohibitively costly to exclude anyone from consuming national defense (not excludable).

Another example of a public good is a flood control project. A flood control project would allow all the people who live in the flood plain area to enjoy the protection of the new program simultaneously. It would also be very difficult to exclude someone who lived in the middle of the project who said she did not want to pay. Like national defense, the good is nonrival in consumption—everyone within the flood project enjoys the protection simultaneously. Other examples of public goods include outdoor fireworks (not stadium) displays and tornado sirens in small towns. You cannot easily keep someone from seeing the fireworks or hearing the siren (not excludable). Also, when one person gets the benefits of the fireworks display or the siren warning it does not reduce the benefits to anyone else (not rival).

Voters may disagree on whether we have too much or too little, but most agree that we must have national defense. If national defense were provided privately and people were asked to pay for the use of national defense, many would be free riders, knowing they could derive the benefits of the good without paying for it. For this reason, the government provides important public goods, such as national defense.

STOCKTREK/PHOTODISC/GETTY IMAGES

Public Goods and the Free-Rider Problem

The fact that a public good is not rival and not excludable makes the good difficult to produce privately. Some would know they could derive the benefits from the good without paying for it, because once it is produced, it is too difficult to exclude them. Some would try to take a *free ride*—derive benefits from something they did not pay for. Let's return to the example of national defense. Suppose the private protection of national defense is actually worth $100 to you. Assume that 100 million households in the United States are willing to make a $100 contribution for national defense. These contributions would add up to $10 billion. You might write a check for $100, or you might reason as follows: "If I don't give $100 and everybody else does, I will be equally well protected plus derive the

free rider
deriving benefits from something not paid for

benefits of $100 in my pocket." Taking the latter course represents a rational attempt to be a **free rider**. The rub is that if everyone attempts to take a free ride, the ride will not exist.

The free-rider problem prevents the private market from supplying the efficient amounts of public goods. That is, no private firm would be willing to supply national defense because people can consume it without paying for it—the free rider problem. Therefore, the government provides important public goods such as national defense.

The Government and Benefit-Cost Analysis

Everything the government provides has an opportunity cost. What is the best level of national defense? More national defense means less of something else that society may value more, like health care or Social Security. To be efficient, additional goods from the public sector must also follow the rule of rational choice—pursue additional government activities if and only if the expected marginal benefits exceed the expected marginal costs. It all comes back to the adage—there are no free lunches.

In addition, there is also the problem of assessing the value of these goods. Consider the case of a new highway. Before it builds the highway, the appropriate government agency will undertake a benefit-cost analysis of the situation. In this case, it must evaluate consumers' willingness to pay for the highway against the costs that will be incurred for construction and maintenance. However, those individuals that want the highway have an incentive to exaggerate their desire for it. At the same time, individuals who will be displaced or otherwise harmed by the highway have an incentive to exaggerate the harm that will be done to them. Together, these elements make it difficult for the government to accurately assess need. Ultimately, their evaluations are reduced to educated guesses about the

net impact, weighing both positive and negative effects, of the highway on all parties concerned.

Common Resources and the Tragedy of the Commons

In many cases we do not have exclusive private property rights to things such as the air around us or the fish in the sea. They are common resources—goods that are owned by everyone and therefore not owned by anyone. When a good is not owned by anyone, individuals feel little incentive to conserve or use the resource efficiently.

Business News

in the news   The Tragedy of the Commons

—BY DANIEL MCFADDEN

Immigrants to New England in the 17th century formed villages in which they had privately owned homesteads and gardens, but they also set aside community-owned pastures, called commons, where all of the villagers' livestock could graze. Settlers had an incentive to avoid overuse of their private lands, so they would remain productive in the future. However, this self-interested stewardship of private lands did not extend to the commons. As a result, the commons were overgrazed and degenerated to the point that they were no longer able to support the villagers' cattle. This failure of private incentives to provide adequate maintenance of public resources is known to economists as "the tragedy of the commons."

Contemporary society has a number of current examples of the tragedy of the commons: the depletion of fish stocks in international waters, congestion on urban highways, and the rise of resistant diseases due to careless use of antibiotics. However, the commons that is likely to have the greatest impact on our lives in the new century

is the digital commons, the information available on the Internet through the portals that provide access. The problem with digital information is the mirror image of the original grazing commons: Information is costly to generate and organize, but its value to individual consumers is too dispersed and small to establish an effective market. The information that is provided is inadequately catalogued and organized. Furthermore, the Internet tends to fill with low-value information: The products that have high commercial value are marketed through revenue-producing channels, and the Internet becomes inundated with products that cannot command these values. Self-published books and music are cases in point....

The solutions that resolve the problem of the digital commons are likely to be ingenious ways to collect money from consumers with little noticeable pain, and these should facilitate the operation of the Internet as a market for goods and services. Just don't expect it to be free.

SOURCE: Daniel McFadden, "The Tragedy of the Commons," *Forbes*, 10 September 2001, pp. 61–63. Daniel McFadden won the Nobel Prize for economics in 2000.

A **common resource** is a rival good that is nonexcludable; that is, nonpayers cannot be easily excluded from consuming the good, and when one unit is consumed by one person, it means that it cannot be consumed by another. Fish in the vast ocean waters are a good example of a common resource. They are rival

common resource
a rival good that is nonexcludable

because fish are limited—a fish taken by one person is not available for others. They are nonexcludable because it is prohibitively costly to keep anyone from catching them—almost anyone with a boat and a fishing rod could catch one. Common resources can lead to tragedy—see the In the News story.

SECTION CHECK

1. A public good is both nonrivalrous in consumption (one person's usage of it does not diminish another's ability to use it) and nonexclusive (no one can be excluded from using it).
2. A free rider is someone who attempts to enjoy the benefits of a good without paying for it.
3. The free-rider problem prevents the private market from supplying the efficient amount of public goods.
4. A common resource good is rival in consumption but nonexcludable.
5. The failure of private incentives to maintain public resources leads to the tragedy of the commons.

---

1. How are public goods different from private goods?
2. Why does the free-rider problem arise in the case of public goods?
3. In what way can government provision of public goods solve the free-rider problem?
4. What is a common resource?
5. What is the tragedy of the commons?

SECTION 8.3   Asymmetric Information

* What is asymmetric information?
* What is adverse selection?
* What is moral hazard?

What Is Asymmetric Information?

When the available information is initially distributed in favor of one party relative to another, **asymmetric information** is said to exist. Suppose you bought a new car for $25,000 and about a month later you decide that you would be much happier with your old car and the money. So you call your salesperson and ask what your car is worth—perfect condition and less than 1,000 miles on the odometer. The salesperson tells you about $20,000. Why did your "new" car depreciate $5,000 in just one month? The problem is that a potential buyer is going to be skeptical. Why is that new car being sold? Is it a lemon?

asymmetric information
occurs when the available information is initially distributed in favor of one party relative to another in an exchange

Sellers are at an information advantage over potential buyers when selling a car because they have more information about the car than does the potential buyer. However, potential buyers know that sellers are more likely to sell a lemon. As a result, potential buyers will offer a lower price than they would if they could be certain of the quality. This is known as the lemon problem. Without incurring significant quality detection costs, such as having it inspected by a mechanic, the potential buyer is at an informational disadvantage relative to the seller. It is rational for the seller to claim that the car is in good shape and has no known defects, but the potential buyer cannot detect whether the car is a lemon or not

When players get traded from one team to another, a potential asymmetric information and adverse selection problem occurs—especially with pitchers. The team that is trading the pitcher knows more about his medical past, his pitching mechanics, his demeanor on and off the field, and so on, than the team that is trading for him. Even though trades are not finalized until the player passes a physical, many ailments or potential problems may go undetected.

without incurring costs. If the quality detection costs are sufficiently high, a solution is to price all used cars as if they are average quality. That is, used cars of the same year, make, and model generally will be offered at the same price, regardless of their known conditions. The seller of a lemon will then receive a payment that is more than the car is worth, and the seller of a relatively high-quality car will receive less than the car is worth. However, if a seller of a high-quality car does *not* receive what the car would sell for if the potential buyer knew its quality, the seller will rationally withdraw the offer to sell the car. Given the logical response of sellers of higher-than-average quality cars, the average quality of used cars on the market will fall, and consequently, many people will avoid buying in the used car market. In other words, the bad cars will drive the good cars out of the market. Thus, fewer used cars are bought and sold because fewer good cars are offered for sale. That is, information problems reduce economic efficiency. A situation where an informed party benefits in an exchange by taking advantage of knowing more than the other party is called **adverse selection**.

This distortion in the used car market resulting from adverse selection can be reduced by the buyer

adverse selection
a situation where an informed party benefits in an exchange by taking advantage of knowing more than the other party

acquiring more information so that the buyer and seller have equal information. In the used car example, it might mean that an individual buyer would demand that an independent mechanic do a detailed inspection of the used car or that the dealership provide an extended warranty. A warranty provides a credible signal that this dealer is not selling lemons. In addition, new services such as carfax.com allow you to pay to find the history of a used car before you buy it. These services help in eliminating the adverse selection problem because buyers would have more information about the product they are buying.

The least-cost solution would have sellers reveal their superior information to potential buyers. The problem is that it is not individually rational for the seller to provide a truthful and complete disclosure, a point that is known by a potential buyer. Only if the seller is punished for not truthfully revealing exchange-relevant information will a potential buyer perceive the seller's disclosure as truthful.

Adverse selection also occurs in the insurance market. Imagine an auto insurance company that has a one-size-fits-all policy for their insurance premiums. Careful drivers would be charged the same premium as careless drivers. The company would assess the average risk of accidents for all drivers and then set the premium. Of course, this would be very appealing to careless drivers, who are more likely to get in an accident; but not very appealing to careful drivers who have a much lower probability of getting in an accident. Under this pricing scheme, the bad drivers would drive the good drivers out of the market. Good drivers would be less likely to buy a policy, thinking that they are paying too much, since they are less likely to get in an accident than a careless driver. Many good drivers would exit the market, leaving a disproportionate share of bad drivers—exactly what the insurance companies do not want—people with a higher risk of getting in accidents. So what do they do?

Insurance companies set premiums according to the risk associated with particular groups of drivers, so good drivers do not exit the market. One strategy they use for dealing with adverse selection is called *screening*, where they use observable information about people to reveal private information. For example, a 17-year-old male driving a sports car will be charged a much higher premium than a 40-year-old female driving a minivan, even if he is a careful driver. Or someone with a good driving record or good grades gets a discount on his insurance. Insurance companies have data on different types of drivers and the probability of those drivers being in accidents, and they use this data to set insurance premiums. They may be wrong on an individual case (the teenager may be accident-free for years), but they are likely to be correct on average.

Reputation and Standardization

Asymmetric information is also present in other markets like rare stamps, coins, paintings, and sports memorabilia where the dealer (seller) knows more about the product than does the potential buyer. Potential buyers want to be assured that these items are authentic, not counterfeits. Unless the seller can successfully provide evidence of the quality of the product, bad products will tend to drive good products out of the market, resulting in a market failure.

One method that sellers can use to convince potential buyers that their products are high quality is *reputation*. For example, if a supermarket has a reputation of selling fresh produce, you are more likely to shop there. The same is true when you choose an electrician, plumber, or physician. In the used car market, the dealer might advertise how long he has been in business. This provides a signal that he has many satisfied customers. Therefore, he is likely to sell more used cars at a higher price. In short, if there is a reputation of high quality, it will minimize the market failure problem.

However, there may be cases where it is difficult to develop a reputation. For example, take a restaurant or a motel on a desolate highway. These establishments may not receive repeat customers. Customers have little idea of the quality of food, the probability of bedbugs, and so on. In this case, *standardization* is important. A national restaurant or a motel chain provides standardization. While you may not frequent McDonald's when you are at home, when confronted with the choice between a little known restaurant and McDonald's, you may pick the McDonald's because of the standardized products backed by a large corporation.

Asymmetric Information and Job Market Signaling

Why does non-job-related schooling raise your income? Why would salaried workers work longer hours—putting in 60 to 70 hours a week? The reason is this behavior provides a useful signal to the employer about the person's intelligence and work ethic.

Signaling is important because it reduces information costs associated with asymmetric information; the seller of labor (potential employee) has more information about her work ethic and reliability than the buyer of labor (potential employer). Imagine how costly it

would be to try out 150 potential employees for a job. In short, signals provide a measure that can help reduce asymmetric information and lower hiring costs.

There are strong signals and weak signals. Wearing a nice suit to work would be a weak signal because it does not necessarily distinguish a high productivity worker from a low productivity worker—a lazy worker can dress well too. To provide a strong signal, it must be harder for a low productivity worker to give the signal than a high productivity worker. Education is a strong signal in labor markets because it requires effort that many low productivity workers may find too difficult to obtain. The education signal is also relatively easy to measure—years of education, grade point average, highest degree attained, reputation of the university of college, rigor of courses attempted, and so on. Education can clearly improve a person's productivity; even if it did not, however, it would be a useful signal because more productive people find it easier to obtain education than lazy people. Furthermore, productive people are more likely to attain more education in order to signal to their employer that they are productive. So it may not just be the knowledge obtained from a college education, it may be the effort that you are signaling—something you presumably already had before you entered college. So according to the signaling model, workers go to college, not for the knowledge gained, but to send the important signal that they are highly productive.

In all likelihood, education provides knowledge and enhances productivity. However, it also sends an important signal. For example, many firms will not hire managers without an MBA because of the knowledge potential employees gained in courses like finance and economics, but also because an MBA sends a powerful signal that the worker is disciplined and hard working.

Durable Goods, Signals, and Warranties

Why are people reluctant to buy durable goods like televisions, refrigerators, and cameras without a warranty? Warranties are a signal. Honest and reliable firms find it less expensive to provide a warranty than dishonest firms. The dilemma for consumers is that they are trying to distinguish the good brands from the bad brands. One way to do this is to see what kind of warranty the producer offers. Low-quality items would require more frequent and expensive servicing than high-quality items. Thus, producers of low-quality items will tend to not offer extensive warranties. In short, extensive warranties signal high quality, while low-quality items without extensive warranties signal poor quality. With this knowledge, consumers will pay more for high-quality products with good warranties.

MONKEYBUSINESSIMAGES/ISTOCKPHOTO.COM

Asymmetric information occurs when the available information is initially distributed in favor of one party relative to another. In the used car market, the problem of asymmetric information can be reduced if a private seller can show records of regular maintenance and service and dealers can offer extended warranties.

What Is Moral Hazard?

Another information problem is associated with the insurance market and is called moral hazard. If an individual is fully insured for fire, theft, auto, life, and so on, what incentives will this individual have to take additional precautions from risk? For example, a person with auto insurance may drive less cautiously than would a person without auto insurance.

Insurance companies do, however, try to remedy the adverse selection problem by requiring regular checkups, discounts for nonsmokers, charging different deductibles and different rates for different age and occupational groups, and so on.

Additionally, those with health insurance may devote less effort and resources to staying healthy than those who are not covered. The problem, of course, is that if the insured are behaving more recklessly than they would if they were not insured, the result might be much higher insurance rates. The **moral hazard** arises from the fact that it is costly for the insurer to monitor the behaviors of the insured party. Suppose an individual knew that his car was protected with a "bumper to bumper" warranty. He might have less incentive to take care of the car, despite the manufacturer's contract specifying that the warranty was only valid under "normal wear and tear." It would be too costly for the manufacturer

moral hazard
taking additional risks because you are insured

winner's curse
a situation that arises in certain auctions where the winner is worse off than the loser because of an overly optimistic value placed on the good

to detect if a product failure was the consequence of a manufacturing defect or the abuse of the owner-user.

Adverse Selection versus Moral Hazard

Don't confuse adverse selection and moral hazard. Adverse selection is the phenomenon that occurs when one party in the exchange takes advantage of knowing more than the other party. Moral hazard involves the action taken *after* the exchange, such as if you were a nonsmoker who had just bought a life insurance policy and then started smoking heavily.

Winner's Curse

Suppose you and five other classmates were asked to bid on a jar of pennies. Nobody knows how many pennies are in the jar and you are not allowed to open the jar. The winner gets the jar of pennies. Let's say there are 500 pennies ($5) in the jar and you win by bidding $7. You are happy you won the bid until they count the pennies and you realize you just paid $7 for $5 worth of pennies. A common-value auction is where the auctioned item has the same value for all buyers but the value is unknown prior to the bidding. We call this a winner's curse because in this case the "winner" is overly optimistic and bids more for an item than its worth. Therefore, the winner could end up being worse off (cursed) than the loser.

The problem also occurs because value is subjective. In some cases bidders have a difficult time establishing an item's value. Without complete information, participants with limited skill in establishing valuation may overpay for an item. Historically, we have seen this when speculative bubbles in the stock or real estate markets occur. Then, investors with little skill in valuation and incomplete information tend to push prices beyond their true value.

However, an actual overpayment will generally occur only if the winner fails to account for the winner's curse when bidding. So despite its dire-sounding name, the winner's curse does not necessarily have ill effects.

The severity of the winner's curse tends to increase with the number of bidders. This is because the more bidders, the more likely it is that some of them have overestimated the auctioned item's value. The more serious your error of overbidding, the more likely you are to win. However, if you win you probably made a serious error. The best strategy may be to underbid. If the winner normally overestimates the true value by 20 percent then you might offer 80 percent of what you

ADVERSE SELECTION

Q If individuals know a lot more about their health condition than an insurance company, do we have a case of adverse selection?

A Yes. Even after a medical examination, individuals will know more about their health than the insurance company. That is, the buyers of health insurance have a better idea about their overall body conditions and nutritional habits than the seller, the insurance company. People with greater health problems tend to buy more health insurance than those who are healthy. This tendency drives up the price of health insurance to reflect the costs of sicker-than-average people, which drives people of average health out of the market. So the people who end up buying insurance will be the riskiest group.

think the item is worth. That way, if you happen to win by overbidding you won't "get taken to the cleaners." You might also choose not to participate in auctions likely to generate a winner's curse.

There is often confusion that winner's curse applies to the winners of all auctions. However, it is worth repeating here that for auctions based on the private value someone places on a good (i.e., when the item is desired independent of its value in the market), the winner's curse does not arise.

The winner's curse can also occur with underbidding, where people offer to do a job for less than other bidders. Imagine you need to hire a landscaper, so you get estimates from various landscapers. Who is likely to win? Probably, the landscaper with the lowest estimate. However, he may not think he won if he underestimated the amount of work required in your yard.

THE WINNER'S CURSE—OIL FIELD ECONOMICS AND BASEBALL

I t's the middle of winter. Right now baseball General Managers (GMs) are hitting the phones talking to player agents, trying to sign the men they think will push them over the top next season. The fans enter the season with great expectations. Yet so many times the player thought to be a savior to the team ends up not being worth the money it took to sign him. Is it because free agents lose their edge after signing their big-money contracts? Seeing as many of these guys were set for life before they switched teams, this explanation doesn't seem to work. To find the real answer, we have to drill for oil.

Back in the 1950s the players in the American petroleum industry turned their eyes to the Gulf of Mexico. With newer technology it was possible to drill offshore. So the race began and the oil companies bid for drilling rights and set up operations. There was only one problem. These offshore oil wells weren't turning a profit. Is drilling on the seabed harder than drilling on dry land? Sure, but that wasn't the difficulty. The real problem was the bidding process

(continued)

given the uncertainties in information available to the oil companies. This was explained in an article published in the *Journal of Petroleum Technology* titled "Competitive bidding in high risk situations," by Capen, Clapp and Campbell of the Atlantic Richfield Company (ARCO) in 1971. Here they coined the term "winner's curse."

Suppose you have four oil companies all interested in the same patch of offshore property. Back in the 1950s the methods available for determining the amount of liquid gold under a few hundred feet of water were primitive. This led to a large spread in the estimations of the value of the oil, and hence the drilling rights. Suppose that after all the costs of drilling were accounted for there was $10M worth of oil in the ground. Company A might determine that there was only $5M worth of oil. On the other hand, Company B might nail it at $10M, Company C could value the oil at $12M and Company D could make a gross overestimation and believe that there was $20M worth of oil in the ground.

Now we come to the bidding for the drilling rights. At $5M, Company A drops out of the competition. At $10M, we lose Company B. At $12M Company C bows out, and Company D is very happy because they have paid $12M for property they believe is worth $20M. But since there is only $10M worth of oil in the ground, Company D is in the red for $2M. They have suffered the winner's curse. In an auction, the prize goes to whoever has the most optimistic view of the value of the object being bid upon. In many cases, this also means that the winner is the person who has overestimated the most.

Is a baseball player really like an oil well? He is in that some estimation to his value can be made with the data available, but his future value (what the owners are bidding on) is in many cases an open question. How much will a thirty-year-old outfielder with a .280 batting average and 30 homers a year be worth over the span of his next contract? $5M a year? $7M a year? It's hard to guess, especially when the future free-market value of his competition is factored in. How fast will the average salary rise over the next three years? (Note that the oil companies

need to make a similar calculation—they need to not only estimate the amount of oil in the ground, but they also have to make an estimation of the future price of oil.) It's easy to see how several different teams could make very different estimations of the value of this player. And the team that signs him in the end is the team that was the most optimistic about his value. Like an oil company, this optimism could leave them well in the red.

So what solutions exist to the winner's curse? Information and caution are two big factors. Improving technology allowed oil companies to get a better grasp on how much oil is in the ground. Obviously a company that had better information made smarter bids, and was less likely to overbid. After the winner's curse phenomenon became better understood, oil companies were more cautious and started bidding fractions of what they thought the drilling rights were worth in order to avoid the curse. If all of the oil companies were bidding .75 what they thought the true value of the drilling rights were worth, they were much less likely to be bitten. A higher-risk operator might be willing to bid .8 the estimated value, whereas a more conservative player might only bid .65. The problem that quickly surfaced is that newcomers to the industry often did not factor in the fractional weighting when making their bids. Well, these newcomers were often bitten by the winner's curse, and while the newcomers might have annoyed the older companies, in the long run it was mainly the newcomers that were hurt.

In baseball more information will also lead to a better bid. A team that understands statistics will probably realize that a certain slugger's gaudy RBI (Runs Batted In) totals are due to his high-OBP (on base percentage) table-setters, while a team that doesn't analyze the situation as well will drool over the RBIs and adjust their bid accordingly. A team that understands how aging affects performance is less likely to overbid for the thirty-five-year-old shortstop. Caution also comes into play. A GM can estimate a player's value, discount it by a fraction as would an oil executive, and then bid accordingly. The problem is the newcomers. How often do we

Use what you've
LEARNED

THE WINNER'S CURSE—OIL FIELD ECONOMICS AND BASEBALL (cont.)

see a new owner come in and make a big splash in the free agent market? This is the case of the new oil company that hasn't figured out how the modified bidding works to fight against the winner's curse.

Sadly, the baseball owners can't just sit back and watch the new guy squirm under the burden of his foolish purchases. Because of the salary arbitration process the winner's curse becomes everyone's curse. The grossly overpaid shortstop can be used as evidence against all the other teams in baseball when the arbitration process sets the next year's salaries. Perhaps when new owners are initiated into baseball and taught the secret handshake, they also need to be given a short course on the history of oil field economics.

SOURCE: From http://economics.about.com/cs/baseballeconomics/a/winnerscurse .htm. Used by permission of the author.

SECTION CHECK

1. Asymmetric information occurs when the available information is initially distributed in favor of one party relative to another in an exchange.

2. Adverse selection is a situation where an informed party benefits in an exchange by taking advantage of knowing more than the other party.

3. Moral hazard occurs when one party to a contract passes on the cost of its behavior to the other party.

4. Asymmetric information, adverse selection, and moral hazard are information problems that can distort market signals.

5. Asymmetric information leads to signaling behavior.

6. Auctions for goods of uncertain value may suffer from the winner's curse. In the winner's curse the most optimistic buyer wins, but may overpay as a result, leaving the winner worse off.

---

1. How do substantial warranties offered by sellers of used cars act to help protect buyers from the problem of asymmetric information and adverse selection? Why might too extensive a warranty lead to a moral hazard problem?

2. If where you got your college degree acted as a signaling device to potential employers, why would you want the school from which you graduated to raise its academic standards after you leave?

3. Why might withdrawals in several classes send a poor signal to potential employers?

4. Why is the winner's curse less likely for repeat-purchase items?

Interactive Chapter Summary

Fill in the blanks:

1. Sometimes the market system fails to produce efficient outcomes because of side effects economists call _____.

2. Whenever an activity has physical impacts on individuals not directly involved in the activity, if the impact on the outside party is negative, it is called a _____; if the impact is positive, it is called a _____.

3. If a firm can avoid paying the external costs it imposes on others, it _____ its own costs of production but not the _____ cost to society.

4. If the government taxed a manufacturer by the amount of those external costs it imposes on others, it would force the manufacturer to _____ the costs.

5. The benefits of a product or service that spill over to an outside party not involved in producing or consuming the good are called _____.

6. If suppliers are unaware of or not responsible for the external costs created by their production, the result is a(n) _____ of scarce resources to the production of the good.

7. Because producers are unable to collect payments from all who are benefiting from the good or service, the market has a tendency to _____ goods with external benefits.

8. In the case of either external benefits or external costs, buyers and sellers are receiving the wrong signals: The apparent benefits or costs of some actions differ from the _____ benefits or costs.

9. Unlike the consumption of private goods, the consumption of public goods is both _____ and _____.

10. If once a good is produced it is prohibitively costly to exclude anyone from consuming the good, consumption of that good is called _____.

11. If everyone can consume a good simultaneously, it is _____.

12. When individuals derive the benefits of a good without paying for it, it is called a(n) _____.

13. The government may be able to overcome the free-rider problem by _____ the public good and imposing taxes to pay for it.

14. Goods that are owned by everyone and therefore not owned by anyone are called _____ resources.

15. A common resource is a _____ good that is _____.

16. Fish in the vast ocean are a good example of a _____ resource.

17. The failure of private incentives to provide adequate maintenance of public resources is known to economists as the _____.

18. When the available information is initially distributed in favor of one party relative to another, _____ is said to exist.

19. The existence of _____ may give rise to signaling behavior.

20. When one party enters into an exchange with another party that has more information, we call it _____ selection.

21. A college education can provide a _____ about a person's intelligence and perseverance.

22. Good warranties are an example of _____ behavior that takes place because the _____ may know the actual quality of durable goods better than the _____.

23. _____ arises from the cost involved for the insurer to monitor the behaviors of the insured party.

24. The _____ occurs when the winner of an auction overpays.

25. The winner's curse is less likely for items that are purchased _____/infrequently and where there is a larger/_____ number of bidders.

Answers: 1. externalities 2. negative externality; positive externality 3. lowers; true 4. internalize (bear) 5. positive externalities 6. overallocation 7. underproduce 8. true social 9. nonexcludable; nonrivalrous 10. nonexcludable 11. nonrivalous 12. free ride 13. providing 14. common 15. rival; nonexcludable 16. common 17. tragedy of the commons 18. asymmetric information 19. asymmetric information 20. adverse 21. signal 22. signaling; sellers; buyers 23. Moral hazard 24. winner's curse 25. frequently; smaller

Key Terms and Concepts

externality 210
positive externality 210
negative externality 210
public good 216

private good 216
free rider 217
common resource 219
asymmetric information 219

adverse selection 220
moral hazard 222
winner's curse 222

Section Check Answers

8.1 Externalities

1. Why are externalities also called spillover effects?

An externality exists whenever the benefits or costs of an activity impact individuals outside the market mechanism. That is, some of the effects spill over to those who have not voluntarily agreed to bear them or compensate others for them, unlike the voluntary exchange of the market.

2. How do external costs affect the price and output of a polluting activity?

If the owner of a firm that pollutes does not have to bear the external costs of pollution, she can ignore those real costs of pollution to society. The result is that the private costs she must pay are less than the true social costs of production, so that the market output of the polluting activity is greater, and the resulting market price less, than it would be if producers did have to bear the external costs of production.

3. How can the government intervene to force producers to internalize external costs?

If the government could impose on producers a tax or fee, equal to the external costs imposed on people without their consent, producers would have to take into account those costs. The result would be that those costs were no longer external costs, but internalized by producers.

4. How do external benefits affect the output of an activity that causes them?

External benefits are benefits that spill over to others, because the party responsible need not be paid for those benefits. Therefore, some of the benefits of an activity to society will be ignored by the relevant decision makers in this case, and the result will be a smaller output and a higher price for goods that generate external benefits to others.

5. How can the government intervene to force external benefits to be internalized?

Just as taxes can be used to internalize external costs imposed on others, subsidies can be used to internalize external benefits generated for others.

6. Why do most cities have more stringent noise laws for the early morning and late evening hours than for during the day?

The external costs to others from loud noises in residential areas early in the morning and late in the evening are higher, because most residents are home and trying to sleep, than when many people are gone at work or are already awake in the daytime. Given those higher potential external costs, most cities impose more restrictive noise laws for nighttime hours to reduce them.

8.2 Public Goods

1. How are public goods different from private goods?

Private goods are rival in consumption (we can't both consume the same unit of a good) and exclusive (nonpayers can be prevented from consuming the good unless they pay for it). Public goods are nonrival in consumption (more than one person can consume the same good) and nonexclusive (nonpayers can't be effectively kept from consuming the good, even if they don't voluntarily pay for it).

2. Why does the free-rider problem arise in the case of public goods?

The free-rider problem arises in the case of public goods because people cannot be prevented from enjoying the benefits of public goods once they are provided. Therefore, people have an incentive to not voluntarily pay for those benefits, making it difficult or even impossible to finance the efficient quantity of public goods through voluntary market arrangements.

3. In what way can government provision of public goods solve the free-rider problem?

The government can overcome the free-rider problem by forcing people to pay for the provision of a public good through taxes.

4. What is a common resource?

A common resource good is rival in consumption but nonexcludable.

5. What is the tragedy of the commons?

Common resource goods often lead to overuse because if no one owns the resource, they are not likely to consider the cost of their use of the resource on others. This is the so-called tragedy of the commons. This problem has led to overfishing. Of course, you could remove the common and make the resource private property, but assigning private property rights to a vast ocean area would be virtually impossible.

8.3 Asymmetric Information

1. **How do substantial warranties offered by sellers of used cars act to help protect buyers from the problem of asymmetric information and adverse selection? Why might too extensive a warranty lead to a moral hazard problem?**

   In the used car market, the seller has superior information about the car's condition, placing the buyer at an information disadvantage. It also increases the chance that the car being sold is a "lemon." A substantial warranty can provide the buyer with valuable additional information about the condition of the car, reducing both asymmetric information and adverse selection problems.

   Too extensive a warranty (e.g., an unlimited "bumper to bumper" warranty) will give the buyer less incentive to take care of the car, because the buyer is effectively insured against the damage that lack of care would cause.

2. **If where you got your college degree acted as a signaling device to potential employers, why would you want the school from which you graduated to raise its academic standards after you leave?**

   If an employer used your college's academic reputation as a signal of your likely "quality" as a potential employee, you want the school to raise its standards after you graduate, because it would improve the average quality of its graduates, improving the quality it signals about you to an employer.

3. **Why might withdrawals in several classes send a poor signal to potential employers?**

   It would indicate a failure to stick to difficult tasks relative to other students.

4. **Why is the winner's curse less likely for repeat-purchase items?**

   Repeat purchases reveal good information on the actual value of items.

True or False:

1. A negative externality is when the action of one party imposes a cost on another party.

2. A positive externality is when the action of one party benefits another party.

3. In the case of external costs, firms tend to produce too little from society's standpoint, causing an efficiency loss due to an underallocation of scarce resources to the production of the good.

4. If government could impose a pollution tax equal to the exact size of the external costs imposed by a firm, then the firm would produce at the socially desired level of output.

5. The tax revenues raised by a pollution tax could be used to compensate those who have suffered damages from the pollution.

6. Alternatives to pollution taxes include the government prohibiting certain types of activities that cause pollution and forcing firms to clean up their emissions.

7. Because the decision makers involved ignore some of the real social benefits, the private market does not provide enough of goods that generate external benefits.

8. In the case of external benefits, if we could add the benefits that are derived by nonpaying consumers, the demand curve would shift to the right, increasing output.

9. In the case of external benefits, a tax equal to external benefits would result in an efficient level of output.

10. Externality problems always require the intervention of government.

11. In the case of goods where all those affected benefit simultaneously and it is prohibitively costly to exclude anyone from consuming them, market failures tend to arise.

12. In the case of public goods, when people act as free riders, some goods having benefits greater than costs will not be produced.

13. If quality detection costs are high, high-quality products will tend to be withdrawn from the market, and the average quality will rise.

14. Asymmetric information exists when the available information is initially distributed in favor of one party to a transaction relative to another.

15. In adverse selection situations, it is rational for a seller with more information about a product to provide a truthful and complete disclosure and make that fact known to a potential buyer.

16. Warranty agreements that limit the responsibility of the insurer in certain situations can be one method of controlling moral hazard problems.

17. In the market for insurance, the adverse selection problem leads those most likely to collect on insurance to buy it.

18. In the market for insurance, moral hazard can lead those who buy insurance to take fewer precautions to avoid the insured risk.

19. The winner's curse is more likely when a large number of bidders is involved.

20. Repeat purchasers are less likely to suffer from the winner's curse than one-time purchasers.

Multiple Choice:

1. The presence of negative externalities leads to a misallocation of societal resources because
   a. whenever external costs are imposed on outside parties, the good should not be produced at all.
   b. less of the good than is ideal for society is produced.
   c. some costs are associated with production that the producer fails to take into consideration.
   d. the government always intervenes in markets when negative externalities are present, and the government is inherently inefficient.

2. A tax equal to the external cost on firms that emit pollutants would
   a. provide firms with the incentive to increase the level of activity creating the pollution.
   b. provide firms with the incentive to decrease the level of activity creating the pollution.
   c. provide firms with little incentive to search for less environmentally damaging production methods.
   d. not reduce pollution levels at all.

3. In the case of a good whose production generates negative externalities,
   a. those not directly involved in the market transactions are harmed.
   b. internalizing the externality would tend to result in a greater output of the good.
   c. too little of the good tends to be produced.
   d. a subsidy would be the appropriate government corrective action.
   e. all of the above are true.

4. If firms were required to pay the full social costs of the production of goods, including both private and external costs, other things being equal, there would probably be
   a. an increase in production.
   b. a decrease in production.
   c. a greater misallocation of resources.
   d. a decrease in the market price of the product.

5. Which of the following will most likely generate positive externalities of consumption?
   a. a hot dog vendor
   b. public education
   c. an automobile
   d. a city bus
   e. a polluting factory

6. Assume that production of a good imposes external costs on others. The market equilibrium price will be _____ and the equilibrium quantity _____ for efficient resource allocation.
   a. too high; too high
   b. too high; too low
   c. too low; too high
   d. too low; too low

7. Assume that production of a good generates external benefits of consumption. The market equilibrium price of the good will be _____ and the equilibrium quantity _____ for efficient resource allocation.
   a. too high; too high
   b. too high; too low
   c. too low; too high
   d. too low; too low

8. Socially inefficient outcomes may occur in markets that have
   a. free riders.
   b. negative externalities.
   c. asymmetric information problems.
   d. positive externalities.
   e. any of the above.

9. In the case of externalities, appropriate government corrective policy would be
   a. taxes in the case of external benefits and subsidies in the case of external costs.
   b. subsidies in the case of external benefits and taxes in the case of external costs.
   c. taxes in both the case of external benefits and the case of external costs.
   d. subsidies in both the case of external benefits and the case of external costs.
   e. none of the above; the appropriate thing to do would be to do nothing.

10. The market system fails to provide the efficient output of public goods because
    a. people place no value on public goods.
    b. private firms cannot restrict the benefits from those goods to consumers who are willing to pay for them.
    c. public enterprises can produce those goods at lower cost than private firms.
    d. public goods create widespread spillover costs.

11. Public goods, like national defense, are usually funded through government because
    a. no one cares about them, because they are public.
    b. it is prohibitively difficult to withhold national defense from someone unwilling to pay for it.

c. they cost too much for private firms to produce them.

d. they provide benefits only to individuals, and not firms.

12. Adverse selection refers to
   a. the phenomenon that occurs when one party in an exchange takes advantage of knowing more than another party.
   b. the tendency for individuals to alter their behavior once they are insured against loss.
   c. the tendency for individuals to engage in insurance fraud.
   d. both b and c.

13. Which of the following is not true of adverse selection?
   a. It can result when both parties to a transaction have little information about the quality of the goods involved.
   b. It can cause the quality of goods traded to fall, if quality detection costs are high.
   c. It can be a difficult problem to overcome, because it is not individually rational for the transactor with the superior information to provide a truthful and complete disclosure.
   d. All of the above are true.

14. If a company offers a medical and dental care plan that offers benefits to all of the members of each employee's family for a given monthly premium, an employee who is a mother of five children and who has bad teeth who elects that plan would be an illustration of
   a. the moral hazard problem.
   b. the free-rider problem.
   c. the adverse selection problem.
   d. the "lemon" problem.

15. If, after you buy a car with air bags, you start to drive recklessly, it would be an illustration of
   a. the moral hazard problem.
   b. the free-rider problem.
   c. the adverse selection problem.
   d. the "lemon" problem.

16. In the market for insurance, the moral hazard problem leads
   a. those most likely to collect on insurance to buy it.
   b. those who buy insurance to take fewer precautions to avoid the insured risk.
   c. those with more prior insurance claims to be charged a higher premium.
   d. to none of the above.

17. The winner's curse
   a. is more likely the fewer the bidders.
   b. is more likely the more frequently a good is purchased.
   c. is more likely when a good is being purchased because of its expected future market value.
   d. is a myth.

18. In the analysis of the winner's curse
   a. a bidder who realizes he might be in a winner's curse situation may bid less as a result.
   b. it can be better to lose an auction than to win it.
   c. a good bought for its value to the bidder is less likely to be subject to the winner's curse than a good bought for its expected future market value.
   d. all of the above are true.

Problems:

1. Indicate which of the following activities create a positive externality, a negative externality, or no externality at all:
   a. During a live theater performance, an audience member's cell phone loudly rings.
   b. You are given a flu shot.
   c. You purchase and drink a soda during a break from class.
   d. A college fraternity and sorority clean up trash along a two-mile stretch on the highway.
   e. A firm dumps chemical waste into a local water reservoir.
   f. The person down the hall in your dorm plays loud music while you are trying to sleep.

2. Draw a standard supply and demand diagram for televisions, and indicate the equilibrium price and output.
   a. Assuming that the production of televisions generates external costs, illustrate the effect of the producers being forced to pay a tax equal to the external costs generated, and indicate the equilibrium output.
   b. If instead of generating external costs, television production generates external benefits, illustrate the effect of the producers being given a subsidy equal to the external benefits generated, and indicate the equilibrium output.

3. For each of the following goods, indicate whether they are nonrival and/or nonexclusive. Indicate whether they are private or public goods.
   a. hot dogs
   b. cable TV
   c. broadcast TV
   d. automobiles
   e. national defense
   f. pollution control
   g. parking in a parking structure
   h. a sunset
   i. admission to a theme park

4. Is a lighthouse a public good if it benefits many ship owners? What if it primarily benefits ships going to a port nearby?

5. Why do you think buffaloes became almost completely extinct on the Great Plains but cattle did not? Why is it possible that you can buy a buffalo burger in a store or diner today?

6. What kind of problems does the government face when trying to perform a cost-benefit analysis of whether or how much of a public project to produce?

7. How does a TV broadcast have characteristics of a public good? What about cable services such as HBO?

8. In order to get a license to practice in the United States, foreign-trained veterinarians must take an exam given by the American Veterinary Association. Only 48 people per year are allowed to take the exam, which is administered at only two universities. The fee for the exam, which must be booked at least 18 months in advance, was recently raised from $2,500 to $6,000. What effects does this clinical competency exam have on the number of veterinarians practicing in the United States? Do you think it improves the quality of veterinary services?

9. How would the adverse selection problem arise in the insurance market? How is it like the "lemon" used-car problem?

10. In terms of signaling behavior:
    a. Why is wearing a suit a weaker signal of ability than higher educational achievement?
    b. Why do some majors in college provide more powerful signals to future employers than others?
    c. Why could double-majoring provide a more powerful labor market signal than having a single major?
    d. How would you explain why students might be said to "overinvest" in grades as opposed to learning course material?

11. In terms of winner's curse:
    a. Why is the winner's curse unlikely for frequently purchased goods?
    b. Why would the winner's curse be more likely as the number of bidders increases?
    c. Why would we except there to be no winner's curse for goods desired for their own private value, unlike the case of purchases based on a good's market value to others?

12. In terms of moral hazard:
    a. Why does someone's willingness to pay a large deductible on an insurance policy tell an insurer something valuable about the seriousness of the moral hazard problem they might expect from the policyholder?
    b. Why does car insurance which explicitly excludes insuring the car for commercial use act to reduce moral hazard?
    c. Why does vehicle insurance based in part on miles driven reduce moral hazard problems?
    d. Why would a GPS monitor that can record the location and the speed a rental car is driven help reduce the moral hazard problem that rental companies are exposed to?

Public Sector and Public Choice

9

In the last chapter, we discussed the role of government in the case of externalities and public goods. We argued that the government can sometimes improve economic well-being by remedying externalities through pollution taxes, regulation and subsidies, and providing public goods.

However, in this chapter, we cover other important facets of the public sector—protecting property rights, providing a legal system, intervention in cases of insufficient competition, income redistribution, and promoting stability and growth in the economy. In this chapter, we will see how the government obtains revenues through taxation to provide these goods and services. We also examine the different types of taxation. The last section of the chapter is on public choice economics, the application of economic principles to politics. ∎

Other Functions of Government

* What are private property rights?
* What is the role of the legal system?
* How does government discourage insufficient competition?

* What tools does the government use to redistribute income?

Property Rights and the Legal System

In a market economy, private individuals and firms own most of the resources. For example, when consumers buy houses, cars, or pizzas, they have purchased the right to use these goods in ways they, not someone else, see fit. These rights are called **private property rights**. Property rights are the rules of our economic game. If well-defined, property rights give individuals the incentive to use their property efficiently. That is, owners with property rights have a greater incentive to maintain, improve, and even conserve their property to preserve or increase its value.

Markets, just like baseball, need umpires. It is the government that plays this role when it defines and protects the rights of people and their property through the legal system and police protection. That is, by providing rules and regulations, government makes markets work more efficiently. Private enforcement is possible, but as economic life becomes more complex, political institutions have become the major instrument for defining and enforcing property rights.

The government defines and protects property rights through the legal system and policy protection. The legal system ensures the rights of private ownership, the enforcement of contracts, and the legal status for businesses. The legal system serves as the referee and imposes penalties on violators of our legal rules. Property rights also include intellectual property—the property rights that an owner receives through patents, copyrights, and trademarks. These rights give the owner long-term protection that encourages individuals to write books, music, and software programs and invent new products (see the

private property rights consumers' right to use their property as they see fit

In the News story on song swapping on the Net). In short, well-defined property rights encourage investment, innovation, exchange, conservation, and economic growth.

Insufficient Competition in Markets

Another justification given for government intervention is to correct cases of insufficient competition that arise in the marketplace. As we discussed in Chapter 2, monopoly, or one-supplier, situations result in higher prices and lower quantities traded than in a competitive market. When such conditions of restricted competition arise, the communication system of the marketplace is disrupted, causing the market to function inefficiently, to the detriment of consumers. For this reason, since the 1880s, the federal government has engaged in antitrust activities designed to encourage competition and discourage monopoly conditions. Specifically, the Antitrust Division of the Department of Justice and the Federal Trade Commission attempt to increase competition by attacking monopolistic practices.

Income Redistribution

Not only does the market determine what goods are going to be produced, and in what quantities, but it also determines, through the interaction of demand and supply for productive resources, the distribution of output among members of society. Some argue that the market distribution of income may produce disparities

in the news   Song Swapping on the Net

If you were a rock star, would you want to put a stop to bootlegged music on the Internet?

❋ Yes, it violates copyright laws and cheats the artist.

❋ Yes, but unlicensed music sharing is inevitable.

❋ No, it will only increase the size of my audience.

❋ No, it hurts only record companies, which charge too much anyway.

Song swapping on the Net allows you to search for almost any song you can think of, find the song on a fellow enthusiast's hard drive, and then download it for yourself, right now—for the unbeatable cost of zero, free, nada, gratis.

consider this:

Song swapping on the Net has set the stage for an interesting battle over copyright laws and intellectual property rights. Is sharing songs with others on the Internet underground piracy, or is it sharing someone's purchased possession? Is

it a "personal use" right to share music online—like sharing a CD with a friend?

Napster and Grokster may be gone, but "free" music and videos are alive and well. The network is still wide open. It is a tough war to win, and the people trading music illegally online have little chance of being caught. Also, many young music lovers do not see downloading music without paying the copyright as a crime. The industry must innovate its way out. One reason that illegal downloading took off was because the industry did not keep up with the technology. The music industry continued to sell CDs and tapes when buyers had the technology to download songs.

A 2007 study by the Institute for Policy Innovation concludes that the "piracy" of recorded music costs the U.S. recording industries billions of dollars annually in lost revenue and profits. In addition, the study states that recorded music piracy costs American workers significant losses in jobs and earnings, and lost tax revenues to the government.

Incentives play an important part in this story, too. If the price is zero, the probability of being caught is close to zero, and people do not view it as illegal, then you would expect many to download music illegally rather than purchase. However, the flipside of the story is that when talented producers and artists do not get royalties for their artistic work, you will see a lot less of it—especially quality music. Incentives matter.

that violate a common sense of equity or fairness and government should intervene to reduce income inequality. Others argue that high incomes are a result of hard work and greater skills. They believe that higher taxes designed to redistribute income only reduce incentives to work hard, save, and invest. Ultimately, the decision on how much redistribution will occur is a normative issue. Economists can estimate the benefits and costs of these efforts, but society must decide.

Government redistributes income in three major ways: taxes, subsidies, and transfer payments. We will now briefly examine each of these methods in turn.

Taxes

In addition to being one of the primary ways that the government finances its activities, taxes are an important tool for redistributing income. Specifically, one type of tax, a progressive tax, is designed to take a larger percentage of higher incomes as compared to lower incomes. In this way, progressive taxes help to reduce income disparities. The federal income tax is an example of a progressive tax. The progressive tax and other types of taxes will be discussed in greater detail in the next section.

Government Subsidies

A second way that governments can help the less affluent is by the use of governmental revenues to provide low-cost public services. Inexpensive public housing, subsidized public transport, and even public parks are services that probably serve the poor to a greater extent than the rich. "Free" public education is viewed by many as an equalizing force in that it opens opportunities for children of less prosperous members of society to obtain the skills necessary for employment that could improve their economic status.

Transfer Payments

A third means by which income redistribution can be carried out by government is through direct transfer payments. Cash transfer payments are made by the government, particularly to the poor and aged, for which no goods or services are exchanged. Transfer payments include Social Security, unemployment compensation benefits, welfare (temporary assistance for needy families, or TANF), and veteran payments.

Noncash transfers, such as food stamps, Medicaid, school lunch programs, and housing subsidies, for example, are designed to raise the living standards of the poor.

SECTION CHECK

1. The government defines and protects property rights through the legal system and police protection.
2. Well-defined property rights encourage investment, innovation, exchange, conservation, and economic growth.
3. Government encourages competition and discourages monopoly, or one-supplier conditions, through its antitrust activities.
4. The government redistributes income through taxes, subsidies, and transfer payments.

1. Why do owners with clear property rights have incentives to use their property efficiently?
2. How does the government use taxes, subsidies, and transfer payments to redistribute income toward lower-income groups?
3. Why would the government want to prevent market conditions of insufficient competition?

SECTION
9.2

Government Spending and Taxation

* How does government finance its spending?
* On what does the public sector spend its money?
* What are progressive and regressive taxes?
* What is a flat tax?

* What is the ability to pay principle?
* What is vertical equity?
* What is the benefits received principle?
* What is a consumption tax?

Growth in Government

Government plays a large role in the economy; and its role increased markedly from 1929 to 1975, as may be seen in Exhibit 1. Although it is true that federal spending has changed little since 1960, the composition of government spending has changed considerably. National defense spending fell from roughly 9 percent of GDP in 1960 to 2.9 percent in 2000. However, the aftermath of the terrorist attacks of September 11, 2001, and the wars in Iraq and Afghanistan, led to increases in defense spending. It rose to 4.7 percent of GDP in 2009. Areas of government growth can be identified at least in part by looking at statistics on the types of government spending.

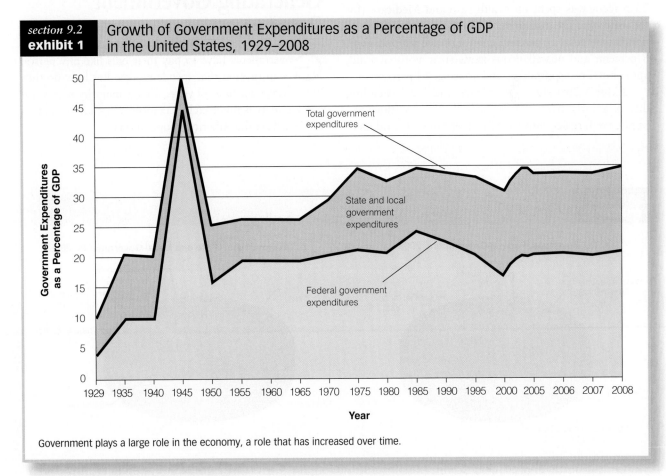

section 9.2 **exhibit 1**   Growth of Government Expenditures as a Percentage of GDP in the United States, 1929–2008

Government plays a large role in the economy, a role that has increased over time.

SOURCE: *Economic Report of the President,* 2009.

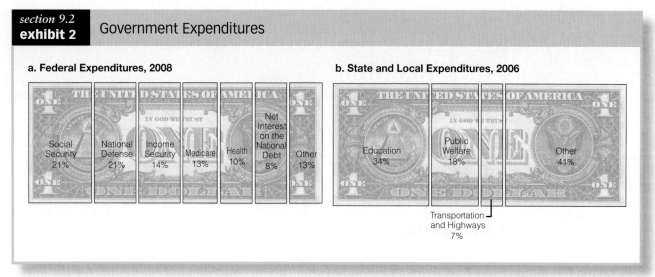

SOURCE: *Economic Report of the President,* 2009.

The share of GDP devoted to Social Security and Medicare rose from about 2.5 percent in 1960 to more than 7 percent today. Exhibit 2(a) shows that 35 percent of federal government spending in 2008 went to Social Security and income security programs. Another 23 percent was spent on health care and Medicare (for the elderly). The remaining federal expenditures were national defense, 21 percent; interest on the national debt, 8 percent; and miscellaneous items such as foreign aid, agriculture, transportation, and housing, 13 percent.

Exhibit 2(b) shows that state and local spending differs greatly from federal spending. Education and public welfare account for 52 percent of state and local expenditures. Other significant areas of state and local spending include highways, utilities, and police and fire protection.

Generating Government Revenue

Governments have to pay their bills like any person or institution that spends money. But how do they obtain revenue? In most years, a large majority of government activity is financed by taxation. What kinds of taxes are levied on the American population?

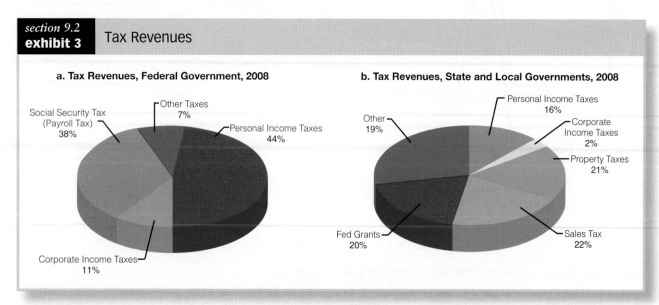

section 9.2
exhibit 3   Tax Revenues

a. Tax Revenues, Federal Government, 2008

Social Security Tax (Payroll Tax) 38%
Other Taxes 7%
Personal Income Taxes 44%
Corporate Income Taxes 11%

b. Tax Revenues, State and Local Governments, 2008

Personal Income Taxes 16%
Corporate Income Taxes 2%
Property Taxes 21%
Sales Tax 22%
Fed Grants 20%
Other 19%

SOURCE: *Economic Report of the President and Bureau of Economic Analysis,* 2009.

At the federal level, most taxes or levies are on income. Exhibit 3 shows that 55 percent of tax revenues come in the form of income taxes on individuals and corporations, called personal income taxes and corporate income taxes, respectively. Most of the remaining revenues come from payroll taxes, which are levied on work-related income, that is, payrolls. These taxes are used to pay for Social Security and compulsory insurance plans such as Medicare. Payroll taxes are split between employees and employers. The Social Security share of federal taxes has steadily risen as the proportion of the population over age 65 has grown and as Social Security benefits have been increased. Consequently, payroll taxes have risen significantly in recent years. Other taxes, on such items as gasoline, liquor, and tobacco products, provide for a small proportion of government revenues, as do customs duties, estate and gift taxes, and some minor miscellaneous taxes and user charges.

The U.S. federal government relies more heavily on income-based taxes than nearly any other government in the world. Most other governments rely more heavily on sales taxes, excise taxes, and customs duties.

A Progressive Tax

One effect of substantial taxes on income is that the "take home" income of Americans is significantly altered by the tax system. **Progressive taxes,** of which the federal income tax is one example, are designed so that those with higher incomes pay a greater proportion of their income in taxes. A progressive tax is one tool that the government can use to redistribute income. It should be noted, however, that certain types of income are excluded from income for taxation purposes, such as interest on municipal bonds and income in kind—food stamps or Medicare, for example.

progressive tax
tax designed so that those with higher incomes pay a greater proportion of their income in taxes

regressive tax
as a person's income rises, the amount his or her tax as a proportion of income falls

excise tax
a sales tax on individual products such as alcohol, tobacco, and gasoline

A Regressive Tax

Payroll taxes, the second most important source of income for the federal government, are actually **regressive taxes;** that is, they take a greater proportion of the income of lower-income groups than of higher-income groups. The reasons for this are simple. Social Security, for example, is imposed as a fixed proportion (now 6.2 percent on employees and an equal amount on employers) of wage and salary income up to $106,800 as of 2009. Also, wealthy persons have relatively more income from sources such as dividends and interest that

are not subject to payroll taxes, and earnings above a certain level are not subject to some payroll taxes.

At first glance it appears that employers and employees split the burden of Social Security tax (called the Federal Insurance Contribution Act, or FICA). However, recall our discussion of elasticity and its burden of taxation. Most labor economists believe the labor supply curve is relatively inelastic compared to the demand curve for labor, so employers will pass on most of the tax in the form of lower wages to employees. So, if workers are relatively unresponsive to a decrease in the wage rate (they have a relatively inelastic labor supply curve), then employers can pass most of the tax on in the form of lower wages, as seen in Exhibit 4. Congress may have intended a 50-50 split on the payroll tax between workers and firms. However, we have learned that the burden of the tax does not depend whether it is levied on the buyer or the seller but rather it depends on the price elasticity of supply and demand.

An Excise Tax

Some consider an **excise tax**—a sales tax on individual products such as alcohol, tobacco, and gasoline—to be the most unfair type of tax because it is generally the most regressive. Excise taxes on specific items impose a far greater burden, as a percentage of income, on the poor and middle classes than on the wealthy, because low-income families generally spend a greater proportion of their income on these items than do high-income families.

In addition, excise taxes may lead to economic inefficiencies. By isolating a few products and subjecting them to discriminatory taxation, excise taxes subject economic choices to political manipulation, which leads to inefficiency.

Financing State and Local Government Activities

Historically, the primary source of state and local revenue has been property taxes. In recent decades, state and local governments have relied increasingly on sales and income taxes for revenues (see Exhibit 3). Today, sales taxes account for roughly 19 percent of revenues, property taxes account for 17 percent, and personal and corporate income taxes account for another 14 percent. Approximately 22 percent of state and local revenues come from the federal government

section 9.2
exhibit 4   Payroll Tax

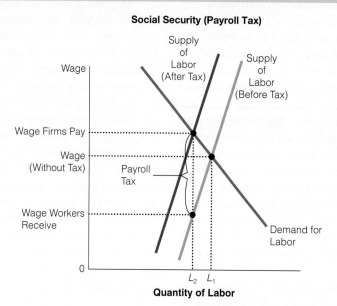

A payroll (FICA) tax puts "a wedge" between the wage firms pay and the wage workers receive. The wedge does not depend on whether the tax was imposed on the buyers or sellers. But the effects depend on elasticity of supply and demand. If, as most labor economists believe the supply of labor is less elastic than the demand for labor. The worker (not the firm) bears most of the burden of the payroll tax.

as grants. The remaining share of revenues comes from license fees and user charges (e.g., payment for utilities, occupational license fees, tuition fees) and other taxes.

Should We Have a Flat Tax?

Some politicians and individuals believe that we should scrap the current progressive income tax and replace it with a **flat tax**. A flat tax, also called a proportional tax, is designed so that everybody would be charged the same percentage of their income. How would a flat tax work? What do you think would be the advantages and disadvantages of a flat tax?

> **flat tax**
> a tax that charges all income earners the same percentage of their income

With a flat tax, a household could simply report its income, multiply it by the tax rate, and send in the money. Because no deductions are involved, the form could be a simple page! But most flat tax proposals call for exempting income to a certain level—say, the poverty line.

Actually, if the flat tax plan allowed individuals to deduct a standard allowance of, say, $20,000 from their wages, the tax would still be progressive. Here's how it would work: If you were earning less than $20,000 a year, you would not have to pay any income taxes.

However, if you earned $50,000 a year, and the flat tax rate was 15 percent, after subtracting your $20,000 allowance you would be paying taxes on $30,000. In this system, you would have to pay $4,500 in taxes (0.15 × $30,000) and your average tax rate would be 9 percent ($4,500/$50,000 = 0.09). Now, say you made $100,000 a year. After taking your $20,000 allowance, you would have to pay a 15 percent tax on $80,000, and you would owe the government $12,000. Notice, however, that your average tax rate would be higher: 12 percent ($12,000/$100,000 = 0.12) as opposed to 9 percent. So if the flat tax system allows individual taxpayers to take a standard allowance, like most flat tax proposals, then the tax is actually progressive. That is, lower- and middle-income families will pay, on average, a smaller average tax rate, even though everyone has the same tax rate over the stipulated allowance.

The advantages of the flat tax are that all of the traditional exemptions, like entertainment deductions, mortgage interest deductions, business travel expenses, and charitable contribution deductions, would be out the door, along with the possibilities of abuses and misrepresentations that go with tax deductions. Taxpayers could fill out tax returns in the way they did in the old days, in a space about the size of a postcard. Advocates

in the news   Social Security: A Ponzi Scheme?

The offer to double your money in 90 days seemed too good to be true. But once the first people to sign up were paid the promised return on their investment, more and more punters queued up in Boston to put their money into the "Securities Exchange Company." Charles Ponzi had devised a classic fraud: extravagant payouts to the first investors were easily financed by the growing numbers of those who followed. But not indefinitely. Once the fraud was uncovered in 1920, Ponzi was sent to jail.

Prosperous Ponzi

Fifteen years later the American president of the day, Franklin Roosevelt, signed the law establishing Social Security, the name America gives to its public pension system. The first pensioner to benefit was Ida May Fuller, a spinster from Vermont, who had paid the grand sum of $24.75 in contributions. Her first monthly Social Security check in January 1940 was for almost as much. Miss Fuller lived to be 100 and received benefits totaling $22,889.

As it happens, the pension scheme that proved so beneficial to Miss Fuller relies on much the same principle as the Ponzi scam. America's Social Security scheme is the pay-as-you-go [PAYG] sort in which today's workers pay for today's pensioners. The first few generations of pensioners received much more in benefits than they had paid in contributions. These windfall gains arguably continued until quite recently because the PAYG system was extended to cover more and more workers, and contribution rates kept going up.

Paul Samuelson, a Nobel-prize-winning economist, pinpointed the Ponzi characteristics of pay-as-you-go pensions back in 1967. "The beauty of social insurance is that it is actuarially unsound. Everyone who reaches retirement age is given benefit privileges that far exceed anything he has paid in. . . . Always there are more youths than old folks in a growing population. More important, with real incomes growing at some 3% a year, the taxable base upon which benefits rest in any period are much greater than the taxes paid historically by the generation now retired. . . . A growing nation is the greatest Ponzi game ever contrived."

After the second world war, politicians in most developed countries joined in the game with gusto. In the 1960s and 1970s, they made state PAYG pensions even more unsound by introducing big hikes in benefits. To this day, PAYG schemes remain the main form of pension provision the world over. They are especially important in the EU, where they account for nearly 90% of total pension income. Even in Britain, where the PAYG scheme is much less generous than in most of continental Europe, it accounts for 60% of total pension income.

Yet all the while the foundations of PAYG schemes were being undermined. As Mr. Samuelson had pointed out, the underlying return from this kind of pension comes from the growth in the workforce and its real earnings. But in the 1970s, the post-war baby boom gave way to a baby bust that put an end to the indefinite prospect of "more youths than old folks." Besides, those "old folks" were living longer because of an unprecedented rise in life expectancy at older ages. At the same time the postwar surge in productivity and hence real wages gave way to much more pedestrian growth rates.

What has saved PAYG schemes so far is that demographic developments take a long time to work their way through the system. The schemes are still benefiting from the large number of post-war baby boomers in the working-age population, most of whom won't reach retirement for another decade or so.

(continued)

in the news   Social Security: A Ponzi Scheme? (cont.)

Today's problems arise largely from overgenerous increases in pension benefits that have already pushed contribution rates to the limit.

The worst is yet to come. Over the next 30 years, western populations will age at a record rate. The ratio of the over-65s to those aged 20–64 will double. Japan's working-age population, already declining, will shrink drastically. Something will have to give. Either benefits must halve in relation to average incomes; or contribution rates—already oppressively high in many countries—must double; or the retirement age must go up.

If governments were to leave matters as they are, they would eventually have to borrow to bridge the gap between future pension outlays and tax revenue. . . .

consider this:

Rumor has it that most young people believe that there is a greater chance that they will see an unidentified flying object (UFO) in their lifetime than a Social Security payment.

We are often told that Social Security is a retirement program. However, it is really a tax plan that transfers money from workers to the elderly. Social Security is a pay-as-you-go system—payments to current retirees are derived from payroll taxes imposed on current workers.

SOURCE: From "Snares and Delusions", 'The Economist', February 14, 2002 ©. The Economist Newspaper Limited, London 2002. Reprinted with permission.

The Social Security Trust Fund is slowly going broke, and if it is not fixed, it is predicted to go belly up by 2037 (and some say serious problems could occur as soon as 2016). At that point, retirees would only get 75 percent of their promised benefits. The problem is that many baby boomers will begin to retire in the next several years, and simply not enough workers are contributing part of their incomes to pay for these new retirees. Currently, the system has 3.3 workers for each Social Security beneficiary. By 2031, that ratio changes to only an estimated 2.2 workers for each beneficiary. In addition, demographers' forecasts of declining birth rates and longer life expectancies only make matters worse.

In 1940, the life expectancy of a 65-year-old was 12.5 years; today it is 17.5 years. According to the Social Security Administration, in 30 years, the number of older Americans will be nearly twice what it is today—an increase from 36 million to almost 74 million in 2034. Another serious problem stems from indexing initial benefits to wages rather than prices. Wages rise almost 1 percent per year faster than prices. According to Greg Mankiw, former chair of the Council of Economic Advisers, "A person, with average wages, retiring at age 65 this year gets an annual benefit of about $14,000, but a similar person retiring in 2050 is scheduled to get over $20,000 in today's dollars. In other words, even after adjusting for inflation, a typical person's benefits are scheduled to rise by over 40 percent."

argue that the government could collect the same amount of tax revenues, but the tax would be much more efficient, as many productive resources would be released from looking for tax loopholes to doing something productive from society's standpoint.

Of course, some versions of the flat tax will hurt certain groups. Not surprisingly, realtors and home-owners, who like the mortgage interest deductions, and tax accountants, who make billions every year preparing tax returns, will not be supportive of a flat tax with no deductions. And, of course, many legitimate questions would inevitably arise, such as: What would happen to the size of charitable contributions if the charitable contribution deduction was eliminated? And how much will the housing sector be hurt if the mortgage interest deduction was eliminated or phased out? After all, the government's intent of the tax break was to increase home ownership. And the deductions for hybrid cars are intended to get drivers into cleaner, more fuel-efficient cars. These deductions could be gone in most flat tax proposals. In addition, the critics of the flat tax believe that the tax is not progressive enough to eliminate the inequities in income and are skeptical of the tax-revenue–raising capabilities of a flat tax.

ability to pay principle
belief that those with the greatest ability to pay taxes should pay more than those with less ability to pay

vertical equity
different treatment based on level of income and the ability to pay principle

Taxes: Efficiency and Equity

In the last few chapters, we talked about efficiency—getting the most out of our scarce resources. However, taxes for the most part are *not* efficient (except for internalizing externalities and providing public goods) because they change incentives and distort the values that buyers and sellers place on goods and services. That is, decisions made by buyers and sellers are different from what they would be without the tax. Taxes can be inefficient because they may lead to less work, less saving, less investment, and lower output.

Economists spend a lot of time on issues of efficiency, but policymakers (and economists) are also concerned about other goals, such as fairness. Income redistribution through taxation may also lead to greater productivity for low-income workers through improvements in health and education. Even though what is fair to one person may not be fair to another, most people would agree that we should have a fair tax system based on either ability to pay or benefits received.

Ability to Pay Principle and Vertical Equity The **ability to pay principle** is simply that those with the greatest ability to pay taxes (richer people) should pay more than those with the least ability to pay taxes (poorer people). This concept is known as **vertical equity**—people with different levels of income should be treated differently. The federal income tax is a good example of the ability to pay principle because the rich pay a larger percentage of their income in taxes. That is, high-income individuals will pay a higher percentage of their income in taxes than low-income individuals. The richest 20 percent of households in the United States make slightly more than 60 percent of the income but pay roughly 85 percent of the federal income tax; the poorest 40 percent actually have a negative tax (many in the group receive tax credits). When you add payroll taxes (Social Security) and Medicare, the tax system becomes less progressive than the federal income tax: 40 percent of the low-income taxpayers pay about 3 percent and the

Use what you've LEARNED   THE BURDEN OF THE CORPORATE INCOME TAX

Corporate income taxes are generally popular among voters because they think the tax comes from the corporation. Of course, it does write the check to the IRS, but that does not mean that the corporation (and its stockholders) bears the burden of the tax. Some of the tax burden (perhaps a great deal) is passed on to consumers in the form of higher prices. It will also impact investors' rates of return. Less investment leads to less capital for workers which lowers workers' productivity and wages. The key here is to be careful to distinguish between who pays the tax and who incurs the burden of the tax.

POLICY application   A CONSUMPTION TAX?

Some economists believe the current system of taxation creates a disincentive to save. They would replace the income tax with a **consumption tax**: that is, tax the amount that is spent rather than what is earned. Under a consumption tax, saved income is not taxed. Europeans tax consumption more than the United States. Former chair of the Federal Reserve, Alan Greenspan, encouraged policymakers to look at consumption taxes rather than income taxes because of its positive impact on saving and capital formation.

The theory behind a consumption tax is that people are taxed based on what they take out of the economy, not on what they put in. The reason: When they save and invest, those dollars add to the capital stock and raise workers' productivity. A consumption tax, such as a sales tax, provides more incentive to save and invest than does an income tax. Saving provides the funds that business uses to engage in investment, which in turn leads to more capital stock, greater output and productivity, and higher real wages.

According to UC Berkeley economist, Alan Auerbach, a consumption tax could raise the same

> **consumption tax**
> tax collected based on a taxpayer's spending

amount of revenue as the current tax system and increase GDP by 9 percent in the long run, as production increases with increased saving and capital formation.

SOURCE: Alan Auerbach, "A Consumption Tax," *Wall Street Journal*, August 25, 2005.

consider this:

Although many economists believe that a consumption tax is a good idea, the transition from an income tax to a consumption tax would be challenging. Others argue that low-income individuals save a small percentage of their income and spend a large fraction of their income, so they would benefit little from a consumption tax. Moving from an income tax to a consumption tax would also shift tax burdens to older generations that would have to pay a consumption tax on spending with income on which they had already paid income taxes. In addition, individual retirement accounts (IRAs) are already similar to a consumption tax. With IRA accounts, taxpayers can put a limited amount of their savings away and not have it taxed until retirement.

top 20 percent of income earners pay slightly less than 70 percent. Sales taxes are not a good example of the ability to pay principle, because low-income individuals pay a larger percentage of their income in such taxes.

Benefits Received Principle

The *benefits received principle* means that the individuals receiving the benefits are those who pay for them. Take the gasoline tax: the more miles one drives on the highway, the more gasoline used and the more taxes collected. The tax revenues are then used to maintain the highways. Or those who benefit from a new airport or an opera house should be the ones who pay for such public spending. Although this principle may work for some private goods, it does not work well for public goods such as national defense and the judicial system. Because we collectively consume national defense, it is not possible to find out who benefits and by exactly how much.

Administration Burden of Taxation

The administration burden of the income tax also leads to another deadweight loss. Imagine if everyone filled out a one-page tax form that took no more than 5 minutes. Instead the opportunity cost of the hours of time and services used in tax preparation is in the billions of dollars. The government also spends a great deal to enforce these taxes. A simplified tax system would reduce the deadweight loss.

Social Policy of Taxes

Taxes and subsidies can be efficiency enhancing when used to correct for externalities. For example, the government may view it as good social policy to subsidize cleaner, more efficient hybrid vehicles. Or they may want to put a high tax on cigarettes in an attempt to reduce teen smoking. In other words, taxes on alcohol and cigarettes may be used to discourage these activities—sometimes we call these "sin taxes."

SECTION CHECK

1. Over a third of federal spending goes toward pensions and income security programs.
2. A progressive tax takes a greater proportion of the income of higher-income groups than of lower-income groups.
3. A regressive tax takes a greater proportion of the income of lower-income groups than of higher-income groups.
4. A flat tax charges all income earners the same percentage of their income.
5. The ability to pay principle is the belief that those with the greatest ability to pay taxes should pay more than those with less ability.
6. Vertical equity is the concept that people with different levels of income should be treated differently.
7. The benefits received principle means that individuals receiving the benefits are those who pay for them.
8. A consumption tax is a tax collected based on the taxpayer's spending.

1. Has federal government spending as a fraction of GDP changed much since the 1960s?
2. What finances the majority of federal government spending?
3. What happens to the proportion of income paid as taxes when income rises, for a progressive tax? What is an example of such a progressive tax?
4. Why are excise taxes on items such as alcohol, tobacco, and gasoline considered regressive taxes?
5. How could a flat tax also be a progressive tax?
6. Why is the federal income tax an example of the ability to pay principle?
7. How is a gas tax an example of the benefits received principle?

SECTION 9.3   Public Choice

* What is public choice theory?
* What is the median voter model?
* What is rational ignorance?
* Why do special interest groups arise?

When the market fails, as in the case of an externality or public good, it may be necessary for the government to intervene and make public choices. However, it is possible for government actions in response to externalities to make matters worse. That is, just because markets have failed to generate efficient results does not necessarily mean that government can do a better job—see Exhibit 1. One explanation for this outcome is presented by public choice theory.

behavior of individuals in politics, as in the marketplace, will be influenced by self-interest. Bureaucrats, politicians, and voters make choices that they believe will yield them expected marginal benefits that will be greater than their expected marginal costs. Of course, the private sector and the public sector differ when it comes to the "rules of the game" that they must follow. The self-interest assumption is, however, central to the analysis of behavior in both arenas.

What Is Public Choice Theory?

Public choice theory is the application of economic principles to politics. Public choice economists believe that government actions are an outgrowth of individual behavior. Specifically, they assume that the

Scarcity and the Public Sector

The self-interest assumption is not the only similarity between the market and public sectors. For example, scarcity is present in the public sector as well as in the private sector. Public schools and public libraries come at the

section 9.3 exhibit 1	Do People in Government Waste Tax Money? 1970–2004 (percent of population agreeing)																	
	'70	'72	'74	'76	'78	'80	'82	'84	'86	'88	'90	'92	'94	'96	'98	'00	'02	'04
A Lot	69	66	74	74	77	78	66	65	**	63	67	67	70	59	61	59	48	61
Some	26	30	22	20	19	18	29	29	**	33	30	30	27	39	34	38	49	37
Not Very Much	4	2	1	3	2	2	2	4	**	2	2	2	2	1	4	3	3	2
Don't Know	1	2	2	3	2	2	3	2	**	2	1	1	1	0	1	1	0	1

**No data available for 1986 and 2006.

SOURCE: The American National Election Studies, 2009, http://www.electionstudies.org.

expense of something else. Competition is also present in the public sector, as different government agencies compete for government funds and lobbyists compete with each other to get favored legislation through Congress.

The Individual Consumption-Payment Link

In private markets, when a shopper goes to the supermarket to purchase groceries, the shopping cart is filled with many different goods that the consumer presumably wants and is willing to pay for; the shopping cart reflects the individual consumption-payment link. The link breaks down when an assortment of political goods is decided on by majority rule. These political goods might include such items as additional national defense, additional money for the space program, new museums, new public schools, increased foreign aid, and so on. Even though an individual may be willing to pay for some of these goods, it is unlikely that she will want to consume or pay for everything placed in the political shopping cart. However, if the majority decides that these political goods are important, the individual will have to purchase the goods through higher taxes, whether she values the goods or not.

Majority Rule and the Median Voters

In a two-party system, the candidate with the most votes wins the election. Because voters are likely to vote for the candidate who holds views similar to theirs, candidates must pay close attention to the preferences of the majority of voters.

For example, in Exhibit 2, we assume a normal distribution, with a continuum of voter preferences from the liberal left to the conservative right. We can see from the figure that only a few are extremely liberal or extremely conservative. A successful campaign would have to address the concerns of the median voters (those in the middle of the distribution in Exhibit 2), resulting in moderate policies. For example, if one candidate ran a fairly conservative campaign, attracting voters at and to the right of V_1, an opponent could win by a landslide by taking a fairly conservative position just to the left of this candidate. Alternatively, if the candidate takes a liberal position, say V_2, then the

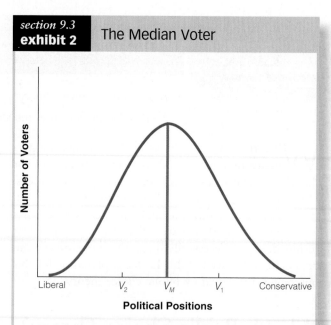

section 9.3 exhibit 2	The Median Voter

The median voter model predicts a strong tendency for both candidates to pick a position in the middle of the distribution, such as V_M, and that the election will be close.

Is this person selecting the items she wants? Do taxpayers always want what they have to pay for?

opponent can win by campaigning just to the right of that position. In this case, it is easy to see that the candidate who takes the median position, V_M, is least likely to be defeated. Of course, the distribution does not have to be normal or symmetrical; it could be skewed to the right or left. Regardless of the distribution, however, the successful candidate will still seek out the median voters. In fact, the median voter model predicts a strong tendency for both candidates to choose a position in the middle of distribution, and therefore the election will be close.

Of course, this model does not mean that all politicians will find or even attempt to find the median. Politicians, for example, may take different positions because they have arrived at different predictions of voter preferences or have merely misread public sentiment; or they may think they have the charisma to change voter preferences.

> **median voter model**
> a model that predicts candidates will choose a position in the middle of the distribution
>
> **rational ignorance** lack of incentive to be informed

Voters and Rational Ignorance

Representative democracy provides a successful mechanism for making social choices in many countries. But some important differences are evident in the way democracy is ideally supposed to work and how it actually works.

One of the keys to an efficiently working democracy is a concerned and informed electorate. Everyone is supposed to take time to study the issues and candidates and then carefully weigh the relevant information before deciding how to vote. Although an informed citizenry is desirable from a social point of view, it is not clear that individuals will find it personally desirable to become politically informed.

Obtaining detailed information about issues and candidates is costly. Many issues are complicated, and a great deal of technical knowledge and information is necessary to make an informed judgment on them. To find out what candidates are really going to do requires a lot more than listening to their campaign slogans. It requires studying their past voting records, reading a great deal that has been written either by or about them, and asking them questions at public meetings. Taking the time and trouble to do these things—and more—is the cost that each eligible voter has to pay personally for the benefits of being politically informed. These costs may help to explain why the majority of Americans cannot identify their congressional representatives and are unlikely to be acquainted with their representatives' views on Social Security, health care, tariffs, and agricultural policies.

For many people the costs of becoming politically informed are high, whereas the benefits are low. As a result, they limit their quest for political information to listening to the radio on the way to work, talking with friends, casual reading, and other things they would normally do anyway. Even though most people in society might be better off if everyone became more informed, it isn't worth the cost for most individuals to make the requisite effort to become informed themselves. Public choice economists refer to this lack of incentive to become informed as rational ignorance. People will generally make much more informed decisions as buyers than as voters. For example, you are likely to gather more information when making a decision on a car purchase than when you are deciding between candidates in an upcoming election. An uninformed decision on a car purchase will most likely affect your life much more than an uninformed decision on a candidate, especially when your vote will most likely not alter the outcome of the election.

The fact that one vote, especially in a state or national election, is highly unlikely to affect the outcome of the election may explain why some citizens choose not to vote. Many factors may determine the net benefits for voting, including candidates and issues on the ballot, weather, and distance to the polling booths. For example, we would certainly expect fewer voters to turn out at the polls on the day of a blizzard; the blizzard would change the net benefits. We would also expect more voters at the polls if the election were predicted to be a close one, with emotions running higher and voter perception that their individual vote is more significant.

If the cost of being an informed voter is high and the benefits low, why do people vote? Many people vote for reasons other than to affect the outcome of the election. They vote because they believe in the democratic process and because of civic pride. In other words, they perceive that the benefits they derive from being involved in the political process outweigh the costs.

Furthermore, rational ignorance does not imply that people should not vote; it is merely one explanation for why some people do not vote. The point that public choice economists are making is that some people will vote only if they think that their vote will make a difference; otherwise, they will not vote.

special interest groups groups with an intense interest in particular voting issues that may be different from that of the general public

Special Interest Groups

Even though many voters may be uninformed about specific issues, others may feel a strong need to be politically informed. Such individuals may be motivated to organize a **special interest group.**

These groups may have intense feelings about and a degree of interest in particular issues that is at variance with the general public. However, as a group these individuals are more likely to influence decision makers and have a far greater impact on the outcome of a political decision than they would with their individual votes.

If a special interest group is successful in getting everyone else to pay for a project that benefits them, the cost will be spread over so large a number of taxpayers that the amount any one person will have to pay is negligible. Hence, the motivation for an individual citizen to spend the necessary time and effort to resist an interest group is minimal, even if she had a guarantee that this resistance would be effective.

For example, many taxpayers and consumers are unaware of the federal subsidy to sugar growers. The subsidy is estimated to cost consumers more than $1 billion a year, which is less than $5 per person. However, the gain from the subsidy is estimated to be over $100,000 per sugar grower. At that price, few customers are going to invest the time and money to fight this issue. However, the effort to keep the subsidy is surely enough to get sugar growers to make trips to Washington, D.C., and help in political campaigns.

SECTION CHECK

1. Public choice theory holds that the behavior of individuals in politics, as in the marketplace, is influenced by self-interest.
2. The median voter model predicts that a candidate will choose a position in the middle of the distribution.
3. Rational ignorance is the condition in which voters tend to be relatively uninformed about political issues because of the high information costs and low benefits of being politically informed.
4. A special interest group is a political pressure group formed by individuals with a common political objective.
5. Special interest groups are more likely to have an impact on the outcome of a social decision than their members would if they voted individually.

1. What principles does the public choice analysis of government behavior share with the economic analysis of market behavior?
2. Why is the tendency strong for candidates to choose positions in the middle of the distribution of voter preferences?
3. Why is it rational to be relatively less informed about most political choices than about your own market choices?
4. Why can't the majority of citizens effectively counter the political power of special interest groups?

Interactive Chapter Summary

Fill in the blanks:

1. _____ are the rules of our economic game.

2. Government redistributes income in three ways: _____, _____, and _____.

3. The market mechanism does not always assure fulfillment of some macroeconomic goals: _____, _____, and _____.

4. Governments obtain revenue through two major avenues: _____ and _____.

5. The government share of GDP changed _____ between 1970 and 2000, but its composition has changed _____.

6. From 1968 to 2005, national defense spending as a fraction of GDP _____.

7. By the mid-1970s, for the first time in history, roughly half of government spending in the United States was for _____.

8. Income transfer payments _____ in the 1980s and 1990s.

9. _____ and _____ account for roughly half of state and local government expenditures.

10. At the federal level, _____ half of taxes are from personal income taxes and corporate income taxes.

11. The United State relies _____ heavily on income-based taxes than most other developed countries in the world.

12. If a higher-income person paid the same taxes as a lower-income person, that tax would be considered _____.

13. Excise taxes are considered regressive because lower-income people spend a _____ fraction of their incomes on such taxes than do higher-income people.

14. Sales taxes account for _____ state and local tax revenue than property taxes.

15. Most people agree that the tax system should be based on either _____ or _____.

16. When people with different levels of income are treated differently, it is called _____ equity.

17. Federal income tax is a good example of the _____ principle.

18. The _____ principle means that the individuals receiving the benefits are those who pay for them.

19. The _____ burden of a tax leads to a deadweight loss.

20. With a _____ tax, individuals are taxed on what they take out of the economy, not on what they put in.

21. Public choice theory is the application of _____ principles to politics.

22. Public choice economists believe that the behavior of individuals in politics, as in the marketplace, will be influenced by _____.

23. The amount of information that is necessary to make an efficient decision is much _____ in political markets than in private markets.

24. In private markets, an individual _____ link indicates that the goods consumers get reflect what they are willing to pay for.

25. Even though actors in both the private and public sectors are _____, the _____ are different.

26. A successful political campaign would have to address the concerns of the _____ voters.

27. _____ implies that most private-sector buyers will tend to be more informed than voters on a given issue.

28. If voters were _____ informed, special-interest groups would have less influence on political results, other things being equal.

29. Compared to private-sector decisions, acquiring information to make public-sector decisions will tend to have _____ benefits and _____ costs.

30. _____ positions tend to win in elections decided by majority votes.

Answers: 1. Property rights 2. taxes; subsidies; transfer payments 3. full employment; stable prices; economic growth 4. taxation; borrowing 5. little; considerably 6. fell 7. social concerns 8. increased 9. Education; public welfare 10. more than 11. more 12. regressive 13. larger 14. more 15. ability to pay; benefits received 16. vertical 17. ability to pay 18. benefits received 19. administrative 20. consumption 21. economic 22. self-interest 23. greater 24. consumption-payment 25. self-interested; "rules of the game" 26. median 27. Rational ignorance 28. more 29. smaller; larger 30. Middle-of-the-road

Key Terms and Concepts

private property rights 234
progressive tax 239
regressive tax 239
excise tax 239

flat tax 240
ability to pay principle 243
vertical equity 243
consumption tax 244

median voter model 247
rational ignorance 247
special interest groups 248

Section Check Answers

9.1 Other Functions of Government

1. **Why do owners with clear property rights have incentives to use their property efficiently?**

   Private property rights mean that owners will capture the benefits and bear the costs of their choices with regard to their property, making it in their self-interest to use it efficiently, in ways for which the benefits are expected to exceed the costs.

2. **How does the government use taxes, subsidies, and transfer payments to redistribute income toward lower-income groups?**

   Taxes, particularly progressive ones such as the individual income tax, are borne more heavily by higher-income citizens than lower-income citizens, while most subsidy and transfer payment programs are primarily focused on lower-income citizens.

3. **Why would the government want to prevent market conditions of insufficient competition?**

   When there is insufficient or restricted competition, outputs are lower and prices paid by consumers are higher than they would be with more effective competition. By encouraging competition and discouraging monopoly, then, consumers can benefit.

9.2 Government Spending and Taxation

1. **Has federal government spending as a fraction of GDP changed much since the 1960s?**

   Overall federall government spending as a fraction of GDP has not changed much since the 1960s. However, the composition of federal government spending has changed, with substantial decreases in national defense spending and substantial increases in income security spending, such as for Social Security and Medicare.

2. **What finances the majority of federal government spending?**

   The majority of federal government spending is financed by taxes on personal and corporate incomes, although payroll taxes have risen substantially in recent years.

3. **What happens to the proportion of income paid as taxes when income rises, for a progressive tax? What is an example of such a progressive tax?**

   A progressive tax is one that takes an increasing proportion of income as income rises. The personal income tax is an example because higher-income earners pay a larger proportion of their incomes than lower-income earners.

4. Why are excise taxes on items such as alcohol, tobacco, and gasoline considered regressive taxes?

Lower-income people pay a larger fraction of their incomes for such items, so that they pay a larger fraction of their incomes for taxes on those items, even though all users pay the same tax rate on them.

5. How could a flat tax also be a progressive tax?

With a standard allowance or deduction amount, a proportional tax on taxable income would represent a larger fraction of total income for a high-income earner than for a low-income earner.

6. Why is the federal income tax an example of the ability to pay principle?

Higher-income people, with a greater ability to pay, pay a larger fraction of their income in taxes.

7. How is a gas tax an example of the benefits received principle?

Those who drive more benefit more from the highway system, but they also pay more in total gasoline taxes.

9.3 Public Choice

1. What principles does the public choice analysis of government behavior share with the economic analysis of market behavior?

Public choice analysis of government behavior is based on the principle that the behavior of individuals in politics, just like that in the marketplace, is influenced by self-interest. That is, it applies basic economic theory to politics, looking for differences in incentives to explain people's behavior.

2. Why is the tendency strong for candidates to choose positions in the middle of the distribution of voter preferences?

This is what we would predict from the median voter model, because the candidate closer to the median is likely to attract a majority of the votes.

3. Why is it rational to be relatively less informed about most political choices than about your own market choices?

It is rational to be relatively less informed about most political choices because the costs of becoming more informed about political issues tend to be higher and the benefits of becoming more informed about political choices tend to be lower than for your own market choices.

4. Why can't the majority of citizens effectively counter the political power of special interest groups?

The majority of citizens can't effectively counter the political power of special interest groups because even if a special interest group is successful in getting everyone else to pay for a project that benefits that group, the cost to each citizen will be small. In fact, this cost is very likely to be far smaller than the cost to a member of the majority of becoming sufficiently informed and active to successfully oppose it.

True or False:

1. Government spending as a percentage of GDP has changed little since 1970, but the composition of government spending has changed considerably.

2. The composition of state and local spending is different from that of federal spending.

3. A large majority of government activity is financed by borrowing.

4. Neither the composition of U.S. federal government spending nor its share of GDP has changed much since 1970.

5. Taxpayers in other parts of the developed world have heavier tax burdens than those in the United States.

6. Taxes on gasoline, liquor, and tobacco products provide a substantial portion of federal tax revenues.

7. The share of federal taxes going to Social Security and Medicare has risen significantly in recent years.

8. Most other countries rely less heavily on income-based taxes than the United States.

9. If a higher-income person pays more in total taxes than a lower-income person, those taxes would be considered progressive.

10. Excise taxes, such as those on alcohol, tobacco, and gasoline, tend to be the most regressive taxes.

11. Excise taxes can lead to economic inefficiency.

12. A larger share of state and local government revenues are from the federal government in grants than from state and local personal and corporate income taxes.

13. For the most part taxes are inefficient because they change incentives and alter the true value buyers and sellers place on goods and services.

14. Most taxes provide incentives for individuals to work hard, save, and invest.

15. The ability to pay principle states that those with the least ability to pay taxes should pay more than those with the greatest ability to pay taxes.

16. The gasoline tax is a good example of the benefits received principle.

17. In public choice analysis, bureaucrats, politicians, and voters are assumed to make choices that they believe will yield to the public expected marginal benefits greater than their expected marginal costs.

18. Scarcity and competition are present in the public sector as well as in the private sector.

19. The individual consumption-payment link breaks down when goods are decided on by majority rule.

20. The median voter result implies that when those with extreme political views become more extreme, it will have a large effect on the majority voting outcome.

21. The majority of Americans cannot identify their congressional representatives.

22. The benefits of casting a well-informed vote are generally far greater than the cost of doing so for most voters.

23. An election that is expected to be close would tend to increase voter turnout.

Multiple Choice:

1. Which of the following are important roles of the government?
   a. protecting property rights
   b. providing a legal system
   c. intervention when insufficient competition occurs in the marketplace
   d. promoting stability and economic growth
   e. all of the above

2. Social Security and Medicare are financed by
   a. personal income taxes.
   b. payroll taxes.
   c. excise taxes.
   d. corporation income taxes.
   e. none of the above taxes.

3. Who must legally pay Social Security and Medicare taxes?
   a. employers
   b. employees
   c. both employers and employees
   d. neither employers nor employees

4. Expenditures on _____ comprise the largest component of state and local government budgets.
   a. education
   b. public safety
   c. public infrastructure (such as roads and water works)
   d. public welfare (such as food stamps and income supplemental programs)

5. _____ taxes are designed to take a larger percentage of high incomes as compared to lower incomes.
   a. Progressive
   b. Regressive
   c. Proportional
   d. Negative

6. An example of a proportional tax would be
   a. a state sales tax.
   b. a local property tax.
   c. a flat rate income tax.
   d. the current U.S. income tax.

7. The largest single source of revenue for the federal government is the
   a. corporate income tax.
   b. federal excise tax.
   c. personal income tax.
   d. Social Security tax.

8. Which is the largest single component of federal expenditures?
   a. interest on the national debt
   b. defense spending
   c. Social Security
   d. foreign aid

9. The U.S. federal income tax is an example of a
   a. progressive tax.
   b. proportional tax.
   c. regressive tax.
   d. value-added tax.

10. The gasoline tax is an example of
    a. progressive taxation.
    b. neutral taxation.
    c. proportional taxation.
    d. regressive taxation.

11. The ability to pay principle states:
    a. Those with the greatest ability to pay taxes should pay more.
    b. Those with the least ability to pay taxes should pay more.
    c. Individuals receiving the benefits should pay for them.
    d. All of the above are true.

12. The amount of information that is necessary to make an efficient choice is generally _____ in the public sector than in the private sector.
    a. less
    b. more
    c. the same
    d. None of the above is true.

13. Voters will tend to be _____ informed about their political choices than their private market choices, other things being equal.
    a. more
    b. equally
    c. less
    d. Any of the above are equally likely to be true.

14. The median voter result implies that
    a. elections will often be very close.
    b. elections will usually be landslides for the same party year after year.
    c. elections will usually be landslides, with victories alternating between parties each year.
    d. when the preferences of most voters change substantially, winning political positions will also tend to change.
    e. both a and d are true.

15. For a voter to become more informed on a political issue is likely to have _____ benefits and _____ costs than for similar market decisions, other things being equal.
    a. smaller; larger
    b. smaller; smaller
    c. larger; larger
    d. larger; smaller

16. Which of the following would tend to raise voter turnout?
    a. a blizzard or heavy rainstorm on election day
    b. an election that is expected to be a landslide
    c. the longer the wait is expected to be at the voting locations
    d. a feeling that the candidates are basically running on the same platforms
    e. None of the above would tend to raise voter turnout.

17. If there are far fewer sugar growers than sugar consumers,
    a. the growers are likely to be more informed and influential on policy than voters.
    b. the consumers are likely to be more informed and influential on policy than voters.
    c. individual sugar growers are likely to have more at stake than individual sugar consumers.
    d. individual sugar consumers are likely to have more at stake than individual sugar growers.
    e. a is likely to be true because c is likely to be true.

Problems:

1. Why does favoring market mechanisms over command and control mechanisms *not* mean that a person wants no government whatsoever?

2. Why would means-tested transfer payments (such as food stamps, in which benefits are reduced as income rises) act like an income tax facing recipients?

3. Why are income taxes more progressive than excise taxes such as those on alcohol, tobacco, and gasoline?

4. Why is the Social Security payroll tax considered regressive?

5. Could the burdens of a regulation be either progressive or regressive, like the effects of a tax?

6. Is a gas tax better described as reflecting the ability to pay principle or the benefits received principle? What about the federal income tax?

7. Why would the benefits received principle be difficult to apply to national defense and the provision of the justice system?

8. Illustrate the median voter model graphically and explain it.

9. Why would a candidate offering "a choice, not an echo," run a risk of losing in a landslide?

10. Why might the party favorites at a political convention sometimes be harder to elect than more moderate candidates?

11. How can you be forced to pay for something you do not want to "buy" in the political sector? Is this sometimes good?

12. Why does the creation of a government program create a special interest group, which makes it difficult to reduce or eliminate it in the future?

13. Why are college students better informed about their own teachers' and schools' policies than about national education issues?

14. Why do you think news reporters are more informed than average citizens about public policy issues?

PART 4 HOUSEHOLDS AND MARKET STRUCTURE

TAKE OUT

10 Consumer Choice Theory

In this chapter, we discuss how individuals allocate their income between different bundles of goods. This decision involves trade-offs—if you buy more of one good, you cannot afford as much of other goods.

Why do consumers buy more of a product when the price falls and less of a product when the price rises? How do consumers respond to rising income? Falling income? How do we as consumers choose certain bundles of goods with our available budget to fit our desires? We address these questions in this chapter to strengthen our understanding of the law of demand. ■

SECTION
10.1

Consumer Behavior

* What is the substitution effect?
* What is the income effect?

* Can we make interpersonal utility comparisons?
* What is diminishing marginal utility?

As you may recall from Chapter 4, the law of demand is intuitive. Put simply, at a higher price, consumers will buy less (a decrease in the quantity demanded); at a lower price, consumers will buy more (an increase in quantity demanded), *ceteris paribus*. However, the downward-sloping demand curve has three other explanations: (1) the income and substitution effects of a price change, (2) the law of diminishing marginal utility, and (3) an interpretation using indifference curves and budget lines (in the appendix).

Let's start with out first explanation of a downward-sloping demand curve—the substitution and income effects of a price change. For example, if the price of pizza increases, the quantity of pizza demanded will fall because some consumers might switch out of pizza into hamburgers, tacos, burritos, submarine sandwiches, or some other foods that substitute for pizza. This behavior is called the **substitution effect** of a price change. In addition, a price increase for pizza will reduce the quantity of pizza demanded because it reduces a buyer's purchasing power. The buyer cannot buy as many pieces of pizza at higher prices as she could at lower prices, which is called the **income effect** of a price change.

The second explanation for the negative relationship between price and quantity demanded is what economists call **diminishing marginal utility.** In a given time period, a buyer will receive less satisfaction from each successive unit consumed. For example, a second ice cream cone will yield less satisfaction than the first, a third less satisfaction than the second, and so on. It follows from diminishing marginal utility that if people are deriving less satisfaction from successive units, consumers would buy added units only if the price were reduced. Let's now take a closer look at utility theory.

substitution effect
a consumer's switch to another similar good when the price of the preferred good increases

income effect
reduction in quantity demanded of a good when its price increases because of a consumer's decreased purchasing power

diminishing marginal utility
a good's ability to provide less satisfaction with each successive unit consumed

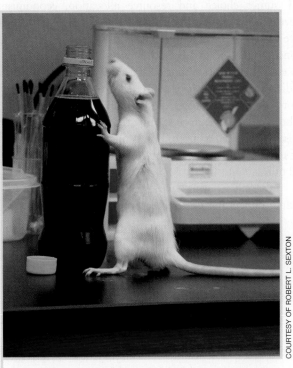

COURTESY OF ROBERT L. SEXTON

Economists conducted an experiment with rats to see how they would respond to changing prices of different drinks (changing the number of times a rat had to press a bar). Rats responded by choosing more of the beverage with a lower price, showing they were willing to substitute when the price changed. That is, even rats seem to behave rationally—responding to incentives and opportunities to make themselves better off.

Wants Versus Needs

The law of demand puts the concept of basic human "needs," at least as an analytical tool, to rest. Needs are those things that you must have at any price. That is, there are no substitutes. There are usually plenty of substitutes for any good, some better than others. The law of demand, with its inverse relationship between price and quantity demanded, implies that even so-called needs can be more or less urgent, depending on the circumstances (opportunity costs). Whenever you hear somebody say, "I need a new car," "I need a new laptop" or "I need new clothes," always be sure to ask: What does the person really mean? At what price does that person "need" the good? What is someone willing to give up to buy a new car—a trip to Hawaii? tuition? rent? That is, the cost of the new car is the items that you could have purchased if you did not buy the car. There are many substitutes for a new car—a used car, the bus, a motorcycle, carpooling, or moving within walking distance to work. The relevant question is whether the marginal benefits of buying a new car exceed the marginal cost, which is very different than saying you need a new car.

Economic goods are scarce and the amount people consume depends on the prices they are willing and able to pay. To need a good implies that we are willing to give up anything for it; need as a concept ignores scarcity and the fact that choices may change with circumstances and trade-offs.

Do We Need More Freeways?

Commuters are constantly complaining about how long it takes to drive to work. Do we *need* more freeways?

Perhaps many commuters would like to see more taxpayer dollars going toward freeways instead of museums, schools, or parks. Remember, the concept of need implies some type of urgency and conveys the message: "I will give up anything to get it." The real question is: At what price do we want more freeways? Would we need more freeways if the price of downtown parking was $1,000 a day? Probably not. Train yourself to think that we want different amounts of goods and services at different opportunity costs and that costs are more than just dollars and cents. For example, a person who normally does not speed while driving may do so if the relevant benefit of speed rises—for example, if he is late for his final exam or wedding, or if she is on her way to the hospital to deliver her baby.

Should There Be a Lane Reserved for Urgent Needs on Our Freeways?

During rush hour there are often very congested freeways. Perhaps we should have an express lane for people who have urgent needs. What do you think of this idea? Imagine the number of people that would develop what they felt were urgent needs if the "urgent need" lane was much shorter than the other lanes. It would be inevitable that the system would fall apart. In fact, it would be fun to guess what might be defined as an urgent need. It might include: "I am really in a hurry because I have to get home to clean up my apartment" or "I need to get back to the dorm to type my overdue term paper." "Oh shoot, I left the dog in the house." Many people would perceive their needs as more urgent than other people's urgent needs. This is a reason that the concept of needs falls apart as a means of explaining behavior. It is impossible to make the concept of need useful analytically when it is so hard to define or compare those "needs" among people.

Utility

To more clearly define the relationship between consumer choice and resource allocation, economists developed the concept of **utility**—a measure of the relative levels of satisfaction that consumers get from the consumption of goods and services. Defining one **util** as equivalent to one unit of satisfaction, economists can indicate relative levels of consumer satisfaction that result from alternative choices. For example, for a java junkie who wouldn't dream of starting the day without a strong dose of caffeine, a cup of coffee might generate 150 utils of satisfaction while a cup of herb tea might only generate 10 utils.

Inherently, utility varies from individual to individual depending on specific preferences. For example, Jason might get 50 utils of satisfaction from eating his first piece of apple pie, while Brittany may only derive 4 utils of satisfaction from her first piece of apple pie.

In fact, a whole school of thought called utilitarianism, based on utility theory, was developed by Jeremy Bentham. Bentham believed that society should seek the greatest happiness for the greater number. (See Bentham's biography on page 259.)

utility
a measure of the relative levels of satisfaction consumers get from consumption of goods and services

util
one unit of satisfaction

Utility Is a Personal Matter

Economists recognize that it is not really possible to make interpersonal utility comparisons. That is, they know that it is impossible to compare the relative satisfactions of different persons. The relative

GREAT ECONOMIC
THINKERS   JEREMY BENTHAM (1748–1832)

Jeremy Bentham was born in London in 1748. He was a gifted child, reading history and other "serious" books at age 3, playing the violin at age 5, and studying Latin and French when he was only 6. At 12, he entered Queens College, Oxford, where he studied law. In his late teens, Bentham decided to concentrate on his writings. With funding provided by his father, he wrote a series of books on philosophy, economics, and politics. He would often write for 8 to 12 hours a day, a practice that continued through his life, leaving scholars material to compile for years to come. Most of his writings were not published until well over a century after his death.

According to Bentham, "pain and pleasure are the sovereign masters governing man's conduct": People will tend to pursue things that are pleasurable and avoid things that are painful. To this day, the rule of rational choice—weighing marginal benefits against marginal costs—has its roots in the earlier works of Jeremy Bentham. That is, economists predict human behavior on the basis of people's responses to changing incentives; people make choices on the basis of their expected marginal benefits and their expected marginal costs.

Although Bentham was most well known for utilitarianism, a philosophy stemming from his rational-choice ideas, he also had much to say on the subjects of prison reform, religion, relief to the poor, international law, and animal welfare. He was an ardent advocate of equality. Good humored, meditative, and kind, he was thought to be a visionary and ahead of his time, and he attracted the leading thinkers of the day to his company.

Bentham died in London in 1832. He left behind a strange legacy. At his request, his body was dissected, his skeleton padded and fully clothed, and his head preserved in the manner of South American headhunters. He asked that this "auto-icon," as it is now called, be seated in a glass case at the University College in London, and that his remains should be present at all meetings for the board. The auto-icon is still there today, although the mummified head, which did not preserve well, has been replaced by a wax head. The real head became an easy target for students and one story has the head being used at soccer practice! No one is quite sure why Bentham desired such an odd afterlife for his body; explanations range from it being a testament to an inflated sense of self-worth to a statement about religion or a practical joke.

satisfactions gained by two people drinking cups of coffee, for example, simply cannot be measured in comparable terms. Likewise, although we might be tempted to believe that a poorer person would derive greater utility from finding a $100 bill than would a richer person, we should resist the temptation. We simply cannot prove it. The poorer person may be "monetarily" poor because money and material things are not important to her, and the rich person may have become richer because of his lust for the things money can buy.

Total Utility and Marginal Utility

Economists recognize two different dimensions of utility: total utility and marginal utility. **Total utility** is the total amount of satisfaction derived from the

How many utils is this woman deriving from this cup of coffee? Can we accurately compare her satisfaction of a cup of coffee with another person's?

COURTESY OF ROBERT L. SEXTON

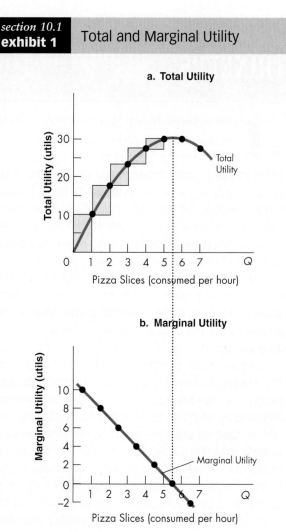

section 10.1
exhibit 1   Total and Marginal Utility

a. Total Utility

b. Marginal Utility

As you can see in (a), the total utility from pizza increases as consumption increases. In (b) marginal utility decreases as consumption increases. That is, as you eat more pizza, your satisfaction from each additional slice diminishes.

Slices of Pizza (per day)	Total Utility (utils)	Marginal Utility (utils)
0	0	
1	10	10
2	18	8
3	24	6
4	28	4
5	30	2
6	30	0
7	28	−2

consumption of a certain number of units of a good or service. In comparison, **marginal utility** is the extra satisfaction generated by an additional unit of a good that is consumed in a particular time period. For example, eating four slices of pizza in an hour might generate a total

total utility
total amount of satisfaction derived from the consumption of a certain number of goods or services

marginal utility
extra satisfaction generated by consumption of an additional good or service during a specific time period

of 28 utils of satisfaction. The first three slices of pizza might generate a total of 24 utils, while the last slice generates only 4 utils. In this case, the total utility of eating four slices of pizza is 28 utils, and the marginal utility of the fourth slice is 4 utils. Notice in Exhibit 1(a) how total

DIMINISHING MARGINAL UTILITY

Q Why do most individuals take only one newspaper from covered, coin-operated newspaper racks when it would be so easy to take more? Do you think potato chips, candy, or sodas could be sold profitably in the same kind of dispenser? Why or why not?

A Although ethical considerations keep some people from taking additional papers, the law of diminishing marginal utility is also at work here. The second newspaper adds practically zero utility to most individuals on most days, so they typically feel no incentive to take more than one. The exception to this case might be on Sundays, when supermarket coupons are present. In that instance, while the marginal utility is still lower for the second paper than for the first, the marginal utility of the second paper may be large enough to tempt some individuals to take additional copies.

On the other hand, if putting money in a vending machine gave access to many bags of potato chips, candy bars, or sodas, the temptation to take more than one might be too great for some people. After

Why are newspaper racks different from vending machines?

all, the potato chip bags would still be good tomorrow. Therefore, vending machines with foods and drinks only dispense one item at a time, because it is likely that, for most people, the marginal utility gained from another unit of food or drink is higher than for a second newspaper.

utility increases as consumption increases (we see more total utility after the fourth slice of pizza than after the third). But notice, too, that the increase in total utility from each additional unit (slice) is less than the unit before, which indicates the marginal utility. In Exhibit 1(b) we see how the marginal utility falls as consumption increases.

Diminishing Marginal Utility

Although economists believe that total utility increases with additional consumption, they also argue that the incremental satisfaction—the marginal utility—that results from the consumption of additional

diminishing marginal utility
the concept that states that as an individual consumes more and more of a good, each successive unit generates less and less utility (or satisfaction)

units tends to decline as consumption increases. In other words, each successive unit of a good that is consumed generates less satisfaction than did the previous unit. This concept is traditionally referred to as the **diminishing marginal utility.** Exhibit 1(b) demonstrates this graphically, where the marginal utility curve has a negative slope.

It follows from the law of diminishing marginal utility that as a person uses more and more units of a good to satisfy a given want, the intensity of the want, and the utility derived from further satisfying that want, diminishes. Think about it: If you are starving, your desire for that first piece of pizza will be great, but as you eat, you gradually become more and more full, reducing your desire for yet another piece.

Use what you've LEARNED

THE DIAMOND-WATER PARADOX: MARGINAL AND TOTAL UTILITY

"Nothing is more useful than water: but it will not purchase scarce anything. . . . Diamond, on the contrary, has scarce any value in use; but a very great quantity of other goods may frequently be had in exchange for it."

—ADAM SMITH, *Wealth of Nations*, 1776

Q Use the concept of marginal utility to evaluate the social value of water versus diamonds.

A The classic diamond-water paradox is the observation that sometimes those things that are necessary for life, like water, are inexpensive, and those items that are not necessary for life, like diamonds, are expensive. This paradox puzzled philosophers for centuries. The answer lies in making the distinction between total utility and marginal utility. The amount of total utility is indeed higher for water than for diamonds because of its importance for survival. But price is not determined by total utility, it is determined by marginal utility. Total utility measures the total amount of satisfaction someone derives from a good, whereas marginal utility determines the price. Market value—the value of the last, or marginal, unit traded—depends on both supply and demand. Thus, the limited supply of diamonds relative to the demand generates a high price, but an abundant supply of water relative to the demand results in a low price. The total utility (usefulness) for water is very large compared to the marginal utility. Because the price of water is so

Why is water, which is so critical to life, priced lower than diamonds which are less useful?

low, we use so much water that the marginal utility we receive from the last glass of water is small. Diamonds have a much smaller total utility (usefulness) relative to water, but because the price of diamonds is so high, we buy so few diamonds that they have a high marginal utility. Could water ever have a higher marginal utility than diamonds? Yes, if you had no water and no diamonds, your first cup of water would give you a much higher marginal value than your first cup of diamonds. Furthermore, if diamonds were very plentiful and water was very scarce, which would have the higher marginal utility? In this case, water would be expensive and diamonds would be inexpensive.

in the news   What Can "Neuroeconomics" Teach Us About How We Shop?

This morning, I had a remarkable experience: I strolled into a delicatessen and bought some delicious Stilton [a cheese produced in England]. What made the shopping trip unusual was that I was wearing a brain scanner while I did it. My costume consisted of an electroencephalograph cap, which looks like a polka-dot shower cap with wires plugged into it; a pair of wraparound glasses with a tiny video camera attached; a clothes peg on one finger to measure my heart rate; two other finger monitors that function like a lie detector; a thermometer patch on a fourth finger; and a satchel to hold a computer gathering the data.

Most of these devices, or their equivalent, can be hidden under clothes or baseball caps so that the wearer looks as if they are sporting only shades and an iPod, but in my case the boffins hadn't bothered, and so I entered the deli looking like an extra from a 1970s episode of Doctor Who.

This was all part of my efforts to understand "neuroeconomics," a new, controversial, and eclectic marriage between economics, marketing, and various branches of physiology and brain science. With very different aims, economists and marketers are attempting to tap into the dramatic advances in our understanding of the brain that have taken place over the past 15 years. Their tools encompass mood-altering drugs, tests for hormone levels, animal studies, and fMRI scans (which use immobile scanners to measure blood flows deep inside the brain).

"Neuromarketing" is the simplest application, and the one in which I was participating. David Lewis, a neurophysiologist at the Mind Lab, a spinoff from the University of Sussex, showed me how the physiological readings could be viewed alongside output from my camera to provide a simple but—presumably—useful demonstration of what really grabbed my attention in the deli. Among Lewis' findings are that eating chocolate is more exciting than making out (at least, making out in an electrical shower cap while surrounded by men with clipboards) and that, subconsciously, young men are more interested in sneakers than in the wares on display in an Ann Summers sex shop.

While the possible applications for marketers are obvious enough, such trials are hardly unlocking the deepest secrets of thought. It remains to be seen whether neuroscience has much to contribute to economics itself, a subject that has long focused on the decisions people make, without relying on any particular theory of how they make them. It is also hard to point to anything terribly interesting that the neuroeconomists have discovered, although neuroeconomics may contribute more as time goes by.

Neuroeconomics may provide more shape to the older and more famous field of behavioral economics. A mixture of economics and psychology, behavioral economics has used laboratory experiments to expose a bewildering number of exceptions to the traditional economic theory of rational choice. At present, though, there is little pattern to what the behavioral economists are observing, and it's possible that a greater understanding of how the brain works might help to provide one.

Yet neuroscience might also help reinforce the traditionalists. Wolfram Schultz, a neuroscientist at Cambridge who studies how the brain processes risk and reward, says that just as the brain registers sensations such as sight, he can now see it registering rewards. There was no reason to expect that the mathematically convenient economists' fantasy of "utility" had any real analogue in the brain—but it seems that it might, after all. There's a thought.

SOURCE: *State* Magazine Tim Harford Posted Saturday, Nov. 1, 2008, at 7:55 A.M. Tim Harford is a columnist for the *Financial Times*. He is the author of *The Undercover Economist*, and his latest book is *The Logic of Life*.

SECTION ✓ CHECK

1. A substitution effect occurs when a consumer switches to another similar good when the price of the preferred good increases.
2. The income effect occurs when there is a reduction in quantity demanded of a good when its price increases because of a consumer's decreased purchasing power.
3. Utility is the amount of satisfaction an individual receives from consumption of a good or service.
4. Economists recognize that it is not possible to make interpersonal utility comparisons.
5. Total utility is the amount of satisfaction derived from all units of goods and services consumed. Total utility increases as consumption increases.
6. Marginal utility is the change in utility from consuming one additional unit of a good or service.
7. According to the law of diminishing marginal utility, as a person consumes additional units of a given good, marginal utility declines.

---

1. What is the substitution effect of a price change?
2. What is the income effect of a price change?
3. How do economists define utility?
4. Why can't interpersonal utility comparisons be made?
5. What is the relationship between total utility and marginal utility?
6. Why could you say that a millionaire gets less marginal utility from a second piece of pizza than from the first piece, but you couldn't say that the millionaire derives more or less marginal utility from a second piece of pizza than someone else who has a much lower level of income?
7. Are you likely to get as much marginal utility from your last piece of chicken at an all-you-can-eat restaurant as at a restaurant where you pay $2 per piece of chicken?

SECTION 10.2   The Consumer's Choice

* How do consumers maximize satisfaction?
* What is the connection between the law of demand and the law of diminishing marginal utility?

What Is the "Best" Decision for Consumers?

We established the fact that marginal utility diminishes as additional units of a good are acquired. But what significance does this idea have for consumers? Remember, consumers try to add to their own total utility, so when the marginal utility generated by the purchase of additional units of one good drops too low, it can become rational for the consumer to purchase other goods rather than purchase more of the first good. In other words, a rational consumer will avoid making purchases of any one good beyond the point at which other goods will yield greater satisfaction for the amount spent—the "bang for the buck."

Marginal utility, then, is an important concept in understanding and predicting consumer behavior, especially when combined with information about prices. By comparing the marginal utilities generated by units of the goods that they desire as well as the prices, rational consumers seek the combination of goods that maximizes their satisfaction for a given amount spent. In the next section, we will see how this concept works.

Consumer Equilibrium

To reach consumer equilibrium, consumers must allocate their incomes in such a way that the marginal utility per dollar's worth of any good is the same for every good. That is, the "bang for the buck" must be equal for all goods at consumer equilibrium. When this goal is realized, one dollar's worth of additional gasoline will yield the same marginal utility as one dollar's worth of additional bread or apples or movie tickets or soap. This concept will become clearer to you as we work through an example illustrating the forces present when consumers are not at equilibrium.

Given a fixed budget, if the marginal utilities per dollar spent on additional units of two goods are not the same, you can increase total satisfaction by buying more of one good and less of the other. For example, assume that the price of a loaf of bread is $1, the price of a bag of apples is $1, the marginal utility of a dollar's worth of apples is 1 util, and the marginal utility of a dollar's worth of bread is 5 utils. In this situation, your total satisfaction can be increased by buying more bread and fewer apples, because bread is currently giving you greater satisfaction per dollar than apples—5 utils versus 1 util, for a net gain of 4 utils to your total satisfaction. By buying more bread, though, you alter the marginal utility of both bread and apples. Consider what would happen if, next week, you buy one more loaf of bread and one less bag of apples. Because you are consuming more of it now, the marginal utility for bread will fall, say to 4 utils. On the other hand, the marginal utility for apples will rise, perhaps to 2 utils, because you now have fewer apples.

A comparison of the marginal utilities for these goods in week 2 versus week 1 would look something like this:

Week 1

$$MU_{bread}/\$1 > MU_{apples}/\$1$$

$$5 \text{ utils}/\$1 > 1 \text{ util}/\$1$$

Week 2

$$MU_{bread}/\$1 > MU_{apples}/\$1$$

$$4 \text{ utils}/\$1 > 2 \text{ utils}/\$1$$

Notice that although the marginal utilities of bread and apples are now closer, they are still not equal. Because of this difference, it is still in the consumer's interest to purchase an additional loaf of bread rather than the last bag of apples; in this case, the net gain would be 2 utils (3 utils for the unit of bread added at a cost of 1 util for the apples given up). By buying yet another loaf of bread, you once again push further down your marginal utility curve for bread, and as a result, the marginal utility for bread falls. With that change, the relative value to you of apples increases again, changing the ratio of marginal utility to dollar spent for both goods in the following way:

> **consumer equilibrium**
> allocation of consumer income that balances the ratio of marginal utility to the price of goods purchased

Week 3

$$MU_{bread}/\$1 = MU_{apples}/\$1$$

$$3 \text{ utils}/\$1 = 3 \text{ utils}/\$1$$

What this example shows is that, to achieve maximum satisfaction—**consumer equilibrium**—consumers have to allocate income in such a way that the ratio of the marginal utility to the price of the goods is equal for all goods purchased. In other words, in a state of consumer equilibrium,

$$MU_1/P_1 = MU_2/P_2 = MU_3/P_3 = \cdots MU_N/P_N$$

In this situation, each good provides the consumer with the same level of marginal utility per dollar spent.

The Law of Demand and the Law of Diminishing Marginal Utility

The law of demand states that when the price of a good is reduced, the quantity of that good demanded will increase. But why is this the case? By examining the law of diminishing marginal utility in action, we can determine the basis for this relationship between price and quantity demanded. Indeed, the demand curve merely translates marginal utility into dollar terms.

For example, let's say that you are in consumer equilibrium when the price of a personal-sized pizza is $4 and the price of a hamburger is $1. Further, in equilibrium, the marginal utility on the last pizza consumed is 40 utils, and the marginal utility on the last hamburger is 10 utils. So in consumer equilibrium, the *MU/P* ratio for both the pizza and the hamburger is 10 utils per dollar:

$$MU_{pizza} (40 \text{ utils})/\$4 = MU_{hamburger} (10 \text{ utils})/\$1$$

Now suppose the price of the personal-sized pizza falls to $2, *ceteris paribus*. Instead of the *MU/P* ratio of the pizza being 10 utils per dollar, it is now 20 utils per dollar (40 utils/$2). This calculation implies, *ceteris paribus*, that you will now buy more pizza at the lower price because you are getting relatively more satisfaction for each dollar you spend on pizza.

$$MU_{pizza} (40 \text{ utils})/\$2 > MU_{hamburger} (10 \text{ utils})/\$1$$

In other words, because the price of the personal-sized pizza fell, you are now willing to purchase more pizzas and fewer hamburgers.

MARGINAL UTILITY

A consumer is faced with choosing between hamburgers and milkshakes that are priced at $2 and $1, respectively. He has $11 to spend for the week. The marginal utility derived from each of the two goods is as follows:

If you did not have a budget constraint, you would choose 5 hamburgers and 5 milkshakes because you would maximize your total utility (68 + 34 = 102); that is, adding up all the marginal utilities for all hamburgers (68 utils) and all milkshakes (34 utils). And that would cost you $15; $10 for the 5 hamburgers and $5 for the 5 milkshakes. However, you can only spend $11; so what is the best way to spend it? Remember economic decisions are made at the margin. This idea is the best "bang for the buck" principle, we must equalize the marginal utility per dollar spent. Looking at the table, we accomplish this at 4 hamburgers and 3 milkshakes per week.

Or

$$MU_H/P_H = MU_M/P_M$$

$$10/\$2 = 5/\$1$$

$$(Q_H \times P_H) + (Q_M \times P_M) = \$11$$

$$(4 \times \$2) + (3 \times \$1) = \$11$$

Marginal Utility from Last Hamburger	Quantity of Hamburgers Consumed Each Week	(MU_H/P_H)
20	1	10
16	2	8
14	3	7
10	4	5
8	5	4

Marginal Utility from Last Milkshake	Quantity of Milkshakes Consumed Each Week	(MU_M/P_M)
12	1	12
10	2	10
5	3	5
4	4	4
3	5	3

SECTION CHECK

1. To maximize consumer satisfaction, income must be allocated so that the ratio of the marginal utility to the price is the same for all goods purchased.

2. If the marginal utility per dollar of additional units is not the same, a person can increase total satisfaction by buying more of some goods and less of others.

---

1. What do economists mean by consumer equilibrium?

2. How could a consumer raise his total utility if the ratio of his marginal utility to the price for good A was greater than that for good B?

3. What must be true about the ratio of marginal utility to the price for each good consumed in consumer equilibrium?

4. How does the law of demand reflect the law of diminishing marginal utility?

5. Why doesn't consumer equilibrium imply that the ratio of total utility per dollar is the same for different goods?

6. Why does the principle of consumer equilibrium imply that people would tend to buy more apples when the price of apples is reduced?

7. Suppose the price of walnuts is $6 per pound and the price of peanuts is $2 per pound. If a person gets 20 units of added utility from eating the last pound of peanuts she consumes, how many utils of added utility would she have to get from eating the last pound of walnuts in order to be in consumer equilibrium?

in the news   **Behavioral Economics**

Today there is a growing school of economists who are drawing on a vast range of behavioural traits identified by experimental psychologists which amount to a frontal assault on the whole idea that people, individually or as a group, mostly act rationally.

A quick tour of the key observations made by these psychologists would make even Mr. Spock's head spin. For example, people appear to be disproportionately influenced by the fear of feeling **regret**, and will often pass up even benefits within reach to avoid a small risk of feeling they have failed. They are also prone to **cognitive dissonance**: holding a belief plainly at odds with the evidence, usually because the belief has been held and cherished for a long time. Psychiatrists sometimes call this "denial."

And then there is **anchoring**: people are often overly influenced by outside suggestion. People can be influenced even when they know that the suggestion is not being made by someone who is better informed. In one experiment, volunteers were asked a series of questions whose answers were in percentages—such as what percentage of African countries is in the United Nations? A wheel with numbers from one to 100 was spun in front of them; they were then asked to say whether their answer was higher or lower than the number on the wheel, and then to give their answer. These answers were strongly influenced by the randomly selected, irrelevant number on the wheel. The average guess when the wheel showed 10 was 25%; when it showed 65 it was 45%.

Experiments show that most people apparently also suffer from **status quo bias**: they are willing to take bigger gambles to maintain the status quo than they would be to acquire it in the first place. In one common experiment, mugs are allocated randomly to some people in a group. Those who have them are asked to name a price to sell their mug; those without one are asked to name a price at which they will buy. Usually, the average sales price is considerably higher than the average offer price.

Expected-utility theory assumes that people look at individual decisions in the context of the big picture. But psychologists have found that, in fact, they tend to **compartmentalize**, often on superficial grounds. They then make choices about things in one particular mental compartment without taking account of the implications for things in other compartments.

There is also a huge amount of evidence that people are persistently, and irrationally, **overconfident**. Asked to answer a factual question, then asked to give the probability that their answer was correct, people typically overestimate this probability. This may be due to a **representativeness heuristic**: a tendency to treat events as representative of some well-known class or pattern. This gives people a sense of familiarity with an event and thus confidence that they have accurately diagnosed it. This can lead people to "see" patterns in data even where there are none. A closely related phenomenon is the **availability heuristic**: people focus excessive attention on a particular fact or event, rather than the big picture, simply because it is more visible or fresher in their mind.

Another delightfully human habit is **magical thinking**: attributing to one's own actions something that had nothing to do with them, and thus assuming that one has a greater influence over events than is actually the case. For instance, an investor who luckily buys a share that goes on to beat the market may become convinced that he is a skillful investor rather than a merely fortunate one. He may also fall prey to **quasi-magical thinking**— behaving as if he believes his thoughts can influence events, even though he knows that they can't.

Most people, say psychologists, are also vulnerable to **hindsight bias**: once something happens, they overestimate the extent to which they could have predicted it. Closely related to this is memory bias: when something happens people often persuade themselves that they actually predicted it, even when they didn't.

Finally, who can deny that people often become **emotional**, cutting off their noses to spite their faces. One of the psychologists' favorite experiments is the

(continued)

Behavioral Economics (cont.)

"ultimatum game" in which one player, the proposer, is given a sum of money, say $10, and offers some portion of it to the other player, the responder. The responder can either accept the offer, in which case he gets the sum offered and the proposer gets the rest, or reject the offer in which case both players get nothing. In experiments, very low offers (less than 20% of the total sum) are often rejected, even though it is rational for the responder to accept any offer (even one cent!) which the proposer makes. And yet responders seem to reject offers out of sheer indignation at being made to accept such a small proportion of the whole sum, and they seem to get more satisfaction from taking revenge on the proposer than in maximizing their own financial gain. Mr. Spock would be appalled if a Vulcan made this mistake.

The psychological idea that has so far had the greatest impact on economics is "prospect theory." This was developed by Daniel Kahneman of Princeton University and the late Amos Tversky of Stanford University. It brings together several aspects of psychological research and differs in crucial respects from expected-utility theory—although, equally crucially, it shares its advantage of being able to be modeled mathematically. It is based on the results of hundreds of experiments in which people have been asked to choose between pairs of gambles.

What Messrs Kahneman and Tversky claim to have found is that people are "loss averse": they have an asymmetric attitude to gains and losses, getting less utility from gaining, say, $100 than they would lose if they lost $100. This is not the same as "risk aversion," any particular level of which can be rational if consistently applied. But those suffering from loss aversion do not measure risk consistently. They take fewer risks that might result in suffering losses than if they were acting as rational utility maximizers. Prospect theory also claims that people regularly miscalculate probabilities: they assume that outcomes which are very probable are less likely than they really are, that outcomes which are quite unlikely are more likely than they are, and that extremely improbable, but still possible, outcomes have no chance at all of happening. They also tend to view decisions in isolation, rather than as part of a bigger picture.

© BLUEFLY/ALAMY

Several real-world examples of how this theory can explain human decisions are reported in a forthcoming paper, "Prospect Theory in the Wild," by Colin Camerer, an economist at the California Institute of Technology. Many New York taxi drivers, points out Mr. Camerer, decide when to finish work each day by setting themselves a daily income target, and on reaching it they stop. This means that they typically work fewer hours on a busy day than on a slow day. Rational labor-market theory predicts that they will do the opposite, working longer on the busy day when their effective hourly wage-rate is higher, and less on the slow day when their wage-rate is lower. Prospect theory can explain this irrational behavior: failing to achieve the daily income target feels like incurring a loss, so drivers put in longer hours to avoid it, and beating the target feels like a win, so once they have done that, there is less incentive to keep working.

Racing and the Equity Premium

People betting on horse races back long-shots over favorites far more often than they should. Prospect theory suggests this is because they attach too low a probability to likely outcomes and too high a probability to quite unlikely ones. Gamblers also tend to shift their bets away from favorites towards long-shots as the day's racing nears its end. Because of the cut taken by the bookies, by the time later races are run most racegoers have lost some money. For many of them, a successful bet on an outsider would probably turn a losing day into a winning one. Mathematically, and rationally, this should not matter. The last race of the day is no different from the first race of the next day. But most racegoers close their "mental account" at the end of each racing day, and they hate to leave the track a loser.

Perhaps the best-known example of prospect theory in action is in suggesting a solution to the "equity-premium puzzle." In America, shares have long delivered much higher returns to investors relative to bonds than seems justified by the difference in riskiness of shares and bonds. Orthodox economists have ascribed this simply to the fact that people have less appetite for risk than expected. But prospect theory suggests that if investors, rather like racegoers, are averse to losses during any given year, this might justify such a high equity premium. Annual losses on shares are much more frequent than annual losses on bonds, so investors demand a much higher premium for holding shares to compensate them for the greater risk of suffering a loss in any given year.

A common response of believers in homo economicus is to claim that apparently irrational behaviour is in fact rational. Gary Becker, of the University of Chicago, was doing this long before behavioral economics came along to challenge rationality. He has won a Nobel prize for his work, which has often shed light on topics from education and family life to suicide, drug addiction and religion. Recently, he has developed "rational" models of the formation of emotions and of religious belief.

Rationalists such as Mr. Becker often accuse behavioralists of picking whichever psychological explanation happens to suit the particular alleged irrationality they are explaining, rather than using a rigorous, consistent scientific approach. Caltech's Mr. Camerer argues that rationalists are guilty of exactly the same error. For instance, rationalists explain away people's fondness for betting on long-shots in horse races by claiming that most are simply more risk-loving than expected, and then claim precisely the opposite about investors to explain the equity premium. Both are possible, but as explanations they leave something to be desired.

Being irrational may even be rational, according to some rationalists. Irrationality can be a good to be consumed like any other, argues Bryan Caplan, an economist at George Mason University—in the sense that the less it costs a person, the more of it they buy. A peculiar feature of beliefs about politics and religion, he says, is that the costs to an individual of error are "virtually non-existent, setting the private cost of irrationality at zero; it is therefore in these areas that irrational views are most apparent." Maybe, although Mr. Caplan may grow sick of having those views read back to him for eternity should he ever end up in hell.

In his book, "Alchemies of the Mind: Rationality and the Emotions," Jon Elster of New York's Columbia University prefers to look at the other side of the same coin. Observing that "those who are most likely to make unbiased cognitive assessments are the clinically depressed," he argues that the "emotional price to pay for cognitive rationality may be too high."

In fact, the battle between rationalists and behavioralists may be largely in the past. Those who believe in homo economicus no longer routinely ignore his emotional and spiritual dimensions. Nor do behavioralists any longer assume people are wholly irrational. Instead, most now view them as "quasi-rational": trying as hard as they can to be rational but making the same mistakes over and over.

Robert Shiller, an economist at Yale who is writing a book on psychology and the stockmarket, and is said to have prompted Mr. Greenspan's "irrational exuberance" remark, argues that "conventional efficient-markets theory is not completely out the window. . . . Doing research that is sensitive to lessons from behavioral research does not mean entirely abandoning research in the conventional expected-utility framework."

Mr. Kahneman, the psychologist who inspired much of the economic research on irrationality, goes further: "as a first approximation, it makes sense to assume rational behaviour." He believes that economists cannot give up the rational model entirely. "They will be doing it one assumption at a time. Otherwise the analysis will very soon become intractable; the great strength of the rational model is that it is very tractable."

Rational Taxi Drivers!
What seems certain is that economics will increasingly embrace the insights of other disciplines, from

(continued)

in the news   Behavioral Economics (cont.)

psychologists to biologists. Andrew Lo, an economist at Massachusetts Institute of Technology, is hopeful that natural scientists will help social scientists by discovering the genetic basis for different attitudes to risk-taking. Considerable attention will be paid to discoveries about how people form their emotions, tastes and beliefs. Understanding better how people learn will also be a priority. Strikingly, even New York taxi drivers seem to become less irrational over time: with experience, they learn to do more work on busy days and less when things are slow. But how representative are they of the rest of humanity?

Richard Thaler was an almost lone pioneer in the use of psychology in financial economics during the 1980s and early 1990s. Today he is a professor at the University of Chicago, the high temple of rational economics. He believes that in the future, "economists will routinely incorporate as much 'behaviour' into their models as they observe in the real world.

After all, to do otherwise would be irrational." Mr. Spock could not have said it better.

consider this:

Henry Farber, an economist at Princeton University, has analyzed data for New York taxicab drivers and shows that traditional economic models offer important insights into taxicab drivers behavior. In short, he found that daily income and hitting one's target had only a *small* effect on a driver's decisions. Drivers responded positively to the prospect of higher pay. He found that drivers put in more hours when the pickings are rich, say during a convention or a theater season, and take more leisure when business is slow. What was important was the cumulative number of hours already worked that day, which is a vastly different result than the conclusions of the behavioral economists.

SOURCE: From "Rethinking Thinking", 'The Economist', December 16, 1999. © The Economist Newspaper Limited, London 1999. Reprinted with permission.

Interactive Chapter Summary

Fill in the blanks:

1. The _____ effect explains why the quantity of pizza demanded decreases as its price goes up, because some people switch to substitute goods that become relatively cheaper as a result.

2. The _____ effect explains why the quantity of pizza demanded decreases as its price goes up, because it reduces buyers' purchasing power.

3. _____ utility implies that people will derive less satisfaction from successive units.

4. You would expect a third ice cream cone to provide _____ additional utility, or satisfaction, on a given day, than the second ice cream cone the same day.

5. _____ is the satisfaction or enjoyment derived from consumption.

6. The relative satisfaction gained by two people drinking cups of coffee _____ be measured in comparable terms.

7. _____ is the total amount of satisfaction derived from the consumption of a certain number of units of a good.

8. _____ utility is the extra satisfaction generated by an additional unit of a good that is consumed in a given time period.

9. If the first of three slices of pizza generates 24 utils and four slices of pizza generates 28 utils, then the marginal utility of the fourth slice of pizza is _____ utils.

10. Marginal utility _____ as consumption increases, which is called the law of _____.

11. Market prices of goods and services are determined by _____ utility.

12. If total utility fell for consuming one more unit of a good, the marginal utility for that good would be _____.

13. To reach _____, consumers must allocate their incomes in such a way that the marginal utility per dollars' worth of any good is the same for every good.

14. If the last dollar spent on good A provides more marginal utility per dollar than the last dollar spent on good B, total satisfaction would increase if _____ was spent on good A and _____ was spent on good B.

15. As an individual approaches consumer equilibrium, the ratio of marginal utility per dollar spent on different goods gets _____ apart across goods.

16. In consumer equilibrium, if the price of good A is three times that of the price of good B, then the

marginal utility from the last unit of good A will be _____ times the marginal utility from the last unit of good B.

17. Starting in consumer equilibrium, when the price of good A falls, it makes the marginal utility per dollar spent on good A _____ relative to that of other goods, leading to a _____ quantity of good A purchased.

Answers: 1. substitution 2. income 3. Diminishing marginal 4. less 5. Utility 6. cannot 7. Total utility 8. Marginal 9. 4 10. declines; diminishing marginal utility 11. marginal 12. negative 13. consumer equilibrium 14. more; less 15. less far 16. three 17. rise; larger

Key Terms and Concepts

substitution effect 259
income effect 259
diminishing marginal utility 259

utility 260
util 260
total utility 262

marginal utility 262
diminishing marginal utility 263
consumer equilibrium 267

Section Check Answers

10.1 Consumer Behavior

1. What is the substitution effect of a price change?

The substitution effect of a price change occurs when a consumer switches to another similar good when the price of the preferred good increases.

2. What is the income effect of a price change?

The income effect of a price change occurs when there is a reduction in the quantity demanded of a good when its price increases because of a consumer's decreased purchasing power.

3. How do economists define utility?

Economists define utility as the level of satisfaction or well-being an individual receives from consumption of a good or service.

4. Why can't interpersonal utility comparisons be made?

We can't make interpersonal utility comparisons because it is impossible to measure the relative satisfaction of different people in comparable terms.

5. What is the relationship between total utility and marginal utility?

Marginal utility is the increase in total utility from increasing consumption of a good or service by one unit.

6. Why could you say that a millionaire gets less marginal utility from a second piece of pizza than from the first piece, but you couldn't say that the millionaire derives more or less marginal utility from a second piece of pizza than someone else who has a much lower level of income?

Both get less marginal utility from a second piece of pizza than from the first piece because of the law of diminishing marginal utility. However, it is impossible to measure the relative satisfaction of different people in comparable terms, even when we are comparing rich and poor people, so we cannot say who got more marginal utility from a second slice of pizza.

7. Are you likely to get as much marginal utility from your last piece of chicken at an all-you-can-eat restaurant as at a restaurant where you pay $2 per piece of chicken?

No. If you pay $2 per piece, you only eat another piece as long as it gives you more marginal utility than spending the $2 on something else. But at an all-you-can-eat restaurant, the dollar price of one more piece of chicken is zero, so you consume more chicken and get less marginal utility out of the last piece of chicken you eat.

10.2 The Consumer's Choice

1. What do economists mean by consumer equilibrium?

Consumer equilibrium means that a consumer is consuming the optimum, or utility maximizing, combination of goods and services, for a given level of income.

2. How could a consumer raise his total utility if the ratio of his marginal utility to the price for good A was greater than that for good B?

Such a consumer would raise his total utility by spending less on good B, and more on good A, because a dollar less spent on B would lower his utility less than a dollar more spent on A would increase it.

3. What must be true about the ratio of marginal utility to the price for each good consumed in consumer equilibrium?

In consumer equilibrium, the ratio of marginal utility to price for each good consumed must be the same, otherwise the consumer could raise his total utility by changing his consumption pattern to increase consumption of those goods with higher marginal utility per dollar and decrease consumption of those goods with lower marginal utility per dollar.

4. How does the law of demand reflect the law of diminishing marginal utility?

In consumer equilibrium, the marginal utility per dollar spent is the same for all goods and services consumed. Starting from that point, reducing the price of one good increases its marginal utility per dollar, resulting in increased consumption of that good. But that is what the law of demand states—that the quantity of a good demanded will increase, the lower its price, *ceteris paribus*.

5. Why doesn't consumer equilibrium imply that the ratio of total utility per dollar is the same for different goods?

It is the additional, or marginal, utility per dollar spent for different goods, not the total utility you get per dollar spent, that matters in determining whether consuming more of some goods and less of others will increase total utility.

6. Why does the principle of consumer equilibrium imply that people would tend to buy more apples when the price of apples is reduced?

A fall in the price of apples will increase the marginal utility per dollar spent on the last apple a person was willing to buy before their price fell. This means a person could increase his or her total utility for a given income by buying more apples and less of some other goods.

7. Suppose the price of walnuts is $6 per pound and the price of peanuts is $2 per pound. If a person gets 20 units of added utility from eating the last pound of peanuts she consumes, how many utils of added utility would she have to get from eating the last pound of walnuts in order to be in consumer equilibrium?

Since consumer equilibrium requires that the marginal utility per dollar spent must be the same across goods that are consumed, the last pound of walnuts would have to provide 60 units of added or marginal utility in this case (60/6 = 20/2).

True or False:

1. Utility is the satisfaction or enjoyment derived from consumption.

2. Economists do *not* think it is possible to compare the relative satisfaction derived from consumption across individuals.

3. Marginal utility is the satisfaction received from all units of a good that are consumed.

4. When marginal utility begins to diminish, total utility always diminishes.

5. If a consumer is maximizing utility, she will purchase quantities of output to the point where the marginal utility per dollar spent on consumption is equal across all goods.

6. As long as the marginal utility of the last unit consumed is positive, total utility will fall if a person consumes less of a good.

7. As long as a person had to pay a positive price for a good, he would never consume to the point where his marginal utility was falling with additional consumption.

8. A person could receive a higher marginal utility from the last diamond she purchases than from the last ounce of water she purchases, yet receive less total utility from diamonds than from water.

9. If total utility from consuming five cups of cocoa is 13, 25, 35, 44, and 52 utils, respectively, the marginal utility of the fourth cup of coffee is 9.

10. If Phil says, "You would have to pay me to eat another cookie now," it would imply that his marginal utility from consuming one more cookie now was negative.

Multiple Choice:

1. The increase in total utility that one receives from eating an additional piece of sushi is called
   a. marginal utility.
   b. interpersonal utility.
   c. marginal cost.
   d. average utility.
   e. average cost.

2. Marginal utility is
   a. the total satisfaction derived from consuming all goods.
   b. always the total satisfaction derived from consuming the first unit of a good.
   c. always positive.
   d. always negative.
   e. the change in total satisfaction derived from consuming one more unit of a particular good.

3. As one eats more and more oranges
   a. his total utility falls, but the marginal utility of each orange rises.
   b. his marginal utility rises as long as the total utility derived from the oranges remains positive.
   c. his total utility rises, as does the marginal utility of each orange.
   d. his total utility rises as long as the marginal utility of the oranges is positive, but the marginal utility of each additional orange likely falls.

4. The marginal utility from a hot fudge sundae
   a. is always increasing.
   b. is always greater than the average utility derived from all hot fudge sundaes consumed.
   c. generally depends on how many hot fudge sundaes the consumer has already consumed.
   d. is always equal to the price paid for the hot fudge sundae.

5. Total utility will decline when
   a. marginal utility is falling.
   b. marginal utility is rising.
   c. marginal utility equals zero.
   d. marginal utility is constant.
   e. marginal utility is negative.

6. When total utility is at its maximum
   a. marginal utility is negative.
   b. marginal utility is positive.
   c. marginal utility is at its maximum.
   d. marginal utility equals zero.
   e. marginal utility stops decreasing and starts increasing.

7. The total utility from consuming five slices of pizza is 11, 18, 24, 29, and 32 utils, respectively. The marginal utility of the third slice of pizza is
   a. 11.
   b. 7.
   c. 18.
   d. 6.
   e. 53.

8. The total utility from consuming five sushi rolls is 12, 23, 33, 42, and 45 utils, respectively. Marginal utility begins to diminish *after* consuming the _____ sushi roll.
   a. first
   b. second
   c. third
   d. fourth
   e. None of the above are correct; marginal utility does not diminish.

9. The law of diminishing marginal utility implies that the more of a commodity you consume, the
   a. more you value additional units of output.
   b. less you value additional units of output.
   c. happier you are.
   d. higher the price that is paid for the commodity.

10. When a consumer spends her income on goods and services in such a way that her utility is maximized, she reaches
    a. monetary equilibrium.
    b. market equilibrium.
    c. consumer equilibrium.
    d. marginal equilibrium.

11. Hamburgers cost $2 and hot dogs cost $1, and Juan is in consumer equilibrium. What must be true about the marginal utility of the last hamburger Juan consumes?
    a. The marginal utility of the last hamburger consumed must be less than that of the last hot dog.
    b. The marginal utility of the last hamburger consumed must be equal to that of the last hot dog.
    c. The marginal utility of the last hamburger consumed must be greater than that of the last hot dog.
    d. The marginal utility of the last hamburger consumed must be equal to zero.

12. Melissa spent the week at an amusement park and used all of her money on rides and popcorn. Both rides and bags of popcorn are priced at $1 each. Melissa realizes that the last bag of popcorn she consumed increased her utility by 40 utils, while the marginal utility of her last ride was only 20 utils. What should Melissa have done differently to increase her satisfaction?
    a. reduced the number of bags of popcorn she consumed and increased the number of rides
    b. increased the number of bags of popcorn she consumed and reduced the number of rides
    c. decreased both the number of bags of popcorn and rides consumed
    d. increased both the number of bags of popcorn and rides consumed
    e. nothing, as her utility was maximized

13. The fact that a gallon of gasoline commands a higher market price than a gallon of water indicates that
    a. gasoline is a scarce good but water is not.
    b. the total utility of gasoline exceeds the total utility of water.
    c. the marginal utility of a gallon of gasoline is greater than the marginal utility of a gallon of water.
    d. the average utility of a gallon of gasoline is greater than the average utility of a gallon of water.

14. The total utility derived from consuming scoops of ice cream can be found by
    a. multiplying the marginal utility of the last scoop consumed by the number of scoops consumed.
    b. multiplying the marginal utility of the last scoop consumed by the price of a scoop of ice cream.
    c. dividing the marginal utility of the last scoop consumed by its price.
    d. summing the marginal utilities of each scoop consumed.
    e. multiplying together the marginal utilities of each scoop of ice cream consumed.

15. In consumer equilibrium
    a. the marginal utility from consumption is the same across all goods.
    b. individuals consume so as to maximize their total satisfaction, given limited income.
    c. the ratio of the marginal utility of each good divided by its price is equal across all goods consumed.
    d. all of the above are true.
    e. all of the above are generally true except a.

Problems:

1. Why can we *not* say that two people who chose to buy the same quantity of a good at the same price have the same marginal utility?

2. If someone said, "You would have to pay me to eat one more bite," what do we know about her marginal utility? What do we know about her total utility?

3. Why would you not continue to consume a good in the range where there was diminishing total utility?

4. The following table shows Rene's total utility from eating escargot. Fill in the blanks that show the marginal utility that Rene derives from eating escargot.

Escargot Per Day	Total Utility	Marginal Utility
1	10	_____
2	18	_____
3	24	_____
4	28	_____
5	30	_____
6	30	_____

5. Plot both Rene's total and marginal utility curves on graphs.

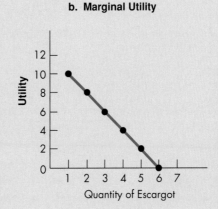

a. Total Utility

b. Marginal Utility

6. Suppose it is "All You Can Eat" Night at your favorite restaurant. Once you've paid $9.95 for your meal, how do you determine how many helpings to consume? Should you continue eating until your food consumption has yielded $9.95 worth of satisfaction? What happens to the marginal utility from successive helpings as consumption increases?

7. Suppose you currently spend your weekly income on movies and video games such that the marginal utility per dollar spent on each activity is equal. If the price of a movie ticket rises, how will you reallocate your fixed income between the two activities? Why?

8. Brandy spends her entire weekly budget of $20 on soda and pizza. A can of soda and a slice of pizza are priced at $1 and $2, respectively. Brandy's marginal utility from soda and pizza consumption is 6 utils and 4 utils, respectively. What advice could you give Brandy to help her increase her overall satisfaction from the consumption of soda and pizza? What will happen to the marginal utility per dollar from soda consumption if Brandy follows your advice? What will happen to the marginal utility per dollar from pizza consumption?

9. Suppose you were studying late one night and you were craving a Papa John's pizza. How much marginal utility would you receive? How much marginal utility would you receive from a pizza that was delivered immediately after you finished a five-course Thanksgiving dinner? Where would you be more likely to eat more pizza in a single setting, at home or at a crowded party (particularly if you are not sure how many pizzas have been ordered)? Use marginal utility analysis to answer the last question.

10. The Consumer Price Index (CPI) measures changes in the cost of living by comparing the cost of buying a certain bundle of goods and services over time. The quantities of each commodity remain the same from year to year but their prices change, so changes in the index reflect the weighted average of changes in the prices of goods and services. Explain how the behavior assumed in the CPI conflicts with the way consumers actually respond to price changes. Do you think the CPI overestimates or underestimates the effect of price changes on consumers?

11. A restaurant offers a free dinner with a six-pound steak, potatoes, and all the trimmings, but only if the patron can eat it all. Otherwise, he must pay $80 for the steak dinner. What does this say about the likely marginal utility most people expect to get from the sixth pound of steak during that dinner?

12. How does the water-diamond paradox explain why there is such a poor correlation between the price of a good and the total utility a person receives from it?

13. Explain the income and substitution effects of a price reduction of a good.

14. Explain the book's distinction between newspaper racks, where the price allows you access to multiple papers, and food vending machines, where you can only get one of the items purchased. Would you expect the policy used by newspaper racks to change if each newspaper routinely included hundreds of dollars of valuable coupons?

In this appendix, we will develop a slightly more advanced set of tools using indifference curves and budget lines to aid in our understanding of the theory of consumer choice. These approaches allow us to express our total utility as a function of two goods. The tools developed here allow us to see how the optimal combination changes in response to changing prices and income. Let's begin with indifference curves.

Indifference Curves

On the basis of their tastes and preferences, consumers must subjectively choose the bundle of goods and services that yield the highest level of satisfaction given their money income and prices.

What Is an Indifference Curve?

A consumer's indifference curve, shown in Exhibit 1, contains various combinations of two commodities, and each combination of goods (like points A, B, and C) on the indifference curve will yield the same level of total utility to this consumer. The consumer is said to be indifferent between any combination of the two goods along an individual indifference curve because she receives the same level of satisfaction from each bundle.

The Properties of the Indifference Curve

Indifference curves have the following three properties: (1) Higher indifference curves represent greater satisfaction, (2) they are negatively sloped, and (3) they are convex from the origin.

Higher Indifference Curves Represent Greater Satisfaction

Although consumers are equally happy with any bundle of goods along the indifference curve, they prefer to be on the highest indifference curve possible. This preference follows from the assumption that more of a good is preferred to less of a good. For example, in Exhibit 2, the consumer would prefer I_2 to I_1. The higher indifference curve represents more satisfaction. As you can see in Exhibit 2, bundle D gives the consumer more of both goods than does bundle C, which is on a lower indifference curve. Bundle D is also preferred to bundle A because there is more than enough extra food to compensate the consumer for the loss of clothing; total utility has risen because the consumer is now on a higher indifference curve.

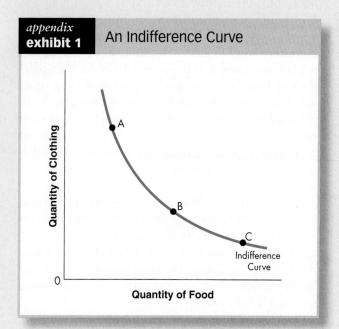

appendix exhibit 1 — An Indifference Curve

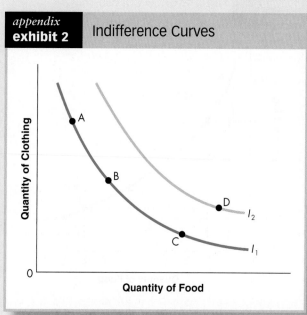

appendix exhibit 2 — Indifference Curves

Indifference Curves Are Negatively Sloped

Indifference curves must slope downward from left to right if the consumer views both goods as desirable. If the quantity of one good is reduced, the quantity of the other good must be increased to maintain the same level of total satisfaction.

Indifference Curves Are Convex from the Origin

The slope of an indifference curve at a particular point measures the marginal rate of substitution (*MRS*), the rate at which the consumer is willing to trade one good to gain one more unit of another good. If the indifference curve is steep, the marginal rate of substitution is high. The consumer would be willing to give up a large amount of clothing for a small amount of food because she would still maintain the same level of satisfaction; she would remain on the same indifference curve, as at point A in Exhibit 3. If the indifference curve is flatter, the marginal rate of substitution is low. The consumer is only willing to give up a small amount of clothing in exchange for an additional unit of food to remain indifferent, as seen at point B in Exhibit 3. A consumer's willingness to substitute one good for another depends on the relative quantities he consumes. If he has lots of something, say food relative to clothing, he will not value the prospect of getting even more food very highly, which is just the law of demand, which is based on the law of diminishing marginal utility.

Complements and Substitutes

As we learned in Chapter 4, many goods are complements to each other; that is, the use of more units of one encourages the acquisition of additional units of the other. Gasoline and automobiles, baseballs and baseball bats, snow skis and bindings, bread and butter, and coffee and cream are examples of complementary goods. When goods are complements, units of one good cannot be acquired without affecting the want-satisfying power of other goods. Some goods are substitutes for one another; that is, the more you have of one, the less you desire the other. (The relationship between substitutes is thus the opposite of the relationship between complements.) Examples of substitutes include coffee and tea, sweaters and jackets, and home-cooked and restaurant meals.

The degree of convexity of an indifference curve—that is, the extent to which the curve deviates from a straight line—depends on how easily the two goods can be substituted for each other. If two commodities are perfect substitutes—one $10 bill and two $5 bills, for example—the indifference curve is a straight line (in this case, the line's slope is −1). As depicted in Exhibit 4(a), the marginal rate of substitution is the same regardless of the extent to which one good is replaced by the other.

At the other extreme are two commodities that are not substitutes but are perfect complements, such as left and right shoes. For most people, these goods are never used separately but are consumed only together. Because it is impossible to replace units of one with units of the other and maintain satisfaction, the marginal rate of substitution is undefined; thus, the indifference curve is a right angle, as shown in Exhibit 4(b). Because most people only care about pairs of shoes, 4 left shoes and 2 right shoes (bundle B) would yield the same level of satisfaction as 2 left shoes and 2 right shoes (bundle A). Two pairs of shoes (bundle A) are also as good as 4 right shoes and 2 left shoes (bundle C). That is, bundles A, B, and C all lie on the same indifference curve and yield the same level of satisfaction. But the combination of three right shoes and three left shoes (bundle D) is preferred to any combination of bundles on indifference curve I_1.

If two commodities can easily be substituted for one another, the nearer the indifference curves will approach a straight line; in other words, it will maintain more closely the same slope along its length throughout. The greater the complementarity between the two goods, the nearer the indifference curves will approach a right angle.

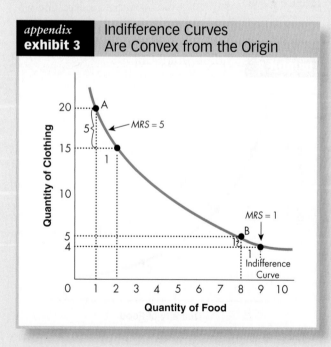

appendix exhibit 3 — Indifference Curves Are Convex from the Origin

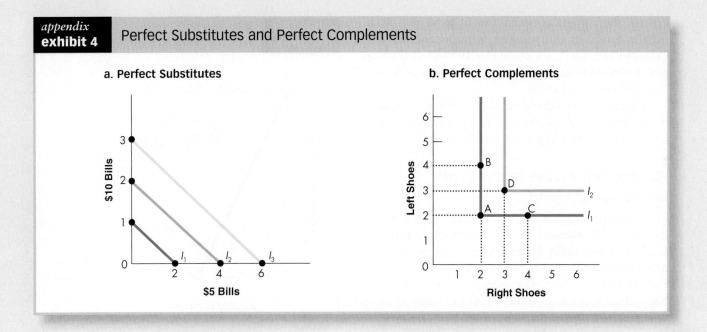

appendix
exhibit 4   Perfect Substitutes and Perfect Complements

a. Perfect Substitutes

b. Perfect Complements

The Budget Line

A consumer's purchase opportunities can be illustrated by a budget line. More precisely, a budget line represents the various combinations of two goods that a consumer can buy with a given income, holding the prices of the two goods constant. For simplicity, we only examine the consumer's choices between two goods. We recognize that this example is not completely realistic, as a quick visit to the store shows consumers buying a variety of different goods and services. However, the two-good model allows us to focus on the essentials, with a minimum of complication.

First, let's look at a consumer who has $50 of income a week to spend on two goods—food and clothing. The price of food is $10 per unit, and the price of clothing is $5 per unit. If the consumer spends all her income on food, she can buy 5 units of food per week ($50/$10 = 5). If she spends all her income on clothing, she can buy 10 units of clothing per week ($50/$5 = 10). However, it is likely that she will spend some of her income on each. Six of the affordable combinations are presented in the table in Exhibit 5. In the graph in Exhibit 5, the horizontal axis measures the quantity of food and the vertical axis measures the quantity of clothing. Moving along the budget line we

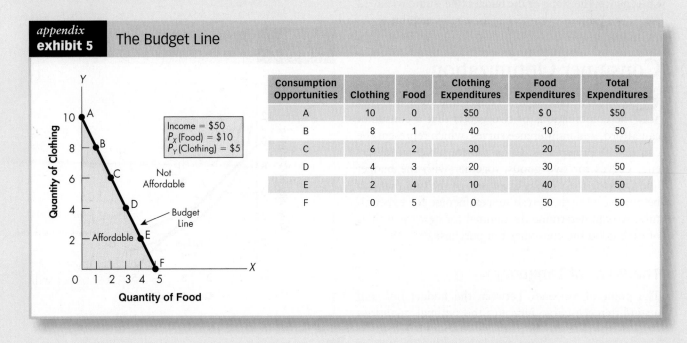

appendix
exhibit 5   The Budget Line

Consumption Opportunities	Clothing	Food	Clothing Expenditures	Food Expenditures	Total Expenditures
A	10	0	$50	$ 0	$50
B	8	1	40	10	50
C	6	2	30	20	50
D	4	3	20	30	50
E	2	4	10	40	50
F	0	5	0	50	50

Income = $50
P_X (Food) = $10
P_Y (Clothing) = $5

can see the various combinations of food and clothing the consumer can purchase with her income. For example, at point A, she could buy 10 units of clothing and 0 units of food; at point B, 8 units of clothing and 1 unit of food; and so on.

Of course, any other combination along the budget line is also affordable. However, any combination of goods beyond the budget line is not feasible.

Finding the *X*- and *Y*-Intercepts of the Budget Line

The intercept on the vertical Y-axis (the clothing axis) and the intercept on the horizontal X-axis (the food axis) can easily be found by dividing the total income available for expenditures by the price of the good in question. For example, if the consumer has a fixed income of $50 a week and clothing costs $5 per unit, we know that if he spends all his income on clothing, he can afford 10 (Income/P_Y = $50/$5 = 10); so 10 is the intercept on the Y-axis. Now if he spends all his $50 on food and food costs $10 per unit, he can afford to buy 5 (Income/P_X = $50/$10 = 5); so 5 is the intercept on the X-axis, as shown in Exhibit 6.

Finding the Slope of the Budget Line

The slope of the budget line is equal to $-P_X/P_Y$. The negative coefficient of the slope indicates that the budget line is negatively sloped (downward sloping), reflecting the fact that you must give up some of one good to get more of the other. For example, if the price of X (food) is $10 and the price of Y (clothing) is $5, then the slope is equal to −10/5, or −2. That is, 2 units of Y can be obtained by forgoing the purchase of 1 unit of X; hence, the slope of the budget line is said to be −2 (or 2, in absolute value terms) as seen in Exhibit 6.

Consumer Optimization

So far, we have seen a budget line, which shows the combinations of two goods that a consumer can afford, and indifference curves, which represent the consumer's preferences. Given the consumer's indifference curves for two goods, together with the budget line showing the various quantities of the two that can be purchased with a given money income for expenditure, we can determine the optimal (or best) quantities of each good the consumer can purchase.

The Point of Tangency

The point of tangency between the budget line and an indifference curve indicates the optimal quantities

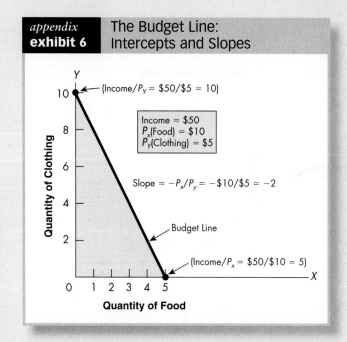

appendix exhibit 6   The Budget Line: Intercepts and Slopes

of each good that will be purchased to maximize total satisfaction. At that point of tangency, $-MRS$ (the slope of the indifference curve) will be equal to $-P_X/P_Y$ (the slope of the budget line). Exhibit 7 shows the consumer's optimal combination of clothing and food. The optimum occurs where the budget line is tangent to indifference curve I_2, at point A: The consumer will acquire 2 units of food and 6 units of clothing.

To maximize satisfaction, the consumer must acquire the most preferred attainable bundle—that is, reach the highest indifference curve that can be reached with a given level of income. The highest curve that can be reached is the one to which the budget line is tangent, at point A. Any other possible combination of the two

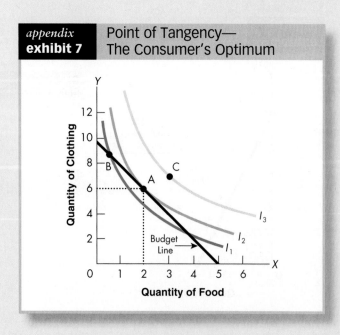

appendix exhibit 7   Point of Tangency— The Consumer's Optimum

goods either would be on a lower indifference curve and thus yield less satisfaction or would be unobtainable with the given income. For example, point B is affordable but would place the consumer on a lower indifference curve. In other words, if the consumer were at point B, she could be made better off moving to point A by consuming less clothing and more food. How about point C? That move would be nice because it is on a higher indifference curve and would yield greater total utility, but unfortunately it is unattainable with the current budget line.

Changes in the Budget Line

So far, we have seen how the prices of goods along with a consumer's income determine a budget line. Now let us examine how the budget line can change as a result of a change in the income level or the price of either good.

The Position of the Budget Line If Income Rises

An increase in income, holding relative prices constant, will cause the curve to shift outward, parallel to the old curve. As seen in Exhibit 8, a richer person can afford more of both goods than a poorer person because of the higher budget line. Suppose you just received an inheritance from a relative; this money will allow you to now buy more of the things that you want. The change in income, holding relative prices constant, is

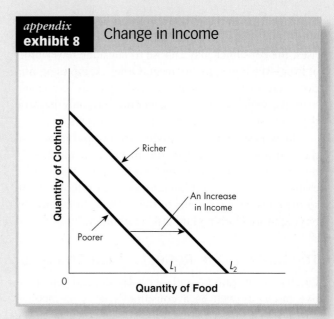

appendix
exhibit 8   Change in Income

called the income effect and it causes this parallel shift in the budget line.

With a given pattern of indifference curves, larger amounts available for spending will result in an income-consumption curve (*ICC*) connecting the best consumption points (tangencies) at each income level.

Consider what happens to consumer purchases with a rise in income. In Exhibit 9(a), the rise in income shifts the budget line outward. If both goods, clothing and food, are normal goods in this range, then the consumer will buy more of both goods as seen in Exhibit 9(a). If income rises and the consumer buys less of one good, we say that good is an inferior good. In Exhibit 9(b), we

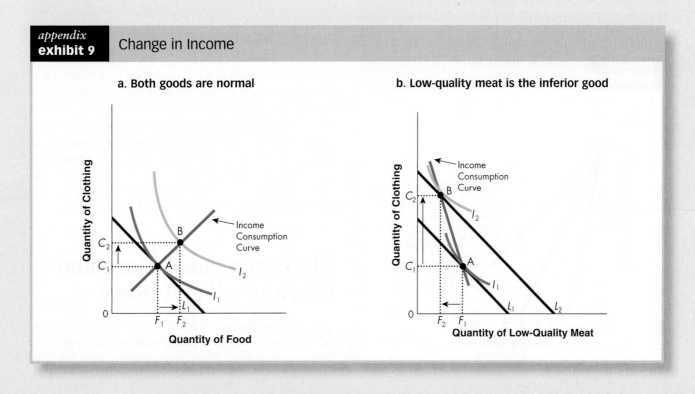

appendix
exhibit 9   Change in Income

a. Both goods are normal

b. Low-quality meat is the inferior good

see that the consumer buys more clothing (normal good) but less liver (inferior good). In this example, as income rises, the consumer may choose to consume fewer units of liver—the lower quality meat. Other examples of inferior goods include secondhand clothing or do-it-yourself haircuts, which consumers generally buy only because they cannot afford more expensive substitutes.

In Exhibit 9(a), both goods are normal goods, so the consumer responds to the increase in income by buying more of both clothing and food. In Exhibit 9(b), clothing is normal and hamburger is an inferior good, so the consumer responds to the increase in income by buying more clothing and less hamburger.

The Budget Line Reflects Price Changes

Purchases of goods and services depend on relative prices as well as a consumer's level of income. However, when the price of one good changes, holding income and the price of the other good constant, it causes a relative price effect. Relative prices affect the way consumers allocate their income among different goods. For example, a change in the price of the good on either the Y- or X-axis will cause the budget line to rotate inward or outward from the budget line's intercept on the other axis.

Let's return to our two-good example—clothing and food. Say the price of food falls from $10 to $5. This decrease in price comes as good news to consumers because it expands their buying opportunities— rotating the budget line outward, as seen in Exhibit 10. Thus, a consumer who spends all his income on food can now buy 10 units of food, as Income/P_X = $50/$5 = 10. If the price per unit of food rose from

$10 to $25, it would contract the consumer's buying opportunities and rotate the budget line inward; so the consumer who spends all his income on food would be able to buy only 2 units of food, as Income/P_X = $50/$25 = 2.

The tangency relationship between the budget line and the indifference curve indicates the optimal amounts of each of the two goods the consumer will purchase, given the prices of both goods and the consumer's total available income for expenditures. At different possible prices for one of the goods, given the price of the other and given total income, a consumer would optimally purchase different quantities of the two goods.

A change in the price of one of the goods will alter the slope of the budget line because a different amount of the good can be purchased with a given level of income. If, for example, the price of food falls, the budget line becomes flatter because the consumer can purchase more food with a given income than she previously could. As shown in Exhibit 11, the new budget line rotates outward, from L_1 to L_2, as a result of the price reduction. Thus, the new point of tangency with an indifference curve will be on a higher indifference curve. In Exhibit 11(a), the point of tangency moves from point A to point B as a result of the decline in price of food from $10 to $5; the equilibrium quantity of food purchased increases from 2 to 5 units.

A relation known as the price-consumption curve (PCC) may be drawn through these points of tangency, indicating the optimum quantities of food (and clothing) at various possible prices of food (given the price of clothing). From this price-consumption curve, we can derive the usual demand curve for the good. Thus, Exhibit 11(a) shows that if the price of food is $10, the consumer will purchase 5 units. These data may be plotted, as in Exhibit 11(b), to derive a demand curve of the usual form. Notice that in Exhibit 11(b) the price of food is measured on the vertical axis and the quantity purchased on the horizontal axis, whereas the axes of Exhibit 11(a) refer to quantities of the two goods. Notice also that the quantities demanded, as shown in Exhibit 11(b), are those with the consumer's expenditures in equilibrium (at her optimum) at the various prices. Essentially, the demand curve is made up of various price and quantity optimum points.

The Income and Substitution Effects of a Price Change

With indifference curves, we can easily see the two ways in which a price reduction influences the quantity demanded. When the price of a good falls, the

appendix exhibit 10 Change in the Relative Price of Food

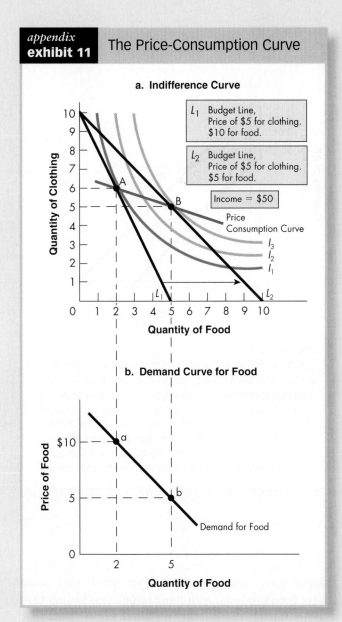

appendix exhibit 11 — The Price-Consumption Curve

appendix exhibit 12 — The Income and Substitution Effects

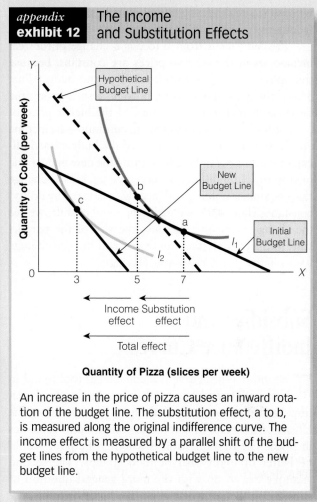

An increase in the price of pizza causes an inward rotation of the budget line. The substitution effect, a to b, is measured along the original indifference curve. The income effect is measured by a parallel shift of the budget lines from the hypothetical budget line to the new budget line.

income effect enables the person to buy more of this good (or other goods) with a given income; the price reduction has the same effect as an increase in money income. That is, the consumer can now move onto a higher indifference curve.

The second influence of the price decline on the quantity demanded is the substitution effect. The lower price encourages the consumer to buy larger quantities of this good. *The substitution effect is always negative.* That is, price and quantity demanded are negatively correlated; lower prices mean higher quantities demanded, and vice versa.

Exhibit 12 shows the income and substitution effects for an *increase* in the price of pizza. Because the relative price of pizza increases, the budget line rotates inward. (Note that the Y-intercept did not change, because neither income nor the price of pizza changed.

Hence if all income is spent on Coke before and after the price increase of pizza, the same amount of Coke can be purchased). The total effect of the increase in the price of pizza is indicated by point c; that is, a reduction in the quantity of pizza from 7 slices of pizza to 3 slices of pizza.

Within the total effect are the substitution effect and the income effect. First consider how much of the total effect is substituting away from the now higher-priced good, pizza. This comparison can easily be made by taking the new budget line and drawing a new hypothetical budget line parallel to the new budget line but tangent to the old indifference curve I_1. Why? It shows the effect of the new relative price on the old indifference curve—in effect, the consumer is compensated for the loss of welfare associated with the price rise by enough income to return to the original indifference curve, I_1. Remember that as long as the new budget line and the hypothetical budget line are parallel, the relative prices are the same; the only difference is the level of income. Thus, we are able to isolate the one effect—the amount of substitution that would prevail without the real income effect—which is the movement from a to b, or the substitution effect.

The movement from b to c is a change in the real income when the relative prices are constant, because this move requires a parallel shift in the budget line. Thus, the movement from b to c results from the decrease in real income because of the higher price of pizza while all other prices remain constant—the income effect. Remember that the slope of the budget line indicates relative prices; thus, by shifting the new budget line next to the old indifference curve, we can see the change that took place holding real income (measured by utility) constant. Then when we make the parallel shift, we see the change in income, because the size of the parallel shift measures only the amount of real income change, with relative prices remaining constant.

Subsidies and Indifference Curves

The indifference curve is a convenient tool to aid in our understanding of subsidies. In this final section, we will consider two examples demonstrating the effects of subsidies in income as compared to subsidies in price. The first question is whether the poor would be better off with cash or food stamps. The second example has to do with the more general question of subsidizing the price of a good like buses or trains.

Using the indifference curve approach, we can show that the poor would be at least equally as well off receiving cash rather than a subsidy like food stamps.

In Exhibit 13, if the individual's initial position is at bundle a (consuming F_1 amount of food, an amount deemed insufficient by society), the introduction of a food stamp program that allowed the recipient to spend an additional $100 per month exclusively on food would make the consumer better off (bundles of indifference curve I_2 are preferred to those on I_1). However, for the same expense, this individual might be made even better off by receiving $100 in cash. The reason is that the shaded triangle is unobtainable to the recipient of food stamps but not to those receiving a cash payment. Unless the individual intended to spend *all* of the next $100 of additional income on food, he or she would be better off with a choice.

Similarly, subsidizing the price of a good (like education, postal services, mass transportation, or medical services) is usually *not* the best method to assure that society's scarce resources are properly allocated. If the price of a good is subsidized, it distorts market signals and results in output levels of the subsidized

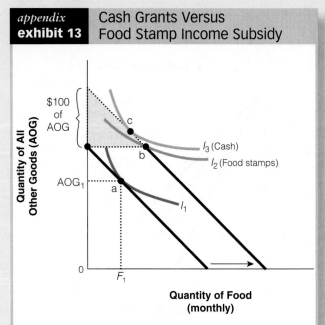

appendix exhibit 13   Cash Grants Versus Food Stamp Income Subsidy

With no government assistance, the consumer chooses bundle a. The availability of food stamps increases the budget and allows the buyer to purchase bundle b, consuming more food and more other goods and attaining a higher level of utility. A cash grant, however, expands the budget set further. The recipient would purchase bundle c, which contains more nonfood items and less food than bundle b. The consumer reaches a higher level of utility with a cash grant than with food stamps.

good that are inefficiently large. In other words, the opportunity cost of forgone other goods that could have been produced with those resources is greater than the (marginal) value of the subsidized good. (Recall the ordinary supply and demand diagram for a subsidy from your elementary economics course.) Exhibit 14 shows that if the whole budget constraint is shifted parallel by an amount equivalent to the price subsidy, ab (ab = cd), then a higher indifference curve can be reached, I_2 rather than I_1. Because reaching the highest indifference curve subject to the budget constraint maximizes consumer satisfaction, this simple diagram shows that it is better to subsidize income (parallel shift) than to subsidize price (altering the slope), if one is interested in making some group better off. Of course, if you want certain groups (say, the poor) to consume more of *particular goods* (housing or food), rather than just raising their utility, you may not wish to give unconstrained income subsidies. Recall that economists can never, in their role as economists, recommend one approach over the other but they can point out the implications of alternative choices.

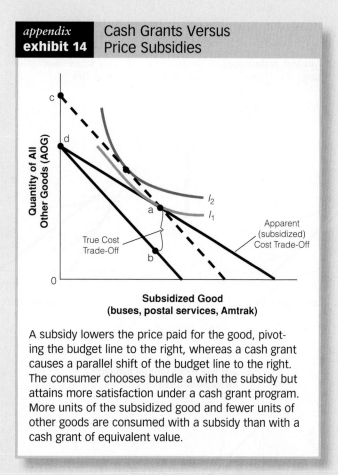

appendix
exhibit 14

Cash Grants Versus
Price Subsidies

A subsidy lowers the price paid for the good, pivot-
ing the budget line to the right, whereas a cash grant
causes a parallel shift of the budget line to the right.
The consumer chooses bundle a with the subsidy but
attains more satisfaction under a cash grant program.
More units of the subsidized good and fewer units of
other goods are consumed with a subsidy than with a
cash grant of equivalent value.

Problems:

1. If you had a budget of $200, and the P_Y is $5 and the P_X is $10, draw the budget line. Draw the budget lines when the P_X falls to $8. Show the budget line when the money available for expenditures increases to $400. What is the slope of the budget line when P_Y is $5 and P_X is $10? How about when P_X falls to $8?

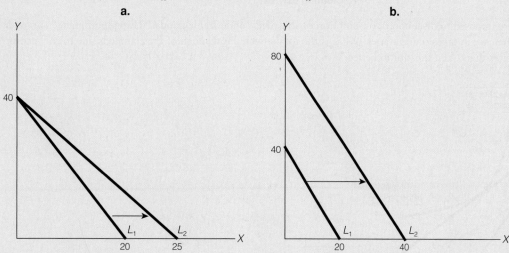

2. Joe buys more clothes than Jim.
   a. Using indifference curves, show how Jim's consumption of clothing and food may differ from Joe's because they have different tastes, *ceteris paribus*.
   b. Suppose that Jim and Joe have the same tastes and income. Joe's father manages a clothing store, and Joe is able to buy all his clothes at wholesale prices. Show why Jim's choices of food and clothing differ from Joe's in this situation.

c. Now suppose that Jim and Joe have the same tastes and face the same prices, but that Joe has more money to spend than Jim. Demonstrate how this difference affects Joe's consumption pattern compared with Jim's.

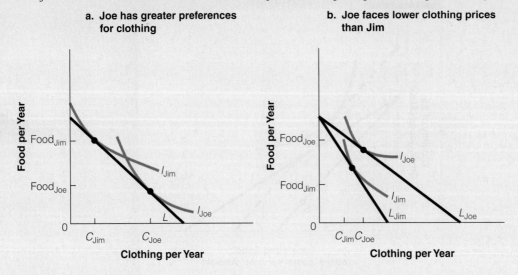

a. Joe has greater preferences for clothing

b. Joe faces lower clothing prices than Jim

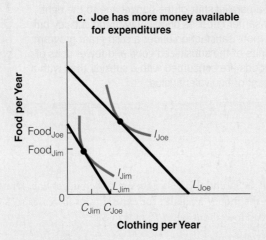

c. Joe has more money available for expenditures

3. Cigarette taxes are imposed to discourage consumption of so-called "undesirable goods." Using indifference curves, show the effect of an increase in taxes on cigarettes. What is the total effect? How much of the change is due to the income effect? How much is due to the substitution effect?

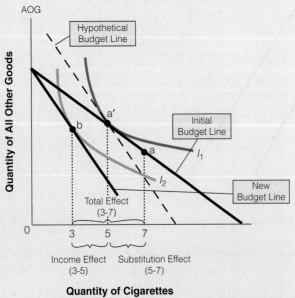

The Firm: Production and Costs

11

Costs exist because resources are scarce and have competing uses—to produce more of one good means forgoing the production of another good. The cost of producing a good is measured by the worth of the most valuable alternative that was given up to obtain the resource, which is called the *opportunity cost*.

In Chapter 3, the production possibilities curve highlighted this trade-off. Recall that the opportunity cost of producing additional shelter was the units of food that had to be sacrificed. Other examples of opportunity costs abound: Paper used in this book could have been used in newspapers or magazines; the steel used in the construction of a new building could have been used in the production of an automobile or a washing machine.

In this chapter, we examine the firm's costs in more detail—what really lies behind the firm's supply curve? A firm's costs are a key determinant in pricing and production decisions. A caveat to this chapter—it is a very important building block for the theory of the firm.

But what exactly makes up a firm's cost of production? Let's begin by looking at the two distinct components of a firm's total cost: explicit costs and implicit costs. ■

SECTION 11.1

Firms and Profits: Total Revenues Minus Total Costs

* What are explicit and implicit costs?
* What are accounting profits?
* What are economic profits?
* What are sunk costs?

Explicit Costs

Explicit costs are the input costs that require a monetary payment—the out-of-pocket expenses that pay for labor services, raw materials, fuel, transportation, utilities, advertising, and so on. It is important to note that the explicit costs are opportunity costs to the firm. For example, money spent on electricity cannot be used for advertising. Remember that in a world of scarcity we are always giving up something to get something else. Trade-offs are pervasive. The costs discussed so far are relatively easy to measure, and an economist and an accountant would most likely arrive at the same figures. However, that will not always be the case.

> **explicit costs**
> the opportunity costs of production that require a monetary payment
>
> **implicit costs**
> the opportunity costs of production that do not require a monetary payment
>
> **profits**
> the difference between total revenues and total costs

What explicit and implicit costs might the owner of this salon incur? His explicit costs include chairs, rent for the shop, scissors, the rinse sinks, electricity, blow dryers, and so on. The implicit costs include the salary he could make at another job or the leisure he could enjoy if he retired.

Implicit Costs

Some of the firm's (opportunity) costs of production are implicit. Implicit costs do not require an outlay of money. Here is where the economist's and accountant's ideas of costs diverge, because accountants do not include implicit costs. For example, whenever an investment is made, opportunities to invest elsewhere are forgone. This lost opportunity is an implicit cost that economists include in the firm's total cost even though no money is expended. A typical farmer or small business owner may perform work without receiving formal wages, but the value of the alternative earnings forgone represents an implicit opportunity cost to the individual. Because other firms could have used the resources, what the resources could have earned elsewhere is an implicit cost to the firm. It is important to emphasize that whenever we are talking about costs—explicit or implicit—we are talking about opportunity costs.

Profits

Economists generally assume that the ultimate goal of every firm is to maximize its **profits**. In other words, firms try to maximize the difference between what they give up for their inputs—their total costs (explicit and implicit)—and the amount they receive for their goods and services—their total revenues. Like revenues and costs, profits refer to flows over time. When we say that a firm earned $5 million in profit, we must specify the period in which the profit was earned—a week, month, year, and so on.

Are Accounting Profits the Same as Economic Profits?

A firm can make profits in the sense that the total revenues it receives exceed the explicit costs it incurs in the process of doing business. We call

Q True or false? If a company owns its own building in a growing urban area, it can protect itself from rising rents.

A False. The company cannot avoid implicit costs. If the company owned the building and rents increased, so would the opportunity cost of owning the building. That is, by occupying the building, the company is giving up the new, higher rents it could receive from renters if it leased out the space. Even though the firm pays zero rent by owning the building, the rent it could receive by leasing it to another company is a real economic cost (but not an accounting cost) to the firm.

these profits **accounting profits**. Profits as accountants record them are based on total revenues and explicit costs and do not include implicit costs.

Economists prefer an alternative way of measuring profits; they are interested in total revenues minus total costs (both explicit and implicit).

> **accounting profits**
> total revenues minus total explicit costs

Economists include the implicit costs—as well as the explicit costs—when calculating the total costs of the firm.

Summing up, measured in terms of accounting profits such as those reported in real-world financial statements, a firm has a profit if its

Q Emily, an energetic 10-year-old, set up a lemonade stand in front of her house. One Saturday, she sold 50 cups of lemonade at 50 cents apiece to her friends, who were hot and thirsty from playing. These sales generated $25 in total revenues for Emily. Emily was pleased because she knew her total costs—for lemonade, mix, cups, and so on—was only $5. As she was closing up shop for the day, her neighbor, an accountant, stopped by to say hello. Emily told him about her successful day. He said, "What a great job! You made a $20 profit!" Excited, Emily rushed into the house to tell her mother, an economist, the great news. Will Emily's mother

agree with the accountant's calculation of Emily's profits? If not, why?

A No, Emily's mother will not agree with the accountant, because he forgot to include the implicit costs when calculating Emily's profits. That is, he neglected to take into account what Emily could have been doing with her time if she had not been selling lemonade. For example, she could have been playing with her friends, cleaning her room, or perhaps helping her friends make money at their garage sale. These lost opportunities are implicit costs that should be included in the calculation of Emily's economic profits.

section 11.1
exhibit 1
Accounting Profits Versus Economic Profits

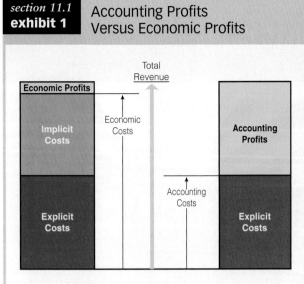

Economic profits equal total revenues minus economic costs (explicit plus implicit costs). Accounting profits equal total revenues minus accounting costs (explicit costs).

total revenues exceed its explicit costs. In terms of **economic profits**, a firm has profits if its total revenues exceed its total opportunity costs—both its explicit costs and implicit costs. Exhibit 1 illustrates the difference between accounting profits and economic profits.

A Zero Economic Profit Is a Normal Profit

As we just discussed, an economic profit is less than an accounting profit because an economic profit includes implicit as well as explicit costs. In fact, an economist considers a zero economic profit a normal profit. A zero economic profit means that the firm is covering both explicit and implicit costs—the total opportunity costs of its resources. In other words,

economic profits
total revenues minus explicit and implicit costs

sunk costs
costs that have been incurred and cannot be recovered

the firm's total revenues are sufficient to compensate for the time and money that owners put in the business. This view is clearly different from making a zero accounting profit, when revenues would not cover the implicit costs.

Sunk Costs

We just saw how opportunity costs are often hidden, as in the case of implicit costs, and that economists believe they should be taken into account when making economic decisions. Another type of cost should also be discussed: sunk costs. **Sunk costs** have already been incurred and cannot be recovered. These costs are visible but should be ignored when making economic decisions. Suppose, for example, that you buy a DVD that sounds interesting but when you get home and play it, you regret your purchase. Now your friend comes over and says he likes that DVD and will buy it from you for $5. You say "no way" because you paid $15 for the DVD. Are you acting rationally? Economists believe that what you paid for the DVD is now irrelevant. Now you must simply decide whether you would rather have the $5 or the DVD. If you decide to keep the DVD, the cost is the $5 you could have received from your friend—the rest is sunk.

Or suppose a donut shop has a one-year lease, but after three months the owner decides that the shop would do much better by relocating to a new mall that just opened. Should the donut shop just stay put until the end of the year because it is legally obligated to pay the 12-month lease? No, the nonrefundable lease payment is sunk and irrelevant to the decision to relocate. The decision to relocate should be based on the prospects of future profits, regardless of the length of the current lease.

In short, sunk costs are irrelevant for any future action because they have already been incurred and cannot be recovered.

6. Economic profits are total revenues minus total opportunity costs—both explicit and implicit costs.

7. Sunk costs have already been incurred and cannot be recovered.

1. What is the difference between explicit costs and implicit costs?

2. Why are both explicit costs and implicit costs relevant in making economic decisions?

3. How do we measure profits?

4. Why is it important to look at all the opportunity costs of production?

5. If you turn down a job offer of $45,000 per year to work for yourself, what is the opportunity cost of working for yourself?

SECTION 11.2 Production in the Short Run

* What is the difference between the short run and the long run?

* What is a production function?

* What is diminishing marginal product?

The Short Run Versus the Long Run

Of fundamental importance for cost and production behavior is the extent to which a firm is able to adjust inputs as it varies output. Because it takes more time to vary some inputs than others, we must distinguish between the short run and the long run. The **short run** is defined as a period too brief for some inputs to be varied. For example, a firm cannot alter the current size of its plant in a day, and it cannot obtain new equipment overnight. If demand increases for the firm's product and the firm chooses to produce more output in the short run, it must do so with its existing equipment and factory. Inputs such as buildings and equipment that do not change with output are called *fixed* inputs.

The **long run** is a period in which a firm can adjust all inputs. That is, in the long run, all inputs to the firm are *variable,* changing as output changes. The long run can vary considerably from industry to industry. For a chain of coffeehouses that wants to add a few more stores, the long run may only be a few months. In other industries, such as automobiles or steel, the long run might be a couple of years, as a new plant or factory in this type of industry takes much longer to build.

short run
a period too brief for some production inputs to be varied

long run
a period over which all production inputs are variable

production function
the relationship between the quantity of inputs and the quantity of outputs

total product (TP)
the total output of a good produced by the firm

Production in the Short Run

Exhibit 1 shows how the quantity of bagels produced by Moe's Bagel Shop per hour varies with the number of workers. This relationship between the quantity of inputs (workers) and the quantity of outputs (bagels) is called the **production function.** Suppose that Moe's has just one input that is variable (labor) and the size of the bagel shop is fixed in the short run. What will happen to **total product (TP)**, the total amount of output (bagels) generated by Moe's, as the level of the variable input, labor, rises? Common sense suggests that total product will start at a low level and increase—perhaps rapidly at first and then more slowly—as the amount of the variable input increases. It will continue to increase until the quantity of the variable input (labor) becomes so large in relation to the quantity of other inputs—the size of the bagel shop, for example—that further increases in output become more and more difficult or even impossible. In the second column of Exhibit 1, we see that as Moe increases the number of workers in his bagel shop, the number of bagels Moe is able to produce increases. The addition of the first worker results in a total output of

section 11.2
exhibit 1

Variable Input Labor (Workers)	Total Output (Bagels per hour) Q	Marginal Product of Labor (Bagels per hour) $\Delta Q/\Delta V$
0	0	
		10
1	10	
		14
2	24	
		12
3	36	
		10
4	46	
		4
5	50	
		1
6	51	

section 11.2 exhibit 1 Moe's Production Function with One Variable, Labor

in Exhibit 1 and in the total product curve shown in Exhibit 2(a).

Diminishing Marginal Product

The **marginal product** (MP) of any single input is defined as the change in total product resulting from a small change in the amount of input used. This concept is shown in the final column in Exhibit 1 and is illustrated by the *MP* curve in Exhibit 2(b). As you can see in Exhibit 2(b), the *MP* curve first rises and then falls.

The Rise in Marginal Product

The initial rise in the marginal product is the result of more effective use of fixed inputs as the number of workers increases. For example, certain types of capital equipment may require a minimum number of workers for efficient operation, or perhaps any operation at all. With a small number of workers (the variable input), some machines cannot operate at all, or only at a low level of efficiency. As additional workers are added, machines are brought into efficient operation and thus the marginal product of the workers rises. Similarly, if one person tried to operate a large department store alone—doing all the types of work necessary in the store—her energies would

10 bagels per hour. When Moe adds a second worker, bagel output climbs to 24, an increase of 14 bagels per hour. Total product continues to increase even with the sixth worker hired; but you can see that it has slowed considerably, with the sixth worker only increasing total product by 1 bagel per hour. Beyond this point, additional workers may even result in a decline in total bagel output as workers bump into each other in the small bagel shop. This outcome is evident both

marginal product (MP)
the change in total output of a good that results from a one-unit change in input

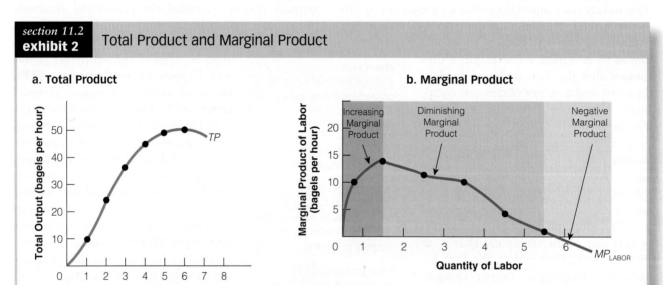

section 11.2 exhibit 2   Total Product and Marginal Product

a. Total Product

b. Marginal Product

In (a), we see that total output increases as the amount of the variable input, labor, is increased—usually more rapidly at first and then more slowly. In (b), we see that the marginal product first rises (increasing marginal product) as workers are added to the fixed input (a machine, for example), which is thus used more efficiently. Then the marginal product falls; the crowding of the fixed input with more and more workers causes marginal product to fall. Finally, negative marginal product occurs as additional inputs cause output to fall.

How many workers could be added to this jackhammer and still be productive (not to mention safe)? If more workers were added, how much output would be derived from each additional worker? Slightly more total output might be realized from the second worker, because the second worker would be using the jackhammer while the first worker was taking a break from "the shakes." However, the fifth or sixth worker would clearly not create any additional output, as workers would just be standing around for their turn. That is, the marginal product (additional output) would eventually fall because of diminishing marginal product.

lead to **diminishing marginal product**. Specifically, as the amount of a variable input is increased, with the amount of other (fixed) inputs held constant, a point will ultimately be reached beyond which marginal product will decline. Beyond this point, output increases but at a decreasing rate. It is the crowding of the fixed input with more and more workers that causes the decline in the marginal product.

The point of this discussion is that production functions conform to the same general pattern as that shown by Moe's Bagel Shop in the third column of Exhibit 1 and illustrated in Exhibit 2(b). In the third column of Exhibit 1, we see that as the number of workers in Moe's Bagel Shop increases, Moe is able to produce more bagels. The first worker is able to produce 10 bagels per hour. When Moe adds a second worker, total bagel output climbs to 24, an increase of 14 bagels per hour. When Moe hires a third worker, bagel output still increases. However, a third worker's marginal production (12 bagels per hour) is less than that of the second worker. In fact, the marginal product continues to drop as more and more workers are added to the bagel shop. This example shows diminishing marginal product at work. Note that it is not because the third worker is not as "good" as the second worker that marginal product falls. Even with identical workers, the increased "crowding" of the fixed input eventually causes marginal output to fall.

be spread so thin in so many directions that total output (sales) might be less than if she were operating a smaller store (working with less capital). As successive workers are added, up to a certain number, each worker adds more to total product than the previous one, and the marginal product rises. This relationship is seen in the shaded area of Exhibit 2(b) labeled "Increasing Marginal Product."

diminishing marginal product
as a variable input increases, with other inputs fixed, a point will be reached where the additions to output will eventually decline

A firm never *knowingly* allows itself to reach the point where the marginal product becomes negative—the situation in which the use of additional variable input units actually reduces total product. In such a situation, having so many units of the variable input—inputs with positive opportunity costs—actually impairs efficient use of the fixed input units. In such a situation, *reducing* the number of workers would actually *increase* total product.

The Fall in Marginal Product

Too many workers in a store make it more difficult for customers to shop; too many workers in a factory get in each other's way. Adding more and more of a variable input to a fixed input will eventually

---

SECTION   CHECK

1. The short run is defined as a period too brief for some inputs to be varied. Inputs such as buildings and equipment that do not change with output are called fixed inputs.
2. The long run is a period of time long enough to allow the firm to adjust all inputs. That is, in the long run, all costs are variable and will change as output changes.
3. The production function is the relationship between the quantity of inputs and the quantity of outputs.
4. A diminishing marginal product occurs when the amount of a variable input keeps increasing while the amount of fixed inputs holds constant; eventually, the marginal product declines.

(continued)

1. What is the difference between fixed and variable inputs?
2. Why are all inputs variable in the long run?
3. What relationship does a production function represent?
4. What is diminishing marginal product? What causes it?

SECTION 11.3 Costs in the Short Run

* What are fixed costs?
* What are variable costs?
* What are marginal costs?

* What are average fixed, average variable, and average total costs?

In the last section, we discussed the relationship between a firm's inputs and its level of output. But that relationship is only one part of the discussion; we must also consider how much it will cost the firm to use each of these inputs in production. In this section, we examine the short-run costs of the firm—what they are and how they vary with the output levels that are produced. The short-run total costs of a business fall into two distinct categories: fixed costs and variable costs.

Fixed Costs, Variable Costs, and Total Costs

Fixed costs are those costs that do not vary with the level of output. For example, the rent on buildings or equipment is usually fixed, at least for some period; whether the firm produces lots of output or little output, the rent stays the same. Insurance premiums, property taxes, and interest payments on debt used to finance capital equipment are other examples of fixed costs; they have to be paid even if no output is produced. In the short run, fixed costs cannot be avoided. The sum of the firm's fixed costs is called the **total fixed cost (TFC)**.

Variable costs vary with the level of output. As more variable inputs such as

fixed costs
costs that do not vary with the level of output

total fixed cost (TFC)
the sum of the firm's fixed costs

variable costs
costs that vary with the level of output

total variable cost (TVC)
the sum of the firm's variable costs

total cost (TC)
the sum of the firm's total fixed costs and total variable costs

average total cost (ATC)
a per-unit cost of operation; total cost divided by output

average fixed cost (AFC)
a per-unit measure of fixed costs; fixed costs divided by output

average variable cost (AVC)
a per-unit measure of variable costs; variable costs divided by output

labor and raw materials are added, output increases. The variable cost (expenditures for wages and raw materials) increases as output increases. The sum of the firm's variable costs is called the **total variable cost (TVC)**. The sum of the total fixed costs and total variable costs is called the firm's **total cost (TC)**.

Average Total Costs

Although we are often interested in the total amount of costs incurred by the firm, sometimes we find it convenient to discuss these costs on a per-unit-of-output, or an average, basis. For example, if Pizza Shack Company has a total fixed cost of $1,600 and a total variable cost of $2,400, its total cost is $4,000. If it produces 800 pizzas in the period in question, its total cost per unit of output equals $5 ($4,000 total cost ÷ 800 units of output = $5). We call this per-unit cost the **average total cost (ATC)**. Likewise, we might talk about the fixed cost per unit of output, or **average fixed cost (AFC)**. In the case of Pizza Shack, the average fixed cost, or *AFC*, would equal $2 ($1,600 fixed cost ÷ 800 units of output = $2). Similarly, we can speak of the per-unit variable cost, or **average variable cost (AVC)**. In this example, the average variable cost would equal $3 ($2,400 variable cost ÷ 800 units of output = $3).

Marginal Costs

Up to this point, six different short-run cost concepts have been introduced: total cost, total fixed cost, total variable cost, average total cost, average fixed cost, and average variable cost. All these concepts are relevant to a discussion of firm behavior and profitability. However, the most important single cost concept has yet to be mentioned: marginal (or additional) cost. You may recall this concept from Chapter 2, where we highlighted the importance of using marginal analysis—that is, analysis that focuses on *additional* or marginal choices. Specifically, **marginal cost (MC)** shows the change in total cost (TC) associated with a change in output (Q) by one unit ($\Delta TC/\Delta Q$). Put a bit differently,

> **marginal cost (MC)**
> the change in total costs resulting from a one-unit change in output

marginal cost is the cost of producing one more unit of output. As such, looking at marginal cost is a useful way to view variable cost—cost that varies as output varies. Marginal cost represents the added labor, raw materials, and miscellaneous expenses incurred in making an additional unit of output. Marginal cost is the additional, or incremental, cost associated with the "last" unit of output produced.

How Are These Costs Related?

Exhibit 1 summarizes the definitions of the seven different short-run cost concepts introduced in this chapter. To further clarify these concepts and to

illustrate the relationships between them, let's return to our discussion of the costs faced by Pizza Shack.

Exhibit 2 presents the costs incurred by Pizza Shack at various levels of output. Notice that the total fixed cost is the same at all output levels and that at low output levels (four or fewer units in the example), total fixed cost is the dominant portion of total costs. At high output levels (eight or more units in the example), total fixed cost becomes quite small relative to total variable cost. As the firm increases its output, it spreads its total fixed cost across more units; as a result, the average fixed cost declines continuously.

It is often easier to understand these cost concepts by examining graphs that show the levels of the various

section 11.3 exhibit 1 A Summary of the Short-Run Cost Concept

Concept	Abbreviation	Definition
Total fixed cost	TFC	Costs that are the same at all output levels (e.g., insurance, rent)
Total variable cost	TVC	Costs that vary with the level of output (e.g., hourly labor, raw materials)
Total cost	TC	Sum of the firm's total fixed costs and total variable costs at a level of output ($TC = TFC + TVC$)
Marginal cost	MC	Added cost of producing one more unit of output; change in TC associated with one more unit of output ($\Delta TC/\Delta Q$)
Average total cost	ATC	TC per unit of output; TC divided by output (TC/Q)
Average fixed cost	AFC	TFC per unit of output; TFC divided by output (TFC/Q)
Average variable cost	AVC	TVC per unit of output; TVC divided by output (TVC/Q)

section 11.3 exhibit 2 Cost Calculations for Pizza Shack Company

(1) Hourly Output (Q)	(2) Total Fixed Cost (TFC)	(3) Total Variable Cost (TVC)	(4) Total Cost (TC = TVC + TFC)	(5) Average Fixed Cost (AFC = TFC/Q)	(6) Average Variable Cost (AVC = TVC/Q)	(7) Average Total Cost (ATC = TC/Q or AFC + AVC)	(8) Marginal Cost (MC = ΔTC/ΔQ)
0	$40	$0	$40	—	—	—	—
1	40	10	50	$40.00	$10.00	$50.00	$10
2	40	18	58	20.00	9.00	29.00	8
3	40	25	65	13.33	8.33	21.66	7
4	40	33	73	10.00	8.25	18.25	8
5	40	43	83	8.00	8.60	16.60	10
6	40	56	96	6.67	9.33	16.00	13
7	40	73	113	5.71	10.43	16.14	17
8	40	94	134	5.00	11.75	16.75	21
9	40	120	160	4.44	13.33	17.77	26
10	40	152	192	4.00	15.20	19.20	32

section 11.3
exhibit 3 Total and Fixed Costs

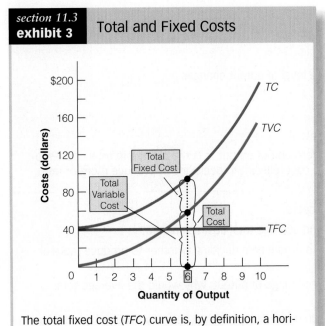

The total fixed cost (*TFC*) curve is, by definition, a horizontal line. The total cost (*TC*) curve is the vertical summation of the total variable cost (*TVC*) and total fixed cost (*TFC*) curves. Notice that *TVC* = 0 when *Q* = 0 and that *TFC* = $40 even when no output is being produced.

a horizontal line because, by definition, fixed costs are the same at all output levels—even at zero level of output. In Exhibit 3, notice that $TVC = 0$ when $Q = 0$; if no output is being produced, no variable costs are incurred.

The total cost (TC) curve is the summation of the total variable cost (TVC) and total fixed cost (TFC) curves. Because the total fixed cost curve is horizontal, the total cost curve lies above the total variable cost curve by a fixed (vertical) amount.

Exhibit 4 shows the average fixed cost curve, the average variable cost curve, the average total cost curve, and the associated marginal cost curve. In this exhibit, notice how the average fixed cost (AFC) curve constantly declines, approaching but never reaching zero. Remember, AFC is simply TFC/Q, so as output expands, AFC declines, because the total fixed cost is being spread over successively larger volumes of output. Also observe how the marginal cost (MC) curve crosses the average variable cost (AVC) and average total cost (ATC) curves at their lowest points. At higher output levels, high marginal costs pull up the average variable cost and average total cost curves, while at low output levels, low marginal costs pull the curves down. In the next section, we will explain why the marginal cost curve intersects the average variable cost curve and the average total cost curve at their minimum points.

costs at different output levels. The graph in Exhibit 3 shows the first three cost concepts: fixed, variable, and total costs. The total fixed cost (*TFC*) curve is always

section 11.3
exhibit 4 Average and Marginal Costs

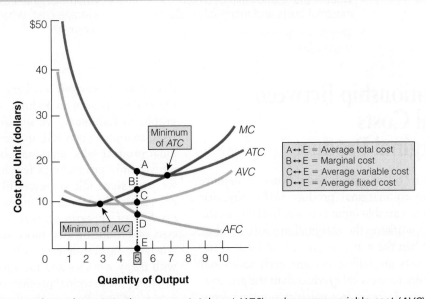

The marginal cost (*MC*) curve always intersects the average total cost (*ATC*) and average variable cost (*AVC*) curves at those curves' minimum points. Average fixed cost (*AFC*) curves always decline and approach—but never reach—zero. The *ATC* curve is the vertical summation of the *AFC* and *AVC* curves; it reaches its minimum (lowest unit cost) point at a higher output than the minimum point of the *AVC* curve.

1. Fixed costs do not change with the level of output.

2. Variable costs are not fixed. Variable costs change as the level of output changes.

3. Average total cost (*ATC*) is total cost divided by output.

4. Average fixed cost (*AFC*) is fixed cost divided by output.

5. Average variable cost (*AVC*) is variable cost divided by output.

6. Marginal cost (*MC*) is the added cost of producing one more unit of output; it is the change in total cost associated with one more unit of output. Marginal cost is the cost relevant to decisions to produce more or less.

---

1. What is the difference between fixed costs and variable costs?

2. How are the average fixed cost, average variable cost, and average total cost calculated?

3. Why is marginal cost the relevant cost to consider when a producer is deciding whether to produce more or less of a product?

4. If the average variable cost curve were constant over some range of output, why would the average total cost be falling over that range of output?

5. If your season batting average going into a game was .300 (three hits per ten at bats) and you got two hits in five at bats during the game, would your season batting average rise or fall as a result?

The Shape of the Short-Run Cost Curves

* What is the relationship between marginal costs and marginal product?

* Why is the average total cost curve U-shaped?

* When marginal cost is greater than average cost, what happens to the average?

The Relationship Between Marginal Costs and Marginal Product

The behavior of marginal costs bears a definite relationship to marginal product (*MP*). Say, for example, that the variable input is labor. Initially, as the firm adds more workers, the marginal product of labor tends to rise. When the marginal product of labor is rising, marginal costs are falling, because each additional worker adds more to the total product than the previous worker. Thus, the increase in total cost resulting from the production of another unit of output—marginal cost—falls. However, when marginal product of labor is declining, marginal costs are rising, because additional workers are adding less to total output. In sum, if an additional worker's marginal product is lower (higher)

than that of previous workers, marginal costs increase (decrease), as seen in Exhibit 1. In area a of the two graphs in Exhibit 1, we see that as marginal product rises, marginal costs fall; in area b, we see that as marginal product falls, marginal costs rise. For example, if we are only producing a few bagels in our bagel shop we have some idle resources like the equipment; toasters, cash registers and so on. At this point, the marginal product of an extra worker is large and the marginal cost of producing one more bagel is small. However, when the bagel shop is crowded, producing many bagels with many workers and the equipment is being used to capacity, the marginal product of hiring another worker is low. Why? Because the new worker has to work in crowded conditions where she may be bumping into other workers as she waits to use the toasters and cash register. In short, when the number of bagels produced is high, the marginal product of another worker is low and the marginal cost of an additional bagel is large.

section 11.4
exhibit 1 Marginal Product
and Marginal Costs

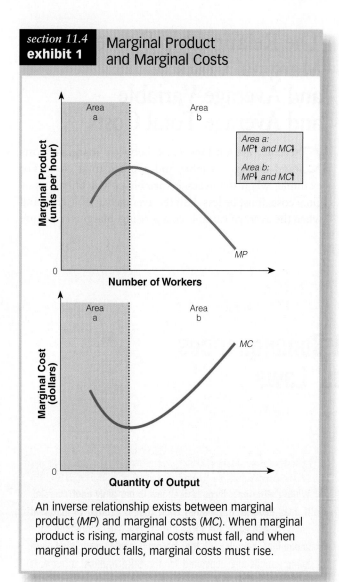

An inverse relationship exists between marginal product (*MP*) and marginal costs (*MC*). When marginal product is rising, marginal costs must fall, and when marginal product falls, marginal costs must rise.

section 11.4
exhibit 2 U-Shaped Average
Total Cost Curve

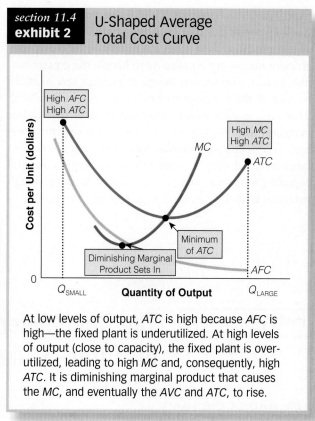

At low levels of output, *ATC* is high because *AFC* is high—the fixed plant is underutilized. At high levels of output (close to capacity), the fixed plant is over-utilized, leading to high *MC* and, consequently, high *ATC*. It is diminishing marginal product that causes the *MC*, and eventually the *AVC* and *ATC*, to rise.

The Relationship Between Marginal and Average Amounts

The relationship between the marginal and the average is simply a matter of arithmetic; when a number (the marginal cost) being added into a series is smaller than the previous average of the series, the new average will be lower than the previous one. Likewise, when the marginal number is larger than the average, the average will rise. For example, if you have taken two economics exams and received a 90 percent on your first exam and an 80 percent on your second exam, you have an 85 percent average. If, after some serious studying, you get a 100 percent on the third exam (the marginal exam), what happens to your average? It rises to 90 percent. Because the marginal is greater than the average, it "pulls" the aver-

age up. However, if the score on your third (marginal) exam is lower—a 70 percent—your average will fall to 80 percent, because the marginal is below the average. Or a baseball or softball player will improve on their batting average if the next trip to the plate is a hit or the average will fall if they strike out.

Why Is the Average Total Cost Curve U-Shaped?

Why is the average total cost curve usually U-shaped, as seen in Exhibit 2? At very small levels of output and very large levels of output, average total cost is very high. The reason for the high average total cost when the firm is producing a very small amount of output is the high average fixed cost—when the output rate of the plant is small relative to its capacity, the plant is being underutilized. But as the firm expands output beyond this point, the average total cost falls. Why? Remember that *ATC* = *AFC* + *AVC*, and average fixed cost always falls when output expands, because the fixed costs are being spread over more units of output. Thus, it is the declining *AFC* that is primarily responsible for the falling *ATC*.

The average total cost rises at high levels of output because of diminishing marginal product. For example, as more and more workers are put to work using a fixed quantity of machines, the result may be crowded working conditions and/or increasing maintenance costs as equipment is used more intensively or as older, less-efficient machinery is called on to handle the greater output. In fact, diminishing marginal product sets in at the bottom of the marginal cost curve, as seen in Exhibit 2. That is, it is diminishing marginal product that causes marginal costs to increase, eventually causing the average variable cost and average total cost curves to rise. At large levels of output, where the plant approaches full capacity, the fixed plant is overutilized, leading to high marginal costs that cause a high average total cost.

The Relationship Between Marginal Costs and Average Variable and Average Total Costs

Certain relationships exist between marginal costs and average variable and average total costs. For example, when the average variable cost is falling, marginal costs must be less than the average variable cost; and when the average variable cost is rising, marginal costs are

in the news   The Unintended Consequences of 'Three-Strikes' Laws

—BY RADHA IYENGAR

Strong sentences are common "tough on crime" tool[s] used to reduce the incentives for individuals to participate in criminal activity. However, the design of such policies often ignores other margins along which individuals interested in participating in crime may adjust. I use California's Three Strikes law to identify several effects of a large increase in the penalty for a broad set of crimes. Using criminal records data, I estimate that Three Strikes reduced participation in criminal activity by 20 percent for second-strike eligible offenders and a 28 percent decline for third-strike eligible offenders. However, I find two unintended consequences of the law. First, because Three Strikes flattened the penalty gradient with respect to severity, criminals were more likely to commit more violent crimes. Among third-strike eligible offenders, the probability of committing violent crimes increased by 9 percentage points. Second, because California's law was more harsh than the laws of other nearby states, Three Strikes had a beggar-thy-neighbor effect increasing the migration of criminals with second and third-strike eligibility to commit crimes in neighboring states. The high cost of incarceration combined with the high cost of violent crime relative to non-violent crime implies that Three Strikes may not be a cost-effective means of reducing crime.

consider this:

While California's three strikes law is certainly controversial, it does have an interesting twist that is related to marginal costs. Specifically, the three strikes law has unintended consequences because of the marginal costs associated with being caught and convicted for the third criminal offense. It is the third offense, no matter what it is, violent or nonviolent, that will put the convicted two-striker away for 25 years to life. Because the marginal cost of the third crime is so high, two-striker might take extreme actions to avoid being caught—perhaps even murdering a witness or a police officer to go undetected. The Fresno Police Department reported a 48 percent increase in assaults on police officers after the passage of the three strikes law. In addition, the number of high-speed chases has increased. There is even the possibility that prisons may become less safe, because three-striker will not be paroled for good behavior. This puts prison staff and fellow prisoners at higher risk.

NBER Working Paper No. W13784

SOURCE: Iyengar, Radha, I'd Rather Be Hanged for a Sheep than a Lamb: The Unintended Consequences of 'Three-Strikes' Laws (February 2008). NBER Working Paper No. W13784. Available at SSRN: http://ssrn.com/abstract=1091419.

greater than the average variable cost. Marginal costs are equal to the average variable cost at the lowest point of the average variable cost curve, as seen in Exhibit 3. In the left-hand (shaded) portion of Exhibit 3, marginal costs are less than the average variable cost, and the average is falling. On the right side, marginal costs are greater than the average variable cost, and the average is rising. The same relationship holds for the marginal cost curve and the average total cost curve. In the left-hand (shaded) portion of Exhibit 4, marginal costs are less than the average total cost, and the average is falling. On the right side, marginal costs are greater than the average total cost, and the average is rising. So it is the marginal cost curve that determines the U-shape of the AVC and ATC curves.

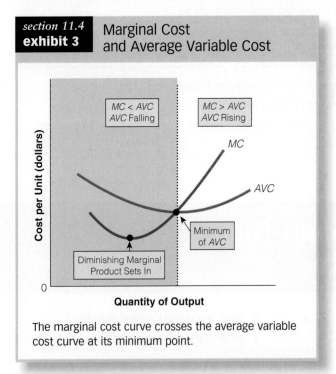

section 11.4
exhibit 3 Marginal Cost and Average Variable Cost

The marginal cost curve crosses the average variable cost curve at its minimum point.

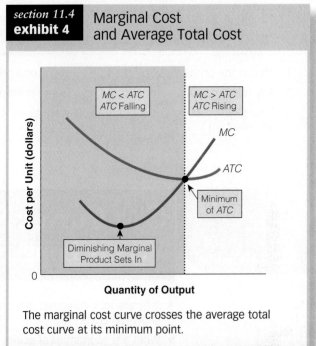

section 11.4
exhibit 4 Marginal Cost and Average Total Cost

The marginal cost curve crosses the average total cost curve at its minimum point.

Use what you've LEARNED   MARGINAL VERSUS AVERAGE AMOUNTS

Q If a small horse-racing jockey decided to join your economics class of 10 students, what would happen to the *average* height of the class?

A The marginal addition, the jockey, would presumably be smaller than the average person in the class, so the average height of the class would fall. Now, if the star seven-foot center on the basketball team joined your class, the average height would rise, because the newer marginal member would presumably be taller than the average person. In sum, if the margin is greater (less) than the average, the average will rise (fall).

If Yao Ming (7′5″) joined your class of 10 students, what would happen to the average class height?

SECTION / CHECK

1. Average total cost declines as output expands but then increases again as output expands still further beyond a certain point.

2. Declining *AFC* is primarily responsible for the *ATC*. The *ATC* rises at high levels of output because of the diminishing marginal product.

3. When marginal costs are less than the average variable cost, the average variable cost must be falling; when marginal costs are less than the average total cost, the average total cost must be falling.

4. When marginal costs are greater than the average variable cost, the average variable cost must be rising; when marginal costs are greater than the average total cost, the average total cost must be rising.

---

1. What is the primary reason that the average total cost falls as output expands over low output ranges?

2. Why does the average total cost rise at some point as output expands further?

3. If marginal costs are less than the average total cost, why does *ATC* fall? If *MC* is greater than *ATC*, why does *ATC* rise?

SECTION

11.5 Cost Curves: Short-Run Versus Long-Run

* Why are long-run costs different than short-run costs?

* What are economies of scale?

* What are diseconomies of scale?

* What are constant returns to scale?

Why Are Long-Run Cost Curves Different from Short-Run Cost Curves?

Over long enough periods, firms can vary all of their productive inputs. That is, time provides an opportunity to substitute lower-cost capital, like larger plants or newer, more sophisticated equipment, for more expensive labor inputs. However, in the short run a firm cannot alter its plant size and equipment. These inputs are fixed in the short run, so the firm can only expand output by employing more variable inputs (e.g., workers and raw materials) in order to get extra output from the existing factory. If a company has to pay many workers overtime wages to expand output in the short run, over the long run firms may opt to invest in new equipment to conserve on expensive labor. That is, in the long run, the firm can expand its factories, build new ones, or shut down unproductive ones. Of course, the time it takes for a firm to get to the long run varies from firm to firm. For example, it may take only a couple of months to build a new coffee shop,

Larger plants may be built in the long run.

BRAND X PICTURES/GETTY IMAGES

while it may take a few years to build a new automobile plant.

In Exhibit 1, we see that the long-run average total cost (*LRATC*) curve lies equal to or below the short-run average total cost (*SRATC*) curves. The reason for the difference between the firm's long-run total cost curve and the short-run total cost curve is that in the long run,

Short- and Long-Run Average Total Costs

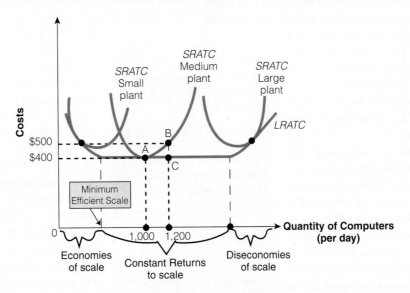

In the long run, firms can increase their capital inputs (fixed in the short run) as well as their inputs that are variable in the short run, in some cases lowering average costs per unit and overcoming the cost-increasing effects of the law of diminishing marginal product. The long-run average total cost curve is thus less U-shaped than short-run average total cost curves. Still, at very low output levels, some reduction of average costs per unit are obtainable by expanding output and productive capacity; in those output ranges, economies of scale exist. At high output ranges, average costs per unit may start rising if the firm enters an output range characterized by diseconomies of scale.

Large automobile manufacturers can produce at a lower average total cost as a result of economies of scale considerations.

AP IMAGES

costs are lower because firms have greater flexibility in changing inputs that are fixed in the short run. Exhibit 1 presents three short-run average total cost curves, representing small, medium, and large plant sizes.

It also shows the long-run average total cost curve. In the *short run*, the firm is restricted to the current plant size, but in the long run it can choose the short-run cost curve for the level of production it is planning on producing. As the firm moves along the long-run average total cost curve, it is adjusting the size of the factory to the quantity of production.

For example, in Exhibit 1, if Apple computer wanted to expand output in the medium plant size from 1,000 computers per day to 1,200 computers per day it has no choice but to hire more workers in the short run, moving from point A to point B. Because of diminishing marginal product (adding more workers to fixed plant size), the short-run average total cost rises from $400 to $500. However, in the long run, Apple can expand its factory size and workforce and the average total cost returns to $400, moving from point A to point C.

What Are Economies of Scale?

By examining the long-run average total cost curve for a firm, we can see three possible production patterns. In Exhibit 1, we see that extremely small firms experience economies of scale, falling per-unit costs as output expands. These firms, then, are functioning inefficiently from a long-run perspective. The **minimum efficient scale** is the output level in which the economies of scale are exhausted and the long-run average total costs are minimized. Similarly, firms that expand beyond a certain point encounter **diseconomies of scale**; that is, they incur rising per-unit costs as their output grows. In more intermediate output ranges, firms of varying sizes can compete on a roughly equal basis as far as costs are concerned because they all exhibit approximately **constant returns to scale.** That is, their per-unit costs remain stable as output grows. In this example Apple computers have economies of scale at low levels of output, construct returns to scale at intermediate levels of output, and diseconomies of very high levels of output.

economies of scale
occur in an output range where *LRATC* falls as output increases

minimum efficient scale
the output level where economies of scale are exhausted and constant returns to scale begin

diseconomies of scale
occur in an output range where LRATC rises as output expands

constant returns to scale
occur in an output range where LRATC does not change as output varies

producing at lower levels of output. For example, workers might experience greater proficiency gains if they concentrated on a few specific tasks rather than on many different tasks. That is, people who try to do everything may end up doing nothing very well.

Recall that diseconomies of scale exist when there is an increase in the firm's long-run average costs as output expands. This may occur as the firm finds it increasingly difficult to handle the complexities of large-scale management. For example, information and coordination problems tend to increase when a firm becomes very large. This is why the *LRATC* is usually U-shaped. At low levels of output, firms generally benefit from increased size because they can take advantage of specialization. However, at high levels of output, the gains from specialization have already occurred but coordination and bureaucratic problems increase.

Why Do Economies and Diseconomies of Scale Occur?

As we have just seen, economies of scale exist when there is a reduction in the firm's long-run average costs as output expands. This may occur because the firm can capture gains from specialization that might not be possible if the firm were

© ERIK DREYER/TAXI/GETTY IMAGES

By having several screens in one complex, the cinema company can cut down on advertising and employee costs as well as rent. Because of economies of scales, it may be less expensive to have eight screens in one building with one concession area than eight separate theaters, each with one screen and a concession area.

SECTION CHECK

1. At low output levels, when all inputs can be varied, some firms will experience economies of scale, where their per-unit costs are decreasing as output increases.
2. Firms that expand all inputs beyond a certain point will encounter diseconomies of scale, incurring rising per-unit costs as output grows in the long-run.
3. In intermediate output ranges, firms may exhibit roughly constant returns to scale; in this range, their per-unit costs remain stable as output increase.

1. What are economies of scale, diseconomies of scale, and constant returns to scale?
2. How might cooking for a family dinner be subject to falling average total cost in the long run as the size of the family grows?
3. What may cause economies or diseconomies of scale?

Interactive Chapter Summary

Fill in the blanks:

1. Profits are defined as _____ minus _____.

2. The cost of producing a good is measured by the worth of the _____ alternative that was given up to obtain the resource.

3. Explicit costs are input costs that require a(n) _____ payment.

4. Whenever we talk about cost—explicit or implicit—we are talking about _____ cost.

5. Economists generally assume that the ultimate goal of a firm is to _____ profits.

6. Accounting profits equal actual revenues minus actual expenditures of cash (explicit costs), so they do not include _____ costs.

7. Economists consider a zero economic profit a normal profit because it means that the firm is covering both _____ and _____ costs—the total opportunity cost of its resources.

8. _____ costs are costs that have already been incurred and cannot be recovered.

9. Because it takes more time to vary some inputs than others, we must distinguish between the _____ run and the _____ run.

10. The long run is a period of time in which the firm can adjust _____ inputs.

11. In the long run, all costs are _____ costs and will change as output changes.

12. The total product schedule shows the total amount of _____ generated as the level of the variable input increases.

13. The marginal product of any single input is the change in total product resulting from a(n) _____ change in the amount of that input used.

14. As the amount of a variable input is increased, the amount of other fixed inputs being held constant, a point will ultimately be reached beyond which marginal product will decline. This point is called _____.

15. The short-run total costs of a business fall into two distinct categories: _____ costs and _____ costs.

16. Fixed costs are costs that _____ with the level of output.

17. In the short run, fixed costs cannot be avoided without _____.

18. The sum of a firm's fixed costs is called its _____.

19. Costs that are not fixed are called _____ costs.

20. The sum of a firm's variable costs is called its _____.

21. The sum of a firm's total _____ costs and total _____ costs is called its total cost.

22. Average total cost equals _____ divided by the _____ produced.

23. Average fixed cost equals _____ divided by the _____ produced.

24. _____ equals total variable cost divided by the level of output produced.

25. Marginal costs are the _____ costs associated with the "last" unit of output produced.

26. A fixed cost curve is always a(n) _____ line because, by definition, fixed costs are the same at all output levels.

27. The reason for high average total costs when a firm is producing a very small amount of output is the high _____ costs.

28. The average total cost curve rises at high levels of output because of _____ product.

29. When AVC is falling, MC must be _____ than AVC; and when AVC is rising, MC must be _____ than AVC.

30. In the _____ run, a company cannot vary its plant size and equipment, so the firm can only expand output by employing more _____ inputs.

31. The $LRATC$ curve is often called a(n) _____ curve because it represents the cost data relevant to a firm when it is planning policy relating to scale of operations, output, and price over a long period of time.

32. When *LRATC* falls as output expands, _____ of scale occur. When the *LRATC* does not vary with output, the firm faces _____ to scale. When the *LRATC* rises as output expands, _____ of scale occur.

33. At the _____ scale, a plant has exhausted its economies of scale and the long-run average total costs are minimized.

34. Any particular cost curve is based on the assumption that _____ prices and _____ are constant.

35. _____ may occur as a firm finds it increasingly difficult to handle the complexities of large-scale management.

Answers: 1. total revenues; total costs 2. most valuable 3. monetary 4. opportunity 5. maximize 6. implicit 7. implicit; explicit 8. Sunk 9. short; long 10. all 11. variable 12. output 13. small 14. diminishing marginal product 15. fixed; variable 16. do not vary 17. going out of business 18. total fixed cost 19. variable 20. total variable cost 21. fixed; variable 22. total cost; level of output 23. total fixed cost; level of output 24. Average variable cost 25. additional 26. horizontal 27. average fixed 28. diminishing marginal 29. less; more 30. short; variable input; technology 34. input; technology 33. minimum efficient 35. Diseconomies of scale
31. planning 32. economies; constant returns; diseconomies

Key Terms and Concepts

explicit costs 290
implicit costs 290
profits 290
accounting profits 291
economic profits 292
sunk costs 292
short run 293
long run 293
production function 293

total product (TP) 293
marginal product (MP) 294
diminishing marginal product 295
fixed costs 296
total fixed cost (TFC) 296
variable costs 296
total variable cost (TVC) 296
total cost (TC) 296
average total cost (ATC) 296

average fixed cost (AFC) 296
average variable cost (AVC) 296
marginal cost (MC) 297
economies of scale 306
minimum efficient scale 306
diseconomies of scale 306
constant returns to scale 306

Section Check Answers

11.1 Firms and Profits: Total Revenues Minus Total Costs

1. What is the difference between explicit costs and implicit costs?

Explicit costs are those costs readily measured by the money spent on the resources used, such as wages. Implicit costs are those that do not represent an explicit outlay of money, but do represent opportunity costs, such as the opportunity cost of your time when you work for yourself.

2. Why are both explicit costs and implicit costs relevant in making economic decisions?

In making economic decisions, where expected marginal benefits must be weighed against expected marginal costs, all relevant costs must be included, whether they are explicit or implicit.

3. How do we measure profits?

Profit is measured as total revenue minus total cost.

4. Why is it important to look at all the opportunity costs of production?

Economic profit equals total revenue minus both explicit and implicit costs, including the opportunity

cost (forgone earnings) of financial resources invested in the firm. All of your owned inputs—including your own time, equipment, structures, land, and so on—have opportunity costs that aren't revealed in explicit dollar payments. Correctly assigning implicit costs to all these owned inputs is necessary so that a correct measure of economic profits can be made. To be earning economic profits means that a firm is earning an above-normal rate of return.

5. If you turn down a job offer of $45,000 per year to work for yourself, what is the opportunity cost of working for yourself?

Other things being equal, you incur a $45,000 per year implicit cost of working for yourself in this case, because it is what you give up when you choose to turn down the alternative job offer. If you turned down even better offers, your opportunity cost of working for yourself would be even higher.

11.2 Production in the Short Run

1. What is the difference between fixed and variable inputs?

Fixed inputs are those, such as plants and equipment, that cannot be changed in the short run, while variable inputs are those, such as hourly labor, that can be changed in the short run.

2. **Why are all inputs variable in the long run?**

    All inputs are variable in the long run by definition, because the long run is defined as that time period necessary to allow all inputs to be varied.

3. **What relationship does a production function represent?**

    A production function represents the relationship between different combinations of inputs and the maximum output of a product that can be produced with those inputs, with given technology.

4. **What is diminishing marginal product? What causes it?**

    Diminishing marginal product means that as the amount of a variable input is increased—the amount of other inputs being held constant—a point will ultimately be reached beyond which marginal product will decline. It is caused by reductions in the amount of fixed inputs that can be combined with each unit of a variable input, as the amount of that variable input used increases.

11.3 Costs in the Short Run

1. **What is the difference between fixed costs and variable costs?**

    Fixed costs are the expenses associated with fixed inputs (that therefore only exist in the short run), which are constant regardless of output. Variable costs are the expenses associated with variable inputs, which change as the level of output changes.

2. **How are the average fixed cost, average variable cost, and average total cost calculated?**

    For a given level of output, any average cost is calculated as the relevant total cost divided by the level of output. Average fixed cost is therefore total fixed cost divided by output; average variable cost is total variable cost divided by output; and average total cost is total cost (fixed cost plus variable cost) divided by output.

3. **Why is marginal cost the relevant cost to consider when a producer is deciding whether to produce more or less of a product?**

    Marginal cost is the additional cost of increasing output by one unit. That is, it is the cost relevant to the choice of whether to produce and sell one more unit of a good. For producing and selling one more unit of a product to increase profits, the addition to revenue from selling that output (marginal revenue) must exceed the addition to cost from producing it (marginal cost).

4. **If the average variable cost curve were constant over some range of output, why would the average total cost be falling over that range of output?**

    Average total cost is the sum of average variable cost and average fixed cost. Average fixed costs fall over the entire possible range of output. Therefore, if the average variable cost curve were constant over a range of output, the average total cost curve must be falling over that range of output.

5. **If your season batting average going into a game was .300 (three hits per ten at bats) and you got two hits in five at bats during the game, would your season batting average rise or fall as a result?**

    Your "marginal" batting average in the game was .400 (two hits per five at bats), which was higher than your previous batting average. As a consequence, because that game's marginal results were above your previous average, it raises your season batting average as a result.

11.4 The Shape of the Short-Run Cost Curves

1. **What is the primary reason that the average total cost falls as output expands over low output ranges?**

    The primary reason average total cost falls as output expands over low output ranges is that average fixed cost declines sharply with output at low levels of output.

2. **Why does the average total cost rise at some point as output expands further?**

    Average total cost begins to rise at some point as output expands further, because of the law of diminishing marginal product, also called the law of increasing costs. Over this range of output, adding more variable inputs does not increase output by the same proportion, so the average cost of production increases over this range of output.

3. **If marginal costs are less than the average total cost, why does *ATC* fall? If *MC* is greater than *ATC*, why does *ATC* rise?**

    When the marginal cost of a unit of output is less than its average total cost, including the lower-cost unit will lower the average (just as getting lower marginal grades this term will decrease your GPA). When the marginal cost of a unit of output exceeds its average total cost, including the higher-cost unit will raise the average (just as getting higher marginal grades this term will increase your GPA).

11.5 Cost Curves: Short-Run Versus Long-Run

1. Why does the *LRATC* curve have a shallower U-shape than the *SRATC*?

In the short run, some inputs are fixed, like the size of the physical plant or certain machinery. Once a firm has chosen its plant size it is fixed in the short run. In the long run, firms can increase their capital inputs (fixed in the short run) as well as their inputs that are variable in the short run. So the short-run costs are at least as high as the long-run costs and higher if the wrong level of capital is chosen in the short run. Thus, the long-run curve has a shallower U-shape curve than the short run. Remember, the firm can adjust all factors in the long run which allows it to keep its costs lower.

2. What are economies of scale, diseconomies of scale, and constant returns to scale?

Each of these terms refers to average or per-unit costs as output expands. Economies of scale means that long-run average cost falls as output expands; diseconomies of scale means that long-run average cost rises as output expands; and constant returns to scale means that long-run average cost is constant as output expands.

3. How might cooking a family dinner be subject to falling average total cost in the long run as the size of the family grows?

Once the appropriate larger-scale cooking technology has been adopted (i.e., in the long run, when all inputs can be varied), such as larger cooking pots, pans, and baking sheets, larger ovens, dishwashers, and so on, and more family members can be involved, each specializing in fewer tasks, this larger scale can reduce the average cost per meal served.

4. What may cause economies or diseconomies of scale?

Economies of scale can result when expanding output allows the use of mass production techniques such as assembly lines or allows gains from further labor specialization that may not be possible at lower levels of output. Diseconomies of scale can result when a firm finds it increasingly difficult to handle the complexity as well as the information and coordination problems of large-scale management.

True or False:

1. Explicit costs include both wages paid to workers and the opportunity cost of using one's own land, labor, or capital.

2. Because implicit costs do not represent an explicit outlay of money, they are not real costs.

3. When economists say firms try to maximize profits, they mean that firms try to maximize the difference between what they receive for their goods and services in total revenue and what they give up for their inputs in total costs (explicit and implicit).

4. Economic profits equal actual revenues minus all explicit and implicit costs.

5. Economists consider a zero economic profit to be less than a normal profit rate.

6. Earning zero economic profit is different from earning zero accounting profit.

7. Sunk costs are irrelevant for any future action.

8. The short run is defined as a period too brief for some inputs to be varied.

9. In the long run, the inputs that do not change with output are called fixed inputs or fixed factors of production.

10. The long run can vary considerably in length from industry to industry.

11. Total product will typically start at a low level and increase slowly at first and then more rapidly as the amount of the variable input increases.

12. Marginal product first rises as the result of more effective use of fixed inputs and then falls.

13. Diminishing marginal product stems from the crowding of the fixed inputs with more and more of the variable input.

14. A firm never knowingly allows itself to reach the point where the marginal product becomes negative.

15. If a firm were producing at the level where the marginal product of an input was negative, its profits would be lower as a result.

16. Fixed costs for a given period have to be paid only if a firm produces output in that period.

17. Variable costs vary with the level of output, while fixed costs do not.

18. Marginal cost shows the change in total costs associated with a change in output by one unit, or the cost of producing one more unit of output.

19. Marginal costs are really just a useful way to view changes in fixed costs as output changes.

20. The total cost curve is the summation of the total variable cost and total fixed cost curves.

21. The average fixed cost curve is always a horizontal line, because fixed costs do not change with output.

22. The marginal cost curve crosses the average variable cost and average total cost curves at those curves' lowest points.

23. At output levels where average total cost is rising, marginal cost must be greater than average total cost.

24. The average fixed cost curve declines whether the marginal cost curve is rising or falling.

25. The average total cost curve is usually U-shaped.

26. The declining average variable cost curve is primarily responsible for the falling segment of the average total cost curve.

27. Diminishing marginal product first sets in at the minimum point of the average total cost curve.

28. Diminishing marginal product causes the marginal cost curve to increase, eventually causing the average variable cost and average total cost curves to rise.

29. *MC* is equal to *AVC* at the lowest point on the *AVC* curve, and it is equal to *ATC* at the lowest point on the *ATC* curve.

30. Over long enough time periods, firms can vary all of their productive inputs.

31. As we move along the *LRATC*, the factory size changes with the quantity of output.

32. A typical firm experiences economies of scale at low levels of output, constant returns to scale at higher levels of output, and diseconomies of scale at still higher levels of output.

33. Diseconomies of scale may exist because a firm can use mass production techniques or capture gains from further labor specialization not possible at lower levels of output.

Multiple Choice:

1. An explicit cost
   a. is an opportunity cost.
   b. is an out-of-pocket expense.
   c. does not require an outlay of money.
   d. is characterized by both a and b.
   e. is characterized by both a and c.

2. Which of the following is false?
   a. Explicit costs are input costs that require a monetary payment.
   b. Implicit costs do not represent an explicit outlay of money.
   c. Both implicit and explicit costs are opportunity costs.
   d. Sunk costs are irrelevant for any future action.
   e. All of the above are *true*.

3. Which of the following is false?
   a. Profits are a firm's total revenue minus its total costs.
   b. Accounting profits are actual revenues minus actual expenditures of money.
   c. Economic profits are actual revenues minus all explicit and implicit costs.
   d. If a firm has any implicit costs, its economic profits exceed its accounting profits.
   e. All of the above are *true*.

4. The crucial difference between how economists and accountants analyze the profitability of a business has to do with whether or not _____ are included when calculating total production costs.
   a. implicit costs
   b. cash payments
   c. sunk costs
   d. explicit costs

5. Which of the following is true?
   a. If a firm's implicit costs are zero, accounting profits equal economic profits.
   b. If a firm's implicit costs are positive, accounting profits exceed economic profits.
   c. If a firm's implicit costs are positive, economic profits exceed accounting profits.
   d. Both a and b are true.
   e. Both a and c are true.

6. Cassie produces and sells 300 jars of homemade jelly each month for $3 each. Each month, she pays $200 for jars, pays $150 for ingredients, and uses her own time, with an opportunity cost of $300. Her economic profits each month are
   a. $250.
   b. $400.
   c. $550.
   d. $600.
   e. minus $350.

7. Sunk costs
   a. should be included when weighing the marginal costs of production against the marginal benefits received.
   b. have already been incurred and cannot be recovered.
   c. plus variable costs equal the total costs of production.
   d. are relevant to future decisions and should be carefully considered.

8. The short run
   a. is a period too brief for any inputs to be varied.
   b. is a period that involves no fixed costs.
   c. is normally a period of one year.
   d. is none of the above.

9. The long run
   a. is a period in which a firm can adjust all its inputs.
   b. can vary in length from industry to industry.
   c. is a period in which all costs are variable costs.
   d. is characterized by all of the above.

10. The long-run production period
    a. is a time when all inputs are variable.
    b. varies in length according to how capital goods are specialized.
    c. is likely to be longer for a steel manufacturer than for a retailer who sells watches off a cart at the local mall.
    d. is characterized by all of the above.

11. Which of the following most accurately describes the long-run period?
    a. The long run is a period of time in which a firm is unable to vary some of its factors of production.
    b. In the long run, a firm is able to expand output by utilizing additional workers and raw materials, but not physical capital.
    c. The long run is of sufficient length to allow a firm to alter its plant capacity and all other factors of production.
    d. The long run is of sufficient length to allow a firm to transform economic losses into economic profits.
    e. Both a and b most accurately describe the long-run period.

12. Production in the short run
    a. is subject to the law of diminishing marginal product.
    b. involves some fixed factors.
    c. can be increased by employing another unit of a variable input, as long as the marginal product of that input is positive.
    d. is characterized by all of the above.
    e. is characterized by none of the above.

13. A production function shows the relationship between
    a. variable inputs and fixed inputs.
    b. variable inputs and output.
    c. costs and output.
    d. inputs and costs.
    e. production and sales revenue.

14. Diminishing marginal product
    a. occurs in the long run but not in the short run.
    b. occurs in the short run but not in the long run.
    c. occurs both in the long run and the short run.
    d. occurs in neither the long run nor the short run.

15. Diminishing marginal productivity in a frozen-pizza company means that
    a. hiring additional workers causes the total output of pizza to fall.
    b. hiring additional workers does not change the total output of pizza produced.
    c. hiring additional workers adds fewer and fewer pizzas to total output.
    d. the average total cost of production must be decreasing.

16. If the marginal product of a firm's only variable input is negative,
    a. its total product is growing at a decreasing rate.
    b. it will use more of the variable input until its marginal product is again positive.
    c. it will reduce its use of the variable input.
    d. its total product is minimized.
    e. none of the above would be true.

17. Total fixed costs
    a. do not vary with the level of output.
    b. cannot be avoided in the short run without going out of business.
    c. do not exist in the long run.
    d. are characterized by all of the above.

18. Which of the following is most likely a variable cost for a business?
    a. the loan payment on funds borrowed when a new building is constructed
    b. payments for electricity
    c. the lease payment on a warehouse used by the business
    d. the opportunity cost of the heavy equipment installed in a factory

19. The change in total cost that results from the production of one additional unit of output is called
    a. marginal revenue.
    b. average variable cost.
    c. marginal cost.
    d. average total cost.
    e. average fixed cost.

20. Which short-run curve typically declines continuously as output expands?
    a. average variable cost
    b. average total cost
    c. average fixed cost
    d. marginal cost
    e. none of the above

21. Which of the following is true?
    a. The short-run ATC exceeds the short-run AVC at any given level of output.
    b. If the short-run ATC curve is rising, the short-run AVC curve is also rising.
    c. The short-run AFC is always falling with increased output, whether the short-run MC curve is greater or less than short-run AFC.
    d. If short-run MC is less than short-run AVC, short-run AVC is falling.
    e. All of the above are true.

22. Which of the following is false in the short run?
    a. ATC is usually U-shaped.
    b. Declining $AFCs$ are the primary reason ATC decreases at low levels of output.
    c. ATC increases at high levels of output because of diminishing marginal product.
    d. Diminishing marginal product sets in at the minimum point of ATC.
    e. All of the above are true in the short run.

23. Typically, what is the shape of the average total cost curve for a firm in the short run?
    a. Typically, an average total cost curve is U-shaped.
    b. Typically, an average total cost curve constantly slopes upward as output expands and eventually approaches an infinite dollar amount at high rates of output.
    c. Typically, an average total cost curve is a vertical line.
    d. Typically, an average total cost curve slopes downward as output expands and approaches the X-axis when output is very large.

24. Which of the following is true in the short run?
    a. MC equals ATC at the lowest point of ATC.
    b. MC equals AVC at the lowest point of AVC.
    c. When AVC is at its minimum point, ATC is falling.
    d. When ATC is at its minimum point, AVC is rising.
    e. All of the above are true.

25. Which of the following is always true?
    a. When marginal cost is less than average total cost, average total cost is increasing.
    b. When average fixed cost is falling, marginal cost must be less than average fixed cost.
    c. When average variable cost is falling, marginal cost must be greater than average variable cost.
    d. When marginal cost is greater than average total cost, average total cost is increasing.

26. When marginal product is increasing,
    a. marginal cost is increasing.
    b. marginal cost is decreasing.
    c. average variable cost is increasing.
    d. average total cost is increasing.
    e. total cost is decreasing.

27. If a taxi service is operating in the region of diminishing marginal product and more taxi service is added in the short run, what will happen to the marginal cost of providing the additional service?
    a. It is impossible to say anything about marginal cost with the information provided.
    b. Marginal cost will decrease.
    c. Marginal cost will increase.
    d. Marginal cost will stay the same.

28. If the Burger Hut's city permit to operate rose by $3,000 per year,
    a. its *MC* curve would shift upward.
    b. its *AVC* curve would shift upward.
    c. its *ATC* curve would shift upward.
    d. its *MC, AVC,* and *ATC* curves would shift upward.

29. If a firm's *ATC* is falling in the long run, then
    a. it is subject to economies of scale over that range of output.
    b. it is subject to diseconomies of scale over that range of output.
    c. it is subject to constant return to scale over that range of output.
    d. it has reached the minimum efficient scale of production.
    e. both c and d are true.

30. In the long run,
    a. the average fixed cost curve is U-shaped.
    b. average fixed cost exceeds the average variable cost of production.
    c. all costs are variable.
    d. all costs are fixed.
    e. none of the above is correct.

31. When a firm experiences economies of scale in production,
    a. long-run average total cost declines as output expands.
    b. long-run average total cost increases as output expands.
    c. marginal cost increases as output expands.
    d. the marginal product of an input diminishes with increased utilization.

32. The lowest level of output at which a firm's goods are produced at minimum long-run average total cost is called
    a. the point of zero marginal cost.
    b. the point of diminishing returns.
    c. the minimum total product.
    d. the minimum efficient scale.
    e. plant capacity.

Problems:

1. What happens to the cost of growing strawberries on your own land if a housing developer offers you three times what you thought your land was worth?

2. As a farmer, you work for yourself using your own tractor, equipment, and farm structures, and you cultivate your own land. Why might it be difficult to calculate your profits from farming?

3. The salmon fishery in Alaska's Bristol Bay has historically been one of the world's richest. Over the past few years, poor returns of salmon to the bay and competition from farm-raised salmon have reduced the economic returns to the fishermen. One response to lower revenues has been for fishermen to use family members instead of hiring crew "in order to reduce their costs." Evaluate this business strategy. Will employing relatives really keep profits from falling? Under what conditions is this a good strategy?

4. Use the table below for a–c.

   Willie's Water Park Short-Run Production Function

Labor (workers)	Total Product (visitors per hour)	Marginal Product
0	_____	
1	_____	10
2	_____	12
3	_____	9
4	_____	8
5	_____	4
6	_____	−2

   a. Fill in the Total Product column.
   b. Willie's Water Park experiences diminishing marginal product beginning with which worker?
   c. Willie's Water Park experiences diminishing total product beginning with which worker?

5. Harry's Hat Company makes hats using the technology described in the following data:

   With Three Machines

Labor	Total Product (hats)	Marginal Product (hats)
1 day	8	_____
2 days	18	_____
3 days	30	_____
4 days	45	_____
5 days	57	_____
6 days	67	_____
7 days	72	_____

   With Four Machines

Labor	Total Product (hats)	Marginal Product (hats)
1 day	9	_____
2 days	20	_____
3 days	35	_____
4 days	55	_____
5 days	76	_____
6 days	88	_____
7 days	95	_____

   a. Fill in the Marginal Product columns of these tables.
   b. At what point does diminishing marginal product set in with three machines? With four?
   c. Why is the point of diminishing marginal product different in each case?

6. Fill in the rest of the production function for Candy's Candies from the information provided.

Labor (workers)	Total Product (pounds)	Marginal Product (pounds)
0	_____	_____
1	20	_____
2	44	_____
3	62	_____
4	_____	12
5	_____	6
6	78	_____

a. Candy's Candies begins to experience diminishing marginal product with which worker?

b. Does Candy's Candies ever experience negative marginal product? If so, with the addition of which worker?

7. Draw a typically shaped total product curve and the marginal product curve derived from it, and indicate the ranges of increasing, diminishing, and negative marginal product.

8. Say that your firm's total product curve includes the following data: one worker can produce 8 units of output; two workers, 20 units; three workers, 34 units; four workers, 50 units; five workers, 60 units; six workers, 70 units; seven workers, 76 units; eight workers, 78 units; and nine workers, 77 units.

a. What is the marginal product of the seventh worker?

b. When does the law of diminishing product set in?

c. Under these conditions, would you ever choose to employ nine workers?

9. Why does the law of diminishing marginal product imply the law of increasing costs?

10. Complete the following table describing the short-run daily costs of the Attractive Magnet Co. for 2009.

Total Product (magnets)	Total Fixed Costs	Total Variable Costs	Total Costs	Average Fixed Costs	Average Variable Costs	Average Total Costs	Marginal Costs
1	$100	$ 30	$130	$100	$30	$130	$30
2	_____	_____	_____	_____	25	_____	_____
3	_____	_____	_____	_____	20	_____	_____
4	_____	_____	_____	_____	16	_____	_____
5	_____	_____	_____	_____	18	_____	_____
6	_____	_____	_____	_____	21	_____	_____
7	_____	_____	_____	_____	24	_____	_____
8	_____	218	318	_____	_____	_____	_____

11. A one-day ticket to visit the Screaming Coasters theme park costs $36, but you can also get a two-consecutive-day ticket for $40. What is the average cost per day for the two-day ticket? What is the marginal cost of the second consecutive day?

12. As a movie exhibitor, you can choose between paying a flat fee of $5,000 to show a movie for a week or paying a fee of $2 per customer. Will your choice affect your fixed and variable costs? How?

13. What is likely to happen to your marginal costs when adding output requires working beyond an eight-hour day, if workers must be paid time-and-a-half wages beyond an eight-hour day?

14. If your university pays lecture note takers $20 per hour to take notes in your economics class and then sells subscriptions for $15 per student, is the cost of the lecture note taker a fixed or variable cost of selling an additional subscription?

15. The Lighthouse Safety Vest Co. makes flotation vests for recreational boaters. They currently employ 50 people and produce 12,000 vests per month. Lighthouse managers know that when they hire one more person, monthly vest production will increase by 200 vests. They pay workers $1,600 per month.
    a. What is the marginal product of the 51st worker?
    b. What is the marginal cost to produce one more vest? (*Hint:* Think of the marginal cost as the additional worker's pay divided by the changes in output.)
    c. If labor is the only variable factor of production, will the average variable cost of production rise or fall as a result of hiring a 51st worker? Why?
    d. What happens to the marginal cost of a vest when the 52nd worker is added and the marginal product drops to 160 vests per month?

16. Illustrate how the shape of the marginal product curve relates to the shape of the marginal cost curve.

17. Use the graph to answer the following questions.
    a. Curve A represents which cost curve?
    b. Curve B represents which cost curve?
    c. Curve C represents which cost curve?
    d. Curve D represents which cost curve?

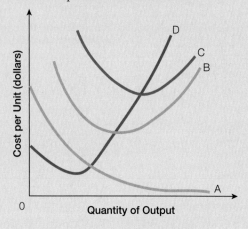

    e. Why must curve D pass through the minimum points of both curve B and curve C?
    f. What significance does the point where curve A intersects curve D have?

18. Fill in the rest of the cost function for Bob's Bowling Balls.

Output	Total Fixed Costs	Total Variable Costs	Total Costs	Average Fixed Cost	Average Variable Cost	Average Total Cost	Marginal Cost
1	$200	$ 60	$_____	$_____	$_____	$_____	$_____
2	_____	100	_____	_____	_____	_____	_____
3	_____	120	_____	_____	_____	_____	_____
4	_____	128	_____	_____	_____	_____	_____
5	_____	180	_____	_____	_____	_____	_____
6	_____	252	_____	_____	_____	_____	_____
7	_____	316	_____	_____	_____	_____	_____
8	_____	436	_____	_____	_____	_____	_____

19. Buffalo Bill has a potato chip company, Buffalo's chips. He is currently losing money on every bag of chips he sells. Mrs. Bill, who has just completed an economics class, tells Buffalo Bill he could make a profit if he adds more machines and produces more chips. How could this be possible? What is Mrs. Bill assuming about the output range in which Buffalo Bill is currently producing?

20. You have the following information about long-run total cost for the following firms:

Quantity	Arnold's Apples *LRTC*	Belle's Bananas *LRTC*	Cam's Cantaloupes *LRTC*
1	120	33	42
2	140	72	68
3	160	117	98
4	180	168	132
5	200	225	170
6	220	288	212
7	240	357	258

   a. Do any of these firms experience constant returns to scale? How do you know?
   b. Do any of these firms experience diseconomics of scale? How do you know?
   c. Do any of these firms experience economics of scale? How do you know?

21. Refer to the cost curve in the following exhibit:

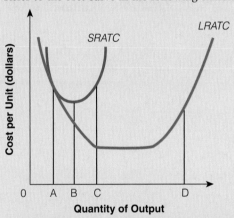

   a. What is the lowest level of output at which the efficient scale of production is reached in the long run?
   b. In the short run described by *SRATC*, what is the efficient output level?
   c. When the firm is producing at the level of output described by D, will it be experiencing constant returns to scale, economies of scale, or diseconomies of scale?

Optimal Factor Combinations: Two Variable Inputs

If the production manager had to deal with just one variable input, decision problems would be relatively easy. Given the output target, the production manager would purchase the minimum quantity of input needed to produce the assigned output and would inform the output manager of the costs incurred. However, the production manager's job becomes much more complicated when the output can be produced with several

isoquant
curve showing the various factor combinations that can produce a given level of output

alternative combinations of inputs. For the sake of simplicity, we shall confine ourselves to two variable inputs, capital and labor.

The Isoquant

The various combinations of two factors that allow the firm to produce a given quantity of output can be illustrated graphically. The curve showing the various factor combinations that can produce a given level of output is known as an **isoquant**. Exhibit 1 shows that units of capital are measured on the vertical axis, and units

| *appendix* **exhibit 1** | Isoquant Showing Various Combinations of Labor and Capital That Can Be Used to Produce 20 Units of Output per Day |

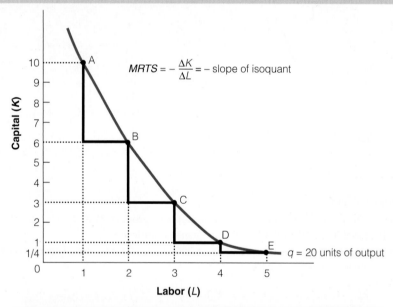

$$MRTS = -\frac{\Delta K}{\Delta L} = -\text{ slope of isoquant}$$

$q = 20$ units of output

Combination	Labor (L)	Capital (K)	Marginal Rate of Technical Substitution
A	1	10	
B	2	6	4
C	3	3	3
D	4	1	2
E	5	1/4	3/4

The isoquant q indicates that 20 units of output can be produced with 10 units of capital and 1 unit of labor (combination A), or 3 units of capital and 3 units of labor (combination C). All other combinations of capital and labor capable of producing 20 units of output are also charted along isoquant q.

of labor on the horizontal axis; isoquant q shows the various combinations of capital and labor that allow the firm to produce a given level (20 units) of output.

Isoquants, like indifference curves, have several important properties. Isoquants are negatively sloped, nonintersecting, convex, and they increase in value as we move in a northeast direction from the origin. However, unlike indifference curves, isoquants are measured cardinally. That is, an output of 40 is twice as large as an output of 20.

The Marginal Rate of Technical Substitution

Explanation of the optimal factor combination can be facilitated by discussing the concept of the **marginal rate of technical substitution of labor for capital (MRTS)** (to distinguish it from the marginal rate of substitution along an indifference curve). The slope of the isoquant is the number of units of one factor necessary to replace a unit of another factor, in order to maintain the same level of output, $-\Delta K/\Delta L$. If we remove the negative sign on the slope we have the *MRTS*.

Suppose that various combinations of labor and capital (together with given quantities of other factors) are used to produce a given level of output, as illustrated in Exhibit 1. Various combinations will produce 20 units of output per day; for example, if 2 units of labor are used, 6 units of capital will be needed (Combination B); and if 3 units of labor are used, then 3 units of capital will be required (Combination C). Note that the various combinations are alternative possibilities for the production of a given quantity of the product, 20 units of output per day in this example.

The *MRTS* measures the quantity of capital that can be given up by using one additional unit of labor, while still producing the same level of output. For example, if 2 units of labor (and 6 units of capital) are now being used, 3 units of capital can be given up by using 1 additional unit of labor.

As the data in Exhibit 1 illustrate, the isoquants are convex. That is, the *MRTS* diminishes as we move down along the isoquant. We also see that labor becomes more abundant and capital more scarce. Hence, it becomes increasingly difficult to substitute even more labor for capital.

As the quantity of one factor, say labor, is increased relative to the quantity of the other, say capital, output being constant, the number of units of capital that can be replaced by one unit of labor falls. In other words, the marginal product of labor falls as we use more of

it, and the marginal product of capital rises as we use less of it.

Under ordinary circumstances, the isoquant will be convex to the point of origin, because of the principle of diminishing marginal rate of technical substitution. The greater the quantity of labor used, the smaller is the quantity of the capital needed to replace a unit of labor and maintain output. Thus, the right-hand portion of the isoquant is almost parallel to the horizontal axis, while the left-hand portion is almost parallel to the vertical axis.

The marginal rate of technical substitution is equal to $-\Delta K/\Delta L$, which is the slope of the isoquant. Recall that all combinations on a given isoquant yield the same level of output. Thus, if labor is substituted for capital, with output remaining constant, we know that:

$$(\Delta K)(MP_K) + (\Delta L)(MP_L) = 0$$

Rearranging the terms in this equation we have:

$$MRTS = -(\Delta K)/(\Delta L) = MP_L/MP_K$$

That is, the slope of the isoquant at any point is equal to the ratio of the marginal product of labor to the marginal product of capital.

The *MRTS* is a measure of the extent to which the two factors are substitutes for each other. If they are perfect substitutes—that is, if either factor can be used equally well to produce the product—the marginal rate of technical substitution will be a constant. If capital and labor can be used equally well, the *MRTS* will remain unchanged, regardless of the extent to which substitution is carried in either direction, as seen in Exhibit 2. For example, a woven rug or a sweater could either be done almost exclusively by machine or with a few tools and hand labor.

At the other extreme, two factors may not be substitutes for a particular purpose (such as carpenters and hammers or taxicab drivers and taxicabs). Here, the *MRTS* is undefinable, because output cannot be maintained if one factor is replaced by the other. If this relationship exists between all factors the firm uses, the factor combination the firm employs is dictated entirely by technological conditions, and no substitution is possible. The curve in Exhibit 3 is a right angle indicating that the same output would be forthcoming if more of either (but not more of both!) of the inputs were used. That is, you are equally well off producing q_1 output using factor combination A as you would be using factor combination B. However, you can clearly produce more output, q_2, if you increase both labor and capital, a move from A to C. This type of

marginal rate of technical substitution of labor for capital (MRTS)
the quantity of capital that can be given up by using one additional unit of labor while producing the same level of output

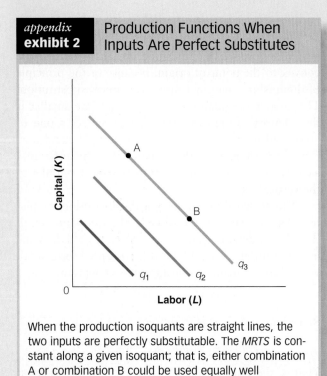

appendix **exhibit 2** Production Functions When Inputs Are Perfect Substitutes

When the production isoquants are straight lines, the two inputs are perfectly substitutable. The *MRTS* is constant along a given isoquant; that is, either combination A or combination B could be used equally well to produce q_3.

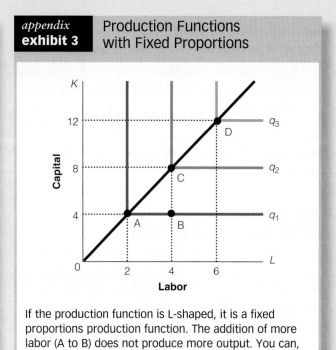

appendix **exhibit 3** Production Functions with Fixed Proportions

If the production function is L-shaped, it is a fixed proportions production function. The addition of more labor (A to B) does not produce more output. You can, however, produce more output (q_2) if you increase both labor and capital (A to C).

production relationship is called **fixed-proportions production function.**

Cost Schedules with Long-Run Adjustments Completed

The long-run period has been defined as a period sufficiently long for a firm to adjust all factors of production. The long run, as emphasized earlier, is always a *planning period,* because at any moment, firms are inevitably in some short-run situation. In the long run, however, a firm can choose any short-run plant configuration. The actual time interval depends on the nature of the production processes and particularly on the extent to which specialized capital equipment, requiring a substantial period to construct and having a certain lifespan, are used. The time a firm needs to adjust all factors is much greater for a steel mill or a railroad than for a service station or a grocery store. Over a long-run period, because all factors are adjustable, all costs are variable.

In the long run, the firm can alter all its inputs. Thus, the manager must choose among alternative

fixed-proportions production function
when it is impossible to substitute one input for another so inputs must be used in fixed proportions

isocost (equal cost) lines
graphical display of the various possible quantities of the two factors that can be purchased with a given outlay of money

inputs that minimize the cost of producing a given output. In addition we need to obtain information on long-run costs and output levels.

Isocost Lines and the Optimum Factor Combination

The optimal factor combination can be shown graphically by combining isoquants with **isocost (equal cost) lines,** each of which shows the various possible quantities of the two factors that can be purchased with a given outlay of money. Exhibit 4 shows isoquants when isocost lines are added. Specifically, Exhibit 4 shows the various quantities of capital and labor that can be purchased with a given outlay of money, assuming that the prices of labor and capital are $5 and $10 per hour, respectively. If the given outlay is $600, for example, the isocost line is represented in Exhibit 4 by line B, which indicates that 60 units of capital can be purchased if only capital is purchased, 120 units of labor if only labor is purchased, and 60 units of labor if 30 units of capital are used. The isocost relation is a straight line as a matter of mathematical necessity as long as prices paid for factor units are the same regardless of the quantities purchased.

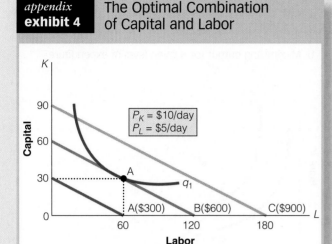

appendix
exhibit 4

The Optimal Combination of Capital and Labor

$P_K = \$10/day$
$P_L = \$5/day$

The isocost lines contain factor combinations that can be hired at the same expense. Minimizing the cost of producing q_1 output involves choosing a factor combination that coincides with q_1 output. The optimum input combination occurs at point A, where 60 units of labor and 30 units of capital are utilized to produce q_1 output.

The various possible isocost lines, one for each potential level of outlay on factors, are parallel to each other (see lines A, B, and C in Exhibit 4). The farther to the right an isocost line is located, the higher is the level of outlay that it represents.

Minimum cost is achieved when the firm chooses the least expensive combination of factor inputs for a given level of output. This combination is represented graphically by the lowest isocost line (the farthest one to the left) that touches the isoquant representing the quantity to be produced. Thus, the **optimum factor combination** is represented by a point of tangency between the given isoquant and the lowest possible isocost line, point A in Exhibit 4.

optimum factor combination
a point of tangency between the given isoquant and the lowest possible isocost line

The isocost line that is just tangent to the isoquant allows a firm to acquire the necessary factor units with the lowest possible outlay.* Any lower line would not allow the firm to purchase enough factors to produce the desired output, while any higher isocost line would entail unnecessarily high factor costs. At any point on the isoquant other than the point of tangency, the outlay on the factors to produce the given output would be higher than that at the tangency point. At the tangency, the slope of the isoquant (which represents the marginal rate of technical substitution between the two

factors) is equal to the slope of the isocost line (which represents the ratio of the prices of the two factors), and thus the marginal rate of technical substitution is equal to the ratio of the factor prices.

Therefore at the tangency points, the isoquant and the isocost line will have identical slopes. The slope of the MRTS is equal to the ratio of the factor prices:

$$MRTS_{LK} = w/r.$$

where

$w = $ wages (the price of labor)
$r = $ rental rate of capital

For example, in Exhibit 5(a), to minimize the cost of producing 100 units of output, the firm should produce at point A, where the isoquant is tangent to the isocost line. Point B is an input combination that can produce 100 units of output. However, B costs more than A. Point C represents a cheaper factor combination, but it is impossible to produce 100 units of output with so few inputs. Exhibit 5(b) illustrates the alternative optimization process, maximizing output for a given level of costs. The producer attempts to reach the highest isoquant for a given isocost line. Again point A, the tangency point between the isoquant and the isocost line, gives the optimum factor combination. Point B is feasible, but produces a lower level of output. Greater output is attained at point C, but costs are too high. Hence, both strategies result in the same optimization conditons: the isoquant and the isocost line are tangent, and the MRTS equals the ratio of input prices.

Recall that MRTS is a measure of the extent to which the two factors are substitutes for each other. Also recall that the MRTS is equal to the ratio of the marginal product of labor to capital. So we can rewrite our previous equation as:

$$(\text{slope of the isoquant}) - MP_L/MP_K = -w/r \text{ (slope of the isocost line)}$$

or

$$MP_L/MP_K = w/r$$

Rearranging our terms, we find that

$$MP_{L/w} = MP_{K/r}$$

In other words, at the tangency solution, the ratio of the marginal product to input price must be the same for all inputs used in production.

The Expansion Path

In Exhibit 6, the optimal factor bundles are presented for different levels of output. For example,

---

*Remember that an isoquant shows the various quantities of the two factors necessary to produce a given output, while each isocost line shows the various quantities of two factors which can be acquired with the expenditure of a given sum of money.

appendix
exhibit 5   Equivalent Optimization Solutions

a. Minimizing the cost of producing a given output level

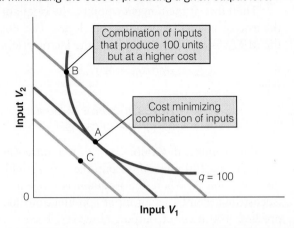

b. Maximizing output for a given level of expenditure

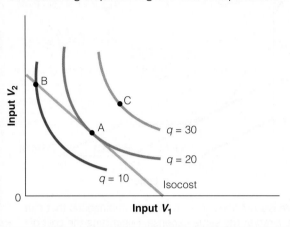

the least-cost method for producing 100 units of output is using L_1 units of labor and K_1 units of capital, while the least-cost method of producing 120 units of output would be combining L_2 units of labor and K_2 units of capital. The

expansion path
shows the least-cost input solutions for providing a given output

expansion path is the line that connects these least-cost input combinations, holding input prices constant.

The **expansion path** provides us information regarding the long-run total cost curve. Specifically, it shows

appendix
exhibit 6   The Expansion Path

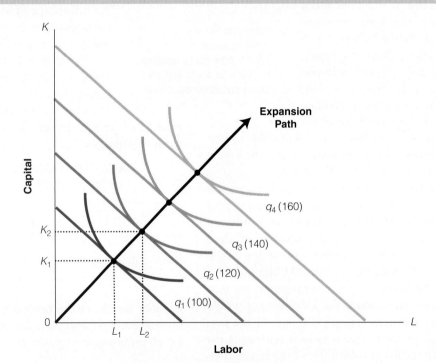

An expansion path connects the firm's least-cost input combinations of producing each level of output in the long run, when all inputs can be varied. The least-cost input combination for producing 120 units of output is K_2 units of capital and L_2 units of labor.

appendix
exhibit 7   Deriving *LRTC* from an Isoquant-Isocost Map

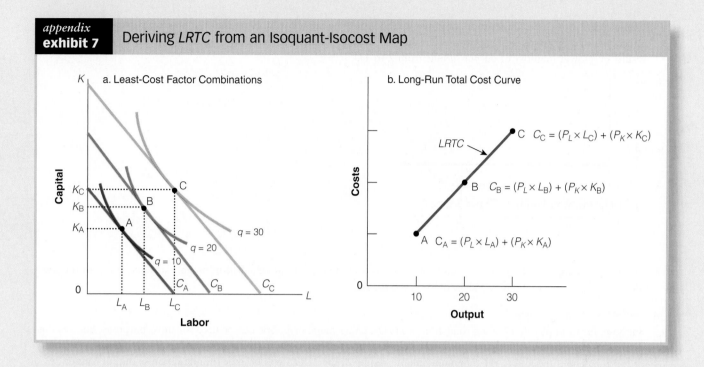

the least-cost input solutions for providing a given output, or equivalently, the lowest long-run total cost for producing each level of output. The connection between long-run total cost and the expansion path is seen in Exhibit 7. Points A, B, and C are the cost minimizing input combinations along the expansion path

in part (a). The corresponding points on the long-run total cost curve are A, B, and C in part (b). Long-run total cost is simply the optimum amount of labor times the wage plus the optimum amount of capital times the price of capital.

Key Terms and Concepts

isoquant 320
marginal rate of technical substitution
    of labor for capital (MRTS) 321

fixed-proportions production
    function 322
isocost (equal cost) lines 322

optimum factor combination 323
expansion path 324

Problems:

1. Would a firm ever choose a factor combination on a positively sloped portion of an isoquant? Explain.

   Answer

   The following figure reveals two isoquants with positively sloped sections. If the amount of input V_2 is fixed at V_2, 1 unit of output can be produced at either V_1 or V_1''. The input combination at point C would clearly be less efficient than at point A because C uses more of input V_1 and would be more costly. Note that the positively sloped segment of an isoquant corresponds to stage three of production because an increase in V_1 from V_1' to V_1'' when V_2 is fixed at V_2 results in a lower quantity of output (q falls from 2 to 1).

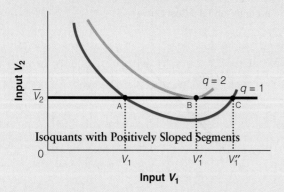

Isoquants with Positively Sloped Segments

2. If two factors are partial substitutes for one another, will the marginal rate of substitution vary as factor proportions are altered, ranging from infinity to values of, or equal to, zero? Explain.

Answer

Suppose, for example, that in the production of DVDs, either metal or plastic can be used for most purposes, but metal is essential for some purposes because plastic lacks sufficient strength for performing the task. In this case, once the quantity of metal has been reduced to the minimum amount required, the *MRTS* will become infinite, because output cannot be maintained if substitution is carried further.

3. A firm is producing 50 units of output. The marginal rate of technical substitution at the current usage rates of V_1 and V_2 is 1. The price of V_1 = \$8 per unit, and the price of V_2 = \$9 per unit. Should the firm change its purchases of V_1 and V_2?

Answer

The firm can substitute one unit of V_1 for one unit of V_2 and still produce the same output level, but the price of V_1 is less than the price of V_2. Thus, the firm should decrease the amount of V_2 and increase the amount of V_1. The situation is depicted in the following graph. The input price ratio, 8/9, is less than the *MRTS*, 1, which is demonstrated by the flatter slope of the isocost than the isoquant at point A, the current factor combination. The firm can, however, lower its expenditure by moving to point B and hiring more V_1 and less V_2.

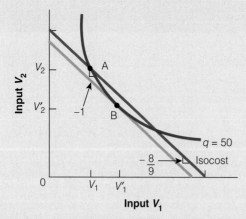

4. Suppose a union raises earnings for workers, and management decides to continue to produce the same output level. How will the firm's optimum combination of labor and capital change, assuming only two inputs? Illustrate graphically. Under what conditions will the effect be large?

Answer

The original factor combination is L and K at point A in the figure. A pay raise increases the slope of the isocost line, the price of labor divided by the price of capital. If the firm continues to produce along the same isoquant, the new quantities of labor and capital are L' and K''. If labor and capital are roughly equally good substitutes over a wide range of input combinations the isoquant will have little curvature, and the substitution of capital for labor will be great.

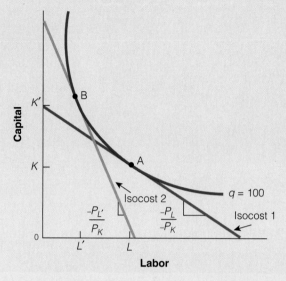

5. Use isoquants to demonstrate how a technological advance allows a firm to produce the same level of output with fewer inputs.

Answer

In the following figure, a technological advance is illustrated by the inward shift of the isoquant from $q = 100$ to $q' = 100$. Both isoquants represent the same level of output, but q' demonstrates that the new technology requires fewer inputs to do so. Thus, the same level of output can be produced at lower costs.

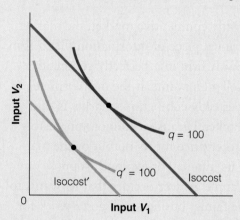

12 Firms in Perfectly Competitive Markets

A firm must answer two critical questions: What price should we charge for the goods and services we sell, and how much should we produce? The answers to these two questions will depend on the market structure.

The behavior of firms will depend on the number of firms in the market, the ease with which firms can enter and exit the market, and the ability of firms to differentiate their products from those of other firms. There is no typical industry. An industry might include one firm that dominates the market, or it might consist of thousands of smaller firms that each produce a small fraction of the market supply. Between these two end points are many other industries. However, because we cannot examine each industry individually, we break them into four main categories: perfect competition, monopoly, monopolistic competition, and oligopoly.

In a perfectly competitive market, the market price is the critical piece of information that a firm needs to know. A firm in a perfectly competitive market can sell all it wants at the market price. A firm in a perfectly competitive market is said to be a price taker, because it cannot appreciably affect the market price for its output or the market price for its inputs. For example, suppose a Washington apple grower decides that he wants to get out of the family business and go to work for Microsoft. Because he may be one of 50,000 apple growers in the United States, his decision will not appreciably change the price of the apples, the production of apples, or the price of inputs. ■

SECTION 12.1 A Perfectly Competitive Market

* What are the characteristics of a firm in a perfectly competitive market?
* What is a price taker?

A Perfectly Competitive Market

This chapter examines perfect competition, a market structure characterized by (1) many buyers and sellers, (2) identical (homogeneous) products, and (3) easy market entry and exit. Let's examine these characteristics in greater detail.

Many Buyers and Sellers

In a perfectly competitive market, there are *many buyers and sellers;* perhaps thousands or conceivably millions. Because each firm is so small in relation to the industry, its production decisions have no impact on the market—each regards price as something over which it has little control. For this reason, perfectly competitive firms are called price takers: They must take the price given by the market because their influence on price is insignificant. If the price of apples in the apple market is $2 a pound, then individual apple farmers will receive $2 a pound for their apples. Similarly, no single buyer of apples can influence the price of apples, because each buyer purchases only a small amount of the apples traded. We will see how this relationship works in more detail in Section 12.2.

Identical (Homogeneous) Products

Consumers believe that all firms in perfectly competitive markets *sell identical (or homogeneous) products.* For example, in the wheat market, it is not possible to determine any significant and consistent qualitative differences in the wheat produced by different farmers. Wheat produced by Farmer Jones looks, feels, smells, and tastes like that produced by Farmer Smith. In short, a bushel of wheat is a bushel of wheat. The products of all the firms are considered to be perfect substitutes.

Easy Entry and Exit

Product markets characterized by perfect competition *have no significant barriers to entry or exit.* Therefore it is fairly easy for entrepreneurs to become suppliers of the product or, if they are already producers, to stop supplying the product. "Fairly easy" does not mean that any person on the street can instantly enter

Can the owner of this orchard charge a noticeably higher price for apples of similar quality to those sold at the orchard down the road? What if she charges a lower price for apples of similar quality? How many apples can she sell at the market price?

BRUCE HEINEMANN/PHOTODISC/GETTY IMAGES

the business but rather that the financial, legal, educational, and other barriers to entering the business are modest, enabling large numbers of people to overcome the barriers and enter the business if they so desire in any given period. If buyers can easily switch from one seller to another and sellers can easily enter or exit the industry, then they have met the perfectly competitive condition of easy entry and exit. Because of this easy market entry, perfectly competitive markets generally consist of a large number of small suppliers.

A perfectly competitive market is approximated most closely in highly organized markets for securities and agricultural commodities, such as the New York Stock Exchange or the Chicago Board of Trade. Wheat, corn, soybeans, cotton, and many other agricultural products are sold in perfectly competitive markets. Although all the criteria for a perfectly competitive market are rarely met, a number of markets come close to satisfying them. Even when all the assumptions don't hold, it is important to note that studying the model of perfect competition is useful because many markets resemble perfect competition—that is, markets in which firms face highly elastic (flat) demand curves and relatively easy entry and exit. The model also gives us a standard of comparison. In other words, we can make comparisons with the perfectly competitive model to help us evaluate what is going on in the real world.

CHICAGO BOARD OF TRADE

At the Chicago Board of Trade (CBOT), prices are set by thousands of buyers interacting with thousands of sellers. The goods in question are typically standardized (e.g., grade A winter wheat), and information is readily available. Every buyer and seller in the market knows the price, the quantity, and the quality of the wheat. Transaction costs are negligible. For example, if a news story breaks on an infestation in the cotton crop, the price of cotton will rise immediately. CBOT price information is used to determine the value of a particular commodity all over the world.

SECTION CHECK

1. A perfectly competitive market is characterized by many buyers and sellers, an identical (homogeneous) product, and easy market entry and exit.

2. Consumers believe that all firms in perfectly competitive markets sell virtually identical (homogeneous) products. The products of all firms are considered to be perfect substitutes.

3. In markets with so many buyers and so many sellers, neither buyers nor sellers have any control over price in perfect competition. They must take the going price and hence are called price takers.

4. Firms in perfectly competitive markets have no significant barriers to entry. That is, the barriers are significantly modest, so that many sellers can enter or exit the industry.

---

1. Why do firms in perfectly competitive markets involve homogeneous goods?

2. Why does the absence of significant barriers to entry tend to result in a large number of suppliers?

3. Why does the fact that perfectly competitive firms are small relative to the market make them price takers?

An Individual Price Taker's Demand Curve

* Why won't individual price takers raise or lower their prices?

* Can individual price takers sell all they want at the market price?

* Will the position of individual price takers' demand curves change when market price changes?

An Individual Firm's Demand Curve

Perfectly competitive firms are **price takers**; that is, they must sell at the market-determined price, where the market price and output are determined

price takers
a perfectly competitive firm that takes the price it is given by the intersection of the market demand and market supply curves

by the intersection of the market supply and demand curves, as seen in Exhibit 1(b). Individual wheat farmers know that they cannot dispose of their wheat at any figure higher than the current market price; if they attempt to charge a higher price, potential buyers will simply make their purchases from

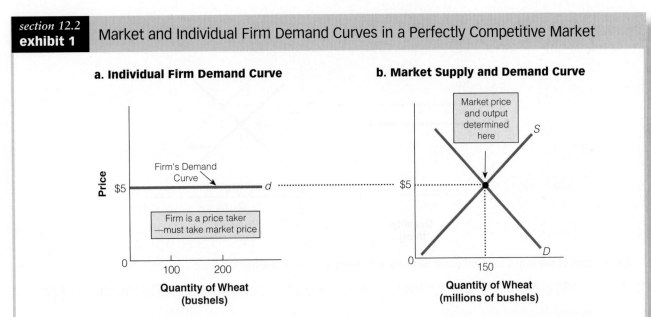

At the market price for wheat, $5, the individual farmer can sell all the wheat he wishes. Because each producer provides only a small fraction of industry output, any additional output will have an insignificant impact on market price. The firm's demand curve is perfectly elastic at the market price.

other wheat farmers. Further, the farmers certainly would not knowingly charge a lower price, because they could sell all they want at the market price.

Likewise, in a perfectly competitive market, individual sellers can change their outputs, and it will not alter the market price. The large number of sellers who are selling identical products make this situation possible. Each producer provides such a small fraction of the total supply that a change in the amount he offers does *not* have a noticeable effect on market equilibrium price. In a perfectly competitive market, then, an individual firm can sell as much as it wishes to place on the market at the prevailing price; the demand, as seen by the seller, is perfectly elastic.

It is easy to construct the demand curve for an individual seller in a perfectly competitive market. Remember, she won't charge more than the market price because no one will buy it, and she won't charge less because she can sell all she wants at the market price. Thus, the farmer's demand curve is horizontal over the entire range of output that she could possibly produce. If the prevailing market price of the product is $5, the farmer's demand curve will be represented graphically by a horizontal line at the market price of $5, as shown in Exhibit 1(a).

A Change in Market Price and the Firm's Demand Curve

To say that producers under perfect competition regard price as a given is not to say that price is constant. The *position* of the firm's demand curve varies with every change in the market price. In Exhibit 2, we see that when the market price for wheat increases, say as a result of an increase in market demand, the price-taking firm will receive a higher price for all its output. Or when the market price decreases, say as a result of a decrease in market demand, the price-taking firm will receive a lower price for all its output.

In effect, sellers are provided with current information about market demand and supply conditions as a result of price changes. It is an essential aspect of the perfectly competitive model that sellers respond to the signals provided by such price movements, so they must alter their behavior over time in the light of actual experience, revising their production decisions to reflect changes in market price. In this respect, the perfectly competitive model is straightforward; it does not assume any knowledge on the part of individual buyers and sellers about market demand and supply—they only have to know the price of the good they sell.

section 12.2
exhibit 2   Market Prices and the Position of a Firm's Demand Curve

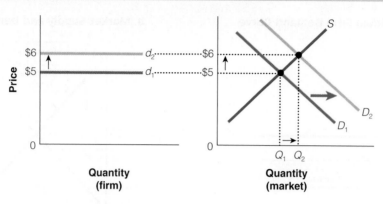

The position of the firm's demand curve will vary with every change in the market price.

SECTION CHECK

1. An individual seller won't sell at a higher price than the going price, because buyers can purchase the same good from someone else at the going price.

2. Individual sellers won't sell for less than the going price, because they are so small relative to the market that they can sell all they want at the going price.

3. The position of the individual firm's demand curve varies directly with the market price.

---

1. Why would a perfectly competitive firm not try to raise or lower its price?

2. Why can we represent the demand curve of a perfectly competitive firm as perfectly elastic (horizontal) at the market price?

3. How does an individual perfectly competitive firm's demand curve change when the market price changes?

4. If the marginal cost facing every producer of a product shifted upward, would the position of a perfectly competitive firm's demand curve be likely to change as a result? Why or why not?

SECTION
12.3   Profit Maximization

* What is total revenue?
* What is average revenue?
* What is marginal revenue?

* Why does the firm maximize profits where marginal revenue equals marginal costs?

Revenues in a Perfectly Competitive Market

The objective of the firm is to maximize profits. To maximize profits, the firm wants to produce the amount that maximizes the difference between its total revenues and total costs. In this section, we will examine the different ways to look at revenue in a perfectly competitive market: total revenue, average revenue, and marginal revenue.

Total Revenue

Total revenue (TR) is the revenue that the firm receives from the sale of its products. Total revenue from a product equals the price of the good (P) times the quantity (q) of units sold ($TR = P \times q$). For example, if a farmer sells 10 bushels of wheat a day for $5 a bushel, his total revenue is $50 ($5 × 10 bushels). (*Note:* We will use the lowercase letter q to denote the single firm's output and reserve the uppercase letter Q for the output of the entire market. For example, q would be used to represent the output of one lettuce grower, while Q would be used to represent the output of all lettuce growers in the lettuce market.)

> **total revenue (TR)**
> the product price times the quantity sold
>
> **average revenue (AR)**
> total revenue divided by the number of units sold
>
> **marginal revenue (MR)**
> the increase in total revenue resulting from a one-unit increase in sales

Average Revenue and Marginal Revenue

Average revenue (AR) equals total revenue divided by the number of units sold of the product ($TR \div q$, or $[P \times q] \div q$). For example, if the farmer sells 10 bushels at $5 a bushel, total revenue is $50 and average revenue is $5 per bushel ($50 ÷ 10 bushels). Thus, in perfect competition, average revenue is equal to the price of the good.

Marginal revenue (MR) is the additional revenue derived from the production of one more unit of the good. In other words, marginal revenue represents the increase in total revenue that results from the sale of one more unit ($MR = \Delta TR \div \Delta q$). In a perfectly competitive market, because additional units of output can be sold without reducing the price of the product, marginal revenue is constant at all outputs and equal to average revenue. For example, if the price of wheat per bushel is $5, the marginal revenue is $5. Because total revenue is equal to price multiplied by quantity ($TR = P \times q$), as we add one additional unit of output, total revenue will always increase by the amount of the product price, $5. Marginal revenue facing a perfectly competitive firm is equal to the price of the good.

In perfect competition, then, we know that marginal revenue, average revenue, and price are all equal: $P = MR = AR$. These relationships are clearly illustrated in the calculations presented in Exhibit 1.

How Do Firms Maximize Profits?

Now that we have discussed the firm's cost curves (in Chapter 11) and its revenues, we are ready to see how a firm maximizes its profits. A firm's profits equal its total revenues minus its total costs. However, at what output level must a firm produce and sell to maximize profits? In all types of market environments, the firm will maximize its profits at the output that maximizes the difference between total revenue and total cost, which is at the same output level at which marginal revenue equals marginal cost.

Equating Marginal Revenue and Marginal Cost

The importance of equating marginal revenue and marginal cost is seen in Exhibit 2. As output expands beyond zero up to q^*, the marginal revenue derived from each unit of the expanded output exceeds the marginal cost of that unit of output; so

section 12.3 **exhibit 1**	Revenues for a Perfectly Competitive Firm			
Quantity **(q)**	**Price** **(P)**	**Total Revenue** **(TR = P × q)**	**Average Revenue** **(AR = TR/q)**	**Marginal Revenue** **(MR = ΔTR/Δq)**
1	$5	$5	$5	
2	5	10	5	$5
3	5	15	5	5
4	5	20	5	5
5	5	25	5	5

Finding the Profit-Maximizing Level of Output

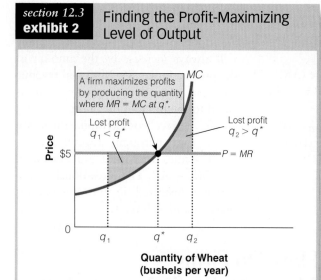

A firm maximizes profits by producing the quantity where $MR = MC$ at q^*.

At any output below q^*—at q_1, for example—the marginal revenue (MR) from expanding output exceeds the added costs (MC) of that output, so additional profits can be made by expanding output. Beyond q^*—at q_2, for example—marginal costs exceed marginal revenue, so output expansion is unprofitable and output should be reduced. The profit-maximizing level of output is at q^*, where the profit-maximizing output rule is followed—the firm should produce the level of output where $MR = MC$.

at q^*, where $MR = MC$, is the output level just right—not too large, not too small. Further expansion of output beyond q^* will lead to losses on the additional output (i.e., decrease the firm's overall profits), because $MC > MR$. For example, if the firm produces q_2, the firm incurs losses on the output produced beyond q^*; the firm should reduce its output. Only at output q^*, where $MR = MC$, can we find the **profit-maximizing level of output**.

Be careful not to make the mistake of focusing on profit per unit rather than total profit. That is, you might think that at q_1, if MR is much greater than MC, the firm should not produce more because the profit per unit is high at this point. However, that would be a mistake because a firm can add to its total profits as long as $MR > MC$—that is, all the way to q^*.

The Marginal Approach

We can use the data from the table in Exhibit 3 to find Farmer Jones's profit-maximizing position. Columns 5 and 6 show the marginal revenue and marginal cost, respectively. We see that output levels of 1 and 2 bushels produce outputs that have marginal revenues that exceed marginal cost—Farmer Jones wants to produce those units and more. That is, as long as marginal revenue exceeds marginal cost, producing and selling those units add more to revenues than to costs; in other words, they add to profits. However, once he expands production beyond four units of output, Farmer Jones's costs are less than his marginal revenues, and his profits begin to fall. Clearly, Farmer Jones should not produce beyond 4 bushels of wheat.

the expansion of output creates additional profits. This addition to profit is shown as the leftmost shaded section in Exhibit 2. As long as marginal revenue exceeds marginal cost, profits continue to grow. For example, if the firm decides to produce q_1, the firm sacrifices potential profits, because the marginal revenue from producing more output is greater than the marginal cost. Only

> **profit-maximizing level of output**
> a firm should always produce at the output where $MR = MC$

Let's take another look at profit maximization, using the table in Exhibit 3. Comparing columns 2 and 3—the calculations of total revenue and total cost, respectively—we

Cost and Revenue Calculations for a Perfectly Competitive Firm

Quantity (1)	Total Revenue (2)	Total Cost (3)	Profit ($TR - TC$) (4)	Marginal Revenue ($\Delta TR/\Delta q$) (5)	Marginal Cost ($\Delta TC/\Delta q$) (6)	Change in Profit ($MR - MC$) (7)
0	$0	$2	$-2			
1	5	4	1	$5	$2	$3
2	10	7	3	5	3	2
3	15	11	4	5	4	1
4	20	16	4	5	5	0
5	25	22	3	5	6	-1

see that Farmer Jones maximizes his profits at output levels of 3 or 4 bushels, where he will make profits of $4. In column 4—profit—you can see that there is no higher level of profit at any of the other output levels. Producing 5 bushels would reduce profits by $1, because marginal revenue, $5, is less than the marginal cost, $6. Consequently, Farmer Jones would not produce this bushel of output. If $MR > MC$, Farmer Jones should increase production; if $MR < MC$, Farmer Jones should decrease production.

In the next section we will use the profit-maximizing output rule to see what happens when changes in the market cause the price to fall below average total cost and even below average variable costs. We will introduce the three-step method to determine whether the firm is making an economic profit, minimizing its losses, or should be temporarily shut down.

SECTION CHECK

1. Total revenue is price times the quantity sold ($TR = P \times q$).
2. Average revenue is total revenue divided by the quantity sold ($AR = TR/q = P$).
3. Marginal revenue is the change in total revenue from the sale of an additional unit of output ($MR = \Delta TR/\Delta q$). In a competitive industry, the price of the good equals both the average revenue and the marginal revenue.
4. As long as the marginal revenue exceeds marginal costs, the seller should expand production, because producing and selling those units adds more to revenues than to costs; that is, it increases profits. However, if the marginal revenue is less than the marginal cost, the seller should decrease production.
5. The profit-maximizing output rule says a firm should always produce where $MR = MC$.

---

1. How is total revenue calculated?
2. How is average revenue derived from total revenue?
3. How is marginal revenue derived from total revenue?
4. Why is marginal revenue equal to price for a perfectly competitive firm?

SECTION 12.4 Short-Run Profits and Losses

* How do we determine whether a firm is generating an economic profit?
* How do we determine whether a firm is experiencing an economic loss?
* How do we determine whether a firm is making zero economic profits?
* Why doesn't a firm produce when price is below average variable cost?

In the previous section, we discussed how to determine the profit-maximizing output level for a perfectly competitive firm. How do we know whether a firm is actually making economic profits or losses?

The Three-Step Method

What Is the Three-Step Method?

Determining whether a firm is generating economic profits, economic losses, or zero economic profits at the profit-maximizing level of output, q^*, can be done in three easy steps. First, we will walk through these steps, and then we will apply the method to three situations for a hypothetical firm in the short run in Exhibit 1.

1. Find where marginal revenue equals marginal cost and proceed straight down to the horizontal quantity axis to find q^*, the profit-maximizing output level.
2. At q^*, go straight up to the demand curve and then to the left to find the market price, P^*. Once you have identified P^* and q^*, you can find total revenue at the profit-maximizing output level, because $TR = P \times q$.

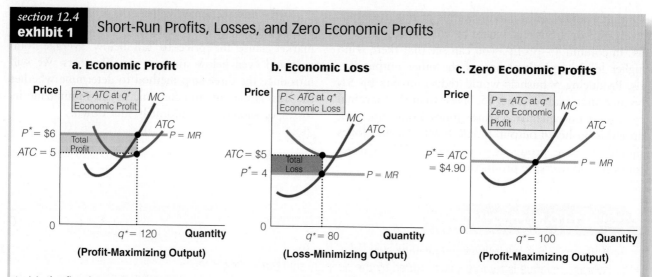

section 12.4
exhibit 1   Short-Run Profits, Losses, and Zero Economic Profits

In (a), the firm is earning short-run economic profits of $120. In (b), the firm is suffering losses of $80. In (c), the firm is making zero economic profits, with the price just equal to the average total cost in the short run.

3. The last step is to find the total cost. Again, go straight up from q^* to the average total cost (ATC) curve and then left to the vertical axis to compute the average total cost *per unit*. If we multiply average total cost by the output level, we can find the total cost ($TC = ATC \times q$).

If total revenue is greater than total cost at q^*, the firm is generating economic profits. If total revenue is less than total cost at q^*, the firm is generating economic losses. If total revenue is equal to total cost at q^*, there are zero economic profits (or a normal rate of return).

Alternatively, to find total economic profits, we can take the product price at P^* and subtract the average total cost at q^*. This will give us per-unit profit. If we multiply this by output, we will arrive at total economic profit. Or $(P^* - ATC) \times q^* = $ total economic profit.

Remember, the cost curves include implicit and explicit costs—that is, we are covering the opportunity costs of our resources. Therefore, even with zero economic profits, no tears should be shed, because the firm is covering both its implicit and explicit costs. Because firms are also covering their implicit costs, or what they could be producing with these resources in another endeavor, economists sometimes call this zero economic profit *a normal rate of return*. That is, the owners are doing as well as they could elsewhere, in that they are getting the normal rate of return on the resources they invested in the firm.

The Three-Step Method in Action

Exhibit 1 shows three different short-run equilibrium positions; in each case, the firm is producing at a level where marginal revenue equals marginal cost. Each of these alternatives shows that the firm is maximizing profits or minimizing losses in the short run.

Assume that three alternative prices—$6, $5, and $4—are available for a firm with given costs. In Exhibit 1(a), the firm receives $6 per unit at an equilibrium level of output ($MR = MC$) of 120 units. Total revenue ($P \times q^*$) is 6×120, or $720. The average total cost at 120 units of output is $5, and the total cost ($ATC \times q^*$) is $600. Following the three-step method, we can calculate that this firm is earning a total economic profit of $120. Or we can calculate total economic profit by using the following equation: $(P^* - ATC) \times q^* = (\$6 - \$5) \times 120 = \$120$.

In Exhibit 1(b), the market price has fallen to $4 per unit. At the equilibrium level of output, the firm is now producing 80 units of output at an average total cost of $5 per unit. The total revenue is now $320 ($4 \times 80$), and the total cost is $400 ($5 \times 80$). We can see that the firm is now incurring a total economic loss of $80. Or we can calculate total economic profit by using the following equation: $(P^* - ATC) \times q^* = (\$4 - \$5) \times 80 = -\$80$.

In Exhibit 1(c), the firm is earning zero economic profits, or a normal rate of return. The market price is $4.90, and the average total cost is $4.90 per unit for 100 units of output. In this case, economic profits are zero, because total revenue, $490, minus total cost, $490, is equal to zero. This firm is just covering all its costs, both implicit and explicit. Or we can calculate total economic profit by using the following equation: $(P^* - ATC) \times q^* = \$4.90 - \$4.90 \times 100 = \$0$.

Evaluating Economic Losses in the Short Run

A firm generating an economic loss faces a tough choice: Should it continue to produce or should it shut down its operation? To make this decision, we need to add another variable to our discussion of economic profits and losses: average variable cost. Variable costs are costs that vary with output—for example, wages, raw material, transportation, and electricity. If a firm cannot generate enough revenues to cover its variable costs, it will have larger losses if it operates than if it shuts down (when losses are equal to fixed costs). That is, the firm will shut down if its total revenue ($p \times q$) is less than its variable costs (VC). If we divide $p \times q$ by q, we get p, and if we divide VC by q we get AVC, so if $p < AVC$, a profit-maximizing firm will shut down. Thus, a firm will not produce at all unless the price is greater than its average variable cost.

Operating at a Loss

At price levels greater than or equal to the average variable cost, a firm may continue to operate in the short run even if its average total cost—variable and fixed costs—is not completely covered. That is, the firm may continue to operate even though it is experiencing an economic loss. Why? Because fixed costs continue whether the firm produces or not; it is better to earn enough to cover a portion of fixed costs than to earn nothing at all.

In Exhibit 2, price is less than average total cost but more than average variable cost. In this case, the firm produces in the short run, but at a loss. To shut down would make this firm worse off, because it can cover at least *some* of its fixed costs with the excess of revenue over its variable costs.

The Decision to Shut Down

Exhibit 3 illustrates a situation in which the price a firm is able to obtain for its product is below its average variable cost at all ranges of output. In this case, the firm is unable to cover even its variable costs in the short run. Because the firm is losing even more than the fixed costs it would lose if it shut down, it is more logical for the firm to cease operations. Hence, if $P < AVC$, the firm can cut its losses by shutting down.

The Short-Run Supply Curve

As we have just seen, at all prices above the minimum AVC, a firm produces in the short run even if average total cost (ATC) is not completely covered;

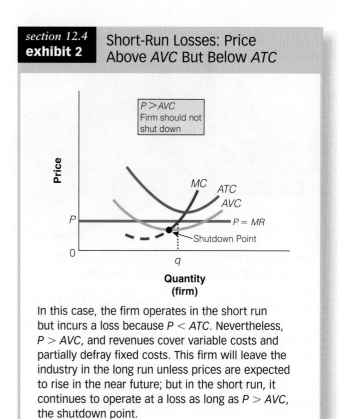

Short-Run Losses: Price Above *AVC* But Below *ATC*

In this case, the firm operates in the short run but incurs a loss because $P < ATC$. Nevertheless, $P > AVC$, and revenues cover variable costs and partially defray fixed costs. This firm will leave the industry in the long run unless prices are expected to rise in the near future; but in the short run, it continues to operate at a loss as long as $P > AVC$, the shutdown point.

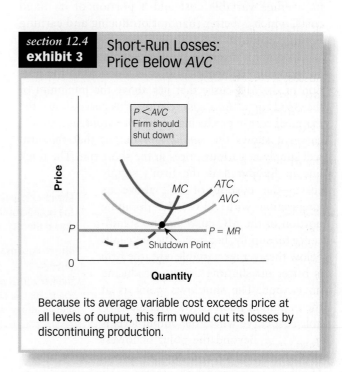

Short-Run Losses: Price Below *AVC*

Because its average variable cost exceeds price at all levels of output, this firm would cut its losses by discontinuing production.

and at all prices below the minimum AVC, the firm shuts down. The firm produces above the minimum AVC even if it is incurring economic losses because it can still earn enough in total revenues to cover all

COURTESY OF ROBERT L. SEXTON

Because the demand for summer camps will be lower during the off-season, it is likely that revenues may be too low for the camp to cover its variable costs and the owner will choose to shut down. Remember, the owner will still have to pay the fixed costs: property tax, insurance, the costs associated with the building and land. However, if the camp is not in operation during the off-season, the owner will at least not have to pay the variable costs: salaries for the camp staff, food, and electricity.

---

section 12.4
exhibit 4   ## The Firm's Short-Run Supply Curve

[Graph showing Price on vertical axis and Quantity on horizontal axis, with Short-Run Supply, MC, ATC, and AVC curves. P_{MIN} marked on the price axis. A box labeled "Firms shut down if P < AVC". $q_{SHUT\ DOWN}$ marked on the quantity axis.]

If price is less than average variable cost, the firm's losses would be smaller if it shut down and stopped producing. That is, if $P < AVC$, the firm is better off producing zero output. Hence, the firm's short-run supply curve is the marginal cost curve above average variable cost.

---

its average variable cost and a portion of its fixed costs, which is better than not producing and earning nothing at all.

In graphical terms, the **short-run supply curve** of an individual competitive seller is identical to the portion of the *MC* curve that lies above the minimum of the *AVC* curve. As a cost relation, this curve shows the marginal cost of producing any *given output;* as a supply curve, it shows the *equilibrium output* that the firm will supply at various prices in the short run. The thick line in Exhibit 4 is the firm's supply curve—the portion of *MC* above its intersection with *AVC*. The declining portion of the *MC* curve has no significance for supply, because if the price falls below the average variable cost, the firm is better off shutting down—producing no output. The shutdown point is at the minimum point on the average variable cost curve where the output level is $q_{SHUT\ DOWN}$. Beyond the point of lowest *AVC*, the marginal costs of successively larger amounts of output are progressively greater, so the firm will supply larger and larger amounts only at higher prices. The absolute maximum that the firm can supply, regardless of price, is the maximum quantity that it can produce with the existing plant.

short-run supply curve
the portion of the *MC* curve above the *AVC* curve

short-run market supply curve
the horizontal summation of the individual firms' supply curves in the market

Deriving the Short-Run Market Supply Curve

The short-run market supply curve is the summation of all the individual firms' supply curves (that is, the portion of the firms' *MC* above *AVC*) in the market. Because the short run is too brief for new firms to enter the market, the market supply curve is the summation of *existing* firms. For example, in Exhibit 5, at P_1, each of the 1,000 identical firms in the industry produces 500 bushels of wheat per day at point a, in Exhibit 5(a); and the quantity supplied in the market is 500,000 bushels of wheat, point A, in Exhibit 5(b). We can again sum horizontally at P_2; the quantity supplied for each of the 1,000 identical firms is 800 bushels of wheat per day at point b in Exhibit 5(a), so the quantity supplied for the industry is 800,000 bushels of wheat per day, point B in Exhibit 5(b). Continuing this process gives us the market supply curve for the wheat market. In a market of 1,000 identical wheat farmers, the market supply curve is 1,000 times the quantity supplied by each firm, as long as the price is above *AVC*.

section 12.4
exhibit 5   Deriving the Short-Run Market Supply Curve

a. Individual Firm Supply Curve for Wheat   **b. Market Supply Curve for Wheat**

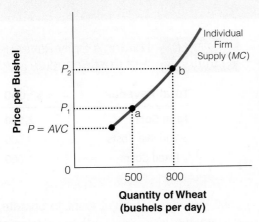

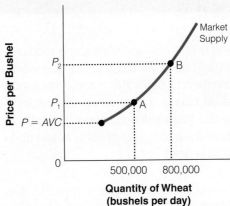

The short-run supply curve is the horizontal summation of the individual firms' supply curves (each firm's marginal cost curve above *AVC*), shown in (a). In a market of 1,000 identical wheat farmers, the market supply curve is 1,000 times the quantity supplied by each firm, shown in (b).

Use what you've
LEARNED   REVIEWING THE SHORT-RUN OUTPUT DECISION

xhibit 6 shows the firm's short-run output at these various market prices: P_1, P_2, P_3, and P_4.

At the market price of P_1, the firm would not cover its average variable cost—the firm would produce zero output, because the firm's losses would be smaller if it shut down and stopped producing. At the market price of P_2, the firm would produce at the loss-minimizing output of q_2 units. It would operate rather than shut down, because it could cover all its average variable costs and some of its fixed costs. At the market price of P_3, the firm would produce q_3 units of output and make zero economic profit (a normal rate of return). At the market price of P_4, the firm would produce q_4 units of output and be making short-run economic profits.

section 12.4
exhibit 6   The Short-Run Output Decision

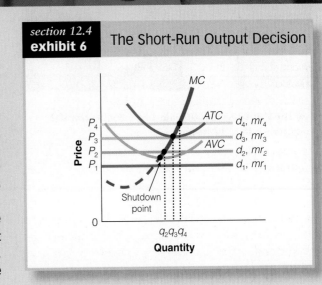

Use what you've LEARNED   EVALUATING SHORT-RUN ECONOMIC LOSSES

Q Lei-ann is one of many florists in a medium-size urban area. That is, we assume that she works in a market similar to a perfectly competitive market and operates, of course, in the short run. Lei-ann's cost and revenue information is shown in Exhibit 6. Based on this information, what should Lei-ann do in the short run, and why?

A Fixed costs are unavoidable unless the firm goes out of business. Lei-ann really has two decisions in the short run—either to operate or to shut down temporarily. In Exhibit 6, we see that Lei-ann makes $2,000 a day in total revenue, but her daily costs (fixed and variable) are $2,500. She has to pay her workers, pay for fresh flowers, and pay for the fuel used by her drivers in picking up and delivering flowers. She must also pay the electricity bill to heat her shop and keep her refrigerators going to protect her flowers. That is, every day, poor Lei-ann is losing

section 12.4 exhibit 7	Lei-ann's Daily Revenue and Cost Schedule
Total Revenue	**$2,000**
Total Costs	2,500
Variable Costs	1,500
Fixed Costs	1,000

$500; but she still might want to operate the shop despite the loss. Why? Lei-ann's average variable cost (comprising flowers, transportation, fuel, daily wage earners, and so on) amounts to $1,500 a day; her fixed costs (insurance, property taxes, rent for the building, and refrigerator payments) are $1,000 a day. Now, if Lei-ann does not operate, she will save on her variable cost—$1,500 a day—but she will be out the $2,000 a day she makes in revenue from selling her flowers. Thus, every day she operates, she is better off than if she had not operated at all. That is, if the firm can cover the average variable cost, it is better off operating than not operating. But suppose Lei-ann's *VC* were $2,100 a day. Then Lei-ann should not operate, because every day she does, she is $100 worse off than if she shut down altogether. In short, a firm will shut down if $TR < VC$ or $(P \times q) < VC$. If we divide both sides by q, the firm will shut down if $P < AVC$ or $(P \times q)/q < VC/q$.

Why does Lei-ann even bother operating if she is making a loss? Perhaps the economy is in a recession and the demand for flowers is temporarily down, but Lei-ann thinks things will pick up again in the next few months. If Lei-ann is right and demand picks up, her prices and marginal revenue will rise, and she may have a chance to make short-run economic profits.

If Lei-ann cannot cover her fixed costs, will she continue to operate?

COURTESY OF ROBERT L. SEXTON

1. How is the profit-maximizing output quantity determined?

2. How do we determine total revenue and total cost for the profit-maximizing output quantity?

3. If a profit-maximizing perfectly competitive firm is earning a profit because total revenue exceeds total cost, why must the market price exceed average total cost?

4. If a profit-maximizing perfectly competitive firm is earning a loss because total revenue is less than total cost, why must the market price be less than average total cost?

5. If a profit-maximizing perfectly competitive firm is earning zero economic profits because total revenue equals total cost, why must the market price be equal to the average total cost for that level of output?

6. Why would a profit-maximizing perfectly competitive firm shut down rather than operate if price was less than its average variable cost?

7. Why would a profit-maximizing perfectly competitive firm continue to operate for a period of time if price was greater than average variable cost but less than average total cost?

SECTION 12.5
Long-Run Equilibrium

* When an industry is earning profits, will it encourage the entry of new firms?

* Why do perfectly competitive firms make zero economic profits in the long run?

Economic Profits and Losses Disappear in the Long Run

If farmers are able to make economic profits producing wheat, what will their response be in the long run? Farmers will increase the resources that they devote to the lucrative business of producing wheat. Suppose Farmer Jones is making an economic profit (he is earning an above-normal rate of return) producing wheat. To make even more profits, he may take land out of producing other crops and plant more wheat. Other farmers or people who are holding land for speculative purposes may also decide to plant wheat on their land.

As word gets out that wheat production is proving profitable, it will cause a supply response—the market supply curve will shift to the right as more firms enter

the industry and existing firms expand as shown in Exhibit 1(b). With this shift, the quantity of wheat supplied at any given price is greater than before. It may take a year or even longer, of course, for the complete supply response to take place, simply because it takes some time for information on profit opportunities to spread and still more time to plant, grow, and harvest the wheat. Note that the effect of increasing supply, other things being equal, is a reduction in the equilibrium price of wheat.

Suppose that, as a result of the supply response, the price of wheat falls from P_1 to P_2. The impact of the change in the market price of wheat, over which Farmer Jones has absolutely no control, is simple. If his costs don't change, he moves from making a profit $(P_1 > ATC)$ to zero economic profits $(P_2 = ATC)$, as shown in Exhibit 1(a). In long-run equilibrium, perfectly competitive firms make zero economic profits.

Remember, a zero economic profit means that the firm actually earns a normal return on the use of its capital. Zero economic profit is an equilibrium or stable situation because any positive economic (above-normal) profit signals resources into the industry, beating down prices and therefore revenues to the firm.

Any economic losses signal resources to leave the industry, causing supply reductions that lead to increased prices and higher firm revenues for the remaining firms. For example, in Exhibit 2 we see a firm that continues to operate despite its losses—ATC is greater than P_1 at q_1. With losses, however, some

---

Profits Disappear with Entry

a. Individual Firm

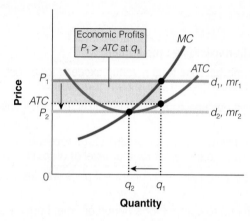

b. Market

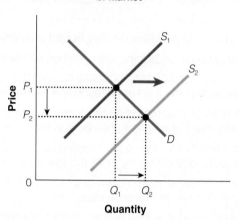

As the industry-determined price of wheat falls in (b), Farmer Jones's marginal revenue curve shifts downward from mr_1 to mr_2 in (a). A new profit-maximizing ($MC = MR$) point is reached at q_2. When the price is P_1, Farmer Jones is making a profit, because $P_1 > ATC$. When the market supply increases, causing the market price to fall to P_2, Farmer Jones's profits disappear, because $P_2 = ATC$.

Losses Disappear with Exit

a. Individual Firm

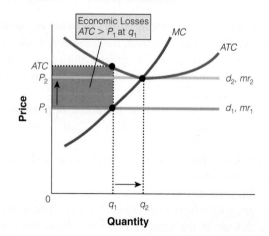

b. Market

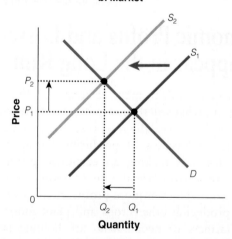

When firms in the industry suffer losses, some firms will exit in the long run, shifting the market supply curve to the left from S_1 to S_2. This shift causes market price to rise from P_1 to P_2 and market output to fall from Q_1 to Q_2. When the price is P_1, the firm is incurring a loss, because ATC is greater than P_1 at q_1. When the market supply increases from S_1 to S_2, it causes the market price to rise and the firm's losses disappear, because $P_2 = ATC$.

firms will exit the industry, causing the market supply curve to shift from S_1 to S_2 and driving up the market price to P_2. This price increase reduces the losses for the firms remaining in the industry, until the losses are completely eliminated at P_2. The remaining firms will maximize profits by producing at q_2 units of output, where profits and losses are zero. Only at zero economic profits is there no tendency for firms to either enter or leave the industry.

The Long-Run Equilibrium for the Competitive Firm

The long-run competitive equilibrium for a perfectly competitive firm is illustrated graphically in Exhibit 3. At the equilibrium point, e (where $MC = MR$), short-run and long-run average total costs are also equal. The average total cost curves touch the marginal cost and marginal revenue (demand) curves at the equilibrium output point. Because the marginal revenue curve is also the average revenue curve, average revenue and average total cost are equal at the equilibrium point. The long-run equilibrium in perfect competition depicted in Exhibit 3 has an interesting feature. Note that the equilibrium output occurs at the lowest point on the average total cost curve. As you may recall, this occurs because the marginal cost curve must intersect the average total cost curve at the latter curve's lowest point. Hence, the equilibrium condition in the long run in perfect competition is for each firm to produce at the output that minimizes average total cost—that is, the firm is operating at its minimum

efficient scale. At this long-run equilibrium, all firms in the industry earn zero economic profit; consequently, new firms have no incentive to enter the market, and existing firms have no incentive to exit the market.

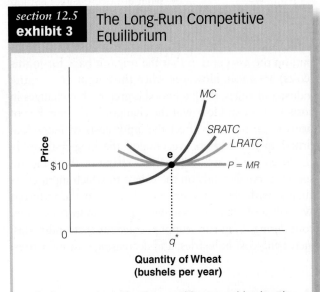

section 12.5
exhibit 3　The Long-Run Competitive Equilibrium

In the long run in perfect competition, a stable situation or equilibrium is achieved when economic profits are zero. In this case, at the Profit-maximizing point where $MC = MR$, short-run and long-run average total costs are equal. Industrywide supply shifts would change prices and average revenue, wiping out any losses or profits that develop in the short run and leading to the situation depicted in the exhibit.

Long-Run Supply

* What are constant-cost industries?
* What are increasing-cost industries?
* What are decreasing-cost industries?

* What is productive efficiency?
* What is allocative efficiency?

The preceding sections considered the costs for an individual, perfectly competitive firm as it varies output, on the assumption that the prices it pays for inputs (costs) are given. However, when the output of an entire industry changes, the likelihood is greater that changes in costs will occur. How will the changes in the number of firms in an industry affect the input costs of individual firms? In this section, we develop the long-run supply (*LRS*) curve. As we will see, the shape of the long-run supply curve depends on the extent to which input costs change with the entry or exit of firms in the industry. We will look at three possible types of industries when considering long-run supply: constant-cost industries, increasing-cost industries, and decreasing-cost industries.

A Constant-Cost Industry

In a **constant-cost industry**, the prices of inputs do not change as output is expanded. The industry may not use inputs in sufficient quantities to affect input prices. For example, say the firms in the industry use a lot of unskilled labor but the industry is small. Therefore, as output expands, the increase in demand for unskilled labor will not cause the market wage for unskilled labor to rise. Similarly, suppose a paper clip maker decides to double its output. It is highly unlikely that its demand for steel will have an impact on steel prices, because its demand for the input is so small.

Once long-run adjustments are complete, by necessity each firm operates at the point of lowest long-run average total cost, because supply shifts with entry and exit, eliminating profits. Therefore, each firm supplies the market with the quantity of output that it can produce at the lowest possible long-run average total cost.

In Exhibit 1, we can see the impact of an unexpected increase in market demand. Suppose that recent reports show that blueberries can lower cholesterol, lower blood pressure, and significantly reduce the risk of all cancers. The increase in market demand for blueberries leads to a price increase from P_1 to P_2 as the firm increases output from q_1 to q_2, and blueberry industry output increases

from Q_1 to Q_2, as seen in Exhibit 1(b). The increase in market demand generates a higher price and positive profits for existing firms in the short run. The existence of economic profits will attract new firms into the industry, causing the short-run supply curve to shift from S_1 to S_2 and lowering price until excess profits are zero. This shift results in a new equilibrium, point C in Exhibit 1(c). Because the industry is one with constant costs, industry expansion does not alter firms' cost curves, and the industry long-run supply curve is horizontal. That is, the long-run equilibrium price is at the same level that prevailed before demand increased; the only long-run effect of the increase in demand is an increase in industry output, as more firms enter that are just like existing firms [shown in Exhibit 1(c)]. The long-run supply curve is horizontal when the market has free entry and exit, there is a large number of firms with identical costs and input prices are constant. Because these strong assumptions do not generally hold, we will now discuss when the long run supply curve has a positive or negative slope.

constant-cost industry
an industry where input prices (and cost curves) do not change as industry output changes

increasing-cost industry
an industry where input prices rise (and cost curves rise) as industry output rises

An Increasing-Cost Industry

In an **increasing-cost industry**, a more likely scenario, the cost curves of individual firms rise as the total output of the industry increases. Increases in input prices (upward shifts in cost curves) occur as larger quantities of factors are employed in the industry. When an industry utilizes a large portion of an input whose total supply is not huge, input prices will rise when the industry uses more of the input.

Increasing cost conditions are typical of "extractive" industries, such as agriculture, fishing, mining, and lumbering, which utilize large portions of the total supply of specialized natural resources such as land or mineral deposits. As the output of such an industry expands, the increased demand for the resources raises the prices that must be paid for their use. Because additional resources of giving quality cannot be produced, greater supplies can be obtained (if at all) only by luring them away

Demand Increase in a Constant-Cost Industry

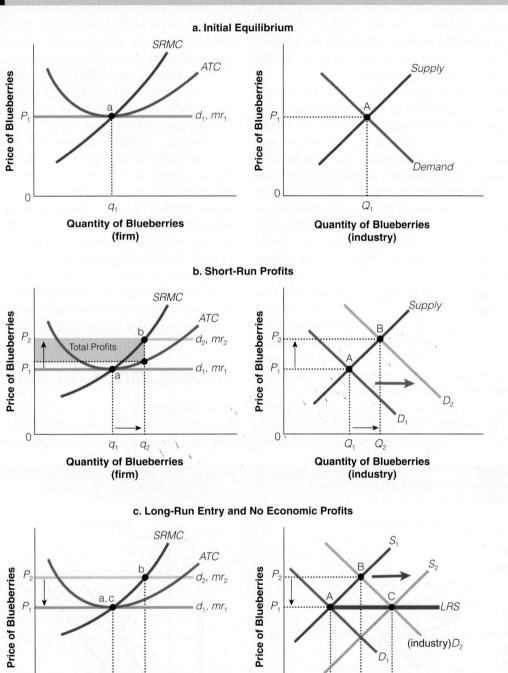

An unexpected increase in market demand for blueberries leads to an increase in the market price in (b). The new market price leads to positive profits for existing firms, which attracts new firms into the industry, shifting market supply from S_1 to S_2 in (c). This increased short-run industry supply curve intersects D_2 at point C. Each firm (of a new, larger number of firms) is again producing at q_1 and earning zero economic profits.

from other industries, or by using lower-quality (and less-productive, thus higher-cost) resources.

Wheat production is a typical example of an increasing-cost industry. As the output of wheat increases, the demand for land suitable for the production of wheat rises, and thus the price paid for the use of land of any given quality increases.

If there were a construction boom in a fully employed economy, would it be more costly to get additional resources like skilled workers and raw materials? Yes, if this is an increasing-cost industry, the industry can only produce more output if it gets a higher price because the firm's costs of production rise as output expands. As new firms enter and output expands, the increase in demand for inputs causes the price of inputs to rise— the cost curves of all construction firms shift upward as the industry expands. Or consider a downtown building boom where the supply of workers that are willing to work on tall skyscrapers is very small; a very steep supply of labor curve. The high demand for these few workers causes their wages to rise sharply and the cost of skyscrapers to rise. The industry can produce more output but only at a higher price, enough to compensate the firm for the higher input costs. In an increasing-cost industry, the long-run supply curve is upward sloping.

For example, in Exhibit 2, we see that an unexpected increase in the market demand for wheat will shift the market demand curve from D_1 to D_2, in panel (b). Consequently, price will increase from P_1 to P_2 in the short run and the industry output increases from Q_1 to Q_2. The typical firm (farm) will have positive short-run profits and expand output from q_1 to q_2 as seen in panel (a). With the presence of short-run economic profits, new firms will enter the industry, shifting the short-run market supply curve to the right from S_1 to S_2. The prices of inputs, like farm land, fertilizer, seed, farm machinery, and so on, will be bid up by competing farmers, causing the firm's marginal and long-run average cost curves to rise.

Another example is provided by the airlines. Growth in the airline industry results in more congestion of airports and airspace. That is, as the output of the airline industry increases, the firm's cost increases, *ceteris paribus*. This situation of an upward sloping long-run industry supply curve is what economists call *external diseconomies of scale*—factors that are beyond, the firm's control (that is, external) raise the firm's costs as industry output expands. In contrast, recall the discussion of diseconomies of scale in the last chapter where the costs were internal to the firm— increased costs due to managing a larger firm.

A Decreasing-Cost Industry

It is also possible that an expansion in the output of an industry can lead to a reduction in input costs and shift the MC and ATC curves downward, and

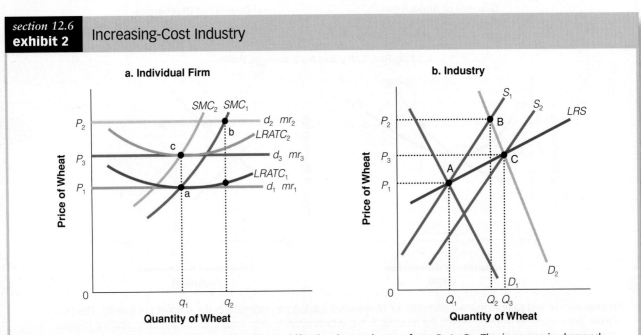

section 12.6
exhibit 2 Increasing-Cost Industry

a. Individual Firm

b. Industry

In (b) the unexpected increase in demand for wheat shifts the demand curve from D_1 to D_2. The increase in demand leads to higher prices from P_1 to P_2. In (a) firms increase output from q_1 to q_2 and experience short-run economic profits (P_2 > LRATC$_1$ at q_2). The short-run economic profits induce other firms to enter the industry. This causes the short-run supply curve to shift right, from S_1 to S_2. As new firms enter and output expands, the increase in demand for inputs causes the price of inputs to rise, leading to higher cost curves for the firm—SMC$_1$ to SMC$_2$ and LRATC$_1$ to LRATC$_2$. The new long-run equilibrium is at P_3 and q_1. The LRS is positively sloped. This means the industry must receive a higher market price to produce more output, Q_3, because the increased output causes input prices to rise.

the market price falls because of *external economies of scale*. We use the term external because the cost decreases are external to the firm; no one firm can gain by its own expansion. That is, the gains occurs when the total industry's output expands. The new long-run market equilibrium has more output at a lower price—that is, the long-run supply curve for a *decreasing-cost industry* is downward sloping (not shown).

Consider a new mining region, developed in an area remote from railroad facilities back in the days before motor vehicles. So long as the total output of the mines was small, the ore was hauled by wagon, an extremely expensive form of transportation. But when the number of mines increased, and the total output of the region rose substantially, it became feasible to construct a railroad to serve the area. The railroad lowered transportation costs and reduced the costs of all firms in the industry. As a practical matter, decreasing-cost industries are rarely encountered, at least over a large range of output. However, some industries may operate under decreasing-cost conditions in the short intervals of output expansion when continued growth makes possible the supply of materials or services at reduced cost. A larger industry might benefit from improved transportation or financial services, for example.

> **productive efficiency**
> where a good or service
> is produced at the lowest
> possible cost

This situation might occur in the computer industry. The firms in the industry may be able to acquire computer chips at a lower price as the industry's demand for computer chips rises. Why? Perhaps it is because the computer chip industry can employ cost-saving techniques that become more economical at higher levels of output. That is, the marginal and average costs of the firm fall as input prices fall because of expanded output in the industry.

Perfect Competition and Economic Efficiency

In this chapter, we have seen that a firm in a perfectly competitive market produces at the minimum of the *ATC* curve in the long run and charges a price consistent with that cost. Because competitive firms are producing using the least-cost method, the minimum amount of resources is being used to produce a given level of output. This leads to lower product prices for consumers. In short, **productive efficiency** requires that firms produce goods and services in the least costly way, where $P =$ Minimum *ATC*, as seen in Exhibit 3 in section 12.5 on page 341. However, productive efficiency alone does not guarantee that

---

| section 12.6 **exhibit 3** | Allocative Efficiency and Perfect Competition |

a. Producing Less Than the Competitive Level of Output Lowers Welfare

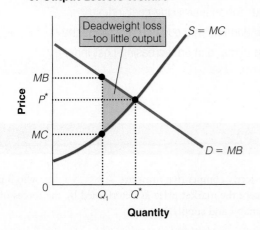

b. Producing More Than the Competitive Level of Output Lowers Welfare

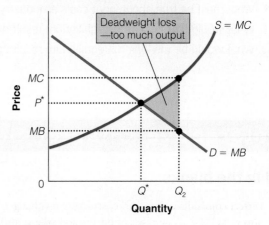

The demand curve measures the marginal benefits to the consumer and the supply curve measures the marginal cost to the sellers. At *P** and *Q**, resources are being allocated efficiently—the marginal benefits of these resources are equal to the marginal cost of these resources. If Q_1 is produced, then the marginal benefits from producing additional units are greater than the marginal costs. Society gains from expending output up to the point where *MB = MC* at *Q**. If output is expanded beyond *Q** (*MC > MB*) society gains from a reduction in output back to *Q**.

markets are operating efficiently—society must also produce the goods and services that society wants most. This leads us to what economists call allocative efficiency.

We say that the output that results from equilibrium conditions of market demand and market supply in perfectly competitive markets achieve an efficient allocation of resources.

At the intersection of market supply and market demand, we find the competitive equilibrium price, P^*, and the competitive equilibrium output, Q^*. In competitive markets, market supply equals market demand, and $P = MC$. When $P = MC$, buyers value the last unit of output by the same amount that it cost sellers to produce it. If buyers value the last unit by more than the marginal cost of production, resources are not being allocated efficiently, as at Q_1 in Exhibit 3(a). Think of the demand curve as the marginal benefit curve ($D = MB$) and the supply curve as the marginal cost curve ($S = MC$). According to the

allocative efficiency
where $P = MC$ and production will be allocated to reflect consumer preferences

rule of rational choice, we should pursue an activity as long as the expected marginal benefits are greater than the expected marginal costs. For example, in Exhibit 3(a), if Q_1 is produced, then the marginal benefits from producing additional units are greater than the marginal costs. The shaded area is deadweight loss. That is, at Q_1, resources are not being allocated efficiently, and output should be expanded.

We can also produce too much output. For example, if output is expanded beyond Q^* in Exhibit 3(b), the cost to sellers for producing the good is greater than the marginal benefit to consumers. The shaded area is deadweight loss. Society would gain from a reduction in output back to Q^*. Once the competitive equilibrium is reached, the buyers' marginal benefit equals the sellers' marginal cost. That is, in a competitive market, producers efficiently use their scarce resources (labor, machinery, and other inputs) to produce what consumers want. In this sense, perfect competition achieves **allocative efficiency.**

SECTION CHECK

1. In constant-cost industries, the cost curves of the firm are not affected by changes in the output of the entire industry. Such industries must be small demanders of resources in the market.

2. In an increasing-cost industry, the cost curves of the individual firms rise as total output increases. This case is the most typical.

3. A decreasing-cost industry has a downward-sloping long-run supply curve. Firms experience lower cost as industry expands.

4. Productive efficiency occurs in perfect competition because the firm produces at the minimum of the *ATC* curve.

5. Allocative efficiency occurs when $P = MC$; production is allocated to reflect consumers' wants.

---

1. What must be true about input costs as industry output expands for a constant-cost industry?
2. What must be true about input costs as industry output expands for an increasing-cost industry?
3. What would be the long-run equilibrium result of an increase in demand in a constant-cost industry?
4. What would be the long-run equilibrium result of an increase in demand in an increasing-cost industry?

Interactive Chapter Summary

Fill in the blanks:

1. Perfect competition is a market structure involving a(n) _____ number of buyers and sellers, a(n) _____ product, and _____ market entry and exit.

2. Perfectly competitive firms are _____, who must accept the market price as determined by the forces of demand and supply.

3. Because perfectly competitive markets have _____ buyers and sellers, each firm is so

_____ in relation to the industry that its production decisions have no impact on the market.

4. Because consumers believe that all firms in a perfectly competitive market sell _____ products, the products of all the firms are perfect substitutes.

5. Because of _____ market entry and exit, perfectly competitive markets generally consist of a(n) _____ number of small suppliers.

6. In a perfectly competitive industry, each producer provides such a(n) _____ fraction of the total supply that a change in the amount he or she offers does not have a noticeable effect on the market price.

7. Because perfectly competitive sellers can sell all they want at the market price, their demand curve is _____ at the market price over the _____ range of output that they could possibly produce.

8. The objective of a firm is to maximize profits by producing the amount that maximizes the difference between its _____ and _____.

9. Total revenue for a perfectly competitive firm equals the _____ times the _____.

10. _____ equals total revenue divided by the number of units of the product sold.

11. _____ is the additional revenue derived from the sale of one more unit of the good.

12. In perfect competition, we know that _____ and price are equal.

13. In all types of market environments, firms will maximize profits at that output which maximizes the difference between _____ and _____, which is the same output level where _____ equals _____.

14. At the level of output chosen by a competitive firm, total cost equals _____ times quantity, while total revenue equals _____ times quantity.

15. If total revenue is greater than total costs at its profit-maximizing output level, a firm is generating _____. If total revenue is less than total costs, the firm is generating _____. If total revenue equals total costs, the firm is earning _____.

16. If a firm cannot generate enough revenues to cover its _____ costs, then it will have larger losses if it operates than if it shuts down in the short run.

17. The loss a firm would bear if it shuts down would be equal to _____.

18. When price is less than _____ but more than _____, a firm produces in the short run, but at a loss.

19. The short-run supply curve of an individual competitive seller is identical with that portion of the _____ curve that lies above the minimum of the _____ curve.

20. The short-run market supply curve is the horizontal summation of the individual firms' supply curves, providing that _____ are not affected by increased production by existing firms.

21. If perfectly competitive producers are currently making economic profits, the market supply curve will shift to the right over time as more firms _____ and existing firms _____.

22. As entry into a profitable industry pushes down the market price, producers will move from a situation where price _____ average total cost to one where price _____ average total cost.

23. Only at _____ is the tendency for firms either to enter or leave the business eliminated.

24. The long-run equilibrium output in perfect competition occurs at the lowest point on the average total cost curve, so the equilibrium condition in the long run in perfect competition is for firms to produce at that output that minimizes the _____.

25. The shape of the long-run supply curve depends on the extent to which _____ change with the entry or exit of firms in the industry.

26. In a constant-cost industry, the prices of inputs _____ as output is expanded.

27. In an increasing-cost industry, the cost curves of the individual firms _____ as the total output of the industry increases.

28. There is a _____ efficiency in perfect competition because the firm produces at the minimum of the ATC curve.

29. There is _____ efficiency in perfect competition because $P = MC$ and production is allocated to reflect consumers' wants.

30. Once the competitive equilibrium is reached, the buyers' _____ equals the sellers' _____.

Answers: 1. large; homogeneous (standardized); easy 2. price takers 3. many; small 4. identical (homogeneous) 5. easy; large 6. small 7. horizontal; entire 8. total revenues; total costs 9. market price; quantity of units sold 10. Average revenue 11. Marginal revenue 12. marginal revenue 13. total revenue; total costs; marginal revenue; marginal costs 14. average total cost; the market price 15. economic profits; economic losses; zero economic profits 16. variable 17. fixed costs 18. average total costs; average variable costs 19. marginal cost; average variable cost 20. input prices 21. enter the industry; expand 22. exceeds; equals 23. zero economic profits 24. average total cost curve 25. input costs 26. do not change 27. rise 28. productive 29. allocative 30. marginal benefit; marginal cost

Key Terms and Concepts

price takers 330
total revenue (TR) 333
average revenue (AR) 333
marginal revenue (MR) 333

profit-maximizing level of output 334
short-run supply curve 338
short-run market supply curve 338
constant-cost industry 344

increasing-cost industry 344
productive efficiency 347
allocative efficiency 348

Section Check Answers

12.1 A Perfectly Competitive Market

1. Why do firms in perfectly competitive markets involve homogeneous goods?

For there to be a large number of sellers of a particular good, so that no seller can appreciably affect the market price (i.e., sellers are price takers), the goods in question must be the same, or homogeneous.

2. Why does the absence of significant barriers to entry tend to result in a large number of suppliers?

With no significant barriers to entry, it is fairly easy for entrepreneurs to become suppliers of a product. With such easy entry, as long as an industry is profitable it will attract new suppliers, typically resulting in large numbers of sellers.

3. Why does the fact that perfectly competitive firms are small relative to the market make them price takers?

If a perfectly competitive firm sells only a small amount relative to the total market supply, even sharply reducing its output will make virtually no difference in the market quantity supplied; therefore, it will make virtually no difference in the market price. In this case, a firm is able to sell all it wants at the market equilibrium price but is unable to appreciably affect that price; therefore, it takes the market equilibrium price as given—that is, it is a price taker.

12.2 An Individual Price Taker's Demand Curve

1. Why would a perfectly competitive firm not try to raise or lower its price?

A perfectly competitive firm is able to sell all it wants at the market equilibrium price. Therefore, it has no incentive to lower prices (sacrificing revenues and therefore profits) in an attempt to increase sales. Because other firms are willing to sell perfect substitutes for each other's product (because goods are homogeneous) at the market equilibrium price, trying to raise price

would lead to the firm losing all its sales. Therefore, it has no incentive to try to raise its price, either.

2. Why can we represent the demand curve of a perfectly competitive firm as perfectly elastic (horizontal) at the market price?

If a perfectly competitive firm can sell all it would like at the market equilibrium price, the demand curve it faces for its output is perfectly elastic (horizontal) at that market equilibrium price.

3. How does an individual perfectly competitive firm's demand curve change when the market price changes?

If a perfectly competitive firm can sell all it would like at the market equilibrium price, it faces a perfectly elastic demand curve at the market equilibrium price. Therefore, anything that changes the market equilibrium price (any of the market demand curve shifters or the market supply curve shifters) will change the price at which each perfectly competitive firm's demand curve is perfectly elastic (horizontal).

4. If the marginal cost facing every producer of a product shifted upward, would the position of a perfectly competitive firm's demand curve be likely to change as a result? Why or why not?

Yes. If the marginal cost curves facing each producer shifted upward, a decrease (leftward shift) would occur in the industry supply curve. This shift would result in a higher market price that each producer takes as given, which would shift each producer's horizontal demand curve upward to that new market price.

12.3 Profit Maximization

1. How is total revenue calculated?

Total revenue is equal to the price times the quantity sold. However, because the quantity sold at that price must equal the quantity demanded at that price (to sell a product you need a willing buyer), it can also be described as price times quantity demanded at that price.

2. **How is average revenue derived from total revenue?**

   Average or per-unit revenue for a given quantity of output is just the total revenue from that quantity of sales divided by the quantity sold.

3. **How is marginal revenue derived from total revenue?**

   Marginal revenue is the change in total revenue from the sale of one more unit of output. It can be either positive (total revenue increases with output) or negative (total revenue decreases with output).

4. **Why is marginal revenue equal to price for a perfectly competitive firm?**

   If a perfectly competitive seller can sell all it would like at the market equilibrium price, it can sell one more unit at that price without having to lower its price on the other units it sells (which would require sacrificing revenues from those sales). Therefore, its marginal revenue from selling one more unit equals the market equilibrium price, and its horizontal demand curve therefore is the same as its horizontal marginal revenue curve.

12.4 Short-Run Profits and Losses

1. **How is the profit-maximizing output quantity determined?**

   The profit-maximizing output is the output where marginal revenue equals marginal cost (because profits increase for every unit of output for which marginal revenue exceeds marginal cost).

2. **How do we determine total revenue and total cost for the profit-maximizing output quantity?**

   At the profit-maximizing quantity, total revenue is equal to average revenue (price) times quantity (because average revenue is total revenue divided by quantity), and total cost is equal to average cost times quantity (because average cost equals total cost divided by quantity).

3. **If a profit-maximizing perfectly competitive firm is earning a profit because total revenue exceeds total cost, why must the market price exceed average total cost?**

   If total revenue exceeds total cost, total revenue divided by the quantity of output, which is average revenue or price, must also exceed total cost divided by the same quantity of output, which is average total cost, for that level of output.

4. **If a profit-maximizing perfectly competitive firm is earning a loss because total revenue is less than total cost, why must the market price be less than average total cost?**

   If total revenue is less than total cost, total revenue divided by the quantity of output, which is average revenue or price, must also be less than total cost divided

by the same quantity of output, which is average total cost, for that level of output.

5. **If a profit-maximizing perfectly competitive firm is earning zero economic profits because total revenue equals total cost, why must the market price be equal to the average total cost for that level of output?**

   If total revenue equals total cost, total revenue divided by the quantity of output, which is average revenue or price, must also be equal to total cost divided by the same quantity of output, which is average total cost, for that level of output.

6. **Why would a profit-maximizing perfectly competitive firm shut down rather than operate if price was less than its average variable cost?**

   If a firm shuts down, its losses will equal its fixed costs (because it has no revenue or variable costs). If a firm operates, and revenues exactly cover variable costs, it will also suffer losses equal to fixed costs. But if a firm cannot cover even all its variable costs with its revenues, it will lose its fixed costs plus part of its variable costs. But because these losses are greater than the losses from shutting down, a firm would choose to shut down rather than continue to operate in this situation.

7. **Why would a profit-maximizing perfectly competitive firm continue to operate for a period of time if price was greater than average variable cost but less than average total cost?**

   If price was greater than average variable cost but less than average total cost, a firm would be earning losses and would eventually go out of business if that situation continued. However, in the short run, as long as revenues more than covered variable costs, losses from operating would be less than the losses from shutting down (these losses equal total fixed cost), as at least part of fixed costs would be covered by revenues; so a firm would continue to operate in the short run in this situation.

12.5 Long-Run Equilibrium

1. **Why do firms enter profitable industries?**

   Profitable industries generate a higher rate of return to productive assets than other industries. Therefore, firms will enter such industries in their search for more profitable uses for their assets.

2. **Why does entry eliminate positive economic profits in a perfectly competitive industry?**

   Entry eliminates positive economic profits (above-normal rates of return) in a perfectly competitive industry because entry will continue as long as economic profits remain positive (rates of return are higher than in other industries); that is, until no more positive economic profits can be earned.

3. **Why do firms exit unprofitable industries?**

Unprofitable industries generate lower rates of return to productive assets than other industries. Therefore, firms will exit such industries in their search for more profitable uses for their assets elsewhere.

4. **Why does exit eliminate economic losses in a perfectly competitive industry?**

Exit eliminates negative economic profits (below-normal rates of return) in a perfectly competitive industry because exit will continue as long as economic profits remain negative (rates of return are lower than in other industries); that is, until no firms are experiencing economic losses.

5. **Why is a situation of zero economic profits a stable long-run equilibrium situation for a perfectly competitive industry?**

A situation of zero economic profits is a stable long-run equilibrium situation for a perfectly competitive industry because that situation offers no profit incentives for firms to either enter or leave the industry.

12.6 Long-Run Supply

1. **What must be true about input costs as industry output expands for a constant-cost industry?**

Input costs remain constant as industry output expands for a constant-cost industry (which is why it is a constant-cost industry).

2. **What must be true about input costs as industry output expands for an increasing-cost industry?**

Input costs increase as industry output expands for an increasing-cost industry (which is why it is an increasing-cost industry).

3. **What would be the long-run equilibrium result of an increase in demand in a constant-cost industry?**

The long-run equilibrium result of an increase in demand in a constant-cost industry is an increase in industry output with no change in price, because output will expand as long as price exceeds the constant level of long-run average cost.

4. **What would be the long-run equilibrium result of an increase in demand in an increasing-cost industry?**

The long-run equilibrium result of an increase in demand in an increasing-cost industry is an increase in industry output (but a smaller increase than in the constant-cost case) and a higher price. Output will expand as long as price exceeds long-run average cost; but that expansion of output increases costs by raising input prices, so in the long run prices just cover the resulting higher costs of production.

True or False:

1. In perfect competition, no single firm produces more than an extremely small proportion of output, so no firm can influence the market price.

2. Perfectly competitive firms are price takers because their influence on price is insignificant.

3. It is difficult for entrepreneurs to become suppliers of a product in a perfectly competitive market structure.

4. A perfectly competitive market is approximated most closely in highly organized markets for securities and agricultural commodities.

5. A perfectly competitive firm cannot sell at any figure higher than the current market price and would not knowingly charge a lower price, because it could sell all it wants at the market price.

6. In a perfectly competitive market, individual sellers can change their output without altering the market price.

7. In a perfectly competitive industry, the market demand curve is perfectly elastic at the market price.

8. Because perfectly competitive firms are price takers, each firm's demand curve remains unchanged even when the market price changes.

9. The perfectly competitive model does not assume any knowledge on the part of individual buyers and sellers about market demand and supply—they only have to know the price of the good they sell.

10. In a perfectly competitive market, marginal revenue is constant and equal to the market price.

11. For a perfectly competitive firm, as long as the price derived from expanded output exceeds the marginal cost of that output, the expansion of output creates additional profits.

12. Producing at the profit-maximizing output level means that a firm is actually earning economic profits.

13. A competitive firm earning zero economic profits will be unable to continue in operation over time.

14. A firm will not produce at all unless the price is greater than its average variable costs.

15. A perfectly competitive firm will operate in the short run only at price levels greater than or equal to average total costs.

16. The *MC* curve above minimum *AVC* shows the marginal cost of producing any given output, as well as the equilibrium output that the firm will supply at various prices in the short run.

17. Because the short run is too brief for new firms to enter the market, the market supply curve is the vertical summation of the supply curves of existing firms.

18. As new firms enter an industry where sellers are earning economic profits, the result will include a reduction in the equilibrium price.

19. In long-run equilibrium, perfectly competitive firms make zero economic profits, earning a normal return on the use of their capital.

20. For a perfectly competitive firm, the long-run equilibrium will be the point at which price equals marginal cost as well as short-run average total cost and long-run average cost.

21. In a constant-cost industry, the industry does not use inputs in sufficient quantities to affect input prices.

22. In a constant-cost competitive industry, industry expansion does not alter a firm's cost curves, and the industry long-run supply curve is upward sloping.

23. In a constant-cost competitive industry, the only long-run effect of an increase in demand is an increase in industry output.

24. When an industry utilizes a large portion of an input, input prices will rise when the industry uses more of that input as it expands output.

Multiple Choice:

1. Which of the following is false about perfect competition?
   a. Perfectly competitive firms sell homogeneous products.
   b. A perfectly competitive industry allows easy entry and exit.
   c. A perfectly competitive firm must take the market price as given.
   d. A perfectly competitive firm produces a substantial fraction of the industry output.
   e. All of the above are true.

2. An individual perfectly competitive firm
   a. may increase its price without losing sales.
   b. is a price maker.
   c. has no perceptible influence on the market price.
   d. sells a product that is differentiated from those of its competitors.

3. When will a perfectly competitive firm's demand curve shift?
   a. never
   b. when the market demand curve shifts
   c. when new producers enter the industry in large numbers
   d. when either b or c occurs

4. In a market with perfectly competitive firms, the market demand curve is _____ and the demand curve facing each individual firm is _____.
   a. upward sloping; horizontal
   b. downward sloping; horizontal
   c. horizontal; downward sloping
   d. horizontal; upward sloping
   e. horizontal; horizontal

5. The marginal revenue of a perfectly competitive firm
   a. decreases as output increases.
   b. increases as output increases.
   c. is constant as output increases and is equal to price.
   d. increases as output increases and is equal to price.

6. A perfectly competitive firm seeking to maximize its profits would want to maximize the difference between
   a. its marginal revenue and its marginal cost.
   b. its average revenue and its average cost.
   c. its total revenue and its total cost.
   d. its price and its marginal cost.
   e. either a or d.

7. If a perfectly competitive firm's marginal revenue exceeded its marginal cost,
   a. it would cut its price in order to sell more output and increase its profits.
   b. it would expand its output but not cut its price in order to increase its profits.
   c. it is currently earning economic profits.
   d. both a and c are true.
   e. both b and c are true.

8. A perfectly competitive firm maximizes its profit at an output in which
   a. total revenue exceeds total cost by the greatest dollar amount.
   b. marginal cost equals the price.
   c. marginal cost equals marginal revenue.
   d. all of the above are true.

9. In perfect competition, at a firm's short-run profit-maximizing output,
   a. its marginal revenue equals zero.
   b. its average revenue could be greater or less than average cost.
   c. its marginal revenue will be falling.
   d. both b and c will be true.

10. In perfect competition, at the firm's short-run profit-maximizing output, which of the following need *not* be true?
    a. Marginal revenue equals marginal cost.
    b. Price equals marginal cost.
    c. Average revenue equals average cost.
    d. Average revenue equals marginal revenue.
    e. All of the above would have to be true.

11. The minimum price at which a firm would produce in the short run is the point at which
    a. price equals the minimum point on its marginal cost curve.
    b. price equals the minimum point on its average variable cost curve.
    c. price equals the minimum point on its average total cost curve.
    d. price equals the minimum point on its average fixed cost curve.

12. A profit-maximizing perfectly competitive firm would never operate at an output level at which
    a. it would lose more than its total fixed costs.
    b. it was not earning a positive economic profit.
    c. it was not earning a zero economic profit.
    d. it was not earning an accounting profit.

13. If a perfectly competitive firm finds that price is greater than *AVC* but less than *ATC* at the quantity where its marginal cost equals the market price,
    a. the firm will produce in the short run but may eventually go out of business.
    b. the firm will produce in the short run, and new entrants will tend to enter the industry over time.
    c. the firm will immediately shut down.
    d. the firm will be earning economic profits.
    e. both b and d are true.

Use the following diagram to answer questions 14–17.

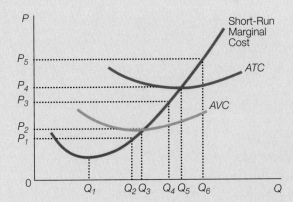

14. When the market price equals P_1, the firm should produce output
    a. Q_1.
    b. Q_2.
    c. Q_3.
    d. Q_4.
    e. none of the above.

15. When the market price equals P_3, the firm should produce output
    a. Q_3, operating at a loss.
    b. Q_4, operating at a loss.
    c. Q_4, earning an economic profit.
    d. Q_5, operating at a loss.
    e. Q_5, earning a normal profit.

16. When the market price equals P_4, the firm should produce output
    a. Q_4, operating at a loss.
    b. Q_4, earning an economic profit.
    c. Q_5, operating at a loss.
    d. Q_5, earning a normal profit.
    e. Q_5, earning a positive economic profit.

17. When the market price equals P_5, the firm should produce output
    a. Q_5, operating at a loss.
    b. Q_5, earning an economic profit.
    c. Q_6, operating at a loss.
    d. Q_6, earning a normal profit.
    e. Q_6, earning a positive economic profit.

18. The short-run supply curve of a perfectly competitive firm is
    a. its MC curve.
    b. its MC curve above the minimum point of AVC.
    c. its MC curve above the minimum point of ATC.
    d. none of the above.

19. Darlene runs a fruit-and-vegetable stand in a medium-sized community where many such stands operate. Her weekly total revenue equals $3,000. Her weekly total cost of running the stand equals $3,500, consisting of $2,500 of variable costs and $1,000 of fixed costs. An economist would likely advise Darlene to
    a. shut down as quickly as possible in order to minimize her losses.
    b. keep the stand open because it is generating an economic profit.
    c. keep the stand open for a while longer because she is covering all of her variable costs and some of her fixed costs.
    d. keep the stand open for a while longer because she is covering all of her fixed costs and some of her variable costs.

20. The entry of new firms into an industry will likely
    a. shift the industry supply curve to the right.
    b. cause the market price to fall.
    c. reduce the profits of existing firms in the industry.
    d. do all of the above.

21. Which of the following statements concerning equilibrium in the long run is incorrect?
    a. Firms will exit the industry if economic profits equal zero.
    b. Firms are able to vary their plant sizes in the long run.
    c. Economic profits are eliminated as new firms enter the industry.
    d. The market price equals both marginal cost and average total cost.

22. In long-run equilibrium under perfect competition, price does not equal which of the following?
    a. long-run marginal cost
    b. minimum average total cost
    c. average fixed cost
    d. marginal revenue
    e. average revenue

23. If the domino-making industry is a constant-cost industry, one would expect the long-run result of an increase in demand for dominos to include
  a. a greater number of firms and a higher price.
  b. a greater number of firms and the same price.
  c. the same number of firms and a higher price.
  d. the same number of firms and the same price.

24. In an increasing-cost industry, an unexpected increase in demand would lead to what result in the long run?
  a. higher costs and a higher price
  b. higher costs and a lower price
  c. no change in costs or prices
  d. impossible to determine from the information given

Problems:

1. Which of the following are most likely to be perfectly competitive?
  a. Chicago Board of Trade
  b. fast-food industry
  c. computer software industry
  d. New York Stock Exchange
  e. clothing industry

2. Using the following information, which of the industries described are perfectly competitive? Check the perfectly competitive market characteristics each industry possessed and determine whether it is a perfectly competitive industry.

Industry	Many Firms and Buyers	Identical Products	Ease of Entry and Exit	Perfectly Competitive Market?
New York taxi business: City issues a limited number of permits.	☐	☐	☐	____
Commercial aircraft industry: The costs of starting such a business are significant.	☐	☐	☐	____
Window washing business: Low cost of entry and limited specialized training.	☐	☐	☐	____
Fast-food business: Restaurant chains produce meals that are distinct	☐	☐	☐	____
Broccoli farming: There are many producers of broccoli, which requires no special growing conditions.	☐	☐	☐	____

3.

Output	Total Cost	Total Revenue
0	$ 30	$ 0
1	45	25
2	65	50
3	90	75
4	120	100
5	155	125

Given these data, determine AR, MR, P, and the short-run profit-maximizing (loss-minimizing) level of output.

4. Illustrate the *SRATC, AVC, MC,* and *MR* curves for a perfectly competitive firm that is operating at a loss. What is the output level that minimizes losses? Why is it more profitable to continue producing in the short run rather than shut down?

5. Industry councils promote the consumption of particular types of farm products. These groups urge us to "Drink Milk" or "Eat Apples." Very little advertising is done by individual farmers. Using your understanding of the perfectly competitive market, explain this advertising strategy.

6. Complete the following table and identify the profit-maximizing output.
   a.

Quantity	Price	Total Revenue	Marginal Revenue	Marginal Cost	Total Profit
10	$12	$120	$12	$8	$25
11	12	___	___	9	___
12	12	___	___	11	___
13	12	___	___	12	___
14	12	___	___	14	___

   b. What is true about marginal revenue and marginal costs when profit is maximized?
   c. What would be the profit-maximizing level of output if price fell to $9?

7. Explain why the following conditions are typical under perfect competition in the long run.
   a. $P = MC$
   b. $P = $ minimum ATC

8. Discuss the following questions.
   a. Why must price cover AVC if firms are to continue to operate?
   b. If the firm is covering its AVC but not all its fixed costs, will it continue to operate in the short run? Why or why not?
   c. Why is it possible for price to remain above the average total cost in the short run but not in the long run?

9. At a price of $5 the profit-maximizing output for a perfectly competitive firm is 1,000 units per year. If the average total cost is $3 per unit, what will be the firm's profit? If the average total cost is $6 per unit, what will be the firm's profit? What is the relationship between profit, price, and average total cost?

10. Use the following diagram to answer a, b, and c.

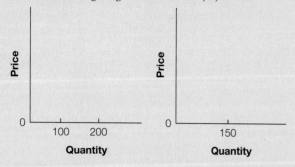

   a. Illustrate the relationship between a perfectly competitive firm's demand curve and the market supply and demand curve.
   b. Illustrate the effects of an increase in market demand on a perfectly competitive firm's demand curve.
   c. Illustrate the effects of a decrease in market demand on a perfectly competitive firm's demand curve.

11. Complete the following table for a perfectly competitive firm, and indicate its profit-maximizing output.

Quantity	Price	Total Revenue	Marginal Revenue	Total Cost	Marginal Cost	Total Profit
6	$10	$ ___	$ ___	$30	$3	$30
7	___	___	___	35	___	___
8	___	___	___	42	___	___
9	___	___	___	51	___	___
10	___	___	___	62	___	___
11	___	___	___	75	___	___
12	___	___	___	90	___	___

12. Use the following diagram to answer a–d.

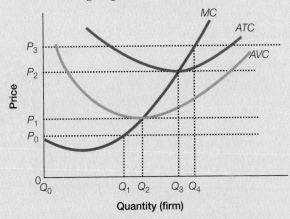

a. How much would a perfectly competitive firm produce at each of the indicated prices?
b. At which prices is the firm earning economic profits? Zero economic profits? Negative economic profits?
c. At which prices would the firm shut down?
d. Indicate what this firm's supply curve would be.

13. Use the following diagrams to answer a and b.

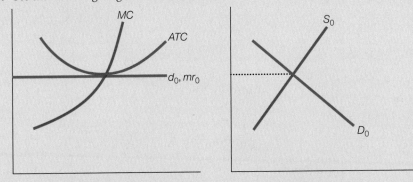

a. Show the effect of an increase in demand on the perfectly competitive firm's price, marginal revenue, output, and profits in the short run.
b. Show the long-run effects of an increase in demand for the industry, and the effects on a perfectly competitive firm's price, marginal revenue, output, and profits for a constant-cost industry.

14. In The *Wealth of Nations*, Adam Smith wrote, "Every individual endeavors to employ his capital so that its produce may be of greatest value. He generally neither intends to promote the public interest, nor knows how much he is promoting it. He intends only his own security, only his own gain. And he is led by an invisible hand to promote an end which was no part of his intention. By pursuing his own interest he frequently promotes that of society more effectively than when he really intends to promote it." How does the story of long-run equilibrium in a perfectly competitive industry illustrate Adam Smith's invisible hand?

15. Graph and explain the adjustments to long-run equilibrium when market demand decreases in a constant-cost industry.

16. Evaluate the following statements. Determine whether each is true or false and explain your answer.
    a. If economic profits are zero, firms will exit the industry in the long run.
    b. A firm cannot maximize profits without minimizing costs.
    c. If a firm is minimizing costs, it must be maximizing profits.

17. Describe what would happen to the industry supply curve and the economic profits of the firms in a competitive industry if those firms were currently earning economic profits. What if they were currently earning economic losses?

18. Given the industry description, identify each of the following as an increasing- or constant-cost industry.
    a. Major League Baseball: Uses the majority of pitchers. As the number of pitchers used increased, the quality declines.
    b. Fast-food restaurants: Uses a relatively small share of land and unskilled labor in most cities.
    c. Trucking industry: Uses a large portion of the trained and experienced drivers, especially long-distance drivers.

Monopoly and Antitrust

13

Monopoly is at the other end of the spectrum from perfect competition. Pure monopoly is a market with a single seller. Because it is the sole supplier, a monopoly faces the market demand curve for its product.

Consequently, the monopolist has control over the market price—it is a price maker. The monopolist can choose any combination of price and quantity along its market demand curve. But do not confuse ability with incentive. The monopolist, just like the perfectly competitive firm, will maximize profits (or minimize losses) by producing at the output level where $MR = MC$.

A pure monopoly, with literally one seller, is rare in the real world. But situations in which a few firms compete with each other are quite common. For example, Microsoft's Windows system, certain patented prescription drugs, the DeBeers diamond company, and your cable company are all examples of near monopolies. All of these firms have some monopoly power—control over prices and output.

In this chapter, we will see how a monopolist determines the profit-maximizing price and output. We will also compare monopoly and perfect competition to see which is more efficient. Does the monopoly equilibrium solution lead to higher prices and lower output levels than the perfectly competitive equilibrium solution? If so, what can the government do about it? ■

Monopoly: The Price Maker

* What is a monopoly?
* Why is pure monopoly rare?

* What are the sources of monopoly power?
* What is a natural monopoly?

What Is a Monopoly?

A true or pure **monopoly** exists when a market consists of only one seller of a product with no close substitute and natural or legal barriers to prevent entry competition. The reason a monopoly is the only firm in the market is because other firms cannot enter—there are barriers to entry. In monopoly, the firm and "the industry" are one and the same. Consequently, the firm sets the price of the good, because the firm faces the industry demand curve and can pick the most profitable point on that demand curve. Monopolists are price makers (rather than price takers) that try to pick the price that will maximize their profits.

Pure Monopoly Is a Rarity

Few goods and services truly have only one producer. One might think of a small community with a single bank, a single newspaper, or even a single grocery store. Even in these situations, however, most people can bank out of town, use a substitute financial institution, buy out-of-town newspapers or read them on the Web, go to a nearby town to buy groceries, and so on. Near-monopoly conditions exist, but absolutely pure monopoly is unusual.

One market in which there is typically only one producer of goods and services within an area is public utilities. In any given market, usually only one company provides natural gas or supplies water. Moreover, governments themselves provide many services for which they are often the sole provider—sewer services, fire and police protection, and military protection. Most of these situations resemble a pure monopoly. However, for most of these goods and services, substitute goods and services are available. People heating their homes with natural gas can switch to electric heat (or vice versa). In some areas, residents can even substitute home-collected rainwater or well water for what the local water company provides.

Even though the purist may correctly deny the existence of monopoly, the number of situations where monopoly conditions are closely approximated is numerous enough to make the study of monopoly more than a theoretical abstraction; moreover, the study of monopoly is useful in clarifying certain desirable aspects of perfect competition.

Barriers to Entry

A monopolist can use several ways to make it virtually impossible for other firms to overcome barriers to entry. For example, a monopolist might prevent potential rivals from entering the market by establishing legal barriers, taking advantage of economies of scale, or controlling important inputs.

Legal Barriers

In the case of legal barriers, the government might franchise only one firm to operate an industry, as is the case for postal services in most countries. The government can also provide licensing designed to ensure a certain level of quality and competence. Workers in many trade industries must obtain government licensing—hair stylists, bartenders, contractors, electricians, and plumbers, for instance.

Also, the government could award patents that encourage inventive activity. It can cost millions of dollars to develop a new drug or computer chip, for example, and without a patent to recoup some of the costs, a company would certainly be less motivated to pursue inventive activity. As long as the patent is in effect, the company has the potential to enjoy monopoly profits for many years. After all, why would a firm engage in costly research if any company could take a free ride on their discovery and produce and sell the new drug or computer chip?

Economies of Scale

The situation in which one large firm can provide the output of the market at a lower cost than two or more smaller firms is called a **natural monopoly**. With a natural monopoly, it is more efficient to have one firm produce the good. The reason for the cost advantage

> **monopoly**
> the single supplier of a product that has no close substitute
>
> **natural monopoly**
> a firm that can produce at a lower cost than a number of smaller firms can

is economies of scale; that is, *ATC* falls as output expands throughout the relevant output range, as seen in Exhibit 1. Public utilities, such as water, gas, and electricity, are examples of natural monopoly. It is less costly for one firm to lay down pipes and distribute water than for competing firms to lay down a maze of competing pipes. That is, a single water company can supply the town water more efficiently than a large number of competing firms.

Control Over an Important Input

Another barrier to entry could exist if a firm had control over an important input. For example, from the late nineteenth century to the early 1940s, the Aluminum Company of America (Alcoa) had a monopoly in the production of aluminum. Its monopoly power was guaranteed because of its control over an important ingredient in the production of aluminum—bauxite. Similarly, the DeBeers diamond company of South Africa has monopoly power because it controls roughly 75 percent of the world's output of diamonds.

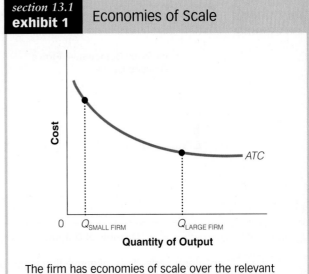

section 13.1
exhibit 1   Economies of Scale

The firm has economies of scale over the relevant range of output with declining average total costs. When one firm can produce the total output at a lower cost than several small firms, it is called a natural monopoly.

SECTION CHECK

1. A pure monopoly exists in a market with only one seller of a product for which no close substitute is available.
2. Pure monopolies are rare because few goods and services have only one existing producer.
3. Sources of monopoly power include legal barriers, economies of scale, and control over important inputs.
4. A natural monopoly occurs when one firm can provide the good or service at a lower cost than two or more smaller firms.

---

1. Why does monopoly depend on the existence of barriers to entry?
2. Why is a pure monopoly a rarity?
3. Why does the government grant some companies, such as public utilities, monopoly power?

SECTION 13.2

Demand and Marginal Revenue in Monopoly

* How does the demand curve for a monopolist differ from that for a perfectly competitive firm?
* Why is marginal revenue less than price in monopoly?

In monopoly, the market demand curve may be regarded as the demand curve for the firm's product because the monopoly firm *is* the market for that particular product. The demand curve indicates the quantities that the firm can sell at various possible prices. In monopoly, the demand curve for the firm's product declines as

section 13.2 exhibit 1   Comparing Demand Curves: Perfect Competition Versus Monopoly

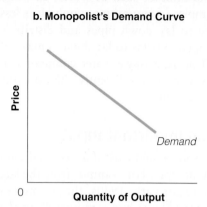

The demand curve for a perfectly competitive firm is perfectly elastic; competitive firms can sell all they want at the market price. The firm is a price taker. The demand curve for a monopolist is downward sloping; if the monopolist raises its price it will lose some but not all of its customers. The monopolist is a *price maker*. Because a monopoly has no close competitors, it can change the product price by adjusting its output.

additional units are placed on the market—the demand curve is downward sloping. In monopoly, the firm cannot set both its price and the quantity it sells. That is, a monopolist would love to sell a larger quantity at a high price, but it can't. If the monopolist raises the price, the amount sold will fall; if the monopolist lowers the price, the amount sold will rise.

Recall that in perfect competition, many buyers and sellers of homogeneous goods (resulting in a perfectly elastic demand curve) mean that competitive firms can sell all they want at the market price. They face a horizontal demand curve. The firm takes the price of its output as determined by the market forces of supply and demand. Monopolists, and all other firms that are price makers, face a downward-sloping demand curve. If the monopolist raises its price, it will lose some—but not all—of its customers. The two demand curves are displayed side by side in Exhibit 1.

In Exhibit 2, we see the price of the good, the quantity of the good, the *total revenue*, which is the quantity sold times the price ($TR = P \times Q$), and the *average revenue*, that is, the amount of revenue the firm receives per unit sold ($AR = TR \div Q$). The average revenue is simply the price per unit sold, which is exactly equal to the market demand curve, and the *marginal revenue* (MR)—the amount of revenue the firm receives from selling an additional unit—is equal to $\Delta TR \div \Delta Q$.

Taking the information from Exhibit 2, we can create the demand and marginal revenue curves as seen in Exhibit 3. We see that the marginal revenue is always less than the price of the good. To understand why, suppose the firm cuts its price from $4 to $3.

To induce a third daily customer to purchase the good, the firm must cut its price to $3. In doing so, it gains $3 in revenue from the newest customer—the output effect. However, it loses $2 in revenue because each of the first

section 13.2 exhibit 2   Total, Marginal, and Average Revenue

Price	Quantity	Total Revenue ($TR = P \times Q$)	Average Revenue ($AR = TR/Q$)	Marginal Revenue ($MR = \Delta TR/\Delta Q$)
$6	0	—	—	
5	1	$5	$5	
				$3
4	2	8	4	
				1
3	3	9	3	
				−1
2	4	8	2	
				−3
1	5	5	1	

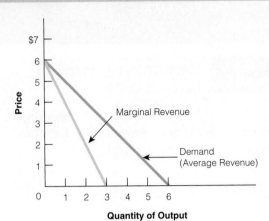

Demand and Marginal Revenue for the Monopolist

To sell more output, the monopolist must accept a lower price on all units sold—the price effect; the monopolist receives additional revenue from the new unit sold—the output effect, but less revenue on all the units it was previously selling. Thus, the marginal revenue curve for the monopolist always lies below the demand curve.

two customers are now paying $1 less than previously—the price effect. The marginal revenue is $1 ($3 − $2), which is less than the price of the good ($3).

Exhibit 3 graphs the relationship between the demand curve and the marginal revenue curve for a monopolist. Because *a monopolist's marginal revenue is always less than the price,* the marginal revenue curve will always lie below the demand curve, as shown in Exhibit 3. Recall that in perfect competition, the firm could sell all it wanted at the market price, and the price was equal to marginal revenue. However, in monopoly, if the seller wants to expand output, it will have to lower the price on *all* units; the monopolist receives additional revenue from the new unit sold—the output effect, but will receive less revenue on all the units it was previously selling—the price effect. Thus, when the monopolist cuts the price to attract new customers, the old customers benefit.

In Exhibit 4, we can compare marginal revenue for the competitive firm with marginal revenue for the monopolist. The firm in perfect competition can sell another unit of output without lowering its price; hence, the marginal revenue from selling its last unit of output is the market price. However, the monopolist

Marginal Revenue—Competitive Firm Versus Monopolist

a. Perfect Competitive Firm's Demand Curve

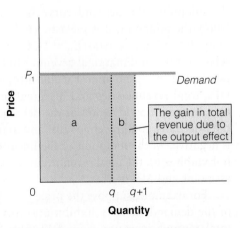

b. Monopolist's Demand Curve

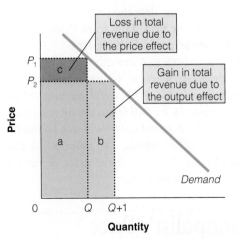

Area b in (a) represents the marginal revenue from an extra unit of output ($q + 1$) for the firm in perfect competition. The competitive firm's marginal revenue (area b) is equal to the market price, P_1 ($P_1 \times 1$). In (b), we see that the monopolist's marginal revenue from an extra unit ($Q + 1$) is less than the price by area b minus area c, because the monopolist must lower its price to sell another unit of output. That is, area b is the gain in revenue from the output effect and area c is the loss in revenue from the price effect. Notice there is no price effect for the perfectly competitve firm.

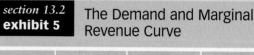

Use what you've LEARNED — DEMAND AND MARGINAL REVENUE

Q Using the concepts of total revenue and marginal revenue, show why marginal revenue is less than price in a monopoly situation. Suppose a monopolist wants to expand output from one unit to two units. To sell two units rather than one, the monopolist must lower its price from $10 to $8, as shown in Exhibit 5. Will the marginal revenue be less than the price?

A In Exhibit 5, we see that to sell two units, the monopolist will have to lower the price on both units to $8. That is, the seller doesn't receive $10 for unit one and $8 for unit two but receives $8 for both units. Therefore, what happens to marginal revenue? This answer involves two parts: First, a loss in revenue, $2, occurs from selling the first unit at $8 instead of $10. Second, the gain in revenue from the additional output—the second unit—is $8. Thus, the marginal revenue is $6 ($8 − $2), which is less than the price of the good, $8. The monopolist's marginal revenue will always be less than the price of the downward-sloping demand curve.

section 13.2 exhibit 5 The Demand and Marginal Revenue Curve

Price	Quantity	Total Revenue	Marginal Revenue
$10	1	$10	
8	2	16	$6
6	3	18	2

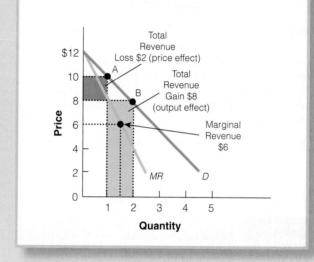

has a downward-sloping demand curve. To sell an extra unit of output, the price falls from P_1 to P_2, and the monopolist loses area c in Exhibit 4(b).

It is important to note that even though a monopolist can set its price anywhere it wants, it will not set its price as high as possible—be careful not to confuse ability with incentive. As we will see in the next section, some prices along the demand curve will not be profitable for a firm. In other words, the monopolist can enhance profits by either lowering the price or raising it, depending on the circumstances.

The Monopolist's Price in the Elastic Portion of the Demand Curve

The relationships between the elasticity of demand and the marginal and total revenue are shown in Exhibit 6. In Exhibit 6(a), elasticity varies along a

linear demand curve. Recall from Chapter 6 that above the midpoint, the demand curve is elastic ($E_D > 1$); below the midpoint, it is inelastic ($E_D < 1$); and at the midpoint, it is unit elastic ($E_D = 1$). How does elasticity relate to total and marginal revenue? In the elastic portion of the curve shown in Exhibit 6(b), when the price falls, total revenue rises and marginal revenue is positive. In the inelastic region of the demand curve, when the price falls, total revenue falls, and marginal revenue is negative. At the midpoint of the linear demand curve in Exhibit 6(b), the total revenue curve reaches its highest point and $MR = 0$.

For example, suppose the price falls on the top half of the demand curve in Exhibit 6(a) from $90 to $80; total revenue increases from $90 ($90 × 1) to $160 ($80 × 2), and marginal revenue is positive at $70. Because a reduction in price leads to an increase in total revenue, the demand curve is elastic in this region. Now suppose the price falls from $20 to $10 on the lower portion of the demand curve; total revenue falls from $160 ($20 × 8) to $90 ($10 × 9), and marginal

The Relationship Between the Elasticity of Demand and Total and Marginal Revenue

a. Demand and Marginal Revenue

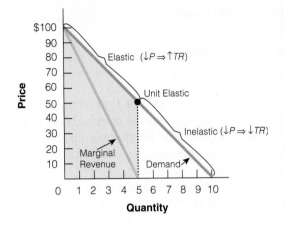

b. Total Revenue

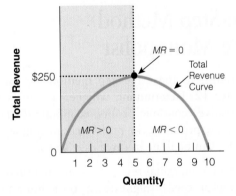

In (a), we see that along a linear demand curve, the elastic segment lies above the midpoint, the inelastic segment lies below the midpoint, and at the midpoint the demand is unit elastic. When demand is elastic, a decline in price will increase total revenue; when demand is inelastic, a decline in price will lead to a decrease in total revenue. In (b), we see that over the range from 0 to 5 units, total revenue is rising, so marginal revenue is positive. Over the range from 5 units to 10 units, total revenue is falling, so marginal revenue is negative. At 5 units of output, total revenue is maximized at $250 ($50 × 5), so marginal revenue is zero.

revenue is negative at −$70. Because a reduction in price leads to a decrease in total revenue, the demand curve is inelastic in this region.

A monopolist will never knowingly operate on the inelastic portion of its demand curve, because increased output will lead to lower total revenue in this region. Not only are total revenues falling, but total costs will rise as the monopolist produces more output. Similarly, if the monopolist were to lower its output, it could increase its total revenue and lower its total costs (because it costs less to produce fewer units), leading to greater economic profits.

SECTION CHECK

1. The monopolist's demand curve is downward sloping because it is the market demand curve. To produce and sell another unit of output, the firm must lower its price on *all* units sold. As a result, the marginal revenue curve lies below the demand curve.

2. The monopolist cannot set both the price and the quantity it sells. If the monopolist reduces output, the price will rise, and if the monopolist expands output, the price will fall.

3. The monopolist's marginal revenue will always be less than the price because of its downward-sloping demand curve. In order to sell more output, the monopolist must accept a lower price on all units sold; the monopolist will receive additional revenue from the new unit sold but will receive less revenue on all of the units it was previously selling.

4. The monopolist will operate on the elastic portion of its demand curve.

---

1. Why are the market and firm demand curves the same for a monopoly?

2. Why is a monopoly a price maker, but a perfectly competitive firm a price taker?

3. Why is marginal revenue less than price for a profit-maximizing monopolist?

4. Why would a monopolist never knowingly operate in the inelastic portion of its demand curve?

The Monopolist's Equilibrium

* How does the monopolist decide what output to produce?
* How does the monopolist decide what price to charge?
* How do we know whether the monopolist is making a profit?
* How do we know whether the monopolist is incurring a loss?
* Can the monopolist's economic profits last into the long run?

How Does the Monopolist Determine the Profit-Maximizing Output?

In the preceding section, we saw how a monopolist could choose any point along a demand curve. However, the monopolist's decision as to what level of output to produce depends on more than the marginal revenue derived at various outputs. The firm faces production costs; and the monopolist, like the perfect competitor, will maximize profits at that output where $MR = MC$. This point is demonstrated graphically in Exhibit 1.

As you can see in Exhibit 1, at output level Q_1, the marginal revenue exceeds the marginal cost of production, so it is profitable for the monopolist to expand output. Profits continue to grow until output Q_M is reached. Beyond that output, say at Q_2, the marginal cost of production exceeds the marginal revenue from production, so profits decline. The monopolist should cut production back to Q_M. Therefore, the equilibrium output is Q_M. At this output, marginal cost and marginal revenue are equal.

Three-Step Method for the Monopolist

Let's return to the three-step method we used in Chapter 12. Determining whether a firm is generating positive economic profits, economic losses, or zero economic profits at the profit-maximizing level of output, Q_M, can be done in three easy steps.

1. Find where marginal revenue equals marginal cost and proceed straight down to the horizontal (quantity) axis to find Q_M, the profit-maximizing output level for the monopolist.
2. At Q_M, go straight up to the demand curve and then to the left to find the market price, P_M. Once you have identified P_M and Q_M, you can find total revenue at the profit-maximizing output level, because $TR = P \times Q$.
3. The last step is to find total cost. Again, go straight up from Q_M to the average total cost (ATC) curve and then left to the vertical axis to compute the average total cost at Q_M. If we multiply average total cost by the output level, we can find the total cost $(TC = ATC \times Q)$.

Profits for a Monopolist

Exhibit 1 does not show what profits, if any, the monopolist is actually making. This missing information is found in Exhibit 2, which shows the

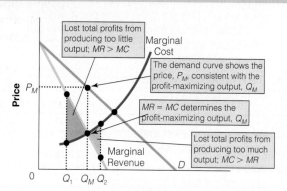

**section 13.3
exhibit 1**   Equilibrium Output and Price for a Monopolist

The monopolist maximizes profits at that quantity where $MR = MC$, that is, at Q_M. At Q_M the monopolist finds P^* by extending a vertical line up to the demand curve and over to the vertical axis to find the price. Rather than charging a price equal to marginal cost or marginal revenue at their intersection, however, the monopolist charges the price that customers are willing to pay for that quantity as indicated on the demand curve at P_M. At Q_1, $MR > MC$, and the firm should expand output. At Q_2, $MC > MR$, and the firm should cut back production.

section 13.3
exhibit 2   **A Monopolist's Profits**

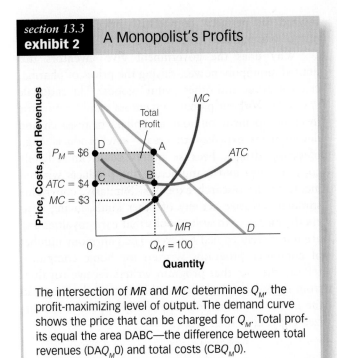

The intersection of *MR* and *MC* determines Q_M, the profit-maximizing level of output. The demand curve shows the price that can be charged for Q_M. Total profits equal the area DABC—the difference between total revenues (DAQ_M0) and total costs (CBQ_M0).

section 13.3
exhibit 3   **A Monopolist's Losses**

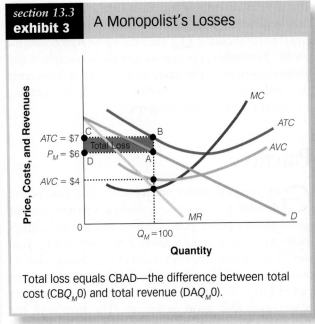

Total loss equals CBAD—the difference between total cost (CBQ$_M$0) and total revenue (DAQ$_M$0).

equilibrium position for a monopolist, this time adding an average total cost (*ATC*) curve. As we just discussed, the firm produces where *MC* = *MR*, at output Q_M. At output Q_M (100) and price P_M ($6) the firm's total revenue is equal to DAQ$_M$0, which is $P_M \times Q_M$ ($600). At output Q_M, the firm's total cost is CBQ$_M$0, which is $ATC \times Q_M$ ($400). In Exhibit 2, we see that total revenue is greater than total cost, so the firm has a total profit of area DABC. Or, $P_M - ATC$ (price minus average total cost) is the per-unit profit, $2. The width of the box (segment CB) is the quantity sold (0 to Q_M), 100 units. Hence, the area of the box is the monopoly firm's total profit, $200 (per-unit profit × quantity sold).

In perfect competition, profits in an economic sense will persist only in the short run. In the long run, new firms will enter the industry and increase industry supply, thereby driving down the price of the good and eliminating profits. In monopoly, however, profits are not eliminated, because one of the conditions for monopoly is that barriers to entry exist. Other firms cannot enter, so economic profits persist in the long run.

Losses for the Monopolist

It is easy to imagine a monopolist ripping off consumers by charging prices that result in long-run economic profits. However, many companies with monopoly

power have gone out of business. Imagine that you received a patent on a bad idea such as a roof ejection seat for a helicopter, or that you had the sole rights to turn an economics textbook into a screenplay for a motion picture. Although you may be the sole supplier of a product, you are not guaranteed that consumers will demand your product. Even without a close substitute for your product, you will always face competition for the consumer dollar, and other goods may provide greater satisfaction.

Exhibit 3 illustrates loss in a monopoly situation. In this graph, notice that the demand curve is below the average total cost curve. In this case, the monopolist will incur a loss, because of insufficient demand to cover the average total cost at any price and output combination along the demand curve. At Q_M, total cost, CBQ$_M$0, is greater than total revenue, DAQ$_M$0, so the firm incurs a total loss of CBAD. Or, total revenue is $600 ($P_M \times Q_M$ = $6 × 100) and total cost is $700 ($ATC \times Q_M$ = $7 × 100), for an economic loss of $100. Notice that the total revenue is great enough to cover the variable costs of $400 ($TVC$ = $4 × 100). That is, the firm can reduce its losses by operating rather than shutting down in the short run. However, in monopoly as in perfect competition, a firm will go out of business in the long run if it cannot generate enough revenue to cover its total costs.

In summary, if total revenue is greater than total cost at Q_M, the firm generates a total economic profit;

and if total revenue is less than total cost at Q_M, the firm generates a total economic loss. If total revenue is equal to total cost at Q_M, the firm earns zero economic profit. Remember, the cost curves include implicit and explicit costs, so in this case, the monopolist is covering the total opportunity costs of its resources and earning a normal profit or rate of return.

Patents

Governments confer one form of monopoly power through patents and copyrights. A patent puts the government's police power behind the patent-holder's exclusive right to make a product for a specified period (up to 20 years) without anyone else being able to make an identical product. As Exhibit 4 suggests, the patent gives the supplier at least temporary monopoly power over that good or service. The firm with the patent can then price its product well above marginal costs, at P_M. Notice that the marginal cost curve is flat. The reason is that most of the cost of drugs is in the development stage. Once the drug is available for the market, the marginal costs are close to constant—flat. When the patent expires, the price of the patented good or service usually falls substantially with the entry of competing firms into the market. The price will fall toward the perfectly competitive price P_{PC}, and the output will increase toward Q_{PC}.

Why does the government give inventors this limited monopoly power, raising the prices of pharmaceutical drugs and other "vital" goods? The rationale is simple. Without patents, inventors would have little incentive to incur millions of dollars in research and development expenses to create new products (e.g., lifesaving drugs), because others could immediately copy the idea and manufacture the products without incurring the research expenses. Similarly, copyrights stimulate creative activity of other kinds, giving writers the incentive to write books that earn royalties and are not merely copied for free. The enormous number of computer programs written for home computers reflects the fact that program writers receive royalties from the sale of each copy sold; that is why they and the firms they work for vehemently oppose unauthorized copying of their work.

Without patents, would some lifesaving drugs have been invented? Some drugs cost millions of dollars in research. Without the protection of a patent, the firm might not have been able to make profits from its inventive activity for very long, which is why the government issues patents that last up to 20 years. However, after the patent expires, many popular drugs soon lose their protection; Prozac lost its patent in February 2001 and Claritin lost its patent in April 2004. In most cases, less costly generic drugs hit the market soon after patent expiration; and prices then move closer to the competitive price, although perhaps not all the way to the competitive level, as some companies are able to keep customers through brand loyalty.

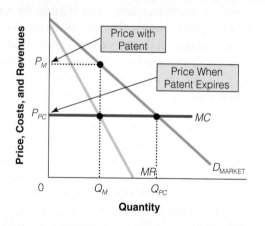

section 13.3 exhibit 4   Impact of Patent Protection on Equilibrium Price and Quantity

Patent power allows the firm to charge the higher monopoly price, P_M, which is well above the marginal cost of producing that good. However, when the patent expires, the price falls to a position closer to the perfectly competitive price, P_{PC}.

1. The monopolist, like the perfect competitor, maximizes profits at that output where marginal revenue equals marginal cost.
2. The monopolist sets the price according to the demand for the product at the profit-maximizing output.
3. Monopoly profits can be found by comparing the price per unit and average total cost per unit at Q^*. If $P > ATC$, a firm realizes economic profits. If $P < ATC$, it has economic losses.
4. Monopolists' profits can last into the long run, because of a monopoly's barriers to entry.

---

1. What is a monopolist's principle for choosing the profit-maximizing output?
2. How do you find the profit-maximizing price for a monopolist?
3. For a monopolist making positive economic profits, what must be true about the relationship between price and average total cost?
4. For a monopolist making negative economic profits, what must be true about the relationship between price and average total cost?
5. Why, unlike perfectly competitive firms, can a monopolist continue to earn positive economic profits in the long run?

SECTION 13.4

Monopoly and Welfare Loss

* How does monopoly lead to inefficiencies?
* What is the welfare loss in monopoly?
* Does monopoly retard innovation?

Does Monopoly Promote Inefficiency?

Monopoly is often considered to be bad. Two main objections form the basis for concerns about the establishment of monopoly power. First, on equity grounds, many people feel that it is not "fair" for monopoly owners to have persistent economic profits when they work no harder than other firms. However, to most economists, the more serious objection is that monopolies result in market inefficiencies. That is, monopoly leads to a lower output and higher prices than would exist under perfect competition. Exhibit 1 demonstrates why. In monopoly, the firm produces output Q_M and charges price P_M. Suppose, however, that perfect competition exists and the industry is characterized by many small firms that could produce output with the same efficiency (at the same cost) as one large firm. Then the marginal cost curve shown in Exhibit 1 is the sum of all the individual marginal cost curves of the individual firms, which is the industry supply curve.

In the perfectly competitive market, the equilibrium price and quantity would be determined where the marginal cost (or supply) curve intersects with the demand curve, at output Q_{PC} and price P_{PC}. Thus, the competitive equilibrium solution provides for more output and lower prices than the solution prevailing in monopoly, which leads to the major efficiency objection to monopoly: Monopolists charge higher prices and produce less output. This situation may also be viewed as "unfair," in that consumers are burdened more than under the alternative competitive arrangement.

Welfare Loss in Monopoly

In addition to the monopolist producing lower levels of output at higher prices, notice that the monopolist produces at an output where the price (P_M) is greater than the marginal cost (MC_M). Because $P > MC$, the value to society from the last unit produced is greater than its costs (MC_M). That is, the monopoly is *not* producing enough of the good from society's perspective. We call the area c + e in Exhibit 1 the welfare or deadweight loss due to monopoly. In perfect competition, the equilibrium is P_{PC} and the equilibrium quantity is Q_{PC}. Consumer surplus is area a + b + c, and the product surplus is area d + e + f. In monopoly, the equilibrium

section 13.4
exhibit 1 Perfect Competition Versus Monopoly

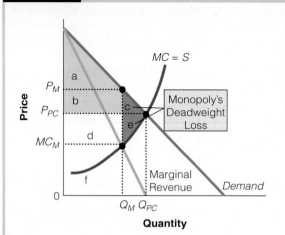

Compared with perfect competition, the monopolist's equilibrium price is higher, P_M, and its equilibrium output is lower, Q_M. Also notice that P_M is greater than MC_M, which means that the value of the last unit produced by the monopolist (P_M) is greater than the cost (MC_M), so from society's point of view the monopolist is producing too little output. Under monopoly, consumer surplus is area a, producer surplus is area b + d + f, and the deadweight loss of monopoly is c + e.

	Perfect Competition	**Monopoly**	**Change**
Consumer Surplus	a + b + c	a	− b − c
Producer Surplus	d + e + f	b + d + f	b − e
Welfare	a + b + c + d + e + f	a + b + d + f	− c − e

Use what you've LEARNED THE WELFARE COST OF MONOPOLY

Q The output level set by the monopolist is inefficient from society's standpoint, but the profits are not. Why?

A The net loss resulting from lower output is what economists call the welfare cost of monopoly. However, society as a whole does not lose from monopoly profits. Why? Because the income is not lost, but it is transferred from consumers to producers (stockholders and workers). The monopolist gains at the expense of consumers who pay a higher price for a monopolist's product than they would if the product were produced by a perfectly competitive firm. This situation is depicted in Exhibit 2.

The welfare loss is graphically represented by area cde. It is the difference between how much consumers value quantity Q_1 minus Q_0, which is Q_0ceQ_1, and how much they would have to give up for it, Q_0deQ_1. You may recall from Chapter 7 that this area represents *consumer surplus.* Under perfectly competitive conditions, however, area abdc would also be part of

section 13.4
exhibit 2 The Welfare Cost of Monopoly

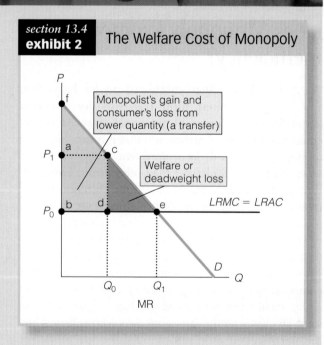

the consumer's surplus. In sum, the loss to society from monopoly is area cde, and area abdc is merely a transfer of consumer surplus to monopoly profits.

price is higher at P_M and the equilibrium quantity is lower at Q_M. Under monopoly, consumer surplus is area a, producer surplus is area b + d + f, and lost welfare or the deadweight loss of monopoly is c + e.

The actual amount of the welfare loss in monopoly is of considerable debate among economists. Estimates vary from between one-tenth of 1 percent to 6 percent of national income. The variation depends on the researchers' estimates of elasticity of demand, whether firm or industry data were used, whether adjustments for profits were made (for the inclusion of royalties and intangibles), and whether the researcher included some proxy for scarce resources used in attempting to create the monopoly.

Does Monopoly Retard Innovation?

Another argument against monopoly is that a lack of competition tends to retard technological advancement. Monopolists become comfortable, reaping their monopolistic profits, so they do not work hard at product improvement, technical advances designed to promote efficiency, and so forth. The American railroad is some-

times cited as an example of this situation. Early in the last century, railroads had strong monopoly power, but they did not spend much on research or development; they did not aggressively try to improve rail transport. Consequently, technical advances in substitute modes of transportation—like cars, trucks, and airplanes—led to a loss of monopoly power for the railroads.

However, the notion that monopoly retards all innovation can be disputed. Many near monopolists are, in fact, important innovators. Companies such as Microsoft, International Business Machines (IBM), Polaroid, and Xerox have all, at one time or another, had strong market positions, in some instances approaching monopoly secured by patent protection, but they were also important innovators. Indeed, innovation helps firms initially obtain a degree of monopoly status, because patents can give a monopoly to new products and/or cost-saving technology. Even the monopolist wants more profits, and any innovation that lowers costs or expands revenues creates profits for the monopolist. In addition, because patents expire, a monopolist may be expected to innovate in order to obtain additional patents and preserve its monopoly power. Therefore, the incentive to innovate might well exist in monopolistic market structures.

SECTION CHECK

1. Monopoly results in smaller output and a higher price than would be the case under perfect competition.

2. The monopolist produces at an output where $P > MC$ and the value to society of the last unit produced is greater than its cost. In other words, the monopoly is not producing enough output from society's standpoint.

3. Monopoly may lead to greater concentration of economic power and could retard innovation.

---

1. Why does the reduced output under monopoly cause inefficiency?

2. Does monopoly power retard innovation? Why or why not?

3. What does the welfare cost of monopoly represent? How is it measured?

4. How can economies of scale lead to monopoly? How could it result in monopoly increasing rather than decreasing market output, relative to the competitive market structure?

5. Can monopoly be the result of a new innovation that leaves consumers better off than before? Why or why not?

SECTION 13.5 Monopoly Policy

* What is the objective of antitrust policy?
* What is regulation?
* What is average cost pricing?

Because monopolies pose certain problems with respect to efficiency, equity, and power, the public, through its governments, must decide how to

deal with the phenomenon. Two major approaches to dealing with such problems are commonly employed: antitrust policies and regulation. It should be pointed

POLICY application COLLUSION

Ivy League schools have been charged with illegally colluding to fix the price of scholarships. Ivy League schools wanted to make sure they did not get into a "scholarship war," so the participating schools collectively met and fixed scholarship packages. Students would then pick their schools on the basis of academic quality, not the size of the scholarship package. These activities guaranteed that any student applying to more than one of these schools would be offered the same financial package. The Justice Department charged the eight Ivy League schools and MIT with an illegal conspiracy to set prices and required these schools to stop their collusion on tuition, salaries, and financial aid by signing a consent order.

out that in these discussions, the word *monopoly* is sometimes used in a loose, general sense to refer to imperfectly competitive markets, not just to "pure" monopoly.

Antitrust Policies

Perhaps the most obvious way to deal with monopoly is to make it illegal. The government can bring civil lawsuits or even criminal actions against businesspeople or corporations engaged in monopolistic practices. By imposing costs on monopolists that can be either monetary or nonmonetary (such as the fear of lawsuits or even jail sentences), antitrust policies reduce the profitability of monopoly.

Antitrust Laws

The first important law regulating monopoly was the Sherman Antitrust Act. The Sherman Act prohibited "restraint of trade"—price fixing and collusion—but narrow court interpretation of the legislation led to a number of large mergers, such as U.S. Steel. Some important near-monopolies were broken up, however. For example, in 1911, the Standard Oil Trust, which controlled most of the country's oil refining, and the American Tobacco Co., which had similar dominance in tobacco, were both forcibly divided up into smaller companies.

Antitrust Acts Strengthened

Antitrust efforts were strengthened by subsequent legislation, the most important of which was the Clayton Act in 1914. Additional legislation in the same year created the Federal Trade Commission (FTC), which became the second government agency concerned with antitrust actions. The Clayton Act made it illegal to engage in predatory pricing—setting prices to drive out competitors or deter potential entrants in order to ensure higher prices in the future. The Clayton Act also prohibited mergers if it led to weakened competition. Not all of the later legislation actually served to enhance competition. A case in point is the Robinson-Patman Act of 1936 (forbidding most forms of price discrimination) and the Cellar-Kefauver Act in 1950, legislation that toughened restrictions on mergers that reduced competition.

However, antitrust laws may have costs as well as benefits because mergers may lead to lower costs and greater efficiency. A number of banks recently merged, lowering costs. So, good antitrust policy must be able to recognize which mergers are desirable and which are not.

Promoting More Price Competition

Many professional associations restrict the promotion of price competition by prohibiting advertising among their members. Recently, both the FTC and the Justice Department successfully attacked these types of restrictions on the grounds that they violate the antitrust laws. They have been spurred on in their efforts by consumer groups who noticed that prices tend to be much lower

in the news   Is Microsoft a Monopoly?

Government prosecutors argued that Microsoft engaged in a pattern of using its monopoly power to crush its rivals and prevent real competition from developing. In June 2001, a federal appeals court unanimously threw out a lower court order to break Microsoft into two companies. However, the appeals court did find that the company repeatedly abused its monopoly power in the software business.

According to competitor Larry Ellison, "They repeatedly broke the law. They said to Compaq: If you want to get a good price for Windows, you better not put Netscape on that computer. That is using an existing monopoly, Windows, to obtain a new monopoly in browsers. That's an explicit violation of the Sherman Antitrust Act. They did it over and over again."

A settlement was finally reached in November 2002 that led to some restrictions on Microsoft's business practices.

SOURCE: Staff, "Is Microsoft a Monopoly," *Business Week,* 26 February 2001.

consider this:

It appears that the Microsoft case has less to do with the degree of monopoly power and more to do with the abuse of that power. Specifically, antitrust is about actions taken to form, extend, or maintain the monopoly. However, we have to ask the question: Are consumers necessarily worse off as a result of a few powerful computer companies that temporarily dominate the industry? Because of potential economies of scale in production and technology, the monopoly may be short lived. Are the barriers to entry in the computer industry insurmountable? The history of the computer industry includes several success stories of individuals with great ideas who have successfully broken into the industry. In addition, Microsoft and Intel are at least partially responsible for making computer power what it is today—providing consumers with low-priced, innovative products. By bundling its internet browser (Internet Explorer) into its Windows operating system the government claimed that Microsoft was expanding its market power in the computer industry. This apparently allowed Windows to win the browser wars knocking out Netscape Navigator and in the office suite market knocking out Word Perfect. The government believed there would have been more competition if Microsoft had not bundled their package and given their browser away for "free." Every Windows user had a copy of Internet Explorer.

When the dust settled Microsoft had to agree to some business restrictions but was allowed to keep their browser as part of their operating system.

In 2005, European Union cracked down on Microsoft because they bundled their media player with its Windows operation system. They were fined and required to offer both bundled and unbundled versions of their operating system.

when price competition is allowed to flourish. Thus, optometrists were prodded to advertise the price of eyeglasses; pharmacists, the price of commonly prescribed drugs; and even lawyers, the price of a divorce.

Have Antitrust Policies Been Successful?

The success of antitrust policies can be debated. It is true that few giant monopolies were disbanded as a consequence of antitrust policies. Studies showed little change in the degree of monopoly/oligopoly power in the first 100 years or so of U.S. antitrust legislation.

Manufacturing, as a whole, actually became more concentrated; that is, fewer firms are now in the industry. However, it is likely that at least some anticompetitive practices were prevented simply by the existence of laws prohibiting monopoly-like practices. Although the laws were probably enforced in an imperfect fashion, on balance they impeded monopoly influences to some degree, at least.

Government Regulation

Government regulation is an alternative approach to dealing with monopolies. Under regulation, a company would not be allowed to charge any price it wants. Suppose the government does not want to break up a natural monopoly in the water or power industry. Remember that natural monopolies occur when one large firm can produce as much output as many smaller firms but at a lower average cost per unit. The government may decide to regulate the monopoly price; but what price does it let the firm charge? The goal is to achieve the efficiency of large-scale production without permitting the high monopoly prices and low output that can promote allocative *inefficiency*.

The basic policy dilemma that regulators often face in attempting to fix maximum prices can be illustrated rather easily. Consider Exhibit 1. Without regulation, say the profit-maximizing monopolist operates at point A—at output Q_M and price P_M. At this output, the price exceeds the average total cost, so economic profits exist, as seen in Exhibit 1. However, the monopolist is producing relatively little output and is charging a relatively high price; and it is producing at a point where price is above marginal cost. This point is not the best from society's perspective.

Allocative Efficiency

From society's point of view, what would be the best price and output position? As we discussed in Chapter 12, the best position is at the competitive equilibrium output, where $P = MC$, because the equilibrium price represents the marginal value of output. The marginal cost represents society's opportunity costs of making the good as opposed to something else. Where price equals marginal cost, society matches marginal value and marginal cost—that is, it achieves allocative efficiency, as seen at point C in Exhibit 1.

Can the Regulated Monopolist Operate at *P = MC*?

Unfortunately, the natural monopoly cannot operate profitably at the allocative efficient point, where $P = MC$, indicated as point C in Exhibit 1. At point C, the intersection of the demand and marginal cost curves, average total cost is greater than price. The optimal output, then, is an output that results in losses for the producer. Any regulated business that produced for long at this "optimal" output would go bankrupt; it would be impossible to attract new capital to the industry.

Therefore, the "optimal" output from a welfare perspective is not really viable, because firms incur losses. The regulators cannot force firms to price their products at P_{MC} and to sell Q_{MC} output, because they would go out of business. Indeed, in the long run, the industry's capital would deteriorate as investors failed to replace old capital as it became worn out or

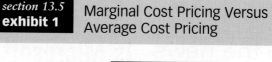

section 13.5 exhibit 1   Marginal Cost Pricing Versus Average Cost Pricing

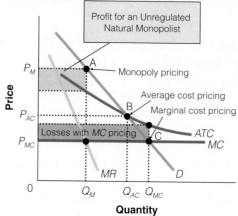

The marginal cost (*MC*) curve is less than the average total cost (*ATC*) curve for the natural monopolist as the average cost falls. If the monopolist is unregulated, it could produce a relatively small level of output, Q_M, at a relatively high price, P_M, and make an economic profit. If regulators require the natural monopolist to use marginal cost pricing, the monopoly will lose money, because P_{MC} is less than *ATC*. Average cost pricing (at point B) would permit firms to make a normal rate of return, where $P_{AC} = ATC$. The monopolist's unregulated output at point A is not optimal from society's standpoint, and the optimal output at point C is not feasible.

obsolete. If the monopolist's unregulated output at point A is not optimal from society's standpoint, and the short-run optimal output at point C is not feasible from the monopolist's standpoint, where should the regulated monopolist be allowed to operate?

One possible solution to the problem is for the government to subsidize the losses associated with marginal cost pricing. However, the burden of this solution would ultimately fall on the taxpayers, as the government would have to raise the money to pay for the losses.

The Compromise: Average Cost Pricing

A compromise between monopoly pricing and marginal cost pricing is found at point B in Exhibit 1, at output Q_{AC}, which is somewhere between the excessively low output and high prices of an unregulated monopoly and the excessively high output and low prices achieved when prices are equated with marginal cost pricing. At point B, price equals average total cost. The monopolist is permitted to price the product where economic profit is zero, earning a normal economic profit or rate of return, such as firms experience in perfect competition in the long run. This compromise is called **average cost pricing.**

In the real world, regulators often permit utilities to receive a "fair and reasonable" return that is a rough approximation to that suggested by average cost pricing, at point B. Point B would seem "fair" in that the monopolist is receiving rewards equal to those that a perfect competitor would ordinarily receive—no more, no less. Point B permits more output at a significantly lower price than is possible at point A, where the monopolist is unregulated, even though output is still somewhat less and price somewhat more than that suggested by point C, the socially optimum or best position.

> **average cost pricing**
> setting price equal to average total cost

Difficulties in Average Cost Pricing

Inaccurate Calculations of Costs

The actual implementation of a rate (price) that permits a "fair and reasonable" return is more difficult than the analysis suggests. The calculations of costs and values are difficult. In reality, the firm may not know exactly what its demand and cost curves look like, which forces regulatory agencies to use profits, another somewhat ambiguous target, as a guide. If profits are "too high," lower the price; if profits are "too low," raise the price. In addition, what if the regulated firm has more information than the regulators about its firm, workers and technology—asymmetric information? If the firm can persuade regulators that its average cost is higher than it actually is; the regulated price could be set higher, closer to the monopoly price.

No Incentives to Keep Costs Down

Another problem is that average cost pricing offers the monopolist no incentive to reduce costs. That is, if the firm's costs rise from ATC_1 to ATC_2 in Exhibit 2, the price will rise from P_1 to P_2. If costs fall, the firm's price will fall. In either scenario, the firm will still be earning a normal rate of return. In other words, if the regulatory agency sets the price at any point where the ATC curve intersects the demand curve, the firm will earn a normal rate of return. Thus, if the agency is going to set the price wherever ATC intersects the demand curve, the firm might just think, Why not let average costs rise? Why not let employees fly first class and dine in the finest restaurants? Why not buy concert tickets and season tickets to sporting events? And if the regulated monopolist knows that the regulators will reduce

prices if costs fall, the regulated monopolist does not benefit from lower costs. Regulators have tackled this problem by allowing the regulated firm to keep some of the profits that come from lower costs; that is, they do not adhere strictly to average cost pricing.

Special Interest Groups

In the real world, consumer groups are constantly battling for lower utility rates, while the utilities themselves are lobbying for higher rates so they can approach the monopoly profits indicated by point A in Exhibit 1. Decisions are not always made in a calm, objective, dispassionate atmosphere free from outside involvement. It is precisely the political economy of rate setting that disturbs some critics of this approach to dealing with the monopoly problem. For example, a rate-making commissioner could become friendly with a utility company, believing that he could obtain a nice job after his tenure as a regulator expires. The temptation would be great for the commissioner to be generous to the utilities. On the other hand, the tendency might be for regulators to bow to pressure from consumer groups. A politician who wants to win votes can almost always succeed by attacking utility rates and promising rate "reform" (lower rates). If zealous rate regulators listen too closely to consumer groups and push rates down to a level indicated by point C

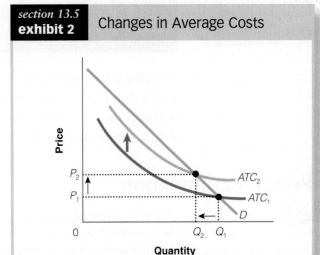

section 13.5
exhibit 2   Changes in Average Costs

An increase in average total cost leads to a higher price and lower output (P_2Q_2); lower average total cost leads to a lower price and greater output (P_1Q_1). However, both situations lead to a normal rate of return. Because the regulated firm has little incentive to minimize costs, average total cost would have a tendency to rise.

in Exhibit 1, the industry might be too unstable to attract capital for expansion.

In recent years, we have seen a trend away from regulation toward competition; for example, after AT&T was broken up by the courts in 1982, the long-distance market became very competitive, and local telephone service is much more competitive now than in the past. Technological advances now allow us to separate the production of electronic power or natural gas from the distributor, which will ultimately lead to greater competition in these markets. Some states have already started deregulation in the electricity market.

SECTION CHECK

1. Antitrust policies are government policies designed to reduce the profitability of a monopoly and push production closer to the social optimum.
2. Privately owned monopolies may be allowed to operate if under regulation by a government agency.
3. Average cost pricing sets price equal to average total cost, where the demand curve intersects average total costs.

---

1. What alternative ways of dealing with the monopoly problem are commonly used?
2. How do antitrust laws promote greater price competition?
3. What price and output are ideal for allocative efficiency for a regulated natural monopolist? Why is an unregulated natural monopolist unlikely to pick this solution?
4. What is average cost pricing? How is it different from marginal cost pricing?
5. What are some difficulties encountered when regulators try to implement average cost pricing for natural monopolies?
6. Why might a job with a regulated natural monopolist that is allowed to earn a "fair and reasonable" return have more perks (noncash forms of compensation) than a comparable job in a nonregulated firm?

SECTION 13.6

Price Discrimination and Peak Load Pricing

* What is price discrimination?
* Why does price discrimination exist?
* Does price discrimination work when reselling is easy?
* What is peak load pricing?

Price Discrimination

Sometimes sellers will charge different customers different prices for the same good or service when the cost of providing that good or service does not differ among customers. This practice is called price discrimination. Under certain conditions, the monopolist finds it profitable to discriminate among various buyers, charging higher prices to those who are more willing to pay and lower prices to those who are less willing to pay.

> **price discrimination**
> the practice of charging different consumers different prices for the same good or service

Conditions for Price Discrimination

The ability to practice price discrimination is not available to all sellers. To practice price discrimination, the following three conditions must hold:

Monopoly Power

Price discrimination is possible only with monopoly or where members of a small group of firms (firms that are not price takers) follow identical pricing policies. In cases with a large number of competing firms, discrimination is less likely because competitors tend to undercut the high prices charged by the firms that are engaging in price discrimination.

Market Segregation

Price discrimination can only occur if the demand curves for markets, groups, or individuals are different. If the demand curves are not different, a profit-maximizing monopolist would charge the same price in both markets. In short, price discrimination requires the ability to separate customers according to their willingness to pay.

No Resale

For price discrimination to work, the person buying the product at a discount must have difficulty in reselling the product to customers being charged more. Otherwise, those getting the items cheaply would want to buy extra amounts of the product at the discounted price and sell it at a profit to others. Price differentials between groups erode if reselling is easy.

Why Does Price Discrimination Exist?

Price discrimination results from the profit-maximization motive. Our graphical analysis of monopoly described the demand curve for the product and the corresponding marginal revenue curve. Sometimes, however, different groups of people have different demand curves and therefore react differently to price changes. A producer can make more money by charging these different buyers different prices. For example, if the price of a movie is increased from $7 to $10, many kids who would attend at $7 may have to stay home at $10, as they (and perhaps their parents) balk at paying the higher price. The impact of raising prices on attendance may be less, however, for adults, who have higher incomes in the first place and for whom the ticket price may represent a smaller part of the expenses of an evening out.

Thus, a different demand curve applies for those, say, under 2, as opposed to those who are older. Specifically, the elasticity of demand with respect to price is greater for children than for adults, meaning that the demand and marginal revenue curves for children is different from the curves for adults. Assume, for simplicity, that the marginal cost is constant. The

Disneyland practices price discrimination. During the off-season, locals are charged less than out-of-town visitors. If nonlocals have a greater willingness to pay (a less elastic demand curve) for the park hopper ticket (which is good for both Disneyland and its next door neighbor, California Adventure) than locals do, Disneyland can increase its profits with this pricing strategy as long as it can prevent reselling.

profit-maximizing movie theater owner will price where the constant marginal costs equal marginal revenue for each group. As you can see in Exhibit 1(a), the demand curve for children is relatively elastic—firms will charge these customers a lower price. The adult demand curve, shown in Exhibit 1(b), is less elastic; firms will charge adult customers a higher price. But in order for price discrimination to be feasible, the seller must be able to successfully distinguish members of targeted groups.

Examples of Price Discrimination

Other examples of price discrimination in the United States are plentiful. Here are just a few.

Price Discrimination in Movie Ticket Prices

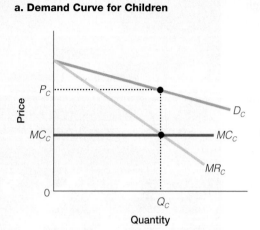
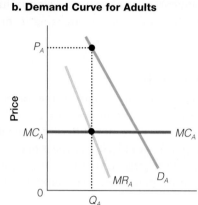

a. Demand Curve for Children

b. Demand Curve for Adults

If the movie theaters in the area have some monopoly power and if children have a lower willingness to pay than adults, then movie theaters can increase profits by price discriminating. Because the demand curve for children is relatively more elastic than the demand curve for adults, the firm finds it profitable to charge the two different groups a different price. To maximize profit, the firm charges the group with the less elastic demand curve (adults) a higher price and the group with the more elastic demand curve (children) a lower price.

Airline Tickets

Seats on airplanes usually go for different prices. They sell high-priced, no-strings-attached fares, and they sell restricted fares—tickets that require Saturday night layovers or must be purchased weeks in advance. This airline pricing strategy allows the airlines to discriminate against business travelers, who usually have little advance warning, travel on the weekdays, and are not as willing to spend their weekends away from home and family. Because business travelers have a high willingness to pay (a relatively inelastic demand curve), the airlines can charge them higher prices. If the airlines were to cut prices for these clients, their revenues would fall. On the other hand, the personal traveler (perhaps a vacationer) can choose among many substitutes, such as other modes of transportation and different times. In short, the personal traveler has a lower willingness to pay (a relatively elastic demand curve). Thus, the airlines can clearly make more money by charging a higher price to those who have a higher willingness to pay (less elastic demand) and a lower price to those who have a lower willingness to pay (more elastic demand)—those who are willing to book in advance and stay over on Saturday nights. If the airlines charged a higher single price to everyone, those with a lower willingness to pay would not travel; if they charged a lower single price to everyone, they would lose profits by receiving less revenue from those who were willing to pay more.

Coupons

The key to price discrimination is observing the difference in demand curves for different customers. The coupon cutter, who spends an hour looking through the Sunday paper for coupons, will probably have a relatively more elastic demand curve than, say, a busy and wealthy physician or executive. Consequently, firms charge a lower price to customers with a lower willingness to pay (more elastic demand)—the coupon cutter—and a higher price to those who don't use coupons (less elastic demand).

College and University Tuition

Another example of price discrimination is the financial aid packages given by many colleges and universities. That is, even though colleges do not charge different tuitions to different students, they do offer different financial aid packages. Furthermore, to receive financial aid, parents must disclose their family income and wealth. In short, students who are well off financially tend to pay more for their education than do students who are less well off.

Quantity Discounts

Another form of price discrimination occurs when customers buy in large quantities, as with public utilities and wholesalers. But even stores will sell a six-pack

Use what you've LEARNED — PRICE DISCRIMINATION OVER TIME

Q Why do people pay a lot more for a hardcover book than a paperback book?

A Sometimes firms engage in price discrimination over time to increase their profits. Although a hardcover book is only slightly more expensive to publish, the real reason for the price differential between hardcover and paperback books is the price elasticity of demand. Some people are willing to pay a higher price to be among the first to read a book; the demand curve is relatively inelastic for these devoted fans. Other individuals have a more elastic demand curve for these goods and are willing to wait for the book to come out in paperback. Other customers, such as libraries, find that paperbacks are not durable enough to be good substitutes for hardbacks. Sellers are able to profit from this difference in elasticities of demand by charging more to those

Why do hardcover texts come out before the paperback version?

who are more willing to pay and charging a lower price to those who are less willing to pay. Thus, book publishers are able to profit.

of soda for less than six single cans. For example, the local bagel shop might sell you a baker's dozen, where you get 13 bagels for the price of 12. This type of price discrimination allows the producer to charge a higher price for the first unit than for, say, the 20th. This form of price discrimination is effective because a buyer's willingness to pay declines as additional units are purchased.

The Welfare Effects of Price Discrimination

In Exhibit 2 on page 384, we analyze the welfare effects of perfect price discrimination using consumer and producer surplus and then compare this with perfect competition and single-price monopoly. When the firm is able to perfectly price discriminate, each unit is sold at its **reservation price**; that is, the firm sells each unit at the maximum amount that the customer would be willing to pay. Because

reservation price
the maximum amount a customer would be willing to pay for a unit of output

Why is the price a lot higher to launder a woman's blouse than a man's shirt? Why are women charged more for haircuts than are men? Are these differences based on costs—perhaps it is more costly to launder a delicate blouse or cut longer hair? Or is it a form of price discrimination where one group may have a greater willingness to pay than the other group?

in the news   The Dynamics of Pricing Tickets for Broadway Shows

–BY HAL R. VARIAN

EVERY night in New York, about 25,000 people, on average, attend Broadway shows.

As avid theatergoers know, ticket prices have been rising inexorably. The top ticket price for Broadway shows has risen 31 percent since 1998. But the actual price paid has gone up by only 24 percent.

The difference is a result of discounting. Savvy fans know that there are deals available for even the most popular shows, with the most popular discounts being offered through coupons, two-for-one deals, special prices for students, and through the TKTS booth in Times Square.

Why so much discounting? The value of a seat in a theater, like a seat on an airplane, is highly perishable. Once the show starts or the plane takes off, a seat is worth next to nothing.

In both industries, sellers use a variety of strategies to try to ensure that the seats are sold to those who are willing to pay the most.

This phenomenon was examined recently by a Stanford economist, Phillip Leslie, in an article, "Price Discrimination in Broadway Theater," published in the autumn 2004 issue of the *RAND Journal of Economics*.

Mr. Leslie was able to collect detailed data on a 1996 Broadway play, "Seven Guitars." Over 140,000 people saw this play, and they bought tickets in 17 price categories. Some price variation was due to the quality of the seats—orchestra, mezzanine, balcony and so on—while other price differences were a result of various forms of discounting.

The combination of quality variation and discounts led to widely varying ticket prices. The average difference of two tickets chosen at random on a given night was about 40 percent of the average price. This is comparable to the price variation in airline tickets.

The highest price, for full-price orchestra seats, was about $55, while the lowest-price balcony seats were about $17. The average price over all performances was about $36.

The ticket promotions also varied over the 199 performances of the show. Targeted direct mail was used early on, while two-for-one tickets were not introduced until about halfway through the run.

The tickets offered for sale at the TKTS booth in Times Square are typically orchestra seats, the best category of seats available. But the discounted tickets at TKTS tend to be the lower-quality orchestra seats. They sell at a fixed discount of 50 percent, but are offered only for performances that day.

Mr. Leslie's goal was primarily to model the behavior of the theatergoer. The audience for Broadway shows is highly diverse. About 10 percent, according to a 1991 survey conducted by Broadway producers, had household incomes of $25,000 or $35,000 while an equal number had incomes over $150,000 (in 1990 dollars).

The prices and discounting policy set by the producers of Broadway shows try to use this heterogeneity to get people to sort themselves by their willingness to pay for tickets.

You probably will not see Donald Trump waiting in line at TKTS; presumably, those in his income class do not mind paying full price. But a lot of students, unemployed actors and tourists do use TKTS.

Yes, it is inconvenient to wait in line at TKTS. But that is the point. If it weren't inconvenient, everyone would do it, and this would result in substantially lower revenues for Broadway shows.

Mr. Leslie uses some advanced econometric techniques to estimate the values that different income groups put on the various categories of tickets. He finds that Broadway producers do a pretty good job, in general, at maximizing revenue. The average price set—which is different than the average price paid—was about $55. According to Mr. Leslie's estimates, the best price to maximize revenue would be about $60.

Mr. Leslie was also able to examine what would happen if the producers changed the way tickets were sold. For example, suppose the producers moved to flat-rate pricing, where they sold every ticket at the same price. In this case, his model predicts that the average price set would be about $50.

Mr. Leslie also looked at various possibilities involving the TKTS booth. He found that the current

STEPHEN CHERNIN/GETTY IMAGES

benefit from the low prices and the variety of choice offered by the Times Square booth.

There are other variations in ticket pricing that could be considered. For example, rather than sell good orchestra seats at full prices and not-so-good seats at half price at the TKTS booth, why not split these seats into two categories? It is difficult to estimate the impact of such a change with the data Mr. Leslie used, but theater owners might want to consider such an experiment.

We are likely to see more and more goods and services sold using the same sort of differential pricing. As more and more transactions become computer-mediated, it becomes easier for sellers to collect data, to experiment with pricing and to analyze the results of those experiments.

This, of course, makes life more complicated for us consumers. The flip side is that pricing variations make those good deals more likely.

Last time I was in New York, I was pleased that I managed to get a ticket to "The Producers" for half price. It almost made up for the fact that I had to book my airline ticket two weeks in advance and stay over a Saturday night.

50 percent discount is too low if the goal is to maximize revenue. He calculates that a 30 percent discount would raise revenue by about 7 percent, albeit at the cost of reducing attendance by about 1.6 percent.

Of course, this estimate is based on data from only one show.

The availability of the TKTS booth stimulates attendances at dozens of shows. Even though any single show might wish for a lower discount and higher revenue, the overall industry could easily

each customer pays exactly the amount he is willing to pay, the marginal revenue is the same as the demand curve.

In Exhibit 2, we see that the firm sells its first unit at P_1 to the customer who is willing to pay the most. The marginal cost for producing that good is MC, so the firm makes $P_1 - MC$ on that unit. For each successive unit, the firm receives a lower price (moving down the demand curve) and has a higher marginal cost (moving up the marginal cost curve). The firm will continue to sell units as long as price exceeds marginal cost. Perfect price discrimination leads to an economically efficient level of output because price equals marginal cost on the last unit sold. However, what is efficient may not always be viewed as fair. In particular, consumers may not be happy with the outcome because the entire sur-

plus (a + b + c + d + e) goes to the monopolist in the form of producer surplus. Consumer surplus is zero because each consumer pays exactly the amount she is willing to pay—her reservation price.

In Exhibit 2, we see that in the competitive market, the equilibrium is established at the intersection of the demand curve and the marginal cost curve, where the equilibrium price is P_{PC} and the equilibrium quantity is Q_{PC}. The perfectly competitive market is efficient because price equals marginal cost. Consumer surplus is a + b + c, producer surplus is d + e, and total welfare is maximized (a + b + c + d + e). The deadweight loss is zero.

We can also see in Exhibit 2 that if the monopolist charges a single price (the monopoly price), deadweight loss is area c + e; that is, some potential buyers value

Use what you've LEARNED   PRICE DISCRIMINATION AND COUPONS

Q Bill loves to go through the Sunday paper and cut out supermarket coupons. How do you think Bill's coupon-clipping habits apply to the concept of price discrimination?

A Often the key to price discrimination is observing the differences in customers' demand curves. For example, Bill, a full-time student who finds it relaxing to look through the Sunday paper for coupons, may have a relatively more elastic demand curve than, say, a wealthy neurosurgeon who enjoys sailing and golfing on Sundays.

© MYRLEEN FERGUSON CATE/PHOTO EDIT

---

section 13.6
exhibit 2   The Welfare Effects of Perfect Price Discrimination

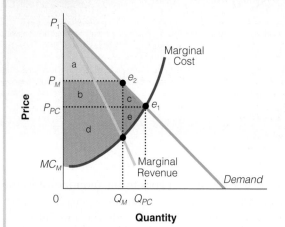

In perfect competition, the market equilibrium price is P_{PC} and the market equilibrium quantity is Q_{PC}. Consumer surplus is area a + b + c, producer surplus is area d + e, and there is no deadweight loss. In a single-price monopoly, the monopoly equilibrium price is P_M and the equilibrium quantity is Q_M. Compared with perfect competition, consumer surplus falls to area a, producer surplus is area b + d, and the deadweight loss is area c + e. In perfect price discrimination, the monopolist sells each unit at the buyer's reservation price—the consumer surplus falls to zero, producer surplus increases to area a + b + c + d + e, and there is no deadweight loss.

	Perfect Competition	Single Price Monopoly	Perfect Price Discrimination
Customer Surplus	a + b + c	a	0
Producer Surplus	d + e	b + d	a + b + c + d + e
Total Welfare	a + b + c + d + e	a + b + d	a + b + c + d + e
Deadweight Loss	0	c + e	0

PERFECT PRICE DISCRIMINATION

Q Why does no social-welfare loss occur when a monopolist practices perfect price discrimination?

A A perfect price discriminating monopolist obtains the maximum price along the demand curve for each unit of output. For example, in Exhibit 3, the monopolist charges $10 for the first unit of output, $9 for the second, $8 for the third, and so on. The demand curve represents the firm's marginal revenue curve, and profits are maximized at the output level at which the *LRMC* equals *MR*, or in this case, *LRMC* equals *P*. (Constant costs are assumed for simplicity.) The marginal social benefits, represented by the demand price of the last unit sold ($5), equal marginal social costs, *LRMC*, and social welfare cannot be improved by increasing or decreasing output. Thus, the perfect price discriminating monopolist charges the competitive price, $5, on only the last unit sold and produces the competitive output level, 6 units. The consumer surplus that would have arisen in perfect competition, area ABC (the difference

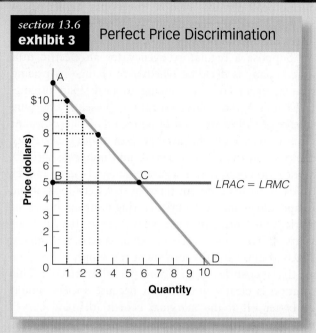

section 13.6
exhibit 3 Perfect Price Discrimination

between what consumers are willing to pay and what they actually pay), is transferred to the monopolist as a profit.

---

the good at more than the marginal cost but are not able to buy the good at the monopoly price. The market is not efficient because $P > MC$ at Q_M. In this market, the consumer surplus is area a, and the producer surplus is area b + d. While consumers receive the most consumer surplus from perfect competition, they are better off with the single-price monopoly than with perfect price discrimination, where consumer surplus is totally eliminated.

Market conditions obviously do not permit perfect price discrimination to be carried out to any significant extent. It is much too difficult to know each consumer's demand curve. However, rough approximations of perfect price discrimination are possible. Lawyers, accountants, and doctors might try to figure out whether their customers are rich or poor and charge accordingly. Car dealers might try to figure out how much a prospective buyer is willing to pay. We do know that price discrimination increases the monopolist's profits;

peak load pricing
when producers charge different prices during different periods because the demand and the cost of producing a product vary over time

otherwise, it would simply charge a single uniform price to all its customers.

Peak Load Pricing

In our earlier discussion of price discrimination, we assumed that the marginal costs associated with selling output over time were constant, but this assumption is not always true. Sometimes producers will charge different prices during different periods because the demand and the cost of producing the product vary over time. For a number of goods and services, demand peaks at particular times—bridges, roads, and tunnels during rush hour traffic; telephone services during business hours; electricity during late summer afternoons; movie theaters on weekend evenings; and amusement parks and ski resorts during holidays.

In price discrimination, we saw that prices reflected different demands from buyers. With **peak load pricing**, demand levels and costs are different. Peak load pricing leads to greater efficiency because consumer prices reflect the higher marginal costs of production during peak periods. That is, buyers pay higher prices for goods and services during peak periods and lower prices during nonpeak periods.

Suppose a regulatory agency for an electric utility company is deciding whether to change its pricing strategy from constant pricing to peak load pricing. In Exhibit 4, the utility company is presently charging 4 cents per kilowatt-hour 24 hours a day. This constant price is based on the average cost to the electricity company in the combined peak and nonpeak periods. Notice, however, that a separate demand curve applies for each of two different times of day. Let's look at the nonpeak demand curve first. During nonpeak hours, at a price of 4 cents, customers will purchase 200,000 kilowatts. If we look at the marginal cost of producing 200,000 kilowatts (by looking at the supply curve), we see that it costs less than 3 cents per kilowatt-hour. This solution is clearly not efficient because society would be better off if the marginal benefit (demand curve) was equal to the marginal cost (supply curve), which is where supply intersects demand—at a price of 3 cents and a quantity of 300,000 kilowatt-hours (point C).

Now let's look at the demand curve during peak hours. Notice that if the company stuck with its price of 4 cents per kilowatt-hour, it would sell 600,000 kilowatts. However, how much does it cost to produce 600,000 kilowatts? Looking at the supply curve, we see that the marginal cost is more than 6 cents per kilowatt-hour. This solution is not efficient because, once again, society would be better off if the marginal benefit (demand curve) equaled the marginal cost (supply curve), which is where supply intersects

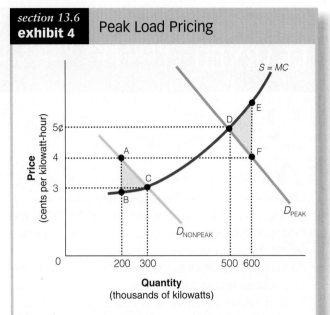

section 13.6
exhibit 4   Peak Load Pricing

Demand for some goods and services fluctuates considerably and predictably between peak and nonpeak periods. It is more efficient to charge a higher price, 5 cents, during peak periods (when marginal costs are higher) and a lower price, 3 cents, during nonpeak periods (when marginal costs are lower) compared with charging a single price, 4 cents, at all times.

demand—at a price of 5 cents and a quantity of 500,000 kilowatt-hours (point D).

In sum, the most economically efficient solution is to charge the lower price during the nonpeak period and the higher price during the peak period. The gain from peak load pricing, compared with constant pricing, can be seen graphically as the sum of the two shaded triangles in Exhibit 4. With this pricing strategy, consumers have an incentive to give their appliances a rest during the peak period when the cost of providing electricity is the highest.

SECTION CHECK

1. When producers charge different prices for the same good or service when no cost difference exists, it is called price discrimination.

2. Price discrimination occurs if demand differs among buyers and the seller can successfully identify group members, because producers can make profits by charging different prices to each group.

3. Price discrimination would not work well if the person buying the product could easily resell the product to another customer at a higher profitable price.

---

1. How do we define price discrimination?

2. Why does price discrimination arise from the profit-maximization motive?

3. Why is preventing resale the key to successful price discrimination?

4. Why is it generally easier to price discriminate for services than for goods?

5. What principle will a profit-maximizing monopolist use in trying to price discriminate among different groups of customers?

6. How can offering quantity discounts increase a producer's profits?

7. Why does perfect price discrimination lead to the economically efficient level of output while reducing consumer surplus to zero?

8. What does perfect price discrimination do to the deadweight cost of monopoly?

9. Why is peak load pricing more efficient than constant pricing for a good with sharp swings in demand over time?

Interactive Chapter Summary

Fill in the blanks:

1. A true or pure monopoly exists in cases of only _____ seller of a product for which no close substitute is available.

2. Monopolists are _____ rather than price takers.

3. A monopolist's barriers to entry can include _____, _____, and _____.

4. _____ include franchising, licensing, and patents.

5. The situation in which one large firm can provide the output of the market at a lower cost than two or more smaller firms is called a(n) _____.

6. A barrier to entry is control over an important _____, such as Alcoa's control over bauxite in the 1940s and DeBeers' control over much of the world's output of diamonds.

7. In monopoly, the market demand curve may be regarded as the demand curve for the _____ because it is the market for that particular product.

8. If a monopolist reduces output, the price will _____; if the monopolist expands output, the price will _____.

9. In monopoly, if the seller wants to expand output, it will have to lower its price on _____ units.

10. The monopolist, like the perfect competitor, will maximize profits at that output where _____ = MC.

11. The monopolist, unlike the perfect competitor, will not maximize profits at that output where _____ = MC.

12. If at a monopolist's profit-maximizing price and output, the price is less than _____, the monopolist is generating economic losses.

13. In monopoly, economic profits are not eliminated by entry, because one of the conditions for monopoly is that _____ exist.

14. Patents and copyrights are examples of _____ power designed to provide an incentive to develop new products.

15. The major efficiency objection to monopoly is that a monopolist charges _____ prices and produces _____ output than would exist under perfect competition.

16. A monopolist produces at an output where the price is _____ than its marginal cost, so the value to society from the last unit produced is _____ than its marginal cost.

17. An argument against monopoly is that a lack of competition tends to retard _____ advance; but, in fact, many near monopolists are important innovators.

18. Three major approaches to dealing with the monopoly problem are commonly used: _____ policies, _____, and _____ ownership.

19. It is likely that at least some anticompetitive practices have been prevented by _____ policies simply by their prohibition of monopoly-like practices.

20. The goal of government regulation as an alternative approach to dealing with monopolies is to achieve the efficiency of large-scale production without permitting the _____ monopoly prices and _____ output that can cause allocative inefficiency.

21. From society's point of view, allocative efficiency occurs where the price of the good is equal to _____. But with natural monopoly, at the "optimal" level of output for allocative efficiency, _____ are incurred.

22. A compromise between unregulated monopoly and marginal cost pricing is _____ pricing, where

the monopolist is permitted to price the product where price equals _____.

23. Average cost pricing _____ the incentives for a monopolist to find ways to reduce its costs.

24. _____ occurs when sellers charge different customers different prices for the same good or service when the cost does not differ.

25. In the case of a number of competing firms, price discrimination is _____ likely because competitors tend to undercut the _____ prices charged.

26. A profit-maximizing seller will charge a(n) _____ price for more inelastic demanders and a(n) _____ price for more elastic demanders.

27. The profit-maximizing rule for a price discriminating monopolist is to price where _____ equals _____ for each different group of demanders.

28. For price discrimination to work, the person buying the product at a discount must have difficulty in _____ the product to customers being charged more.

29. _____, which allow sellers to charge a higher price for the first unit than for later units, are another form of price discrimination.

Answers: 1. one 2. price makers 3. legal barriers; economies of scale; control of important inputs 4. Legal barriers to entry 5. natural monopoly 6. input 7. firm 8. rise; fall 9. all 10. MR 11. P 12. average total cost 13. barriers to entry 14. barriers to entry 15. higher; less 16. greater; greater 17. technological 18. antitrust; regulation; public 19. antitrust 20. high; low 21. marginal costs; losses 22. average cost; average total cost 23. reduces 24. Price discrimination 25. less; high 26. higher; lower 27. marginal revenue; marginal cost 28. reselling 29. Quantity discounts

Key Terms and Concepts

monopoly 362
natural monopoly 362

average cost pricing 377
price discrimination 378

reservation price 381
peak load pricing 385

Section Check Answers

13.1 Monopoly: The Price Maker

1. Why does monopoly depend on the existence of barriers to entry?

If a monopoly were unusually profitable (earning a higher than normal rate of return), entry by other firms would occur, driving its economic profits down and increasing the number of sellers, unless some barrier to entry prevented it.

2. Why is a pure monopoly a rarity?

Pure monopolies are a rarity because there are very few goods or services for which there are no close substitutes and for which there is only one producer.

3. Why does the government grant some companies, such as public utilities, monopoly power?

In some industries, it is inherently inefficient to have more than one firm producing the good or service (i.e., the good or service is a natural monopoly).

13.2 Demand and Marginal Revenue in Monopoly

1. Why are the market and firm demand curves the same for a monopoly?

The market and firm demand curves are the same for a monopoly because a monopoly is the only seller of the product under consideration. Since a monopolist is the only seller in the industry, its demand curve is the industry or market demand curve.

2. Why is a monopoly a price maker, but a perfectly competitive firm a price taker?

A perfectly competitive firm is a price taker because it cannot appreciably change the quantity offered for sale on a market, and therefore it cannot change the equilibrium market price appreciably. However, since a monopoly controls the quantity offered for sale, it can alter the price by changing its output—it "makes" the price through its decision of how much to produce.

3. Why is marginal revenue less than price for a profit-maximizing monopolist?

For a monopolist, selling an additional unit requires it to reduce its price, and reducing its price reduces its revenues from units it was selling before at its previous higher price. Therefore, the monopolist's marginal revenue equals price minus this lost revenue from the reduced price on other units, and is less than price as a result.

4. Why would a monopolist never knowingly operate in the inelastic portion of its demand curve?

To maximize its profits, a monopolist will produce the output where marginal revenue equals marginal cost. But since marginal cost will be positive, this requires that marginal revenue is also positive at the profit-maximizing level. Since a positive marginal revenue means that total revenue increases as quantity sold increases along a demand curve, and this only occurs if demand is relatively elastic (the elasticity of demand is greater than one), this means that a monopolist will always choose to operate on the elastic portion of its demand curve.

13.3 The Monopolist's Equilibrium

1. **What is a monopolist's principle for choosing the profit-maximizing output?**

   A monopolist's principle for choosing the profit-maximizing output is the same as for a perfectly competitive firm: Produce all those units for which marginal revenue exceeds marginal cost, resulting in a profit-maximizing equilibrium quantity where marginal revenue equals marginal cost. The differences between a monopoly and a perfectly competitive firm arise because marginal revenue also equals price for a perfectly competitive firm, but marginal revenue is less than price for a monopolist.

2. **How do you find the profit-maximizing price for a monopolist?**

   A monopolist produces the quantity where marginal revenue equals marginal cost. The height of its demand curve at that quantity indicates the price at which that profit-maximizing quantity can be sold.

3. **For a monopolist making positive economic profits, what must be true about the relationship between price and average total cost?**

   Just as with a perfectly competitive firm, for a monopoly to be earning economic profits, its total revenue must exceed total cost at the profit-maximizing output. But this means that price (average revenue) must also exceed average cost at the profit-maximizing output level for positive economic profits to be earned.

4. **For a monopolist making negative economic profits, what must be true about the relationship between price and average total cost?**

   Just as with a perfectly competitive firm, for a monopoly to be earning negative economic profits, its total revenue must be less than its total cost at the profit-maximizing output. But this means that price (average revenue) must also be less than average cost at the profit-maximizing output level for negative economic profits to be earned.

5. **Why, unlike perfectly competitive firms, can a monopolist continue to earn positive economic profits in the long run?**

   Unlike perfectly competitive firms, a monopolist can continue to earn positive economic profits in the long run, because barriers to entry keep entrants, whose entry would erode those economic profits, from entering the industry.

13.4 Monopoly and Welfare Loss

1. **Why does the reduced output under monopoly cause inefficiency?**

   The reduced output and higher prices under monopoly cause inefficiency because some units for which the marginal value (indicated by willingness to pay along the demand curve) exceeds the marginal cost are no longer exchanged (unlike in perfect competition), eliminating the net gains that such trades would have generated.

2. **Does monopoly power retard innovation? Why or why not?**

   Monopoly has been claimed to retard innovation, but many near-monopolists are important innovators. Therefore the incentive to innovate exists in monopolistic as well as competitive market structures.

3. **What does the welfare cost of monopoly represent? How is it measured?**

   The welfare cost of monopoly represents the net gains from trade (the difference between the marginal values of those goods indicated by the demand curve and the marginal costs of producing them) from those units of a good that would have been traded, but are no longer traded because of the output restriction of monopoly. It is measured by the area between the demand curve and the marginal cost curve for those units that are no longer traded because of the monopoly output restriction.

4. **How can economies of scale lead to monopoly? How could it result in monopoly increasing rather than decreasing market output, relative to the competitive market structure?**

   Economies of scale can lead to monopoly because output can be produced at lower costs on a larger scale than on a smaller scale, and this efficiency (cost) advantage can result in a larger firm outcompeting smaller firms. Industries with economies of scale over the entire range of industry output therefore tend toward monopoly. But if the production cost savings are greater than the price increasing effect of monopoly output restriction, the result of such a monopoly would be a lower price and a higher quantity than would be the case with a larger number of firms (i.e., a more competitive market structure).

5. **Can monopoly be the result of a new innovation that leaves consumers better off than before? Why or why not?**

   A new innovation may result in its innovator having a monopoly on it, which would give its creator incentives to raise prices and reduce outputs like any other monopoly. But for that monopoly innovator to attract customers away from the products customers currently purchase, those customers must expect to be made better off buying the product at the price charged. This means that such a monopoly has no ability to harm consumers compared to their earlier situation, but can make them better off.

13.5 Monopoly Policy

1. What alternative ways of dealing with the monopoly problem are commonly used?
The monopoly problem (with respect to efficiency, equity, and power) is commonly dealt with through antitrust policies, regulation, and public ownership.

2. How do antitrust laws promote greater price competition?
Antitrust laws promote more price competition by making monopolistic practices and restrictions on price competition illegal.

3. What price and output are ideal for allocative efficiency for a regulated natural monopolist? Why is an unregulated natural monopolist unlikely to pick this solution?
The efficient price and output are where demand (marginal value) equals marginal cost, since this guarantees that every mutually beneficial trade takes place. However, with economies of scale (falling average cost curves), marginal cost is less than average cost for a natural monopolist, so that marginal cost prices would result in economic losses. An unregulated natural monopolist would not choose such a solution.

4. What is average cost pricing? How is it different from marginal cost pricing?
Average cost pricing is a regulatory approach to natural monopoly that permits the regulated natural monopolist to earn a normal rate of return on capital investment (zero economic profits). Zero economic profits requires that total revenues equal total (opportunity) costs, which requires that average revenue, or price, equals average cost. Forcing such a natural monopolist to charge prices equal to marginal cost would require a price below average cost, because marginal cost is less than average cost for a natural monopolist, implying losses to the producer, which is not sustainable over the long run.

5. What are some difficulties encountered when regulators try to implement average cost pricing for natural monopolies?
Difficulties encountered when regulators try to implement average cost pricing include difficulties in calculating costs, eroded incentives for regulated firms to keep costs down, and the risk that the regulatory agency will make decisions on a political rather than on an economic basis.

6. Why might a job with a regulated natural monopolist that is allowed to earn a "fair and reasonable" return have more perks (noncash forms of compensation) than a comparable job in a nonregulated firm?
A regulated natural monopolist that is allowed to earn a "fair and reasonable" rate of return has little or no incentive to keep costs down, since reducing costs won't allow them to earn higher profits as a result. Those potential profits the monopolist is not allowed to keep get converted instead into business expenses that benefit the management, such as lavish perks (first class air travel, hotels, meals, etc.).

13.6 Price Discrimination and Peak Load Pricing

1. How do we define price discrimination?
Price discrimination is defined as charging different customers different prices for the same good or service.

2. Why does price discrimination arise from the profit-maximization motive?
Price discrimination arises from the profit-maximization motive because different customers react differently to price changes (i.e., they have different elasticities of demand). Therefore, profit-maximization implies treating these different customers differently.

3. Why is preventing resale the key to successful price discrimination?
If customers who are being charged different prices for the same goods can resell the goods among themselves, the lower price group will resell to the higher price group, undermining the seller's ability to charge a higher price to the groups with more inelastic demand curves.

4. Why is it generally easier to price discriminate for services than for goods?
Preventing resale is a key to successful price discrimination, and it is typically easier to prevent resale of services provided directly to customers than for goods sold to them (e.g., it is harder to resell a gall bladder surgery or plumbing repairs than to resell a computer).

5. What principle will a profit-maximizing monopolist use in trying to price discriminate among different groups of customers?
A profit-maximizing monopolist will attempt to charge higher prices to those who are more willing to pay (more inelastic demanders), and lower prices to those who are less willing to pay (more elastic demanders).

6. How can offering quantity discounts increase a producer's profits?
Quantity discounts can allow a producer to charge a lower price for additional units, without having

to reduce the price on the earlier units; it is effective because a buyer's willingness to pay declines as additional units are purchased.

7.   Why does perfect price discrimination lead to the economically efficient level of output while reducing consumer surplus to zero?

Perfect price discrimination allows a seller to sell each unit for a price equal to the buyer's reservation price, which eliminates any consumer surplus. But since a perfect price discriminating monopolist need not lower its price on previous units when it sells more, its marginal revenue is the same as its price, so when it produces to the output level where marginal revenue equals marginal cost, it also produces to the output level where price equals marginal cost, which is the efficient level of output.

8.   What does perfect price discrimination do to the deadweight cost of monopoly?

Since perfect price discrimination makes marginal revenue equal to price for each unit sold, such a monopolist has no reason to restrict output to increase profits; with no incentive to reduce output below the efficient level, there would be no deadweight cost.

9.   Why is peak load pricing more efficient than constant pricing for a good with sharp swings in demand over time?

A constant price would result in price being too low in the peak demand period, and too high in the low demand period; both of these pricing "errors" would cause a deadweight cost that could be avoided by peak load pricing.

True or False:

1. In terms of the number of firms in an industry, monopoly is at the other end of the spectrum from perfect competition.

2. As long as market demand curves are downward sloping, the demand curves faced by monopolists will be downward sloping.

3. For a pure monopoly, the firm and the industry are one and the same.

4. A monopoly firm is a price maker, and it will pick a price that is the highest point on its demand curve.

5. Pure monopolies are a rarity because few goods and services truly have only one producer.

6. The cost advantage of a natural monopoly is due to economies of scale throughout the relevant output range.

7. As in perfect competition, in monopoly the demand curve for the firm's product is downward sloping.

8. The marginal revenue curve for a monopolist lies below the demand curve.

9. For a monopoly to get revenue from marginal customers, the firm has to lower the price so that marginal revenue is always less than price.

10. When a monopolist cuts prices to attract new customers, its existing customers benefit.

11. Along the inelastic portion of the demand curve, when the price falls, total revenue rises, so that marginal revenue is positive.

12. Along the elastic portion of the demand curve, when the price falls, total revenue rises, so that marginal revenue is positive.

13. A monopolist will never knowingly operate in the inelastic portion of its demand curve, because increased output will lead to lower total revenue and higher total cost in that region.

14. For a monopolist, the profit-maximizing price is indicated by the height of the demand curve at the profit-maximizing quantity of output.

15. If, at a monopolist's profit-maximizing price and output, the price is greater than average total cost, the monopolist is generating economic losses.

16. Economic profits cannot persist in the long run for a monopolist.

17. A monopolist will incur a loss if demand is insufficient to cover average total costs at any price and output combination along its demand curve.

18. Having monopoly guarantees economic profits.

19. Perfect competition leads to lower output and higher prices than would exist under monopoly.

20. Monopoly creates a welfare loss because a monopoly does not produce enough of a good from society's perspective.

21. Economists widely agree about the size of the welfare loss from monopoly.

22. By imposing monetary and nonmonetary costs on monopolists, antitrust policies aim to reduce the profitability of monopoly.

23. Government regulation of monopolies aims to achieve the efficiency of large-scale production without permitting the monopolists to charge monopoly prices, which would reduce output.

24. With natural monopoly, the efficient, or optimal, output is one that produces zero economic profits for the producer where price equals marginal cost.

25. Any regulated business that produced for long at the optimal, or efficient, output would go bankrupt.

26. Under average cost pricing, a regulated monopoly is permitted to earn a normal return such as firms experience in perfect competition in the long run.

27. Price discrimination is possible only with monopoly or where members of a small group of firms follow identical pricing policies.

28. When different groups of customers have predictably different willingness to pay, a monopolist could earn higher profits by charging those different buyers different prices, if it could prevent resale of the product among customers.

29. Price differentials between groups will erode if reselling is easy, which is why price discrimination is usually limited to services and to some goods where it is inherently difficult to resell or where the producer can effectively prevent resale.

Multiple Choice Questions:

1. Pure monopoly is defined as
   a. an industry consisting of a single seller.
   b. a market structure that involves many substitute products.
   c. a market in which many rival firms compete for sales.
   d. a market structure consisting of a single buyer.

2. For a true, or pure, monopoly,
   a. there is only one seller of the product.
   b. no close substitutes are available.
   c. the firm and the industry are the same.
   d. it must be virtually impossible for other firms to overcome barriers to entry.
   e. all of the above are true.

3. Which of the following is inconsistent with monopoly?
   a. a single seller
   b. economies of scale
   c. $MR < P$
   d. free entry and exit
   e. selling in the elastic portion of the demand curve in order to maximize profits

4. For a natural monopoly, which of the following is false?
   a. It is more efficient to have a single firm produce the good.
   b. Production of the good must involve economies of scale throughout the relevant output range.
   c. It would typically result from a firm's possession of an exclusive patent.
   d. One large firm can produce at lower cost than two or more smaller firms.

5. Which of the following is potentially a barrier to entry into a product market?
   a. patent protection on the design of the product
   b. economies of scale in the product market
   c. government licensing of the product's producers
   d. the control of a crucial input necessary to produce the product
   e. all of the above

6. A profit-maximizing monopolist sets
   a. the product price where marginal cost equals marginal revenue.
   b. output where marginal cost equals marginal revenue.
   c. output where marginal cost equals average revenue.
   d. output where demand equals average total cost.
   e. price equal to the highest dollar amount that any customer is willing to pay.

7. For a monopolist,
   a. its demand curve is downward sloping.
   b. its marginal revenue is less than price.
   c. existing economic profits can be sustained over time.
   d. all of the above are true.

8. If a profit-maximizing monopolist is currently charging a price on the inelastic portion of its demand curve, it should
   a. raise price and decrease output.
   b. lower price and increase output.
   c. reduce both output and price.
   d. hold output constant and raise price.
   e. do none of the above.

9. If a monopolist had a zero marginal cost of production, it would maximize profits by choosing to produce a quantity where
   a. demand was inelastic.
   b. demand was unit elastic.
   c. demand was elastic.
   d. It is impossible to determine where along a demand curve such a monopolist would choose to produce.

10. Tom is the monopoly provider of a town's TV cable service, whose current subscription price is $20.00 per month. In order to attract one more subscriber, he has to lower his price to $19.95. What is true of Tom's marginal revenue from that additional subscriber?
    a. Tom's marginal revenue equals $19.95.
    b. Tom's marginal revenue is greater than $19.95.
    c. Tom's marginal revenue is less than $19.95.
    d. Tom's marginal revenue is between $19.95 and $20.00.

11. Rob owns the only race-car track in the entire region. When he lowers his price, the track attracts more customers, but its total revenue falls. Which of the following is true of Rob?
    a. He is a monopolist operating in the inelastic region of his demand curve.
    b. He is a monopolist operating in the elastic region of his demand curve.
    c. He would not choose to lower his price in such a situation.
    d. He is a price taker.
    e. Both a and c are true of Rob.

12. Which of the following is *not* true about a profit-maximizing monopolist?
    a. The monopolist faces the downward-sloping market demand curve.
    b. The monopolist always earns an economic profit.
    c. The price of output exceeds marginal revenue.
    d. The monopolist chooses output where marginal revenue equals marginal cost.
    e. All of the above are true.

13. Which of the following is true for a firm that is a monopolist?
    a. The firm will definitely make an economic profit in the short run.
    b. The firm will produce a smaller quantity of output than what would be best from the viewpoint of ideal economic efficiency.
    c. The additional revenue that can be generated from an increase in output will exceed the firm's price.
    d. The firm can charge whatever it wants for its product, because consumers have no alternatives.

14. Monopolists are like perfectly competitive firms in that
    a. both maximize profits at the output level where marginal revenue equals marginal cost.
    b. both could be earning either profits or losses in the short run.
    c. both are in industries with downward-sloping demand curves.
    d. all of the above are true of both of them.
    e. a and b are true of both of them, but not c.

15. Monopoly is unlike perfect competition in that
    a. a monopolist's price is greater than marginal cost.
    b. there are no barriers to entry into a monopoly industry.
    c. a monopolist earns an economic profit only if its price is greater than *ATC*.
    d. all of the preceding are ways in which monopoly is unlike perfect competition.
    e. a and b, but not c, are ways in which monopoly is unlike perfect competition.

16. A price-taking firm and a monopolist are alike in that
    a. price equals marginal revenue for both.
    b. both maximize profits by choosing an output where marginal revenue equals marginal cost, provided that price exceeds average variable cost.
    c. price exceeds marginal cost at the profit-maximizing level of output for both.
    d. in the long run, both earn zero economic profits.

17. Which of the following is true of perfect competition but not true of monopoly?
    a. The firm's average total cost curve is U-shaped.
    b. Marginal revenue is equal to price.
    c. A profit-maximizing firm chooses output where marginal revenue equals marginal cost.
    d. Profits may exist in the short run.

18. Objections to monopolies do *not* include which of the following?
    a. They reduce output below the efficient level of output that would be produced in perfect competition.
    b. They reduce the price below what would be charged in perfect competition.
    c. They charge a price that is greater than marginal cost.
    d. They create a welfare cost.
    e. All of the preceding are objections to monopolies.

19. A natural monopoly is defined as an industry in which
    a. one firm can produce the entire industry output at a lower average cost than can two or more firms.
    b. a single firm controls crucial inputs to the production process.
    c. one firm is especially large relative to other firms that could enter the industry.
    d. a single seller exists as a result of patent protection.

20. If regulators set a price according to marginal cost pricing, the firm will
    a. earn positive economic profits.
    b. make zero economic profits.
    c. suffer an economic loss.
    d. earn the same level of profits as it would absent regulation.

21. Average cost pricing for a natural monopoly will
    a. result in the socially efficient level of output.
    b. result in a less than socially efficient level of output.
    c. result in a greater than socially efficient level of output.
    d. result in the firm suffering economic losses.
    e. result in the firm earning economic profit.

22. Under average cost pricing by a natural monopoly,
    a. price is greater than marginal cost.
    b. a welfare cost will be incurred.
    c. the producer will earn a normal rate of return.
    d. a producer experiences little or no incentive to hold down costs.
    e. all of the preceding are true.

23. Which of the following is not a limitation that regulators face when they implement average cost pricing?
    a. Average cost pricing provides little or no incentive for firms to keep costs down.
    b. The accurate calculation of a firm's costs is difficult.
    c. Decisions are political and often influenced by special interests.
    d. All of the preceding are limitations faced by regulators implementing average cost pricing.

24. A price-discriminating monopolist will
    a. price where marginal revenue equals marginal cost for each different group of demanders.
    b. charge a higher price to those with a greater willingness to pay (the more inelastic demanders).
    c. have to face customers who have a difficult time reselling the good to others who were charged more.
    d. do all of the preceding.

25. A price-discriminating monopolist will tend to charge a lower price to students if it believes that student demand is
    a. more elastic than that of other demanders.
    b. more inelastic than that of other demanders.
    c. unit elastic.
    d. graphically represented by a vertical curve.

26. Which of the following is *not* true of successful price discriminators?
    a. They could make greater profits by charging everyone a higher, uniform price.
    b. Their customers must differ in their willingness to pay.
    c. Their customers must have difficulty reselling the good to other customers.
    d. They must have monopoly power.

27. Price discrimination may be a rational strategy for a profit-maximizing monopolist when
    a. it has no opportunity for reselling across market segments.
    b. it has a substantial opportunity for reselling across market segments.
    c. consumers are unable to be segmented into identifiable markets.
    d. the willingness to pay is the same across all customers.

Problems:

1. Which of the following could be considered a monopoly?
    a. Kate Hudson (an actress)
    b. DeBeers diamond company
    c. the only doctor in a small town
    d. Ford Motor Company

2. Barriers to entry are important in the creation of monopolies because they keep competitors out of the industry. Although many types of barriers exist, historically, ownership of an essential resource, government patents and licenses, and large entry costs have served as the primary barriers to entry. For each of the following cases, indicate which type of barrier created the monopoly.
    a. In the 1940s, Aluminum Company of America owns all of the world's known bauxite deposits.
    b. The local cable TV company has the only government issued license to supply services in the area.
    c. The pharmaceutical company, MAXCO, invented and patended a new baldness drug.
    d. In the 1950s, AT&T provided long-distance telephone service by stringing millions of miles of copper wiring across the United States.

3. Is it optimal for the monopolist to operate on the inelastic portion of the demand curve? Why or why not?

4. Fill in the missing data in the following table for a monopolist.

Quantity	Price	Total Revenue	Marginal Revenue	Demand Elastic or Inelastic?
1	$11	_____	_____	_____
2	10	_____	_____	_____
3	9	_____	_____	_____
4	8	_____	_____	_____
5	7	_____	_____	_____
6	6	_____	_____	_____
7	5	_____	_____	_____
8	4	_____	_____	_____
9	3	_____	_____	_____
10	2	_____	_____	_____
11	1	_____	_____	_____

5. Assume that the monopolist in problem 4 had fixed costs of $10 and a constant marginal cost of $4 per unit. Add columns to the above table for Total Cost, Marginal Cost, and profit.

6. The Mobile Phone Company has served Mobile, Alabama, since the 1930s as a government-authorized natural monopoly. The following table describes a portion of the demand curve for long-distance service facing Mobile Phone Company.
   a. Complete the table.

MOBILE PHONE COMPANY DEMAND FOR PHONE HOURS

Quantity	Price	Total Revenue	Marginal Revenue	Elastic or Inelastic?
30	$3.65	_____	_____	_____
31	3.58	_____	_____	_____
32	3.50	_____	_____	_____
33	3.43	_____	_____	_____
34	3.35	_____	_____	_____
35	3.27	_____	_____	_____
36	3.20	_____	_____	_____
37	3.12	_____	_____	_____
38	3.05	_____	_____	_____
39	2.97	_____	_____	_____
40	2.89	_____	_____	_____
41	2.82	_____	_____	_____
42	2.74	_____	_____	_____
43	2.67	_____	_____	_____
44	2.59	_____	_____	_____
45	2.51	_____	_____	_____
46	2.44	_____	_____	_____
47	2.36	_____	_____	_____
48	2.29	_____	_____	_____
49	2.21	_____	_____	_____
50	2.13	_____	_____	_____

   b. How does the company's marginal revenue change as the price changes? What is the relationship between marginal revenue and price?
   c. At what price does demand become inelastic?
   d. What will happen to the elasticity of demand when a new company, Mobile Phones of Mobile, starts a competing wireless phone company?

7. The following table shows the demand for water and cost conditions for the New South Springdale Water Utility, a pure monopoly.
   a. Complete the table.

Quanity (gallons)	Price (per gallon)	Total Revenue	Marginal Revenue	Marginal Costs	Average Total Costs	Profit
100	$1.28	_____	_____	$0.15	$1.252	_____
101	$1.27	_____	_____	$0.18	$1.241	_____
102	$1.26	_____	_____	$0.21	$1.231	_____
103	$1.25	_____	_____	$0.23	$1.221	_____
104	$1.24	_____	_____	$0.26	$1.212	_____

   b. What is true about the relationship between marginal revenue and marginal costs when profit is the greatest?
   c. Suppose the government imposed a tax on the firm of $103, which the firm had to pay even if it went out of business. What would be the profit-maximizing level of output? What would happen to profits? Would the firm stay in business?

8. A patent gives a firm a monopoly in production of the patented good. While the monopoly profits provide an incentive for firms to innovate, the monopoly power imposes a cost on consumers. Why do consumers suffer a cost? Is it greater than the profits earned by the monopolist?

9. Use the accompanying diagram to answer a–c.

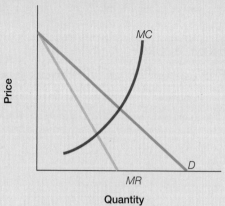

a. Assuming the monopolist indicated in the diagram produced at all, indicate its profit-maximizing quantity and price.
b. Add an *ATC* curve that would show this monopolist earning an economic profit.
c. Add an *ATC* curve that would show this monopolist experiencing an economic loss.

10. If economic profits were zero, would a monopolist ever stay in business? Why might it be possible for a monopolist to earn positive economic profits in the long run?

11. What is meant by "the welfare loss" of monopoly? Why does no welfare loss occur if a monopolist successfully practices perfect price discrimination?

12. Consider the data in the following table:

Price	Quantity	Fixed Cost	Variable Cost
$100	0	$60	$0
90	1	60	25
80	2	60	40
70	3	60	50
60	4	60	70
50	5	60	100
40	6	60	140
30	7	60	190
20	8	60	250

A simple monopolist with these fixed and variable cost schedules maximizes profits at what level of output?

13. Explain how each of the following is a form of price discrimination.
a. a student discount at the movie theater
b. long-distance phone service that costs 15 cents per minute for the first 10 minutes and 5 cents per minute after 10 minutes
c. a psychic who charges each customer his or her maximum reservation price for palm readings
d. a senior citizen breakfast discount at a local restaurant
e. coupon discounts on laundry detergent

14. In October of 1999, Coca-Cola announced that it was considering testing a new vending machine that was temperature sensitive. The price of the soft drinks in the machines would be higher on hot days. The *Miami Herald* story read "Soda

Jerks." How is this practice a form of price discrimination? How can the placement of the vending machines create a monopoly? What if other vending machines are close by and are not owned by Coca-Cola?

15. Compare the size of the welfare (deadweight) loss under monopoly in the case of perfect price discrimination and under the standard case of simple monopoly. Explain.

16. Use the accompanying diagram to answer a–c.

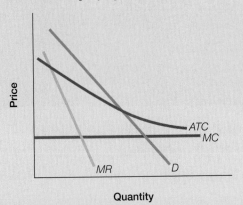

a. Indicate the efficient result on the graph.
b. Illustrate the profits or losses from the efficient result in a.
c. Show the average cost-pricing solution. What profits are earned with that approach?

17. Governments around the world are allowing competition in the production of goods and services that have historically been considered natural monopolies. Competition has been introduced in industries such as the local telephone service and electricity provision. Why might the introduction of competition increase the efficiency of these industries?

18. The Mississippi Bridge Authority operates a toll bridge that crosses the river near St. Louis. Traffic over the bridge includes tourist traffic and commercial traffic. It also includes commuters who work in St. Louis but live on the Illinois side of the river.
a. Would you expect demand for bridge use to differ at different times during the day? Why?
b. How might costs differ in these time periods?
c. What would be the effects of charging a higher toll to cross the bridge during busy times?

14 Monopolistic Competition and Product Differentiation

Restaurants, clothing stores, beauty salons, video stores, hardware stores, and coffee houses have elements of both competitive and monopoly markets.

Recall that the perfectly competitive model includes many buyers and sellers; coffee houses can be found in almost every town in the country. You can even find Starbucks in Barnes & Noble bookstores and grocery stores. In addition, the barriers to entry of owning an individual coffee shop are relatively low. However, monopolistically competitive firms sell a differentiated product and thus each firm has an element of monopoly power. Each coffee store is different. It might be different because of its location or décor. It might be different because of its products. It might be different because of the service it provides. Monopolistically competitive markets are common in the real world. They are the topic of this chapter. ■

Monopolistic Competition

* What are the distinguishing features of monopolistic competition?

* How can a firm differentiate its product?

What Is Monopolistic Competition?

Monopolistic competition is a market structure where many producers of somewhat different products compete with one another. For example, a restaurant is a monopoly in the sense that it has a unique name, menu, quality of service, location, and so on; but it also has many competitors—others selling prepared meals. That is, monopolistic competition has features in common with both monopoly and perfect competition, even though this explanation may sound like an oxymoron—like "jumbo shrimp" or "civil war." As with monopoly, individual sellers in monopolistic competition believe that they have some market power. But monopolistic competition is probably closer to competition than monopoly. Entry into and exit out of the industry is unrestricted, and consequently, the industry has many independent sellers. In virtue of the relatively free entry of new firms, the long-run price and output behavior, and zero long-run economic profits, monopolistic competition is similar to perfect competition. However, the monopolistically competitive firm produces a product that is different (that is, *differentiated* rather than identical or homogeneous) from others, which leads to some degree of monopoly power. In a sense, sellers in a monopolistically competitive market may be regarded as "monopolists" of their own particular brands; but unlike firms with a true monopoly, competition occurs among the many firms selling similar (but not identical) brands. For example, a buyer living in a city of moderate size and in the market for books, CDs, toothpaste, furniture, shampoo, video rentals, restaurants, eyeglasses, running shoes, movie theaters, super markets, and music lessons has many competing sellers from which to choose.

> **monopolistic competition**
> a market structure with many firms selling differentiated products

> **product differentiation**
> goods or services that are slightly different, or perceived to be different, from one another

The Three Basic Characteristics of Monopolistic Competition

The theory of monopolistic competition is based on three characteristics: (1) product differentiation, (2) many sellers, and (3) free entry.

Product Differentiation

One characteristic of monopolistic competition is product differentiation—the accentuation of unique product qualities, real or perceived, to develop a specific product identity.

The significant feature of differentiation is the buyer's belief that various sellers' products are not the same, whether the products are actually different or not. Aspirin and some brands of over-the-counter cold medicines are examples of products that are similar

Restaurants can be very different. A restaurant that sells tacos and burritos competes with other Mexican restaurants, but it also competes with restaurants that sell burgers and fries. Monopolistic competition has some elements of competition (many sellers) and some elements of monopoly power (differentiated products).

DAVID BLUMENFELD/GETTY IMAGES NEWS/GETTY IMAGES

in the news   Is a Beer a Beer?

To show that some differentiation is perceived rather than real, blind taste tests on beer were conducted on 250 participants.

Four glasses of identical beer, each with different labels, were presented to the subjects as four different brands of beer. In the end, all the subjects believed that the brands of beer were different and that they could tell the difference between them. Another interesting result came out of the taste tests—most of the participants commented that at least one of the beers was unfit for human consumption.

SOURCE: Russell L. Ackoff and James R. Emshoff, "Advertising Research at Anheuser. Busch, Inc. (1963–1968)," *Sloan Management Review* 16 (Winter 1975): 1–15.

COURTESY OF ROBERT L. SEXTON

consider this:

Product differentiation, whether perceived or real, can be effective. Take another example: In blind taste testing, few people can consistently distinguish between Coca-Cola and Pepsi, yet each brand has many loyal customers. Sometimes the key to product differentiation is that consumers believe they are different.

or identical but have different brand names. Product differentiation leads to preferences among buyers dealing with or purchasing the products of particular sellers.

Physical Differences Physical differences constitute a primary source of product differentiation. For example, brands of ice cream (such as Dreyer's and Breyers), running shoes (such as Nike and Asics), or fast-food Mexican restaurants (such as Taco Bell and Del Taco) differ significantly in taste to many buyers.

Prestige Prestige considerations also differentiate products to a significant degree. Many people prefer to be seen using the currently popular brand, while others prefer the "off" brand. Prestige considerations are particularly important with gifts— Cuban cigars, Montblanc pens, beluga caviar,

Godiva chocolates, Dom Perignon champagne, Rolex watches, and so on.

Location Location is a major differentiating factor in retailing. Shoppers are not willing to travel long distances to purchase similar items, which is one reason for the large number of convenience stores and service station mini-marts. Most buyers realize brands of gasoline do not differ significantly, which means the location of a gas station might influence their choice of gasoline. Location is also important for restaurants. Some restaurants can differentiate their products with beautiful views of the city lights, ocean, or mountains.

Service Service considerations are likewise significant for product differentiation. Speedy and friendly service or lenient return policies are important to many people. Likewise, speed and quality of service may significantly influence a person's choice of restaurants.

The Impact of Many Sellers

When many firms compete for the same customers, any particular firm has little control over or interest in what other firms do. That is, a restaurant may change prices or improve service without a retaliatory move on the part of other competing restaurants, because the time and effort necessary to learn about such changes may have marginal costs that are greater than the marginal benefits.

The Significance of Free Entry

Entry in monopolistic competition is relatively unrestricted in the sense that new firms may easily start the production of close substitutes for existing products, as happens with restaurants, styling salons, barber shops, and many forms of retail activity. Because of relatively free entry, economic profits tend to be eliminated in the long run, as is the case with perfect competition.

SECTION CHECK

1. The theory of monopolistic competition is based on three primary characteristics: product differentiation, many sellers, and free entry.
2. The many sources of product differentiation include physical differences, prestige, location, and service.

---

1. How is monopolistic competition a mixture of monopoly and perfect competition?
2. Why is product differentiation necessary for monopolistic competition?
3. What are some common forms of product differentiation?
4. Why are many sellers necessary for monopolistic competition?
5. Why is free entry necessary for monopolistic competition?

SECTION 14.2

Price and Output Determination in Monopolistic Competition

* How are short-run economic profits and losses determined?
* Why is marginal revenue less than price?
* How is long-run equilibrium determined?

The Firm's Demand and Marginal Revenue Curve

Suppose the Coffee Bean decides to raise its price on caffè lattes from $2.75 to $3.00, as seen in Exhibit 1. The Coffee Bean is one of many places to get caffè lattes in town (Starbucks, Diedrich's, Peet's, and others). At the higher price, $3.00, a number of Coffee Bean customers will switch to other places in town for their caffè lattes, but not everyone. Some may not switch; perhaps because of the location, the ambience, the selection of other drinks, or the quality of the coffee. Because there are many substitutes and the fact that some will not change, the demand curve will be very elastic (flat) but not horizontal, as

seen in Exhibit 1. That is, unlike the perfectly competitive firm, a monopolistically competitive firm faces a downward-sloping demand curve. The increase in price from $2.75 to $3.00 leads to a reduction in caffè lattes sold from 2,400 per month to 800 per month.

Let's continue our example with the Coffee Bean. In the table in Exhibit 2, we will show how a monopolistically competitive firm must cut its price to sell more and why its marginal revenue will therefore lie below its demand curve. For simplicity, we will use caffè lattes sold per hour. The first two columns in the table show the demand schedule. If the Coffee Bean charges $4.00 for a caffè latte, no one will buy it and will buy their caffè lattes at another store. If it charges $3.50, it will sell one caffè latte per hour. And if the Coffee Bean wants to sell 2 caffè lattes, it must lower the price to

Downward-Sloping Demand
for Caffè Lattes
at the Coffee Bean

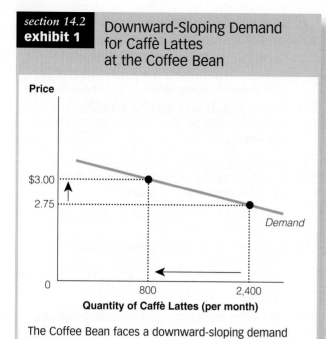

The Coffee Bean faces a downward-sloping demand curve. If the price of coffee increases at the Coffee Bean, some but not all of its customers will leave. In this case, an increase in its price from $2.75 to $3.00 leads to a reduction in caffè lattes sold from 2,400 per month to 800 per month.

1 unit. For example, when the Coffee Bean sells 2 caffè lattes its total revenue is $6.00. Increasing output to 3 caffè lattes will increase total revenue to $7.50. Thus, the marginal revenue is $1.50; $7.50 − $6.00.

It is important to notice in Exhibit 3 that the marginal revenue curve is below the demand curve. That is, the price on all units must fall if the firm increases its production; consequently, marginal revenue must be less than price. This is true for all firms that face a downward-sloping demand curve. Recall from the Monopoly chapter, when the firm sells more output there are two effects; the output effect and the price effect. For example, in Exhibit 4, we see that if the Coffee Bean wants to sell 4 caffè lattes rather than 3 caffè lattes it will have to lower its price on all 4 caffè lattes from $2.50 to $2.00. This is the *price effect*; the lower price leads to a loss in total revenue ($0.50 × 3 = $1.50). There is also an *output effect*; more output is sold when the Coffee Bean lowers its price ($2 × 1 = $2). That is, more output is sold which increases total revenue. It is the price effect that leads to lower revenue; consequently, marginal revenue is less than price for all firms that face a downward-sloping demand curve. Marginal revenue can become negative when the price effect on revenue is greater than the output effect. Recall, there is no price effect in perfectly competitive markets because the firm can sell all it wants at the going market price.

$3.00, and so on. If we were to graph these numbers, we would get a downward-sloping demand curve.

The third column presents the *total revenue*—the quantity sold (column 1) times the price (column 2). The fourth column shows the firm's *average revenue*—the amount of revenue the firm receives per unit sold. We compute average revenue by dividing total revenue (column 3) by output (column 1) or $AR = TR/q$. In the last column, we show the marginal revenue the firm receives for each additional caffè latte. We find this by looking at the change in total revenue when output changes by

Determining Short-Run Equilibrium

Because monopolistically competitive sellers are price makers rather than price takers, they do not regard price as a given by market conditions like perfectly competitive firms.

Demand and Marginal Revenue for Caffè Lattes at the Coffee Bean

Caffè Lattes Sold (q)	Price (P)	Total Revenue (TR = P × q)	Average Revenue (AR = TR/q)	Marginal Revenue (MR = ΔTR/Δq)
0	$4.00	$ 0	—	
1	3.50	3.50	$3.50	$ 3.50
2	3.00	6.00	3.00	2.50
3	2.50	7.50	2.50	1.50
4	2.00	8.00	2.00	0.50
5	1.50	7.50	1.50	−0.50
6	1.00	6.00	1.00	−1.50

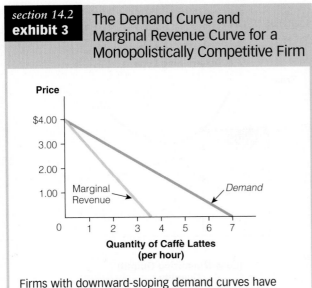

section 14.2
exhibit 3   The Demand Curve and Marginal Revenue Curve for a Monopolistically Competitive Firm

Firms with downward-sloping demand curves have marginal revenue curves that are below the demand curve. Because the price of all units sold must fall if the firm increases production, marginal revenue is less than price.

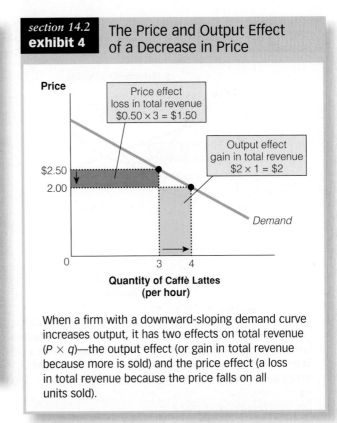

section 14.2
exhibit 4   The Price and Output Effect of a Decrease in Price

When a firm with a downward-sloping demand curve increases output, it has two effects on total revenue ($P \times q$)—the output effect (or gain in total revenue because more is sold) and the price effect (a loss in total revenue because the price falls on all units sold).

The cost and revenue curves of a typical seller are shown in Exhibit 5; the intersection of the marginal revenue and marginal cost curves indicates that the short-run profit-maximizing output will be q^*. Now, by observing how much will be demanded at that output level, we find our profit-maximizing price, P^*. That is, at the equilibrium quantity, q^*, we go vertically to the demand curve and read the corresponding price on the vertical axis, P^*.

Three-Step Method for Monopolistic Competition

Let us return to the same three-step method we used in Chapters 12 and 13. Determining whether a firm is generating economic profits, economic losses, or zero economic profits at the profit-maximizing level of output, q^*, can be done in three easy steps.

1. Find where marginal revenues equal marginal costs and proceed straight down to the horizontal quantity axis to find q^*, the profit-maximizing output level.

2. At q^*, go straight up to the demand curve then to the left to find the market price, P^*. Once you have identified P^* and q^*, you can find total revenue at the profit-maximizing output level, because $TR = P \times q$.

3. The last step is to find total costs. Again, go straight up from q^* to the average total cost (ATC) curve then left to the vertical axis to compute the average total cost *per unit*. If we multiply average total costs by the output level, we can find the total costs ($TC = ATC \times q$).

If total revenue is greater than total costs at q^*, the firm is generating total economic profits. And if total revenue is less than total costs at q^*, the firm is generating total economic losses.

Or, if we take the product price at P^* and subtract the average cost at q^*, this will give us per-unit profit. If we multiply this by output, we will arrive at total economic profit, that is, $(P^* - ATC) \times q^* =$ total profit.

Remember, the cost curves include implicit and explicit costs—that is, even at zero economic profits the firm is covering the total opportunity costs of its resources and earning a normal profit or rate of return.

Short-Run Profits and Losses in Monopolistic Competition

Exhibit 5(a) shows the equilibrium position of a monopolistically competitive firm. As we just discussed, the firm produces where $MC = MR$, or output

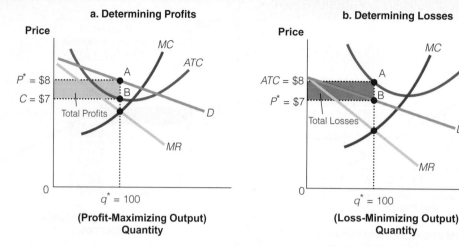

a. Determining Profits

b. Determining Losses

In (a) the firm is making short-run economic profits because the firm's total revenue ($P^* \times q^*$ = $800) at output q^* is greater than the firm's total cost ($ATC \times q^*$ = $700). Because the firm's total revenue is greater than total cost, the firm has a total profit of $100; $TR - TC$ = $800 - $700. In (b) the firm is incurring a short-run economic loss because at q^*, price is below average total cost. At q^*, total cost ($ATC \times q^*$ = $800) is greater than total revenue ($P^* \times q^*$ = $700), so the firm incurs a total loss ($TR - TC$ = $700 - $800 = -$100).

q^*. At output q^* and price P^*, the firm's total revenue is equal to $P^* \times q^*$, or $800. At output q^*, the firm's total cost is $ATC \times q^*$, or $700. In Exhibit 5(a), we see that total revenue is greater than total cost so the firm has a total economic profit. That is, TR ($800) − TC ($700) = total economic profit ($100) or P^* ($8) − ATC ($7) $\times q^*$ (100) = $100.

In Exhibit 5(b), at q^*, price is below average total cost, so the firm is minimizing its economic loss. At q^*, total cost ($800) is greater than total revenue ($700). So the firm incurs a total loss ($100) or P^* ($7) − ATC ($8) $\times q^*$ (100) = total economic losses (−$100).

Determining Long-Run Equilibrium

The short-run equilibrium situation, whether involving profits or losses, will probably not last long, because entry and exit occur in the long run. If market entry and exit are sufficiently free, new firms will have an incentive to enter the market when there are economic profits, and exit when there are economic losses.

What Happens to Economic Profits When Firms Enter the Industry?

In Exhibit 6(a), we see the market impact as new firms enter to take advantage of the economic profits. The result of this influx is more sellers of similar products, which means that each new firm will cut into the demand of the existing firms. That is, the demand curve for each of the existing firms will fall. With entry, not only will the firm's demand curve move inward but it also becomes relatively more elastic due to each firm's products having more substitutes (more choices for consumers). We see this situation in Exhibit 6(a) when demand shifts leftward from D_{SR} to D_{LR}. This decline in demand continues to occur until the average total cost (ATC) curve becomes tangent with the demand curve, and economic profits are reduced to zero.

What Happens to Losses When Some Firms Exit?

When firms are making economic losses, some firms will exit the industry. As some firms exit, it means fewer firms in the market, which increases the demand for the remaining firms' product, shifting their demand curves to the right, from D_{SR} to D_{LR} as seen in

section 14.2
exhibit 6 Market Entry and Exit in the Long Run

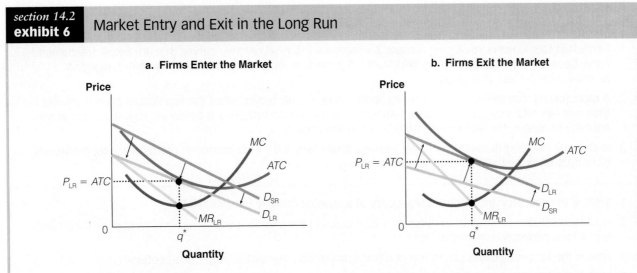

In (a), excess profits attract new firms into the industry. As a result, the firm's share of the market declines and demand shifts down. Profits are eliminated when P_{LR} = ATC, that is, when the ATC curve is tangent to D_{LR}. In (b), some firms exit because of economic losses. Their exit increases the demand for existing firms, shifting D_{SR} to D_{LR}, where all losses have been eliminated.

Exhibit 6(b). When firms exit not only will the firm's demand curve move outward but it also becomes relatively more inelastic due to each firm's products having fewer substitutes (less choices for consumers). The higher demand results in smaller losses for the existing firms until all losses finally disappear where the ATC curve is tangent to the demand curve.

Achieving Long-Run Equilibrium

Long-run equilibrium will occur when demand is equal to average total costs for each firm at a level of output at which each firm's demand curve is just tangent to its ATC curve. The point of tangency will always occur at the same level of output as that at which marginal cost is equal to marginal revenue, as seen in Exhibit 7. At this equilibrium point, there are zero economic profits and there are no incentives for firms to either enter or exit the industry.

However, complete adjustment toward equality of price with average cost may be checked by the strength of reputation built up by established firms. Those firms that are particularly successful in their selling efforts may create such strong consumer preferences that newcomers—even though they are able to enter the industry freely and cover their own costs—will not take sufficient business away from the well-established firms to eliminate their excess profits.

section 14.2
exhibit 7 Long-Run Equilibrium for a Monopolistically Competitive Firm

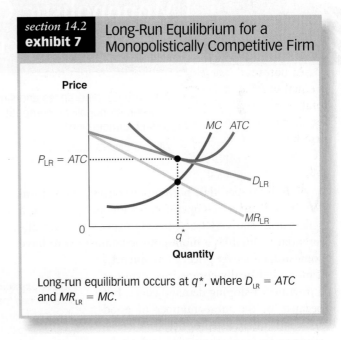

Long-run equilibrium occurs at q*, where D_{LR} = ATC and MR_{LR} = MC.

Thus, a restaurant that has been particularly successful in promoting customer goodwill may continue to earn excess profits long after the entry of new firms has brought about equality of price and average cost for the others, or even losses. Adjustments toward a final equilibrium situation involving equality of price and average cost do not proceed with the certainty that is supposed to be characteristic of perfect competition.

1. Firms that face downward-sloping demand curves have marginal revenue curves that are below the demand curve because the price on all units sold must fall if the firm increases production. Therefore, marginal revenue must be less than price.

2. A monopolistic competitive firm is making short-run economic profits when the equilibrium price is greater than average total costs at the equilibrium output; when equilibrium price is below average total cost at the equilibrium output, the firm is minimizing its economic loss.

3. In the long run, equilibrium price equals average total costs. With that, economic profits are zero, eliminating incentives for firms to either enter or exit the industry.

1. What is the short-run profit-maximizing policy of a monopolistically competitive firm?

2. How is the choice of whether to operate or shut down in the short run the same for a monopolistic competitor as for a perfectly competitive firm?

3. How is the long-run equilibrium of monopolistic competition like that of perfect competition?

4. How is the long-run equilibrium of monopolistic competition different from that of perfect competition?

SECTION 14.3

Monopolistic Competition Versus Perfect Competition

* What are the differences and similarities between monopolistic competition and perfect competition?

* What is excess capacity?

* Why does the monopolistically competitive firm fail to meet productive efficiency?

* Why does the monopolistically competitive firm fail to meet allocative efficiency?

We have seen that both monopolistic competition and perfect competition have many buyers and sellers and relatively free entry. However, product differentiation enables a monopolistic competitor to have some influence over price. Consequently, a monopolistically competitive firm has a downward-sloping demand curve, but because of the large number of good substitutes for its product, the curve tends to be much more elastic than the demand curve for a monopolist.

excess capacity
occurs when the firm produces below the level where average total cost is minimized

The Significance of Excess Capacity

Because in monopolistic competition the demand curve is downward sloping, its point of tangency with the *ATC* curve will not and cannot be at the lowest level of average cost. What does this statement mean? It means that even when long-run adjustments are complete, firms are not operating at a level that permits the lowest average cost of production—the efficient scale of the firm. The existing plant, even though optimal for the equilibrium volume of output, is not used to capacity; that is, excess capacity exists at that level of output. Excess capacity occurs when the firm produces below the level where average total cost is minimized.

Unlike a perfectly competitive firm, a monopolistically competitive firm could increase output and lower its average total cost, as shown in Exhibit 1(a). However, any attempt to increase output to attain lower average cost would be unprofitable,

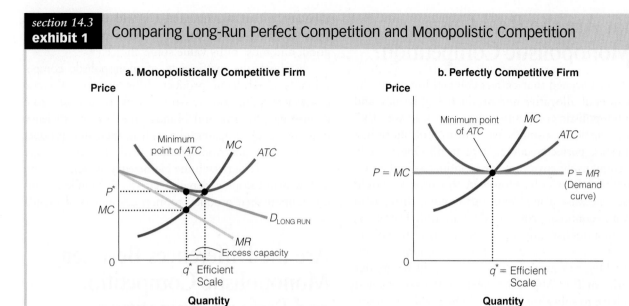

Comparing the differences between perfect competition and monopolistic competition, we see that the monopolistically competitive firm fails to meet both productive efficiency, minimizing costs in the long run, and allocative efficiency, producing output where $P = MC$.

because the price reduction necessary to sell the greater output would cause marginal revenue to fall below the marginal cost of the increased output. As we can see in Exhibit 1(a), to the right of q^*, marginal cost is greater than marginal revenue. Consequently, in monopolistic competition, the tendency is too many firms in the industry, each producing a volume of output less than what would allow lowest cost. Economists call this tendency a failure to reach productive efficiency. For example, the market may have too many grocery stores or too many service stations, in the sense that if the total volume of business were concentrated in a smaller number of sellers, average cost, and thus price, could in principle be less.

Failing to Meet Allocative Efficiency, Too

Productive inefficiency is not the only problem with a monopolistically competitive firm. Exhibit 1(a) shows a firm that is not operating where price is equal to marginal costs. In the monopolistically competitive model, at the intersection of the *MC* and *MR*

curves (q^*), we can clearly see that price is greater than marginal cost. Society is willing to pay more for the product (the price, P^*) than it costs society to produce it (MC at q^*). In this case, the firm is failing to reach allocative efficiency, where price equals marginal cost. Because the price is greater than the marginal cost, it would be profitable for the monopolistically competitive firm to sell to another customer. If it were a perfectly competitive firm it would not care because price is equal to marginal cost and the extra profit from another customer would be zero.

In short, firms are not producing at the minimum point of ATC, failing to meet productive efficiency and firms are not charging a price equal to marginal cost; failing to meet allocative efficiency. Note that in Exhibit 1(b), the perfectly competitive firm has reached both productive efficiency ($P = ATC$ at the minimum point on the *ATC* curve) and allocative efficiency ($P = MC$).

However, in defense of monopolistic competition, the higher average cost and the slightly higher price and lower output may simply be the price firms pay for differentiated products—variety. That is, just because monopolistically competitive firms have not met the conditions for productive and allocative efficiency, it is not obvious that society is not better off.

What Are the Real Costs of Monopolistic Competition?

We just argued that perfect competition meets the tests of allocative and productive efficiency and that monopolistic competition does not. Can we "fix" a monopolistically competitive firm to look more like an efficient, perfectly competitive firm? One remedy might entail using government regulation, as in the case of a natural monopoly. However, this process would be costly because a monopolistically competitive firm makes no economic profits in the long run. Therefore, asking monopolistically competitive firms to equate price and marginal cost would lead to economic losses, because long-run average total cost would be greater than price at $P = MC$. Consequently, the government would have to subsidize the firm. Living with the inefficiencies in monopolistically competitive markets might be easier than coping with the difficulties entailed by regulations and the cost of the necessary subsidies.

We argued that the monopolistically competitive firm does not operate at the minimum point of the *ATC* curve while the perfectly competitive firm does. However, is this comparison fair? A monopolistic competition involves differentiated goods and services, while a perfect competition does not. In other words, the excess capacity that exists in monopolistic competition is the price we pay for product differentiation. Have you ever thought about the many restaurants, movies, and gasoline stations that have "excess capacity"? Can you imagine a world where all firms were working at full capacity? After all, choice is a good, and most of us value some choice.

In short, the inefficiency of monopolistic competition is a result of product differentiation. Because consumers value variety—the ability to choose from competing products and brands—the loss in efficiency must be weighed against the gain in increased product variety. The gains from product diversity can be large and may easily outweigh the inefficiency associated with a downward-sloping demand curve. Remember, firms differentiate their products to meet consumers' demand.

Are the Differences Between Monopolistic Competition and Perfect Competition Exaggerated?

The significance of the difference between the relationship of marginal cost to price in monopolistic competition and in perfect competition can easily be exaggerated. As long as preferences for various brands are not extremely strong, the demand for a firm's products will be highly elastic (flat). Accordingly, the points of tangency with the *ATC* curves are not likely to be far above the point of lowest cost, and excess capacity will be small, as illustrated in Exhibit 2. Only if differentiation is strong will the difference between the long-run

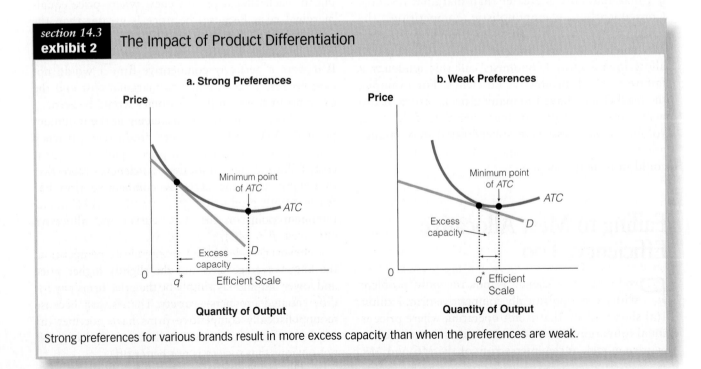

section 14.3
exhibit 2   The Impact of Product Differentiation

Strong preferences for various brands result in more excess capacity than when the preferences are weak.

price level and the price that would prevail under perfectly competitive conditions be significant.

Remember this little caveat: The theory of the firm is like a road map that does not detail every gully, creek, and hill but does give directions to get from one geographic point to another. Any particular theory of the firm may not tell precisely how an individual firm will operate, but it does provide valuable insight into the ways firms will tend to react to changing economic conditions such as entry, demand, and cost changes.

SECTION CHECK

1. Both the competitive firm and the monopolistically competitive firm may earn short-run economic profits, but these profits will be eliminated in the long run.

2. Because monopolistically competitive firms face a downward-sloping demand curve, average total cost is not minimized in the long run, after entry and exit have eliminated profits. Monopolistically competitive firms fail to reach productive efficiency, producing at output levels less than the efficient output.

3. The monopolistically competitive firm does not achieve allocative efficiency, because it does not operate where the price is equal to marginal costs, which means that society is willing to pay more for additional output than it costs society to produce additional output.

---

1. Why is a monopolistic competitor's demand curve relatively elastic (flat)?

2. Why do monopolistically competitive firms produce at less than the efficient scale of production?

3. Why do monopolistically competitive firms operate with excess capacity?

4. Why does the fact that price exceeds marginal cost in monopolistic competition lead to allocative inefficiency?

5. What is the price we pay for differentiated goods under monopolistic competition?

6. Why is the difference between the long-run equilibriums under perfect competition and monopolistic competition likely to be relatively small?

SECTION 14.4   Advertising

* Why do firms advertise?
* Is advertising good or bad from society's perspective?

* Will advertising always increase costs?
* Can advertising increase demand?

Why Do Firms Advertise?

Advertising is an important nonprice method of competition that is commonly used in industries where the firm has market power. It would make little sense for a perfectly competitive firm to advertise its products. Recall that the perfectly competitive firm sells a homogeneous product and can sell all it wants at the market price—so why spend money to advertise to encourage consumers to buy more of its product? Why do some firms advertise? The reason is simple: By advertising, firms hope to increase the demand and create a less elastic demand curve for their products, thus enhancing revenues and profits. In short, this is how monopolistically competitive firms can differentiate their products to appeal to consumers. Advertising is part of our life, whether we are watching television, listening to the radio, reading a newspaper or magazine, or simply driving down the highway. Firms that sell differentiated products can spend between 10 and 20 percent of their revenue on advertising. Advertising to differentiate products is also important in oligopoly, as we will see in the next chapter.

QWhy is it so important for monopolistically competitive firms to advertise?

AOwners of fast-food restaurants must compete with many other restaurants, so they often must advertise to demonstrate that their restaurant is dif-
ferent. Advertising may convince customers that a firm's products or services are better than others, which then may influence the shape and position of the demand curve for the products and potentially increase profits. Remember, monopolistically competitive firms are different from competitive firms because of their ability, to some extent, to set prices.

Is Advertising "Good" or "Bad" from Society's Perspective?

What Is the Impact of Advertising on Society?

This question elicits sharply different responses. Some have argued that advertising manipulates consumer tastes and wastes billions of dollars annually creating "needs" for trivial products. Advertising helps create a demonstration effect, whereby people have new urges to buy products previously unknown to them. In creating additional demands for private goods, the ability to provide needed public goods (for which little advertising is needed to create demand) is potentially reduced. Moreover, sometimes advertising is based on misleading claims, so people find themselves buying products that do not provide the satisfaction or results promised in the ads. Finally, advertising itself requires resources that raise average costs and increase prices.

On the other hand, who is to say that the purchase of any product is frivolous or unnecessary? If one believes that people are rational and should be permitted freedom of expression, the argument against advertising loses some of its force. In addition, advertisers might be focusing in on what consumer's want rather than what producers want to sell.

Furthermore, defenders of advertising argue that firms use advertising to provide important information about the price and availability of a product, the location and hours of store operation, and so on. For example, a real estate ad might state when a rental unit is available, the location, the price, the number of bedrooms and bathrooms, wood floors, and proximity to mass transit, freeways, or schools. This information allows for customers to make better choices and allows markets to function more efficiently. An

expensive ad on television or in the telephone book *may signal* to consumers that this product may come from a relatively large and successful company. Finally, a nationally recognized *brand name* will provide consumers with confidence about the quality of its product. It will also distinguish its product from others. For example, brand names such as Ritz-Carlton, Double Tree, or Motel 6 will provide the buyer with information about the quality of the accommodations more so than the No-Tell Motel. Or consider a national chain restaurant such as McDonald's or Burger King versus the Greasy Spoon Coffee Shop—consumers expect consistent quality from a chain restaurant. The chain name may also send a *signal* to the buyer that the company expects repeat business and, therefore, it has an important reputation to uphold. This aspect may help it assume even greater quality in the consumers' eyes.

Will Advertising Always Increase Costs?

Even though it is true that advertising may raise the average total cost, it is possible that when substantial economies of scale exist, the average production cost will decline more than the amount of the per-unit cost of advertising. In other words, average total cost, in some situations, actually declines after extensive advertising, because advertising may allow the firm to operate closer to the point of minimum cost on its ATC curve. Specifically, notice in Exhibit 1 that the average total cost curve before advertising is $ATC_{BEFORE\ ADVERTISING}$. After advertising, the curve shifts upward to $ATC_{AFTER\ ADVERTISING}$. If the increase in demand resulting from advertising is significant, economies of scale from higher output levels may offset the advertising costs. Average total cost may fall from C_1 to C_2, a movement from point A to point B, and allow the firm to sell its product at a lower price. Therefore, it is possible for the decline in production costs (through specialization and division of labor in the short run and/or economies of scale in the long run) to exceed the added advertising cost, per unit of output, thus allowing the firm to sell its product at a lower price; Toys"R"Us versus a smaller, owner-operated toy store provides an example.

However, it also is possible that an advertising war between two firms, say Burger King and McDonald's, will result in higher advertising costs for both and no gain in market share (increased output) for either. This possibility is shown as a movement from point A to point C in Exhibit 2. Output remains at q_1, but average total cost rises from C_1 to C_3.

Firms in monopolistic competition are not likely to experience substantial cost reductions as output increases. Therefore, they probably will not be able to offset advertising costs with lower production costs, particularly if advertising costs are high. Even if advertising does add to total cost, however, it is true that advertising conveys information. Through advertising, customers become aware of the options available to them in terms of product choice. Advertising helps customers choose products that best meet their needs, and it informs price-conscious customers about the costs of products. In this way, advertising lowers information costs, which is one reason that the Federal Trade Commission opposes bans on advertising.

What If Advertising Increases Competition?

The idea that advertising reduces information costs leads to some interesting economic implications. For example, say that as a result of advertising, we know about more products that may be substitutes for the products we have been buying for years. That is, the more goods that are advertised, the more consumers are aware of "substitute" products, which leads to increasingly competitive markets. Studies in the eyeglass,

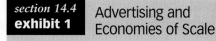

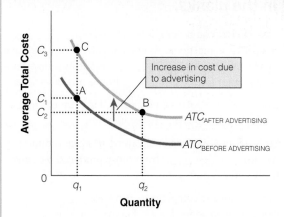

section 14.4
exhibit 1
Advertising and Economies of Scale

The average total cost before advertising is shown as $ATC_{BEFORE\ ADVERTISING}$. After advertising, the curve shifts to $ATC_{AFTER\ ADVERTISING}$. If the increase in demand resulting from advertising is significant, economies of scale from higher output levels may offset the advertising costs, lowering average total cost. The movement from point A to point B allows the firm to sell its product at a lower price. However, when two firms engage in an advertising war, it is possible that neither will gain market share (increased output) but each will incur higher advertising costs. This possibility is shown as a movement from point A to point C—output remains at q_1, but average total cost rises from C_1 to C_3.

toy, and drug industries have shown that advertising increases competition and leads to lower prices in these markets. In short, critics of advertising argue that impedes competition, alters consumer's tastes and may lead to "irrational" brand loyalty. But defenders believe it can increase competition and quality and often provides valuable product and service information.

SECTION CHECK

1. With advertising, a firm hopes it can alter the elasticity of the demand for its product, making it more inelastic and causing an increase in demand that will enhance profits.

2. To some, advertising manipulates consumer tastes and creates "needs" for trivial products. However, if one believes that people act rationally, this argument loses some of its force.

3. Where substantial economies of scale exist, it is possible that average production costs will decline more than the amount of per-unit costs of advertising in the long run. Even in the short run, specialization and division of labor may cause advertising to decrease average costs.

4. By making consumers aware of different "substitute" products, advertising may lead to more competitive markets and lower consumer prices.

1. How can advertising make a firm's demand curve more inelastic?

2. What are the arguments made against advertising?

3. What are the arguments made for advertising?

4. Can advertising actually result in lower costs? How?

Interactive Chapter Summary

Fill in the blanks:

1. Monopolistic competition is similar to both _____ and perfect competition. As in monopoly, firms have some control over market _____, but as in perfect competition, they face _____ from many other sellers.

2. Due to the free entry of new firms, long-run economic profits in monopolistic competition are _____.

3. Firms in monopolistic competition produce products that are _____ from those produced by other firms in the industry.

4. In monopolistic competition, firms use _____ names to gain some degree of control over price.

5. The theory of monopolistic competition is based on three characteristics: (1) product _____, (2) many _____, and (3) free _____.

6. Product differentiation is the accentuation of _____ product qualities to develop a product identity.

7. Monopolistic competitive sellers are price _____ and they do not regard price as given by the market. Because products in the industry are slightly different each firm faces a(n) _____ sloping demand curve.

8. In the short run, equilibrium output is determined where marginal revenue equals marginal _____. The price is set equal to the _____ the consumer will pay for this amount.

9. When price is greater than average total costs, the monopolistic competitive firm will make an economic _____.

10. Barriers to entry do not protect monopolistic competitive firms in the _____ run. Economic profits will _____ new firms to the industry. Similarly, firms will leave when there are economic _____.

11. Long-run equilibrium in a monopolistic competitive industry occurs when the firm experiences _____ economic profits or losses, which eliminates incentive for firms to _____ or _____ the industry.

12. Because it faces competition, a monopolistically competitive firm has a (n) _____ sloping demand curve that tends to be more _____ than the demand curve for a monopolist.

13. Even in the long run, monopolistically competitive firms do not operate at levels that permit the full realization of _____ of scale.

14. Unlike a perfectly competitive firm in long-run equilibrium, a monopolistically competitive firm will produce with _____ capacity. The firm could lower average costs by increasing output, but this move would reduce _____.

15. In monopolistic competition the tendency is toward too _____ firms in the industry. Monopolistically competitive industries will not reach _____ efficiency, because firms in the industry do not produce at the _____ per-unit cost.

16. In monopolistic competition, firms operate where price is _____ than marginal cost, which means that consumers are willing to pay _____ for the product than it costs society to produce it. In this case, the firm fails to reach _____ efficiency.

17. Although average costs and prices are higher under monopolistic competition than they are under perfect competition, society gets a benefit from monopolistic competition in the form of _____ products.

18. Advertising is an important type of _____ competition that firms use to _____ the demand for their products.

19. Advertising may not only increase the demand facing a firm, it may also make the demand facing the firm more _____ if it convinces buyers the product is truly different. A more inelastic demand curve means price changes will have relatively _____ effects on the quantity demanded of the product.

20. Critics of advertising assert that it _____ average total costs while manipulating consumers' tastes. However, if people are _____, this argument loses some of its force.

21. When advertising is used in industries with significant economies of _____, per-unit costs may decline by more than per-unit advertising costs.

22. An important function of advertising is to lower the cost of acquiring _____ about the availability of substitutes and the _____ of products.

23. By making information about substitutes and prices less costly to acquire, advertising will increase the _____ in industries, which is good for consumers.

Key Terms and Concepts

monopolistic competition   401   product differentiation   401   excess capacity   408

Section Check Answers

14.1 Monopolistic Competition

1. How is monopolistic competition a mixture of monopoly and perfect competition?

Monopolistic competition is like monopoly in that sellers' actions can change the price. It is like competition in that it is characterized by competition from substitute products, many sellers, and relatively free entry.

2. Why is product differentiation necessary for monopolistic competition?

Product differentiation is the source of the monopoly power each monopolistically competitive seller (a monopolist of its own brand) has. If products were homogeneous, others' products would be perfect substitutes for the products of any particular firm, and such a firm would have no market power as a result.

3. What are some common forms of product differentiation?

Forms of product differentiation include physical differences, prestige differences, location differences, and service differences.

4. Why are many sellers necessary for monopolistic competition?

Many sellers are necessary in the monopolistic competition model because it means that a particular firm has little control over what other firms do; with only a few firms in an industry, they would begin to consider competitors as individuals (rather than only as a group) whose policies will be influenced by their own actions.

5. Why is free entry necessary for monopolistic competition?

Free entry is necessary in the monopolistic competition model because entry in this type of market is what tends to eliminate economic profits in the long run, as in perfect competition.

14.2 Price and Output Determination in Monopolistic Competition

1. What is the short-run profit-maximizing policy of a monopolistically competitive firm?

A monopolistic competitor maximizes its short-run profits by producing the quantity (and corresponding price along the demand curve) at which marginal revenue equals marginal cost.

2. How is the choice of whether to operate or shut down in the short run the same for a monopolistic competitor as for a perfectly competitive firm?

Because a firm will lose its fixed costs if it shuts down, it will shut down if price is expected to remain below average variable cost, regardless of market structure, because operating in that situation results in even greater losses than shutting down.

3. How is the long-run equilibrium of monopolistic competition like that of perfect competition?

The long-run equilibrium of monopolistic competition is like that of perfect competition in that entry, when the industry makes short-run economic profits, and exit, when it makes short-run economic losses, drives economic profits to zero in the long run.

4. How is the long-run equilibrium of monopolistic competition different from that of perfect competition?

For zero economic profits in long-run equilibrium at the same time each seller faces a downward-sloping demand curve, a firm's downward-sloping demand curve must be just tangent to its average cost curve (because that is the situation where a firm earns zero economic profits and that is the best the firm can do), resulting in costs greater than the minimum possible average cost. This same tangency to long-run cost curves characterizes the long-run zero economic profit equilibrium in perfect competition; but because firm demand curves are horizontal in perfect competition, that tangency comes at the minimum point of firm average cost curves.

14.3 Monopolistic Competition Versus Perfect Competition

1. Why is a monopolistic competitor's demand curve relatively elastic (flat)?

A monopolistic competitor has a downward-sloping demand curve because of product differentiation; but because of the large number of good substitutes for its product, its demand curve is very elastic.

2. **Why do monopolistically competitive firms produce at less than the efficient scale of production?**

Because monopolistically competitive firms have downward-sloping demand curves, their long-run zero-profit equilibrium tangency between demand and long-run average total cost must occur along the downward-sloping part of the long-run average total cost curve. Because this level of output does not allow the full realization of all economies of scale, it results in a less than efficient scale of production.

3. **Why do monopolistically competitive firms operate with excess capacity?**

Monopolistically competitive firms operate with excess capacity because the zero-profit tangency equilibrium occurs along the downward-sloping part of a firm's short-run average cost curve, so the firm's plant has the capacity to produce more output at lower average cost than it is actually producing.

4. **Why does the fact that price exceeds marginal cost in monopolistic competition lead to allocative inefficiency?**

The fact that price exceeds marginal cost in monopolistic competition leads to allocative inefficiency because some goods for which the marginal value (measured by willingness to pay along a demand curve) exceeds their marginal cost are not traded and the net gains that would have resulted from those trades are therefore lost. However, the degree of that inefficiency is relatively small because firms face a very elastic demand curve so the resulting output restriction is small.

5. **What is the price we pay for differentiated goods under monopolistic competition?**

Under monopolistic competition, excess capacity can be considered the price we pay for differentiated goods, because it is the "cost" we pay for the value we get from the additional choices and variety offered by differentiated products.

6. **Why is the difference between the long-run equilibriums under perfect competition and monopolistic competition likely to be relatively small?**

Even though monopolistically competitive firms face downward-sloping demand curves, which is the cause of the excess capacity and higher than necessary costs in these markets, those demand curves are likely to be highly elastic because of the large number of close substitutes. Therefore, the deviation from perfectly competitive results is likely to be relatively small.

14.4 Advertising

1. **How can advertising make a firm's demand curve more inelastic?**

Advertising is intended to increase a firm's demand curve by increasing consumer awareness of the firm's products and improving its image. It is intended to make its demand curve more inelastic by convincing buyers that its products are truly different (better) than alternatives (remember that the number of good substitutes is the primary determinant of a firm's elasticity of demand).

2. **What are the arguments made against advertising?**

Some people argue that advertising manipulates consumer tastes and creates artificial "needs" for unimportant products, taking resources away from more valuable uses.

3. **What are the arguments made for advertising?**

The essential argument for advertising is that it conveys valuable information to potential customers about the products and options available to them and the prices at which they are available, helping them to make choices that better match their situations and preferences.

4. **Can advertising actually result in lower costs? How?**

Advertising can lower costs by increasing sales, thereby lowering production costs if a company can realize economies of scale. Overall costs and prices may be lowered as a result, if the savings in production costs are greater than the additional costs of advertising.

True or False:

1. Monopolistic competition is a mixture of monopoly and perfect competition.

2. All firms in monopolistically competitive industries earn economic profits in the long run.

3. By differentiating their products and promoting brand-name loyalty, firms in monopolistic competition can raise prices without losing all their customers.

4. In monopolistic competition, as in perfect competition, all firms in an industry charge the same price.

5. Competitive firms and monopolistic competitive firms follow the same general rule when deciding how much to produce.

6. A monopolistic competitor's demand curve is relatively inelastic (steep).

7. Unlike perfectly competitive firms, firms in monopolistic competition will operate with excess capacity, even in the long run.

8. Although certain inefficiencies are associated with monopolistic competition, society receives a benefit from monopolistic competition in the form of differentiated goods and services.

9. Even though advertising will add to the cost of production, it may lead to significant economies of scale that may lower the per-unit total cost.

10. Misleading claims and preposterous bragging about products are a type of advertising that will result in increased demand for a firm's products.

Multiple Choice:

1. Which of the following is *not* a source of product differentiation?
   a. physical differences in products
   b. differences in quantities that firms offer for sale
   c. differences in service provided by firms
   d. differences in location of sales outlets

2. Which of the following characteristics do monopolistic competition and perfect competition have in common?
   a. Individual firms believe that they can influence market price.
   b. Firms sell brand-name products.
   c. Firms are able to earn long-run economic profits.
   d. Competing firms can enter the industry easily.

3. Firms in monopolistically competitive industries cannot earn economic profits in the long run because
   a. government regulators, whose first interest is the public good, will impose regulations that limit economic profits.
   b. the additional costs of product differentiation will eliminate long-run economic profits.
   c. economic profits will attract competitors whose presence will eliminate profits in the long run.
   d. whenever one firm in the industry begins making economic profits, others will lower their prices, thus eliminating long-run economic profits.

4. Maria's West Side Bakery is the only bakery on the west side of the city. She is a monopolistic competitor and she is open for business. Which of the following *cannot* be true of Maria's profits?
   a. She is making an economic profit.
   b. She is making neither an economic profit nor a loss.
   c. She is making an economic loss that is less than her fixed cost.
   d. She is making an economic loss that is greater than her fixed cost.

5. Claire is considering buying the only Hungarian restaurant in Boise, Idaho. The restaurant's unique food means that it faces a negatively sloped demand curve and is currently earning an economic profit. Why shouldn't Claire assume that the current profits will continue when she makes her decision?
   a. Claire will not earn those profits right away because she doesn't know much about cooking.
   b. The firm is a monopolist, which attracts government regulation.
   c. Current economic profits will be eliminated by the entry of competitors.
   d. While economic profits are positive, accounting profits may be negative.

Use the accompanying diagram to answer questions 6–7.

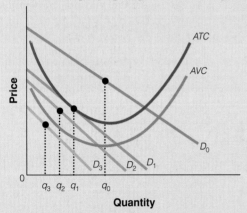

6. Which of the demand curves represents a long-run equilibrium for the firm?
   a. D_0
   b. D_1
   c. D_2
   d. D_3

7. Which of the demand curves will result in the firm shutting down in the short run?
   a. D_0
   b. D_1
   c. D_2
   d. D_3

8. In the long run, firms in monopolistic competition do not attain productive efficiency because they produce
   a. at a point where economic profits are positive.
   b. at a point where marginal revenue is less than marginal cost.
   c. at a point to the left of the low point of their long-run average total cost curve.
   d. where marginal cost is equal to long-run average total cost.

9. In the long run, firms in monopolistic competition do not attain allocative efficiency because they
   a. operate where price equals marginal cost.
   b. do not operate where price equals marginal cost.
   c. produce more output than society wants.
   d. charge prices that are less than production costs.

10. Compared to perfect competition, firms in monopolist competition in the long run produce
    a. less output at a lower cost.
    b. less output at a higher cost.
    c. more output at a lower cost.
    d. more output at a higher cost.

11. If Rolf wants to use advertising to reduce the elasticity of demand for his chiropractic services, he must make sure the advertising
    a. clearly states the prices he charges.
    b. shows that he is producing a product like that of the other chiropractors in town.

c. shows why his services are truly different from the other chiropractors in town.

d. explains the hours and days that he is open for business.

12. Advertising about prices by firms in an industry will make an industry more competitive because it

a. reduces the cost of finding a substitute when one producer raises his price.

b. assures the consumers that prices are the same everywhere.

c. increases the cost for all firms because of the existence of economies of scale.

d. reduces the number of firms because of the existence of economies of scale.

Problems:

1. Which of the following markets are perfectly competitive or monopolistically competitive. Why?
   a. soy market
   b. retail clothing stores
   c. Spago's Restaurant Beverly Hills

2. List three ways in which a grocery store might differentiate itself from its competitors.

3. What might make you choose one gas station over another?

4. If Frank's hot dog stand was profitable when he first opened, why should he expect those profits to fall over time?

5. Draw a graph showing a monopolistically competitive firm in a short-run equilibrium where it is earning positive economic profits. What must be true of price versus average total cost for such a firm? What will happen to the firm's demand curve as a result of the short-run profits?

6. Draw a graph showing a monopolistically competitive firm in a short-run equilibrium where it is earning economic losses. What must be true of price versus average total cost for such a firm? What will happen to the firm's demand curve as a result of the short-run losses?

7. How are monopolistically competitive firms and perfectly competitive firms similar? Why don't monopolistically competitive firms produce the same output in the long run as perfectly competitive firms, which face similar costs?

8. Can you explain why some restaurants are highly profitable while other restaurants in the same general area are going out of business?

9. Suppose that half the restaurants in a city are closed so that the remaining eateries can operate at full capacity. What "cost" might restaurant patrons incur as a result?

10. How is price related to marginal and average total cost for monopolistically competitive firms in the following situations?
    a. a short-run equilibrium where it is earning positive economic profits
    b. a short-run equilibrium where it is earning negative economic profits
    c. a short-run equilibrium where it is earning zero economic profits
    d. a long-run equilibrium

11. What is meant by the price of variety? Graph and explain.

12. How does Starbucks differentiate its product? Why does Starbucks stay open until late at night but a donut or bagel shop might close at noon?

13. How are monopolistically competitive firms and perfectly competitive firms similar? Why don't monopolistically competitive firms produce the same output in the long run as perfectly competitive firms, which face similar costs?

14. Why is advertising more important for the success of chains such as Toys "R" Us and Office Depot than for the corner barbershop?

15. Think of your favorite ads on television. Do you think that these ads have an effect on your spending? These ads are expensive; do you think they are a waste from society's standpoint?

16. Product differentiation is a hallmark of monopolistic competition, and the text lists four sources of such differentiation: physical differences, prestige, location, and service. How do firms in the industries listed here differentiate their products? How important is each of the four sources of differentiation in each case? Give the most important source of differentiation in each case.
    a. fast-food restaurants
    b. espresso shops/carts
    c. hair stylists
    d. soft drinks
    e. wine

17. As you know, perfect competition and monopolistic competition differ in important ways. Show your understanding of these differences by listing the following terms under either "perfect competition" or "monopolistic competition."

		Perfect Competition	Monopolistic Competition
standardized product	productive efficiency	_____	_____
differentiated product	horizontal demand curve	_____	_____
allocative efficiency	downward-sloping demand curve	_____	_____
excess capacity	no control over price	_____	_____

18. In what way is the use of advertising another example of Adam Smith's "Invisible Hand," according to which entrepreneurs pursuing their own best interest make consumers better off?

19. How does advertising intend to shift demand? How does it intend to change the elasticity of demand?

Oligopoly and Strategic Behavior

Oligopoly is a market structure where a few large firms dominate an industry. Examples of oligopolistic markets include commercial airlines, oil, automobiles, steel, breakfast cereals, computers, cigarettes, tobacco, and sports drinks.

In all of these instances, the market is dominated by anywhere from a few to several big companies, although they may have many different brands (e.g., General Motors, General Foods, Apple Computers). In this chapter, we will learn about the unique characteristics of firms in this industry. ■

SECTION 15.1 Oligopoly

* What is oligopoly?
* What is mutual interdependence?
* Are economies of scale a major barrier to entry?

* Why is it so difficult for the oligopolist to determine its profit-maximizing price and output?

What Is Oligopoly?

As we discussed in Chapter 12, oligopolies exist, by definition, where relatively few firms control all or most of the production and sale of a product ("oligopoly" = few sellers). The products may be homogeneous or differentiated, but the barriers to entry are often high, which makes it difficult for firms to enter into the industry. Consequently, long-run economic profits may be earned by firms in the industry.

Mutual Interdependence

Oligopoly is characterized by **mutual interdependence** among firms; that is, each firm shapes its policy with an eye to the policies of competing firms. Oligopolists must strategize, much like good chess or bridge players who are constantly observing and anticipating the moves of their rivals. Oligopoly is likely to occur whenever the number of firms in an industry is so small that any change in output or price by one firm appreciably impacts the sales of competing firms. In this situation, it is almost inevitable that competitors will respond directly to these actions in determining their own policy.

mutual interdependence
when a firm shapes its policy with an eye to the policies of competing firms

Why Do Oligopolies Exist?

Primarily, oligopoly is a result of the relationship between the technological conditions of production and potential sales volume. For many products, a firm cannot obtain a reasonably low cost of production unless it is producing a large fraction of the market output. In other words, substantial economies of scale are present in oligopoly markets. Automobile and steel production are classic examples of this. Because of legal concerns such as patents, large start-up costs, and the presence of pronounced economies of scale, the barriers to entry are quite high in oligopoly.

Measuring Industry Concentration

The extent of oligopoly power in various industries can be measured by means of concentration ratios. A concentration ratio indicates the proportion of total industry shipments (sales) of goods produced by a specified number of the largest firms in the industry, or the proportion of total industry assets held by these largest firms. We can use four-firm or eight-firm concentration ratios; most often, concentration ratios are for the four largest firms.

The extent of oligopoly power is indicated by the four-firm concentration ratio for the United States shown in Exhibit 1. Note that for breakfast cereals, to take an example, the four largest firms produce 87 percent of all breakfast cereals produced in the United

section 15.1
exhibit 1   Four-Firm Concentration Ratios, U.S. Manufacturing

Industry	Share of Value of Shipments by the Top Four Firms (%)
Tobacco products	96
Breweries	91
Motor vehicles	90
Electric lightbulbs	89
Small arms ammunition	89
Refrigerators	88
Breakfast cereals	87
Aircraft	85
Soaps, detergents	73
Tires	69
Motorcycles and bicycles	68
Lawn and garden equipment	65
Coffee and tea	58

SOURCE: U.S. Census Bureau.

States. Concentration ratios of 70 to 100 percent are common in oligopolies. That is, a high concentration ratio means that a few sellers dominate the market.

Concentration ratios, however, are not a perfect guide to industry concentration. One problem is that they do not take into consideration foreign competition. For example, the U.S. auto industry is highly concentrated but faces stiff competition from foreign automobile producers. The same is true for motorcycles and bicycles.

Economies of Scale as a Barrier to Entry

Economies of large-scale production make operation on a small scale during a new firm's early years extremely unprofitable. A firm cannot build up

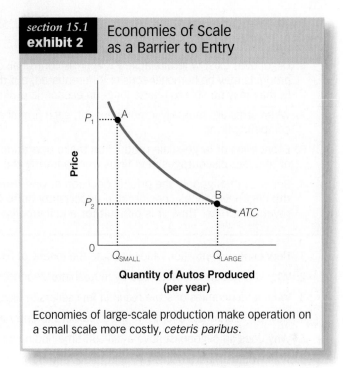

section 15.1 exhibit 2
Economies of Scale as a Barrier to Entry

Economies of large-scale production make operation on a small scale more costly, *ceteris paribus*.

Do you think economies of scale are important in this industry? Unlike home-cooked meals, few cars are "homemade." The barriers to entry in the auto industry are formidable. A new entrant would have to start out as a large producer (investing billions of dollars in plant, equipment, and advertising) to compete with existing firms, which have lower average total costs per unit because of economies of large-scale production.

a large market overnight; in the interim, average total cost is so high that losses are heavy. Recognition of this fact discourages new firms from entering the market, as illustrated in Exhibit 2. We can see that if an automobile company produces quantity Q_{LARGE} rather than Q_{SMALL}, it will be able to produce cars at a significantly lower cost. If the average total cost to a potential entrant is equivalent to point A on the *ATC* curve and the price of automobiles is less than P_1, a new firm would be deterred from entering the industry.

Equilibrium Price and Quantity in Oligopoly

It is difficult to predict how firms will react in situations of mutual interdependence. No firm knows what its demand curve looks like with any degree of certainty, and therefore it has a limited knowledge of its marginal revenue curve. To know anything about its demand curve, the firm must know how other firms will react to its prices and other policies. In the absence of additional assumptions, then, equating marginal revenue and expected marginal cost is relegated to guesswork. Thus, it is difficult for an oligopolist to determine its profit-maximizing price and output.

SECTION CHECK

1. Oligopolies exist where relatively few firms control all or most of the production and sale of a product. The products may be homogeneous or differentiated, but the barriers to entry are often very high and, consequently, they may be able to realize long-run economic profits.

2. When firms are mutually interdependent, each firm shapes its policy with an eye to the policies of competing firms.

3. Economies of large-scale production make operation on a small scale extremely unprofitable. Recognition of this fact discourages new firms from entering the market.

4. Because in oligopoly the pricing decision of one firm influences the demand curve of competing firms, the oligopolist faces considerable uncertainty as to the location and shape of its demand and marginal revenue curves. Thus, it is difficult for an oligopolist to determine its profit-maximizing price and output.

---

1. How can concentration ratios indicate the extent of oligopolies' power?
2. Why is oligopoly characterized by mutual interdependence?
3. Why do economies of scale result in few sellers in oligopoly models?
4. How do economies of scale result in barriers to entry in oligopoly models?
5. Why does an oligopolist have a difficult time finding its profit-maximizing price and output?
6. Why would an automobile manufacturer be more likely than the corner baker to be an oligopolist

---

SECTION 15.2   Collusion and Cartels

* Why do firms collude?
* What is joint profit maximization?

* Why does collusion break down?

Uncertainty and Pricing Decisions

The uncertainties of pricing decisions are substantial in oligopoly. The implications of misjudging the behavior of competitors could prove to be disastrous. An executive who makes the wrong pricing move may force the firm to lose sales or, at a minimum, be forced himself to back down in an embarrassing fashion from an announced price increase. Because of this uncertainty, some believe that oligopolists change their prices less frequently than perfect competitors, whose prices may change almost continually. The empirical evidence, however, does not clearly indicate that prices are in fact always slow to change in oligopoly situations.

Collusion

Because the actions and profits of oligopolists are so dominated by

collude
when firms act together to restrict competition

cartel
a collection of firms that agree on sales, pricing, and other decisions

mutual interdependence, the temptation is great for firms to **collude**—to get together and agree to act jointly in pricing and other matters. If firms believe they can increase their profits by coordinating their actions, they will be tempted to collude. Collusion reduces uncertainty and increases the potential for economic profits. From society's point of view, collusion creates a situation in which goods very likely become overpriced and underproduced, with consumers losing out as the result of a misallocation of resources.

Joint Profit Maximization

Agreements between or among firms on sales, pricing, and other decisions are usually referred to as cartel agreements. A **cartel** is a collection of firms making an agreement.

Cartels may lead to what economists call **joint profit maximization:** Price is based on the marginal revenue function, which is derived from the product's total (or market) demand schedule and the various firms' marginal cost schedules, as shown in Exhibit 1. With outright agreements—necessarily secret because of antitrust laws (in the United States, at least)—firms that make up the market will attempt to estimate demand and cost schedules and then set optimum price and output levels accordingly.

joint profit maximization
determination of price based on the marginal revenue derived from the market demand schedule and marginal cost schedule of the firms in the industry

Equilibrium price and quantity for a collusive oligopoly are determined according to the intersection of the marginal revenue curve (derived from the market demand curve) and the horizontal sum of the short-run marginal cost curves for the oligopolists. As shown in Exhibit 1, the resulting equilibrium quantity is Q^* and the equilibrium price is P^*. Collusion facilitates joint profit maximization for the oligopoly. If the oligopoly is maintained in the long run, it charges a

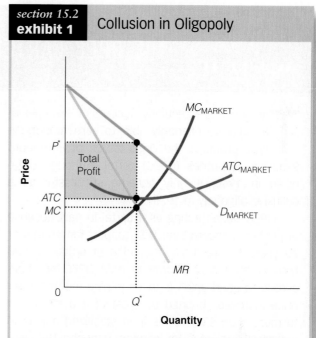

section 15.2
exhibit 1   Collusion in Oligopoly

In collusive oligopoly, the producers would restrict joint output to Q^*, setting their price at P^*. The members of the collusive oligopoly would share the profits in the shaded area.

---

in the news   The Crash of an Airline Collusion

Mr. Crandall: I think it's dumb as @#$% for !@#$%* sake, . . . to sit here and pound the @#$% out of each other and neither one of us making a #!@ !$&* dime. I mean, you know, @!#$, what the @#$!, is the point of it.

Mr. Putnam: Do you have a suggestion for me?

Mr. Crandall: Yes, I have a suggestion for you. Raise your @#$&!$% fares 20 percent. I'll raise mine the next morning. . . . You'll make more money and I will, too.

Mr. Putnam: We can't talk about pricing!

Mr. Crandall: Oh @#$% we can talk about any @#$%&*# thing we want to talk about.

consider this:

At the time of this conversation, Crandall was the president of American Airlines and Putnam was the president of Braniff Airlines. According to the Sherman Antitrust Act, it is illegal for corporate leaders to talk about and propose price fixing with their competitors. Putnam turned the tapes of this conversation over to the Justice Department. After reviewing the tapes, the Justice Department ruled that attempts to fix prices could monopolize the airline industry. American Airlines promised they would not engage in this type of activity again.

SOURCE: Staff, "American Air Accused of Bid to Fix Prices," *The Wall Street Journal,* February 24, 1983, pp. 2, 23.

global WATCH   THE OPEC CARTEL

The most spectacularly successful example of a collusive oligopoly able to earn monopoly-type profits is the Organization of Petroleum Exporting Countries (OPEC) cartel. Although organized in 1960, it only became successful as a collusive oligopoly in 1973.

OPEC began acting as a cartel in part because of political concern over U.S. support for Israel. For 20 years before 1973, the price of crude oil had hovered around $2 a barrel. In 1973, OPEC members agreed to quadruple oil prices in nine months; later price increases pushed the cost of a barrel of oil to more than $20. Prices then stabilized, falling in real terms (adjusted for inflation) between 1973 and 1978 as OPEC sought the profit-maximizing price and politics remained relatively calm. By the early 1980s, however, prices were approaching $40 per barrel. Exhibit 2 illustrates the relative impact of the OPEC cartel on the supply and price of oil.

The OPEC nations were successful with their pricing policies between 1973 and the early 1980s for several reasons. First, the worldwide demand for petroleum was highly inelastic with respect to price in the short run. Second, OPEC's share of total world oil output had steadily increased, from around 20 percent of total world output in the early 1940s to about 70 percent by 1973, when OPEC became an effective cartel. Third, the price elasticity of supply of petroleum from OPEC's competitors was low in the short run: Ability to increase production from existing wells is limited, and it takes time to drill new ones.

From the mid-1980s to the mid-1990s, OPEC oil prices hovered around $20 per barrel because of increases in non-OPEC production and the uncertain willingness of key suppliers (such as Saudi Arabia)

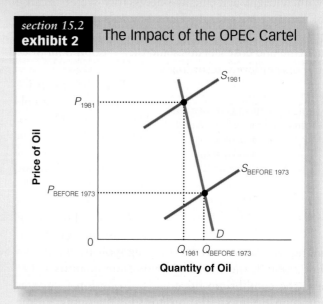

section 15.2 exhibit 2   The Impact of the OPEC Cartel

to restrict supply. Moreover, at the higher prices of the 1970s, long-run substitution possibilities caused oil consumption to fall almost 5 percent per year, with conservation and alternative energy easing the demand for OPEC oil. After adjusting for inflation, oil prices during most of the 1990s was roughly the same as it was before OPEC formed.

OPEC now controls less than one-third of world oil production and surprisingly it still has some clout as a cartel. However, it is not just OPEC. High oil prices still emerge because of growing world demand and the political instability in the Middle East. By July 2006, oil prices had reached $78 per barrel. However, in real terms (adjusted for inflation), a barrel would have to reach $90 to beat the mark it set in 1980. In 2008, in the midst of a worldwide recession, the price of oil fell below $40, despite OPEC's attempts to keep prices higher.

higher price, produces less output, and fails to maximize social welfare, relative to perfect competition, because $P^* > MC$ at Q^*.

The manner in which total profits are shared among firms in the industry depends in part on the relative costs and sales of the various firms. Firms with low costs and large supply capabilities will obtain the largest profits, because they have greater bargaining

power. Sales, in turn, may depend in large measure on consumer preferences for various brands if there is product differentiation. With outright collusion, firms may agree on market shares and the division of profits. The division of total profits will depend on the relative bargaining strength of each firm, influenced by its relative financial strength, ability to inflict damage (through price wars) on other firms if an agreement is not reached, ability to withstand similar actions on the part of other firms, relative costs, consumer preferences, and bargaining skills.

Why Are Most Collusive Oligopolies Short Lived?

Collusive oligopolies are potentially highly profitable for participants but detrimental to society. Fortunately, most strong collusive oligopolies are rather short lived, for two reasons. First, in the United States and in some other nations, collusive oligopolies are strictly illegal under antitrust laws. Second, for collusion to work, firms must agree to restrict output to a level that will support the profit-maximizing price. At that price, firms can earn positive economic profits. Yet a great temptation is for firms to cheat on the agreement of the collusive oligopoly; and because collusive agreements are illegal, the other parties have no way to punish the offender. Why do they have a strong incentive to cheat? Because any individual firm could lower its price slightly and thereby increase sales and profits, as long as it goes undetected. Undetected price cuts could bring in new customers, including rivals' customers. In addition, nonprice methods of defection include better credit terms, rebates, prompt delivery service, and so on.

SECTION CHECK

1. A price leader sends a signal to competing firms about a price change. Competitors that go along with the pricing decisions of the price leader are known as price followers.

2. The mutual interdependence of oligopolists tempts them to collude in order to reduce uncertainty and increase potential for economic profits.

3. Joint profit maximization requires the determination of price based on the market demand for the product and the marginal costs of the various firms.

4. Most strong collusive oligopolies are rather short lived for primarily two reasons: (1) Collusive oligopolies are strictly illegal under U.S. antitrust laws, and (2) there is a great temptation for firms to cheat on the agreement of the collusive oligopoly.

1. Why are collusive agreements typically unstable and short lived?

2. Why is the temptation to collude greater when the industry's demand curve is more inelastic?

SECTION 15.3   Other Oligopoly Models

* What is the kinked demand curve model?
* What happens to the oligopolists' profits if entry is easy?
* How can existing firms deter potential entrants?

The Kinked Demand Curve Model—Price Rigidity

As we have seen, collusion tends to be fragile in oligopoly markets. Prices in some oligopolistic industries tend to be quite stable, or rigid. That is, even if demand or cost changes, firms will be reluctant to change their prices. For example, if demand or costs were to increase, a firm might be tempted to increase its prices but may not because it fears that rivals will not raise their prices and the firm will lose customer sales. The firm may also be reluctant to lower its prices in fear of setting off a round of price warfare. That is, once the collusion outcome has been reached, individual producers have an incentive to be cautious about changing their output—or price.

This idea of price rigidity in oligopoly is the basis of the **kinked demand curve** model. According to the kinked

kinked demand curve
indicates the price rigidity in oligopoly when competitors show a greater tendency to follow price reductions than price increases

section 15.3
exhibit 1   The Kinked Demand Curve

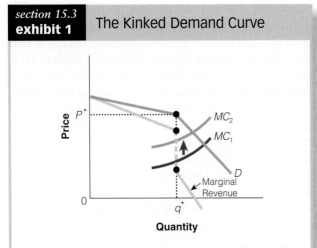

If the firm increases its price from P^*, most firms will not follow, and its demand curve is said to be relatively elastic (that is, a slight increase in price will lead to a more than proportionate fall in the quantity demanded). Conversely, below P^*, demand is relatively inelastic; a slight decrease in price will not lead to a large increase in the quantity demanded because rivals will also lower prices to hold onto their market share. Even if the marginal cost increases from MC_1 to MC_2, the firm will produce the same at the same price, P^*, and at the same output, q^*.

demand curve model, each firm faces a demand curve that is kinked at the collusive market price (P^*) and output (q^*). This kinked demand curve, illustrated in Exhibit 1, is produced by the greater tendency of competitors to follow price reductions than price increases. A price reduction takes business away from other firms and forces them to cut prices in order to protect their sales. A price increase does not necessitate a readjustment because other firms gain customers if one increases its price. At the point of the kink, the MR curve is discontinuous.

The profit-maximizing price, P^*, is indicated in Exhibit 1 by the point at which the demand curve changes slope. At prices higher than P^*, the firm's demand curve is very elastic. The reason for this elasticity is that a price increase would significantly cut revenues, as other rival firms fail to follow the price increase, causing the firm to lose sales and market share. If it lowers the price below P^*, reductions would yield little additional business because most of the other firms are presumed to follow price cuts. That is, sales will only increase if the total market quantity demanded increases due to the lower price. Below P^*, the firm does not capture many rivals' clients as rival firms match the price reduction, so the demand curve

price leader
a large firm in an oligopoly that unilaterally makes changes in its product prices that competitors tend to follow

tends to be relatively inelastic below P^*. A slight decrease in price will not lead to a large increase in quantity demanded because rivals will lower their price to maintain their market share.

One important consequence of the kink in the demand curve is that the firm may be slow to adjust price in response to cost changes. Because of the kink in the demand curve, the marginal revenue curve is discontinuous. Therefore, the MC curve can move up or down over a substantial range without affecting the optimum level of output or price. For example, as the marginal cost increases from MC_1 to MC_2 in Exhibit 1, the firm will continue to produce at the same price, P^*, and at the same output, q^*.

The key feature of the kinked demand curve is that the shape of the firm's demand curve is dependent on the action of competing firms. In the real world, of course, when a firm raises its price, anticipating that other firms will also raise prices but they do not, then the price-raising firm will face the prospect of a major sales decline, and the firm that initiated the price increase will usually retreat from the price increase originally announced. The explanation for the price rigidity comes from the idea that firms do not want to engage in destructive price competition. Game theory is useful in this situation. We will discuss game theory in the context of prisoners' dilemma in Section 15.4.

Not all oligopolies experience price rigidity. For example, during the high inflationary periods of the 1970s, some oligopolists increased their prices frequently. Oligopolists are more likely to experience price rigidity in situations of excess capacity—during a business downturn or a recession, for instance. In such cases, firms are likely to match a price cut but not a price hike—that is, they face a kinked demand curve. Also, if an oligopolist believes that other firms are faced with rising cost, then all the firms in the industry would respond to the change in marginal cost by adjusting their price and output accordingly to maintain their collusive position.

Price Leadership

Over time, an implied understanding may develop in an oligopoly market that a large firm is the price leader, sending a signal to competitors, perhaps through a press release, that they have increased their prices. This approach is not outright collusion because no formal cartel arrangement or formal meetings are used to determine price and output; but this is what

Oligopolists may initiate pricing policies that reduce the entry incentive for new firms, or they may try to drive a competitor out of the industry. For example, it is possible that a small-town drug store might be run out of town by Wal-Mart's "falling prices."

JACK HOLLINGSWORTH/PHOTODISC/GETTY IMAGES

section 15.3
exhibit 2   Long-Run Equilibrium and Deterring Entry

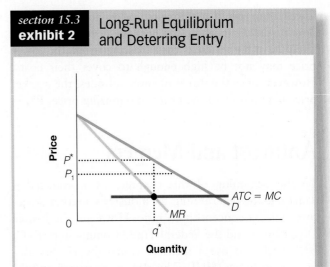

With barriers to entry, oligopolists may earn excess profits in the long run. Theoretically, profit maximization occurs at P^* and q^* in the short run. Empirical work, however, suggests that oligopolists often actually charge a lower price than the short-run profit-maximizing price (such as P_1). This strategy discourages entry because newcomers may have costs higher than P_1.

is called tacit collusion. Any competitor that goes along with the pricing decision of the price leader is called a **price follower.**

Price leadership is most likely to develop when one firm, the so-called dominant firm, produces a large portion of the total output. The dominant firm sets the price that maximizes its profits and the smaller firms, which would have little influence over price anyway, act as if they are perfect competitors—selling all they want at that price. In the past, a number of firms have been price leaders: U.S. Steel and Bethlehem Steel, RJ Reynolds (tobacco), General Motors (automobiles), Kellogg's (breakfast cereals), and Goodyear (tires). In the banking industry, various dominant banks have taken turns being the dominant firm in announcing changes in the prime interest rate—the interest rate that banks charge large corporate clients. Because the prime rate is widely cited in newspapers, it makes it easy for other banks to follow the lead and avoid frequent changes and competitive warfare.

price follower
a competitor in an oligopoly that goes along with the pricing decision of the price leader

price leadership
when a dominant firm that produces a large portion of the industry's output sets a price that maximizes its profits, and other firms follow

with which new firms can enter the industry. When entry is easy, excess profits attract newcomers. New firms may break down existing price agreements by undercutting prices in an attempt to establish themselves in the industry. In response, older firms may reduce prices to avoid excessive sales losses; as a result, the general level of prices will begin to approach average total cost.

What Happens in the Long Run If Entry Is Easy?

Mutual interdependence is, in itself, no guarantee of economic profits, even if the firms in the industry succeed in maximizing joint profits. The extent to which economic profits disappear depends on the ease

How Do Oligopolists Deter Market Entry?

If most firms reach a scale of plant and firm size great enough to allow lowest-cost operation, their long-run positions will be similar to that shown in Exhibit 2. To simplify, we have drawn MC and ATC constant. The equilibrium, or profit-maximizing, price in an established oligopoly is represented by P^*. Typically, the rate of profit in these industries is high, which would encourage entry. However, empirical research indicates that oligopolists often initiate pricing policies that reduce the entry incentive for new firms. Established firms may deliberately hold prices below the maximum profit point at P^*, charging a price of, say, P_1. This lower than profit-maximizing price may discourage newcomers from entering. Because new firms would likely have higher costs than existing firms, the lower price may not be high enough to cover their costs. However, once the threat of entry subsides, the market price may return to the profit-maximizing price, P^*.

Antitrust and Mergers

In the beginning of this chapter, we introduced a method for determining an industry's market structure called a concentration ratio. However, the Justice Department and the Federal Trade Commission (FTC) both prefer to use a measure called the Herfindahl-Hirshman Index (HHI). The HHI is measured by taking the square for each firm's share of market sales summed over the firms in the industry. For example, if the industry has three firms and their market share is 50 percent, 30 percent, 20 percent, respectively, the HHI would be:

$$HHI = 50^2 + 30^2 + 20^2 = 3,800$$

By squaring, the HHI produces a much larger number when industry is dominated by a few firms. According to the Justice Department, an HHI below 1,000 is very competitive, an HHI between 1,000 and 1,800 is somewhat competitive, and an HHI over 1,800 indicates an oligopoly. The HHI takes into account the relative size and distribution of the firms in a market. The HHI is lowest when a market consists of a large number of firms of relatively equal size. The HHI increases both as the number of firms in the market decreases and as the disparity in size between those firms increases.

A potential merger resulting in an HHI over 1,000 will receive close scrutiny. In 2007, for example, Whole Foods made a takeover bid for Wild Oats. Both were organic grocery stores. The FTC argued that the takeover would increase prices and limit competition in the organic food market. Whole Foods argued that it competes with many grocery stores that carry healthy food and organic products. The merger is still in appeal at the time of this writing. Another interesting case is the merger of Ticketmaster and Live Nation (see the In the News box).

Three Types of Mergers

There are three different types of mergers.

1. A *horizontal merger* combines firms that sell similar products; for example, if Motel 6 merges with Holiday Inn or GM merges with Chrysler.

2. A *vertical merger* combines firms at different stages of production; for example, Pepsi merged with Pizza Hut and Taco Bell. Similarly, a hotel chain may merge with a mattress company.

3. A *conglomerate merger* combines firms in different industries. For example, an automobile company might merge with a pharmaceutical company.

Since vertical mergers are not often a threat to competition, they are not usually subject to antitrust probes. They do not reduce competition in other markets. This is also true of conglomerate mergers—when an auto company merges with a pharmaceutical company, neither increases market share. Most of the problems occur with horizontal mergers. For example, an attempted merger between Office Depot and Staples was blocked.

Antitrust and Pricing Strategies

Most economists agree that price fixing should be illegal. However, there are antitrust laws that forbid other types of activities where the effects are not as obvious—predatory pricing, price discrimination, and tying.

Predatory Pricing

If the price is deliberately kept low (below average variable cost) to drive a competitor out of the market, it is called **predatory pricing**. However, both economists and the courts have a difficult time deciding whether or not the price is truly predatory or not. Even if the price is driven down below average variable cost (recall from Chapter 11, that when price is below AVC it is the shutdown point of a firm), the courts still have to determine whether the low price destroyed the rival and kept it out of business. And did the firm raise its price to the monopoly level once the rival had been driven out of the industry? Microsoft, American Airlines, and other companies have been accused of predatory pricing, but not convicted because it is so difficult to distinguish predatory pricing from vigorous competition.

> **predatory pricing**
> setting a price deliberately low in order to drive out competitors

Price Discrimination

Price discrimination, as we studied in Chapter 13, is a common pricing strategy for many businesses. It generally does not reduce competition unless it is part of a strategy to block entry or force a competitor out of the market; therefore, it is not normally challenged by antitrust authorities. However, it can be challenged under the Robinson-Patman Act, which places restrictions on allowable price discrimination.

in the news

Live Nation, Ticketmaster Merger Risks Antitrust Scrutiny

—BY ELIOT VAN BUSKIRK

[T]wo of the biggest forces in live music today—Live Nation and Ticketmaster—are set to merge into a single behemoth of ticketing and promotion that will call itself "Live Nation Entertainment."

The new powerhouse may be able to run from an unpopular brand—"Ticketmaster" is for many synonymous with niggling "convenience" fees and the stress-inducing process of vying for limited supplies of concert tickets, especially since no method of matching supply with demand seems particularly fair.

But it cannot hide from the antitrust scrutiny the deal is virtually certain to attract from governmental agencies since the combination could reduce competition and result in higher ticket prices.

Update: The Justice Department says it will in fact investigate the merger between Live Nation and Ticketmaster.

For Ticketmaster, this is familiar territory: It attracted a healthy dose of interest from antitrust regulators in the '90s for its domination of the concert ticket market. But now it is merging with the largest concert promoter in the world. The combined entity, which would control aspects of booking, promotion, primary ticket sales, secondary (fan-to-fan, or scalped) ticket sales, merchandising, direct marketing and even album sales in some cases, will be doubly attractive as a target for regulators.

"From an antitrust perspective, I do think it's going to get an extensive and thorough investigation by one of the two antitrust agencies—maybe more likely the Justice Department than the FTC, because the Justice Department did a monopoly investigation of Ticketmaster in the '90s," said Marc Schildkraut, a former assistant director of the Federal Trade Commission's Bureau of Competition and partner at merger clearance firm Howrey, LLP, by phone.

The Justice Department closed that investigation in 1999 for undisclosed reasons. Schildkraut said the likely cause was that the government didn't find a sufficient barrier to entry to other companies entering the music-ticketing space, even despite Ticketmaster's exclusive, multiyear venue contracts.

But Live Nation Entertainment would be a completely different animal. The world's largest promoter doubling as its largest ticket seller presents challenges Ticketmaster did not face during its '90s antitrust travails.

"This is both a horizontal and a vertical merger," explained Shildkraut. "Horizontal means they're competitors to each other [due to Live Nation's recent entry into the ticketing market, two years of development] and vertical means they are in adjacent spaces in the market."

By the latter, he's referring to synergy between the company's ticketing and promotion departments. The combined effort could present a barrier to entry to promoters, who would likely have to work with Live Nation Entertainment's ticketing division—not to mention other potential ticket sellers, who would be prevented from ticketing Live Nation Entertainment-promoted shows.

Why merge, if it's going to mean this much scrutiny? According to Live Nation CEO Michael Rapino (who would be CEO of Live Nation Entertainment if the merger goes through) the idea here is merely to sell more tickets, more efficiently. "As every industry observer knows, too many tickets go unsold and too many fans are frustrated with their ticket-buying experiences," he said, adding, "the better job we do of getting the right fan in the right seat at the right time, the more money our clients are going to make."

AP PHOTO/HENNY RAY ABRAMS

Use what you've LEARNED   MUTUAL INTERDEPENDENCE IN OLIGOPOLY

Q Suppose that Firm A is a member of a naive oligopoly, meaning that neither Firm A nor its competitors recognize the mutual interdependence that exists between them. Firm A decides to lower its price to capture a greater market share. What will happen to profits in this market in the long run?

A If an oligopolist believes that its rivals will not respond to pricing policies, it will expect to capture market share by reducing price. In response, rivals will cut prices as well, and if they do not understand the mutual interdependence among firms in oligopoly, they will attempt to undercut prices, as shown in Exhibit 3 in the movement from P_1 to P_2, and so on. This exchange would result in a price war, which could continue until economic profits were zero and price equaled average cost.

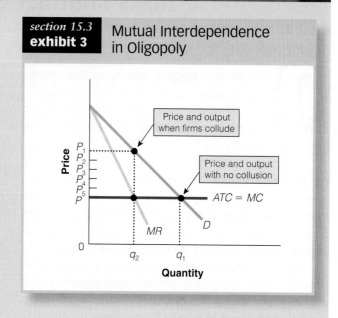

section 15.3
exhibit 3   Mutual Interdependence in Oligopoly

Price and output when firms collude

Price and output with no collusion

Tying

Tie-in-sales *require* that a customer who buys one product (the tying good) must also buy another product (the tied good) that a customer needs to use the first product. Two companies that followed this practice were Xerox and IBM. When Xerox was the largest photocopier producer, they required companies that rented their machines to also buy paper from them. Similarly, IBM required that users of its computers buy IBM computer cards. IBM charged more for the computer cards than other firms would have charged.

Antitrust authorities look for dominant firms that use types of pricing discrimination policies. For example, the Supreme Court ruled that studios could not force theaters to buy an entire package of films in order to get the rights to show a blockbuster movie. That is, tying a blockbuster movie together with a package of not-so-good B movies could allow studios to expand their market power. To economists, the "jury" is still out on whether various forms of price discrimination really impede competition.

SECTION CHECK

1. In the kinked demand curve model, if one firm cuts its price, rivals will follow, but rival firms will not follow the firm if it raises its price.

2. When market entry is easy, excess profits attract newcomers. They may break down existing price agreements, causing older firms to reduce their prices and, ultimately, drive the general level of prices toward average total cost.

3. Firms in an oligopoly may deliberately hold prices below the short-run profit-maximizing point in order to discourage newcomers from entering the market.

4. The Herfindahl-Hirshman Index (HHI), which equals the sum of the squares of the market shares, is a measure of the competitiveness of a market structure, where a lower number indicates a more competitive structure.

5. There are three types of mergers: horizontal (merging firms that produce similar products), vertical (merging firms at different stages of a production process), and conglomerate (merging firms in different industries).

6. Price discrimination, allegations of predatory pricing, and tying sales are also subject to antitrust laws.

1. What explains the kink in the kinked demand curve?

2. What impact does easy entry have on the profitability of oligopolies?

3. Why are barriers to entry necessary for successful, ongoing collusion?

4. Why might oligopolists charge less than their short-run profit-maximizing price when threatened by entry?

5. A group of colluding oligopolists incurs costs of $10 per unit, and their profit-maximizing price is $15. If they know that potential market entrants could produce at a cost of $12 per unit, what price are the colluders likely to charge?

6. Why is price leadership also called tacit collusion?

7. What two factors increase the Herfindahl-Hirshman Index (HHI)?

8. Why do horizontal mergers tend to concern antitrust authorities more than vertical or conglomerate mergers?

9. For someone to be engaged in predatory pricing, what must happen to prices after their predation? Why would potential entry undermine the strategy?

SECTION 15.4

Game Theory and Strategic Behavior

* What is game theory?
* What are cooperative and noncooperative games?

* What is a dominant strategy?
* What is Nash equilibrium?

Some Strategies for Noncollusive Oligopolies

In some respects, noncollusive oligopoly resembles a military campaign or a poker game. Firms take certain actions not because they are necessarily advantageous in themselves but because they improve the position of the oligopolist relative to its competitors and may ultimately improve its financial position. For example, a firm may deliberately cut prices, sacrificing profits either to drive competitors out of business or to discourage them from undertaking actions contrary to the interests of other firms.

What Is Game Theory?

Some economists have suggested that the entire approach to oligopoly equilibrium price and output should be recast. They replace the analysis that assumes that firms attempt to maximize profits with one that examines firm behavior in terms of a strategic game. This point of view, called **game theory**, stresses the tendency of various parties in such circumstances to act in a way that minimizes damage from opponents. This approach involves a set

game theory
firms attempt to maximize profits by acting in ways that minimize damage from competitors

cooperative game
collusion by two firms in order to improve their profit maximizations

noncooperative game
each firm sets its own price without consulting other firms

of alternative actions (with respect to price and output levels, for example); the action that would be taken in a particular case depends on the specific policies followed by each firm. The firm may try to figure out its competitors' most likely countermoves to its own policies and then formulate alternative defense measures.

Each firm will react to the price, quantity, and quality of rival firms. Because each firm is interdependent, each must observe the moves of its rivals.

Cooperative and Noncooperative Games

Games, in interactions between oligopolists, can either be cooperative or noncooperative. An example of a **cooperative game** would be two firms that decide to collude in order to improve their profit-maximization position. However, as we discussed earlier, enforcement costs are usually too high to keep all firms from cheating on collusive agreements. Consequently, most games are **noncooperative games**, in which each firm sets its own price without consulting other firms. The primary difference between cooperative and noncooperative games is the contract.

For example, players in a cooperative game can talk and set binding contracts, while those in noncooperative games are assumed to act independently, with no communication and no binding contracts. Because antitrust laws forbid firms to collude, we will assume that most strategic behavior in the marketplace is noncooperative.

The Prisoners' Dilemma

A firm's decision makers must map out a pricing strategy based on a wide range of information. They must also decide whether their strategy will be effective and whether it will be affected by competitors' actions. A strategy that will be optimal regardless of the opponents' actions is called a **dominant strategy**. A famous game that has a dominant strategy and demonstrates the basic problem confronting noncolluding oligopolists is known as the **prisoners' dilemma**.

Imagine that a bank robbery occurs and two suspects are caught. The suspects are placed in separate cells in the county jail and are not allowed to talk with each other. Four results are possible in this situation: both prisoners confess, neither confesses, Prisoner A confesses but

dominant strategy
strategy that will be optimal regardless of opponents' actions

prisoners' dilemma
the basic problem facing noncolluding oligopolists in maximizing their own profit

payoff matrix
a summary of the possible outcomes of various strategies

Prisoner B doesn't, or Prisoner B confesses but Prisoner A doesn't. In Exhibit 1, we see the **payoff matrix**, which summarizes the possible outcomes from the various strategies. Looking at the payoff matrix, we can see that if each prisoner confesses to the crime, each will serve two years in jail. However, if neither confesses, each prisoner may only get one year because of insufficient evidence. Now, if Prisoner A confesses and Prisoner B does not, Prisoner A will get six months (because of his cooperation with the authorities and his evidence) and Prisoner B six years. Alternatively, if Prisoner B confesses and Prisoner A does not, Prisoner B will get six months and Prisoner A six years. As you can see, then, the prisoners have a dilemma. What should each prisoner do?

Looking at the payoff matrix, we can see that if Prisoner A confesses, it is in the best interest for Prisoner B to confess. If Prisoner A confesses, he will

section 15.4
exhibit 1

The Prisoners' Dilemma Payoff Matrix

		Prisoner B	
		Confesses	**Doesn't Confess**
Prisoner A	**Confesses**	2 years (A) / 2 years (B)	6 months (A) / 6 years (B)
	Doesn't Confess	6 years (A) / 6 months (B)	1 year (A) / 1 year (B)

The sentence depends on the prisoner's decision to confess or remain silent and on the decision made by the other prisoner. When the prisoners follow their dominant strategy and confess, both will be worse off than if each had remained silent—hence, the "prisoners' dilemma."

A pitcher wants to throw a pitch that will surprise this batter. The batter knows that the pitcher wants to fool him. So what does the pitcher throw, knowing the batter expects the pitcher to fool him? Is this a game with strategic interaction?

© GARY I ROTHSTEIN/ICON SMI/CORBIS

© STEPHEN MARKS/THE IMAGE BANK/GETTY IMAGES

get either two years or six months, depending on what Prisoner B does. However, Prisoner B knows the temptation to confess facing Prisoner A, so confessing is also the best strategy for Prisoner B. A confession would mean a lighter sentence for Prisoner B—two years rather than six years.

It is clear that both would be better off confessing *if* they knew for sure that the other was going to remain silent, because that would lead to a six-month sentence for each. However, in each case, can the prisoner take the chance that the co-conspirator will not talk? The dominant strategy, although it may not lead to the best joint outcome, is to confess. That is, the prisoners know that confessing is the way to make the best of a bad situation. No matter what their counterpart does, the maximum sentence will be two years for each, and each understands the possibility of being out in six months. In summary, when the prisoners follow their dominant strategy and confess, both will be worse off than if each had remained silent—hence, the "prisoners' dilemma."

Firms in oligopoly often behave like the prisoners in the prisoners' dilemma, carefully anticipating the moves of their rivals in an uncertain environment. For example, should a firm cut its prices and try to gain more sales by luring customers away from its competitors? What if the firm keeps its price stable and competitors lower theirs? Or what if the firm and its competitors all lower their prices? What if all of the firms decide to raise their prices? Each of these situations will have vastly different implications for an oligopolist, so it must carefully watch and anticipate the moves of its competitors.

Profits Under Different Pricing Strategies

To demonstrate how the prisoners' dilemma can shed light on oligopoly theory, let us consider the pricing strategy of two firms. In Exhibit 2, we present the payoff matrix—the possible profits that each firm would earn under different pricing strategies. Assume that each firm has total production costs of $1 per unit. When both firms set their price at $10 and each sells 1,000 units per week, then each earns a profit of $9,000 a week. If each firm sets its price at $9, each sells 1,100 units per week for a profit of $8,800 [($9 − $1) × 1,100]. However, what if one firm charges $10 and the other firm charges $9? The low-price firm increases its profits through additional sales. It now sells, say, 1,500 units for a profit of $12,000, while the high-price firm sells only 600 units per week for a profit of $5,400.

When the two firms each charge $9 per unit, they are said to have reached a Nash equilibrium (named after Nobel Prize–winning economist and mathematician John Nash). At a Nash equilibrium, each firm is said to be doing as well as it can *given the actions of its competitor.* For example, if each firm believes the other is going to charge $9, then the best strategy for both firms is to charge $9. In this scenario, if Firm A charges $9, the worst possible outcome is a profit of $8,800. However, if Firm A prices at $10 and Firm B prices at $9, Firm A will have a profit of only $5,400. Hence, the choice that minimizes the risk of the worst scenario is $9. The same is true for Firm B; it too

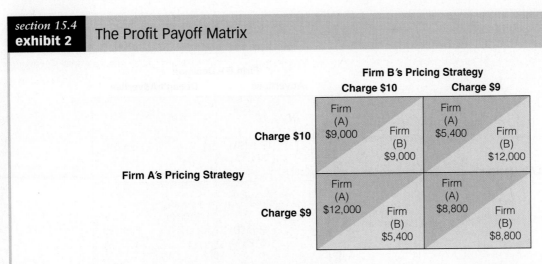

section 15.4
exhibit 2   The Profit Payoff Matrix

		Firm B's Pricing Strategy	
		Charge $10	Charge $9
Firm A's Pricing Strategy	Charge $10	Firm (A) $9,000 — Firm (B) $9,000	Firm (A) $5,400 — Firm (B) $12,000
	Charge $9	Firm (A) $12,000 — Firm (B) $5,400	Firm (A) $8,800 — Firm (B) $8,800

If both firms defect by lowering their prices from the level of joint profit maximization, both will be worse off than if they had colluded, but at least each will have minimized its potential loss if it cannot trust its competitor. This situation is the oligopolists' dilemma.

minimizes the risk of the worst scenario by choosing to price at the Nash equilibrium, $9. In this case, the Nash equilibrium is also the dominant strategy. The Nash equilibrium takes on particular importance because it is a self-enforcing equilibrium. That is, once this equilibrium is established, neither firm has an incentive to move.

In sum, we see that if the two firms were to collude and set their price at $10, it would be in their best interest. However, each firm has a strong incentive to lower its price to $9 if this pricing strategy goes undetected by its competitor. However, if both firms defect by lowering their prices from the level of joint profit maximization, both will be worse off than if they had colluded, but at least each will have minimized its potential loss if it cannot trust its competitor. This situation is the oligopolists' dilemma.

Advertising

Advertising can lead to a situation like the prisoners' dilemma. For example, perhaps the decision makers of a large firm are deciding whether to launch an advertising campaign against a rival firm. According to the payoff matrix in Exhibit 3, if neither company advertises, the two companies split the market, each making $100 million in profits. They also split the market if they both advertise, but their net profits are smaller, $75 million, because they would both incur advertising costs that are greater than any gains in additional revenues from advertising. However, if one advertises and the other does not, the company that advertises takes customers away from the rival. Profits for the company that advertises would be $125 million, and profits for the company that does not advertise would be $50 million.

The dominant strategy—the optimal strategy regardless of the rival's actions—is to advertise. In this game, both firms will choose to advertise, even though both would be better off if no one advertised. But one company can't take a chance and not advertise, because if its competitor then elects to advertise, the competitor could have a big year, primarily at the expense of the firm that doesn't advertise.

Arms Race

The arms race provides a classic example of prisoners' dilemma. During the Cold War (mid 1940s to the early 1990s), the United States and the former Soviet Union were engaged in costly military expansion that hampered both economies. It exacted a greater toll on the Soviets because their economy was not as economically productive as the United States and may have ultimately led to their decline. The United States' power was based on economic and military strength; the USSR's was based solely on military strength. Each country raced to produce more military goods than the other. Representatives from both sides would periodically meet to discuss arms reduction but to no avail. Neither party was willing to risk losing its military superiority.

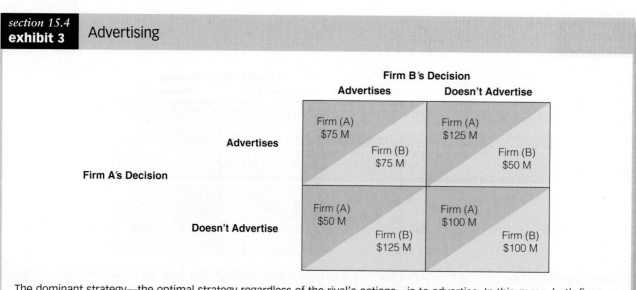

section 15.4
exhibit 3   Advertising

		Firm B's Decision	
		Advertises	**Doesn't Advertise**
Firm A's Decision	**Advertises**	Firm (A) $75 M · Firm (B) $75 M	Firm (A) $125 M · Firm (B) $50 M
	Doesn't Advertise	Firm (A) $50 M · Firm (B) $125 M	Firm (A) $100 M · Firm (B) $100 M

The dominant strategy—the optimal strategy regardless of the rival's actions—is to advertise. In this game, both firms will choose to advertise, even though both would be better off if no one advertised.

The Game Theory of the Bar Scene Problem from *A Beautiful Mind*

The Problem

You and three male friends are at a bar trying to pick up women. Suddenly one blonde and four brunettes enter in a group. What's the individual strategy?

Here are the rules. Each of you wants to talk to the blonde. If more than one of you tries to talk to her, however, she will be put off and talk to no one. At that point it will also be too late to talk to a brunette, as no one likes being second choice. Assume anyone who starts out talking to a brunette will succeed.

The Movie

Nash suggests the group should cooperate. If everyone goes for the blonde, they block each other and no one wins. The brunettes will feel hurt as a second choice and categorically reject advances. Everyone loses.

But what if everyone goes for a brunette? Then each person will succeed, and everyone ends up with a good option.

It's a good thought, except for one question: what about the blonde?

The Equilibrium

The movie is directed so well that it sounds persuasive. But it's sadly incomplete. It misses the essence of noncooperative game theory.

A Nash equilibrium is a state where no one person can improve *given what others are doing*. This means you are picking the best possible action in response to others—the formal term is you are picking a *best response*.

As an example, let's analyze whether everyone going for a brunette is a Nash equilibrium. You are *given* that three of your friends go for brunettes. What is your best response?

You can either go for the brunette or the blonde. With your friends already going for brunettes, you have no competition to go for the blonde. The answer is clear that you would talk to the blonde. That's your best response. Incidentally, this is a Nash equilibrium. You are happy, and your friends cannot

do better. If your friends try to talk to the blonde, they end up with nothing and give up talking to a brunette. So you see, when Nash told his friends to go for the brunettes in the movie, it really does sound like he was leaving the blonde for himself.

The lesson: advice that sounds good for you might really be better for someone else. Be skeptical of the strategic implications.

Now, in practical matters it will be hard to achieve the equilibrium that one person goes for a blonde. There is going to be competition and someone in the group will surely sabotage the mission. So there are two ways you might go about it using strategies outside the game. One is to ignore the current group and wait for another group of blondes (the classic "wait and see" strategy). The second is to let a random group member go for the blonde as the others distract the brunettes (also practiced as "wingman theory").

section 15.4
exhibit 4   Arms Race

section 15.4 exhibit 4   Arms Race

		Country A	
		Spend More on Arms	**Spend Less on Arms**
Country B	**Spend More on Arms**	At risk (A) / At risk (B)	At risk (A) / Safe (B)
	Spend Less on Arms	Safe (A) / At risk (B)	Safe (A) / Safe (B)

For each country the dominant strategy is to build arms. Self interest drives each participant into a noncooperative game that is worse for both.

The dilemma was that each country wanted to achieve military superiority, and building more arms could make that possible, for a given level of arms spending by the other. Each would prefer less spending on the military but each rationally chose to spend more to avoid the risk of becoming militarily inferior. They were trapped in a spending war. Of course, negotiations to spend less would be the preferred outcome for both, if they could be assured the other party would not cheat.

As you can see in the payoff matrix in Exhibit 4, if Country A spends more money on arms, then Country B better do the same or risk military inferiority. If Country A chooses to spend less on arms, then Country B gains military superiority by not following. For each country, the dominant strategy is to build arms, which leads to an inferior outcome—a less safe world. This is similar to the collusion game we examined earlier where self-interest drives each participant to a noncooperative outcome that is worse for both parties.

Repeated Games

In the one-shot, prisoners' dilemma game in Exhibit 1, we saw that the best strategy is to confess regardless of what your opponent does—your behavior does not influence the other player's behavior. In one-shot prisoners' dilemma games, self-interest prevents cooperative behavior and leads to an inferior joint outcome for the participants.

However, cooperation is not impossible because most oligopolistic interactions are not one-shot games. Instead they are repeated games. Most firms assume that they will have repeat customers. For example, if a grocery store fails to provide fresh produce, customers can punish the store by shopping elsewhere in the future. These future consequences change the incentives from those in a one-shot game. All stores might have gained short-run profits from low-quality (and cost) produce, but all may offer high-quality produce because of the adverse future effects of offering lower quality produce. In a repeated game, cooperation occurs as long as others continue to cooperate.

Suppose two firms are both going to be in business for many years. Several studies have shown that, in this type of situation, the best strategy is to do what your opponent did to you earlier. This type of response tends to elicit cooperation rather than competition. This form of strategic behavior is called a **tit-for-tat strategy**.

A repeated game allows the firm to establish a reputation of cooperation. Cooperation may mean maintaining a high price or a certain advertising budget, provided that the other firm did the same in the previous round. In short, a firm has an incentive to cooperate now so there is greater cooperation in the future. However, if your opponent cheats, you cheat in the next round to punish your opponent for a lack of cooperation. You do what your opponent did in the previous round. In the tit-for-tat game, both firms will be better off if they stick to the plan rather than cheating—that is, failing to cooperate. Many cartels appear to employ the tit-for-tat strategy.

tit-for-tat strategy
strategy used in repeated games where one player follows the othe player's move in the previous round; leads to greater cooperation

Use what you've LEARNED   NASH AT THE BEACH

Two ice cream vendors on the beach are selling identical ice cream at the same price. The demanders are uniformly distributed along the beach. To minimize transportation costs, each vendor might strategically set up at the 1/4-mile mark and 3/4-mile mark, each with an advantage of being halfway to its rival. However, the situation in Exhibit 5 is not a stable equilibrium, because if vendor A thinks vendor B is going to stay put, then vendor A will move to the right, closer to vendor B, and capture three-fourths of the market, and vendor B will have the remaining one-fourth. Vendor B would then want to move to the left of vendor A. They would continue to leap frog until they reached the center. That is, a Nash equilibrium will lead to both vendors locating in the middle—doing the best they can given what the competitor is doing.

Recall the discussion of the median voter model in Chapter 8, where the prediction was that the candidates will pick a political position in the middle of the distribution of voters. The ice cream vendor model helps us understand this phenomenon as well as why fast-food restaurants, car dealerships, and motels are often found in close proximity to each other.

section 15.4 exhibit 5   Vendors at the Beach

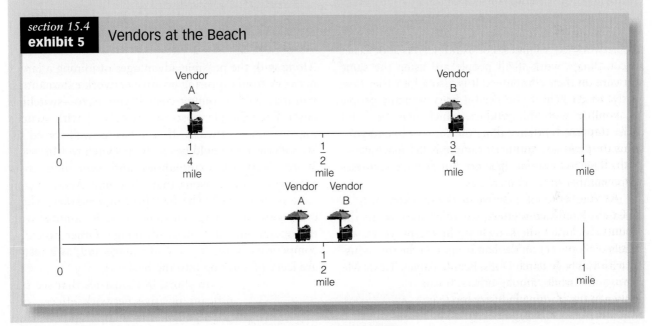

In short, the most effective strategy to promote cooperation is tit-for-tat.

Network Externalities

In our discussion of supply and demand (Chapter 4), we assumed that demand was a function of the price of the good (a change in quantity demanded) and the determinants of demand (the shifters that cause changes in demand). For

network externality
when the number of other people purchasing the good influences quantity demanded

positive network externality
increase in a consumer's quantity demanded for a good because a greater number of other consumers are purchasing the good

example, the amount of ice cream we are willing and able to buy is a function of the price of ice cream, the price of related goods—substitutes like yogurt and complements like hot fudge—income, the number of buyers, tastes, and expectations. However, we did not mention that for some goods, the quantity demanded depends on how many other people purchase the good. This factor is called a **network externality**. A **positive network externality** occurs when a consumer's quantity demanded for a good increases because a greater number of consumers purchase the same good. A **negative network externality** occurs if the consumer's quantity demanded for a good increases because fewer consumers are purchasing the same good. In other words, sometimes an individual's demand curve is influenced by the other people purchasing the good.

Positive Network Externalities

Many examples of network externalities can be found in the communications area, such as with fax machines, telephones, and the Internet. Imagine you had a telephone, but nobody else did; it would be relatively worthless without others with whom to talk. It is also true that if you were the only one to own a compact disc player, it would make little sense for manufacturers to make discs and your CD player would be of little value.

The software industry has many examples of positive network externalities. For example, it is a lot easier to coordinate work if all people are using the same software on their computers. It is also a lot easier (less costly) to get help if you need it because many people are familiar with the product, which may be a lot easier (less costly) than calling the support line to your software package. Another example is fax machines—others have to have one. In short, our demand increases as the number of users increases.

Another type of positive network externality is called the **bandwagon effect**, where a buyer wants the product because others own it. In recent years, we watched people get on the bandwagon in the toy industry with Cabbage Patch Dolls, Beanie Babies, Tickle Me Elmo, and Furbies, among others. It can happen in the clothing industry too (e.g., Tommy Bahama or Ugg boots).

Negative Network Externalities

Other goods and services are subject to negative network externalities, which may be a result of the snob effect. The snob effect is a negative network externality where a consumer wants to own a unique good. For example, a rare baseball card of Shoeless Joe Jackson, a Model T car (a tin lizzy), a Vincent Van Gogh painting, a Rolex watch, or an expensive sports car may qualify as snob goods where the quantity that a particular individual demanded of

negative network externality
increase in a consumer's demand for a good because fewer consumers are purchasing the same good

bandwagon effect
a positive network externality in which a consumer's demand for a product increases because other consumers own it

switching costs
the costs involved in changing from one product to another brand or in changing suppliers

a good increases when fewer other people own it. Firms seek to achieve a snob effect through marketing and advertising, knowing that if they can create a less elastic demand curve for their product they can raise prices.

Negative network externalities can arise from congestion too. For example, if you are a member of a health club, a negative network externality may occur because too many people are in the gym working out at the same time. Even though I may prefer a ski resort with shorter lift lines, others may view these goods as a positive externality and would increase their quantity demanded if more people were in the gym, on the beach, or at the ski slopes. Perhaps they do not want to work out alone, hang out on a lonely beach, or ride up on the chair lift by themselves. That is, whether it is a positive or negative network externality may depend on the consumer's tastes and preferences.

Switching Costs

Along with the possible advantages of joining a larger network from capturing positive network externalities, you may also encounter costs if you leave—switching costs. For example, costs are associated with switching to new software. If you were well-versed in WordPerfect, it would be costly to switch to Microsoft Word. Network externalities and switching costs are two of the reasons that eBay and Amazon.com have done so well. The first firm in a market, where everybody in its large customer base is familiar with the operation, gains huge advantage. Other potential competitors recognize this advantage and, as a result, are leery of entering into the business.

In short, in industries that see significant positive network effects, oligopoly is likely to be present. That is, a small number of firms may be able to secure most of the market. Consumers tend to choose the products that everyone else is using. Thus, behavior may allow these firms to increase their output and achieve economics of scale that smaller firms cannot obtain. Hence, the smaller firms will go out of business or be bought out by larger firms.

You might legitimately ask the question: If perfectly competitive and monopolistic firms are rare and monopolistically competitive and oligopoly firms are common, why did we study the former first? What we learned from the perfectly competitive model about costs, entry, exit, and efficiency are still important concepts for imperfectly competitive firms. In addition, the applications of oligopoly and monopolistic competition theory are still somewhat controversial among economists—so we started with what we know best. Exhibit 6 provides an overview of the various types of market structures.

section 15.4
exhibit 6   Characteristics of the Four Major Market Structures

Characteristic	Perfect Competition	Monopoly	Monopolistic Competition	Oligopoly
Number of firms	Very many	One	Many	A few
Firm role in determining price	No role; price taker	Major role; price maker	Some role	Some role
Close substitutes available	Perfect substitutes	No	Yes	Usually but not always
Barriers to entry or exit from industry	No substantial ones	Extremely great	Minor barriers	Considerable barriers
Type of product	Homogeneous	Homogeneous	Differentiated	Homogeneous or differentiated
Key characteristic	Firms are price takers	Only one firm	Product differentiation	Mutual interdependence

SECTION CHECK

1. Game theory stresses the tendency of various parties to minimize damage from opponents. A firm may try to figure out its competitors' most likely countermoves to its own policies and then formulate alternative defense measures.

2. Players in cooperative games can talk and set binding contracts, while those in noncooperative games are assumed to act independently with no communications and no binding contracts.

3. The prisoners' dilemma is an example of a noncooperative game.

4. A dominant strategy is optimal regardless of the opponents' actions.

5. At a Nash equilibrium, each player is said to be doing as well as it can, given the actions of its competitor.

6. In one-shot games, the participants' self-interest tends to prevent cooperative behavior, but in repeated games, cooperation occurs as long as others continue to cooperate (a tit-for-tat strategy).

7. The arms race is a classic example of prisoners' dilemma.

8. Positive (negative) network externality occurs when a consumer's quantity demanded increases (decreases) because a greater (smaller) number of consumers purchase the same good.

9. In industries with significant positive network externalities, oligopoly is likely to be present.

---

1. How is noncollusive oligopoly like a military campaign or a poker game?

2. What is the difference between cooperative and noncooperative games?

3. How does the prisoners' dilemma illustrate a dominant strategy for noncolluding oligopolists?

4. What is a Nash equilibrium?

5. In the prisoners' dilemma, if each prisoner believed that the other prisoner would deny the crime, would each choose to deny the crime?

6. Why are repeated games more likely to lead to cooperative results than one-shot games?

7. How does a tit-for-tat strategy work?

8. Why would industries with substantial positive network externalities tend to be oligopolies?

Interactive Chapter Summary

Fill in the blanks:

1. Oligopolies exist when only a (n) _____ firms control all or most of the production and sale of a product.

2. In oligopoly, products may be either homogeneous or _____.

3. In oligopoly, _____ to entry are often high, preventing competing firms from entering the market.

4. In oligopoly, firms can earn long-run _____ profits.

5. Oligopoly is characterized by mutual _____ among firms. Oligopolists must _____ because the number of firms in the industry is so small that changes in one firm's price of output will affect the sales of competing firms.

6. In oligopoly, barriers to entry in the form of large start-up costs, economies of scale, or _____ are usually present.

7. The economy of large-scale production _____ new firms from entering a market, because high initial average total costs impose heavy losses on new entrants.

8. Mutual interdependence means that no firm knows with _____ what its demand curve looks like. The demand curve and the profit-maximizing price and output will depend on how others _____ to the firm's policies.

9. Because they are mutually interdependent, oligopolists are tempted to get together and agree to act jointly, or to _____, in order to reduce uncertainty and raise profits.

10. From society's point of view, collusion creates a situation where goods are priced too _____ and outputs too _____.

11. International agreements between firms regarding sales, pricing, and other decisions are called _____ agreements.

12. Although collusive oligopolies may be profitable for participants, they are often short lived because firms have a great temptation to _____ on their fellow colluders.

13. In oligopoly, an understanding may develop under which one large firm will play the role of price_____, sending signals to competitors that they have changed their prices.

14. Competitors that go along with the pricing decisions of a price leader are called price _____.

15. Collusive behavior is no guarantee of economic profits in the _____ run.

16. Without _____ to entry, new firms will be attracted by the economic profits earned when firms act to maximize joint profits.

17. New firms will lower _____ and break down existing pricing agreements. Price competition will result in prices approaching the level of average total _____.

18. Oligopolists may charge a price lower than the profit-maximizing price to _____ new firms from entering the market. This strategy will be effective when new firms face _____ costs than existing firms in the industry do.

19. The idea of price _____ in oligopoly is the basis of the kinked demand curve model.

20. The kinked oligopoly firm's demand curve is produced by the greater tendency of competitors to follow price _____ than price _____.

21. Under the assumptions of the kinked demand curve model, a firm's demand curve is _____ elastic for price increases than for price decreases.

22. The kinked demand curve model implies that firms may be slow to adjust price in response to changes in _____.

23. In some respects, _____ oligopoly resembles a military campaign or poker game.

24. Oligopoly interdependence is often analyzed in terms of _____ theory.

25. Collusion is an example of a _____ game.

26. In _____, each firm sets its policy without consulting other firms.

27. The primary difference between cooperative games and noncooperative games lies in the players' ability to make_____.

28. In game theory, a strategy that will be optimal regardless of one's opponents' actions is called a _____ strategy.

29. In the traditional prisoners' dilemma, a _____ matrix is used to illustrate the various possibilities and results for the two parties.

30. A _____ equilibrium is reached in game theory when each firm is doing as well as it can, given the actions of its competitor.

31. A Nash equilibrium is _____, because once it is established, neither firm has an incentive to change behavior.

32. Repeated games are _____ likely to lead to cooperative results than one-shot games.

33. In a _____ strategy, a game participant does whatever the other participant did during the previous play.

34. A _____ externality occurs when a consumer's quantity demanded increases because a greater number of consumers purchase the same good.

35. Positive network externalities are particularly common in the area of _____.

36. The _____ effect refers to the case where a buyer wants a product because others also own it.

37. Congestion can cause _____ network externalities by overcrowding.

38. Switching costs can give an advantage to the _____ firms in an industry.

Answers: 1. few 2. differentiated 3. barriers 4. economic 5. interdependence; strategize 6. patents 7. discourages 8. certainty; react 9. collude 10. high; low 11. cartel 12. cheat 13. leader 14. followers 15. long 16. barriers 17. prices; costs 18. discourages; higher 19. rigidity 20. reductions; increases 21. more 22. marginal cost 23. noncollusive 24. game 25. cooperative 26. noncooperative games 27. contracts 28. dominant 29. payoff 30. Nash 31. self-enforcing 32. more 33. tit-for-tat 34. positive network 35. communications 36. bandwagon 37. negative 38. first

Key Terms and Concepts

mutual interdependence 422
collude 424
cartel 424
joint profit maximization 425
kinked demand curve 427
price leader 428
price follower 429

price leadership 429
predatory pricing 430
game theory 433
cooperative game 433
noncooperative game 433
dominant strategy 434
prisoners' dilemma 434

payoff matrix 434
tit-for-tat strategy 438
network externality 439
positive network externality 439
negative network externality 440
bandwagon effect 440
switching costs 440

Section Check Answers

15.1 Oligopoly

1. **How can concentration ratios indicate the extent of oligopolies' power?**
Concentration ratios indicate the fraction of total industry output produced by the largest firms in the industry, which is a guide to their ability to increase prices. However, they are imperfect indicators; for instance, they do not reflect foreign competition.

2. **Why is oligopoly characterized by mutual interdependence?**
Because an oligopoly includes few sellers, any change in output or price by one of them is likely to appreciably impact the sales of competing firms. Each of the sellers recognizes this fact, so what each firm should do to maximize its profits depends on what other firms do. Their choices and policies therefore reflect this mutual interdependence.

3. **Why do economies of scale result in few sellers in oligopoly models?**
Where substantial economies of scale are available relative to market demand, reasonably low costs of production cannot be obtained unless a firm produces a large fraction of the market output. If each firm, to produce at low costs, must supply a substantial fraction of the market, the industry has room for only a few firms to produce efficiently.

4. **How do economies of scale result in barriers to entry in oligopoly models?**
Low-cost entry must take place on a large scale in industries with substantial economies of scale. Therefore, existing firms could be profitable at their current prices and outputs without leading to entry. The great increase a large-scale entrant would cause in market output and the resulting decrease in market price could make that entrant unprofitable at those lower post-entry prices, even if current firms are profitable at current prices.

5. **Why does an oligopolist have a difficult time finding its profit-maximizing price and output?**
An oligopolist has a difficult time finding its profit-maximizing price and output because its demand curve is dramatically affected by the price and output policies of each of its rivals. This difficulty causes a great deal of uncertainty about the location and shape of its demand and marginal revenue curves, because they depend on what policies rivals actually adopt.

6. **Why would an automobile manufacturer be more likely than the corner baker to be an oligopolist?**

The automobile industry realizes substantial economies of scale relative to market demand, so lower-cost automobile production can be obtained by a firm that produces a substantial fraction of the market output. As a result, the automobile industry only has room for relatively few efficient-scale producers. In contrast, the bakery industry does not have substantial economies of scale relative to market demand, so the industry has room for a large number of efficient-scale bakeries.

15.2 Collusion and Cartels

1. **Why are collusive agreements typically unstable and short lived?**

Collusive agreements are typically unstable and short lived because they are strictly illegal under antitrust laws in the United States and many other countries and because firms experience a great temptation to cheat on collusive agreements by increasing their output and decreasing prices, which undermines any collusive agreement.

2. **Why is the temptation to collude greater when the industry's demand curve is more inelastic?**

The more inelastic the demand curve, the greater the increase in profits from colluding to jointly restrict output below its current level and raise prices in the industry; and hence the greater the temptation to collude.

15.3 Other Oligopoly Models

1. **What explains the kink in the kinked demand curve?**

The kink is produced by the greater tendency of competitors to follow price reductions than price increases. If a price increase is not met by rivals, a competitor would lose a substantial number of sales to rivals, resulting in a relatively elastic demand for price increases. If, on the other hand, a price decrease is met by rivals, a competitor would not be able to take a substantial number of sales from rivals, resulting in a more inelastic demand curve for price decreases.

2. **What impact does easy entry have on the profitability of oligopolies?**

Economic profits in oligopolistic industries will attract entrants, if entry is easy. Entrants may break down existing price agreements by cutting prices in an attempt to establish themselves in the industry, forcing existing firms to reduce their prices and suffer reduced market shares and thus undermining the profitability of the oligopoly.

3. **Why are barriers to entry necessary for successful, ongoing collusion?**

Because easy entry erodes economic profits where they are positive, barriers to entry are necessary for oligopolists to continue to earn economic profits in the long run.

4. **Why might oligopolists charge less than their short-run profit-maximizing price when threatened by entry?**

When entry threatens to undermine the economic profits of an oligopolistic industry, firms in the industry may lower their prices below the level that would maximize their short-run profits in order to deter entry by making it less profitable.

5. **A group of colluding oligopolists incurs costs of $10 per unit, and their profit-maximizing price is $15. If they know that potential market entrants could produce at a cost of $12 per unit, what price are the colluders likely to charge?**

If the colluding oligopolists are afraid of attracting entrants who will expand market output and reduce market prices and the colluders' profits, they might price below their short-run profit-maximizing price in order to make it unprofitable for new entrants. In this case, colluding oligopolists might well charge $12 or just below rather than the $15 they would otherwise charge.

6. **Why is price leadership also called tacit collusion?**

Price leadership, where one (typically dominant) firm signals how it intends to change its price and other firms follow suit, does not involve explicit agreements to restrict output and raise price. However, it can potentially be used to coordinate firms' behavior to achieve the same ends.

7. **What two factors increase the Herfindahl-Hirshman Index (HHI)?**

The HHI increases as either the number of firms in an industry decreases or the disparity in firm sizes increases.

8. **Why do horizontal mergers tend to concern antitrust authorities more than vertical or conglomerate mergers?**

Only horizontal mergers between makers of similar products increase market shares in a particular market, triggering changes in the HHI.

9. **For someone to be engaged in predatory pricing, what must happen to prices after the predation? Why would potential entry undermine the strategy?**

To reap monetary profits after predatory pricing, a firm would have to raise its prices substantially afterward. Easy entry would tend to make such a price increase unprofitable, as it would attract new competitors.

15.4 Game Theory and Strategic Behavior

1. **How is noncollusive oligopoly like a military campaign or a poker game?**

   Noncollusive oligopoly is like a military campaign, a poker game, or other strategic games in that firms take certain actions, not because they are necessarily advantageous in themselves, but because they improve the position of the oligopolist relative to its competitors, with the intent of improving its ultimate position. Firm actions take into account the likely countermoves rivals will make in response to those actions.

2. **What is the difference between cooperative and noncooperative games?**

   Noncooperative games are those where actions are taken independently, without consulting others; cooperative games are those where players can communicate and agree to binding contracts with each other.

3. **How does the prisoners' dilemma illustrate a dominant strategy for noncolluding oligopolists?**

   The prisoners' dilemma illustrates a dominant strategy for noncolluding oligopolists because it is in each player's interest to make the same choice regardless of the choice of the other player. Where a strategy is optimal regardless of opponents' actions, that strategy will dominate (be chosen over) others.

4. **What is a Nash equilibrium?**

   A Nash equilibrium is one where each firm is doing as well as it can, given the actions of its competitors. It is self-enforcing because once it is established, there is no incentive for any firm to change its policies or its actions.

5. **In the prisoners' dilemma, if each prisoner believed that the other prisoner would deny the crime, would each choose to deny the crime?**

   The prisoners' dilemma illustrates a dominant strategy in which it is in the interest of each of the two prisoners to confess, regardless of whether the other prisoner confesses—Prisoner A gets a lighter sentence if he confesses (2 years) than if he does not (6 years) if Prisoner B confesses, but he also gets a lighter sentence if he confesses (6 months) than if he does not (1 year) when Prisoner B does not confess; and the same is true for Prisoner B. The result is that, given the payoff matrix, each prisoner will confess regardless of what he expects the other prisoner will do.

6. **Why are repeated games more likely to lead to cooperative results than one-shot games?**

   While there are no adverse future consequences from "cheating" in a one-shot game, repeated games introduce these effects into the analysis by influencing the results of future games.

7. **How does a tit-for-tat strategy work?**

   In the first round, you cooperate. Then, in each successive round, you do what the other player did in the previous round. This "rewards" the opponent's current cooperation and "punishes" any choice the opponent makes not to cooperate.

8. **Why would industries with substantial positive network externalities tend to be oligopolies?**

   Consumers' demands are greater the larger the number of consumers. This could allow the more successful firms to grow and increase their output more, letting them achieve economies of scale that others cannot attain.

True or False:

1. Under oligopoly, individual firms produce only an infinitesimal share of total output.

2. The auto industry is an example of oligopoly.

3. Under oligopoly, as in perfect competition and monopolistic competition, firms cannot earn economic profits in the long run.

4. When firms in an oligopolistic industry collude, in the long run they fail to maximize social welfare.

5. When firms collude to set prices, their individual demand curves become relatively more elastic.

6. Although they are difficult to establish, most collusive oligopolies last indefinitely.

7. The new diamond industry in northern Canada will not threaten the economic profits earned by members of the international diamond cartel.

8. By the year 2050 the moon travel business consists of three international firms that create the International Moon Cartel, which restricts output and raises prices. Because this industry is an oligopoly, the existing firms' economic profits will be guaranteed for the long run.

9. Collusion tends to be quite durable in oligopoly markets.

10. In the kinked demand curve model, other firms are assumed to match price reductions because price reductions take business away from rivals, forcing them to cut price to protect their sales.

11. In the kinked demand curve model, an oligopoly firm's marginal revenue is discontinuous (has a gap in it).

12. The kinked demand curve model illustrates how costs can change for some oligopolists without leading to a change in price, even without collusion.

13. Oligopolists are less likely to experience price rigidity when they have excess capacity than when they are near full capacity.

14. The Herfindahl-Hirshman Index (HHI) increases when the number of firms in an industry increases.

15. Horizontal, vertical, and conglomerate mergers all increase a firm's market shares in the industries involved.

16. For predatory pricing to work, a firm would have to be able to raise its prices substantially afterward.

17. In noncooperative games, each firm sets its policy without consulting other firms.

18. A dominant strategy is one that will be optimal regardless of one's opponent's actions.

19. A Nash equilibrium is an example of a game that does not have a dominant strategy.

20. Repeated games are more likely to produce cooperative results than one-shot games.

21. Firms always cooperate in repeated games.

22. All network externalities act to increase consumer demands for products.

23. The area of communications often exhibits positive network externalities.

24. The bandwagon effect can apply to the "hot" toy during the Christmas shopping season.

25. Whether a good is subject to positive or negative network externalities from congestion can depend on a consumer's preferences.

26. Switching costs can be a significant barrier to new entrants in an industry.

27. When significant positive network effects are present, oligopoly is a common market structure.

Multiple Choice:

1. Which of the following is *not* a characteristic of oligopoly?
   a. A few firms control most of the production and sale of a product.
   b. Firms in the industry make price and output decisions with an eye to the decisions and policies of other firms in the industry.
   c. Competing firms can enter the industry easily.
   d. Substantial economies of scale are present in production.

2. Under oligopoly, a few large firms control most of the production and sale of a product because
   a. economies of scale make it difficult for small firms to compete.
   b. diseconomies of scale make it difficult for small firms to compete.
   c average total costs rise as production expands.
   d. marginal costs rise as production expands.

3. In an oligopoly such as the U.S. domestic airline industry, a firm such as United Airlines would
   a. carefully anticipate Delta, American, and Southwest's likely responses before it raised or lowered fares.
   b. pretty much disregard Delta, American, and Southwest's likely responses when raising or lowering fares.
   c. charge the lowest fare possible in order to maximize market share.
   d. schedule as many flights to as many cities as possible without regard to what competitors do.

4. One of the reasons that collusive oligopolies are usually short lived is that
   a. they are unable to earn economic profits in the long run.
   b. they do not set prices where marginal cost equals marginal revenue.
   c. they set prices below long-run average total costs.
   d. parties to the collusion often cheat on one another.

5. In a collusive oligopoly, joint profits are maximized when a price is set based on
   a. its own demand and cost schedules.
   b. the market demand for the product and the summation of marginal costs of the various firms.
   c. the price followers' demand schedules and the price leader's marginal costs.
   d. the price leader's demand schedule and the price followers' marginal costs.

6. During the 1950s, many profitable manufacturing industries in the United States, such as steel, tires, and autos, were considered oligopolies. Why do you think such firms work hard to keep imports from other countries out of the U.S. market?
   a. Without import barriers, excess profits in the United States would attract foreign firms, break down existing price agreements, and reduce profits of U.S. firms.
   b. Without import barriers, foreign firms would be attracted to the United States and cause the cost in the industry to rise.
   c. Without import barriers, foreign firms would buy U.S. goods and resell them in the United States, causing profits to fall.
   d. Without import barriers, prices of goods would rise, so consumers would buy less of the products of these firms.

7. Over the past 20 years, Dominator, Inc., a large firm in an oligopolistic industry, has changed prices a number of times. Each time it does so, the other firms in the industry follow suit. Dominator, Inc., is a
   a. monopoly.
   b. perfect competitor.
   c. price leader.
   d. price follower.

8. In the kinked demand curve model, starting from the initial price, the demand curve assumed to face a firm is relatively _____ for price increases and relatively _____ for price decreases.
   a. elastic; elastic
   b. elastic; inelastic
   c. inelastic; elastic
   d. inelastic; inelastic

9. The kinked demand curve model illustrates
   a. how price rigidity could characterize some oligopoly firms, despite changing marginal costs.
   b. how price increases and price decreases can elicit different responses from rival firms, in oligopoly.
   c. why price rigidity may be more common when firms have excess capacity than when operating near capacity.
   d. the importance of expectations about rival behavior in oligopoly.
   e. all of the above.

10. The Herfindahl-Hirshman Index (HHI) increases as the number of firms _____ or the disparity of firm sizes _____.
    a. increases; increases
    b. increases; decreases
    c. decreases; increases
    d. decreases; decreases

11. The Herfindahl-Hirshman Index (HHI) will increase the most in an industry when
    a. one large firm merges with another large firm.
    b. one large firm merges with a small firm.
    c. two small firms merge.
    d. a large firm separates into two firms.

12. Which kind of merger increases the HHI and thus triggers concerns about competitiveness?
    a. horizontal mergers
    b. vertical mergers
    c. conglomerate mergers
    d. all of the above

13. In game theory
    a. there is not always a dominant strategy.
    b. a Nash equilibrium is a dominant strategy.
    c. collusion is an example of a cooperative game.
    d. all of the above are true.

14. In game theory
    a. cooperative strategies are more likely in repeated games than one-shot games.
    b. cooperative strategies are more likely in one-shot games than repeated games.
    c. cooperative strategies are equally likely in one-shot and repeated games.
    d. we do not know whether cooperative strategies are more likely in one type of game or another.

15. In game theory
    a. a dominant strategy in a noncooperative game does not yield the same result as if players cooperate.
    b. a tit-for-tat strategy is a way to reward cooperation and punish noncooperation in a repeated game.
    c. in a Nash equilibrium, neither firm has an incentive to change behavior.
    d. all of the above are true.

16. Which of the following areas illustrates positive network externalities?
    a. telephones
    b. software
    c. fax machines
    d. the Internet
    e. all of the above

Problems:

1. Which of the following markets are oligopolistic?
   a. corn
   b. funeral services
   c. airline travel
   d. hamburgers
   e. oil
   f. breakfast cereals

2. Which of the following are characteristic of oligopolistic industries?
   a. a large number of firms
   b. few firms
   c. a high degree of product differentiation
   d. high barriers to entry
   e. free entry and exit
   f. mutual interdependence

3. Suppose Farmer Smith from Kansas and Farmer Jones from Missouri agree to restrict their combined output of wheat in an attempt to increase the price and profits. How likely do you think the Smith–Jones cartel is to succeed? Explain.

4. Explain how the joint profit-maximizing price of colluding firms under oligopoly is determined. How about output?

5. Explain how the long-run equilibrium under oligopoly differs from that of perfect competition.

6. Important differences exist between perfect competition and oligopoly. Show your understanding of these differences by listing the following terms under either "perfect competition" or "oligopoly."

		Perfect Competition	Oligopoly
allocative efficiency	large economies of scale	_____	_____
many small firms	productive efficiency	_____	_____
high barriers to entry	horizontal demand curve	_____	_____
few large firms	mutual interdependence	_____	_____
downward-sloping demand curve	no control over price	_____	_____

7. One of the world's most successful cartels has been the Central Selling Organization (CSO), which controls about three-quarters of the world's diamonds. This collusive oligopoly has kept diamond prices high by restricting supply. The CSO has also promoted the general consumption of diamonds through advertising and marketing. New supplies of diamonds have been found in Canada and Russia. These new mines, which are outside the direct control of the CSO, want to sell their diamonds on the open market.
   a. What would you predict will happen in the market for diamonds if these new mines do not cooperate with the cartel?
   b. What do you think will happen to CSO diamond advertising?

8. The U.S. Justice Department has been worried that the nation's four largest air carriers—Delta, Northwest, American, and United—use low prices to limit competition at the busiest airports. Predatory pricing exists when the dominant carrier at an airport matches the low prices of any new low-fare competitor and sells more low-fare seats. The major carrier holds these low prices until the new competition folds. The dominant carrier recovers any short-term losses with increased fares once the competition is eliminated.

   The government thinks that this pricing response is an anticompetitive strategy. The dominant carriers claim that this response is simply a part of competition. Which is it? How would each of the following pieces of information affect your decision as to whether it is an anticompetitive strategy or a competitive response? Check the appropriate column.

	Anticompetitive Strategy	Competitive Response
Large, unrecoverable start-up costs for new airlines.	_____	_____
Many airlines serve the airport.	_____	_____
Dominant airline drops price below average variable cost.	_____	_____
Dominant airline flights have excess capacity before the new airline enters the market.	_____	_____

9. In the kinked demand model, what is assumed about rival responses to price increases? Price decreases? What does that imply about anticipated elasticities of demand as a result?

10. What would the Herfindahl-Hirshman Index (HHI) be in each of the following situations:
   a. 10 firms, each with 10 percent of the market
   b. 4 firms, each with 25 percent of the market
   c. 2 firms, each with 50 percent of the market
   d. 1 firm with a monopoly in the market

11. Why would someone consider how broadly or narrowly the relevant market is considered to be so critical to the results when HHI values are used to evaluate mergers?

12. Assume there are initially 10 firms, each with a 10 percent market share.
   a. What is the initial HHI?
   b. What will the HHI become if two firms merge?
   c. What will the HHI become if three firms merge?

13. Answer questions a–c on HHI.
   a. What would the HHI be for an industry made up of one firm with 30 percent of the market, and 14 firms, each with 5 percent of the market?
   b. What would the HHI be if two of the firms with 5 percent of the market merge?
   c. What would the HHI be if the large (30 percent share) firm merged with one of the smaller (5 percent share) firms?

14. Are the following mergers horizontal, vertical, or conglomerate?
   a. *Newsweek* magazine and *Time* magazine
   b. Tyson Chicken and Popeye's Chicken restaurants
   c. CBS TV and Jerry Bruckheimer Productions (TV show producer)
   d. Alcoa and McDonald's
   e. Alcoa and an aluminum siding company
   f. Sealy Mattress Company and Beautyrest Mattress Company
   g. a bakery and a sandwich chain

15. Two firms compete in the breakfast cereal industry producing Rice Krinkles and Wheat Krinkles cereal, respectively. Each manufacturer must decide whether to promote its product with a large or small advertising budget. The potential profits for these firms are as follows (in millions of dollars):

Firm A
Wheat Krinkles Cereal

		Small Advertising Budget	Large Advertising Budget
Firm B Rice Krinkles Cereal	**Small Advertising Budget**	Firm (A) $50 M / Firm (B) $50 M	Firm (A) $30 M / Firm (B) $100 M
	Large Advertising Budget	Firm (A) $140 M / Firm (B) $20 M	Firm (A) $150 M / Firm (B) $150 M

Describe the nature of the mutual interdependence between the two firms. Is a Nash equilibrium evident?

16. Suppose Pepsi is considering an ad campaign aimed at rival Coca-Cola. What is the dominant strategy if the payoff matrix is similar to the one shown in Exhibit 3 in Section 15.4?

17. Suppose your professor announces that each student in your large lecture class who receives the highest score (no matter how high) on the take-home final exam will get an A in the course. The professor points out that if the entire class colludes successfully everyone could get the same score. Is it likely that everyone in the class will get an A?

18. The following payoff matrix shows the possible sentences that two suspects, who are arrested on suspicion of car theft, could receive. The suspects are interrogated separately and are unable to communicate with one another.

Use the following information to answer the question below.

		Suspect 2	
		Confess	Don't Confess
Suspect 1	Confess	1 — 6 years / 2 — 6 years	1 — 1 year / 2 — 10 years
	Don't Confess	1 — 10 years / 2 — 1 year	1 — 2 years / 2 — 2 years

For the information given in the payoff matrix above:
a. Is there is a dominant strategy?
b. What is the dominant strategy? How do you know?
c. Is there a Nash equilibrium? How do you know?

19. Why are repeated games more likely to be cooperative than one-shot games?

20. Why might shirking on a team project in school be a dominant strategy, but not shirking on a team project at work?

PART 5 INPUT MARKETS AND MICROECONOMIC POLICY ISSUES

16 The Markets for Labor, Capital, and Land

Approximately 75 percent of national income goes to wages and salaries for labor services. So, how are salary levels among those individuals determined?

After laborers take their share, the remaining 25 percent of national income is compensation received by the owners of land and capital and the entrepreneurs who employ these resources to produce valued goods and services.

In labor markets, actor Johnny Depp can make more than $20 million acting in one film. Baseball player Alex Rodriguez of the New York Yankees makes $25 million a year. Singer Madonna's income is many times larger than that of the average college professor or medical

doctor. Female models make more than male models, yet male basketball players make more than female basketball players. Why do these differences occur? To understand the reasons for the wide variation in compensation workers receive for their labors, we must focus on the workings of supply and demand in the labor market.

In this chapter, we also study the relationship between productivity and wages, labor unions, and the markets for land and capital. ■

Input Markets

* How is income distributed among workers, landowners, and the owners of capital?

* What is derived demand?

Determining the Price of a Productive Factor: Derived Demand

Input markets are the markets for the factors of production used to produce output. Output (goods and services)

derived demand
the demand for an input derived from consumers' demand for the good or service produced with that input

markets and input markets have one major difference. In input or factor markets, the demand for an input derived from consumers' demand for the good or service produced with that input is called a derived demand. That is, the demand for an input such as labor is derived from the demand for the good

---

in the news

Demand, Not Higher Salaries, Drives Up Baseball Ticket Prices

Teams that blame escalating salaries for escalating ticket prices are simply using players as a handy scapegoat, University of Chicago economist Allen Sanderson says. . . . "Player salaries have virtually no impact on ticket prices. Ticket prices are set by what the market will bear. After that, it's a matter of who gets the money, [the owners or the players]. . . ."

Remember supply and demand from your economics class? A team would raise ticket prices, regardless of player salaries, only if it believed fans would pay the higher prices. In economic jargon, a team would raise ticket prices only if it believed a demand would remain strong at the higher prices for a fixed supply of seats.

"If I'm an owner and I have to justify this to my season-ticket holders, I have to blame somebody," Sanderson said. "I can't stand up and say, 'The ticket prices are going up 19% next year because you'll pay it. . . .'"

Virtually all economists would support this application of the basic economic theory of supply and demand.

"Anyone who has studied the industry would tell you this is what's going on," said [Roger] Noll [a Stanford economist and a specialist on sports

economics]. . . . "Revenues drive everything, including the degree of vitriol in collective bargaining."

So owners, defending price increases, point fingers at players. But when three national theater chains increased movie prices recently, executives did not point fingers at actors. "There was certainly no reference to . . . we have to do this because Jack Nicholson and Tom Cruise and Michelle Pfeiffer have such high salaries," Sanderson said. "I've never heard anyone say, 'If Tom Cruise would work for $10 million [a movie] instead of $20 million, my ticket would be $6 instead of $7. . . .'"

"Every sports fan, if he wants to see why player salaries are so high should go look in the mirror," Noll said. "If fans were not willing to pay a lot, salaries would not be so high. Everything starts with what consumers are willing to pay."

SOURCE: Bill Shaikin, "Face Value," *Los Angeles Times*, April 1, 1999, p. D1. Copyright © 1999 Los Angeles Times. Reprinted with permission.

consider this:

Baseball salaries are a derived demand. It is the customers' demand for a baseball game that drives baseball salaries. This same reason explains why top women's tennis players make more than top women (and men) professional bowlers.

or service. Thus, consumers do *not* demand the labor directly—it is the goods and services the labor produces that consumers demand. For example, the chef at a restaurant is paid and her skills are in demand because she produces what customers want—great-tasting meals. The "price" of any productive factor is directly related to consumer demand for the final good or service.

SECTION CHECK

1. Supply and demand determine the prices paid to workers, landowners, and capital owners.
2. In factor or input markets, demand is derived from consumers' demand for the final good or service that the input produces.

---

1. Why is the demand for productive inputs derived from the demand for the outputs those inputs produce?
2. Why is the demand for tractors and fertilizer derived from the demand for agricultural products?

SECTION 16.2 Supply and Demand in the Labor Market

* What is the marginal revenue product for an input?
* What is the marginal resource cost of hiring another worker?

* Why is the demand curve for labor downward sloping?
* What is the shape of the supply curve of labor?

Will Hiring That Input Add More to Revenue Than Costs?

Because firms are trying to maximize their profits, they try (by definition) to make the *difference* between total revenue and total cost as large as possible. An input's attractiveness, then, varies with what the input can add to the firm's revenues relative to what the input adds to costs. In a competitive labor market, the demand for labor is determined by its **marginal revenue product (MRP)**, which is the additional revenue that a firm obtains from one more unit of input. Why? Suppose a worker adds $500 per week to a firm's sales by his productivity; he produces 100 units that add $5 each to firm revenue. To determine whether the worker adds to the firm's profits, we would need to calculate the marginal resource cost associated with the worker. The **marginal resource cost (MRC)** is the amount that an extra

> **marginal revenue product (MRP)**
> marginal product times the price of the product
>
> **marginal resource cost (MRC)**
> the amount that an extra input adds to the firm's total cost

input adds to the firm's total costs. In this case, the marginal resource cost is the wage the employer has to pay to entice an extra worker. Assume that the marginal resource cost of the worker, the market wage, is $350 per worker per week. In our example, the firm would find its profits growing by adding one more worker, because the marginal benefit (MRP) associated with the worker, $500, would exceed the marginal cost (MRC) of the worker, $350. So we can see that just by adding another worker to its labor force, the firm would increase its weekly profits by $150 ($500 − $350). Even if the market wage were $490 per week, the firm could slightly increase its profits by hiring the employee, because the marginal revenue product, $500, is greater than the added labor cost, $490. At wage payments greater than $500, however, the firm would not be interested in the worker, because the marginal resource cost would exceed the marginal revenue product, making additional hiring unprofitable.

The Demand Curve for Labor Slopes Downward

The downward-sloping demand curve for labor indicates a negative relationship between wage and the quantity of labor demanded. Higher wages will decrease the quantity of labor demanded, while lower wages will increase the quantity of labor demanded. But why does this relationship exist?

The major reason for the downward-sloping demand curve for labor (illustrated in Exhibit 1) is the law of diminishing marginal product. Remember that the law of diminishing marginal product states that as increasing quantities of some variable input (say, labor) are added to fixed quantities of another input (say, land or capital), output will rise, but at some point it will increase by diminishing amounts.

Consider a farmer who owns a given amount of land. Suppose the farmer is producing wheat, and the relationship between output and labor force requirements is that indicated in Exhibit 2. Output expands as more workers are hired to cultivate the land, but the growth in output steadily slows, meaning that the added output associated with one more worker declines as more workers are added. For example, in Exhibit 2, when a third worker is hired, total wheat output increases from 5,500 bushels to 7,000 bushels, an increase of 1,500 bushels in terms of marginal product. However, when a fourth worker is added, total wheat output only

marginal product (MP)
the change in total output of a good that results from a one-unit change in input

**section 16.2
exhibit 1   The Marginal Revenue Product of Labor**

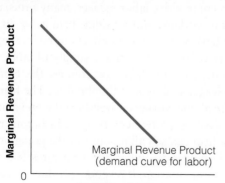

The value of the marginal revenue product of labor shows how the marginal revenue product depends on the number of workers employed. The curve is downward sloping because of the diminishing marginal product of labor.

section 16.2 exhibit 2	**Diminishing Marginal Productivity on a Hypothetical Farm**	
Units of Labor Input (workers)	**Total Wheat Output (bushels per year)**	**Marginal Product of Labor (bushels per year)**
0	—	
1	3,000	3,000
2	5,500	2,500
3	7,000	1,500
4	8,000	1,000
5	8,500	500
6	8,800	300
7	9,000	200

increases from 7,000 bushels to 8,000 bushels, or a marginal increase of 1,000 bushels. Note that the reason for the decline in marginal product is *not* that the workers being added are steadily inferior in terms of ability or quality relative to the first workers. Indeed, for simplicity, we assume that each worker has exactly the same skills and productive capacity. But as more workers are added, each additional worker has fewer of the fixed resources with which to work, and marginal product falls. For example, the fifth worker might merely cultivate the same land more intensively. The work of the fifth worker, then, might only slightly improve output. That is, the **marginal product (MP)**—the number of physical units of added output from the addition of one additional unit of input—falls.

As we discussed earlier, the marginal revenue product (*MRP*) is the change in total revenue associated with an additional unit of input. The marginal revenue product is equal to the marginal product (that is, the units of output added by a worker) multiplied by marginal revenue (*MR*) (that is, the price of the output):

$$MRP = MP \times MR$$

The *MRP* curve takes on different characteristics depending on whether the output market is competitive or imperfectly competitive. In this chapter, we are assuming the product, or output markets, are competitive. Recall from Chapter 12, that in competitive output markets, the firm will sell all its output at the market price. Consequently, the marginal revenue from the sale of an additional unit is also equal to the market price. Therefore, when output markets are perfectly

section 16.2 exhibit 3	Marginal Revenue Product, Output, and Labor Inputs					
Quantity of Labor	Total Output (bushels per week)	Marginal Product of Labor (bushels per week)	Product Price (dollars per bushel)	Marginal Revenue Product of Labor	Wage Rate (MRC) (dollars per week)	Marginal Profit (MRP − W)
0	0					
1	100	100	$10	$1,000	$550	$450
2	190	90	10	900	550	350
3	270	80	10	800	550	250
4	340	70	10	700	550	150
5	400	60	10	600	550	50
6	450	50	10	500	550	−50
7	490	40	10	400	550	−150
8	520	30	10	300	550	−250

competitive, the marginal revenue product of a factor is equal to the marginal product times the price of the product the firm is selling:

$$MRP = MP \times P$$

For example, if an additional worker adds 10 bushels of wheat per day (marginal product) and each of these 10 bushels sells for $10 (price of the product), then the worker's marginal revenue product is $100 per day.

The marginal revenue product of labor declines because of the diminishing marginal product of labor when additional workers are added. This decline in MRP is illustrated in Exhibit 3, which shows various output and revenue levels for a wheat farmer using different quantities of labor. We see in Exhibit 3 that the marginal product, or the added physical volume of output, declines as the number of workers grows, because of diminishing marginal product. Thus, the fifth worker adds only 60 bushels of wheat per week compared with 100 bushels for the first worker.

How Many Workers Will an Employer Hire?

Profits are maximized if the firm hires only to the point where the wage equals the expected marginal revenue product; that is, the firm will hire up to the last unit of input for which the marginal revenue product is expected to exceed the wage. Because the demand curve for labor and the value of the marginal revenue product show the quantity of labor that a firm demands at a given wage in a competitive market, we say that the marginal revenue product (MRP)

is the same as the demand curve for labor for a competitive firm.

Using the data in Exhibit 3, if the market wage is $550 per week, it would pay for the wheat farmer to employ five workers. The fifth worker's marginal revenue product ($600) exceeds the wage, so profits are increased $50 by adding the worker. Adding a sixth worker would be unprofitable, however, as that worker's marginal revenue product of $500 is less than the wage of $550. Hiring the sixth worker would reduce profits by $50.

But what if the market wage increases from $550 to $650? In this case, hiring the fifth worker becomes unprofitable, because the marginal resource cost, $650, is now greater than the marginal revenue product of $600. That is, a higher wage rate, *ceteris paribus*, lowers the employment levels of individual firms.

In a competitive labor market, many firms are competing for workers, and no single firm is big enough by itself to have any significant effect on the level of wages. The intersection of the market supply of labor and the market demand for labor determines the competitive market wage, as shown in Exhibit 4(a). The firm's ability to hire all the workers it wishes at the prevailing wage is analogous to perfect competition in output markets, where a firm can sell all it wants at the going price.

In Exhibit 4(b), when the firm hires less than q^* workers, the marginal revenue product exceeds the market wage, so adding workers expands profits. With more than q^* workers, however, the "going wage" exceeds marginal revenue product, and hiring additional workers lowers profits. With q^* workers, profits are maximized.

In this chapter, we assume that labor markets are competitive, with many buyers and sellers of labor,

a. Market Supply and Demand for Labor

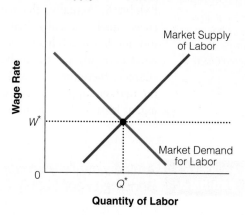

b. Firm's Supply and Demand for Labor

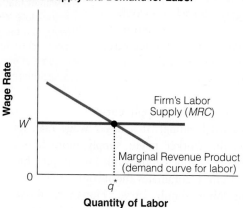

A competitive firm can hire any number of potential workers at the market-determined wage; it is a price (wage) taker. At employment levels less than $q*$, additional workers add profits. At employment levels beyond $q*$, additional workers are unprofitable. At $q*$, profits are maximized.

and no individual worker having an impact on wages. It is generally a realistic assumption because in most labor markets firms compete with each other to attract workers, and workers can choose from many possible employers.

The Market Labor Supply Curve

How much work effort individuals are collectively willing and able to supply in the marketplace is the essence of the market supply curve. Just as was the case in our earlier discussion of the law of supply, a positive relationship exists between the wage rate and the quantity of labor supplied. As the wage rate rises, the quantity of labor supplied increases, *ceteris paribus*; as the wage rate falls, the quantity of labor supplied falls, *ceteris paribus*. This positive relationship is consistent with the evidence that the total quantity of labor supplied by *all* workers increases as the wage rate increases, as shown in Exhibit 5.

An Individual's Labor Supply Curve

Will the quantity of labor supplied by an individual be greater at higher wages than at lower wages? The answer is by no means obvious because workers have another use for their time—namely, leisure. Furthermore, wage increases have two conflicting effects on the quantity of labor supplied:

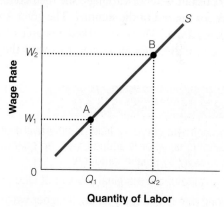

An increase in the wage rate, from A to B, leads to an increase in the quantity of labor supplied, *ceteris paribus*. A decrease in the wage rate, from B to A, leads to a decrease in the quantity of labor supplied, *ceteris paribus*.

1. *Substitution effect:* At a higher wage rate, the cost of forgoing labor time to gain greater leisure time increases, producing a tendency to substitute labor for leisure. In other words, a higher wage rate makes leisure more expensive—its opportunity cost rises.

2. *Income effect:* At a higher wage rate, the quantity of labor supplied tends to decrease because many individuals consider leisure a normal good. So when income increases, people demand more leisure. That is, at some wage rate, some workers feel that they can afford more leisure.

backward-bending labor supply curve
above a certain wage rate, a worker may prefer to enjoy more leisure and less work to meet his or her own personal preferences (the income effect dominates the substitution effect)

the year at Walden Pond, pursuing his pastime of writing and observing nature. In both these cases, the individual's labor supply curve might appear as shown in Exhibit 6. Actually, the market supply curve might actually bend backwards too but at a much higher wage rate than what currently exists. In the rest of this chapter, therefore, we will assume that the market supply curve is upward sloping, at least in the relevant range.

Thus, the individual's labor supply curve might be backward bending. At a lower wage rate, as wages increase, the worker might supply more hours of work to obtain as much money income as possible (the substitution effect dominates the income effect), an upward-sloping labor supply curve. However, above a certain wage rate, a worker might prefer to enjoy more leisure and less work to meet personal preferences (the income effect dominates the substitution effect), a **backward-bending labor supply curve.** That is, if the substitution effect is stronger than the income effect, the individual's labor supply curve is upward sloping. If the income effect is stronger than the substitution effect, the individual's labor supply curve is backward bending. For example, a student working during the summer to earn money for the school year might quit her job once she has reached a certain level of earnings; she then concentrates on leisure for the rest of the summer. The great American writer Henry David Thoreau worked a couple of months each year to make enough money to spend the rest of

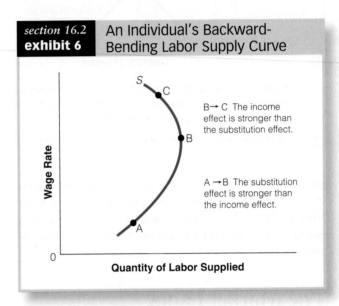

section 16.2
exhibit 6   An Individual's Backward-Bending Labor Supply Curve

B → C The income effect is stronger than the substitution effect.

A → B The substitution effect is stronger than the income effect.

Quantity of Labor Supplied

SECTION CHECK

1. The demand curve for labor is downward sloping because of diminishing marginal product. That is, if additional labor is added to a fixed quantity of land or capital equipment, output will increase, but eventually by smaller amounts.

2. The value of the marginal product of labor is the marginal product times the price of the output.

3. Along a market supply curve, a higher wage rate will increase the quantity supplied of labor and a lower wage rate will decrease the quantity supplied of labor.

4. An individual labor supply curve can be backward bending. When higher wages are offered, the cost of forgoing labor time to gain greater leisure time becomes greater; thus, workers tend to substitute labor for leisure—the substitution effect. At higher wage levels, the income from a given quantity of labor is greater, and a worker may feel that he or she can afford more leisure—the income effect. If the substitution effect is stronger than the income effect, the individual's labor supply curve is upward sloping. If the income effect is stronger than the substitution effect, the individual's labor supply curve is backward bending.

---

1. What is marginal revenue product?

2. Would a firm hire another worker if the marginal revenue product of labor exceeded the market wage rate? Why or why not?

3. Why does the marginal product of labor eventually fall?

4. Why does diminishing marginal product mean that the marginal revenue product will eventually fall?

5. Why is a firm hiring in a competitive labor market a price (wage) taker for a given quality of labor?

6. What is responsible for a backward-bending individual supply curve for labor?

Labor Market Equilibrium

✱ How are the equilibrium wage and employment determined in labor markets?

✱ What shifts the labor demand curve?

✱ What shifts the labor supply curve?

Determining Equilibrium in the Competitive Labor Market

The equilibrium wage and quantity in competitive markets for labor is determined by the intersection of labor demand and labor supply. As shown in Exhibit 1, the equilibrium wage, W^*, and equilibrium employment level, Q^*, are found at that point where the quantity of labor demanded equals the quantity of labor supplied. At any wage higher than W^*—at W_1, for example—the quantity of labor supplied exceeds the quantity of labor demanded, resulting in a surplus of labor. In this situation, unemployed workers are willing to undercut the established wage in order to get jobs, pushing the wage down and returning the market to equilibrium. At a wage below the equilibrium level—at W_2, for example—quantity demanded exceeds quantity supplied, resulting in a labor shortage. In this situation, employers are forced to offer higher wages in order to hire as many workers as they would like. Note that only at the equilibrium wage are both suppliers and demanders able to exchange the quantity of labor they desire.

Shifts in the Labor Demand Curve

In Chapter 4, we demonstrated that the determinants of demand can shift the demand curve for a good or service. In the case of an input such as labor, two important factors can shift the demand curve: increases in labor productivity—caused by technological advances, for instance—or changes in the output price of the good—caused by, say, an increased demand for the firm's product. Exhibit 2 highlights the impact of these changes.

Changes in Labor Productivity

Workers can increase productivity if they have more capital or land with which to work, if technological improvements occur, or if they acquire additional skills or experience (human capital). This increase in productivity will increase the marginal product of the labor and shift the demand curve for labor to the right from D_1 to D_2 in Exhibit 2(a). However, if labor productivity falls, then marginal product will fall, and the demand curve for labor will shift to the left [see Exhibit 2(b)].

Changes in the Demand for the Firm's Product

The greater the demand for the firm's product, the greater the firm's demand for labor or any other variable input (the *derived demand* discussed earlier). The reason for this is that the higher demand for the firm's product increases the firm's marginal revenue, which increases marginal revenue product. That is, the greater

**section 16.3
exhibit 1**

Supply and Demand in the Competitive Labor Market

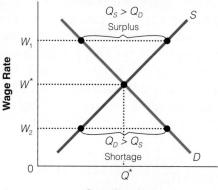

Equilibrium prices and quantities in the competitive labor market are determined in the same way prices and quantities of goods and services are determined: by the intersection of demand and supply. At wages above the equilibrium wage—at W_1, for example—quantity supplied exceeds quantity demanded, and potential workers are willing to supply their labor services for an amount lower than the prevailing wage. At a wage lower than W^*—at W_2, for example—potential demanders overcome the resulting shortage of labor by offering workers a wage greater than the prevailing wage. In both cases, wages are pushed toward the equilibrium value.

section 16.3
exhibit 2 Shifts in the Labor Demand Curve

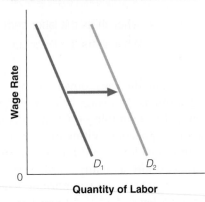

a. Increase in Labor Demand

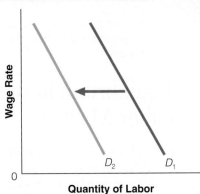

b. Decrease in Labor Demand

An increase in labor demand will shift the demand curve for labor to the right. A decrease in labor demand will shift the demand curve for labor to the left.

Use what you've LEARNED — LABOR SUPPLY AND DEMAND

Q Why do teachers, who provide a valuable service to the community, make millions and millions of dollars less than star basketball players?

A It is the marginal revenue product of additional teachers and the supply of teachers that determine the market wage (regardless of how important we consider the job). A teacher's marginal revenue product is likely to be well below $5 million a year. Most people probably think that teachers are more important than star basketball players, yet teachers make a lot less money. Of course, the reason for this is simple supply and demand. A lot of people enjoy watching star basketball players, but only a few individuals have the skill to perform at that level. Although demand for teachers is large, the number of potential suppliers is also relatively large. As shown in Exhibit 3, this relationship between supply and demand translates into a much lower wage for teachers than for star basketball players.

section 16.3
exhibit 3 Labor Markets for Basketball Players and Teachers

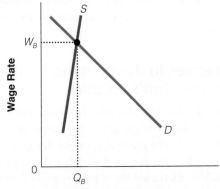

a. Labor Market for Star Basketball Players

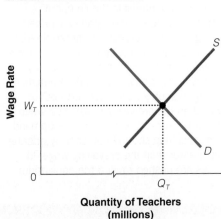

b. Labor Market for Teachers

demand for the product causes prices to rise, and the price of the product is part of the value of the labor to the firm ($MRP = MP \times P$). Therefore, the rising product price shifts the labor demand curve to the right. Of course, if demand for the firm's product falls, the labor demand curve will shift to the left as marginal revenue product falls.

Shifting the Labor Supply Curve

In Chapter 4, we learned that changes in the determinants of supply can shift the supply curve for goods and services to the right or left. Likewise, several factors can cause the labor supply curve to shift. These factors include immigration and population growth, the number of hours workers are willing to work at a given wage (worker tastes or preferences), nonwage income, and amenities. Exhibit 4 illustrates the impact of these factors on the labor supply curve.

Immigration and Population Growth

If new workers enter the labor force, the labor supply curve will shift to the right—from S_1 to S_2 in Exhibit 4(a). Of course, if workers leave the country—and thus the labor force—or the relevant population declines, the supply curve will shift to the left, as shown in Exhibit 4(b).

Number of Hours People Are Willing to Work (Worker Preferences)

If people become willing to work more hours at a given wage (due to changes in worker tastes or preferences), the labor supply curve will shift to the right, as shown in the movement from S_1 to S_2 in Exhibit 4(a). If they become willing to work fewer hours at a given wage, the labor supply curve will shift to the left, as shown in Exhibit 4(b).

Nonwage Income

Increases in income from other sources than employment can cause the labor supply curve to shift to the left. For example, if you just won $20 million in your state's Super Lotto, you might decide to take yourself out of the labor force. Likewise, a decrease in nonwage income might push a person back into the labor force, thus shifting the labor supply curve to the right.

Amenities

Amenities associated with a job or location—such as good fringe benefits, safe and friendly working conditions, a child-care center, and so on—will make for a more desirable work environment, *ceteris paribus*. These amenities will cause an increase in the supply of labor, resulting in a rightward shift of the labor supply curve—from S_1 to S_2 in Exhibit 4(a). If job conditions deteriorate, the labor supply will decrease, shifting the labor supply curve to the left, as shown in Exhibit 4(b).

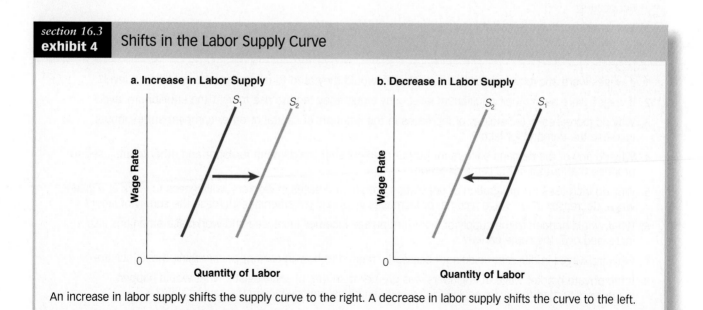

section 16.3 **exhibit 4**   Shifts in the Labor Supply Curve

An increase in labor supply shifts the supply curve to the right. A decrease in labor supply shifts the curve to the left.

Monopsony

So far our discussion assumed that the labor market is competitive—many buyers of labor and many sellers of labor with no one having a marked impact on wages. Recall that, in the case of a single seller of a product or input, we say a monopoly exists. When the market involves a single buyer, however, we say a **monopsony** exists. While monopsony could exist in any single buyer situation, the situation considered most relevant in the real world is the labor market. Monopsony usually refers, then, to circumstances where only one employer is bidding for the services of many laborers. Where monopsony is present, the buyer of labor may have market power and may be able to affect wages. However, pure monopsony, like pure monopoly, is rare. For example, monopsony may arise because a person within a given locality has only a relatively few choices of where to work. However, if the individual was willing to move, or the number of buyers of services potentially is enlarged, then the role of a monopsony is diminished. So monopsony power is more likely to be present where movement and search costs impede workers from seeking employment in different locales.

In the nineteenth century, one or two textile mills often dominated New England mill towns; in other areas, a single mining or manufacturing firm dominated the community to the point that it might be called a company town. Monopsony power existed in such situations and increased the opportunities for monopsonistic exploitation. Even though no fences around the town kept workers from leaving, high transportation and information costs made it expensive, sometimes prohibitively so, for workers to overcome exploitation by moving. The theory suggests that where monopsony exists, fewer workers will be hired at lower wages than if perfect competition prevailed in labor markets. That is, the monopsony firm moves down along the positively sloped labor supply curve it faces, lowering the wages it pays and increasing its profits. In short, workers will work for less than their marginal revenue product—they are in this sense exploited.

monopsony
a market with a single buyer

Today, an example of monopsony power would include the only auto repair shop in a small town—if workers do not want to move. In some professional sports, players are drafted and are assigned to teams until they are eligible to be free agents (after six years in baseball). Because other teams cannot compete for these players, the outcome is lower salaries, as teams exercise their monopsony power. However, for the most part, in most occupations, many potential employers in many different locations compete for workers.

SECTION / CHECK

1. The intersection of the labor demand curve and the labor supply curve determines wages in the labor market.
2. The labor demand curve can shift when a change in productivity or a change in the demand for the final product occurs.
3. The labor supply curve can shift when changes in immigration or population growth, workers' preferences, nonwage income, or amenities occur.

---

1. If wages were above their equilibrium level, why would they tend to fall toward the equilibrium level?
2. If wages were below their equilibrium level, why would they tend to rise toward the equilibrium level?
3. Why do increases in technology or increases in the amounts of capital or other complementary inputs increase the demand for labor?
4. Why do any of the demand shifters for output markets shift the demand for labor and other inputs used to produce that output in the same direction?
5. Why do increases in immigration or population growth, increases in workers' willingness to work at a given wage, decreases in nonwage income, or increases in workplace amenities increase the supply of labor?
6. What would happen to the supply of labor if nonwage incomes increased and workplace amenities also increased over the same period?
7. Why are wages in different fields not necessarily related to how important people think those jobs are?
8. If the private-market wage of engineers was greater than that of sociologists, what would happen if a university tried to pay its engineering faculty and its sociology faculty the same salary?

SECTION 16.4   Labor Unions

* Why do labor unions exist?
* What is the impact of unions on wages?
* Can unions increase productivity?

Labor Unions in the United States

Before the Civil War, when the country was still largely rural and agricultural, labor unions were few, weak, and short-lived. After the Civil War, industrialization grew rapidly. The proportion of the labor force in manufacturing went from 10 percent in 1860 to nearly 30 percent by 1920. Union membership rose after 1880. The rise in labor unions was partially due to the horrendous working conditions in factories—women and children as young as 5 were operating dangerous machinery for 14 hours a day, 7 days a week. In short, early union demands were not only for higher wages but for shorter workweeks and better working conditions too. In the last 60 years, the percentage of workers in union jobs has fallen sharply from 33 percent to 12.4 percent as seen in Exhibit 1. The percentage of workers in the public sector remains high—almost 40 percent of public sector workers are members of a union. In private industry, less than 8 percent are union members. In education, teachers'

organizations such as the National Education Association (NEA) have become powerful labor unions.

Several possible reasons explain the recent decline in labor union membership. First, a shift of U.S. workers shows them moving out of manufacturing into the service sector, where unions typically have a smaller presence. Second, in recent years the federal government deregulated heavily unionized industries such as trucking, railroad, and the airline industry. This deregulation led to increased competition at home and abroad, and consequently, firms hired fewer expensive non-union workers. Third, global competition means many firms must close down plants and lay off workers. This "downsizing" makes it more difficult for unions to gain concessions from firms. Fourth, the federal government passed new laws regarding safer workplaces.

Labor Legislation

Worker alienation and dissatisfaction grew with the rapidly rising unemployment of the early 1930s. Previous depressions in economic activity were accompanied by

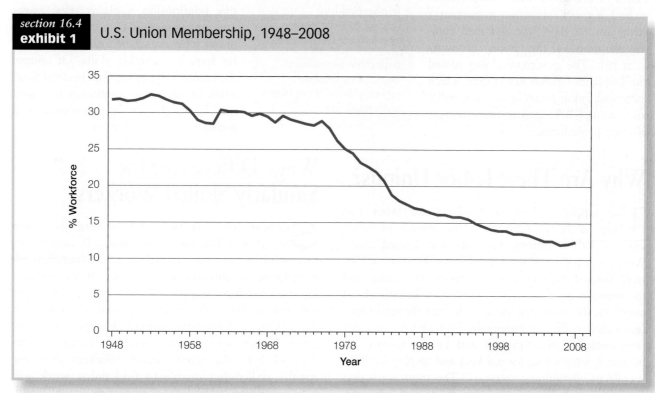

section 16.4
exhibit 1   U.S. Union Membership, 1948–2008

SOURCES: *Union Sourcebook* 1947–1983; U.S. Bureau of Labor Statistics.

a decline in union membership, as unemployed workers dropped their memberships and even employed workers were afraid to stay in unions knowing that the employer could readily "break" the union given the large pool of unemployed. But in the 1930s, the deteriorating economy provided a setting for pro-labor legislation. Several laws were passed that restricted the practices of employers in fighting unions and created a right for employees to engage in collective bargaining.

By far the most important of the labor law reforms of the 1930s was the National Labor Relations Act of 1935, more popularly known as the Wagner Act. The Wagner Act protected the right of workers to organize and bargain collectively. In the late 1930s and early 1940s, most of the heavy mass production industries, such as steel and automobiles, unionized for the first time.

The Taft-Hartley Act (1947) restricted somewhat the power of unions granted by the Wagner Act. The closed shop that required union membership before employment could be obtained was outlawed. The union shop, which permitted nonunion workers to be hired but required them to join the union within 30 days, was permissible. Featherbedding, the practice of adding workers who may not be necessary, was also prohibited by the 1947 law, but it has been difficult to enforce. However, the most famous provision of the Taft-Hartley Act is that it allows the president to seek a court injunction to prevent a strike for 80 days (the so-called cooling off period) if the nation's economy is at risk. The government also passed the Landrum-Griffen Act (1959), which increased union financial accountability and attempted to ensure more regular election procedures.

Wagner Act
legislation enacted in 1935 that protected workers' rights to organize and bargain collectively

Taft-Hartley Act
legislation enacted in 1947 to somewhat restrict the power of unions granted by the Wagner Act

featherbedding
practice of hiring workers who may not be necessary

collective bargaining
negotiations between representatives of employers and unions

more distant from the workers. In small shops or on farms, workers usually have a close relationship with an owner/employer; but in larger enterprises, the workers may only know a supervisor and have no direct contact with either the owner or upper management. Workers realize that acting together, as a union of workers, they have more power in the collective bargaining process than they would acting individually.

Union Impact on Labor Supply and Wages

Labor unions influence the quantity of union labor hired and the wages at which they are hired, primarily through their ability to alter the supply of labor services from what would exist if workers acted independently. One way of influencing supply, of course, is by raising barriers to entry into a given occupation. For example, by restricting membership, unions can reduce the quantity of labor supplied to industry employers from what it otherwise would be. As a result, wages in that occupation will increase, as shown in Exhibit 2(a), from W_1 to W_2. As you can see in the shift from Q_1 to Q_2, some union workers will consequently receive higher wages, but others will become unemployed. Many economists believe that this relationship explains why wages are approximately 15 percent higher in union jobs, even when nonunion workers have comparable skills. Of course, the unions will appropriate some of these gains through dues, initiation fees, and the like, so the workers themselves will not receive the full benefit.

Why Are There Labor Unions?

The supply and demand curves for labor can help us better understand the impact of labor unions. Labor unions such as the United Auto Workers (UAW) and the United Farm Workers (UFW) were formed to increase their members' wages and to improve working conditions. On behalf of its members, the union negotiates with firms through a process called collective bargaining—discussions between representatives of employers and unions focused on balancing what's best for workers and employers. Why is collective bargaining necessary? The argument is that when economies begin to industrialize and urbanize, firms become larger, and often the "boss" becomes

Wage Differences for Similarly Skilled Workers

Suppose you have two labor sectors: the union sector and the nonunion sector. If unions are successful in obtaining higher wages, either through bargaining or threatening to strike or by restricting membership, wages will rise and employment will fall in the union sector, as shown in Exhibit 2(a). With a downward-sloping demand curve for labor, higher wages mean that less labor will be demanded in the union sector. Workers who are equally skilled but unable to find union work will seek nonunion work, thus increasing supply and, in turn, lowering wages in the nonunion sector.

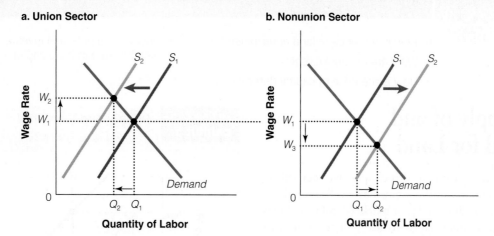

section 16.4
exhibit 2   The Effect of Unions on Wages

Through restrictive membership practices and other means, a union can reduce the labor supply in its industry, thereby increasing the wage rate they can earn (from W_1 to W_2) but reducing employment (from Q_1 to Q_2), as shown in (a). However, as workers unable to get jobs in the union sector join the nonunion sector, the supply of labor in the nonunion sector increases (from Q_1 to Q_2), lowering wages in those industries (from W_1 to W_3), as shown in (b).

This effect is shown in Exhibit 2(b). Thus, comparably skilled workers will experience higher wages in the union sector (W_1) than in the nonunion sector (W_2).

Can Unions Lead to Increased Productivity?

Harvard economists Richard Freeman and James Medoff argue that unions might actually increase worker productivity by increasing marginal productivity. Their argument is that unions provide a collective voice that workers can use to communicate their discontents more effectively, thereby lowering the number of union workers who quit their jobs. Resignations can be particularly costly for firms that invest in training their employees in job-specific skills. In addition, by handling worker's grievances, unions may increase worker motivation and morale. The combined impact of fewer resignations and improved morale could boost productivity.

However, this improvement in worker productivity in the labor sector should show up on the bottom line—the profit statement of the firm. Although the evidence is still preliminary, it appears that unions tend to lower the profitability of firms, not raise it.

SECTION CHECK

1. Workers realize that acting together gives them collective bargaining power.
2. Labor unions try to increase their members' wages and improve working conditions.
3. Through restrictive membership, a union can reduce the labor supply in the market for union workers, thus reducing employment and raising wages. This union "restriction" increases the supply of workers in the nonunion sector and shifts supply to the right, lowering wages for nonunion workers.

---

1. How can acting together as a group increase workers' bargaining power?
2. Why are service industries harder to unionize than manufacturing industries?
3. How do union restrictions on membership or other barriers to entry affect the wages of members?
4. What would increasing unionization do to the wages of those who are not in unions?
5. How can unions potentially increase worker productivity?
6. Why do data indicating that unionization tends to lower firm profits weaken the argument that unions might actually increase worker productivity?

The Markets for Land and Capital

* How is the price of land determined?
* What are economic rents?
* How is the price of capital determined?

* How does a potential investor decide whether to purchase capital or not?

The Supply of and Demand for Land

In the first four sections of this chapter we focused on supply and demand in the labor market. We saw how wages were determined in labor markets and how firms determined how much labor to use and the forces of supply and demand in the union market for workers. However, firms must also decide on the other inputs of production—land and capital: how much capital to employ or how much land to acquire.

You might think of the term *rent* as something you pay at the beginning of the month to compensate the owner for the use of a house or an apartment. But economists use this term in a narrower sense. **Economic rent** is the price paid for land or any other factor that has a fixed supply—a perfectly inelastic supply curve. For example, for the most part, the total supply of land in the country can be viewed as fixed—that is, the supply of land is perfectly inelastic and not at all responsive to prices. The same amount of land will be available at zero price as at a high price. The supply curve does not shift. Only so much land is available.

In Exhibit 1, we see that the price of using land is determined by demand and supply considerations. Because the supply curve is completely inelastic, demand determines the price of the land. If the demand is high, D_{High}, the rental price of the land is high, at R_{High}; if the demand for the land is low, D_{Low}, the rental price of the land is low at R_{Low}. Only changes in the demand for land will change the price of land.

economic rent
the payment for the use of any resource above its opportunity cost

What Causes High Rents?

Rents are high because of a high demand for land, but what causes the demand for land to be high? It is derived from the demand for the products being produced. Suppose an effective advertising campaign promises that cotton is going to keep us looking and feeling cooler. That is, the price of cotton is now higher because of the higher demand for cotton as a result of the advertising campaign. If the supply of land suitable for raising cotton is fixed, an increase in the demand

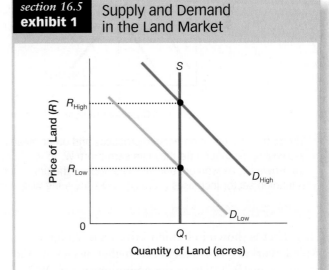

section 16.5 exhibit 1   Supply and Demand in the Land Market

Because the supply of land is perfectly inelastic, demand determines the amount paid to landowners.

for cotton raises the demand (or the MRP) of land, driving up rents.

That same reason explains why rents are high for stores in trendy locations. Rents are bid up as prospective tenants compete with each other for the desirable location. The reason for the bidding wars for the busy locations is that each prospective tenant sees the potential for greater revenue there than elsewhere.

Supply and Demand in the Capital Market

Capital (buildings, machines, and equipment) can be "leased" or "rented" for some stipulated period of time. For example, an airline might lease an airplane or a firm might rent a warehouse. Suppose a company were in the market for a certain type of machine that can be used in making chocolate. Following the law of demand, the lower the rental price of a chocolate-making machine (which would lower the cost of making chocolate), the greater the quantity of chocolate

Why is the price of land so expensive in Malibu? The supply of land is fixed in the short run. That is, no matter whether the price is high or low, only so much land is available in Malibu. It is the demand for living on the beach, good air quality, and closeness to the city of Los Angeles that is high. These features, in turn, increase the demand for land, which drives up the price of land. In Malibu, summer rents of $100,000 a month are not uncommon.

COURTESY OF ROBERT L. SEXTON

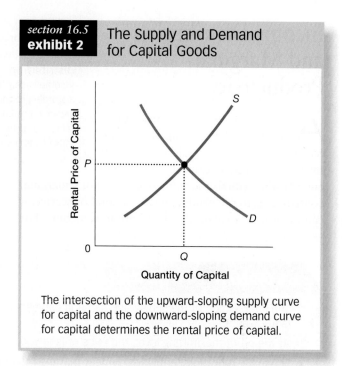

section 16.5
exhibit 2   The Supply and Demand for Capital Goods

The intersection of the upward-sloping supply curve for capital and the downward-sloping demand curve for capital determines the rental price of capital.

machines demanded. Following the law of supply, the greater the rental price of the machine, the more willing owners of chocolate machines are to supply them to entrepreneurs.

Rather than renting a chocolate machine, the company may borrow funds and buy its own machine. In this case, the manufacturer is borrowing funds for the purpose of acquiring capital. The cost of the borrowed funds is usually called **interest**. At lower interest rates, the cost of financing the purchase of the chocolate machine is lower. If a machine costs $1,000 and the interest rate being charged is 10 percent, the interest cost of a chocolate machine is $100 a year ($1,000 × 0.10); if the relevant interest rate is 8 percent, interest costs are only $80 a year ($1,000 × 0.08). At lower interest rates, then, capital costs are lower, and the quantity of funds demanded is greater. Likewise, fund lenders will derive greater income the greater the interest rate, so the benefits to them of making a loan increase as interest rates (the "price" of funds) rise. Thus, the quantity of funds supplied is positively related to interest rates.

The graph in Exhibit 2 is virtually the same whether we are renting the capital equipment or borrowing to pay for that capital. The demand for capital, just like labor, is a derived demand. When a firm increases

interest
the cost of borrowed funds

its capital, the value it receives equals the increase in revenue the firm receives from selling another unit of output by employing the machine. The marginal revenue product curve is the demand curve for capital.

The demand curve for capital is downward sloping, reflecting the fact that as more capital is employed, the value of the marginal product of capital falls. The supply curve for capital is upward sloping, implying that owners of capital face increasing marginal costs and will be more willing to supply at higher prices. The rental price of capital is found at the intersection of the supply and demand curves. At equilibrium, suppliers receive a rental price equal to the marginal revenue product of capital. That is, in equilibrium: The rental price of capital is equal to: the marginal product of capital.

The Interdependence of Input Markets

For simplicity, we treated the labor, capital, and land markets independently. In reality, these markets are interconnected. For example, if wages rise or the rental price of capital falls, machines might be substituted for some workers.

Income Distribution and Marginal Productivity

marginal productivity theory of income distribution
income is distributed according to marginal revenue product of the factors of production individuals own

As we have seen, in competitive equilibrium labor, land, and capital receive a price that equals its marginal revenue product. Because marginal revenue product equals the value of each factor's marginal contribution to the productivity of a good or service, it can be used to explain the distribution of income. For example, workers will receive compensation/wages plus other "fringe benefits" that are equal to their marginal contribution to output. That is, workers are paid for the value of their contribution to output. This is also true of owners of capital and land. The greater quantity and quality an owner of a factor of production possesses, the greater that owner's income. That is, each person receives income for what he or she creates—the marginal revenue product. This theory is called the marginal productivity theory of income distribution.

SECTION CHECK

1. The intersection of the supply and demand curves for land determines the price of land, the compensation to land owners.
2. At the profit-maximizing level, the price of land will equal the value of the marginal product of land.
3. Economic rent represents the payment that the resource owner receives beyond its opportunity cost.
4. The demand and supply curves for capital determine the compensation paid to the owners of capital.
5. In equilibrium, the rental price of capital equals the marginal revenue product of capital.

---

1. If the supply of land was perfectly inelastic, how much would the price of land rise if the price of crops raised on the land doubled, other things equal? What if the supply of land was less than perfectly inelastic?
2. Why is the demand curve for capital downward sloping?
3. Why is the supply curve for capital upward sloping?

Interactive Chapter Summary

Fill in the blanks:

1. In input or factor markets, the demand for an input is a _____ demand—_____ from consumers' demand for the good or service.

2. The demand for labor is determined by its _____, which is the additional revenue that a firm obtains from one more unit of input.

3. The _____ is the amount that an extra input adds to a firm's total costs.

4. A firm would find its profits growing by adding one more worker when the _____ associated with the worker exceeds the _____ of the worker.

5. The law of diminishing marginal product reflects the fact that by adding increasing quantities of a(n) _____ input (e.g., labor) to fixed quantities of another input, output will rise, but at some point it will increase by _____ amounts.

6. Profits are maximized if a firm hires only to the point where the wage equals the expected _____.

7. As the wage rate rises, the quantity of labor supplied _____, *ceteris paribus;* as the wage falls, the quantity of labor supplied _____, *ceteris paribus.*

8. At a wage below the equilibrium level, quantity _____ would exceed quantity _____, resulting in a labor _____. In this situation, employers would be forced to offer higher wages in order to hire as many workers as they would like.

9. Increases in the demand curve for labor may arise from _____ in labor productivity or from _____ in the price of the good.

10. Workers can increase productivity if they have more _____ or land with which to work, if _____ improvements occur, or if they acquire additional _____ or experience.

11. If labor productivity falls, then the demand curve for labor will shift to the _____.

12. If new workers enter the labor force, the labor supply curve will shift to the _____.

13. If unions are successful in raising union wages, the result will be _____ wages in the nonunion sector.

14. When a market consists of a single buyer, we say _____ exists.

15. Monopsony power is more likely to be present when high _____ and _____ costs are involved.

16. Under monopsony, _____ workers will be hired at _____ wages than if perfect competition prevailed in a labor market.

17. Monopsony tends to result in _____ profits for a firm.

18. The percentage of workers in the public sector that are unionized is far _____ than average in the economy.

19. The most important labor law reform of the 1930s was the _____, also known as the Wagner Act.

20. The Taft-Hartley Act outlawed a _____ shop, which required union membership before employment could be obtained.

21. Unions have a much _____ presence in other industrial countries than in the United States.

22. _____ is the price paid for land or any other factor that has a fixed supply.

23. The supply of land is perfectly _____.

24. An increase in the demand for land will _____ the quantity supplied and _____ the price of land.

25. For a given supply of land capable of growing cotton, an increase in the demand for cotton will _____ rents.

26. Economic rent is the payment to a resource in excess of its _____.

27. The cost of borrowed funds is called _____.

28. At _____ interest rates, capital costs are lower.

29. The quantity of funds supplied is _____ related to the interest rate.

30. The intersection of the supply of capital and the demand for capital determines the rental _____ of capital.

31. At equilibrium suppliers of capital receive a rental price equal to the _____.

Answers: 1. derived; derived 2. marginal revenue product 3. marginal resource cost 4. marginal benefit; marginal cost 5. variable; diminishing 6. marginal revenue product 7. increases; decreases 8. demanded; supplied; shortage 9. increases; changes 10. capital; technological; skills 11. left 12. right 13. lower 14. monopsony 15. movement; search 16. fewer; lower 17. higher 18. larger 19. National Labor Relations Act 20. closed 21. larger 22. Economic rent 23. inelastic 24. not change; increase 25. increase 26. opportunity cost 27. interest 28. lower 29. positively 30. price 31. marginal revenue product of capital

Key Terms and Concepts

derived demand 455
marginal revenue product (MRP) 456
marginal resource cost (MRC) 456
marginal product (MP) 457
backward-bending labor
  supply curve 460

monopsony 464
Wagner Act 466
Taft-Hartley Act 466
featherbedding 466
collective bargaining 466

economic rent 468
interest 469
marginal productivity theory of income
  distribution 470

Section Check Answers

16.1 Input Markets

1. Why is the demand for productive inputs derived from the demand for the outputs those inputs produce?

The demand for productive inputs is derived from the demand for the outputs those inputs produce because the value to a firm of the services of a productive input depends on the value of the outputs produced, and the value of the output depends on the demand for that output.

2. Why is the demand for tractors and fertilizer derived from the demand for agricultural products?

The reason farmers demand tractors and fertilizer is that they increase the output of crops they grow. But the value to farmers of the additional crops they can grow as a result is greater, the higher the price of those crops. Therefore, the greater the demand for those crops, other things equal, the higher the price of those crops, which increases the demand for tractors and fertilizer by increasing the value to farmers of the added output they make possible.

16.2 Supply and Demand in the Labor Market

1. What is marginal revenue product?

Marginal revenue product is the additional revenue that a firm obtains from employing one more unit of an input. It is equal to the marginal product multiplied by marginal revenue.

2. Would a firm hire another worker if the marginal revenue product of labor exceeded the market wage rate? Why or why not?

A firm would hire another worker if the marginal revenue product of labor exceeded the market wage rate, because doing so would add more to its total revenue than it would add to its total costs, raising profits.

3. Why does the marginal product of labor eventually fall?

As more and more units of the variable input labor are added to a given quantity of the fixed input, land or capital, the additional output from each additional unit of labor must begin to fall at some point. This is the law of diminishing marginal product.

4. Why does diminishing marginal product mean that the marginal revenue product will eventually fall?

Since marginal revenue product equals marginal product times marginal revenue, the eventually falling marginal product means that the marginal revenue product must also eventually fall, even if the price of the output did not fall with increasing output. If the marginal revenue falls with increasing output, that will also cause marginal revenue product to fall with additional output.

5. Why is a firm hiring in a competitive labor market a price (wage) taker for a given quality of labor?

A perfectly competitive seller cannot by its output choices appreciably affect the market quantity, and thereby the market price of that output, and so it takes the output market price as given. In just the same way, a firm hiring in a competitive labor market cannot by its input (hiring) choices appreciably affect the quantity of that input employed, and therefore the market price of that input, and so it takes the input (labor) market price (wage) as given.

6. What is responsible for a backward-bending individual supply curve for labor?

A backward-bending individual supply curve for labor would result when the income effect of a higher wage (since leisure is a normal good, a higher income leads to a reduction in labor supplied as a result) dominates the substitution effect of a higher wage (at a higher wage, the cost of forgoing labor time for leisure becomes greater, leading to an increase in labor supplied).

16.3 Labor Market Equilibrium

1. If wages were above their equilibrium level, why would they tend to fall toward the equilibrium level?

If wages were above their equilibrium level, the quantity of labor supplied at that price would exceed the quantity of labor demanded at that price. The resulting surplus of labor would lead workers frustrated by their inability to get jobs to compete the wage for those jobs down toward the equilibrium level.

2. If wages were below their equilibrium level, why would they tend to rise toward the equilibrium level?

If wages were below their equilibrium level, the quantity of labor demanded at that price would exceed the quantity of labor supplied at that price. The resulting shortage of labor would lead employers frustrated by their ability to find workers to compete the wage for those jobs up toward the equilibrium level.

3. **Why do increases in technology or increases in the amounts of capital or other complementary inputs increase the demand for labor?**

   Increases in technology or increases in the amounts of capital or other complementary inputs increase the demand for labor by increasing the productivity of labor; as labor productivity increases, the marginal revenue product of labor (the demand for labor) increases.

4. **Why do any of the demand shifters for output markets shift the demand for labor and other inputs used to produce that output in the same direction?**

   When any of the demand shifters for output markets change the price of that output, it changes the marginal revenue product (marginal product times price) of labor and other inputs used to produce that output in the same direction.

5. **Why do increases in immigration or population growth, increases in workers' willingness to work at a given wage, decreases in nonwage income, or increases in workplace amenities increase the supply of labor?**

   Increases in immigration or population growth increase the number of potential workers; increases in willingness to work at a given wage increase hours worked; decreases in nonwage income lower workers' incomes, increasing their willingness to work at any given wage; and an increase in workplace amenities makes working more desirable (less undesirable), also increasing workers' willingness to work at a given wage.

6. **What would happen to the supply of labor if nonwage incomes increased and workplace amenities also increased over the same period?**

   Higher nonwage incomes would reduce the supply of labor, but better workplace amenities would increase the supply of labor. The net effect would depend on which of these effects was of greater magnitude.

7. **Why are wages in different fields not necessarily related to how important people think those jobs are?**

   Wages are determined by the marginal revenue product of labor, and that marginal value which results from the forces of supply and demand does not bear any necessary relationship to how important or critical people consider that job to be in some absolute sense.

8. **If the private-market wage of engineers was greater than that of sociologists, what would happen if a university tried to pay its engineering faculty and its sociology faculty the same salary?**

   Say the university based its salaries on the average salaries elsewhere for all fields. Other things being equal,

the resulting salaries would be below the equilibrium salary level for engineers, resulting in a shortage of engineering professors at that university (e.g., they would lose current engineering faculty and have a hard time hiring new engineering faculty), but above the equilibrium salary level for sociologists, resulting in a surplus of sociology professors at that university (who would never voluntarily leave or retire).

16.4 Labor Unions

1. **How can acting together as a group increase workers' bargaining power?**

   Workers acting together to reduce the competition between them for jobs reduces competition among workers, and therefore gives them increased bargaining power.

2. **Why are service industries harder to unionize than manufacturing industries?**

   Service industries tend to be harder to unionize than manufacturing industries because service industry jobs tend to be less standardized and service industry firms tend to be smaller.

3. **How do union restrictions on membership or other barriers to entry affect the wages of members?**

   Union restrictions on membership or other barriers to entry reduce the quantity of labor services offered to employers, reducing the number of such jobs and increasing their wages.

4. **What would increasing unionization do to the wages of those who were not in unions?**

   Increasing unionization would reduce the number of jobs in industries that became more unionized, increasing the supply of workers in industries that were non-union, and lowering the wages those jobs pay.

5. **How can unions potentially increase worker productivity?**

   Unions can potentially increase worker productivity by providing a collective voice that workers can use to communicate their discontents more effectively, which can reduce the number of workers that quit, reducing employee training costs. They could also improve worker motivation and morale by better handling worker grievances.

6. **Why do data indicating that unionization tends to lower firm profits weaken the argument that unions might actually increase worker productivity?**

   If increased worker productivity was the primary effect of unionization, unionized firms should have lower costs and therefore higher profits than non-union firms. But the data seem to indicate that the opposite is true.

16.5 The Market for Land and Capital

1. **If the supply of land was perfectly inelastic, how much would the price of land rise if the price of crops raised on the land doubled, other things equal? What if the supply of land was less than perfectly inelastic?**

   Because the demand for land is derived from the demand for the products produced on the land, a doubling of the price of the crops raised on land would double the demand for the land. If the supply of land was perfectly inelastic, this would double the price of the land. If the supply of land was less than perfectly elastic, the higher demand would increase the quantity of land supplied, and the doubling of demand would lead the price to rise, but less than double.

2. **Why is the demand curve for capital downward sloping?**

   The demand curve for capital is downward sloping because the lower the interest rate, the lower the opportunity cost of borrowed funds, and the more projects that can profitably be pursued with those funds (there are more capital investment projects with higher rates of return than the opportunity cost of borrowing).

3. **Why is the supply curve for capital upward sloping?**

   The interest rate represents the benefit savers get from saving (deferring consumption). A higher interest rate means an increase in the benefits of saving, resulting in increased saving and therefore an increase in the supply of funds available for capital investment projects.

True or False:

1. By far the largest fraction of national income goes to wages and salaries for labor services.

2. The "price" of a productive factor is directly related to consumer demand for the final good or service.

3. In a competitive labor market, a firm's marginal resource cost is the market wage.

4. Hiring an additional worker would lower profits when the marginal revenue product is greater than the marginal resource cost.

5. The law of diminishing marginal product states that as increasing quantities of a variable input (e.g., labor) are added to fixed quantities of another input, output will rise, but at some point it will increase by diminishing amounts.

6. The marginal revenue product of labor declines, even in the case of competitive output markets, because of the diminishing marginal product of labor.

7. A profit-maximizing firm will hire up to the last unit of input for which the wage is expected to exceed the marginal revenue product.

8. In a competitive labor market, a firm can hire all the labor it wishes at the prevailing wage.

9. Only at the equilibrium wage are both suppliers (workers) and demanders (employers) of labor able to exchange the quantity of labor they desire.

10. Decreases in the demand curve for labor may arise from decreases in labor productivity or from increases in the price of the good produced by that labor.

11. An increase in the demand for a good will increase the demand for labor.

12. A decrease in the nonwage income of workers would shift the labor supply curve to the right.

13. The wage premium paid to union workers shows that all workers benefit from the activity of unions.

14. If unions are successful in obtaining higher wages, it causes employment to rise in the union sector but fall in the nonunion sector.

15. Monopsony as a market structure is considered most relevant to the labor market, in the real world.

16. If a person is willing to move, any employers' monopsony power will be reduced, other things equal.

17. Monopsony power tends to increase wages in a market.

18. Monopsony power tends to reduce output in a market.

19. Before the Civil War, labor unions were few, weak, and short-lived.

20. Early union demands were primarily for higher wages.

21. The Wagner Act protected the rights of workers to organize and bargain collectively.

22. Economic rent arises when a factor of production has a perfectly inelastic supply curve.

23. Because the supply of land is perfectly inelastic, the demand curve for land determines its price.

24. An increase in the demand for land will increase both its price and the quantity of land supplied.

25. The concept of economic rent applies only to land.

26. Economic rent is the payment to a resource above the amount necessary to induce the resource to be supplied.

27. At lower interest rates, the quantity of funds demanded will be greater.

28. At higher interest rates, the quantity of funds supplied will be greater.

29. If the interest rate rose, it would increase the present value of a given flow of future benefits.

30. Falling interest rates lead to greater investment, other things equal.

Multiple Choice:

1. Which of the following is false about input markets?
   a. The greatest fraction of national income goes to wages and salaries for labor services.
   b. The price and quantity of an input traded depends on its supply and demand.
   c. The demand for an input is a derived demand.
   d. The price of an input tends to increase when the demand for the output produced by the input increases.
   e. All of the preceding are true.

2. Marginal revenue product
   a. is the additional revenue that a firm obtains by employing one more unit of an input.
   b. will increase if an input's productivity increases.
   c. will decrease if the price of the output produced by the input falls.
   d. is characterized by all of the preceding.

3. The marginal resource cost of an input
   a. is the amount an added unit of an input adds to a firm's total cost.
   b. exceeds the market wage in a competitive industry.
   c. is less than the market wage in a competitive industry.
   d. is characterized by both a and b.
   e. is characterized by both a and c.

4. If an additional salesclerk is hired to work in a furniture store, the clerk's sales efforts will contribute $700 to the store's total revenue. The store's profits will rise if the additional salesclerk is hired whenever the cost of hiring the clerk is _____ in wages and other costs.
   a. $700
   b. less than $700
   c. more than $700
   d. Not enough information is given to make a determination.

5. A firm will increase its profits by adding one more unit of an input when
   a. $MRP < MRC$.
   b. $MRP = MRC$.
   c. $MRP > MRC$.
   d. none of the above.

6. Assuming competitive markets, a worker's contribution to revenue is given by
   a. the production function.
   b. the marginal revenue product of labor.
   c. the marginal resource cost of labor.
   d. the marginal product minus marginal cost.

7. In a competitive labor market,
   a. a firm is a wage taker.
   b. a firm can hire all the labor it wishes to at the market wage.
   c. a firm hires a small fraction of the total market quantity of labor supplied.
   d. all of the preceding are true.

8. MRP falls as more labor is hired in a competitive labor market because
   a. MRC increases as more labor is hired.
   b. workers that are added are steadily inferior in terms of ability.
   c. of the law of diminishing marginal product.
   d. of all of the preceding.

9. In a competitive labor market in equilibrium,
   a. a firm's $MRP = MP \times MR$.
   b. a firm's $MRP = MP \times P$.
   c. a firm's $MRP = MRC$.
   d. a firm's wage $= MRC$.
   e. all of the preceding are true.

10. At any wage higher than the equilibrium wage, the quantity of labor supplied _____ the quantity of labor demanded, resulting in a _____ of labor.
    a. exceeds; surplus
    b. exceeds; shortage
    c. is less than; surplus
    d. is less than; shortage

11. An increase in the demand for labor can result from
    a. increases in the price of the good produced by the labor.
    b. technological improvements.
    c. improvements in labor productivity.
    d. an increase in the amount of capital available for use by workers.
    e. all of the preceding.

12. Which of the following results in a rightward shift of the market demand curve for labor?
    a. an increase in labor productivity
    b. an increase in demand for the firm's product
    c. an increase in a firm's product price
    d. all of the preceding

13. The market supply of labor resources is affected by
    a. the number of hours workers are willing to work.
    b. the amount of immigration allowed.
    c. changes in a nation's working-age population.
    d. all of the preceding.

14. Differences in monetary wages across jobs may result from
    a. differences in job amenities.
    b. differences in on-the-job hazards.
    c. differences in working conditions.
    d. differences in fringe benefits.
    e. all of the preceding.

15. If labor unions successfully negotiate wage increases for their members,
    a. the wages of nonunion workers increase as well.
    b. the wages in nonunion sectors decrease.
    c. employment likely falls in the union sector.
    d. both a and c occur.
    e. both b and c occur.

16. Monopsony in a market would tend to increase an employer's
    a. wages paid.
    b. profits earned.
    c. output produced.
    d. employment level.

17. Monopsony power will *not* be reduced,
    a. the lower are search costs.
    b. the lower are movement costs.
    c. the more potential employers there are in an area.
    d. by any of these changes.

18. Labor union membership has declined in part due to
    a. a shift in workers from manufacturing to the service sector.
    b. deregulation in unionized industries.
    c. increasing global competition.
    d. all of the preceding.

19. The distinguishing feature of the land market is that
    a. the supply curve is highly inelastic.
    b. the supply curve is highly elastic.
    c. the demand curve is highly inelastic.
    d. the demand curve is highly elastic.

20. The rent paid for land currently used to graze cattle would increase if
    a. the productivity of the land in cattle grazing increased.
    b. people decided to eat more red meat.
    c. oil deposits were discovered under the land.
    d. any of the preceding occurred.

21. An increase in the demand for land will
    a. increase the price of land and increase the quantity of land supplied.
    b. increase the price of land but not change the quantity of land supplied.
    c. increase the quantity of land supplied but not change the price of land.
    d. do none of the preceding.

22. Economic rent
    a. applies as a concept to land.
    b. is the payment to a resource in excess of its opportunity cost.
    c. will increase when the demand for input increases, if supply is perfectly inelastic.
    d. does all of the preceding.

23. At low levels of interest, borrowers will want to borrow _____ and suppliers of funds will want to supply _____.
    a. more; less
    b. less; more
    c. more; more
    d. less; less

Problems:

1. The following table shows the Total Output each week of workers on a perfectly competitive cherry farm. The equilibrium price of a pound of cherries is $4. Complete the Marginal Product of Labor and the Marginal Revenue Product of Labor columns in the table.

Quantity of Labor	Total Output	Marginal Product of Labor	Marginal Revenue Product of Labor
0			
1	250	_____	_____
2	600	_____	_____
3	900	_____	_____
4	1,125	_____	_____
5	1,300	_____	_____
6	1,450	_____	_____
7	1,560	_____	_____

2. Using the table in Problem 1, how many workers will the farmer hire if the equilibrium wage rate is $550 per week? $650 per week?

3. What happens to the demand curve for labor when the equilibrium price of output increases?

4. Which of the following groups are likely to benefit from legislation substantially increasing the minimum wage? Explain why.
    a. unskilled workers seeking jobs but lacking experience and education
    b. skilled workers whose current wages are above the minimum wage
    c. manufacturers of machines that save labor in industries employing large amounts of unskilled labor
    d. unskilled workers who have criminal records
    e. a teenager seeking his or her first job
    f. unskilled workers who retain employment after the minimum wage is raised
    g. regions where almost everybody already earns substantially more than the minimum wage

5. If a competitive firm is paying $8 per hour (with no fringe benefits) to its employees, what would tend to happen to its equilibrium wage if the company began to give on-the-job training or free health insurance to its workers? What would happen to the firm's on-the-job training and workers' health insurance if the government mandated a minimum wage of $9 an hour?

6. Would the owner of University Pizza Parlor hire another worker for $60 per day if that worker added 40 pizzas a day and each pizza added $2 to University Pizza Parlor's revenues? Why or why not?

7. What would happen to the demand for unskilled labor if the demand for hamburgers and fries increased?

8. If all individuals have backward-bending labor supply curves, is the labor supply curve for a particular industry or occupation also backward bending?

9. Professional athletes command and receive higher salaries than teachers. Yet teachers, not athletes, are considered essential to economic growth and development. Why then do athletes receive higher salaries than teachers?

10. The availability of jobs at higher real wages motivates many people to migrate—legally or illegally—to the United States. Other things being equal, what impact would a large influx of immigrants have on real wages? What impact would it have on real wages in the immigrant's home country?

11. The dean at Middle State University knows that poets generally earn less than engineers in the private market; that is, the equilibrium wage for engineers is higher than that for poets. Suppose that all colleges and universities except for Middle State University pay their professors according to their potential private market wage. The administration at Middle State believes that salaries should be equal across all disciplines because its professors work equally hard and because all of the professors have similar degrees—PhDs. As a result, Middle State opts to pay all its professors a mid-range wage, W_{MS}. What do you think is likely to happen to the engineering and poetry programs at Middle State?

12. An entrepreneur considers the following investment opportunity: For an investment of $500 today, he can earn a return of $200 per year over the next three years. Should he undertake the investment if the interest rate is 8 percent? 10 percent?

13. Indicate which point could correspond to the equilibrium wage and quantity hired

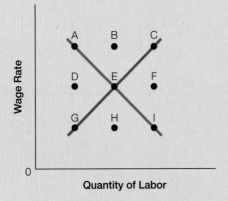

    a. at the initial equilibrium.
    b. if the price of the output produced by the labor increased.

c. if the price of the output produced by the labor decreased.

d. if worker productivity increased and workers' nonwage incomes increased.

e. if worker productivity decreased and population decreased.

f. if the price of output produced by the labor increased and the number of hours workers were willing to work increased.

g. if the price of output produced by the labor decreased and workers' nonwage incomes decreased.

14. Using supply and demand curves, show how each of the following would affect the demand or supply of workers. In each case, label the new equilibrium wage and quantity.

a. Immigration increases dramatically.

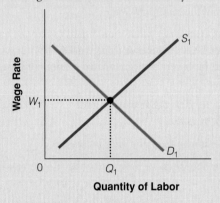

b. Demand for U.S. manufactured goods declines.

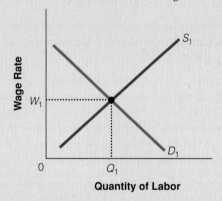

c. New computerized technology increases productivity of U.S. workers.

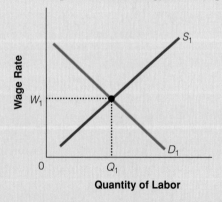

d. U.S. firms increase job amenities for workers.

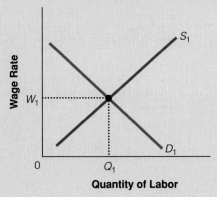

e. U.S. workers choose more leisure.

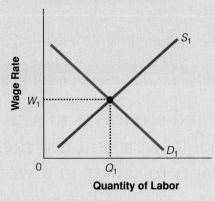

15. Use the following diagrams to answer a–c:

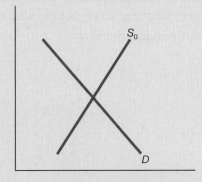
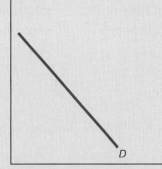

a. If unions are unable to have any effect on wages, draw the supply curve for the nonunion market.
b. If unions become able to restrict the supply of labor in the union sector, indicate what would happen in both the union and nonunion sectors.
c. What happens to the union wage and the number of union workers hired in b? What happens to the nonunion wage and the number of nonunion workers hired in b?

16. If the marginal revenue product for capital increased, what would it do to the demand for capital, the rental price of capital, and the quantity of capital supplied?

17. What is the marginal productivity theory of income distribution?

17 Income and Poverty

The ultimate purpose of producing goods and services is to satisfy the material wants of people. Up to this point, we examined the process by which society decides which wants to satisfy in a world characterized by scarcity; we examined the question of how goods are produced; and we examined the question of how society can fully utilize its productive resources. We did not, however, look carefully into two equally important questions: For whom does society produce consumer goods and services? Why are some people able to consume much more than others? ∎

SECTION 17.1 Income Distribution

* What happened to income distribution since 1935?
* Are income distribution statistics accurate?

* How significant is income mobility?
* How much income inequality exists in other countries?

In many economies, some individuals will have high income and others will have low income. How unequal is the U.S. income distribution? And why do some individuals earn more than others? We will address these and other questions regarding income distribution and poverty in this chapter.

Measuring Income Inequality

Exhibit 1 shows a breakdown of average annual family income by groups of five (or quintiles): the bottom fifth, the second fifth, the third fifth, the fourth fifth, and the top fifth.

Exhibit 2 illustrates the changing distribution of measured income in the United States since 1935. As you can see in this table, the proportion of income received by the richest Americans (top 5 percent) declined sharply after 1935 but has been edging back up since the 1980s. The proportion received by the poorest Americans (the lowest 20 percent) remained virtually unchanged since 1935. Most of the observed changes occurred between 1935 and 1950, probably reflecting the impact of the

Great Depression and new government programs in the 1930s, as well as World War II. From 1950 to 1980, there was little change in the overall distribution of income. Two significant changes occurred since the 1980s: The lowest one-fifth of families have seen their share of measured income fall from 5.3 percent to 4.0 percent of all income, and the top one-fifth of families have seen their share of measured income rise from 41.1 to 47.8 percent of all income.

section 17.1 exhibit 1 — Income Distribution of the United States, 2008

Group	Household Income (Average)
Bottom Fifth	$ 11,656
Second Fifth	$ 29,517
Third Fifth	$ 50,132
Fourth Fifth	$ 79,760
Top Fifth	$171,057

SOURCE: U.S. Bureau of the Census.

section 17.1 exhibit 2 — Income Inequality in the United States

Year	Lowest Fifth	Second Fifth	Third Fifth	Fourth Fifth	Highest Fifth	Highest 5%
1935	4.1%	9.2%	14.1%	20.9%	51.7%	26.5%
1950	4.5	12.0	17.4	23.4	42.7	17.3
1960	4.8	12.2	17.8	24.0	41.3	15.9
1970	5.4	12.2	17.6	23.8	40.9	15.6
1980	5.3	11.6	17.6	24.4	41.1	14.6
1990	4.6	10.8	16.6	23.8	44.3	17.4
2000	4.3	9.8	15.5	22.8	47.4	20.8
2005	4.0	9.6	15.3	22.9	48.1	21.1
2008	4.0	9.6	15.5	23.1	47.8	20.5

SOURCE: U.S. Bureau of the Census, 2009.

The Lorenz Curve

E conomists sometimes use a graphical representation of the distribution of income called the Lorenz curve. The Lorenz curve gives us a visual picture of the difference between the actual distribution of income and perfect equality. In Exhibit 3, we see that along the vertical axis we measure the cumulative percentage of total income and along the horizontal axis we measure the cumulative percentage of households. Moving along the horizontal axis from the left-hand corner to the right-hand corner, we move from 0 percent of the households to 100 percent of the households.

Along the 45-degree line—the line of perfect income equality—the poorest 20 percent of the families would receive 20 percent of total income, 40 percent of the families would receive 40 percent of total income, 60 percent of the families would receive 60 percent of total income, and so on. The curved line on this graph— the Lorenz curve—represents the actual distribution of income. The greater the distance between the Lorenz curve and the 45-degree line—the greater the amount of

inequality. In Exhibit 3, we plot some of the points that make up the Lorenz curve from U.S. data for 1980 and 2008. For example, in 2008, we see the poorest 20 percent of all households received 4 percent of the income, point a′ on the graph. The first 40 percent received 14 percent (4 percent + 10 percent), point b′ on the graph. At point c′ the first 60 percent of households earn 30 percent of the income. At point d′ the first 80 percent of households receive 53 percent of the income or flipping it around—the richest 20 percent receive 47 percent of the income. Notice that the distribution of income was more equal in 1980 because the Lorenz curve is closer to the line of perfect equality.

In Exhibit 4, the shaded area A between the line of perfect income equality and the Lorenz curve measures the amount of income inequality. We derive a Gini coefficient, G, by dividing area A by area A + B. G varies from zero to one. If G is zero, it represents perfect income equality—that is, area A would be zero and the Lorenz curve would overlap the line of perfect income equality. G = 1 means perfect income inequality—if one household earned all the income.

---

section 17.1
exhibit 3   The Lorenz Curve

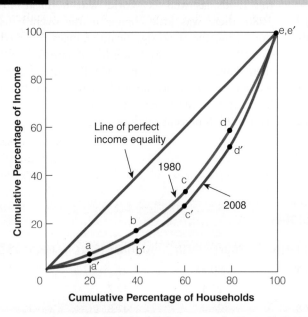

The Lorenz curve is a graphical presentation of the distribution of income. The horizontal axis measures the cumulative percentage of households and the vertical axis measures the cumulative percentage of income. The 45-degree line represents the line of perfect income equality. The further the Lorenz curve is from the line of perfect income equality the more unequal is the distribution of income.

Households			Income 1980			Income 2008		
Point	Percentage	Cumulative Percentage	Point	Percentage	Cumulative Percentage	Point	Percentage	Cumulative Percentage
a	Lowest 20	20%	a	5.3%	5.3%	a′	4%	4%
b	Second 20	40	b	11.6	16.9	b′	10	14
c	Third 20	60	c	17.6	34.5	c′	16	30
d	Fourth 20	80	d	24.4	58.9	d′	23	53
e	Highest 20	100	e	41.1	100.0	e′	47	100

section 17.1
exhibit 4   Gini Coefficient

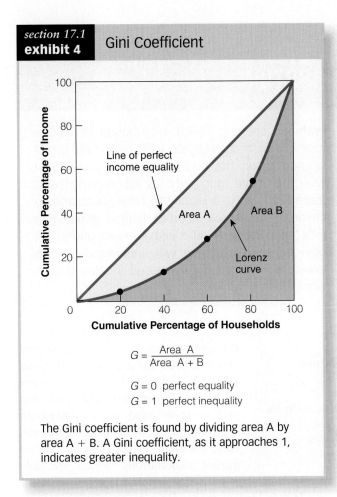

$$G = \frac{\text{Area A}}{\text{Area A} + B}$$

$G = 0$ perfect equality
$G = 1$ perfect inequality

The Gini coefficient is found by dividing area A by area A + B. A Gini coefficient, as it approaches 1, indicates greater inequality.

That is, the closer G is to 1 the greater the degree of income inequality; consequently, area A becomes larger. In the United States, the Gini coefficient was 0.403 in 1980 and 0.466 in 2008, indicating that the distribution of income has become less equal over the last 30 years.

Are We Overstating the Disparity in the Distribution of Income?

Failing to take into consideration differences in age, certain demographic factors, institutional factors, and government redistributive activities have all been identified as elements that influence income distribution data and may suggest that we might be overstating inequality.

Differences in Age

At any moment in time, middle-age people tend to have higher incomes than both younger and older people. Middle age is when most people are at their peak in terms of productivity and

in-kind transfers
in-kind transfers are transfers in the form of goods and services instead of money. In-kind transfers include food stamps, school lunch programs, housing subsidies, and Medicaid, among others.

participate in the labor force to a greater extent than do the very old or very young. Put differently, if every individual earned exactly the same total income over his or her lifetime, we would still observe some inequality at any given moment in time simply because people usually earn more in middle age.

Inequality resulting from this demographic difference overstates the true inequality in the lifetime earnings of people. A typical 50-year-old male earns nearly twice the income of a male in his early 20s and nearly one-third more than workers over 65. Since 1950, the proportion of individuals who are either very young or very old has grown, meaning that in a relative sense, more people are in lower-income age groups.

Other Demographic Trends

Other demographic trends, such as the increased number of divorced couples and the rise of two-income families, also cause the measured distribution of income (which is measured in terms of household income) to appear more unequal. For example, in the 1950s, the overwhelming majority of families had single incomes. Today, many households have two breadwinners instead of one. Suppose their incomes rise from $50,000 a year to roughly $100,000; thus, these households move into a higher-income quintile and create greater apparent income inequality. At the same time, divorces create two households instead of one, lowering income per household for divorced couples; thus, they move into lower-income quintiles, also creating greater apparent income inequality.

Government Activities

Some economists argue that the impact of increased government activity should be considered in evaluating the measured income distribution. Government-imposed taxes burden different income groups in different ways. Also, government programs benefit some groups of income recipients more than others. For example, state-subsidized higher education seems to benefit the high- and middle-income groups more than the poor (because far more students from the higher-income groups go to college), as have such things as government subsidies to airports and airlines, operas, and art museums. Some programs, though, clearly aid the poor more than the rich. Food stamps, school lunch programs, housing subsidies, Medicaid, and several other programs provide recipients with **in-kind transfers**. In-kind transfers are given in the form of goods and services rather than money. When in-kind transfers are included in income distribution data, many economists conclude that they have served to

DEMOGRAPHIC FACTORS AND INCOME DISTRIBUTION

Q What impact do you think higher divorce rates will have on income inequality?

A As you would probably imagine, when one family with two incomes turns into two families with one income each, more families will report less income per family. Often, this situation causes one high-income household to become two middle-income households in the data. However, the most

dramatic changes in the distribution of income may occur in households with one male bread-winner. When the breakup occurs, the woman, who may have little previous job experience, is forced to look for a job. If she receives custody of children, her search might be limited to part-time jobs or low-paying jobs with flexible hours. Her new household income will undoubtedly be far lower, also increasing measured income disparities between families.

---

reduce levels of inequality significantly from the levels suggested by aggregate income statistics.

On balance, the evidence suggests that inequality of money income in the United States declined from 1935 to 1950 and then remained rather stable until 1980. Since then, the distribution of income has become less equal. However, if we consider age distribution, institutional factors, and in-kind transfer programs, it is safe to say that the income distribution is more equal than it appears in Exhibit 2.

Permanent Income Hypothesis

Milton Friedman, a Nobel laureate in economics who taught for many years at the University at Chicago, observed that consumption is related to permanent income rather than to current income levels. This is called the **permanent income hypothesis.** Studies show, for example, that college students often consume more than their total income; the same is true of very old persons. These groups *dissave*. On the other hand, people in their 30s and 40s tend to save quite a bit and consume relatively less of their income (even so, though, a higher-income person of 40 is likely to consume more than a low-income person of 20 or 70). Why? College-age persons expect to earn more income later, and gauge their consumption in part by their expectations of future (lifetime) income. Likewise middle-age persons expect to retire at some future date on a lower income and save for that eventuality. Older, retired persons expect to die and, accordingly, feel justified in drawing down their savings. A highly paid 35-year-old baseball player may consume less than a 35-year-old lawyer with

permanent income hypothesis
the hypothesis that consumption is more closely related to permanent income than current income

the same income, because the baseball player expects his income to fall soon, while the lawyer does not. Farmers have "good" years and "bad" years and save more in good years to maintain consumption in the bad years. People, then, consume on the basis of lifetime income expectations, which are only partly determined by current income.

If standard of living depends on lifetime income rather than current income, people can borrow to smooth out the transitory changes in income that affect all individuals over their "life cycle." Thus, if people save in good years and borrow from their savings in bad years, they can avoid the transitory income changes that can impact standard of living.

That is, to measure inequality it may be more relevant to observe permanent income than current income. The relationship between permanent income and consumption is much more equal because it is less affected by transitory income—wide changes in income that vary from year to year. That is, using permanent income smoothes out the life cycle variation in income and thus leads to less inequality than using the wide variations associated with current income.

How Much Movement Happens on the Economic Ladder?

A study of income mobility during the decade of 1985–1995 found that less than 50 percent of individuals who began in the poorest quintile ended up there a decade later, and almost 30 percent of those in the poorest quintile moved up to the top three quintiles. Although roughly 80 percent of individuals in the richest quintile were still there a decade later, the research does not show that people moving into the top quintile tended to stay there. The middle quintiles appear to experience considerable movement up and down the income ladder. Generational studies also suggest a considerable income mobility—that is, incomes of fathers and sons tend to be only slightly positively correlated. If a father had lifetime income earnings 20 percent above his generation, his son could expect to earn income about 8 percent above his generation. Virtually no positive correlation could be made between the earnings of grandchildren and grandparents. In short, high-income and low-income earners will always be with us, but more than likely they will be different people.

In sum, most Americans experience significant fluctuations in their economic well-being from one year to the next. According to a Census Bureau study in the mid-1990s, about three-fourths of the population see their economic well-being go either up or down by at least 5 percent from one year to the next. Economic well-being can be affected by changes in personal and family circumstances, such as work experience, marital status, and household composition, as well as changes in earnings.

Why Do Some Earn More than Others?

Many reasons explain why some people earn more income than others. Some reasons for income differences include differences in age, skill, human capital (education and training), and preferences toward risk and leisure.

Age

The amount of income people earn varies over their lifetimes. Younger people with few skills tend to make little income when they begin their working careers. Income rises as workers gain experience and on-the-job training. As productivity increases, workers can command higher wages. These wage earnings generally increase up to the age of 50 and fall dramatically at retirement age, around 65.

Skills and Human Capital

Some workers are just more productive than others and therefore earn higher wages. Greater productivity can be a result of innate skills or of improvements in human capital, such as training and education. In Exhibit 5, we

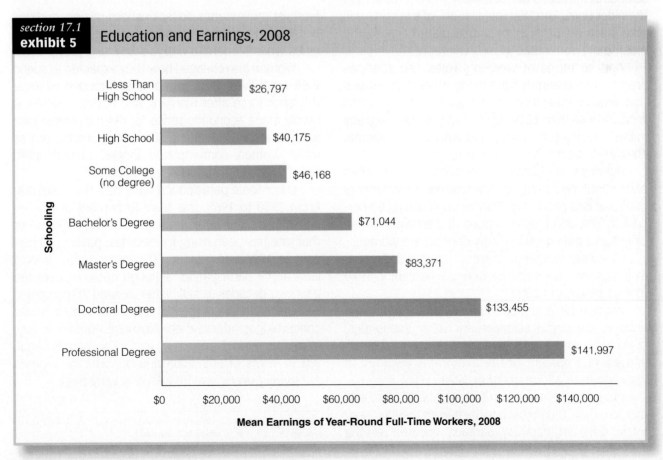

section 17.1 exhibit 5 Education and Earnings, 2008

Schooling	Mean Earnings of Year-Round Full-Time Workers, 2008
Less Than High School	$26,797
High School	$40,175
Some College (no degree)	$46,168
Bachelor's Degree	$71,044
Master's Degree	$83,371
Doctoral Degree	$133,455
Professional Degree	$141,997

Census Bureau, Current Population Survey, 2009.

in the news   Scientists Are Made, Not Born

—BY MICHAEL COX AND RICHARD ALM

Dallas—Do women have what it takes to become scientists?

In our effort to create more female scientists, what matters are the choices and opportunities open to young women at our universities.

Until the last 30 or so years, few women studied the sciences, so there was little mystery about why most people in those professions were men. Over the past generation, however, our research shows, there has been a truly stunning change. As an illustration of the gains by women in historically male disciplines, consider how the percentages of women receiving bachelor's degrees, master's degrees, and doctorates in the sciences increased from 1970 to 2002.

Clearly debating whether women are intellectually equipped for sciences makes little sense. Women themselves have already settled the issue, one degree at a time. The younger generations within the science professions are decidedly more female than the older ones. The "feminimization" of the ranks will take place as a matter of simple math because the older, male-dominated groups will retire.

And, in terms of women's roles, the sciences aren't much different from many other occupations that require education. In the early 1970s, women received less than 10 percent of all graduate degrees in law, medicine, dentistry, and veterinary medicine. They were below 20 percent in pharmacy.

However, as Exhibit 6 indicates, today women earn about two-thirds of the degrees in veterinary medicine and pharmacy. They're approaching 50 percent in law, and they've topped 40 percent in medicine. More than a third of new dentists are women.

Likewise, women's share of master's degrees from business schools rose from 3.6 percent in 1970 to 41.1 percent in 2002.

Women have also greatly expanded their presence in the social sciences, including economics, political science, and sociology. Overall, women earned 46.3 percent of the doctorates awarded in 2002, up from 13.3 percent in 1970.

Women themselves deserve credit for this extraordinary migration into higher education. They made different choices, perhaps because of the

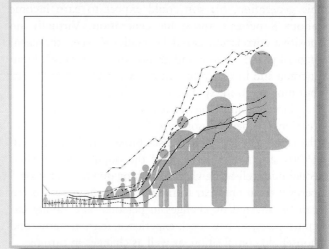

section 17.1 exhibit 6   Percentage Share of Professional Degrees Awarded to Women, 1950–2000

feminist movement's consciousness-raising, perhaps because the growing economy offered new opportunities while barriers to entry fell in many professions.

Women also changed how they expected to spend their adult lives. Back when most intended to leave the labor force after marrying and having children, it hardly made economic sense for them to invest time and money in demanding academic pursuits. But as more women contemplated longer, uninterrupted careers, academic effort began to pay off.

Labor-force participation rates bear this claim out: From 1950 to 1968, less than 40 percent of women age 20 and older were working or looking for jobs. But that rate has been rising for decades, passing 50 percent in 1984 and nearing 60 percent today. (Men's labor force participation, although declining over the past two decades, is still higher, around 75 percent.)

There are of course still a few hot-button issues concerning gender and employment: equality in pay, maternity leave, flexible time for family commitments. But in terms of education and opportunity, women are getting ever closer to a level playing field.

SOURCE: From Michael Cox, "Scientists Are Made, Not Born", 'New York Times', February 28, 2005. Used by permission of the author.

see that college graduates' average earnings are 81 percent greater than high school graduates. The financial rewards for attending college are higher than ever. Why is the gap widening between skilled and unskilled workers? One possibility is that increasing international trade over the last 30 years prompted an increase in domestic demand for skilled workers and a decrease in demand for domestic unskilled workers (unskilled workers are relatively cheap and plentiful in developing countries). That is, the United States tends to import goods produced with unskilled workers and export goods produced with skilled workers. In addition, technological changes to more sophisticated equipment can lead to an increase in demand for skilled workers. Other workers, such as star athletes and rock stars, have specialized talents that are in huge demand, so they make more money than those with fewer skills or with skills that are in less demand.

Worker Preferences

Aside from differences in age, skills, education, and training, people have different attitudes about and preferences regarding their work. Because workaholics (by definition) work longer hours, they earn more than others with comparable skills. Some workers earn more because they work more intensely than others. Still others may choose jobs that pay less but have more amenities—flexible hours, favorable job locations, generous benefit programs, child care, and so on. Some people choose to work less and spend more time pursuing leisure activities, such as traveling, hobbies, or spending time with family and friends. It is not for us to say that one preference is better than another but simply to recognize that these choices lead to differences in earnings.

Job Preferences

Finally, some of the differences in income are the result of the risks or undesirable features of some occupations. Police officers and firefighters are paid higher wages because of the dangers associated with their jobs. The same would be true for window washers on skyscrapers and painters on the Golden Gate bridge. Coal miners and garbage collectors are paid more than other workers with comparable skill levels because of the unpleasantness of the jobs. In short, some workers have higher earnings because they are compensated for the difficult, risky, or unappealing nature of their jobs.

Income Distribution in Other Countries

Is the United States typical of advanced, industrial nations with respect to the distribution of income

among its population? This question is difficult to answer with absolute certainty, given international differences in defining income, difficulties in measuring the impact of taxes, the problem of nonmonetary payments, and so on. Despite these hurdles, international comparisons of income distribution have been made.

Exhibit 7, constructed with data from the World Bank, shows that income inequality is greater in the United States and the United Kingdom than in Sweden and Japan. Japan's ratio of 4.5 means that the richest 10 percent of the population makes 4.5 times as much income as the bottom ten percent. In Brazil, the richest ten percent of the population make 51.3 times as much income as the bottom 10 percent. The table shows that some of the greatest disparities in income are found in developing countries such as Mexico, South Africa, and Brazil.

Although income inequality within nations is often substantial, it is far less than income inequality among nations. A majority of income inequality on Earth reflects differences in living standards among countries rather than disparities within nations. This conclusion is borne out by statistics.

section 17.1 exhibit 7 — Global Income Inequalities

Income Inequality	Country	Gap between Rich and Poor (Ratio)
Most Equal	Japan	4.5
	Sweden	6.2
	Germany	6.9
	India	8.6
	France	9.1
	Canada	9.4
	Russia	12.7
	United Kingdom	13.8
	United States	15.9
	Nigeria	17.8
	China	21.6
	Mexico	24.6
	Chile	33.0
	South Africa	33.1
	Argentina	40.9
Least Equal	Brazil	51.3

NOTE: The ratio of the richest 10% to the poorest 10% gives us the gap between rich and poor. The smaller the ratio the greater the equality.

SOURCE: World Bank

© KAREN KASMAUSKI/CORBIS

The contrasts between rich and poor are more extreme in Brazil than in almost any other country in the world. According to the UN Development Program, nearly half of Brazil's population lives in absolute poverty. Those who are unable to make a living as vendors of newspapers or lottery tickets, shoeshine boys, guards for parked cars, or the like are often forced to earn a living illegally. The number of children who work on the streets, or even live there permanently, is estimated to have reached 10 million.

SECTION CHECK

1. From 1935 to 1980, the distribution of income became more equal. However, since 1980, inequality has increased.

2. Nonmonetary income and privileges to the well-to-do may understate the disparity in income inequality, while demographics, institutional factors, measuring current income rather than permanent income, and government programs may overstate the disparity in income inequality.

3. High-income and low-income earners will always be with us, but they will likely be different people.

4. The level of income inequality differs from country to country.

1. Why might patterns in the measured income distribution give an inaccurate impression?

2. Why might income distribution statistics understate the degree of income inequality?

3. Why might measured income shares overstate the degree of income inequality?

4. How does the fraction of the population that is middle-aged, rather than young or old, affect measurements of income inequality?

5. How does the growth of both two-earner families and divorced couples increase measured income inequality?

6. Why is it important to take account of the substantial mobility of families within the income distribution over time when evaluating the degree of income inequality in America?

Income Redistribution

✴ What is the case for redistribution on the grounds of fairness?

✴ What is the case for efficiency and productivity?

The emphasis to this point has been on describing the amount of income inequality present in the United States and the rest of the world. Little has been said about the impact that inequality has on human welfare. Because of the difficulty of measuring welfare or of comparing the welfare of one person with another, it is impossible to "prove" that a given income distribution is better than another.

At the same time, however, it is clear that political and social changes in the past century or two have generally worked to reduce income inequality. In some cases, revolutions have been fought with income redistribution as a paramount motive—such was the case with the Russian Revolution and probably the French Revolution, not to mention many more recent upheavals in less-developed countries. Why is it generally felt that justice, fairness, and happiness would all be improved by increasing the income of the poor relative to the well-to-do or rich?

Equality

The economic theory supporting policies of income redistribution is derived from the principle of diminishing marginal utility. According to this principle, increases in income generate less additional happiness (utility) at higher levels of income.

Consider Exhibit 1. Suppose a family with an income of $300,000 a year has $30,000 taken from it in the form of a tax on income. The family accordingly reduces its consumption spending, forcing it to cut out some spending on luxuries—perhaps taking less-expensive vacations, forgoing a vacation home, and so on. This lowers the family's daily utility, say, from 27 utils to 25 utils. The marginal utility of the income given up is 2 utils (27 − 25). Now, suppose the income of some family making $10,000 a year is increased by the $30,000 taken from the first, well-to-do family. The poor family was formerly unable to purchase cars or appliances or take vacations. Now their utility is positively influenced by the transfer payment of $30,000, as it increases from 6 to 15 utils a week. The marginal utility to the poor family of the $30,000 in transfer payments is 9 utils (15 − 6). Using the Robin Hood approach—taking from the rich and giving to the poor—could possibly increase society's total utility in this case, because the rich family loses only 2 utils a week while the poor family gains 9 utils.

Thus, a theoretical argument favors income redistribution. Note, however, that the argument is based on the critical assumption that people are alike in how they experience diminishing marginal utility from increasing income, a proposition impossible to prove (economists assume that interpersonal utility comparisons are not possible). Many people believe it is a plausible assumption, but it is merely an assumption nonetheless. It is possible, however, that someone making $20 million a year after taxes would lose little utility if that income was cut to $17 million compared with the gains of the many poor families who could have their income doubled or tripled by receiving a portion of that income.

From time to time, groups have conducted polls asking people, "Are you happy?" Evidence from these polls suggests that, at a moment in time within a country, happiness is positively correlated with income—rich people are generally happier than poor people. This does not necessarily support the existence of diminishing marginal utility, but it might be evidence used by those who argue that income ought to be redistributed simply on the grounds of economic justice and fairness. Many people are able to command high incomes simply because of some inherited physical or mental talents that they develop or because they were, in some other way, "lucky." Why should these people be happier than others simply because of fate? If you believe society should try to equalize happiness among its members, you could argue that some income redistribution makes sense.

section 17.2 exhibit 1 Diminishing Marginal Utility of Income

As income rises, the happiness associated with that income also rises, but the principle of diminishing marginal utility of income means it rises by diminishing amounts. Assuming the two groups have identical marginal utility curves, the decrease in utility that results from taking some income from high-income groups may be less than the increase in utility generated by giving this income to low-income groups. Such redistribution would enhance total utility in society if people have similar preferences for income. The exact utility-income relationship is impossible to state, however, because of our inability to measure utility or to make utility comparisons among individuals.

Income Redistribution Can Reduce Incentives to Work, Invest, and Save

Even if one agreed that income redistribution from the rich to the poor would both tend to equalize happiness and, in the short run, increase the total utility received by the population, one might legitimately oppose some income redistribution on other grounds. If some income redistribution is good, why not go all the way and completely equalize everyone's income, taxing the rich extremely heavily and giving massive subsidies to the poor? Nearly everyone opposes that scenario because our incomes would all be equal but much smaller, providing little incentive to work, invest, and save. Why help make the economic pie (total output) if they will give you a piece if you don't work? Who would take on the risky jobs if everyone were paid the same? Why would you go to school if your investment in human capital was so low? Most of us believe, for efficiency and equity (fairness) reasons, that there ought to be some limits on redistributive efforts. The principal disagreement is not over whether we should have some redistribution, but rather over at what point we should stop in our redistributive efforts. Some believe we should go further than we have, while others think we have already gone too far in attempts to alter the distribution of income in favor of the poor and less affluent.

"Fair" May or May Not Be Fair

What are the arguments against a radical redistribution of income that would eliminate virtually all inequality? The first argument is an equity one. Is it "fair" to take most of the income of hard-working, talented people who earn high incomes, particularly when some of it is given to people who perhaps may be perceived as shiftless and lazy? Not all poor people are automatically good and deserving, nor are all rich people greedy and selfish. Related to that, some income inequality would seem desirable, because consumption needs may well vary with family size, age of family members, and other factors. Total equality of *family* income, for example, would penalize those who choose to have big families, while total equality in *individual* incomes would perhaps penalize those who choose to have small families or live alone.

Indeed, it is possible that the rich are rich largely because of their high marginal utility of income, while many poor may be poor because they care less about goods relative to nonwork activities. As you can see by comparing the shaded areas of Exhibit 2, the rich lose more than the poor gain from the transfer of income. In this situation, then, transferring income from rich to poor actually makes society worse off!

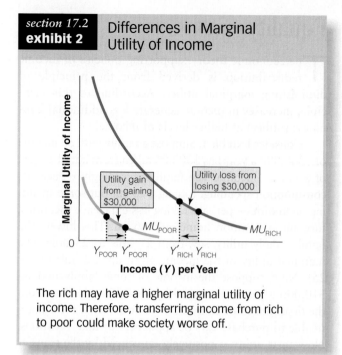

section 17.2
exhibit 2 Differences in Marginal Utility of Income

The rich may have a higher marginal utility of income. Therefore, transferring income from rich to poor could make society worse off.

Revisiting Marginal Productivity Theory

Income derived from payments according to marginal productivity may sound fair, but it may lead to very unequal incomes because ownership of resources is initially divided unequally. For example, individuals have different opportunities to obtain education and training. Some individuals inherit property; in contrast, others may have physical or mental disabilities. In addition, imperfections in labor markets (e.g., unions and licensing restrictions) can lead to factory owners not receiving income according to their marginal productivity. Discrimination can also distort the linkage between income and marginal contribution to output.

SECTION CHECK

1. If the happiness or utility derived from additional income is subject to diminishing marginal utility, then it is possible that income taken from the very rich and given to the very poor might increase total utility. However, this argument is based on the assumption that people are alike in how they experience diminishing marginal utility from increasing income, a proposition that is impossible to prove.

2. Too much income redistribution provides fewer incentives to work, invest, and save.

1. How is the principle of diminishing marginal utility used to justify income redistribution?

2. Why is it not possible to prove the idea that redistributing income from rich to poor will increase society's utility?

3. What are the fairness and incentive arguments against government redistribution of income?

4. If high-income individuals must pay increased income tax rates in order to provide subsidies for low-income individuals (and the subsidies are phased out as income increases), are the productive incentives of both high- and low-income people reduced? Why or why not?

The Economics of Discrimination

* What is job-entry discrimination?
* What is wage discrimination?
* Do earnings differences reflect discrimination or differences in productivity?
* How can we remedy discrimination?

When a worker is denied employment on the basis of some biological feature, such as sex or race, without any regard to productivity, it is called job-entry discrimination. Wage discrimination occurs when a worker is given employment at a wage lower than that of other workers, based on something other than productivity.

Job-Entry Discrimination

In a world where sex and race have absolutely no bearing whatsoever on the employment circumstances of people (e.g., talent, education, willingness and ability to work, move, etc.), every occupation would, apart from random variations, have a workforce with the same sex and race proportions as the population at large. Thus, on average, 51 percent of employees in each occupation would be expected to be female, if women comprised 51 percent of the population, and approximately 12 percent or so would be blacks and other racial minorities, reflecting the proportion of nonwhites to the total population.

In fact, the proportion of females working (46 percent) is slightly less than the proportion of men. Likewise, the proportion of blacks in the workforce is lower than would be expected given the general population percentages. Looking first at females, their less-than-proportionate presence in the workforce might be viewed as a matter of choice; some women may prefer to be engaged in full-time household production rather than work outside the home. On the other hand, others argue that this attitude reflects ingrained sexism; no inherent reason says that the adult male member of the household should not stay at home with the kids as much as the female member. In any case, the proportion of women to men in the workforce has dramatically increased over time—women were only 38 percent of the labor force in 1970, and now they are more than 46 percent.

job-entry discrimination
a worker is denied employment on the basis of some biological feature, such as sex or race, without any regard to productivity

wage discrimination
when a worker is given employment at a wage lower than that of other workers, based on something other than productivity

Job-entry discrimination is further evidenced by the higher proportion of white males with relatively high-paying jobs compared with females and non-whites who make up a relatively larger proportion of employees working in unskilled jobs with low pay and relatively little prestige.

Wage Discrimination

A strong statistical correlation exists between lifetime earnings and years of schooling. High-school graduates earn roughly two-thirds of the salary of college graduates.

Overall, white women make 25 percent to 30 percent less than white men. White males also typically earn 25 percent to 30 percent more than black males. At least part of this wage differential can be explained by differences in educational attainment and does not simply reflect racial prejudice on the part of employers. Blacks and women on average may have acquired fewer years of schooling, less training, and fewer years of experience. For example, although almost 25 percent of whites have college degrees, less than 14 percent of blacks and 10 percent of Hispanics have completed four years of college. Also, compared with 26 percent of men, less than 22 percent of women have completed four years of college. Among females, black women earn 10 percent less than white women. While a major reason women and nonwhites earn less than white males is that they occupy jobs that are lower paying due to their lower skills, it is also possible that they earn less because of wage discrimination—being paid less, strictly because of their race or sex.

Discrimination or Differences in Productivity?

Merely demonstrating that wages are lower for blacks and females does not in itself prove wage discrimination, although it is consistent with the notion

COURTESY OF ROBERT L. SEXTON

Education level has a great impact on earnings potential. Young adults who have completed bachelor's degrees earn substantially more than those with high school diplomas.

that discrimination occurs. However, if occupational and wage differentials are not caused by discrimination, what are the causes?

Several scholars developed statistical models that argue that a great deal of the earnings differentials across the sexes and races can be explained by differences in productivity. In other words, employers hire and pay workers roughly an amount equal to their perceived contributions (marginal revenue product). Now, if the marginal revenue product of blacks and women happens to be lower on average than that of white men, even within occupational groups, then one could argue that employers are not discriminating on the basis of race or sex but rather on the basis of expected productivity. Assuming this reasoning is at least partly true, why might white male workers be more productive than other workers?

Productivity Differences: An Environmental Explanation

The first explanation is that various environmental factors have prevented blacks, Hispanics, and females from gaining the training and skills necessary to achieve high productivity. In the past, blacks and Hispanics often received less schooling than did whites, and the quality of that schooling has often been lower—discrimination in the acquisition of human capital. Even if blacks and Hispanics were

to attend school as long as whites, their quality of schooling is less because of the lack of resources in schools populated with minorities.

Females, because they are far more likely to interrupt their careers to have and care for children, often have less work experience than their male counterparts. This factor may also lower their productivity relative to males. Women may also be more likely to take jobs, such as teaching, that may pay less but have more flexible hours that make it easier to raise children. In other words, some of the wage differences may be job preferences. Also, women who have never been married and have not had any job interruptions earn roughly 10 percent less than their male counterparts. White married women earn roughly 40 percent less than married men. This environmental explanation of productivity differences does not rule out discrimination but rather argues that past discrimination's perverse influences on the environment of females and nonwhites has caused them to have an inferior endowment of human capital now, even if present-day employers were color and sex blind in terms of paying workers. However, unexplained differences between whites and minorities and males and females lead us to believe discrimination is a factor in the labor market.

Why Do People Discriminate?

Why would any employer want to discriminate against an employee on the basis of race or sex? It might appear that discrimination is totally inconsistent with the economist's view of the rational utility-maximizing person. After all, if a firm really wants to maximize profits, it should hire the best person available per dollar of wage expenditure, regardless of age, sex, race, or other attribute of the worker.

Let's take a look at some reasons why discrimination occurs.

Reducing Information Costs

To some extent, discrimination may reflect information costs. Suppose an employer has previously hired 10 green workers and 10 blue workers for a certain type of work, and eight of the green workers performed well while only two of the blue workers did. (The poorer blue worker performance may have reflected poorer training and educational backgrounds.) In this situation, the employer might prefer to hire a green employee for the next job opening, because past experience suggests that the probability is greater that the green worker will perform well. In this case, the color of the worker is used as a screening device, a means of narrowing the list of job candidates.

It costs money and time to evaluate the prospects of every applicant, and race is an imperfect but cheap way of doing some of the screening. A profit-maximizing employer is not overly concerned that by screening workers by color, he discriminates against good blue workers. To this employer, the reduction in information costs achieved by hiring on the basis of color may exceed the perceived benefits from the identification of good blue workers.

Personal Preferences

It is a fact that some people prefer association with others with certain racial and/or sexual attributes. These people may have acquired these preferences out of an ignorance that fosters bigotry and racism, but the preferences are there nonetheless. The utility gained from having the desired racial mix might exceed the loss in income from not having the best

employees. For example, a racially prejudiced business owner might prefer making $900,000 a year in profits from a business with, say, an all-white labor force to making $1,000,000 with a racially mixed force. In the words of the pioneer in the economics of discrimination, Nobel laureate Gary Becker of the University of Chicago, the person has acquired a "taste" for discrimination, just as one might acquire a taste for certain goods. That is, an employer may be willing to trade away some income to satisfy an acquired taste for discrimination.

The Costs of Discrimination

It is also true that in competitive industries, firms that discriminate may lose out ultimately to firms that do not. The nondiscriminating firm can hire the unfavored but equally competent workers and have a cost advantage over firms that discriminate. This cost advantage may allow the nondiscriminating firm to undercut its discriminating competitors' prices and either force them out of business or make them change their hiring practices. That is, in the long run, competition has the potential to reduce discrimination.

SECTION CHECK

1. If a worker is denied employment on the basis of some noneconomic factor like race, religion, sex, or ethnic origin, it is called job-entry discrimination.

2. If a worker is hired at a wage lower than that of other workers on some basis other than productivity differences, it is called wage discrimination.

3. If a firm really wants to maximize its profits, it should minimize costs by hiring the best persons available per dollar of wage expenditure, regardless of age, sex, race, or other attribute of the worker.

4. Discrimination may occur because of information costs or because some workers may prefer to associate with persons with certain racial or sexual attributes.

---

1. What is the difference between job-entry discrimination and wage discrimination?

2. Explain how earnings differences could reflect either discrimination or productivity differences.

3. What is the environmental explanation for differences in earnings across the sexes and races?

4. How do firms' incentives to maximize profits tend to reduce the extent of discrimination?

5. How can discrimination reflect imperfect information and the costs of acquiring more information about potential employees?

6. Say you only hire purple workers. If purple workers strongly prefer to work with one another instead of with other groups, why might you prefer to hire a less productive purple worker than a more productive nonpurple worker at the same wage?

7. Why would subsidizing employers for hiring minority workers rather than imposing implicit quotas give employers greater incentives to expand minority job opportunities?

Poverty

* How do we define poverty?
* How many people live in poverty?
* What is relative income?

At several points in the previous discussion, the words *rich* and *poor* have been used without being defined. Of particular interest is the question of poverty. Our concern over income distribution largely arises because most people believe that those with low incomes have lower satisfaction than those with higher incomes. Thus, the "poor" people are those who, in a material sense, suffer relative to other people. It is desirable, therefore, to define and measure the extent of poverty in the United States.

Defining Poverty

The federal government measures poverty by using a set of money income thresholds that vary by family size to detect who is poor. If the family's total income is less than the established family threshold, then that family, and every individual in it, is considered poor. The poverty thresholds are adjusted annually for inflation. The poverty rate is the percentage of the population who fall below this absolute level, called the **poverty line**. The official poverty rate for the United States is currently set at three times the cost of providing a nutritionally adequate diet—roughly $20,000 for a family of four. The official poverty definition may overstate the level of poverty because it does not include noncash benefits (such as public housing, Medicaid, and food stamps).

The amount of poverty fell steadily in the 1960s, was steady in the 1970s, and rose during the recession in the early 1980s. The poverty rate then fell slightly during the rest of the 1980s and rose again during the recessions of 1990–1991 and the recessions of 2001 and 2008–09. As you would expect, when the economy is in a recession, unemployment rises and poverty tends to increase. Exhibit 1 provides some statistics on the U.S. poverty rate.

poverty rate
the percentage of the population who fall below the poverty line

poverty line
a set of money income thresholds, established by the federal government, that vary by family size and are used to detect who is poor; if a family's total income is less than the established family threshold, then that family, and every individual in it, is considered poor

Poverty rates vary considerably among different races. Exhibit 2 shows that poverty rates for blacks and Hispanics were much higher than for whites. However, poverty rates fell markedly for blacks and Hispanics during the 1990s. Household status also influences poverty. A family headed by a female with no husband present is about five times more likely to experience poverty than a family headed by a married couple. Children are also more likely than average to be members of poor families— see Exhibit 2.

With a definition of poverty that is determined at some fixed, real-income level (that is, an income that has been adjusted for inflation), poverty over time should decline and, indeed, largely disappear, because real incomes generally rise over time with economic growth. Unless lower income groups do not share at all in the rising incomes of the population, some reduction in poverty is inevitable. Thus, one cure for poverty, as defined by some absolute income or standard of living criterion, is economic growth. The greater the rate of economic growth, the more rapidly poverty will be eradicated.

An Alternative Definition of Poverty

Many "poor" individuals in the United States, using the official definition, would be considered well off, even "rich," in many less-developed countries. For example, $15,000 of income a year, while not much in the United States, would make you very rich in a country such as Ethiopia. On the other hand, many Americans with incomes now considered just above the poverty line might be considered poor a generation or two from now, even though their incomes will permit them to buy far more than what today are considered to be the necessities of life. Why?

section 17.4
exhibit 1   Poverty Rate: 1959 to 2008

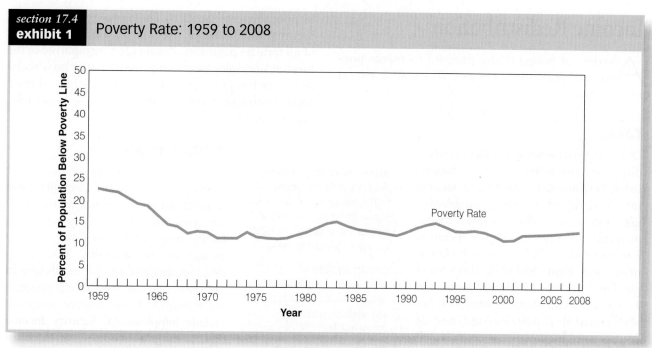

SOURCE: U.S. Census Bureau, Current Population Survey, 2009.

section 17.4
exhibit 2   Poverty Among Different Groups, 2008

Group	Below Poverty Rate
Female household, no husband present	28.7
Black	24.7
Hispanic	23.2
Children (under age 18)	19.0
Male household, no wife present	13.8
All Persons	13.2
Asian	11.8
Elderly (over age 65)	9.7
White, not Hispanic	8.6
Married-couple families	5.5

SOURCE: U.S. Census Bureau.

To most people, being poor means having less income and purchasing power than most other people living in the same community or nation. A person is poor if her income is low relative to the incomes of most other people in the same geographical area, and she is rich if her income exceeds that of most other people in the area. Poverty is therefore often thought of as a relative income concept, rather than being determined by some ability to buy a specific fixed basket of goods and services.

Alternative definitions of poverty have been suggested based on relative income measures. For instance, families that earn less than one-half the median (or middle) family income could be considered poor. Over time, as economic growth proceeds, the income necessary to avoid being considered poor by this measure increases. Using this definition, then, poverty cannot be eradicated by economic growth but only by income redistribution. Even from an equity or fairness point of view, few people favor total income equality, because income needs presumably vary with family size and possibly with the ages of the family members and the cost of living in different cities. It is clear, then, that "poverty," in a relative income sense, will always be with us. We can perhaps reduce the consequences of being poor by policies that raise the incomes of society's lowest-income members to levels closer to the median, but we cannot raise everyone's income to a level equal to or above that median; that is an economic, as well as a statistical, impossibility.

Income Redistribution

A variety of programs are designed to reduce poverty and redistribute income. We examine several of them here.

Taxes

One way to redistribute income to reduce disparities among individuals is through federal income tax. The federal income tax is designed to be a **progressive tax system**—one that imposes higher marginal tax rates on higher incomes. For example in 2006, if individuals made less than $30,650, their marginal tax rate was 15 percent. Income in excess of $30,650 but less than $74,200 was taxed at a marginal tax rate of 25 percent; income between $74,200 and $154,800 was taxed at a marginal tax rate of 28 percent; and income in the range of $154,800 to $336,500 was taxed at a marginal tax rate of 33 percent. Any income earned by an individual over $336,500 was taxed at a marginal tax rate of 35 percent.

Transfer Payments

A second means by which income redistribution can be carried out by the government is through direct transfer payments to the lower part of the income distribution. Transfer payments are payments made to individuals for which goods or services are exchanged. They come in the form of in-kind transfers—direct transfers of goods or services such as food stamps, housing subsidies, and Medicaid—and **cash transfers** of direct cash payments such as welfare, Social Security, and unemployment compensation.

Social Security, Medicare, and Unemployment Compensation Social Security is a cash transfer program that provides income primarily to older persons. Social Security accounts for almost 45 percent of all federal transfer payments. Medicare is an in-kind transfer—a health insurance subsidy program that pays many of the doctor and hospital bills for those over the age of 65. Neither of these programs are considered welfare programs because one does not have to

progressive tax system
tax system that imposes higher marginal tax rates on higher incomes; the federal income tax is designed to be a progressive tax system

cash transfers
direct cash payments like welfare, Social Security, and unemployment compensation

Supplemental Security Income (SSI)
a welfare program designed for the most needy, elderly, disabled, and blind

Temporary Assistance for Needy Families (TANF)
a welfare program designed to help families that have few financial resources

Earned Income Tax Credit (EITC)
a welfare program that allows the working poor to receive income refunds that can be greater than the taxes they paid during the last year

means-tested income transfer program
program in which eligibility is dependent on low income; food stamps, Medicaid, and housing subsidies are examples of means-tested income transfer programs

be poor to receive benefits. These two programs, Social Security and Medicare, account for almost 70 percent of all transfer payments. Benefits for unemployed in the form of unemployment compensation are also a social insurance form of transfer payments. All three of these social insurance programs are event based—job loss, old age, or disability.

Welfare Programs

The social insurance programs (Social Security, Medicare, and Unemployment Compensation) are different from welfare programs, where a person or a family must prove they have a low enough income to qualify. Medicaid, a program designed to give health care to the poor, and the food stamp program are examples. Other welfare programs include **Supplemental Security Income (SSI)**, a program designed for the most needy, elderly, disabled, and blind, and **Temporary Assistance for Needy Families (TANF)**, designed to help families that have few financial resources. The **Earned Income Tax Credit (EITC)** is a program that allows the working poor to receive income refunds that can be greater than the taxes they paid during the last year. It is a **means-tested income transfer program** (eligibility is dependent on low income) like food stamps, Medicaid, and housing subsidies.

Negative Income Tax

A negative income tax collects taxes from high-income families and gives subsidies to low-income families. Thus, it is a tax and a transfer program. It uses the personal income tax system to set up a series of payments to citizens and tax receipts by the U.S. Treasury according to a schedule based on family size and actual income earned. The plan would not require setting up a new system. It could be an extension of the fully computerized system that already exists.

How Does it Work? High-income families would pay a tax; low-income families would receive a subsidy. For example, suppose the government formula for a negative tax is Tax = (25 percent × income) − $10,000. So, if a family earned $100,000 a year it would pay $15,000 in taxes (0.25 × $100,000 = $25,000 − $10,000 =

$15,000). A family that earned $40,000 a year would pay $0.00 in taxes ($0.25 \times \$40,000 = \$10,000 - \$10,000 = \$0$). And a family that earned $20,000 would owe $-\$5,000$ ($0.25 \times \$20,000 = \$5,000 - \$10,000 = -\$5,000$). That is, this family would get $5,000 in return.

The Case for a Negative Income Tax Many economists favor a negative income tax. They point out that it would not require the massive bureaucracy that now exists for administering public assistance, food stamp, and other programs. Hence, many of the resources now spent for this huge bureaucracy could be spent on other priorities, or used to provide the negative tax (the government payment) to needy families. No one would have to demonstrate need. It would not encourage illegitimate births, family break-ups, or many claims the current welfare system does.

The Case Against a Negative Income Tax On the other hand, many economists oppose a negative income tax, pointing out that it might cost "too much." In particular, if for political reasons such current welfare programs as food stamps and subsidized housing cannot be dismantled, then the negative income tax would just be one more facet of the welfare system.

They also contend that any effective negative income tax would have a *work disincentive effect*. That is, the payoff for returning to work would be smaller with an effective negative income tax program, so that many who could work might nevertheless decide not to do so. There is also concern that cash assistance, rather than in-kind welfare (food stamps, housing subsidies, etc.) would lead to poor consumption choices—perhaps drugs and alcohol. However, recipients would substitute food stamps for cash purchases, allowing them to buy whatever they wanted. And some critics say while it subsidizes the unfortunate, it also subsidizes the lazy and undeserving.

Government Subsidies

A third way that governments can help the less affluent is by using government revenues to provide low-cost public services. Inexpensive public housing, subsidized public transport, and even public parks are services that probably serve the poor to a greater extent than the rich. "Free" public education is viewed by many as an equalizing force in that it opens opportunities for children of less prosperous members of society to obtain employment that could improve their economic status. Of course, not all government programs benefit the relatively poor at the expense of the rich. For example, federal government subsidies to commuter railroads primarily lower the cost to affluent suburbanites of getting to work in the central city. Support for public universities may help the middle or even upper income groups more than the poor. In addition, agricultural subsidies often provide large benefits to farmers who already have large incomes.

global WATCH

WHAT'S THE BEST WAY TO REDUCE EXTREME POVERTY? GOOD NEWS ABOUT POVERTY

—BY DAVID BROOKS

I hate to be the bearer of good news, because only pessimists are regarded as intellectually serious, but we're in the 11th month of the most prosperous year in human history. Last week, the World Bank released a report showing that global growth "accelerated sharply" this year to a rate of about 4 percent.

Best of all, the poorer nations are leading the way. Some rich countries, like the U.S. and Japan, are doing well, but the developing world is leading this economic surge. Developing countries are seeing their economies expand by 6.1 percent this year—an unprecedented rate—and, even if you take China,

COURTESY OF KATHERINE SEXTON

(continued)

India and Russia out of the equation, developing world growth is still around 5 percent. As even the cautious folks at the World Bank note, all developing regions are growing faster this decade than they did in the 1980's and 90's.

This is having a wonderful effect on world poverty, because when regions grow, that growth is shared up and down the income ladder. In its report, the World Bank notes that economic growth is producing a "spectacular" decline in poverty in East and South Asia. In 1990, there were roughly 472 million people in the East Asia and Pacific region living on less than $1 a day. By 2001, there were 271 million living in extreme poverty, and by 2015, at current projections, there will only be 19 million people living under those conditions.

Less dramatic declines in extreme poverty have been noted around the developing world, with the vital exception of sub-Saharan Africa. It now seems quite possible that we will meet the United Nations' Millennium Development Goals, which were set a few years ago: the number of people living in extreme poverty will be cut in half by the year 2015. As Martin Wolf of The Financial Times wrote in his recent book, "Why Globalization Works": "Never before have so many people—or so large a proportion of the world's population—enjoyed such large rises in their standard of living."

As other research confirms, these rapid improvements at the bottom of the income ladder are contributing to and correlating with declines in illiteracy, child labor rates and fertility rates. The growth in the world's poorer regions also supports the argument that we are seeing a drop in global inequality.

Economists have been arguing furiously about whether inequality is increasing or decreasing. But it now seems likely that while inequality has grown within particular nations, it is shrinking among individuals worldwide. The Catalan economist Xavier Sala-i-Martin looked at eight measures of global inequality and found they told the same story: after remaining constant during the 70's, inequality among individuals has since declined.

What explains all this good news? The short answer is this thing we call globalization. Over the past decades, many nations have undertaken structural reforms to lower trade barriers, shore up property rights and free economic activity. International trade is surging. The poor nations that opened themselves up to trade, investment and those evil multinational corporations saw the sharpest poverty declines. Write this on your forehead: Free trade reduces world suffering.

Of course, all the news is not good. Plagued by bad governments and AIDS, sub-Saharan Africa has not joined in the benefits of globalization. Big budget deficits in the U.S. and elsewhere threaten stable growth. High oil prices are a problem. Trade produces losers as well as winners, especially among less-skilled workers in the developed world.

But especially around Thanksgiving, it's worth appreciating some of the things that have gone right, and not just sweeping reports like the one from the World Bank under the rug.

It's worth reminding ourselves that the key task ahead is spreading the benefits of globalization to Africa and the Middle East. It's worth noting this perhaps not too surprising phenomenon: As free trade improves the lives of people in poor countries, it is viewed with suspicion by more people in rich countries.

Just once, I'd like to see someone like Bono or Bruce Springsteen stand up at a concert and speak the truth to his fan base: that the world is complicated and there are no free lunches. But if you really want to reduce world poverty, you should be cheering on those guys in pinstripe suits at the free-trade negotiations and those investors jetting around the world. Thanks, in part, to them, we are making progress against poverty. Thanks, in part, to them, more people around the world have something to be thankful for.

TEACH YOUR CHILDREN WELL THE ECONOMIC CASE FOR PRESCHOOL

—BY JOEL WALDFOGEL

Softhearted people always advocate spending more on kids. But according to a new and authoritative synthesis of available evidence, there's a hardheaded case for investing more in young kids over older ones.

In the United States, we've spent trillions of dollars over decades on K–12 schooling in the hopes of making young people more productive, or at least less criminally delinquent. The results have been mixed. About 20 percent of the American workforce is essentially illiterate (compared with 5 to 10 percent in Sweden or Germany), creating a major drag on our international competitiveness. And an astronomical 5.6 million adults in the United States have served time in state or federal prison, with 1.3 million there currently. Their incarceration, along with other costs of crime, costs us around $1.3 trillion a year.

Why doesn't all our spending on education buy better results? Nobel Prize winner James Heckman of the University of Chicago and Dimitriy Masterov of the University of Michigan argue that by waiting until kindergarten, we throw money at kids when it's too late. Their evidence urges shifting educational spending to younger children.

The early investment is needed, the authors argue, to supplement the role of the family. Recent developments in neuroscience have shown that the early years are vital to cognitive development, which in turn is important to subsequent success and productivity in school, life, and work. Early-Childhood nurturing has traditionally been the province of families. But families are deteriorating. Roughly one in six kids was born into poverty or single parenthood or both in 1970. In 2000, the rate was about one in four. What's more, almost 10 percent of children were born to unmarried teenage mothers in 1999; these kids tend to receive especially low levels of emotional and intellectual support and cognitive stimulation. They arrive at kindergarten cognitively disadvantaged, and the gap widens as they get older, eventually leading to early babies, lousy jobs, and elevated crime.

Heckman and Masterov look at a number of pilot programs in early-childhood education that have targeted high-risk kids in disadvantaged families, and studied them into adulthood. These programs are like Head Start, only more intensive. For example, between 1962 and 1967, the Perry Project in Ypsilanti, Mich., provided two years of intensive preschool to a group of disadvantaged 3-year-old black children, chosen from an eligible pool by a coin flip. The program consisted of a daily session of two and a half hours and a weekly 90-minute teacher home visit. In today's dollars, it would cost $10,000 per child per year.

Perry participants have been followed through age 40, and the program has shown substantial benefits in educational achievement and other social outcomes. Participants achieved greater literacy and higher grades, and they were more likely to graduate high school. Later in life, they were more likely to be employed—and to earn more—and less likely to be on welfare. They also committed less crime and had lower rates of teen pregnancy.

The authors estimate the rate of return for programs like the Perry Project to be a substantial 16 percent. While some of this payback accrues directly to the kids, in the form of higher earnings when they're grown up, about three-quarters of it goes to the rest of us in the form of lower crime and savings on prison spending. Heckman and Masterov compare the return from investing in preschool kids with the returns from lower class size in high school (smaller than the return to preschool) and to GED programs (smaller still). They propose that the return on investment declines with age, although they don't offer a ton of quantitative evidence on this point.

The big economic return for intensive preschool for disadvantaged kids has two implications. First, while many people advocate spending on these kids for reasons of fairness or justice, Heckman and Masterov make a different case. They're saying this preschool spending is a sound economic investment. Each dollar we spend on targeted, intensive preschool returns more than a dollar invested in, say, a pretty good mutual fund.

(continued)

POLICY application
TEACH YOUR CHILDREN WELL
THE ECONOMIC CASE FOR PRESCHOOL (CONT.)

Many families already make this investment on their own, either by spending time with their kids or by purchasing high-quality child care. Why involve governments? Well, Heckman and Masterov show that if *your* kid goes to one of these programs, *the rest of us* get most of the benefit. Economists assume that even if parents of disadvantaged kids are rational and forward-looking—as if they didn't have enough to worry about—they will invest in preschool only to boost their kids' earnings and not to reduce crime and prison costs, which are borne by the rest of us. As a result, even conscientious parents will under-invest. So, Economics 101 tells you—granted, in an end-of-semester lecture that you probably skipped—that clearly this is a job for government.

The hardheaded case for Perry-like preschool extends beyond higher pay and reduced crime. Unlike many efforts to boost productivity—think trickle-down—this one would reduce inequality as well, by raising the incomes of the disadvantaged. Investing in preschools can also enhance international

competitiveness. Much of the growth in American standards of living over the past half-century has flowed from our population's ever-increasing educational attainment. But for the generations born since 1950, the growth has stopped. The problem is not that a college education costs too much, but rather that many disadvantaged kids aren't academically ready for college when they finish high school. And Heckman and Masterov argue that it stems from the academic deficits they bring to kindergarten. If preschool whips them into shape, they'll be better prepared for all the other steps along the way.

A sales problem remains: These programs invade the traditional province of the family, and in Heckman and Masterov's conception, they would target disadvantaged populations that are disproportionately minority. Wanted: a credible and sympathetic pitchman. Paging Barack Obama.

SOURCE: Joel Waldfogel is the Ehrenkranz Family Professor of business and public policy at the Wharton School of the University of Pennsylvania. His new book is The Tyranny of the Market: Why you Can't Always Get What You Want.

SECTION CHECK

1. One method of defining poverty is to determine an absolute income level that is necessary to provide the basic necessities of life in minimum quantities. The poverty rate, then, would be the proportion of persons who fail to earn the minimum income standard.

2. An alternative definition of poverty is a relative income measure. For instance, families that earn less than one-half the median (or middle) family income are considered poor. Using this definition, poverty cannot be eradicated by economic growth, but only by income redistribution.

3. A negative income tax (NIT) is a tax and transfer program that collects taxes from higher income families and gives subsidies to lower income families.

1. How are absolute and relative measures of poverty different?

2. Why could economic growth potentially eliminate absolute measures of poverty but not relative measures of poverty?

3. Some people argue that poverty could be eliminated by "rich" countries. Can both absolute and relative poverty be eliminated by rich countries? Why or why not?

4. What are some of the programs designed to reduce poverty and redistribute income?

Interactive Chapter Summary

Fill in the blanks:

1. Since the 1980s, the share of measured income received by the top 5 percent has _____ and that of the lowest fifth of families has _____.

2. People are at their peak in terms of productivity when they are _____.

3. At any moment in time, middle-aged people tend to have _____ incomes than both younger and older people do.

4. An increase in the divorce rate has caused the measured distribution of income in the United States to appear more _____.

5. If we consider age distribution, institutional factors, and in-kind transfer programs, the income distribution is likely considerably more _____ than it appears from measured income.

6. The greater the distance between the Lorenz curve and the 45-degree line, the _____ the amount of inequality.

7. The Gini coefficient, which measures income inequality, varies from _____ for perfect equality to _____ for perfect inequality.

8. Political and social changes in the past century or two have worked to _____ income inequality.

9. The permanent income hypothesis (PIH) indicates that consumption would be _____ likely to exceed income, when one is middle-aged rather than when one is young or old.

10. The economic theory supporting policies of income redistribution is derived from the principle of _____.

11. Diminishing marginal utility implies that increases in income generate _____ additional happiness or utility at higher levels of income.

12. Arguments to justify income redistribution based on diminishing marginal utility must assume that people are _____ in how they experience diminishing marginal utility from increasing income.

13. Heavy taxes on the rich, combined with large subsidies for the poor, would result in little incentive to _____ or _____.

14. Large-scale redistribution from high-income individuals to low-income individuals would likely _____ the level of human capital (education) in society.

15. When a person is denied employment without regard to productivity, it is called _____ discrimination.

16. When a person is given employment at a wage lower than that of other workers, based on something other than productivity, it is called _____ discrimination.

17. The proportion of women to men in the labor force has dramatically _____ over time.

18. A _____ statistical correlation exists between lifetime earnings and years of schooling.

19. The _____ explanation of productivity differences focuses on past discrimination's perverse effect on the environment of females and nonwhites.

20. Discrimination sometimes reflects _____ costs, based on past experiences.

21. Using race or sex is an _____ but cheap way of screening applicants for some jobs.

22. Nondiscriminating firms have a cost _____ compared with firms that discriminate.

23. Differences in _____, certain _____ factors, _____ factors, and government _____ activities have all been identified as elements that influence the income distribution data and suggest that we might be overstating inequality.

24. At any moment in time, middle-aged persons tend to have _____ incomes than younger and older persons because they are at an age when their _____ is at a peak and they are participating in the _____ to a greater extent.

25. The earnings of children of fathers with lifetime earnings 20 percent greater than the average tend to be _____ average.

26. Reasons that some people make more money than others include differences in _____, _____, _____, _____, and _____ towards risk and leisure.

27. A majority of the income inequality on Earth reflects differences in living standards _____ nations rather than disparities _____ nations.

28. _____ discrimination occurs when a worker is denied employment on the basis of some factor without regard to his or her productivity.

29. A great deal of the earnings differentials across the sexes and races can be explained by differences in _____.

30. In competitive industries, firms that do not discriminate can hire the unfavored but equally competent workers and have a(n) _____ advantage, allowing them to _____ discriminating competitors' prices.

31. The poverty rate for the United States is currently set at _____ the cost of providing a nutritionally adequate diet.

32. The greater the rate of economic growth, the _____ rapidly poverty will be eradicated.

33. Using a relative definition of poverty, poverty cannot be eradicated by economic growth but only by _____.

34. Because the federal income tax is _____, it tends to redistribute income in a way that reduces income disparities.

35. Social Security accounts for almost _____ of federal transfer payments and, along with Medicare, accounts for almost _____.

Answers: 1. risen; fallen 2. middle-aged 3. higher 4. unequal 5. equal 6. greater 7. zero; one 8. reduce 9. less 10. diminishing marginal utility 11. less 12. alike 13. works; invest 14. reduce 15. job-entry 16. wage 17. increased 18. strong 19. environmental 20. information 21. imperfect 22. advantage 23. age; demographic; institutional; redistributive 24. higher productivity; labor force 25. above 26. age; skill; education; training; preferences 27. among; within 28. Job-entry 29. productivity 30. costs; undercut 31. three times 32. more 33. income redistribution 34. progressive 35. 45 percent; 70 percent

Key Terms and Concepts

in-kind transfers 485
permanent income hypothesis 486
job-entry discrimination 493
wage discrimination 493
poverty rate 496
poverty line 496

progressive tax system 498
cash transfers 498
Supplemental Security Income (SSI) 498
Temporary Assistance for Needy Families (TANF) 498

Earned Income Tax Credit (EITC) 498
means-tested income transfer program 498

Section Check Answers

17.1 Income Distribution

1. Why might patterns in the measured income distribution give an inaccurate impression?

The measured income distribution may give an inaccurate impression because it does not include all forms of income. For instance, it does not include nonmonetary income.

2. Why might income distribution statistics understate the degree of income inequality?

These statistics may understate the degree of income inequality because they do not include the nonmonetary income and privileges of the relatively well-to-do.

3. Why might measured income shares overstate the degree of income inequality?

Measured income shares may overstate the degree of income inequality because they don't adjust for predictable differences in incomes by age, demographic trends such as the growth of both divorce and two-earner families, taxes, in-kind income from the government (e.g., food stamps), the benefits of government programs, or movement within the income distribution over time.

4. How does the fraction of the population that is middle-aged, rather than young or old, affect measurements of income inequality?

The more people are in their peak earning middle-age years, the higher their earnings appear relative to their lifetime incomes; the more people who are young or old, in their low earning years, the lower their earnings appear relative to their lifetime income.

5. How does the growth of both two-earner families and divorced couples increase measured income inequality?

Combining two incomes as the income of one family and increasing the number of lower-income female-headed households due to divorce increase the number of families counted at both the upper and lower ends of the income distribution, increasing measured income inequality.

6. Why is it important to take account of the substantial mobility of families within the income distribution over time when evaluating the degree of income inequality in America?

The substantial income mobility within the income distribution means that someone who has a low income today will not necessarily have a low income for a long period of time; there may continue to be low-income people, but they are likely to be different people.

17.2 Income Redistribution

1. **How is the principle of diminishing marginal utility used to justify income redistribution?**

   The idea that the marginal utility of income falls with income has been used to argue that by taking income from those with higher incomes (and therefore low marginal utility of income) and giving it to those with lower incomes (and therefore high marginal utility of income), total utility in society could be increased.

2. **Why is it not possible to prove the idea that redistributing income from rich to poor will increase society's utility?**

   Utility is not comparable between people. Even if an individual's marginal utility of income falls with income, that means his marginal utility is lower for higher incomes than for lower incomes; it does not mean that a higher-income person's marginal utility of income is lower than the marginal utility of income of a different person with a lower income.

3. **What are the fairness and incentive arguments against government redistribution of income?**

   The fairness argument against government redistribution of income is that it is unfair to take a substantial part of someone's income (given to him or her voluntarily by others) to give to others. The incentive argument is that there is no way for the government to redistribute income without undermining the incentives to earn income of both those taxed and those subsidized.

4. **If high-income individuals must pay increased income tax rates in order to provide subsidies for low-income individuals (and the subsidies are phased out as income increases), are the productive incentives of both high- and low-income people reduced? Why or why not?**

   Increased income tax rates on high-income people reduce their take-home (after tax) pay from the marginal hours of work involved, giving them less incentive to work those hours. Subsidies to low-income people whose benefits are phased out as their incomes grow act as income taxes (benefit reductions) on low-income people, giving them less incentive to work as well.

17.3 The Economics of Discrimination

1. **What is the difference between job-entry discrimination and wage discrimination?**

   Job-entry discrimination refers to a worker denied employment due to discrimination; wage discrimination refers to those who are employed, but at lower wages, due to discrimination.

2. **Explain how earnings differences could reflect either discrimination or productivity differences.**

   If employers discriminated among workers for reasons other than productivity, that would result in earnings differences. But employers are also willing to pay more to more productive workers (e.g., those with more education), resulting in earnings differences. The difficulty is determining how much each accounts for differences in earnings.

3. **What is the environmental explanation for differences in earnings across the sexes and races?**

   The environmental explanation for differences in earnings across the sexes and races is that women and minorities are not as productive because they have been prevented from gaining the necessary training and skills and because women are more likely to interrupt their careers to have and care for children.

4. **How do firms' incentives to maximize profits tend to reduce the extent of discrimination?**

   A firm that chose not to hire an employee that has a higher marginal revenue product than his or her wage, because of some preference for discrimination, sacrifices profits as a result. Those sacrificed profits make discriminating costly, reducing its extent.

5. **How can discrimination reflect imperfect information and the costs of acquiring more information about potential employees?**

   If an employer's past experience with a particular group has been worse than that with other groups, he or she might prefer not to hire people from that group because the probability that they will perform well is lower. But this use of past experience as a screening device for new employees only makes sense if it is costly for employers to discover the productivity of individual potential employees, rather than the average of some group, prior to hiring them.

6. **Say you only hire purple workers. If purple workers strongly prefer to work with one another instead of with other groups, why might you prefer to hire a less productive purple worker than a more productive nonpurple worker at the same wage?**

   Say each of your 20 current purple workers would demand $1 more per hour to work with a non-purple worker than with another purple worker. You would then have to compare how much more productive your prospective nonpurple worker was at a given wage than a purple worker, or how much less he would have to be paid for a given level of productivity, against how much more you would have to pay your other workers to work next to him. In this case, if the productivity or wage difference exceeds $20 per hour of work, the nonpurple worker would be hired, but if it were less than $20 per hour of work, he would not be hired.

7. **Why would subsidizing employers for hiring minority workers rather than imposing implicit quotas give employers greater incentives to expand minority job opportunities?**

An implicit minority hiring quota would raise employers' costs by making them hire workers they find less productive than those they would otherwise have hired. This reduces the profits of those firms, tending to reduce their size and number, and the number of job opportunities they offer. Subsidizing the hiring of minority workers, however, lowers the cost to employers (they would not hire them unless the subsidy more than compensated them for any reduction in productivity) of hiring minority workers, increasing their profits and expanding the number of job opportunities for minority workers.

17.4 Poverty

1. **How are absolute and relative measures of poverty different?**

An absolute measure of poverty is one based on whether income is sufficient to provide the basic necessities of life (food, clothing, etc.) in minimum quantities; a relative measure of poverty is based on having lower incomes relative to others (e.g., earning half the median income).

2. **Why could economic growth potentially eliminate absolute measures of poverty but not relative measures of poverty?**

Economic growth increases output, making it possible to bring every citizen up to some minimal absolute level of income. It does not, however, eliminate the fact that some will still have relatively lower incomes than others.

3. **Some people argue that poverty could be eliminated by "rich" countries. Can both absolute and relative poverty be eliminated by rich countries? Why or why not?**

Absolute poverty could possibly be eliminated— providing all citizens the basic necessities of life in minimum quantities—by "rich" countries. However, unless a country completely equalized incomes of all its citizens, some would continue to have lower incomes than others, and such relative poverty would persist to some degree.

4. **What are some of the programs designed to reduce poverty and redistribute income?**

These programs include progressive income taxes; transfer payments such as Social Security, Medicare, and unemployment compensation; welfare programs such as Supplementary Security Income and Temporary Assistance to Needy Families; the Earned Income Tax Credit; government subsidies; and minimum wage laws.

True or False:

1. The proportion of income received by the top 5 percent of Americans declined after 1935, but it has been increasing since the 1980s.

2. Differences in age among a population can lead to differences in the distribution of income.

3. Since 1950, the proportion of the population that is very young or very old has fallen.

4. If every individual earned the same total income over his or her lifetime, there would still be observed income inequality because people earn more when they are middle-aged.

5. Inequalities in annual incomes observed at one point in time overstate the degree of income inequality over lifetimes.

6. The distribution of income is more equal when the Lorenz curve is closer to the 45-degree line of perfect equality.

7. The closer the Gini coefficient is to one, the smaller the degree of income inequality.

8. The permanent income hypothesis (PIH) indicates that both college students and the elderly tend to dissave.

9. The PIH indicates that, in recessions, consumption will tend to fall more than proportionately to the fall in current income.

10. It is impossible to prove that a given income distribution is better than another.

11. According to the principle of diminishing marginal utility, increases in income generate greater additional happiness or utility at higher levels of income.

12. Economists assume that interpersonal utility comparisons are not possible.

13. If each person had diminishing marginal utility of income, income redistribution would increase utility in a society.

14. Within a country at a moment in time, happiness is positively correlated with income.

15. If we taxed the rich heavily and gave large subsidies to the poor, our incomes would be more equal but smaller.

16. Large-scale redistribution from high-income people to low-income people would likely result in less overtime being worked in a society.

17. Total equality of family income would result in total equality of individual income.

18. People agree that we should increase the degree of income redistribution in society.

19. Only a weak statistical correlation exists between lifetime earnings and years of schooling.

20. Discovering that wages are lower for blacks and females does not prove wage discrimination.

21. The environmental explanation of productivity differences assumes that there has been no discrimination.

22. Discrimination may reflect information costs, where group characteristics are used as a low-cost screening device.

23. Nondiscriminating firms will have a cost disadvantage over firms that discriminate.

24. If employers can hire equally productive female employees at a lower wage than males, the profit motive will give them a strong incentive to do so.

25. Even if every individual earned exactly the same income over his or her lifetime, there would still be inequality at any given moment in time.

26. The increased proportion of the U.S. population that is either very young or very old has tended to decrease the observed inequality in the distribution of income.

27. Both the increased number of divorced couples and the rise of two-income families have caused the measured distribution of income to appear more unequal.

28. There is virtually no positive correlation between the earnings of grandparents and grandchildren.

29. Other things being equal, workers who prefer more amenities at work or more time for leisure earn less.

30. Income inequality is less in the United States and the United Kingdom than in Sweden and Japan.

31. Some of the greatest disparities in income are found in developing nations.

32. Wage discrimination occurs when workers are given employment at wages lower than other workers on some basis other than productivity differences.

33. The poverty rate reflects a percentage of the population that falls below an absolute value.

34. Economic growth could eliminate poverty in an absolute sense but not poverty in a relative sense.

35. Many "poor" individuals in the United States, using the official definition, would be considered well off, even "rich," in many developing countries.

36. A progressive income tax imposes higher marginal tax rates on individuals with higher incomes.

37. Transfer payments include in-kind transfers but not cash transfers.

38. One argument for a negative income tax is that it would not require any added bureaucracy, unlike other forms of public assistance.

39. The fact that average wages are lower for blacks and females proves wage discrimination.

40. To some extent, discrimination may reflect information costs.

41. In the long run, competition has the potential to reduce discrimination.

42. If poverty is defined as earning less than one-half of the median income, then it cannot be eradicated through economic growth.

43. Poverty can be defined in two ways: using an absolute concept of poverty or a relative concept of poverty.

44. If poverty is defined using an absolute measure, then poverty can never be eliminated.

Multiple Choice:

1. The proportion of income received by the richest 5 percent of Americans has
   a. edged upward since the 1980s.
   b. held steady since the 1980s.
   c. decreased slightly since the 1980s.
   d. decreased significantly since the 1980s.

2. The measured distribution of income may appear more unequal as a result of
   a. an increase in the proportion of young people in the population.
   b. an increase in the number of two-income families.
   c. an increase in the number of divorced couples.
   d. an increase in the proportion of retired older people in the population.
   e. all of the above.

3. Which of the following are over-represented among those with low incomes?
   a. college students working toward their graduate degrees
   b. single-parent families
   c. young, inexperienced workers
   d. all of the above

4. American income inequality data indicate that
   a. most poor families never significantly rise above poverty, but rich families get poorer over time.
   b. most rich families remain rich, but poor families move up substantially through the income distribution over time.
   c. there is substantial movement over time among income groups in America.
   d. rich families stay rich and poor families stay poor in America.

5. Which of the following is false?
   a. The poverty line varies with the size of the family.
   b. The poverty rate is adjusted for inflation.
   c. The poverty rate is set at three times the cost of a nutritionally adequate diet.
   d. The receipt of food stamps cannot lift a recipient family from below the poverty line to above the poverty line.
   e. None of the above is false; all are true.

6. Large-scale income redistribution would make incomes _____ and _____.
   a. more equal; larger
   b. more equal; smaller
   c. less equal; larger
   d. less equal; smaller

7. Large-scale income redistribution would tend to reduce the level of
   a. income inequality.
   b. savings and investment.
   c. human capital (education).
   d. the number of overtime hours worked in society.
   e. all of the above.

8. Which of the following is true?
   a. There is substantial income inequality in the United States, and there has been little change in the distribution of measured income in the past few decades.
   b. There is substantial income inequality in the United States, but there have been appreciable changes in the distribution of measured income in the past few decades.
   c. There is very little income inequality in the United States, and there has been little change in the distribution of measured income in the past few decades.
   d. There is very little income inequality in the United States, but there have been appreciable changes in the distribution of measured income in the past few decades.

9. As more women prepare for careers as professionals,
   a. their level of human capital will more closely approach that of men.
   b. the ratio of female to male earnings will increase.
   c. their number of years of work experience will more closely approach that of men.
   d. all of the above are likely to occur.

10. Evidence suggests that levels of inequality of income _____ from 1935 to 1950, then _____ until 1980, and have since _____.
    a. increased; decreased; increased
    b. increased; remained relatively stable; decreased
    c. decreased; increased; decreased
    d. decreased; remained relatively stable; increased
    e. increased; decreased; remained relatively stable

11. Differences in monetary wages across jobs may result from
    a. differences in job amenities.
    b. differences in on-the-job hazards.
    c. differences in working conditions.
    d. differences in fringe benefits.
    e. all of the above.

12. Diminishing marginal utility
    a. implies that increases in income will give less utility to a rich person than to a poor person.
    b. implies that a given amount of added income would tend to provide less utility to a given individual at higher levels of income than at lower levels of income.
    c. implies that income redistribution from higher- to lower-income persons will give more utility to the lower-income persons than it will take from the higher-income persons.
    d. implies that all of the above are true.

13. The principle of diminishing marginal utility is not enough to guarantee that transferring income from the rich to the poor will increase society's utility because
    a. the total utility of the rich will still be greater.
    b. the rich get richer and the poor get poorer.
    c. it is impossible to make utility comparisons between individuals.
    d. diminishing marginal utility does not hold for everyone.

14. If complete equality of income was legislated, which of the following would be expected to occur?
    a. People, on average, would become richer.
    b. Society would become happier.
    c. Individuals would work longer hours.
    d. The incentive to produce would be largely eliminated.

15. Women earn less on average than men. Which of the following can we conclude as a result?
    a. Women must be less productive.
    b. Men must be highly motivated and productive.
    c. Women must be the victim of discrimination by employers.
    d. Without considering preferences and productivity factors, differences in average earnings do not necessarily imply employment discrimination.

16. Women are more likely than men to
    a. move in order to take a higher-income job.
    b. take jobs with out-of-town travel.
    c. interrupt their careers.
    d. take jobs with uncertain schedules and long hours.

17. Economic theory suggests that when discrimination is based on the personal prejudices of employers
    a. the wages of those who are discriminated against will rise.
    b. it will make no difference to an employer's costs.
    c. profit incentives will tend to reduce discrimination.
    d. it will reduce production costs.

18. Women tend to earn less than men because
    a. women tend to work fewer hours, on average, than men.
    b. women tend to have fewer years of schooling, on average, than men.
    c. women are more likely to prefer jobs that give them flexible hours.
    d. all of the above are true.

19. As more women prepare for careers as professionals,
    a. their level of human capital will more closely approach that of men.
    b. the ratio of female to male earnings will increase.
    c. their number of years of work experience will more closely approach that of men.
    d. all of the above are likely to occur.

20. The poverty rate
    a. is the proportion of persons who fall below the poverty line.
    b. is set at the cost of providing a nutritionally adequate diet.
    c. has been rising since 1960.
    d. All of the above are true.
    e. None of the above is true.

21. Social Security and Medicare
    a. are considered welfare programs.
    b. are only received by senior citizens with low incomes.
    c. together make up the majority of all federal transfer payments.
    d. are both considered in-kind transfer payments.
    e. are characterized by none of the above.

22. Which of the following is *not* a means-tested income transfer program?
    a. Medicare
    b. Food stamps
    c. Temporary Assistance for Needy Families
    d. All of the above are considered means-tested income transfer programs.

23. Which of the following is true?
    a. Job-entry discrimination occurs when a person is denied employment on some basis other than productivity, while wage discrimination involves paying equally productive workers different wages.
    b. Wage discrimination occurs when a person is denied employment on some basis other than productivity, while job-entry discrimination involves paying equally productive workers different wages.
    c. Both wage and job-entry discrimination involve denying some persons employment on some basis other than productivity.
    d. Both wage and job-entry discrimination involve paying equally productive workers different wages.
    e. None of the above is true.

24. The official poverty rate for the United States is currently set at _____ times the cost of providing a nutritionally adequate diet.
    a. two
    b. three
    c. five
    d. eight
    e. ten

25. The official poverty definition may _____ the level of poverty because it does not include _____.
    a. overstate; cash benefits
    b. overstate; noncash benefits
    c. understate; cash benefits
    d. understate; noncash benefits

26. Economic growth has the potential to eliminate:
    a. all unemployment.
    b. relative poverty.
    c. absolute poverty.
    d. both a and b.
    e. both a and c.

27. Because the poverty line is an absolute standard
    a. more families are pushed above the poverty line as economic growth moves the entire distribution of income upward.
    b. the poverty rate has been fairly stable over the last 50 years.
    c. an increase in the price of food will not have an effect on the poverty rate.
    d. the poverty rate increases as an economy grows.

Problems:

1. How might each of the following affect the distribution of income in the near term?
   a. There is a massive influx of low-skilled immigrants.
   b. A new baby boom occurs.
   c. The new baby boomers enter their 20s.
   d. The new baby boomers reach age 65 or older.
   e. There is an increase in cash transfer payments, such as Supplemental Security Income.
   f. There is an increase in in-kind transfer payments, such as food stamps.

2. Using the axes from a Lorenz curve, draw
   a. the Lorenz curve for perfect equality.
   b. the Lorenz curve for perfect inequality.
   c. a Lorenz curve for some inequality.
   d. For the curve used in c, show which ratio of areas equals the Gini coefficient.

3. a. If every individual earned the same total income over his or her lifetime, why would we still see inequality at a given point in time?

   b. Why could means-tested income redistribution be described, at least in part, as redistributing from you to yourself?

4. If the permanent income hypothesis is true, why would inequality measured by current consumption tend to be smaller than inequality measured by current income?

5. If the marginal utility of income falls with added income, why can't we be sure that redistribution from higher to lower income individuals would increase total utility?

6. What factors might explain the differential in average income between males and females?

7. How might a significant reduction in the divorce rate affect the distribution of income?

8. a. How could in-kind transfers, such as food stamps, not reduce measured poverty or inequality?

   b. How could food stamp benefit reductions as income rises cause the program to actually decrease measured incomes of the poor and raise official poverty rates?

9. Consider two economies: one in which there is no redistribution of income by government and one in which the government enforces equality of income among everyone. Evaluate the advantages and disadvantages of each system. Which of these two alternatives would you prefer? Given the choice, would you prefer a system of redistribution of income that lies somewhere between these two extremes?

10. Why would large-scale government redistribution tend to reduce hours worked, savings and investment, and human capital (education)?

11. Why might a regulated utility, which is restricted to keeping profits for less than they could have earned, be more likely to discriminate than if its profits were not limited?

12. If a negative income tax was Tax = (30 percent × income) − $15,000:
    a. What would be the tax/refund for a family earning $100,000 a year?
    b. What would be the tax/refund for a family earning $50,000 a year?
    c. What would be the tax/refund for a family earning $40,000 a year?
    d. What would be the tax/refund for a family earning $10,000 a year?

The Environment

In the 1960s, fish were mysteriously disappearing from thousands of lakes in the northeastern portion of the United States. The culprit was the acid rain from coal-burning power plants that were

releasing sulfur dioxide and nitric oxide into the atmosphere; when combined with water, it created acid rain. Acid rain was not only killing fish but destroying crops and trees as well. Today, acid rain is not the problem it was in the 1960s. The Acid Rain Program introduced an allowance trading system (cap and trade) which is a dramatic departure from traditional command and control regulatory methods. In this chapter, we will examine the economics of pollution: How much pollution should we allow? Why does a market produce too much pollution? What policies can be used to reduce pollution? What are private market solutions to pollution? ▪

SECTION 18.1   Negative Externalities and Pollution

* What are social costs?
* How are negative externalities internalized?

* What is the optimal level of pollution?

What Are Social Costs?

As we learned in Chapter 8, whenever an economic activity has benefits or costs that are shared by individuals other than the demanders or suppliers of a good or service, an externality is involved. If the activity imposes costs on individuals other than the demanders or suppliers of a good or service, it is said to have negative externalities. Put another way, negative externalities exist any time the social costs of producing a good or service exceed the private costs. Social costs refer to costs that spill over to other members of society. Private costs refer to costs incurred only by the producer of the good or service.

Negative Externalities and Pollution

The classic example of a negative externality is pollution. When a steel mill puts soot and other forms of "crud" into the air as a by-product of making steel, it imposes costs on others not connected with the steel mill or with buying or selling steel. The soot requires nearby homeowners to paint their houses more often, entailing costs. Studies show that respiratory diseases are greater in areas with high air pollution, imposing substantial costs, often the shortening of life itself. In addition, the steel mill might discharge chemicals or overheated water into a stream, thus killing wildlife, ruining business for those who make a living fishing, spoiling recreational activities for the local population, and so on.

In deciding how much to produce, the steel makers are governed by demand and supply. They do not worry (unless forced to) about the external costs imposed on members of society, and in all likelihood, the steel makers would not even know the full extent of those costs.

exhibit 1   The Effect of a Negative Externality

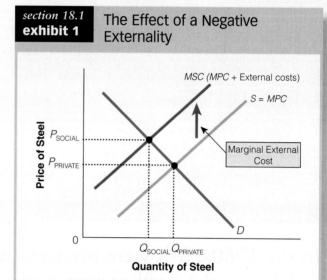

The industry would normally produce where demand equals supply (where supply is equal to the marginal private costs), at output $Q_{PRIVATE}$ and charging price $P_{PRIVATE}$. If, however, the industry were forced to also pay those external costs imposed on others, the industry would produce where demand equals marginal social costs, at output Q_{SOCIAL} and price P_{SOCIAL}. Where firms are not forced to pay for negative externalities, output tends to be larger and prices lower than at the optimal output, where the marginal benefits to society (as measured by demand) equal the marginal costs to society.

Consider the hypothetical steel industry in Exhibit 1. It produces where demand and supply intersect, at output $Q_{PRIVATE}$ and $P_{PRIVATE}$. Let us assume that the marginal social cost of producing the product is indicated by the marginal social cost (MSC) curve, lying above the supply curve, which represents the industry's marginal private costs (MPC). The marginal social costs of production are higher at all output levels, as those costs include all of the industry's private costs plus the costs that spill over to other members of society from the pollution produced by the industry—that is, the external costs.

This factory is clearly polluting the water downstream, creating a negative externality for those who fish downstream. It is possible that the people who fish could try to bargain with the factory, perhaps even pay it to pollute less. However, sometimes private bargaining does not work and the government can provide a solution through regulation or pollution taxes.

were somehow forced to compensate people who endure the costs of its pollution, the firm would produce at output Q_{SOCIAL} and price steel at P_{SOCIAL}. In that case, we would say that the externalities were internalized, because each firm in the industry would now be paying the entire cost to society of making steel. When negative externalities are internalized, steel firms produce less output (Q_{SOCIAL} instead of $Q_{PRIVATE}$) and charge higher prices (P_{SOCIAL} instead of $P_{PRIVATE}$). Optimal output occurs where the marginal social costs are equal to the marginal social benefits. When firms do not pay all of the social costs they incur, and therefore produce too much output, the result is too much pollution. The output of pollution is directly related to the output of the primary goods produced by the firm.

Measuring Externalities

It is generally accepted that in the absence of intervention, the market mechanism will underproduce goods and services with positive externalities, such as education, and overproduce those with negative externalities, such as pollution. But the exact extent of these market misallocations is quite difficult to establish in the real world, because the divergence

At output Q_{SOCIAL}, the marginal social costs to society equal the marginal social benefits (as indicated by the demand curve) from the sale of the last unit of steel. At that output, the price of steel is P_{SOCIAL}. If the firm

internalized externalities
when an industry is forced to compensate those enduring some negative externality caused by its production

---

Use what you've LEARNED — NEGATIVE EXTERNALITIES

Q After months of looking at houses he could not afford, Dean recently bought a home near the airport. After living in his house for only a week, Dean was so fed up with the noise that he decided to organize a group of local homeowners in an effort to stop the noise pollution. Should Dean be compensated for bearing this negative externality?

A Because few people want to live in noisy areas, housing prices and rents in those areas are lower, reflecting the cost of the noise in the area. As a result, fewer people competed with Dean for the purchase of his house relative to houses in quieter neighborhoods, so it is likely he did not pay as much as he might have in another area. Because Dean

paid a lower price for living in a noisier area, he has already been compensated for the noise pollution.

between social and private costs and benefits is often difficult to measure. For example, exactly how much damage at the margin does a steel mill's air pollution do to nonconsumers of the steel? No one really knows, because no market fully measures those costs. Indeed, the costs are partly nonpecuniary, meaning that no outlay of money occurs. Even though we pay dollars to see the doctor for respiratory ailments and pay dollars for paint to repair pollution-caused peeling, we do not make explicit money payments for the visual pollution and undesirable odors that the mill might produce as a by-product of making steel. Nonpecuniary costs are real costs and potentially

have a monetary value that can be associated with them, but assessing that value in practical terms is immensely difficult. You might be able to decide how much you would be willing to pay to live in a pollution-free world, but no current mechanism allows anyone to express the perceived monetary value of having clear air to breathe and smell. Even some pecuniary, or monetary, costs are difficult to truly measure: How much respiratory disease is caused by pollution and how much by other factors such as secondhand cigarette smoke? Environmental economists continue to make progress in valuing these difficult damages.

SECTION CHECK

1. Social costs are those costs that accrue to the total population; private costs are incurred only by the producer of the good or service.
2. If the industry were somehow forced to compensate people who endure the costs of pollution, we would say that the industry had internalized the externality.
3. When negative externalities are internalized, the industry produces less output at a higher price.
4. Optimal output occurs when marginal social benefits are equal to marginal social costs.

---

1. What is the difference between private and social costs?
2. Why do decision makers tend to ignore external costs?
3. How can internalizing the external costs of production move us closer to the efficient level of output?
4. Why is it particularly difficult to measure the value of external costs or benefits?
5. How does pollution control lead to both rising marginal costs and falling marginal benefits?
6. How is the optimal amount of pollution control determined, in principle?

SECTION 18.2
Public Policy and the Environment

* What is the "best" level of pollution?

* What are command and control regulations?

* What is a pollution tax?

* What are transferable pollution rights?

Why Is a Clean Environment Not Free?

In many respects, a clean environment is no different from any other desirable good. In a world of scarcity, we can increase our consumption of a clean environment only by giving up something else. The problem that we face is choosing the combination of goods that does the most to enhance human well-being. Few people would enjoy a perfectly clean environment if they were cold, hungry, and generally destitute. On the other hand, an individual choking to death in smog is hardly to be envied, no matter how great his or her material wealth.

Only by considering the additional cost as well as the additional benefit of increased consumption of all goods, including clean air and water, can decisions on the desirable combination of goods to consume be made properly.

The Costs and Benefits of Pollution Control

It is possible, even probable, that pollution elimination, like nearly everything else, is subject to diminishing returns. Initially, a large amount of pollution can be eliminated fairly inexpensively, but getting rid of still more pollution may prove more costly. Likewise, it is also possible that the benefits from eliminating "crud" from the air might decline as more and more pollution is eliminated. For example, perhaps some pollution elimination initially would have a profound impact on health costs, home repair expenses, and so on, but as pollution levels fall, further elimination of pollutants brings fewer marginal benefits.

The cost-benefit trade-off just discussed is illustrated in Exhibit 1, which examines the marginal social benefits and marginal social costs associated with the elimination of air pollution. In the early 1960s, we had few regulations as a nation on pollution control, and as a result, private firms had little incentive to eliminate the problem. In the context of Exhibit 1, we may have spent Q_1 on controls, meaning that the marginal social benefits of greater pollution control expenditures exceeded the marginal costs associated with having the controls. Investing more capital and labor to reduce pollution is efficient in such a situation.

Optimum pollution control occurs when Q^* of pollution is eliminated. Up to that point, the benefits from the elimination of pollution exceed the marginal costs, both pecuniary and nonpecuniary, of the pollution control. Overly stringent compliance levels force companies to control pollution to the level indicated by Q_2 in Exhibit 1, where the additional costs from the controls far outweigh the environmental benefits. It should be stated, however, that increased concerns about pollution have probably caused the marginal social benefit curve to shift to the right over time, increasing the optimal amount of pollution control. Because of measurement problems, however, it is difficult to state whether we are generally below, at, or above the optimal pollution level.

section 18.2 exhibit 1
Costs and Benefits of Pollution Controls

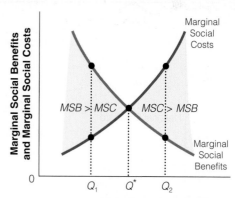

With the principles of diminishing marginal utility and increasing marginal cost at work, the marginal benefits of further expenditures on pollution control will, at some point, fall below the added costs to society imposed by still stricter controls. At output Q_1, pollution control is inadequate; on the other hand, elimination of Q_2 pollution will entail costs that exceed the benefits. Only at Q^* is pollution control expenditure at an optimum level. Of course, in practice, it is difficult to know exactly the position and slope of these curves.

in the news   # Levels of Six Common Pollutants Continue to Decline

* Cleaner cars, industries, and consumer products have contributed to cleaner air for much of the U.S.
* Since 1990, nationwide air quality for six air pollutants for which there are national standards has improved significantly. These air pollutants are ground-level ozone (O_3), particle pollution (PM_{25} and PM_{10}), lead (Pb), nitrogen dioxide (NO_2), carbon monoxide (CO), and sulfur dioxide (SO_2). Nationally, air pollution was lower in 2007 than 1990 for:
  * 8-hour ozone, by 9 percent
  * annual PM_{25} (since 2000), by 11 percent
  * PM_{10}, by 28 percent
  * Lead, by 80 percent
  * NO_2, by 35 percent
  * 8-hour CO, by 67 percent
  * SO_2, by 54 percent

* Despite clean air progress, in 2007, 158.5 million people lived in counties that exceeded any national ambient air quality standard (NAAQS). Ground-level ozone and particle pollution still present challenges in many areas of the country.
* Though PM_{25} concentrations were higher in 2007 than in 2006, partly due to weather conditions, annual PM_{25} concentrations were nine percent lower in 2007 than in 2001.
* 8-hour ozone concentrations were five percent lower in 2007 than in 2001. Ozone levels did not improve in much of the East until 2002, after which there was a significant decline. This decline is largely due to reductions in oxides of nitrogen (NO_x) emissions required by EPA's rule to reduce ozone in the East, the NO_x SIP Call. EPA tracks progress toward meeting these reductions through its NO_x Budget Trading Program.

section 18.2
exhibit 2   National Levels of Six Common Pollutants, 1990-2007

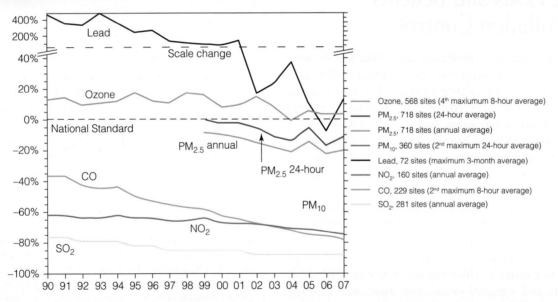

Comparison of national levels of the six common pollutants to national ambient air quality standards, 1990–2007. National levels are averages across all sites with complete data for the time period.

RELATIVE COSTS AND BENEFITS OF POLLUTION CONTROL

Q Pete drives a 1948 pickup truck that has no smog equipment and gets poor gas mileage. He lives and does most of his driving in a sparsely populated area of Wyoming. Do you think Pete should be required to install the same smog equipment on his car as someone with a similar vehicle living in downtown Los Angeles or Denver?

A The economic benefits of pollution control vary by location. In the wide-open, low population density areas of Wyoming, the marginal benefit of pollution cleanup is lower than it would be in a large metropolitan area that already has a large amount of smog. Why? Wyoming has so much space and so few people that the marginal benefit of pollution abatement is quite low. The same would certainly not be true in Los Angeles, where the air is already more polluted by cars and factories. Because so many people are affected and the air is already so saturated with pollutants, the marginal benefit of pollution elimination is much higher in Los Angeles than it would be in rural Wyoming. That is, if a uniform standard is applied, regardless of location, then the car in Wyoming would be overcontrolled and the car in Los Angeles would be undercontrolled. Unfortunately, many of our environmental laws contain this "uniformity" flaw.

Even though measuring externalities, both negative and positive, is often nearly impossible, it does not necessarily mean that it is better to ignore the externality and allow the market solution to operate. As already explained, the market solution will almost certainly result in excessive output by polluters unless some intervention occurs. What form should the intervention take?

Command and Control Policies: Regulation

One approach to dealing with externalities is to require private enterprise to produce their outputs in a manner that would reduce negative externalities below the amounts that would persist in the absence of regulation. For example, the Environmental Protection Agency (EPA) was established by the Clean Air Act of 1970 to serve as a watchdog over the production of goods and services in areas where externalities, especially negative externalities, exist. The EPA's main duty is to enforce environmental standards.

However, the EPA might also require a firm to use a certain technology to reduce emissions. In order to design good policies, the government regulators need information on specific industries and the technologies they could employ. This is not easy information for the government to obtain.

For example, the EPA may identify and then enforce a standard equal to the maximum amount of pollution that firms can produce per unit of output per year. To be effective in pollution reduction, of course, these standards must result in less pollution than would exist in the absence of regulation. The regulations, then, force companies to find less pollution-intensive ways of producing goods and services. Or in the case of consumer products that pollute—such as automobiles, for example—manufacturers have been forced to reduce the emissions from the products themselves. In 1984, the federal government required that auto producers install catalytic converters in new cars to reduce auto emissions.

Pollution (Pigovian) Taxes: A Market-Based Policy

Another means of solving the misallocation problem (relatively too many polluting goods) posed by the existence of externalities is for the government to create incentives for firms to internalize the external costs or benefits resulting from their activities. For example, returning to the case of pollution, suppose that the marginal private cost of making steel was $150 a ton. Suppose further that at the margin, each ton of steel caused $40 in environmental damages per ton. If the government were then to levy a pollution tax—a tax levied on a firm for environmental pollution—on the steel maker equal to $40 per ton, the manufacturer's marginal private cost would rise from $150 to $190; the $190 figure would then be equal to the true marginal social cost of making steel. The firm would accordingly alter its output and pricing decisions to take into account its higher marginal cost, leading ultimately to reduced output (and pollution) and higher prices. The firm also has an incentive to seek new, less pollution-intensive methods of making steel.

Using taxes to internalize external costs is appealing because it allows the relatively efficient private sector to operate according to market forces in a manner that takes socially important spillover costs into account. A major objection to the use of such taxes and subsidies is that, in most cases, it is difficult to measure externalities with any precision. Choosing a tax rate involves some guesswork, and poor guessing might lead to a solution that is far from optimal. But it is likely to be better than ignoring the problem. In spite of the severe difficulties in measurement, however, many economists would like to see greater effort made to force internalization of externalities through taxes rather than using alternative approaches. Why? We know that firms will seek out the least-expensive (in terms of using society's scarce resources) approaches

pollution tax
tax levied by government on a firm for environmental pollution

transferable pollution rights
a right given to a firm to discharge a specified amount of pollution; its transferable nature creates incentive to lower pollution levels

to cleanup because they want more profits. This plan is good for them and good for society, because we can have more of everything that way, including environmental quality.

Transferable Pollution Rights

Economists see an opportunity to control pollution through a government-enforced system of property rights. In this system, the government issues **transferable pollution rights** that give the holder the right to discharge a specified amount (smaller than the uncontrolled amount) of pollution into the air. In this plan, firms have an incentive to lower their levels of pollution because they can sell their permits if they go unused. Specifically, firms that can lower their emissions at the lowest costs will do so and trade their pollution

Pulp and paper mills pollute our environment. The pulp and paper industry is one of the largest and most polluting industries in North America. One of the primary environmental concerns is the use of chlorine-based bleaches and resultant toxic emissions to air, water, and soil.

rights to firms that cannot reduce their pollution levels as easily. That is, each polluter—required either to reduce pollution to the level allowed by the number of rights it holds or buy more rights—will be motivated to eliminate all pollution that is cheaper than the price of pollution rights. The crucial advantage to the pollution rights approach comes from the fact that the rights are private property and can be sold.

It is worth emphasizing that this least-cost pattern of abatement does not require any information about the techniques of pollution abatement on the part of the government—more specifically, the EPA. The EPA does not need to know the cheapest abatement strategy for each and every polluter. Faced with a positive price for pollution rights, each polluter has every motivation to discover and use the cheapest way to reduce pollution. Nor does the EPA need to know anything about the differences in abatement costs among polluters. Each polluter is motivated to reduce pollution as long as the cost of reducing one more unit is less than the price of pollution rights. The information and incentives generated by private ownership and market exchange of these pollution rights automatically leads to the desirable pattern of pollution abatement—namely, having those best at cleaning up doing all the cleanup.

The pollution rights approach also creates an incentive for polluters to develop improved pollution abatement technologies.

The prospect of buying and selling pollution permits would allow firms to move into an area that is already as polluted as allowed by EPA standards. Under the tradable permits policy, the firm can set up operation by purchasing pollution permits from an existing polluter in the area. This type of exchange allows the greatest value to be generated with a given amount of pollution. It also encourages polluters to come up with cheaper ways of reducing pollution, because the firm that reduces pollution is able to sell its pollution credits to others, making pollution reduction profitable.

What Is an Ideal Pollution Control Policy?

What would be the objectives of an ideal pollution control policy? First, and most obviously, we want pollution reduced to the efficient level—the level that maximizes the value of all of our resources. This goal would involve continuing to reduce pollution by one more unit only as long as the value of the improved environmental quality is greater than the value of ordinary goods that are sacrificed.

A second related objective is to reduce pollution as cheaply as possible. Two separate considerations are important here. If pollution is to be reduced as cheaply as possible, it is obvious that each pollution source has to abate at minimum cost. Of the many ways to cut back on pollution, not all are equally costly. But even if all polluters are abating as cheaply as possible, it does not necessarily mean that pollution overall is being reduced at least cost.

The pattern of pollution abatement over all sources is of great importance here. Because some polluters will be more efficient at pollution reduction than others, the least-cost abatement pattern will require some polluters to clean up more than others.

A third objective of a pollution control policy is to establish incentives that will motivate advances in pollution abatement technology. Over the long run, this objective may be even more important than the first two. For example, the cost of controlling pollution can be significantly reduced over time, even if the second objective is not fully realized, if consistent advances are made in the technology of pollution control.

It should be clear that these three objectives—(1) achieving the efficient level of pollution, (2) achieving pollution reduction at least cost, and (3) motivating advances in abatement technology—may never be fully realized, especially the first objective.

ONE ANSWER TO GLOBAL WARMING: A NEW TAX

—BY N. GREGORY MANKIW

In the debate over global *climate change*, there is a yawning gap that needs to be bridged. The gap is not between environmentalists and industrialists, or between Democrats and Republicans. It is between policy wonks and political consultants.

Among policy wonks like me, there is a broad consensus. The scientists tell us that world temperatures are rising because humans are emitting carbon into the atmosphere. Basic economics tells us that when you tax something. You normally get less of it. So if we want to reduce global emissions of carbon, we need a global carbon tax. Q.E.D.

The idea of using taxes to solve problems, rather than merely raise government revenue, has a long history. The British economist Arthur Pigou advocated such corrective taxes to deal with pollution in the early 20th century. In his honor, economics textbooks now call them "Pigovian taxes."

Using a Pigovian tax to address global warming is also an old idea. It was proposed as far back as 1992 by Martin S. Feldstein on the editorial page of *The Wall Street Journal*. Once chief economist to Ronald Reagan, Mr. Feldstein has devoted much of his career to studying how high tax rates distort incentives and impede economic growth. But like most other policy wonks, he appreciates that some taxes align private incentives with social costs and move us toward better outcomes.

Those vying for elected office, however, are reluctant to sign on to this agenda. Their political consultants are no fans of taxes, Pigovian or otherwise. Republican consultants advise using the word "tax" only if followed immediately by the word "cut." Democratic consultants recommend the word "tax" be followed by "on the rich."

Yet this natural aversion to carbon taxes can be overcome if the revenue from the tax is used to reduce other taxes. By itself, a carbon tax would raise the tax burden on anyone who drives a car or uses electricity produced with fossil fuels, which means just about everybody. Some might fear this would be particularly hard on the poor and middle class.

But Gilbert Metcalf, a professor of economics at Tufts, has shown how revenue from a carbon tax could be used to reduce payroll taxes in a way that would leave the distribution of total tax burden approximately unchanged. He proposes a tax of $15 per metric ton of carbon dioxide, together with a rebate of the federal payroll tax on the first $3,660 of earnings for each worker.

The case for a carbon tax looks even stronger after an examination of the other options on the table. Lawmakers in both political parties want to require carmakers to increase the fuel efficiency of the cars they sell. Passing the buck to auto companies has a lot of popular appeal.

Increased fuel efficiency, however, is not free. Like a tax, cost of complying with more stringent regulation will be passed on to consumers in the form of higher car prices. But the government will not raise any revenue that it can use to cut other taxes to compensate for these higher prices. (And don't expect savings on gas to compensate consumers in a meaningful way: Any truly cost-effective increase in fuel efficiency would already have been made.)

More important, enhancing fuel efficiency by itself is not the best way to reduce energy consumption. Fuel use depends not only on the efficiency of the car fleet but also on the daily decisions that people make—how far from work they choose to live and how often they carpool or use public transportation.

A carbon tax would provide incentives for people to use less fuel in a multitude of ways. By contrast, merely having more efficient cars encourages more driving. Increased driving not only produces more carbon, but also exacerbates other problems, like accidents and road congestion.

Another popular proposal to limit carbon emissions is a cap-and-trade system, under which carbon emissions are limited and allowances are bought and sold in the marketplace. The effect of such a system depends on how the carbon allowances are allocated. If the government auctions them off, then the price of a carbon allowance is effectively a carbon tax.

global
WATCH

ONE ANSWER TO GLOBAL WARMING: A NEW TAX (cont.)

But the history of cap-and-trade systems suggests that the allowances would probably be handed out to power companies and other carbon emitters, which would then be free to use them or sell them at market prices. In this case, the prices of energy products would rise as they would under a carbon tax, but the government would collect no revenue to reduce other taxes and compensate consumers.

The international dimension of the problem also suggests the superiority of a carbon tax over cap-and-trade. Any long-term approach to global climate change will have to deal with the emerging economies of China and India. By some reports, China is now the world's leading emitter of carbon, in large part simply because it has so many people. The failure of the Kyoto treaty to include these emerging economies is one reason that, in 1997, the United States Senate passed a resolution rejecting the Kyoto approach by a vote of 95 to zero.

Agreement on a truly global cap-and-trade system, however, is hard to imagine. China is unlikely to be persuaded to accept fewer carbon allowances per person than the United States. Using a historical baseline to allocate allowances, as is often proposed, would reward the United States for having been a leading cause of the problem.

But allocating carbon allowances based on population alone would create a system in which the United States, with its higher standard of living, would buy allowances from China. American voters are not going to embrace a system of higher energy prices, coupled with a large transfer of national income to the Chinese. It would amount to a massive foreign aid program to one of the world's most rapidly growing economies.

A global carbon tax would be easier to negotiate. All governments require revenue for public purposes. The world's nations could agree to use a carbon tax as one instrument to raise some of that revenue. No money needs to change hands across national borders. Each government could keep the revenue from its tax and use it to finance spending or whatever form of tax relief it considered best.

Convincing China of the virtues of a carbon tax, however, may prove to be the easy part. The first and more difficult step is to convince American voters, and therefore political consultants, that "tax" is not a four-letter word.

consider this:

One potentially serious problem with using cap and trade permits that are not auctioned off is that they may be allocated to specific industries in exchange for political support.

Use what you've LEARNED   INCENTIVES AND POLLUTION

Q Brad and Angelina were horrified with the number of abandoned automobiles in their community. Attempting to come up with a solution for this form of visual pollution, they thought maybe something along the line of deposits on bottles might work. Can you help? How would deposits on autos work? How would it affect the incentives of the litterer and the recoverer?

A It is estimated that 15 percent of all automobiles in this country are abandoned at the end of their useful lives along streams, fields, highways, and streets. However, mandatory deposits would provide incentives for both recovery and against the littering of abandoned automobiles. That is, if the deposit is set sufficiently high, people would be less likely to abandon their autos because they would lose their deposits. On the other hand, if someone did decide to abandon an auto, someone else has the incentive to tow it to a recycling center and receive

COURTESY OF ROBERT L. SEXTON

the deposit. This example emphasizes the essential economic reasoning that incentives matter.*

---

*For more details, see D. Lee, P. Graves, and R. Sexton, "Controlling the Abandonment of Automobiles: Mandatory Deposits Versus Fines," *Journal of Urban Economics 31*, no. 1 (January 1992).

SECTION CHECK

1. As with other goods, rational choices about environmental quality involve comparing the marginal benefits to the marginal costs.
2. Command and control policies force companies to find less pollution-intensive ways of producing goods and services.
3. Pollution taxes can be used to force firms to internalize externalities and allow the relatively efficient private sector to operate according to market forces in a manner that takes socially important spillover costs into account.
4. Transferable pollution rights create incentives for the firms that are best at cleaning up to do so.
5. The transferable pollution rights policy encourages polluters to come up with cheaper ways of reducing pollution, because the firm that reduces pollution is able to sell its remaining pollution credits to others.
6. The objectives of pollution control policies are achieving the efficient level of pollution, achieving pollution reduction at least cost, and motivating advances in abatement technology.

---

1. How do command and control policies act to internalize external costs?
2. How could transferable pollution rights lead to pollution being reduced at the lowest possible opportunity cost?
3. What are the objectives of an ideal pollution control policy from the perspective of economists interested in resource allocation?
4. Why might an efficient pollution tax be lower in Fargo, North Dakota, than in Los Angeles, California?

SECTION 18.3 | Property Rights

* What is the relationship between externalities and property rights?

* What is the Coase theorem?

Property Rights and the Environment

The existence of externalities and the efforts to deal with them in a manner that will enhance the social good can be considered a question of the nature of property rights. If the EPA limits the soot that a steel company emits from "its" smokestack, then the property rights of the steel company with respect to its smokestack have been altered or restricted. Similarly, zoning laws restrict how property owners can use their property. Sometimes, to deal with externalities, governments radically alter arrangements of property rights.

Indeed, the entire matter of dealing with externalities ultimately evolves into a question of how property rights should be altered. If no externalities existed in the world, reasons for prohibiting property owners from using their property in any manner they voluntarily chose would be few. Ultimately, then, externalities involve an evaluation of the legal arrangements under which we operate our economy and thus illustrate one area where law and economics merge.

If a rancher lives downstream from a polluting factory and the courts have given the rights to the factory to pollute, economists say that the property rights to pollute are well defined. However, the rancher may be able to negotiate privately and pay the polluting firm to reduce the amount of pollution—and make both parties better off.

The Coase Theorem

In a classic paper, Nobel laureate Ronald Coase observed that when the benefits are greater than the costs for some course of action (say, environmental cleanup), potential transactions can make some people better off without making anyone worse off. This idea is known as the **Coase theorem**. To appreciate this important insight, consider the following problem: A cattle rancher lives downstream from a paper mill. The paper mill dumps waste into the stream, which injures the rancher's cattle. If the rancher is not compensated, an externality exists. The question is, why does the externality persist? Suppose the courts have established (perhaps because the paper mill was there first) that the property rights to use (or abuse) the stream reside with the mill. If the benefits of cleanup are greater than the costs, the rancher should

> **Coase theorem**
> states that where property rights are defined in a clear-cut fashion, externalities are internalized

be willing to pay the mill owner to stop polluting. Let's assume that the rancher's benefits (say $10,000) from the cleanup undertaken by the mill are greater than the cost (say $5,000). If the rancher were to offer $7,500 to the mill owner to clean up the stream, both the rancher and the mill owner would be better off than with continued pollution. If, on the other hand, the rancher had the property rights to the stream, and the mill owner received a sufficiently high benefit from polluting the river, then it would be rational for the mill owner to pay the rancher up to the point where the marginal benefit to the mill owner of polluting equaled the marginal damage to the rancher from pollution.

Transaction Costs and the Coase Theorem

The mill owner and rancher example hinges critically on low transaction costs. Transaction costs are the costs of negotiating and executing an exchange, excluding the cost of the good or service bought. For

POLICY application   PIGOU ON FACEBOOK?

An Old Debate Gets a Makeover in Cyberspace

Arthur Pigou, an early-20th-century British economist, might well have shuddered at the thought of Facebook.com, a student networking site. A hermetic academic, awkward in the company of women, he surely would have balked at the dating and the picture uploads. But what would he have made of the "Pigou Club," which has surfaced on Facebook and is giving him unprecedented—even cultish—exposure?

His appearance on the Internet is due to a contemporary economist clearly at home in cyberspace: Greg Mankiw of Harvard University. For months, Mr. Mankiw, a former adviser to George Bush, has been blogging away in support of "Pigovian taxes" on petrol, believing that a levy of $1 a gallon would not only bring America $100 billion of extra revenue but might also reduce global warming.

With his Pigou Club, Mr. Mankiw has whipped up a following behind an economist whose theories on unemployment came under attack from his colleague, John Maynard Keynes. On Facebook, 600 people have signed up to the Pigou Club. Mostly students, they join other Pigovians such as Larry Summers, Gary Becker, and Kenneth Rogoff.

Pigou advocated taxation as a way to combat the negative externalities, or side-effects, associated with certain activities. These have been used to justify levies on cigarettes, alcohol, and even traffic congestion. Their advocates argue that they could be used to wean Americans off their dependence on petrol, which degrades the environment, props up unsavory regimes, and clogs traffic.

But governments are not perfect arbiters, say opponents of the Pigou Club. In the spirit of Ronald Coase, an intellectual nemesis of Pigou, a NoPigou Club has taken shape on the Internet, with its own Facebook following (though with only 59 supporters so far). Coase claimed that a Pigovian tax would penalize producers and consumers and might have other undesirable side-effects. People should be able to negotiate among themselves when there are side-effects, he said. Terence Corcoran, editor of Canada's *Financial Post*, writes a NoPigou blog, arguing that such taxes are blunt instruments and governments have insufficient information about them to wield them properly.

Pigou did indeed accept that point, albeit rather late in life, so it is unclear how he would have felt about petrol and global warming. One thing, however, is certain: the reclusive outdoorsman would have found the effects of Internet fame decidedly taxing.

consider this:

Taxes, like pollution taxes, that are enacted to correct the effects of a negative externality are called Pigovian taxes, after the economist Arthur Pigou (1877–1959). Pigovian taxes are not just pollution taxes but can be used to reduce any negative externality. Unlike other taxes that distort incentives, Pigovian taxes have the potential to actually move the allocation of resources closer to the social optimum. In short, they could raise revenue and enhance economic efficiency.

example, when buying a car, it is usually rational for the buyer to spend some time searching for the "right" car and negotiating a mutually agreeable price.

Suppose instead that the situation involved 1,000 ranchers and 10 mill owners. Trying to coordinate the activity between the ranch owners and mill owners would be almost impossible. Now imagine the complexities of more realistic cases: 12 million people live within 60 miles of downtown Los Angeles. Each of them is damaged a little by a large number of firms and other consumers (for example, automobile drivers) in Los Angeles.

It thus becomes apparent why the inefficiencies resulting from pollution control are not eliminated by private negotiations. First is the issue of ambiguity regarding property rights in air, water, and other environmental media. Firms that have historically polluted resent controls, giving up their rights to pollute only if bribed, yet consumers feel they have the right to breathe clean air and use clean bodies of water. These conflicting positions must be resolved in court, with the winner being, of course, made wealthier. Second, transaction costs increase greatly with the number of transactors, making it next to impossible for individual firms and citizens to negotiate private agreements. Finally, the properties of air or water quality (and similar public goods) are such that additional people can enjoy the benefits at no additional cost and cannot be excluded from doing so. Hence, in practice, private agreements are unlikely to solve many problems of market failure.

It is, however, too easy to jump to the conclusion that governments should solve any problems that cannot be solved by private actions. No solution may be possible, or all solutions may involve costs that exceed benefits. In any event, the ideas developed in this chapter should enable you to think critically about such problems and the difficulties in formulating appropriate policies.

SECTION CHECK

1. In a world with no externalities, property owners with only a few exceptions, could use their property in any manner they desired. Ultimately, then, externalities involve an evaluation of the legal arrangements in which we operate our economy.

2. The Coase theorem states that where property rights are defined in a clear-cut fashion, externalities are internalized. This condition holds where information and transaction costs are close to zero.

1. Why can externalities be considered a property rights problem?

2. Why, according to the Coase theorem, will externalities tend to be internalized when property rights are clearly defined and information and transaction costs are low?

3. How do transaction costs limit the market's ability to efficiently solve externality problems?

Interactive Chapter Summary

Fill in the blanks:

1. _____ are costs imposed on people other than the suppliers or demanders of a good or service.

2. When a factory puts "crud" in the air as a by-product of its production, it is imposing _____ on others.

3. With external costs, the marginal _____ costs of production are greater than the marginal _____ costs of production.

4. Pollution policy from an efficiency perspective largely seeks ways for external costs to be _____ by decision makers.

5. Where firms are not forced to pay for negative externalities, their output is _____ and their prices are _____ than they would otherwise be.

6. Forcing producers to internalize external costs would _____ their costs of production.

7. Many of the costs of negative externalities are _____ to measure, especially the _____ costs that have no market prices.

8. The goal of compliance standards is to force companies to find less _____-intensive ways to produce.

9. Air quality has _____ in most U.S. cities since 1970.

10. Pollution reduction, like other forms of production, is subject to _____ returns.

11. The marginal cost of pollution abatement _____ with increasing levels of abatement.

12. The optimal quantity of pollution is where the _____ of pollution abatement equals the _____ from pollution abatement.

13. Compliance standards should be stricter where the marginal benefit from pollution reduction is _____.

14. Eliminating nearly all pollution would be economically _____, because the marginal _____ would exceed the marginal _____.

15. The economically ideal tax to impose on a polluter would be _____ the marginal external costs imposed on others by its production.

16. Compared to compliance standards, pollution taxes lead to abatement by firms who can do so at the _____ cost.

17. The imposition of per-unit pollution taxes would likely be _____ costly than compliance standards for the same degree of pollution abatement.

18. Firms buy and sell rights to pollute under a system of _____ rights.

19. Transferable pollution rights _____ work when the EPA does not know the cheapest way for polluters to reduce their emissions, because they make it in polluters' interests to reduce pollution the cheapest way.

20. Under a system of transferable pollution rights, firms with high costs of abatement would likely be _____, and firms with low costs of abatement would be _____.

21. Problems of external costs are largely a question of how _____ should be assigned.

22. _____, the costs of negotiating and executing exchanges, must be low for well-defined property rights to allow externalities to be internalized.

23. According to the Coase theorem, markets can internalize externalities as long as _____ are well-defined and _____ costs are low.

24. When large numbers of individuals are affected by an external cost, the transaction costs of using voluntary negotiation to internalize it is likely to be _____.

Answers: 1. Negative externalities 2. external costs 3. social; private 4. internalized 5. larger; lower 6. raise 7. difficult; nonpecuniary 8. pollution 9. improved 10. diminishing 11. rises 12. marginal benefit; marginal cost 13. greater 14. inefficient; costs; benefits 15. equal to 16. lowest 17. less 18. transferable pollution 19. can 20. buyers; sellers 21. property rights; 22. Transaction costs 23. property rights; transaction 24. large

Key Terms and Concepts

internalized externalities 515
pollution tax 520

transferable pollution rights 520

Coase theorem 525

Section Check Answers

18.1 Negative Externalities and Pollution

1. What is the difference between private and social costs?

Social costs include all the relevant opportunity costs of production, whether they must be paid for by the decision maker or not. Private costs include only those social costs that must be borne by the decision maker.

2. Why do decision makers tend to ignore external costs?

Decision makers pay attention to their private costs because they are forced to compensate others for those costs; they tend to ignore external costs because they are not forced to compensate those who bear the costs.

3. How can internalizing the external costs of production move us closer to the efficient level of output?

A decision maker will produce the quantity where the marginal benefit of production (the price he sells his output for) equals his marginal private costs, in order to maximize profits. But the marginal social costs of those last units, which equal the sum of marginal private and marginal external costs, must exceed their marginal benefits. Internalizing external costs will make the private and social cost of production the same, and will lead profit-maximizing decision makers to reduce their output to the efficient level.

4. Why is it particularly difficult to measure the value of external costs or benefits?

Since there is no market (where people's behavior reveals the relative values they place on goods and services) on which externalities are traded, there are no market prices to reveal those values to us. Therefore, estimating the values of external costs or benefits is much more difficult than for goods traded on markets.

5. How does pollution control lead to both rising marginal costs and falling marginal benefits?

The marginal costs of pollution control rise for the same reason it is true of other goods. Pollution will be reduced in the lowest cost manner first. Once lower cost pollution control methods are exhausted, if we wish to reduce pollution further, we will have to turn to progressively more costly methods. The marginal benefits from pollution controls will fall, because the value of reducing crud in the atmosphere is higher, the more crud there is. As controls reduce the level of crud in the air, the marginal benefit of further crud reductions will fall.

6. How is the optimal amount of pollution control determined, in principle?

In principle, the optimal amount of pollution control is the amount at which the marginal social benefit of pollution reduction equals the marginal cost of pollution reduction. But there is no clear agreement about what those marginal benefits or costs are, leading to disagreements about the optimal amount of pollution.

18.2 Public Policy and the Environment

1. How do command and control policies act to internalize external costs?

By forcing companies to find less pollution-intensive ways of production rather than imposing the costs of additional pollution on others, they are forced to internalize those costs formerly imposed on others.

2. How could transferable pollution rights lead to pollution being reduced at the lowest possible opportunity cost?

Transferable pollution rights would create a market for pollution reduction. Every polluter would then find it profitable to reduce pollution as long as they could do it more cheaply than the price of a pollution right. Therefore, producers would employ the lowest cost pollution control methods for a given amount of pollution reduction.

3. What are the objectives of an ideal pollution control policy from the perspective of economists interested in resource allocation?

An ideal pollution control strategy from the perspective of economists interested in resource allocation would reduce pollution to the efficient level, it would do so at the lowest possible opportunity cost, and it would create incentives to motivate advances in pollution abatement technology.

4. **Why might an efficient pollution tax be lower in Fargo, North Dakota, than in Los Angeles, California?**

The more polluted an area already is and the more people there are breathing that pollution, the greater the marginal social cost of an additional unit of pollution. Therefore, the marginal social benefit from pollution reduction is greater, and therefore the optimal pollution tax will also be greater, in such circumstances.

18.3 Property Rights

1. **Why can externalities be considered a property rights problem?**

If the rights to clean air, water, and so on, were clearly owned, those that infringe on those rights would be forced to compensate the owners. Such costs would be internalized, rather than external, to the relevant decision makers. Therefore, externalities are the result of the absence of clear and enforceable property rights in certain goods.

2. **Why, according to the Coase theorem, will externalities tend to be internalized when property rights are clearly defined and information and transaction costs are low?**

When property rights are clearly defined and information and transaction costs are low, whoever wants to exercise their right faces an opportunity cost of what others would pay for that right. That opportunity cost, represented by the potential payment from others to sell the right, is what forces decision makers to internalize what would otherwise be an externality.

3. **How do transaction costs limit the market's ability to efficiently solve externality problems?**

Transaction costs limit the ability of the market mechanism to internalize externalities, because trading becomes more difficult. The free-rider problem—where those who benefit from some action cannot be forced to pay for it—also hinders the ability for voluntary trade across markets to generate efficient levels of goods such as cleaner air.

True or False:

1. Activities that impose costs on people other than the suppliers or demanders of a good or service are negative externalities.

2. In markets where negative externalities are created, the marginal social cost of production exceeds the marginal private cost of production.

3. In markets where negative externalities are created, the marginal private cost of production exceeds the marginal social cost of production.

4. The marginal social cost of production equals the marginal private cost of production plus the marginal external cost of production.

5. A poultry packing firm breeds, raises, and slaughters chickens for market. The firm's chicken yards and processing plant emit foul odors into the air, which affects surrounding residential neighborhoods. If the poultry packing firm is a perfectly competitive firm producing at a level of output such that the price of a pound of chicken equals the firm's marginal cost, it will produce a socially optimal quantity of chicken.

6. The nonpecuniary (or nonmonetary) costs associated with negative externalities are, in practice, very difficult to assess.

7. The goal of EPA compliance standards is to force companies to find less pollution-intensive ways of producing goods and services.

8. Available evidence suggests that since 1970, compliance standards have not succeeded in reducing U.S. pollution levels.

9. Compliance standards can create situations where the marginal cost of eliminating pollution exceeds the marginal benefit from doing so.

10. Eliminating nearly all pollution would lead to economic efficiency and healthier lifestyles for all.

11. Economists believe that pollution reduction is likely subject to diminishing returns.

12. In practice, it is very difficult to determine the appropriate pollution tax to levy to correct for a negative externality.

13. Under a system of transferable pollution rights, firms with relatively high abatement costs will sell rights to pollute to firms with relatively low abatement costs.

14. In order for a transferable pollution rights system to work, the EPA needs to know the cheapest way for each polluter to reduce pollution.

15. Transaction costs must be low for well-defined property rights to lead to the internalization of externalities.

16. The problem of externalities can be viewed as a question of how property rights should be assigned.

17. According to the Coase theorem, if transaction costs are high it is unlikely that private negotiations can resolve an externality problem and achieve social efficiency.

Multiple Choice:

1. If the production of a good generates a negative externality, then in equilibrium in a perfectly competitive market,
   a. marginal private cost > price.
   b. price > marginal private cost.
   c. marginal private cost > marginal social cost.
   d. marginal social cost > price.

2. Many harmful externalities occur because
   a. persons do not pay the full social cost of using a resource.
   b. persons do not pay the full private cost of using a resource.
   c. companies do not pay the market price for natural resources.
   d. companies pay more than the full social cost of using a resource.

3. A firm is generating harmful externalities when
   a. marginal social cost is less than marginal private cost.
   b. marginal social cost is the same as marginal private cost.
   c. marginal social cost is greater than marginal private cost.
   d. the firm is not producing at the level of output where the *MPC* is minimized.

4. Pollution
   a. is an example of a positive externality.
   b. should be reduced to zero, the socially efficient level.
   c. is not an economic problem.
   d. is an example of a negative externality.
   e. is characterized by both b and d.

5. Pollution control costs lead to
   a. lower prices for goods and services produced by polluting firms.
   b. higher prices for goods and services produced by polluting firms.
   c. a decrease in the cost of production by polluting firms.
   d. an increase in production of output by polluting firms.

6. Which of the following statements is true?
   a. The phasing out of leaded gasoline, which began in 1984, has not had a measurable impact on the levels of lead in our atmosphere.
   b. The EPA's main duty is to collect tax revenue to fund miscellaneous government programs.
   c. Using a compliance standards approach, the EPA identifies and then enforces a standard equal to the maximum amount of pollution that firms can produce per unit of output per year.
   d. Nonpecuniary costs are the out-of-pocket costs of medical bills and environmental cleanup imposed on third parties by polluters.

7. If emissions standards are made more stringent, the privately borne
   a. costs of production would decrease.
   b. costs of production would not be affected.
   c. costs of production would increase.
   d. output prices would decrease.

8. The true extent of a negative externality may be difficult to measure because
   a. firms often keep poor records of their cash outlays.
   b. of the intricacies of accounting rules.
   c. certain costs may be nonpecuniary.
   d. none of the above.

9. If the government were able to force a firm to internalize the external cost of its production, we would expect
   a. the firm to produce more to make up for incurring a higher private cost.
   b. the marginal social cost curve to shift up and the firm to produce more and charge a higher price as a result.
   c. the firm to produce less and charge a higher price as a result of incurring higher marginal private costs.
   d. the firm to lower its price to compensate for incurring a higher private cost.

10. If significant external costs are imposed on third parties by a polluting firm,
    a. the marginal private cost curve overstates the relative importance of the product to society and output should increase.
    b. the marginal private cost curve understates the relative importance of the product to society and output should increase.
    c. the marginal private cost curve overstates the cost to society and output should increase.
    d. the marginal private cost curve understates the cost to society and output should decrease.
    e. the marginal private cost curve accurately reflects the cost to society and output should not change.

11. External costs created by polluting firms
    a. are paid by no one in society.
    b. are typically paid by the consumer purchasing the product.
    c. may be paid by society in the form of nonpecuniary costs, higher medical bills, and/or cleanup costs.
    d. are typically paid by the producer of the pollution.
    e. are typically paid for by the government.

12. It is likely that the marginal cost of pollution abatement
    a. falls the more pollution is reduced.
    b. rises the more pollution is reduced.
    c. is constant as pollution is reduced more.
    d. equals zero.

13. Compliance standards for air pollution
    a. should be the same in Wyoming as in California, since pollution is harmful everywhere.
    b. should probably be stricter in Wyoming, where the marginal benefit of pollution reduction is likely greater than in California.
    c. should probably be stricter in California, where the marginal benefit of pollution reduction is likely greater than in Wyoming.
    d. have not been at all effective in reducing pollution levels.

14. Which of the following is the best example of a nonpecuniary external cost?
    a. wages paid to workers in a steel mill
    b. the medical costs associated with increased asthma caused by steel mill pollution
    c. the cost of repainting cars because of steel mill pollution damage
    d. the cost to steel mill neighbors of suffering from the obnoxious odors from the pollution
    e. Both b and c are good examples of nonpecuniary external costs.

15. There has been a downward trend in the United States since 1980 in the air pollution concentrations of
    a. sulfur dioxide.
    b. carbon monoxide.
    c. lead.
    d. all of the above.

16. Which of the following makes it difficult to achieve the efficient level of pollution reduction?
    a. Property rights are not always well-defined.
    b. It is difficult to accurately measure the costs and benefits of pollution.
    c. It is difficult to determine the level of pollution that is socially optimal.
    d. All of the above.

17. Taxes on the emissions of polluting firms are primarily intended to
    a. encourage firms to reduce product prices.
    b. encourage firms to increase production of output.
    c. raise revenue for general spending needs.
    d. encourage firms to pollute less.

18. An ideal pollution tax
    a. does not affect the quantity of the good produced.
    b. forces a firm to internalize the externality.
    c. causes a polluting firm to increase production to the socially efficient level of output.
    d. leads to a reduction in price to the consumer of the polluting firm's output.

19. Compliance standards that impose emissions limits on polluters
    a. are a fair and efficient way to reduce pollution since all firms are treated equally.
    b. are likely to reduce pollution at a higher cost than would the imposition of per-unit pollution taxes.
    c. are more efficient than the use of pollution taxes since large polluters are less likely to respond to such taxes than are small polluters.
    d. are likely to reduce pollution at a lower cost than would the use of transferable pollution rights.

20. The reason why cleanup costs are lower when the government mandates pollution taxes rather than compliance standards is that
    a. the biggest polluters reduce emissions the most, which is always the lowest cost.
    b. all firms reduce pollution an equal amount.
    c. emissions are reduced most by firms that can do so at the lowest cost.
    d. the smallest polluters reduce emissions the most, which is more cost effective than if large polluters reduce emissions.

21. If compliance standards are too stringent,
    a. the marginal social benefit of pollution reduction may outweigh the marginal social cost of pollution reduction.
    b. the marginal social cost of pollution reduction may outweigh the marginal social benefit of pollution reduction.
    c. the marginal social cost of pollution reduction will just equal the marginal social benefit from pollution reduction.
    d. none of the above is correct.

22. An advantage that emission taxes and tradable emissions permits have over compliance standards is that the former
    a. work well even if pollution output cannot be accurately measured.
    b. result in equal levels of pollution abatement across all firms.
    c. make it in the interests of firms to reduce pollution in the most efficient manner possible.
    d. reduce pollution to zero.

23. A transferable pollution right
    a. would command a price of zero in the free market since pollution is "bad" for society.
    b. could never be resold.
    c. gives a firm the right to emit a certain quantity of pollution.
    d. gives a firm the right to emit an unlimited amount of pollution.

24. Which of the following is *not* an advantage of transferable pollution rights?
    a. They create incentives for polluters to develop cheaper ways to reduce pollution.
    b. They allow the greatest value of output to be produced with a given amount of pollution.
    c. They require polluters to reduce emissions, regardless of the cost.
    d. The rights are private property and may be bought or sold freely.

25. Under a system in which the government grants a fixed number of transferable pollution rights, an increase in demand for the output of firms would
    a. decrease the resale price of pollution rights.
    b. increase the resale price of pollution rights.
    c. increase overall pollution levels.
    d. decrease overall pollution levels.

26. Achieving a 25 percent reduction in pollution is likely to be most costly under
    a. a system of transferable pollution rights.
    b. a compliance standard.
    c. a per-unit pollution tax system.
    d. Costs are the same under all three pollution control policies.

27. Pollution in a free market is more likely when
    a. property rights are not well-defined.
    b. property rights are difficult to enforce.
    c. transaction costs of negotiating private market solutions are high.
    d. any of the above is true.

28. According to the Coase theorem, one way to deal with an externality problem when transaction costs are low is
    a. for the government to impose pollution taxes.
    b. for the government to make certain that property rights are well-defined.
    c. for the government to issue transferable pollution permits.
    d. for the government to impose compliance standards.

29. The Coase theorem suggests that private solutions to externality problems
    a. can lead to an optimal allocation of resources if private parties can bargain at relatively low cost.
    b. result in the efficient outcome under all conditions.
    c. will result in the same distribution of wealth no matter how property rights are assigned.
    d. will result in different efficiency levels of production, depending crucially on how property rights are assigned.

30. In the case of a private solution to the externality problem, the distribution of rights
    a. restricts the ability of private parties to properly price the externalities.
    b. enhances the market incentive to reach an efficient solution.
    c. determines who bears the cost of the solution but does not affect the efficient result.
    d. affects the efficiency of the outcome, but does not determine who bears the cost.

31. It is difficult to identify the efficient level of air pollution because
    a. private ownership of different portions of air is not possible.
    b. there is no way to precisely determine the price that should be paid for fouling an individual's air.
    c. there are no private market transactions over air for politicians to look to when determining the appropriate level of pollution.
    d. of all of the above.

32. Pollution reduction will be achieved for the least cost when
    a. large polluters are required to reduce pollution by a greater extent than small polluters.
    b. small polluters are required to reduce pollution by a greater extent than large polluters.
    c. all firms are required to reduce pollution by a proportionate amount.
    d. all firms are required to reduce pollution by an equal absolute amount.
    e. the cost of reducing pollution by an additional unit is the same for all polluting firms.

33. If the rivers, lakes, and air in the United States could all be privately owned, then
    a. there would be less pollution.
    b. costs of production for many firms would rise.
    c. externalities would be internalized.
    d. a market for the pollution rights would not be needed.
    e. all of the above are correct.

34. Which of the following does not inhibit the ability of voluntary exchange to internalize external costs?
    a. high transaction costs
    b. clear property rights
    c. large numbers of people affected by the external cost, but by a small amount each
    d. the free-rider problem
    e. All of the above do inhibit the ability of voluntary exchange to internalize external costs

35. If there were well-defined property rights in all goods, but positive transaction costs,
    a. there would be no external costs.
    b. external costs would be reduced but not eliminated.
    c. there would be no effect on the magnitude of external costs.
    d. the amount of external costs imposed would increase.

Problems:

1. Say that the last ton of steel produced by a steel company imposes three types of costs: labor costs of $25; additional equipment costs of $10; and the cost of additional "crud" dumped into the air of $15. What costs will the steel company consider in deciding whether to produce another ton of steel?

2. Why can a homeowner make a better argument for compensation for noise pollution if a local airport was built after he moved in than if it was already there when he moved in? Would it matter whether or not he knew it was going to be built?

3. A newly released study demonstrates that populated areas with significant air pollution caused by diesel engines experience a much higher incidence of cancer. If diesel engines were then banned, what sorts of results would you expect?

4. Discuss the incentive effects of each of these policies to reduce air pollution:
    a. a higher tax on gasoline
    b. an annual tax on automobiles based on average emissions
    c. an annual tax on total emissions from a particular model of car

5. Draw a standard supply and demand diagram for widgets, and indicate the equilibrium price and output.

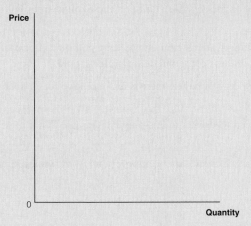

a. Assuming that the production of widgets generates external costs, illustrate the effect of the producer being forced to pay a tax equal to the external costs generated, and indicate the equilibrium output.

b. If instead of generating external costs, widget production generates external benefits, illustrate the effect of the producer being given a subsidy equal to the external benefits generated, and indicate the equilibrium output.

6. a. Why does internalizing externalities with taxes or subsidies sometimes increase the prices of goods and sometimes decrease them?

b. When would workers in an industry benefit from internalizing its externalities?

7. Many communities have launched programs to collect recyclable materials but have been unable to find buyers for the salvaged materials. If the government were to offer a subsidy to firms using recycled materials, how might this affect the market for recycled materials? Illustrate using a demand and supply diagram.

8. What would be the result of taxing an industry that produces external benefits? Subsidizing an industry that produces external cost?

9. If a firm can reduce its sulfur dioxide emissions for $30 per ton, but it owns tradable emissions permits that are selling for $40 per ton, what will the firm want to do if it is trying to maximize profits?

10. A chemical factory dumps pollutants into a nearby river (permissible under the existing laws). In lieu of dumping into the river, the factory could pay for the pollution to be hauled to a toxic waste dump site at a cost of $125,000 per year. A vacation resort located downstream from the factory suffers damages estimated at $200,000 per year. Evaluate whether a change in law is necessary to achieve an efficient outcome in this situation.

11. A factory releases air pollutants that have a negative impact on the adjacent neighborhood (populated by 2,000 households). If the government could assign property rights to the air to either the factory or to the residents of the neighborhood, would this make a difference in the quantity of pollution generated? Explain.

12. Compare a pollution reduction program that permits a certain level of pollution using emissions standards with one that permits the same level of pollution using tradable emissions permits.

13. Evaluate the following toll charges for a stretch of highway frequented by commuters: a $2 toll between 7 A.M. and 10 A.M. and between 3 P.M. and 6 P.M., and a $4 toll at all other times of the day. Do you think these toll charges will help reduce traffic congestion?

14. Evaluate the following statement: "Public health is at stake when drinking water is contaminated by pollution. Local governments should take all measures necessary to ensure that zero pollutants contaminate the water supply."

15. Evaluate the following statement: "If people do not use paper or if they recycle paper, there is less incentive for lumber companies to plant trees on private land."

16. Why does the text argue that lower air pollution taxes should be charged to drivers in less-populated areas? What if air pollution quickly spread throughout the world?

17. If an industry created both external benefits and external cost, would a tax or subsidy be appropriate? Why would someone be hurt by either one?

Health Care

There have been many modern-day successes made possible by tremendous advances in medical knowledge. The twenty-first century will lead to technological progress at a rapid rate, helping to prolong and improve the quality of life of many patients.

Like the production of any other good or service, however, health care involves the use of scarce resources. Not only must the health care sector compete with other sectors for resources, but those resources must also be allocated across patients facing vastly different circumstances.

Where health and survival may be at stake, the question as to how to best allocate limited resources is a particularly complex one. Considerations of ethics and equity cannot be disentangled from decisions as to what quantity and quality of health care to provide and how that care is distributed. How much should be spent to save a life? Is it ethical to deny care on the basis of inability to pay? These questions are difficult to answer. ■

SECTION 19.1

The Rising Cost of Health Care

* How much does the United States spend on health care?

* What are the benefits of investment in health care?

The United States spends more money on health care per person and as a percentage of national income than any other industrialized nation (see Exhibit 1). In 2007, health care expenditures (which includes spending on physician, hospital, nursing home, home care, dental, vision, and other services) in the United States made up approximately 16.2 percent of the total value of the output of goods and services produced in the economy, GDP. This figure is up from 13.3 percent in 2000.

Exhibit 2 shows how health care expenditures as a percentage of GDP varied since 1960. Notice that spending on health care increased significantly over the last several decades, averaging more than 14 percent of GDP since 2000 compared with only 5.1 percent in 1960. Health care spending is roughly 4 times the amount spent on national defense.

Health care is often regarded as if it were a basic "human right." However, it is important to recognize that, as with the consumption of other goods and services, the utilization of medical care involves trade-offs. Scarce resources allocated toward the production of health services cannot be used in the production of other goods and services.

section 19.1 exhibit 1 — Health Care Spending in Selected Countries

Country	Percent of GDP Spent on Health Care
United States	16.2%
Switzerland	11.3
Germany	10.5
France	11
Canada	10
Italy	8.9
United Kingdom	8.4
Japan	8.0
Mexico	6.6

Among industrialized countries, the United States has the highest health care spending as a percentage of GDP.

SOURCES: OECD, 2009; and Center for Medicare and Medicaid Services.

section 19.1 exhibit 2 — U.S. Health Care Expenditures as a Percentage of GDP Since 1960

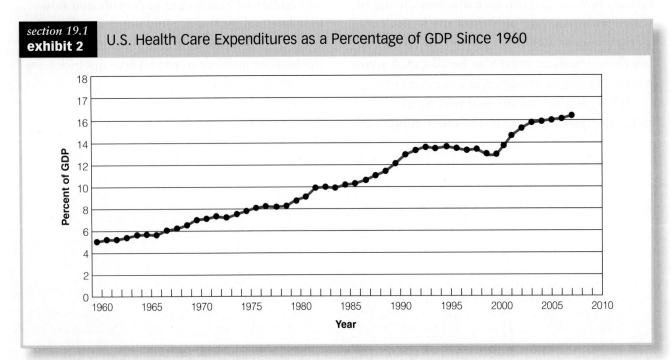

SOURCE: Center for Medicare and Medicaid Services, 2009.

Production Possibilities Curve Between Health Care and All Other Goods

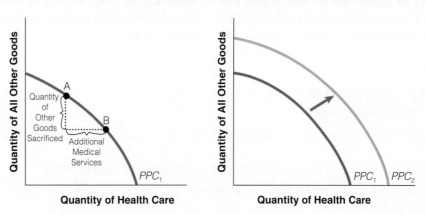

Moving along the production possibilities curve between health care and all other goods from A to B requires sacrificing other goods and services to acquire additional medical care. Over time, however, the production possibilities curve could shift outward from PPC_1 to PPC_2, if worker productivity and/or the labor force increases due to improved health.

Investment in health care, however, does bear similarities to investment in human or physical capital. By promoting health and removing disabilities, medical care can (1) improve the productivity of workers on the job and reduce missed workdays and (2) extend the average number of years that people can participate in the labor force. Increases in the quality and quantity of labor available due to better health care will shift an economy's production possibilities curve outward, as seen in Exhibit 3.

The sources and uses of health care expenditures in the United States during 2007 are illustrated in Exhibit 4(a). Only 12 percent of the nation's health care expenditures are financed by consumers out-of-pocket. Private insurance funds 35 percent of the cost of health care. Public health care expenditures (both federal and state) add up to 47 percent of total U.S. health care expenditures. Health care spending averaged $8,000 per person in 2009. In Exhibit 4(b), most expenditures are for hospital care (31 percent) and physician and clinical services (21 percent).

Part of the increase in health care costs over the last couple of decades may be a measurement problem.

The U.S. Health Dollar, 2007

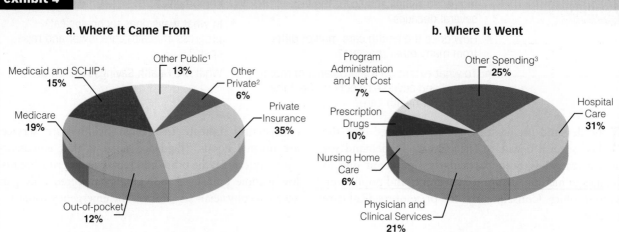

[1] "Other Public" includes programs such as workers' compensation, public health activity, Department of Defense, Department of Veterans Affairs, Indian health services, and state and local hospitals and school health.

[2] "Other Private" includes industrial implant, privately funded construction, and nonpatient revenues including philanthropy.

[3] "Other Spending" includes dental services, other professional services, home health, durable medical products, over-the-counter medicines and sundries, public health, research, and construction.

[4] SCHIP is the State Children's Health Insurance Program designed to help uninsured children for families with low incomes.

SOURCE: Center for Medicare and Medicaid Services, Office of the Actuary, National Health Statistics Group, 2009.

In particular, CPI (the consumer price index which measures the inflation rate) may overestimate the increase in the price of health care because it may not adequately account for improvements in the quality of health care. A heart surgery today is drastically different from one 20 years ago, with fewer complications and a longer and higher-quality life after the operation. In other words, we are not merely paying more for the same service—we are paying more for a better service.

SECTION CHECK

1. Health care spending has increased as a percentage of GDP from roughly 5 percent in 1960 to 16.2 percent in 2007.
2. Among industrialized nations, the United States has the highest health care spending.
3. Health care improves the productivity of workers, reduces the number of missed workdays, and extends the average number of years a person can work.
4. Only 12 percent of health care expenditures are financed by consumers out of pocket.
5. Part of the increase in health care costs may be a measurement problem with the consumer price index (CPI), which may overstate the increase in the price of health care because it may not accurately account for all of the improvements in the quality of health care.

---

1. How is investment in health care like investments in human and physical capital?
2. Who pays for most of the health care?
3. Where are most of the health care dollars spent?
4. Why is it possible that some of the increases in health care costs may be a measurement problem?

SECTION 19.2

The Health Care Market

* Why have expenditures on health care increased significantly over the last several decades?

* How does the health care market differ from many other markets?

* To what extent do the problems of moral hazard and adverse selection affect the market for health care?

* Why are health care markets imperfectly competitive?

* In what ways does technological progress in health care lower and raise costs?

* What are Health Savings Accounts?

The demand for health care has increased over the last several decades. The increase in demand for medical care has been particularly significant due to changes in income, insurance coverage, and population demographics. Consequently, the price of medical care has risen.

Income

Rising U.S. real income has contributed to the increase in demand for medical services. Estimates of the income elasticity of health care vary but consistently indicate that most health care services are normal goods. (Evidence suggests that emergency care services, on the other hand, may be inferior because low-income uninsured individuals can often only gain access to physician services via the emergency room.)

Price Elasticity of Demand

Estimates of the price elasticity of demand for health care are as low as 0.2, indicating significant inelasticity of demand for medical services. That is, a 10 percent increase in price would reduce quantity demanded by only 2 percent. The quantity of medical care demanded appears to be quite insensitive to changes in price. For example, it is hard to imagine that anyone suffering a life-threatening injury would travel from emergency room to emergency room shopping for the lowest-priced care.

Health care is considered a necessity with few good substitutes, particularly when it comes to serious illness. Although vitamins and homeopathic therapies are available to treat minor ailments, few good alternatives to hospital- or physician-guided care are available to treat serious disease or injury. Additionally, many patients in the United States establish long-term relationships with primary care physicians and are reluctant to search for new physicians even if fees increase significantly. Physician services are, in this regard, "experience goods." Average consumers are "brand loyal," often preferring the physician they know and trust to an untried physician (even one with lower fees).

Insurance and Third-Party Payers

The health services market differs from many others in that, because of insurance, the consumer often pays only a fraction of the direct cost of care. Third-party payers, such as insurance companies or health maintenance organizations, play significant roles in this industry. In fact, the structure of the health care payment system has important incentive effects and can alter the behavior of both patients and providers.

In Exhibit 1, we see that approximately 85 percent of the U.S. population is covered by some kind of medical insurance policy. Most of that coverage

(59.3 percent) is sponsored through employers. Despite the fact that the United States spends more on health care per capita than any other nation in the world, over 15 percent of the U.S. population remain uninsured. However, the health care system does provide a safety net whereby the cost of unreimbursed care is shifted to other health care payers. Many of the uninsured are able to receive some care, particularly from public hospitals and clinics.

In Exhibit 2, we see that insurance lowers the price of health care to consumers and increases the quantity of services demanded—a movement down the demand curve. An insurance policy requiring consumers to pay, say, a $20 copayment induces patients to visit physicians more frequently and raises the marginal cost of producing the larger quantity ($150 in Exhibit 2). Total expenditure on office visits increases from $100 million ($100 × 1 million) to $240 million (150 × 1.6 million) as a result.

Moral Hazard

In addition to increasing the quantity demanded of health care by reducing prices, insurance alters the incentive of patients in other ways. Insurance reduces the cost to the insured of undertaking risky activities. In the event of an accident or illness, the burden of health care costs are borne by the insurer. This situation creates what economists call a "moral hazard" problem.

Moral hazard in health care exists whenever insurance makes a person more likely to engage in risky behavior (which could lead to an accident or illness) and less likely to undertake preventative measures against illness. For example, a person covered by a generous insurance plan may be more likely to smoke

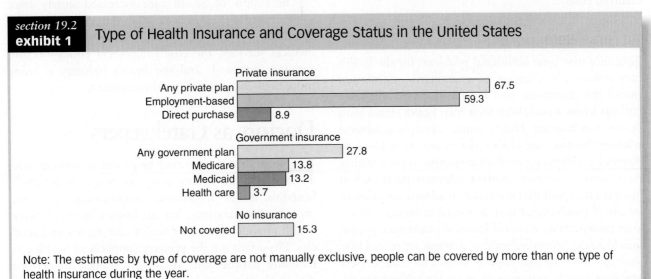

section 19.2 exhibit 1   Type of Health Insurance and Coverage Status in the United States

Private insurance
Any private plan — 67.5
Employment-based — 59.3
Direct purchase — 8.9

Government insurance
Any government plan — 27.8
Medicare — 13.8
Medicaid — 13.2
Health care — 3.7

No insurance
Not covered — 15.3

Note: The estimates by type of coverage are not manually exclusive, people can be covered by more than one type of health insurance during the year.

SOURCE: U.S. Census Bureau, Current Population Survey, 2008

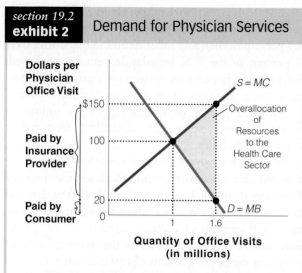

section 19.2
exhibit 2   Demand for Physician Services

Dollars per
Physician
Office Visit

S = MC

$150

Paid by
Insurance
Provider

100

Overallocation
of
Resources
to the
Health Care
Sector

20

0

D = MB

Paid by
Consumer

1   1.6

**Quantity of Office Visits
(in millions)**

Insurance lowers the price of health care to consumers and increases the quantity of services
demanded. An insurance policy requiring consumers
to pay only $20 per office visit lowers the price of
each visit enough to induce patients to visit physicians more frequently. Total expenditure on office
visits increases from $100 million to $240 million as
a result. Because the marginal cost (MC) is greater
than the marginal benefit (MB) at 1.6 million office
visits, an overallocation of resources is made to the
health care sector.

cigarettes or take up motocross racing or skydiving and
less likely to eat a healthy diet and exercise regularly.

Insurance companies or third-party payers attempt
to reduce moral hazard problems by requiring patients
to pay higher deductibles or copayments (thereby
compelling the insured to share a greater proportion of
incurred costs).

Adverse Selection

Insurance may pose additional problems for the health
care industry. A situation of asymmetric information
(recall the discussion in Chapter 8) exists whenever
patients know more about their own health status than
prospective insurers. This situation is known as adverse
selection because the chronically ill are more likely to
demand health insurance than are people in good health.
An insurance company inviting voluntary participation
in a plan may find that it insured an adverse selection of
largely ill patients and may be forced to increase insurance premiums to stave off losses. As insurance premiums increase, however, healthy enrollees are more likely
to drop out of the plan (opting instead for cheaper, less
generous health insurance plans or for self-insurance).
This tendency further exacerbates the adverse selection
problem.

Insurers can reduce adverse selection risk by limiting the period of open enrollment in health insurance
plans, requiring physical exams (so that an individual
cannot purchase insurance after serious illness strikes),
and insuring entire groups (such as all members of a
large employer or union), thereby ensuring a diversity
of health statuses.

Demographic Changes

The aging of the U.S. population is an additional
factor that explains the increase in demand for
health care. In 2007, the elderly composed 12.4 percent of the U.S. population versus 9 percent in 1960.
The elderly segment of the U.S. population is expected
to expand as millions of baby boomers approach
retirement age.

The elderly consume a disproportionate share of
health care services (three to four times as much as
the rest of the population). Illnesses that used to end
life fairly quickly (infections, heart disease, and some
cancers, for example) can now be treated effectively
using expensive new procedures. Thus, the elderly are
living longer, increasingly experiencing chronic disease
(such as emphysema or Alzheimer's disease), and consuming larger total quantities of health care as a result.
However, recent research shows that the aging U.S.
population can only account for roughly 10 percent of
the growth in health care spending.

The Supply of Health Care

The supply of health care increased slowly since
1960 for several reasons: The number of providers increased but has not kept up with the demand for
medical services, the cost of medical education and
training increased, and the health industry is using
more high-cost technological equipment.

Doctors as Gatekeepers

Health care services may be provided through independent physicians, nonprofit hospitals, for-profit
hospitals, health maintenance organizations, preferred
provider organizations, nursing homes, hospices, home
health providers, or other health care agents and agencies. Physicians are the primary suppliers of health care
to ailing patients and are highly trained to perform
diagnostic tests to identify and assess the seriousness
of a patient's illness. Patients depend on their physicians' recommendations as to the appropriate courses

of treatment, leading to a situation of asymmetric information: Doctors are better informed than their patients about health status and appropriate remedies. Primary care physicians act as gatekeepers, controlling access to prescription drugs, hospitals, surgeries, and other treatments. Acting in this capacity, physicians induce demand for additional medical services. If physicians are paid on a fee-for-service basis (as is common), incentives exist for doctors to err on the side of recommending too many services. The suppliers themselves help increase the demand for health care.

Traditional Insurance

Traditional health insurance in the United States provides indemnity coverage (security in the event of illness or injury) on a fee-for-service basis. Patients can freely choose physicians and treatment options in the event of illness. Individuals covered by fee-for-service plans typically pay an annual deductible and a small percentage of all health care costs incurred (called co-insurance) up to an annual limit.

Escalating health care costs over the past decade, however, led to a greater emphasis on cost containment. The result was a proliferation of organizations offering managed care, including health maintenance organizations and preferred provider organizations.

Health Maintenance Organizations

Health maintenance organizations (HMOs) combine two traditionally separated functions: the provision of comprehensive health care and its financing. HMOs seek to contain health care costs by exerting control over patients' treatment options. Patients are often limited to seeking treatment from plan doctors only, whose utilization of services is subject to review. Doctors are typically paid a salary and not reimbursed on a fee-for-service basis. Physicians are generally required to prescribe drugs from an approved list, or formulary, to encourage the substitution of cheaper alternatives for expensive branded products. In some instances, doctors are also provided with financial incentives to limit the utilization of plan services and thereby minimize costs.

Preferred Provider Organizations

A preferred provider organization (PPO) is a network of doctors who agree to provide services to a

indemnity coverage compensation toward the cost of medical services in the event of illness or injury

health maintenance organization (HMO) an organization that contracts with physicians, medical facilities, employers, and individuals to provide medical care to a group of individuals. Health care services are usually provided at a fixed price per patient. The cost of providing care is contained through the rationing of health care resources.

preferred provider organization (PPO) a network of doctors who agree to provide services to a health plan's enrollees at discounted fees

health plan's enrollees at discounted fees. Patients can choose from any of the doctors within the plan. Unlike those enrolled in an HMO, patients in a PPO can generally opt for nonparticipating physicians, but they can do so only by incurring much higher out-of-pocket costs.

Technological Progress and Quality of Care

Medical research and technological progress have vastly improved the quality of medical care. Innovative therapies help reduce disability, improve health, and prolong life. Some innovations undoubtedly reduce the overall cost of health care. For example, cholesterol-reducing drugs can save thousands of dollars in surgical and hospitalization costs while reducing the likelihood of death from coronary heart disease. Other innovations, however, significantly add to the cost of health care. For example, many cancer patients can now be saved through surgery, bone marrow transplants, radiation, and chemotherapy treatments. The availability of these treatment options (where previously little but comfort care would have been provided) adds many thousands of dollars per patient to the cost of treating disease. Magnetic resonance imaging (MRI) scans typically cost from $1,000 to $1,500. Such exams, like an MRI, add cost to a patient's treatment when a cheaper CAT scan ($250 to $300) or X-ray ($100 or less) may suffice.

Technological advances, through interaction with insurance, lead to a significant increase in the demand for medical care. Insured patients who bear a small fraction of health care costs naturally desire the best possible care, contributing to rising health care costs that far exceeds the average level of inflation.

Imperfect Competition

Health care markets are imperfectly competitive for several reasons, including the presence of legal or administrative barriers to entry, economies of scale, collusion, and restrictions on advertising.

Barriers to Entry

Laws requiring the compulsory licensing of physicians help restrict entry into the health care market. Likewise, hospitals sometimes limit privileges to certain physicians. Licensing requirements and limitations on hospital privileges are justified as a means to protect patients from inferior-quality medical care by certifying that physicians possess a certain level of competency. (A voluntary certification program would likely serve the same purpose, however, so it is not clear that compulsory licensing is necessary.) By restricting the supply of physicians, licensing programs and hospital privilege requirements no doubt restrict the quantity of services provided and lead to higher medical prices, as seen in Exhibit 3. In addition, some major metropolitan areas have been dominated by a few hospital systems. The reduced competition can lead to higher prices (as physicians and hospitals leverage market power) and a reduction in quality.

Economies of Scale

Economies of scale are often associated with the provision of health care. Specialty services, such as organ transplants, brain surgery, or treatments of rare diseases, may be used infrequently, which means that even areas with a large population may be served by only a few providers. Likewise, cities and towns are often unable to support a large number of hospitals. Except in densely populated metropolitan areas, it may not be economical for numerous hospitals to compete. Conditions may be such that "natural health care monopolies" exist in many areas.

Collusion Among Sellers

Health care providers possess significant market power, making price discrimination and collusive behavior (such as price fixing) more likely to occur. For example, price discrimination is commonly practiced by the pharmaceutical industry, where large favored buyers (such as hospital networks or health maintenance organizations) are offered drugs at significant discounts. The Federal Trade Commission recently settled four cases against associations of physicians, dentists, surgeons, and chiropractors that had each agreed to boycott health care payers in order to extract higher reimbursement rates.

Advertising Restrictions

Legal restrictions on advertising eyeglasses were shown to reduce price competition. In states that permit price advertising, the prices of glasses were markedly lower. In states with prohibitions against the advertising of eyeglass prices, consumers are less aware of substitute products (due to the high cost of information gathering) and pay on average higher prices for glasses.

Shortages

In Canada, where a national health care program controls prices and strictly rations care, conditions of excess demand for surgery prevail. In 2001, the median waiting time between visiting a primary physician and finally receiving treatment from a specialist was 16.5 weeks, and in 2002, the waiting time was 77 percent higher than in 1995. Consequently, some Canadians travel to the United States and pay for treatment themselves, rather than wait for insurance covered care. Medical referral brokers help match frustrated Canadians with surgical providers in the United States (where fees can vary drastically). In addition, research by Statistics Canada shows that for every one doctor permanently migrating from the United States to Canada, 18 Canadian doctors are migrating permanently to the United States. (The migration to the United States, across all occupations, is found to be grossly disproportionate among those earning $150,000 or more—the most highly skilled.)

Likewise, shortages prevail in the market for organ transplants at zero price, as we can see in Exhibit 4. Ethical considerations leave policymakers reluctant to raise the price of organ transplantation or provide remuneration for organ donations. Trade in body parts is illegal, and few organs become available. Donated organs are rationed according to strict criteria.

section 19.2 exhibit 3   The Market for Physician Services

The market supply of physicians is restricted due to education and licensing requirements, causing the supply curve to shift leftward, *ceteris paribus*. Compared to a market with fewer restrictive licensing requirements, physicians are able to command higher fees. Fewer physician services are used as a result.

section 19.2
exhibit 4 The Market for Human Organs

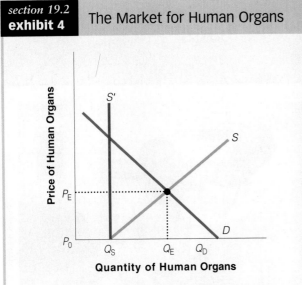

Under the current system, there is a transplantable organ shortage of $Q_S - Q_D$ at zero price. Under a market equilibrium, the price is P_E, and the quantity is Q_E. The demand for transplantable organs far exceeds the supply of organs available at the current price of transplantation services, zero. Because federal law prohibits the sale of organs, no upward pressure is exerted on the price of organs. The result is a persistent shortage of organs for transplant.

The Market for Human Organs

The demand curve for human organs is downward sloping, as seen in Exhibit 4. That is, the quantity demanded for human organs is lower at higher prices and higher at lower prices. Currently, the supply curve for human organs is perfectly inelastic (S' in Exhibit 4)—a fixed quantity of organs is available in the United States because all organs are required to be donated. Notice that in Exhibit 4, at a zero money price, P_0, for human organs, there will be a shortage—donors will supply Q_S organs per year but Q_D will be demanded; resulting in a shortage of $Q_S - Q_D$. That is, many people who want transplantable kidneys, livers, or hearts will not be able to obtain them because of lack of donors.

In 2005, roughly 28,000 organ transplants were made, but 100,000 people remained on the waiting lists. Shortages are so severe that thousands die each year waiting for needed organs. In 1998, 4,557 patients in the United States awaited lung transplants; 485 died. The same year, of the 17,983 U.S. patients waiting for a liver, 1,317 died. The average waiting period for an 18- to 34-year-old needing a lung or a liver transplant in 1997 was 800 days or 273 days, respectively.

Advocates of allowing people to sell their own body parts argue that it would save roughly 6,000 lives a year. In addition, they argue that artificial legs, hips, joints, and hearts are sold, so why not live organs?

Suppose you signed a legal document stating that upon your death you would like to make your organs available for sale. Perhaps you could specify that the proceeds from the sale could go to a loved one, a charity, or a university. We would expect to see an upward-sloping supply curve for human organs—at higher prices, we would expect more people to allow their organs to be sold at death. In Exhibit 4, we present a hypothetical market where S is upward sloping, the market price rises to P_E and the quantity exchanged increases from Q_S to Q_E. In short, the price and quantity would rise, and the shortage would disappear. However, there are several problems with the sale of human organs. First, there may be an asymmetric information problem. When people receive money for their organs, they might hide "adverse" information about their health history. For example, a blood donor might not reveal that he or she has hepatitis, AIDS, or some other virus. However, screening may resolve this problem. After all, there is a market for blood so the problem could not be insurmountable. However, it may be more difficult to detect good kidneys, livers, and hearts than blood. Second, there is the equity issue of allocating human organs on the basis of willingness to pay. But you might ask why are artificial limbs, hearts, and other body parts for sale but kidneys are not? Third, it is also likely to increase health care spending as patients and insurance companies would have to pay a higher price. And increasing demand will only send that price even higher in the future.

Advocates of allowing the sale of human organs argue that the current system is just sending the market underground. Over $1 billion of body parts are purportedly exchanged in the global market. In November 2006, after years of denial, China acknowledged that most of the human organs used in China are taken from executed prisoners. According to rules adopted in 1984, a prisoner's organs can be taken if the relatives of the prisoner are unwilling to take the corpse or if the prisoner or his family agrees to the organ donation. Many of the recipients are foreigners (including those from the United States) who come to China, and pay a hefty sum to avoid the long wait in their home countries for organs.

Health Saving Account (HSA)

The biggest health care problems include the roughly 40 million people who are uninsured and the absence of incentives to cut down on health spending.

Some policies could make health care better. One possibility is a combination of a high-deductible health

global WATCH — PAYING WORKERS TO GO ABROAD FOR HEALTH CARE

With an estimated 750,000 Americans traveling abroad for in-patient and out-patient procedures, insurance plans are beginning to cover treatment overseas. To make travel abroad even more attractive, these plans often throw in a bonus for employees if they agree to undergo elective surgeries abroad, or they offer to split the cost savings between the employer and worker, says the *Wall Street Journal*.

Among the employers jumping on the medical tourism bandwagon are:

❋ Maine-based supermarket chain Hannaford Bros. Co., which began allowing its 18,000 insured workers and dependents to travel to an internationally accredited hospital in Singapore for surgical hip and knee replacements; the company's self-funded plan, administered by Aetna Inc., waives out-of-pocket expenses, saving patients up to $3,000, and reimburses all travel costs.

❋ Corporate Synergies Group Inc., which advises companies on worker benefits, says at least a dozen of its clients with 250 to 2,000 employees are considering adding medical tourism programs in the next few years.

❋ Blue Cross & Blue Shield of South Carolina created a subsidiary for medical tourism called Companion Global Healthcare Inc., which maintains a network of international doctors and hospitals.

❋ Some individual policies offer medical tourism options; however, labor unions have opposed some

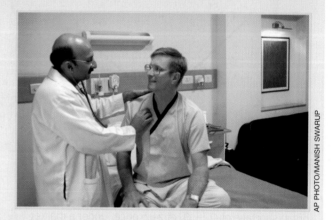

AP PHOTO/MANISH SWARUP

efforts to set up medical tourism plans and Medicare generally doesn't cover treatments abroad.

While medical tourism isn't expected to be a solution to the country's soaring health-care costs, the practice is intended to produce savings for insurers, employers and workers. Open-heart surgery, which can cost roughly $100,000 in the United States, can be done at an internationally accredited hospital in India for just $8,500, for instance.

Proponents note that many international hospitals are staffed with American and European-trained physicians. Many facilities also are accredited by an affiliate of the Joint Commission, a nonprofit group that is the main accrediting body for U.S. hospitals.

SOURCE: M. P. McQueen, "Paying Workers to Go Abroad for Health Care," *Wall Street Journal*, September 30, 2008.

---

care policy and a *health saving account (HSA)* that could replace a traditional health care policy. Health saving accounts allow people to set aside tax-free dollars to pay for medical expenses. People with high health insurance annual deductibles of $1,050 or $2,100 per family would be able to open up an HSA account. Employers can also offer a high-deductible plan that will cover medical expenses once the employee hits the deductible of $1,050 for an individual or $2,100 for a family. Once the employees reach their deductible, they have a copayment. The good news is that the premium is lower.

The HSA account can be used to help pay the high deductible prior to the point when benefits kick in.

Money in the tax-free account must be used for medical expenses or a penalty fee is assessed, plus taxes.

This type of a program is not a panacea, but could help control health care costs because it changes the incentive structure. In short, people will have to spend more of their own money. The plan would require that consumers cover more routine costs out of pocket, and their insurance coverage would primarily protect them against catastrophic expenses. Consequently, health consumers would be more cost conscious and curtail their use of health services.

This system would create incentives for employees to spend less on frivolous medical expenses. As health economist Victor Fuchs states, "When people are

Use what you've LEARNED — HEALTH CARE RATIONING

Q As technological advances continue at a rapid pace, the resulting increased medical costs have forced policymakers to scramble to figure out how to pay for new therapies. How can scarce resources be allocated while equity considerations remain balanced?

A In 1989, the government of the state of Oregon proposed a health care scheme that highlighted the nature of scarcity in the health care market and the rationing problem. The Oregon Basic Health Services Act provided Medicaid health care coverage for all the poorest citizens (nearly doubling the number eligible) but aimed to limit covered services to those offering the greatest cost-benefit ratio. The Oregon plan was an attempt to carefully ration health care by weighing social benefits and costs. The Oregon Health Services Commission produced a list of health services ranked according to relative importance, based on extensive research, surveys, and public hearings. Ailments with the highest priority were acute but potentially fatal; ailments for which treatment would likely result in full recovery. Oregon estimated that it had enough funding to cover the top 587 ailments on the list. Those unfortunate enough to suffer from ailment 588 or below (including congenital birth defects) were to be denied funding for treatment by the state. Although ultimately a less controversial state health plan was adopted, the Oregon plan raised many ethical concerns and brought to the forefront of debate the necessity of making choices when faced with scarcity, even when it comes to medical care.

spending their own money they will tend to use less health care than if somebody else is paying for it."

Critics claim that higher deductibles may lead people to postpone critically needed care or preventive care that could become even more costly if not addressed. Critics also contend that high deductibles and copayments will lead employers to shift health care costs to workers. However, proponents believe that the savings from this policy may be passed on in higher wages to employees. Others, such as MIT professor Jonathan Gruber, believe that the best strategy is through large copayments, not high deductibles, because this strategy reduces the risk of forgoing important health care yet at the same time provides an incentive to be vigilant about costs.

Another benefit of HSAs is that they are portable. Many people lose their company-based health coverage when they become unemployed, which reduces job turnover. This insurance factor results in a less flexible and efficient labor market. In a dynamic economy, when a good job opens up, some qualified applicants might be reluctant to apply because their insurance is not portable.

The Debate over Health Care Reform

A t the time of this writing, policy makers, government officials and their constituents are debating health care reform. Most agree that something must be done but they disagree on the best way to control the escalating health costs.

The Congressional Budget Office estimates that the current House health care proposal will require government medical insurance subsidies of $773 billion from 2013–2019.

On the President's official web page it states that his plan, "will not restrict you to just national health care or private health care. Obama's plan is to make both of these options accessible to you. . . . Health care available to everyone, same coverage as members of congress and no American will be turned down because of their pre-existing conditions. Obama also plans to make premiums, deductibles and co-pays more affordable. . . . You can also choose to purchase private insurance. There will be new rules and practices set forth to help control the private sector. . . . If an employer does not help their employees out with a helpful contribution towards health coverage, they will have to contribute a percentage of their payroll towards the national plan. Some smaller business may be exempt from this part of the plan. Obama's plan will also protect you if you switch jobs. If you switch jobs you will not have to worry about jeopardizing your existing coverage.

Obama's plan will protect private insurers from catastrophic health expenditures that have been the cause of high medical expenses in recent years. The plan would help out these insurers by reimbursing them for a portion of the catastrophic costs that come about, if they promise to reduce the cost of premiums. . . . In order to keep

IT'S NOT YOUR GRANDPA'S MORAL HAZARD ANYMORE
The Problem Goes Corporate

—BY AUSTAN GOOLSBEE

To the despair of almost every informed economist, by New Year's Day, Medicare recipients who want coverage for 2006 will have chosen a prescription drug plan. Even the former chairman of the president's Council of Economic Advisers, R. Glenn Hubbard, says that the costs of the prescription drug benefit are unsustainable in the long term, and perhaps even in the next five years. Meanwhile, a health-care program that many economists love, the Flexible Savings Account, is also approaching a New Year's deadline. By Jan. 1, anyone with an FSA—a tax-free spending account for health care—must spend the money he or she has accumulated in that account or else lose it.

Most economists feel differently about the Medicare drug benefit and FSAs (called Health Savings Accounts in another form) because the two policies represent opposing views of the health market. The FSAs were designed to address what economists call the moral-hazard problem—that if you subsidize people's expenses for something, they will increase the amount they want to spend on it. To contain costs in health care, economists generally argue, we should raise the direct costs that people pay for medicine so they'll feel that they are spending their own money and have more incentive to be frugal. The Medicare benefit, on the other hand, tends to ignore economics and instead embodies a political idea about the social compact: that as a society we should subsidize the expenses of the elderly. A natural fear of that benefit is that the more drugs people can get for free, the more drugs they will take—regardless of how much they really need them—and as a result, spending will spiral out of control. In other words, FSAs were meant to solve the problems created by programs like the Medicare drug benefit.

While the budget analysts panic, though, health economists have begun to disagree over how important moral hazard really is in influencing people's decisions about when to go to the doctor. Older surveys, like the RAND Health Insurance Experiment in the 1970s and 1980s, suggested that patients who don't pay out-of-pocket expenses sought care much more frequently than patients who have to

make co-payments—but alas were not any healthier despite the added expense. Those studies have greatly influenced experts' opinions about the merits of big subsidies like the new Medicare benefit. Some newer studies, however, have downgraded the importance of moral hazard for the choices that individual patients make. A good example is a study by David Grabowski at Harvard and Jon Gruber at MIT. The two economists found that the Medicaid payment rates had no impact on the share of people who went into nursing homes. That means there was no evidence of a moral-hazard problem in this massive segment of the health-care market (it accounted for 7 percent of all health-care spending in the United States in 2000). The traditional economics view would hold that if patient choices aren't driven by more hazard, then we might not have to worry that subsidies like the Medicare drug benefit will impose huge costs.

Unfortunately, the moral-hazard problem isn't gone. It has merely morphed into something more pernicious. The last decade has seen a dramatic consolidation of ownership in much of the health-care industry. Increasingly, it is the few companies left standing, rather than the patients, that are the source of the rapid escalation of health-care costs. With regard to the Medicare prescription drug benefit, the new fear isn't that costs will skyrocket as grandpa goes on a Lipitor buying spree. It's that Medicare spending will skyrocket because Pfizer jacks up Lipitor's price. The moral-hazard problem is more and more about corporations rather than individuals.

The evidence shows that companies are particularly likely to raise prices when the government is footing the bill. Economists Mark Duggan at the University of Maryland and Fiona Scott Morton at Yale studied the prices of the top 200 drugs in the United States from 1997 to 2002. They found that drug makers gamed the government procurement rules that forbid companies from billing Medicaid more for a drug than they bill private consumers. When private-sector demand for a drug is small compared with the demand of Medicaid patients (as is the case, for example, with antipsychotics), drug companies massively inflate the price of the drug for private buyers. Sure, they lose some business from

IT'S NOT YOUR GRANDPA'S MORAL HAZARD ANYMORE
The Problem Goes Corporate (cont.)

that part of the market. But they more than make up for that loss by being able to bill the government at a vastly higher price for the medical patients. Similarly, as the *Wall Street Journal* reported last week, some drug makers are donating money to charities that help patients make their co-pays for expensive drugs. The donations help ensure that the patients will be able to keep taking the drugs—and also keep the official prices high when the bill goes out to insurance companies.

As the moral-hazard problem for medical expenses becomes a corporate rather than individual matter, the solution that economists currently favor—Flexible Savings Accounts—will fail to rein in costs. The FSAs won't fix things because they change the incentives of individuals, not companies. Indeed, as more people get FSAs, we may very well see the companies raise prices even further to capture the tax-free savings in people's accounts. That would be

exactly analogous to what has happened with "529" college savings programs. In 2001, Congress passed a tax break for college savings accounts. As I wrote three years ago, the plans were "supposed to be an enormous federal tax subsidy for education." But the small number of financial firms that are approved to manage the 529 accounts have basically captured that subsidy by raising their investment fees to levels well above those in the regular investment market.

So, as Jan. 1 approaches, we should certainly worry about the potential escalation in drug spending from the new Medicare benefit. But don't think the problem can be solved by forcing Medicare recipients to pay into Flexible Savings Accounts. It's not your grandpa's moral hazard anymore.

SOURCE: Austan Goolsbee is an economics professor at the University of Chicago Graduate School of Business and a senior research fellow at the American Bar Foundation.

our people healthy and provide more efficient treatment we need to promote smart preventative care, like cancer screenings and better nutrition, and make critical investments in electronic health records, technology that can reduce errors while ensuring privacy and saving lives."

Skeptics of a government run health plan want to know if it will have access to taxpayer dollars. Private plans cover expenses with their premiums; shouldn't the government's plan do the same? If it ran into difficulty, would it receive help, like government-sponsored mortgage companies Freddy Mac and Fannie Mae? Further, subsidies to the government plan would not just insure those without previous insurance coverage; it could induce many people to switch from their

private insurance to capture the benefits. In addition, critics point to the history of government programs such as Medicaid, Medicare and Social Security, whose multi-trillion dollar unfunded liabilities are a major reason for current government financial problems. Gregory Mankiw of Harvard University writes, "the health care of the future won't come cheap, but a public option won't make it better."

Recall that living in a world of scarcity requires giving up something to get something else. In order to get more or better health care, we have to sacrifice other goods and services we value. Health care is not free. So the question is whether we value the additional health care more than what we have to give up to obtain it.

SECTION CHECK

1. Factors contributing to the rapid rise in health care costs in recent decades include rising national income, more extensive health insurance coverage, and an aging population.

2. Unlike most other markets, consumers in the health care market often pay only a small fraction of health care costs because of insurance coverage. Insurance essentially lowers the price of care, leading consumers to increase utilization of medical services.

3. Ill consumers are more likely to purchase health insurance than are healthy individuals. Insured individuals may be less likely to take preventive measures against illness. These are problems faced by insurance companies known as adverse selection and moral hazard, respectively.

(continued)

4. Health care markets are imperfectly competitive for several reasons: barriers to entry, economies of scale, collusion among sellers, and advertising restrictions.

5. Health Saving Accounts (HSA) allow people to set aside tax-free dollars to pay for medical expenses.

---

1. Evaluate the following statement: "People are concerned with safety first. Therefore, automobile insurance is unlikely to affect the care with which people drive."

2. What do you think happens to health insurance premiums as a person ages? Why?

3. Why does co-insurance increase the quantity of medical care demanded by a consumer? Why does it increase the demand faced by a physician?

4. If it became easier to sue your doctor, what do you think would happen to the supply and demand curves for medical care? Why? What would happen to the price of medical care?

5. Suppose physicians charge patients $200 per office visit. What is the marginal cost of a physician consultation to a patient who pays no deductible but 20 percent co-insurance? To a patient who pays no deductible but a $10 fee per office visit? Which insurance alternative is likely to exhibit the highest patient utilization of physician services, other things equal?

6. It is often argued that lawyers create demand for more lawyers by filing lawsuits. How do suppliers create their own demand in the medical care market?

Interactive Chapter Summary

Fill in the blanks:

1. Considerations of _____ and _____ cannot be disentangled from decisions about health care provision and distributions.

2. The United States spends approximately _____ percent of GDP on health care, which is _____ than any other industrialized nation.

3. The demand for health care and health care spending have both _____ significantly over the past several decades.

4. Investment in health care would be likely to _____ a society's production possibilities curve over time.

5. The demand for medical care increased because of changes in _____, _____, and _____.

6. When incomes rise, the demand for health care _____, because health care is a _____ good.

7. The demand curve for most health care is relatively _____ with respect to price.

8. Insurance _____ the price of health care to consumers and _____ the quantity of health care services demanded.

9. _____ exists in health care when insurance makes a person more likely to engage in more risky behavior and less likely to take preventative measures against illness.

10. Third-party payers attempt to reduce moral hazard problems with _____ and _____.

11. Asymmetric information, where patients know more about their health status than insurers, leads to the problem of _____.

12. Health insurers try to reduce _____ problems by insuring entire groups.

13. The chronically ill are _____ likely to demand insurance than people in good health.

14. The _____ cause a disproportionate share of health care expenses.

15. The supply of health care has _____ slowly since 1960.

16. Primary care physicians act as _____ to health care.

17. Escalating health care costs have led to a greater emphasis on _____ containment.

18. The interaction of _____ advances and _____ significantly increased the demand for medical care.

19. Health care markets are imperfectly competitive because of legal and administrative barriers to _____, economies of _____, _____, and restrictions on _____.

20. Compulsory _____ of physicians limits entry into the health care market.

21. In countries where medical care prices are controlled and health care is rationed, we would expect _____ of medical care.

22. With health savings accounts, people would have to pay _____ of their own money for health care, making them _____ cost conscious.

23. Because health savings accounts are portable, unlike most employer-provided health insurance, they would _____ flexibility in the job market.

Answers: 1. ethics; equity 2. 16; greater 3. increased 4. increase 5. income; insurance coverage; demographics 6. rises; normal 7. inelastic 8. lowers; increases 9. Moral hazard 10. deductibles; copayments 11. adverse selection 12. adverse selection 13. more 14. elderly 15. increased 16. gatekeepers 17. cost 18. technological; health insurance 19. entry; scale; collusion; advertising 20. licensing 21. shortages 22. more 23. increase

Key Terms and Concepts

indemnity coverage 545

health maintenance organization (HMO) 545

preferred provider organization (PPO) 545

Section Check Answers

19.1 The Rising Cost of Health Care

1. **How is investment in health care like investments in human and physical capital?**
   Improvements in medical care can improve worker productivity, reduce absenteeism, and extend the average number of years that a worker participates in the workforce.

2. **Who pays for most of the health care?**
   Nearly 80 percent of the health care spending is financed by insurance. Private insurance accounts for 36 percent of the funding. Public insurance (Medicare, Medicaid, and Other Public—like workers' compensation, veterans, school health, and state and local hospitals) account for 44 percent of health care spending.

3. **Where are most of the health care dollars spent?**
   Roughly 30 percent of health care dollars is spent on hospitals. Another 21 percent is spent on physician services, while 24 percent is spent on services such as dental services, home care, and eye care.

4. **Why is it possible that some of the increases in health care costs may be a measurement problem?**
   The price of health care over the last couple of decades may not adequately take into account the vast improvements in the quality of health care.

19.2 The Health Care Market

1. **Evaluate the following statement: "People are concerned with safety first. Therefore, automobile insurance is unlikely to affect the care with which people drive."**
   The statement implies that when it comes to safety, the law of demand does not apply. However, safety, as with other goods, involves trade-offs. This statement assumes that people's safety-related behavior is not affected, even at the margin, by the costs to them of an accident. In fact, we would expect people to drive less safely when the cost to them of doing so is lower—the moral hazard problem.

2. **What do you think happens to health insurance premiums as a person ages? Why?**
   The elderly consume a disproportionate share of health care services. Since health insurance premiums are determined by the expected costs of the care provided to members of a group, health insurance premiums increase as a person ages.

3. **Why does co-insurance increase the quantity of medical care demanded by a consumer? Why does it increase the demand faced by a physician?**
   Co-insurance lowers the cost to a patient of physician services for a given market price, increasing the quantity of physician services they demand (moving

them down along their demand curve for physician services). However, that increases the quantity of physician services demanded at any given market price, increasing the demand as seen by physicians.

4. **If it became easier to sue your doctor, what do you think would happen to the supply and demand curves for medical care? Why? What would happen to the price of medical care?**

If it became easier to sue your doctor, the demand curve for medical care would increase, as the benefits of seeing him increase (services otherwise not provided may be provided as a result) and/or the costs fall (some of the costs to patients could be reduced via lawsuits or the threat of lawsuits). However, it would increase the cost to doctors of providing medical care, decreasing the supply curve of medical care. Both of these effects would tend to increase the price of medical care.

5. **Suppose physicians charge patients $200 per office visit. What is the marginal cost of a physician consultation to a patient who pays no deductible but 20 percent co-insurance?**

To a patient who pays no deductible but a $10 fee per office visit? Which insurance alternative is likely to exhibit the highest patient utilization of physician services, other things equal?

The first patient bears a marginal cost of $40 per visit— 20 percent of $200. The second patient bears a marginal cost of $10 per visit—their fee. The second alternative is likely to exhibit the highest patient utilization of physician services, other things equal, because the marginal cost to the patient is lower, increasing the quantity of physician services that will be demanded.

6. **It is often argued that lawyers create demand for more lawyers by filing lawsuits. How do suppliers create their own demand in the medical care market?**

Physicians, particularly primary care physicians, act as gatekeepers, controlling access to prescription drug, hospital, surgical, and other treatments, inducing demand for additional medical services. Especially where physicians are paid on a fee-for-service basis, incentives exist for doctors to err on the side of recommending too many services.

True or False:

1. The United States spends a larger fraction of national income on health care than any other country.

2. Investment in health care, like investment in human and physical capital, can shift a country's production possibilities curve outward over time.

3. If the CPI does not adequately adjust for the increasing quality of medical care, it will result in overestimating increases in the cost of health care.

4. The quality of medical care demanded is quite sensitive to its price.

5. The majority of Americans do not have some kind of medical insurance.

6. Private insurance and public health care expenditures each account for a larger proportion of health care spending than that by consumers paid out of pocket.

7. Insurance coverage is likely to increase the total expenditures on health care from all sources.

8. The chronically ill are more likely to demand insurance than healthy people, because of adverse selection.

9. The chronically ill are more likely to demand insurance than healthy people, because of moral hazard.

10. Physical exams are one way insurers try to reduce their adverse selection risks from health insurance.

11. An increasing share of older people in the population would tend to increase the demand for health care spending.

12. The supply of health care has decreased in recent decades.

13. The demand for health care has increased faster than supply in recent decades.

14. When doctors are paid on a fee-for-service basis, they are more liable to err by recommending too many health care services rather than too few.

15. Because of long-term relationships with primary physicians, people are often reluctant to search for new physicians even when fees increase significantly.

16. The incentives of HMO doctors to provide medical care are greater than those of traditional fee-for-service doctors.

17. Technological advances in providing health care have generally decreased total health care spending in those areas.

18. Insurance lowers the cost to patients of getting "the best possible" care.

19. Economies of scale in health care can limit the number of health care providers in an area.

20. Far more Canadian doctors migrate to the United States than the number of American doctors migrating to Canada.

21. Price controls on medical care cause surpluses of health care.

22. Health savings accounts allow people to set aside tax-free dollars to pay for medical care.

23. Traditional insurance, unlike health savings accounts, is portable, so that workers can take it with them when they change jobs.

24. The demand for health care is thought to be highly elastic.

25. Only about 5 million people in the United States have no health insurance.

Multiple Choice:

1. Investing in health care can
   a. improve worker productivity.
   b. reduce the number of missed workdays.
   c. extend people's working lives.
   d. shift a society's production possibilities curve outward over time.
   e. do all of the above.

2. The largest proportion of health care expenditures comes from which of the following sources?
   a. private insurance funds
   b. public health care expenditures
   c. out-of-pocket expenditures from consumers
   d. emergency room care

3. The demand for health care has increased in recent decades due to
   a. increased income.
   b. increased levels of insurance coverage.
   c. an aging population.
   d. all of the above.

4. Health insurance tends to
   a. reduce the price of health care services to consumers.
   b. increase the quantity of health care services demanded.
   c. increase the total expenditures on health care.
   d. do all of the above.

5. A person covered by more generous health insurance, other things equal, would be
   a. more likely to smoke cigarettes.
   b. more likely to eat a healthy diet.
   c. more likely to exercise regularly.
   d. more likely to do all of the above.

6. Health insurers attempt to reduce the risk from adverse selection by
   a. limiting periods of open enrollment in health care plans.
   b. requiring physical exams.
   c. ensuring large groups.
   d. doing all of the above.

7. Reasons for restricted competition in the health care market do not include
   a. compulsory licensing, which restricts entry into the health care market.
   b. economies of scale in the provision of certain health care services.
   c. collusion among sellers.
   d. the high cost of advertising health care products.

8. Which of the following is not true of health care expenditures over the past few decades?
   a. The share paid for by private insurance companies has fallen.
   b. The share paid for by health care consumers out of pocket has fallen.
   c. The share of health care expenditures spent on the elderly has risen.
   d. Total expenditures on health care from all sources have risen.

9. In the decades following the passage of Medicare and Medicaid, which of the following has not risen?
   a. the share of expenditures on health care in proportion to the economy
   b. the prices of health care services relative to the prices of other goods and services
   c. the share of health care expenditures financed by consumers out of pocket
   d. the share of health care expenditures that are from third-party payers

10. Growth in payments for health care services that come from third-party payers has not tended to be accompanied by
    a. increased incentives for consumers to demand "the best" health care providers.
    b. increased incentives for suppliers to find ways to provide health care at low prices.
    c. decreased sensitivity of health care consumers to the prices of health care services.
    d. increases in the level of medical technology.

11. Given current U.S. health care policy, the growth in the proportion of the population that is elderly will tend to _____ health care demand and _____ the share of health care services financed by third parties.
    a. increase; increase
    b. increase; decrease
    c. decrease; increase
    d. decrease; decrease

12. Which of the following would assist in controlling the growth of future health care expenditures?
    a. an increase in the share of the population that has private health insurance with low copayments
    b. expanding Medicare to include discounts for drugs in the program
    c. an increase in the share of health care paid for by consumers through health savings accounts
    d. a decrease in copayments for the elderly under Medicare

13. Special accounts that people pay into to be used for medical expenses are called
    a. comprehensive insurance plans.
    b. national health insurance plans.
    c. health savings accounts.
    d. health maintenance organizations.

14. Advantages of health savings accounts from an efficiency standpoint include
    a. guaranteeing that no one will every be forced to pay for another medical bill.
    b. giving medical care consumers substantial incentives to economize on their expenditures.
    c. requiring employers to pay a larger fraction of their employees' health care bills.
    d. increasing the flexibility of the labor market by allowing employees to take the accounts with them when they change jobs.
    e. both b and d.

15. _____ spends more money on health care per person than any other industrialized nation.
    a. Canada
    b. The United States
    c. Sweden
    d. France
    e. Germany

16. Spending on health care in the United States over the last several decades has
    a. increased significantly.
    b. decreased significantly.
    c. remained steady.
    d. increased slightly.
    e. decreased slightly.

17. Health care
    a. can be provided to everyone without requiring sacrifices.
    b. improves the productivity of workers.
    c. can extend the number of years a person is able to participate in the labor force.
    d. is characterized by all of the above.
    e. is characterized by b and c only.

18. Over the last several decades, the price of medical care has _____, while the utilization of health care services has _____.
    a. increased; increased
    b. increased; decreased
    c. decreased; decreased
    d. decreased; increased

19. Evidence suggests that the demand for health care
    a. is relatively elastic.
    b. is relatively inelastic.
    c. has decreased over the last decade.
    d. is characterized by both a and b.
    e. is characterized by both b and c.

20. Which of the following statements about health insurance in the United States is true?
    a. Most health insurance policies in the United States are sponsored by the government.
    b. Most health insurance policies in the United States are sponsored through employers.
    c. Over 80 million Americans have no health insurance.
    d. Only 60 percent of the U.S. population is covered by some kind of medical insurance policy.
    e. Both c and d are correct.

21. The safety net in the U.S. health care system is that
    a. anyone without private insurance coverage is automatically covered by Medicaid.
    b. all employers are required to offer employees basic health insurance coverage.
    c. many of the uninsured are able to receive care, for which the cost is often shifted to other health care payers.
    d. physicians are required to provide free services in public clinics to low-income patients in order to renew their medical licenses.

22. Insurance
    a. increases the price of health care to patients and decreases the quantity of services demanded.
    b. decreases the price of health care to patients and decreases the quantity of services demanded.
    c. increases the price of health care to patients and increases the quantity of services demanded.
    d. decreases the price of health care to patients and increases the quantity of services demanded.

23. When insurance increases the likelihood that an individual will engage in risky behavior, it is known as
    a. moral hazard.
    b. adverse selection.
    c. risk selection.
    d. the lemon problem.
    e. both b and d.

24. To reduce the problem of moral hazard, health insurance companies could
    a. decrease required deductible payments.
    b. increase required deductible payments.
    c. increase required copayments.
    d. do both b and c.

25. Adverse selection
    a. arises in situations where there is asymmetric information.
    b. arises because the unhealthy are more likely to purchase health insurance than are the healthy.
    c. problems can be reduced by insuring entire employee groups, rather than individual applicants.
    d. is characterized by all of the above.

26. Health insurers can reduce adverse selection problems by
    a. insuring entire groups.
    b. requiring physical exams as a condition of purchase.
    c. limiting the period of open enrollment in health insurance.
    d. doing all of the above.

27. Since 1960 the elderly proportion of the population has _____ and in the next two decades is expected to _____.
    a. increased; decrease
    b. increased; increase
    c. decreased; decrease
    d. decreased; increase

28. With traditional indemnity insurance coverage,
    a. patients must choose physicians from a limited network.
    b. patients can freely choose physicians.
    c. patients typically pay nothing out of pocket for medical care.
    d. both a and c are correct.
    e. both b and c are correct.

29. Physicians are least likely to limit the utilization of health care services if
    a. they are paid an annual salary for their services.
    b. they are paid on a fee-for-service basis.
    c. they are restricted to choosing treatment options on an approved list.
    d. they are required to contain health care costs as a condition of membership in a physicians' network.

30. Technological advances in medical care
    a. always lead to reductions in the overall cost of treating a disease.
    b. always lead to increases in the overall cost of treating a disease.
    c. can either increase or decrease the overall cost of treating a disease.
    d. decrease the supply of health care.

31. Technological advances in medical care
    a. increase the supply of health care.
    b. increase the demand for health care, since the quality of care increases.
    c. can either increase or decrease the overall cost of treating a disease.
    d. are characterized by all of the above.

32. The supply of health care services is restricted by
    a. the compulsory licensing of physicians.
    b. limitations on hospital privileges of physicians.
    c. a reduction in the wages of health care employees.
    d. all of the above.
    e. only a and b.

33. Natural monopolies may arise in health care
    a. when the government grants exclusive licenses for hospitals to operate in a local area.
    b. when cities and towns are sufficiently small that they are unable to support a large number of hospitals.
    c. when a health care provider holds crucial patents over new medical technologies.
    d. in metropolitan areas with large populations.

34. It has been shown that in states where restrictions are placed on the advertising of eyeglasses
    a. price competition between eyeglass manufacturers increases.
    b. consumers pay, on average, lower prices.
    c. consumers pay, on average, higher prices.
    d. the prices of eyeglasses are unaffected.
    e. both a and b occur.

35. When the price of health care is controlled,
    a. shortages are likely to result.
    b. it may be necessary to ration health care services.
    c. patients may die while waiting for treatment.
    d. all of the above may occur.

Problems:

1. Why would calling health care a basic "human right" make it difficult to effectively analyze health care?

2. How can health care expenditures be viewed as similar to other investments in capital equipment and education (human capital)?

3. Why would the percentage that health care consumers pay out of pocket be an important determinant of how much care they receive?

4. Why would the welfare cost of insurance be smaller, the more inelastic the demand for that type of health care?

5. How does an insurance company inviting voluntary participation in a plan face an adverse selection problem?

6. How can better care for potentially fatal diseases sharply increase the cost of health care?

7. Are the chronically ill more likely to demand health insurance because of moral hazard or adverse selection?

8. Do health care innovations raise or lower the overall cost of health care?

9. If the selling of kidneys were legalized, predict the impact on the market for organ transplants using supply and demand analysis. Why might the quantity supplied increase?

10. Who is most likely to purchase a kidney? Who is most likely to sell a kidney? Would either party be harmed?

11. Decisions as to the allocation of human organs for transplant are based on characteristics such as "blood type, weight, and age; urgency of need; and length of time on the waiting list" (quoted from the Transplant Resource Center of Maryland, http://www.mdtransplant.org/topicsa2.htm). Suppose you were on a transplant committee that was permitted to consider other factors. Do you think that the life of a person who is beloved by many family members and friends should be given greater weight than a person with few friends? Should the chief executive officer of a major corporation be given preferential treatment over someone who is a cook at McDonald's? How about Mickey Mantle, a famous baseball player who battled alcoholism? Do these queries fall into the realm of normative or positive economic analysis?

12. Is it inefficient that the United States spends a larger fraction of income on health care than the fraction spent by other countries?

13. How do higher deductibles act to reduce moral hazard problems, especially for small medical expenses?

14. Why do both adverse selection and moral hazard mean that "lunch insurance," which would pay for lunch if you choose to eat it, is never likely to be a commercial success?

15. How does insuring all the workers at a given firm tend to reduce adverse selection problems? How does requiring physical exams have a similar effect?

16. Why does health insurance increase demand for the highest quality of care?

17. If genetic testing becomes widely practiced, is there an economic reason to fear the discovery of a genetic predisposition toward a serious illness?

PART **6** THE GLOBAL ECONOMY

20 International Trade

Economics is largely about exchange. But up to this point we have focused on trade between individuals within the domestic economy. In this chapter, we extend our coverage to international trade.

Why do countries trade? Hong Kong has no oil—how are they going to get it? What is comparative advantage? Bananas could be grown in the most tropical parts of the United States or in expensive greenhouses, but wouldn't it be easier to import bananas from Honduras?

Stop for a moment and imagine a world without international trade. Chocolate is derived from cocoa beans that are imported from South America and Africa. There are imported cars from Germany and Japan, shoes and sweaters from Italy, shirts from India, and watches and clocks from Switzerland. Consumers love trade because it provides us with more choices. It is good for producers, too; and the speed of transportation and communication has opened up world markets. In addition, lower costs are sometimes the result of economies of scale. Free trade gives firms access to large world markets. It also fosters more competition, which helps to keep prices down.

In this chapter, we will study the theoretical reasons for the importance of trade. We will also look at the arguments for and against trade protection. ■

The Growth in World Trade

* What has happened to the volume of international trade over time?
* Who trades with the United States?
* What does the United States export? Import?

Importance of International Trade

In a typical year, about 15 percent of the world's output is traded in international markets. Of course, the importance of the international sector varies enormously from place to place across the world. Some nations are virtually closed economies (no interaction with other economies), with foreign trade equaling only a small proportion (perhaps 5 percent) of total output, while in other countries, trade is much more important. In the last three decades, the sum of U.S. imports and exports has increased from 11 percent of GDP to roughly 30 percent. In addition, incoming and outgoing investments (capital flows) have risen from less than 1 percent to roughly 3 percent of GDP. In Germany, roughly 30 percent of all output produced is

exported, while Ireland and Belgium each export more than 70 percent of GDP.

U.S. exports include capital goods, automobiles, industrial supplies, raw materials, consumer goods, and agricultural products. U.S. imports include crude oil and refined petroleum products, machinery, automobiles, consumer goods, industrial raw materials, food, and beverages.

Trading Partners

In the early history of the United States, international trade largely took place with Europe and with Great Britain in particular. Now the United States trades with a number of countries, the most important of which are Canada, China, Japan, Mexico, Germany, and the United Kingdom as seen in Exhibit 1.

section 20.1
exhibit 1   Major U.S. Trading Partners

Top Trading Partners—Exports of Goods in 2007			Top Trading Partners—Imports of Goods in 2007		
Rank	Country	Percent of Total	Rank	Country	Percent of Total
1	Canada	21.4%	1	China	16.9%
2	Mexico	11.7	2	Canada	15.7
3	China	5.6	3	Mexico	10.6
4	Japan	5.4	4	Japan	7.4
5	United Kingdom	4.3	5	Germany	4.8
6	Germany	4.3			

SOURCE: CIA, *The World Factbook 2009.*

global WATCH

INTERNATIONAL TRADE MAY REDUCE INEQUALITY IN THE UNITED STATES

Conventional wisdom says globalization has increased US income inequality. This column says that is dead wrong, as China and Wal-Mart have increased the purchasing power of the poor more than the rich....

How rich you are depends on two things: how much money you have and how much the goods you buy cost. If your income doubles but the prices of the goods you consume also double, then you are no better off. Unfortunately, the conventional wisdom on US inequality is based on official measures that only look at the first half, the income differential. National statistics ignore the fact that inflation affects people in different income groups unevenly because the rich and poor consume different baskets of goods.

Inflation differentials between the rich and poor dramatically change our view of the evolution of inequality in America. Inflation of the richest 10 percent of American households has been 6 percentage points higher than that of the poorest 10 percent over the period 1994–2005. This means that real inequality in America, if you measure it correctly, has been roughly unchanged. And the reason is just as dramatic as the result. Why has inflation for the poor been lower than that for the rich? In large part it is because of China and Wal-Mart!

Poor families in America spend a larger share of their income on goods whose prices are directly affected by trade—like clothing and food—relative to wealthier families. By contrast, the higher your income, the more you spend on services, which are less subject to competition from abroad. Since 1994 the price of goods in the U.S. has risen much less than the price of services—and, yes, this includes the recent surge in food prices. Paradoxically, focusing only in the last few quarters of high relative food prices misses the fact that the main trend we have observed for decades is exactly the opposite.

This trend can partly be explained by China. In U.S. stores, prices of consumer goods have fallen the most in sectors where Chinese presence has increased the most. Take canned seafood or cotton shirts, for instance. Exports of China to the rest of the world in these categories have increased

© CHRIS HONDROS/GETTY IMAGES

dramatically over this decade. Inflation in these sectors has been negative over the last decade, while in other sectors with no Chinese presence inflation has been over 20 percent. Moreover, as China produces goods of relatively low quality, sectors with strong Chinese presence are disproportionately consumed by the poor.

The expansion of superstores—like Wal-Mart and Target—has also played an important role in accounting for the inflation differentials between rich and poor. Superstores sell the same products as traditional shops at much lower prices. Today the poor do roughly twice as much of their buying of non-durable goods in these stores than the rich. So poor consumers have been the biggest beneficiaries of Wal-Mart coming to town.

What is really worrying is that, *despite* these facts, we have had a backlash against China and Wal-Mart in America.

We need to remind politicians and the public that the gains from trade are broadly shared. Every time the discussion over trade is diverted towards the problems facing specific producers, be they farmers in France or textile workers in the U.S., we miss the central point. Trading allows everyone, and

especially the poor, to buy things that they could not otherwise afford. Without better public understanding of these facts, governments will not only keep supporting policies aimed against China and Wal-Mart but may receive the uninformed support of many consumers who are benefitting from trade.

SOURCE: Vox, July 3, 2008 http://www.voxeu.org.

SECTION CHECK

1. The volume of international trade has increased substantially in the United States over the last 30 years. During that time, exports and imports have grown from 11 percent to 30 percent of GDP.

2. Our single most important trading partner, Canada, accounts for roughly one-fourth of our exports and almost one-fifth of our imports. Trade with Japan, Mexico, China, Germany, the United Kingdom, France, and Taiwan is also particularly important to the United States.

3. U.S. exports include capital goods, automobiles, industrial supplies, raw materials, consumer goods, and agricultural products. U.S. imports include crude oil and refined petroleum products, machinery, automobiles, consumer goods, industrial raw materials, food, and beverages.

---

1. Why is it important to understand the effects of international trade?

2. Why would U.S. producers and consumers be more concerned about Canadian trade restrictions than Swedish trade restrictions?

SECTION
20.2

Comparative Advantage and Gains from Trade

* Does voluntary trade lead to an improvement in economic welfare?
* What is the principle of comparative advantage?
* What benefits are derived from specialization?

Economic Growth and Trade

Using simple logic, we conclude that the very existence of trade suggests that trade is economically beneficial. Our conclusion is true if we assume that people are utility maximizers and are rational, are intelligent, and engage in trade on a voluntary basis. Because almost all trade is voluntary, it would seem that trade occurs because the participants feel that they are better off because of the trade. Both participants in an exchange of goods and services anticipate an improvement in their economic welfare. Sometimes, of course, anticipations are not realized (because the world is uncertain); but the motive behind trade remains an expectation of some enhancement in utility or satisfaction by both parties.

Granted, "trade must be good because people do it" is a rather simplistic explanation. The classical economist David Ricardo is usually given most of the credit for developing the economic theory that more precisely explains how trade can be mutually beneficial to both parties, raising output and income levels in the entire trading area.

> **comparative advantage** occurs when a person or country can produce a good or service at a lower opportunity cost than others

The Principle of Comparative Advantage

Ricardo's theory of international trade centers on the concept of comparative advantage. Persons, regions, or countries can gain by specializing in the production of the good in which they have a comparative advantage. That is, if they can produce a good or service at a lower opportunity cost than others, we say that they have a **comparative advantage** in the production of that good or service. In other words, a country or a region should specialize in producing and selling those items that it can produce at a lower opportunity cost than other regions or countries.

Comparative advantage analysis does not mean that nations or areas that export goods will necessarily be able to produce those goods or services more cheaply than other nations in an absolute sense. What is important is *comparative* advantage, not *absolute* advantage. For example, the United States may be able to produce more cotton cloth per worker than India can, but this capability does not mean that the United States should necessarily sell cotton cloth to India. For a highly productive nation to produce goods in which it is only marginally more productive than other nations, the nation must take resources from the production of other goods in which its productive abilities are markedly superior. As a result, the opportunity costs in India of making cotton cloth may be less than in the United States. With that, both can gain from trade, despite potential absolute advantages for every good in the United States.

Comparative Advantage, Specialization, and the Production Possibilities Curves

Wendy and Calvin live on opposite ends of a small town. Wendy can produce either food or cloth. On a daily basis, she can produce 10 pounds of food, 5 yards of cloth, or any linear combination between the

two goods along her production possibilities curve in Exhibit 1 (to simplify the calculations we have drawn linear production possibilities curves). If Wendy spends the whole day producing food, she can produce 10 pounds. If she spends the whole day producing cloth, she can produce 5 yards. Recall that the production possibilities curve represents the maximum possible combinations of food and cloth she can produce, given her fixed set of resources and technology.

The negatively sloped production possibilities curve means that when she produces one good, with her fixed resources, she gives up the opportunity to produce another good.

What is Wendy's opportunity cost of producing cloth? It is what Wendy gives up in food production for each unit of cloth production, which is 2 pounds of food per yard of cloth. Therefore, her opportunity cost of producing a yard of cloth is 2 pounds of food. What is the opportunity cost of Wendy producing food? If is what she gives up in cloth production for each unit increase

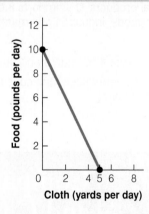

section 20.2
exhibit 1   Wendy's Production Possibilities Curve

$$OC_{CLOTH} = \frac{\text{loss in food}}{\text{gain in cloth}} = \frac{10}{5} = \frac{2 \text{ pounds of food}}{1 \text{ yard of cloth}}$$

$$OC_{FOOD} = \frac{\text{loss in cloth}}{\text{gain in food}} = \frac{5}{10} = \frac{1 \text{ yard in cloth}}{2 \text{ pounds of food}}$$

or

1 yard of cloth costs 2 pounds of food
1 pound of food costs ½ yard of cloth

Wendy can produce either food or cloth along her production possibilities curve. For Wendy, the opportunity cost of producing a yard of cloth is 2 pounds of food; and the opportunity cost of producing a pound of food is ½ yard of cloth.

GREAT ECONOMIC THINKERS

DAVID RICARDO (1772–1823)

© HUTTON ARCHIVE/GETTY IMAGES

David Ricardo was born in London to a wealthy, Jewish immigrant stockbroker, the third of 17 children. His father trained him in the stock brokerage business, which he entered at age 14. At 21, he married a young Quaker woman, leaving the Jewish faith to become a Unitarian. This upset his father, who disowned David. The young Ricardo joined a bank and entered the stock market on his own. He was very successful in this enterprise, making millions of pounds and quickly surpassing the wealth accumulated by his father, with whom he later reconciled. Ricardo retired from the stock exchange business at age 43 and died of an ear infection at 51, leaving behind a large fortune.

Ricardo could accredit much of his success in the stock market to his brilliant ability to predict human nature and public reaction. As a member of the House of Commons, he was also an undaunted advocate of government reform, religious and political freedom, and free trade. A man of firm convictions, he often lobbied for class-leveling policies that conflicted with his personal interests as a landowner and a man of wealth.

In his late 20s, while vacationing in Bath, England, Ricardo picked up a copy of Adam Smith's *The Wealth of Nations* and became interested in economics. It was a few years later that Ricardo, who had no formal education past age 14, improved upon Smith's principle of absolute advantage. Ricardo's ideas, though difficult for many of his fellow politicians to understand, were ingenious.

Smith argued that two countries should engage in trade if one was better at producing one good than the other—absolute advantage. For example, if one country is better at producing hats and the other at producing shoes, the two countries can produce more total output by producing those goods that they can produce best. However, Ricardo demonstrated that even if one country was absolutely more productive than another in making all goods

and services, it would still be mutually beneficial for the two countries to engage in trade, as each had a comparative advantage in one of the goods.

Ricardo argued this point at a time in British history when the wealthy landowners, who had a clutch on parliament, had a virtual monopoly on grain in England in the form of the Corn Laws, passed in 1815. These acts prevented the importation of grain from France, although, as Ricardo argued, France could afford to feed the British for less than it would cost them to feed themselves. Despite Ricardo's argument and the fact that English laborers were spending one-fourth of their income on bread, the Corn Laws persisted until 1846. Ricardo did, however, leave behind a remarkable concept that convinced future economists that free trade is almost always in the best interest of an economy as a whole.

Use what you've LEARNED
COMPARATIVE ADVANTAGE AND ABSOLUTE ADVANTAGE

Q Renee Saunts is a successful artist, who can complete one painting in each 40-hour workweek. Each painting sells for $4,000. As a result of her enormous success, however, Renee is swamped in paperwork. To solve the problem, Renee hires Drake to handle all the bookkeeping and typing associated with buying supplies, answering inquiries from prospective buyers and dealers, writing art galleries, and so forth. Renee pays Drake $300 per week for his work. After a couple of weeks in this arrangement, Renee realizes that she can handle Drake's chores more quickly than Drake does. In fact, she estimates that she is twice as fast as Drake, completing in 20 hours what it takes Drake 40 hours to complete. Should Renee fire Drake?

A Clearly, Renee has an absolute advantage over Drake in both painting and paperwork, because she can do twice as much paperwork in 40 hours as Drake can and Drake can't paint well at all. Still, it would be foolish for Renee to do both jobs. If Renee did her own paperwork, it would take her 20 hours per week, leaving her only 20 hours to paint. Because each watercolor takes 40 hours to paint, Renee's output would fall from one painting per week to one painting per two weeks.

When Drake works for her, Renee's net income is $3,700 per week ($4,000 per painting minus $300 in Drake's wages); when Drake does not work for her, it is only $2,000 per week (one painting every two weeks). Even though Renee is both a better painter and better at Drake's chores than Drake, it pays for her to specialize in painting, in which she has a comparative advantage, and allow Drake to do the paperwork. The opportunity cost to Renee of paperwork is high. For Drake, who lacks skills as a painter, the opportunity costs of doing the paperwork are much less.

in food production = 1 yard of cloth per 2 pounds of food. That is, for each pound of food Wendy produces, she gives up producing ½ yard of cloth.

Calvin, who lives on the other side of town, can also produce food or cloth. On a daily basis, he could produce 3 pounds of food, 4 yards of cloth, or any linear combination between the two along his production possibilities curve in Exhibit 2. When he spends the day producing cloth, he can produce 4 yards. When he spends the day producing food, he can produce 3 pounds. To produce cloth, Calvin must decrease his production of food. What is Calvin's opportunity cost of producing cloth? It is what he gives up in producing food for each unit of cloth production, which is 3 pounds of food per 4 pounds of cloth. Therefore, his opportunity cost of producing cloth is ¾ pound of food. What is Calvin's opportunity cost of producing food? It is what he gives up in cloth production for each unit of food production which is 4 yards of cloth per 3 pounds of food. Therefore, the opportunity cost of producing a pound of food is ⁴⁄₃ yards of cloth per day.

Absolute and Comparative Advantage

Now let's compare Wendy's production possibilities curve to Calvin's production possibilities curve to see

who has an absolute advantage in producing cloth and who has an absolute advantage in producing food. An absolute advantage occurs when one producer can do a task using fewer inputs than the other producer. In Exhibit 3, we see that Wendy is more productive than Calvin at producing food. Along the vertical axis, we can see that if Wendy uses all of her resources to produce food, she can produce 10 pounds of food per day. If Calvin devotes all of his resources to producing food, he can only produce 3 pounds of food per day. We say that Wendy has an absolute advantage over Calvin in the production of food.

Along the horizontal axis in Exhibit 3, we can see that Wendy is also more productive than Calvin at producing cloth. If Wendy devotes all of her resources to producing cloth, she can produce 5 yards of cloth per day. If Calvin devotes all of his resources to producing cloth, he can only produce 4 yards of cloth per day. We say that Wendy also has an absolute advantage over Calvin in the production of cloth. She has an absolute advantage in producing both food and cloth. Therefore, should Wendy produce both food and cloth and Calvin produce nothing? No!

Recall from Chapter 2 that a comparative advantage exists when one person can produce a good at a lower opportunity cost than another person. So who

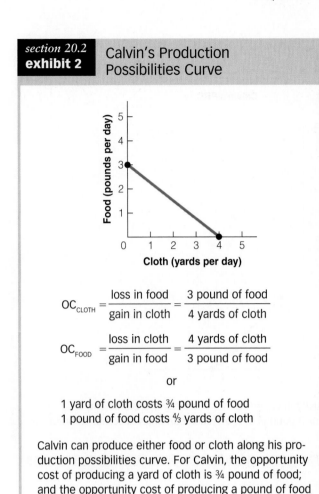

section 20.2 exhibit 2   Calvin's Production Possibilities Curve

$$OC_{CLOTH} = \frac{\text{loss in food}}{\text{gain in cloth}} = \frac{3 \text{ pound of food}}{4 \text{ yards of cloth}}$$

$$OC_{FOOD} = \frac{\text{loss in cloth}}{\text{gain in food}} = \frac{4 \text{ yards of cloth}}{3 \text{ pound of food}}$$

or

1 yard of cloth costs ¾ pound of food
1 pound of food costs 4/3 yards of cloth

Calvin can produce either food or cloth along his production possibilities curve. For Calvin, the opportunity cost of producing a yard of cloth is ¾ pound of food; and the opportunity cost of producing a pound of food is 4/3 yards of cloth.

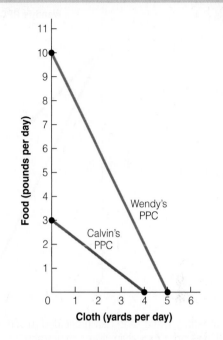

section 20.2 exhibit 3   Absolute and Comparative Advantage

	Cloth (yds/day)	Food (lbs/day)	OC of Cloth	OC of Food
Wendy	5	10	2 lb of food	½ yd of cloth
Calvin	4	3	¾ lbs of food	4/3 yds of cloth

In this case, Wendy has an absolute advantage producing food and cloth. It is easy to see the absolute advantage, because if she devotes all her resources to producing cloth she can produce 10 yards per day, while Calvin could only produce 5 yards. But she also has a comparative advantages because she has a lower opportunity cost of producing cloth, ½ lb of food versus Calvin's ¾ lbs of food.

In addition, if she devotes all her resources to producing food she could produce 5 pounds of food and Calvin could only produce 4 pounds of food.

has the comparative advantage (lowest opportunity cost) in producing food? In this case, Wendy's opportunity cost of producing food is less than Calvin's. Wendy's opportunity cost of producing a pound of food is ½ yard of cloth, whereas Calvin's opportunity cost of producing 1 pound of food is 4/3 yards of cloth. Therefore, Wendy is the more efficient producer of food—she gives up less in cloth when she produces food, compared to Calvin. Remember, comparative advantage is always a relative concept.

Who has the comparative advantage in producing cloth? That is, who can produce cloth at the lowest opportunity cost? That would be Calvin, because he gives up only ¾ pound of food to produce 1 yard of cloth. If Wendy were to produce a yard of cloth, she would have to give up 2 pounds of food. The lowest opportunity cost producer of cloth is Calvin. In other words, to produce one more yard of cloth, Calvin gives up fewer pounds of food than Wendy. Therefore, Calvin is the more efficient producer of cloth—he gives up less

in food when he produces cloth, compared to Wendy. Calvin has a comparative advantage in producing cloth.

Gains from Specialization and Exchange

Suppose Wendy and Calvin meet and decide to specialize in those activities in which they have a comparative advantage. Wendy would specialize in the production of food and Calvin would specialize in the production of

section 20.2	
exhibit 4	The Gains from Specialization and Trade

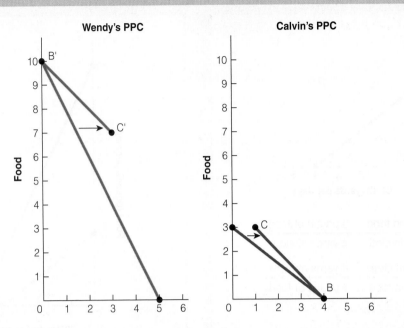

After meeting, Wendy and Calvin decided to specialize in the activity in which each is relatively more efficient; food for Wendy and cloth for Calvin. When they trade 3 pounds of cloth for 3 pounds of food, each can enjoy a combination of food and cloth they could not have produced on their own.

cloth. By specializing, Wendy can produce 10 pounds of food per day (point B' in Exhibit 4) and Calvin can produce 4 yards of cloth per day (point B in Exhibit 4). However, to achieve any of the gains from comparative advantage and specialization, there must be trade.

After specializing in the good in which they have a comparative advantage, suppose Wendy and Calvin agree to trade at the exchange "price" of 1 pound of food for 1 yard of cloth. If Wendy trades 3 pounds of cloth for 3 pounds of food, she can obtain a position along the new production possibilities curve which is beyond her original production possibilities curve, point C in Exhibit 4. Wendy can now have 7 pounds of food and 3 yards of cloth—a combination she could not have obtained without specialization and trade.

Calvin also benefits from specialization and trade. In the trade, he receives 3 pounds of food for 3 yards of cloth and now can enjoy 3 pounds of food and 1 yard of cloth a combination, at point C, he could not have obtained without specialization and trade. In sum, the exchange has allowed both Wendy and Calvin to produce and consume a combination of the two goods beyond what would have been attainable if it were not for specialization and exchange.

Individuals and Nations Gain from Specialization and Trade

Just as Calvin and Wendy benefit from specialization and trade, so do the people of different nations. Because of specialization, according to comparative advantage, both nations can be better off, even if one nation has an absolute advantage in both goods over the other. Furthermore, the greater the difference in opportunity cost between the two trading partners, the greater the benefits from specialization and exchange.

Note that when we say nations trade with nations, we really mean that the people of a nation trade with people of other nations. When China trades clothes to the United States for Boeing 787 jetliners, they both benefit from the exchange, because they are able to obtain them at a lower cost than if they produced those goods themselves. Free trade does not guarantee that each individual will be better off or that everyone will receive the same benefits, but it does mean that collectively, the population of each nation will benefit from the trade. Indeed, unskilled workers in high wage countries may temporarily lose jobs. Recall that when NAFTA was passed, its critics argued that low skilled workers would lose jobs because of U.S. trade with Mexico. However, that does not appear to have happened to any large extent. Instead, consumers have been enjoying lower priced goods because of the trade.

Regional Comparative Advantage

Using a production possibilities curve, we saw how Wendy and Calvin could benefit from specialization and trade. The principle of comparative advantage can be applied to regional markets as well. In fact, trade has evolved in large part because different geographic areas have different resources and therefore different production possibilities. The impact of trade between two areas with differing resources is shown in Exhibit 5. To keep the analysis simple, suppose two trading areas can produce only two commodities, grain and computers. A "trading area" may be a locality, a region, or even a nation, but for our example suppose we think in terms of two hypothetical regions, Grainsville and Techland.

Grainsville and Techland have various potential combinations of grain and computers that they can produce. For each region, the cost of producing more grain is the output of computers that must be forgone, and vice versa. We see in Exhibit 5 that Techland can

section 20.2 **exhibit 5**	Production Possibilities, Techland and Grainsville	

Region	Grain (bushels per day)	Computers (units per day)
Techland	0	100
	10	75
	20	50
	30	25
	40	0
Grainsville	0	30
	6	24
	12	18
	18	12
	24	6
	30	0
Before Specialization		
Techland	10	75
Grainsville	18	12
Total	28	87
After Specialization		
Techland	0	100
Grainsville	30	0
Total	30	100

Use what you've LEARNED   THE SECRET TO WEALTH

Do what you do relatively best. Trade for the rest. In other words, specialize and then trade.

The farmer grows wheat, the baker makes bread, the weaver produces cloth, the tailor sews clothing, the lumberjack harvests wood, the carpenter builds houses. By exchanging the fruits of their labor in the marketplace, they all can enjoy more food, clothing, and shelter than they could if each tried to meet his needs in isolation. . . .

It's a matter of working smarter, not harder.

Societies reaped the benefits of specialization and trade for thousands of years before English economist David Ricardo (1772–1823) finally demonstrated

why it works. His theory of comparative advantage helps explain why the United States exports soybeans to China and imports shoes in return.

Suppose an average American worker can produce 100 bushels of soybeans or five pairs of shoes and a typical Chinese worker can turn out 8 bushels of soybeans or four pairs of shoes. [See Exhibit 6.]

The United States is more productive than China in both industries, but consumers in both countries can still gain from specialization and trade. Shifting a U.S. worker from shoe factory to soybean farm produces a gain of 100 bushels of soybeans at the cost of five pairs of shoes. Shifting two Chinese workers from farm to factory raises shoe output by eight pairs

(continued)

Use what you've LEARNED   THE SECRET TO WEALTH (cont.)

but cuts soybean production by 16 bushels. The net effect is an increase of 84 bushels of soybeans and three pairs of shoes.

Total output of both products reaches a maximum when the United States specializes in soybeans and China in shoes. Through trade, the two countries can divide the added production between themselves, leaving both better off than they were on their own.

In the real world, trade isn't a two-party swap meet. The United States does business with more than 225 other nations—from Albania to Zimbabwe. The dizzying number of potential transactions increases the opportunities to gain from trade.

This potent international division of labor enables America to take advantage of its expertise in such industries as jet-aircraft manufacturing and financial services while other countries exploit their edge in oil production or hand assembly.

Specialization and trade arise out of the profit motive. Except when transaction costs are too high or governments impose barriers, buyers and sellers will find each other. We're not meant to go it alone.

SOURCE: W. Michael Cox and Richard Alm "The Secret to Wealth," 2002 *Annual Report: The Fruits of Free Trade*, Federal Reserve Bank of Dallas.

section 20.2 exhibit 6   The Alchemy of Exchange

	Autarky		Free Trade	
	China	U.S.	China	U.S.
Labor Force	500	100	500	100
Output per worker				
Shoes	4	5	4	5
Soybeans	8	100	8	100
Employment				
Shoes	125	60	500	0
Soybeans	375	40	0	100
Production				
Shoes	500	300	2,000	0
Soybeans	3,000	4,000	0	10,000
Consumption				
Shoes	500	300	1,500	500
Soybeans	3,000	4,000	5,000	5,000
Consumption per person				
Shoes	1	3	3	5
Soybeans	6	40	10	50

Five hundred Chinese workers can each produce four pairs of shoes or 8 bushels of soybeans. One hundred U.S. workers can each produce five pairs or 100 bushels—more productive in both jobs but comparatively more so in farming. Under an autarkic regime—isolated from foreign trade—Chinese workers can afford one pair of shoes each and 6 bushels of soybeans; Americans, three and 40. Trading freely, China will specialize in shoes and America in soybeans, raising world production of shoes from 800 to 2,000 pairs and soybeans from 7,000 to 10,000 bushels. Chinese workers can then afford three pairs of shoes and 10 bushels of soybeans; American workers, five and 50. In this case, the United States trades 10 bushels of soybeans to China for each pair of shoes.

produce more grain (40 bushels) and more computers (100 units) than Grainsville can (30 bushels and 30 units, respectively), perhaps reflecting superior resources (more or better labor, more land, and so on). These numbers mean that Techland has an absolute advantage in both products.

Suppose that, before specialization, Techland chooses to produce 75 computers and 10 bushels of grain per day. Similarly, suppose Grainsville decides to produce 12 computers and 18 bushels of grain. Collectively, then, the two areas are producing 87 computers (75 + 12) and 28 bushels of grain (10 + 18) per day before specialization.

Now, suppose the two nations specialize. Techland decides to specialize in computers and devotes all its resources to making that product. As a result, computer output in Techland rises to 100 units per day, some of which is sold to Grainsville. Grainsville, in turn, devotes all its resources to grain, producing 30 bushels of grain per day and selling some of it to Techland. Together, the two areas are producing more of both grain and computers than before—100 instead of 87 computers and 30 instead of 28 bushels of grain. Both areas could, as a result, have more of both products than before they began specializing and trading.

How can this happen? In Techland, the opportunity cost of producing grain is high—25 computers must be forgone to get 10 more bushels of grain. The cost of one bushel of grain, then, is 2.5 computers (25 divided by 10). In Grainsville, by contrast, the opportunity cost of producing six more units of grain is six units of computers that must be forgone; so the cost of one unit of grain is one unit of computers. In Techland, a unit of grain costs 2.5 computers, while in Grainsville the same amount of grain costs only one computer. Grain is more costly in Techland in terms of the computers forgone than in Grainsville, so Grainsville has the comparative advantage in the production of grain, even though Techland has an absolute advantage in grain.

With respect to computers, an increase in output by 25 units, say from 25 to 50 units, costs 10 bushels of grain forgone in Techland. The cost of one more computer is 0.4 bushel of grain (10 divided by 25). In Grainsville, an increase in computer output of six units, say from 12 to 18, is accompanied by a decrease in grain production by 6 bushels, as resources are converted from grain to computer manufacturing. The cost of one computer is 1 bushel of grain. Computers are more costly (in terms of opportunity cost) in Grainsville and cheaper in Techland, so Techland should specialize in the production of computers.

Thus, by specializing in products in which it has a comparative advantage, an area has the potential of having more goods and services, assuming it trades the additional output for other desirable goods and services that others can produce at a lower opportunity cost. In the scenario presented here, the people in Techland would specialize in computers, and the people in Grainsville would specialize in farming (grain). We can see from this example that specialization increases both the division of labor and the interdependence among groups of people.

SECTION CHECK

1. Voluntary trade occurs because the participants feel that they are better off as a result of the trade.
2. A nation, geographic area, or even a person can gain from trade if the good or service is produced relatively cheaper than anyone else can produce it. That is, an area should specialize in producing and selling those items that it can produce at a lower opportunity cost than others.
3. Through trade and specialization in products in which it has a comparative advantage, a country can enjoy a greater array of goods and services at a lower cost.

---

1. Why do people voluntarily choose to specialize and trade?
2. How could a country have an absolute advantage in producing one good or service without also having a comparative advantage in its production?
3. Why do you think the introduction of the railroad reduced self-sufficiency in the United States?
4. If you can wash the dishes in two-thirds the time it takes your younger sister to wash them, do you have a comparative advantage in washing the dishes with respect to her?

SECTION
20.3 Supply and Demand in International Trade

* What is consumer surplus?
* What is producer surplus?
* Who benefits and who loses when a country becomes an exporter?
* Who benefits and who loses when a country becomes an importer?

The Importance of Trade: Producer and Consumer Surplus

Recall from Chapter 7 that the difference between the most a consumer would be willing to pay for a quantity of a good and what a consumer actually has to pay is called **consumer surplus.** The difference between the lowest price for which a supplier would be willing to supply a quantity of a good or service and the revenues a supplier actually receives for selling it is called **producer surplus.** With the tools of consumer and producer surplus, we can better analyze the impact of trade. Who gains? Who loses? What happens to net welfare?

The demand curve represents the maximum prices that consumers are willing and able to pay for different quantities of a good or service; the supply curve represents the minimum prices suppliers require to be willing to supply different quantities of that good or service. For example, in Exhibit 1, the consumer is willing to pay up to $7 for the first unit of output and the producer would demand at least $1 for producing that unit. However, the equilibrium price is $4, as indicated by the intersection of the supply and demand curves. It is clear that the two would gain from getting together and trading that unit, because the consumer

consumer surplus
the difference between the price a consumer is willing and able to pay for an additional unit of a good and the price the consumer actually pays; for the whole market, it is the sum of all the individual consumer surpluses—the area below the market demand curve and above the market price

producer surplus
the difference between what a producer is paid for a good and the cost of producing that unit of the good; for the market, it is the sum of all the individual sellers' producer surpluses—the area above the market supply curve and below the market price

would receive $3 of consumer surplus ($7 − $4), and the producer would receive $3 of producer surplus ($4 − $1). Both would also benefit from trading the second and third units of output—in fact, from every unit up to the equilibrium output. Once the equilibrium output is reached at the equilibrium price, all the mutually beneficial opportunities from trade between suppliers and demanders will have taken place; the sum of consumer surplus and producer surplus is maximized.

It is important to recognize that the total gain to the economy from trade is the sum of the consumer and the producer surpluses. That is, consumers benefit from additional amounts of consumer surplus, and producers benefit from additional amounts of producer surplus.

section 20.3 exhibit 1 Consumer and Product Surplus

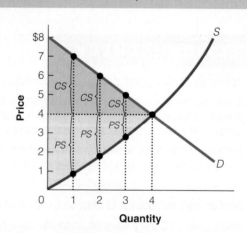

Consumer surplus is the difference between what a consumer has to pay ($4) and what the consumer is willing to pay. For unit 1, consumer surplus is $3 ($7 − $4). Producer surplus is the difference between what a seller receives for selling a good or service ($4) and the price at which the seller is willing to supply that good or service. For unit 1, producer surplus is $3 ($4 − $1).

Free Trade and Exports— Domestic Producers Gain More Than Domestic Consumers Lose

Using the concepts of consumer and producer surplus, we can graphically show the net benefits of free trade. Imagine an economy with no trade, where the equilibrium price, P_{BT}, and equilibrium quantity, Q_{BT}, of wheat are determined exclusively in the domestic economy, as shown in Exhibit 2. Suppose that this imaginary economy decides to engage in free trade. You can see that the world price (established in the world market for wheat), P_{AT}, is higher than the domestic price before trade, P_{BT}. In other words, the domestic economy has a comparative advantage in wheat, because it can produce wheat at a lower relative price than the rest of the world. So this wheat-producing country sells some wheat to the domestic market and some wheat to the world market, all at the going world price.

The price after trade (P_{AT}) is higher than the price before trade (P_{BT}). Because the world market is huge, the demand from the rest of the world at the world price (P_{AT}) is assumed to be perfectly elastic. That is, domestic wheat farmers can sell all the wheat they want at the world price. If you were a wheat farmer in Nebraska, would you rather sell all your bushels of wheat at the higher world price or the lower domestic price? As a wheat farmer, you would surely prefer the higher world price. But this preference is not good news for domestic cereal and bread eaters, who now have to pay more for products made with wheat because P_{AT} is greater than P_{BT}.

Graphically, we can see how free trade and exports affect both domestic consumers and domestic producers. At the higher world price, P_{AT}, domestic wheat producers are receiving larger amounts of producer surplus. Before trade, they received a surplus equal to area e + f; after trade, they received surplus b + c + d + e + f, for a net gain of area b + c + d. However, part of the domestic producers' gain comes at domestic consumers' expense. Specifically, consumers had a consumer surplus equal to area a + b + c before the trade (at P_{BT}), but they now have only area a (at P_{AT})—a loss of area b + c.

Area b reflects a redistribution of income, because producers are gaining exactly what consumers are losing. Is that good or bad? We can't say objectively whether

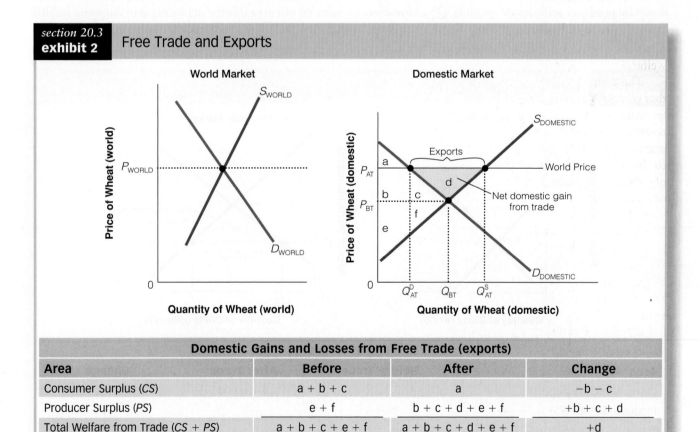

section 20.3
exhibit 2   Free Trade and Exports

Domestic Gains and Losses from Free Trade (exports)			
Area	**Before**	**After**	**Change**
Consumer Surplus (*CS*)	a + b + c	a	−b − c
Producer Surplus (*PS*)	e + f	b + c + d + e + f	+b + c + d
Total Welfare from Trade (*CS* + *PS*)	a + b + c + e + f	a + b + c + d + e + f	+d

Domestic producers gain more than domestic consumers lose from exports when free trade takes place. On net, domestic wealth rises by area d.

consumers or producers are more deserving. However, the net benefits from allowing free trade and exports are clearly visible in area d. Without free trade, no one gets area d. That is, on net, members of the domestic society gain when domestic wheat producers are able to sell their wheat at the higher world price. Although domestic wheat consumers lose from the free trade, those negative effects are more than offset by the positive gains captured by producers. Area d is the net increase in domestic wealth (the welfare gain) from free trade and exports.

Free Trade and Imports— Domestic Consumers Gain More Than Domestic Producers Lose

Now suppose that our economy does not produce shirts as well as other countries of the world. In other words, other countries have a comparative advantage in producing shirts, and the domestic price for shirts is above the world price. This scenario is illustrated in Exhibit 3. At the new, lower world price, the domestic producer will supply quantity Q_{AT}^S. However, at the lower world price, the domestic producers will not produce the entire amount demanded by domestic consumers, Q_{AT}^D. At the world price, reflecting the world supply and demand for shirts, the difference between what is domestically supplied and what is domestically demanded is supplied by imports.

At the world price (established in the world market for shirts), we assume that the world supply to the domestic market curve is perfectly elastic—that the producers of the world can supply all that domestic consumers are willing to buy at the going price. At the world price, Q_{AT}^S is supplied by domestic producers, and the difference between Q_{AT}^D and Q_{AT}^S is imported from other countries.

Who wins and who loses from free trade and imports? Domestic consumers benefit from paying a lower price for shirts. In Exhibit 3, before trade, consumers only received area a in consumer surplus. After trade, the price fell and quantity purchased increased, causing the area of consumer surplus to increase from area a to area a + b + d, a gain of b + d. Domestic producers lose because they are now selling their shirts at the lower world price, P_{AT}. The producer surplus before trade was b + c. After trade, the producer surplus falls to area c, reducing producer surplus by area b. Area b, then, represents a redistribution from producers to consumers; but area d is the net increase in domestic wealth (the welfare gain) from free trade and imports.

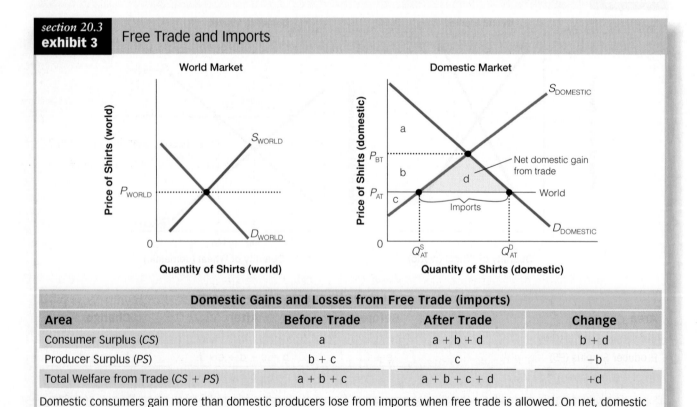

section 20.3
exhibit 3   Free Trade and Imports

Domestic Gains and Losses from Free Trade (imports)			
Area	Before Trade	After Trade	Change
Consumer Surplus (*CS*)	a	a + b + d	b + d
Producer Surplus (*PS*)	b + c	c	−b
Total Welfare from Trade (*CS* + *PS*)	a + b + c	a + b + c + d	+d

Domestic consumers gain more than domestic producers lose from imports when free trade is allowed. On net, domestic wealth rises by area d.

SECTION CHECK

1. The difference between what a consumer is willing and able to pay and what a consumer actually has to pay is called consumer surplus.

2. The difference between what a supplier is willing and able to supply and the price a supplier actually receives for selling a good or service is called producer surplus.

3. With free trade and exports, domestic producers gain more than domestic consumers lose.

4. With free trade and imports, domestic consumers gain more than domestic producers lose.

---

1. How does voluntary trade generate both consumer and producer surplus?

2. If the world price of a good is greater than the domestic price prior to trade, why does it imply that the domestic economy has a comparative advantage in producing that good?

3. If the world price of a good is less than the domestic price prior to trade, why does it imply that the domestic economy has a comparative disadvantage in producing that good?

4. When a country has a comparative advantage in the production of a good, why do domestic producers gain more than domestic consumers lose from free international trade?

5. When a country has a comparative disadvantage in a good, why do domestic consumers gain more than domestic producers lose from free international trade?

6. Why do U.S. exporters, such as farmers, favor free trade more than U.S. producers of domestic products who face competition from foreign imports, such as the automobile industry?

SECTION 20.4 — Tariffs, Import Quotas, and Subsidies

* What is a tariff?
* What are the effects of a tariff?
* What are the effects of an import quota?
* What is the economic impact of subsidies?

Tariffs

A tariff is a tax on imported goods. Tariffs are usually relatively small revenue producers that retard the expansion of trade. They bring about higher prices and revenues for domestic producers, and lower sales and revenues for foreign producers. Moreover, tariffs lead to higher prices for domestic consumers. In fact, the gains to producers are more than offset by the losses to consumers. With the aid of a graph we will see how the gains and losses from tariffs work.

tariff
a tax on imports

The Domestic Economic Impact of Tariffs

The domestic economic impact of tariffs is presented in Exhibit 1, which illustrates the supply and demand curves for domestic consumers and producers of shoes. In a typical international supply and demand illustration, the intersection of the world supply and demand curves would determine the domestic market price. However, with import tariffs, the

section 20.4
exhibit 1   Free Trade and Tariffs

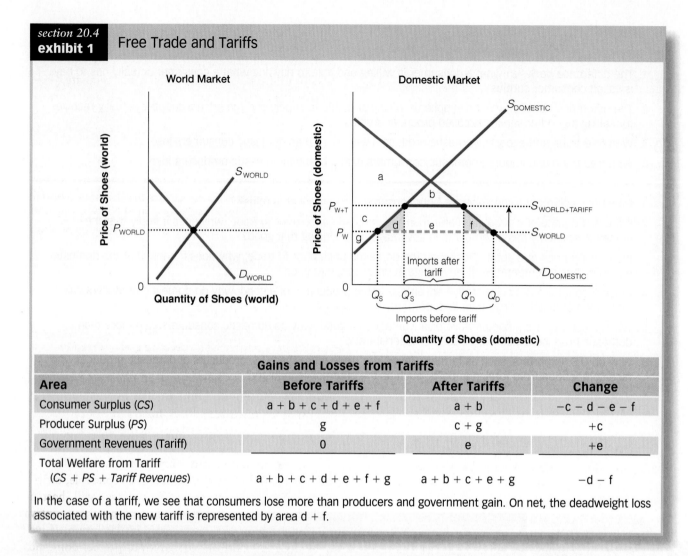

Gains and Losses from Tariffs			
Area	**Before Tariffs**	**After Tariffs**	**Change**
Consumer Surplus (*CS*)	a + b + c + d + e + f	a + b	−c − d − e − f
Producer Surplus (*PS*)	g	c + g	+c
Government Revenues (Tariff)	0	e	+e
Total Welfare from Tariff (*CS + PS + Tariff Revenues*)	a + b + c + d + e + f + g	a + b + c + e + g	−d − f

In the case of a tariff, we see that consumers lose more than producers and government gain. On net, the deadweight loss associated with the new tariff is represented by area d + f.

domestic price of shoes is greater than the world price, as in Exhibit 1. We consider the world supply curve (S_W) for domestic consumers to be perfectly elastic; that is, we can buy all we want at the world price (P_W). At the world price, domestic producers are only willing to provide quantity Q_S, but domestic consumers are willing to buy quantity Q_D—more than domestic producers are willing to supply. Imports make up the difference.

As you can see in Exhibit 1, the imposition of the tariff shifts the perfectly elastic supply curve from foreigners to domestic consumers upward from S_{WORLD} to $S_{WORLD+TARIFF}$, but it does not alter the domestic supply or demand curve. At the resulting higher domestic price (P_{W+T}), domestic suppliers are willing to supply more, Q'_S, but domestic consumers are willing to buy less, Q'_D. At the new equilibrium, the domestic price (P_{W+T}) is higher and the quantity of shoes demanded (Q'_D) is lower. But at the new price, the domestic quantity demanded is lower and the quantity supplied domestically is higher, reducing the quantity of imported shoes. Overall, then, tariffs lead to (1) a smaller total

quantity sold, (2) a higher price for shoes for domestic consumers, (3) greater sales of shoes at higher prices for domestic producers, and (4) lower sales of foreign shoes.

Although domestic producers do gain more sales and higher earnings, consumers lose much more. The increase in price from the tariff results in a loss in consumer surplus, as shown in Exhibit 1. After the tariff, shoe prices rise to P_{W+T}, and, consequently, consumer surplus falls by area c + d + e + f, representing the welfare loss to consumers from the tariff. Area c in Exhibit 1 shows the gain to domestic producers as a result of the tariff. That is, at the higher price, domestic producers are willing to supply more shoes, representing a welfare gain to producers resulting from the tariff. As a result of the tariff revenues, government gains area e. This is the import tariff—the revenue government collects from foreign countries on imports. However, we see from Exhibit 1 that consumers lose more than producers and government gain from the tariff. That is, on net, the deadweight loss associated with the tariff is represented by area d + f.

Arguments for Tariffs

Despite the preceding arguments against trade restrictions, they continue to be levied. Some rationale for their existence is necessary. Three common arguments for the use of trade restrictions deserve our critical examination.

Temporary Trade Restrictions Help Infant Industries Grow

A country might argue that a protective tariff will allow a new industry to more quickly reach a scale of operation at which economies of scale and production efficiencies can be realized. That is, temporarily shielding the young industry from competition from foreign firms will allow the infant industry a chance to grow. With early protection, these firms will eventually be able to compete effectively in the global market. It is presumed that without this protection, the industry could never get on its feet. At first hearing, the argument sounds valid, but it involves many problems. How do you identify "infant industries" that genuinely have potential economies of scale and will quickly become efficient with protection? We do not know the long-run average total cost curves of industries, a necessary piece of information. Moreover, if firms and governments are truly convinced of the advantages of allowing an industry to reach a large scale, would it not be wise to make massive loans to the industry, allowing it to begin large-scale production all at once rather than slowly and at the expense of consumers? In other words, the goal of allowing the industry to reach its efficient size can be reached without protection. Finally, the history of infant industry tariffs suggests that the tariffs often linger long after the industry is mature and no longer in need of protection.

Tariffs Can Reduce Domestic Unemployment

Exhibit 1 shows how tariffs increase output by domestic producers, thus leading to increased employment and reduced unemployment in industries where tariffs have been imposed. Yet the overall employment effects of a tariff imposition are not likely to be positive; the argument is incorrect. Why? First, the imposition of a tariff by the United States on, say, foreign steel is going to be noticed in the countries adversely affected by the tariff. If a new tariff on steel lowers Japanese steel sales to the United States, the Japanese will likely retaliate by imposing tariffs on U.S. exports to Japan, say, on machinery exports. The retaliatory tariff will lower U.S. sales of machinery and thus employment in the U.S. machinery industries. As a result, the gain in employment in the steel industry will be offset by a loss of employment elsewhere.

Even if other countries did not retaliate, U.S. employment would likely suffer outside the industry gaining tariff protection. The way that other countries pay for U.S. goods is by getting dollars from sales to the United States—imports to us. If new tariffs lead to restrictions on imports, fewer dollars will be flowing overseas in payment for imports, which means that foreigners will have fewer dollars available to buy our exports. Other things being equal, this situation will tend to reduce our exports, thus creating unemployment in the export industries.

Tariffs Are Necessary for Reasons of National Security

Sometimes it is argued that tariffs are a means of preventing a nation from becoming too dependent on foreign suppliers of goods vital to national security. That is, by making foreign goods more expensive, we can protect domestic suppliers. For example, if oil is vital to operating planes and tanks, a cutoff of foreign supplies of oil during wartime could cripple a nation's defenses.

The national security argument is usually not valid. If a nation's own resources are depletable, tariff-imposed reliance on domestic supplies will hasten depletion of domestic reserves, making the country even *more* dependent on imports in the future. If we impose a high tariff on foreign oil to protect domestic producers, we will increase domestic output of oil in the short run; but in the process, we will deplete the stockpile of available reserves. Thus, the defense argument is of questionable validity. From a defense standpoint, it makes more sense to use foreign oil in peacetime and perhaps stockpile "insurance" supplies so that larger domestic supplies would be available during wars.

Are Tariffs Necessary to Protect Against Dumping?

Dumping occurs when a foreign country sells its products at prices below their costs or below the prices for which they are sold on the domestic market. For example, the Japanese government has been accused for years of subsidizing Japanese steel producers as they attempt to gain a greater share of the world steel market and greater market power. That is, the short-term losses from selling below cost may be offset by the long-term economic profits from employing this strategy. Some have argued that tariffs are needed to protect domestic producers against low-cost dumpers because they will raise the cost to foreign producers and offset their cost advantage.

The United States has antidumping laws; if a foreign country is found guilty of dumping, the United States can impose antidumping tariffs on that country's products, thereby raising the price of the foreign goods that are being dumped. In practice, however, it is often difficult to prove dumping; foreign countries may simply have lower steel production costs. So what may seem like dumping may in fact be comparative advantage.

Import Quotas

Like tariffs, import quotas directly restrict imports, leading to reductions in trade and thus preventing nations from fully realizing their comparative advantage. The case for quotas is probably even weaker than the case for tariffs. Unlike what occurs with a tariff, the U.S. government does not collect any revenue as a result of the import quota. Despite the higher prices, the loss in consumer surplus, and the loss in government revenue, quotas come about because people often view them as being less protectionist than tariffs—the traditional, most-maligned form of protection.

Besides the rather blunt means of curtailing imports by using tariffs and quotas, nations have devised still other, more subtle means of restricting international trade. For example, nations sometimes impose product standards, ostensibly to protect consumers against inferior merchandise. Effectively, however, those standards may be simply a means of restricting foreign competition. For example, France might keep certain kinds of wine out of the country on the grounds that they are made with allegedly inferior grapes or have an inappropriate alcoholic content. Likewise, the United States might prohibit automobile imports that do not meet certain standards in terms of pollutants, safety, and gasoline mileage. Even if these standards are not intended to restrict foreign competition, the regulations may nonetheless have that impact, restricting consumer choice in the process.

import quota
a legal limit on the imported quantity of a good that is produced abroad and can be sold in domestic markets

rent seeking
efforts by producers to gain profits from government protections such as tariffs and import quotas

The Domestic Economic Impact of an Import Quota

The domestic economic impact of an import quota on autos is presented in Exhibit 2. The introduction of an import quota increases the price from the world

price, P_W (established in the world market for autos) to P_{W+Q}. The quota causes the price to rise above the world price. The domestic quantity demanded falls and the domestic quantity supplied rises. Consequently, the number of imports is much smaller than it would be without the import quota. Compared with free trade, domestic producers are better off but domestic consumers are worse off. Specifically, the import quota results in a gain in producer surplus of area c and a loss in consumer surplus of area c + d + e + f. However, unlike the tariff case, where the government gains area e in revenues, the government does not gain any revenues with a quota. Consequently, the deadweight loss is even greater with quotas than with tariffs. That is, on net, the deadweight loss associated with the quota is represented by area d + e + f. Recall that the deadweight loss was only d + f for tariffs.

If tariffs and import quotas hurt importing countries, why do they exist? The reason they exist is that producers can make large profits or "rents" from tariffs and import quotas. Economists call these efforts to gain profits from government protection **rent seeking**. Because this money, time, and effort spent on lobbying could have been spent producing something else, the deadweight loss from tariffs and quotas will likely understate the true deadweight loss to society.

The Economic Impact of Subsidies

Working in the opposite direction, governments sometimes try to encourage exports by subsidizing producers. With a subsidy, revenue is given to producers for each exported unit of output, which stimulates exports. Although not a barrier to trade like tariffs and quotas, subsidies can distort trade patterns and lead to inefficiencies. How do these distortions happen? With subsidies, producers will export goods not because their costs are lower than those of a foreign competitor but because their costs have been artificially reduced by government action, transferring income from taxpayers to the exporter. The subsidy does not reduce the amounts of actual labor, raw material, and capital costs of production—society has the same opportunity costs as before. The nation's taxpayers end up subsidizing the output of producers who, relative to producers in other countries, are inefficient. The nation, then, is exporting products in which it does

section 20.4
exhibit 2   Free Trade and Import Quotas

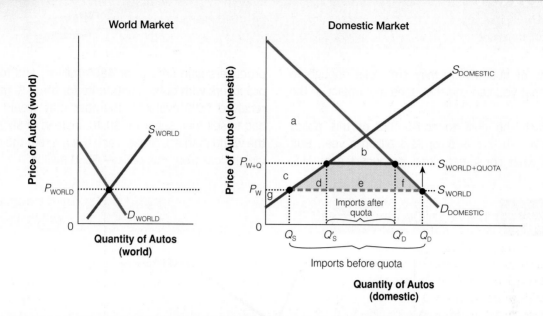

World Market

Domestic Market

Gains and Losses from Import Quotas			
Area	**Before Quota**	**After Quota**	**Change**
Consumer Surplus (*CS*)	a + b + c + d + e + f	a + b	−c − d − e − f
Producer Surplus (*PS*)	g	c + g	+c
Total Welfare (*CS* + *PS*) from Quota	a + b + c + d + e + f + g	a + b + c + g	−d − e − f

With an import quota, the price rises from P_w to P_{w+Q}. Compared with free trade, consumers lose area c + d + e + f, while producers gain area b. The deadweight loss from the quota is area d + e + f. Under quotas, consumers lose and producers gain. The difference in deadweight loss between quotas and tariffs is area d, which the government is not able to pick up with import quotas.

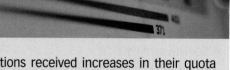

POLICY
application   THE SUGAR QUOTA

The world price of sugar is much lower than the U.S. price. For example, in recent years, the U.S. price of sugar has been as high as 25 cents per pound while the world price was less than a nickel per pound. Why? The reason is that a sugar import quota protects the domestic sugar industry, by controlling how much foreign sugar can enter the country. This policy raised the price of U.S. sugar and helps both domestic producers and those foreign producers who have lobbied successfully for quota allotment. In 2006, five of the largest producing

Caribbean nations received increases in their quota because of the devastation done to the sugar plantations in Louisiana by Hurricane Katrina.

The sugar quota impacts the price of everything from beverages to birthday cakes. As we can see graphically in Exhibit 3, this policy may be good for domestic sugar producers but it is clearly bad for consumers (and those producers who use sugar as an input to further production such as candy makers, several of whom have moved out of the United States). Even though the numbers are hypothetical

(continued)

for ease of quantifying, they are close enough to reality that you can see the monetary impact of the quota.

Notice the cost to consumers of this policy is area a + b + c + d, or $2.1 billion a year. But, part of what consumers lose, producers gain. U.S.

producers gain area a, or $850 million, and foreign producers with quota allotments for the U.S. market received $600 million (remember they would have had to sell their sugar for $0.10, instead of $0.20, on the world market). Areas b and d represent the deadweight loss from this policy—$650 million.

section 20.4
exhibit 3   The Sugar Quota

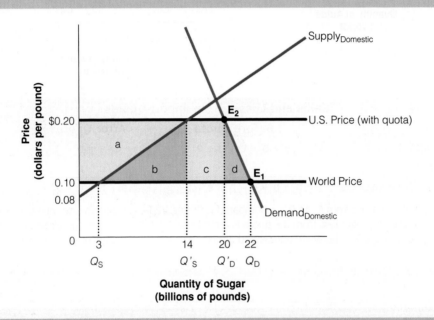

Quantity of Sugar
(billions of pounds)

Gains and Losses Associated with Sugar Quota

Loss of Consumer Surplus	Area a + b + c + d = $2.1 billion
Gain to U.S. Producers of Sugar	Area a = $850 million
Gain to Foreign Sugar Producers with Quota Allotments	Area c = $600 million
Deadweight Loss	Area b + d = $650 million
Area a = $850 million ($0.10 × 11 billion × 0.5) + ($0.10 × 3 billion)	Area c = $600 million ($0.10 × 6 billion)
Area b = $550 million ($0.10 × 11 billion × 0.5)	Area d = $100 million ($0.10 × 2 billion × 0.5)

in the news

True or False: Outsourcing Is a Crisis

—BY EDUARDO PORTER

If you read only the headlines, the future of globalization may seem scary, indeed.

American jobs have already been heading abroad. And as telecommunications and more powerful computers enable companies to take even more jobs overseas, the service sector, which accounts for about 85 percent of the United States work force, will be increasingly vulnerable to competition from the cheap labor pools of the developing world.

So the question looms: Is America on the verge of losing oodles of white-collar jobs?

Probably not. The threat of global outsourcing is easily overstated.

The debate over the global competition for jobs is awash in dire projections. All those legal assistants in New York and Washington, for example, could be replaced with smart young graduates from Hyderabad. Office support occupations—jobs like data entry assistant, file clerk and the entire payroll department - could also be carried out in remote locations. "We are really at the beginning stages of this, and it is accelerating rapidly," said Ron Hira, assistant professor of public policy at the Rochester Institute of Technology.

In a study published this year, two economists at the Organization for Economic Cooperation and Development in Brussels estimated that 20 percent of the developed world's employment could be "potentially affected" by global outsourcing. That could include all American librarians, statisticians, chemical engineers and air traffic controllers, the study said.

What does "potentially affected" mean? Even if offshoring didn't drain away all these jobs, global competition for employment—including workers in developing countries who earn so little by

chart 1
A Variety of Jobs Being Outsourced

Business
11%

Office
53%

Computer
26%

Architecture
3%

Sales
4%

Legal
2%

Art, design
1%

NOTE: Percentages computed on estimates for 2000.

SOURCE: John C. McCarthy (2002), "3.3 Million U.S. Services Jobs to Go Offshore," TechStrategy Research Brief, Forrester Research Inc., November 11.

chart 2
Outsourcing to India Can Net Large Savings

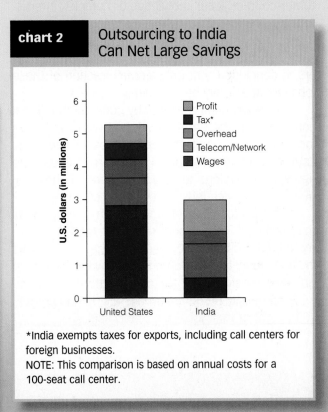

Profit
Tax*
Overhead
Telecom/Network
Wages

U.S. dollars (in millions)

United States   India

*India exempts taxes for exports, including call centers for foreign businesses.

NOTE: This comparison is based on annual costs for a 100-seat call center.

SOURCE: Antonio Riera, Janmejaya Sinha, and Alpesh Shah (2002), "Passage to India: The Rewards of Remote Business Processing," The Boston Consulting Group.

continued

Business News

in the news   True or False: Outsourcing Is a Crisis (cont.)

comparison—could severely dent the livelihoods of American workers. "It isn't going to hurt in terms of jobs," said William J. Baumol, an economics professor at New York University who has studied the costs of globalization. "It is going to hurt in terms of wages."

But even if millions of tasks can be done by cheaper labor on the other side of the planet, businesses won't rush to move every job they can to wherever the cost is lowest. The labor market isn't quite that global, and it's unlikely to be anytime soon.

In a new set of reports, the McKinsey Global Institute, a research group known for its unabashedly favorable view of globalization, argued that 160 million service jobs—about 10 percent of total worldwide employment—could be moved to remote sites because these job functions don't require customer contact, local knowledge or complex interactions with the rest of a business.

Yet after surveying dozens of companies in eight sectors, from pharmaceutical companies to insurers, it concluded that only a small fraction of these jobs would actually be sent away.

The report estimates that by 2008, multinational companies in the entire developed world will have located only 4.1 million service jobs in low-wage countries, up from about 1.5 million in 2003. The figure is equivalent to only 1 percent of the total number of service jobs in developed countries.

Some sectors, like retail and health care, are likely to put very few jobs in poor countries. McKinsey estimated that less than 0.07 percent of health care jobs in 2008 would be outsourced to low-wage countries. But even designers of packaged software, whose work can easily be done abroad, will outsource only 18 percent of their jobs, the report said.

Moving tasks to faraway sites isn't simple. According to McKinsey's study, many business processes are difficult to separate into discrete chunks that can be sent away. Many insurance companies use information technology systems that have been cobbled together over time and would be difficult to manage remotely. Managers can be unwilling or unprepared to work overseas. And sometimes the tasks that can be sent offshore are too small to make the move worthwhile.

To top it off, there aren't that many suitable cheap workers available. Human-resources managers interviewed for the McKinsey study said that for reasons ranging from poor language skills to second-rate education systems, only about 13 percent of the young, college-educated professionals in the big developing countries are suitable to work for multinationals. And competition from local companies reduces this pool.

Sure, there are a billion Indians, but only a tiny percentage of the Indian work force have the appropriate qualifications. "Only a fraction have English as a medium of instruction, and only a fraction of those speak English that you or I can understand," said Jagdish N. Bhagwati, a professor of economics at Columbia University.

Of course, many of these obstacles can be overcome with time. The pool of adequate workers in poorer countries will grow, and companies will eventually iron out many of the logistical complications.

But that is likely to take a while."

© FEDERAL RESERVE BANK OF DALLAS

Buy American. The Job You Save May Be Your Own.
A common myth is that it's better for Americans to spend their money at home than abroad. The best way to expose the fallacy in this argument is to take it to its logical extreme. If it's better for me to spend my money here than abroad, then it's even better to buy in Texas than in New York, better yet to buy in Dallas than in Houston . . . in my own neighborhood . . . within my own family . . . to consume only what I can produce. Alone and poor.

not have a comparative advantage. Gains from trade in terms of world output are eliminated or reduced by such subsidies. Thus, subsidies, usually defended as a means of increasing exports and improving a nation's international financial position, are usually of dubious worth to the world economy and even to the economy doing the subsidizing.

According to the World Bank and the International Monetary Fund (IMF), world trade has benefited enormously from greater openness in trade since 1950. Tariffs on goods have fallen from a worldwide average of 26 percent to less than 9 percent today. On average, trade has grown more than twice as fast as world output.

SECTION CHECK

1. A tariff is a tax on imported goods.

2. Tariffs bring about higher prices and revenues to domestic producers and lower sales and revenues to foreign producers. Tariffs lead to higher prices and reduce consumer surplus for domestic consumers. Tariffs result in a net loss in welfare because the loss in consumer surplus is greater than the gain to producers and the government.

3. Arguments for the use of tariffs include: tariffs help infant industries grow; tariffs can reduce domestic unemployment; new tariffs can help finance our international trade; and tariffs are necessary for national security reasons.

4. Like tariffs, import quotas restrict imports, lowering consumer surplus and preventing countries from fully realizing their comparative advantage. The net loss in welfare from a quota is proportionately larger than for a tariff because it does not result in government revenues.

5. Sometimes government tries to encourage production of a certain good by subsidizing its production with taxpayer dollars. Because subsidies stimulate exports, they are not a barrier to trade like tariffs and import quotas. However, they do distort trade patterns and cause overall inefficiencies.

1. Why do tariffs increase domestic producer surplus but decrease domestic consumer surplus?

2. How do import tariffs increase employment in "protected" industries but at the expense of a likely decrease in employment overall?

3. Why is the national security argument for tariffs questionable?

4. Why is the domestic argument for import quotas weaker than the case for tariffs?

5. Why would foreign producers prefer import quotas to tariffs, even if they resulted in the same reduced level of imports?

6. Why does subsidizing exports by industries without a comparative advantage tend to harm the domestic economy, on net?

Interactive Chapter Summary

Fill in the blanks:

1. In a typical year, about _____ percent of the world's output is traded in international markets.

2. In the global economy, one country's exports are another country's _____.

3. _____ trade implies that both participants in an exchange of goods and services anticipate an improvement in their economic welfare.

4. The theory that explains how trade can be beneficial to both parties centers on the concept of _____.

5. A person, a region, or a country has a comparative advantage over another person, region, or country in producing a particular good or service if it produces a good or service at a lower _____ than others do.

6. What is important for mutually beneficial specialization and trade is _____ advantage, not _____ advantage.

7. Trade has evolved in large part because different geographic areas have _____ resources and therefore _____ production possibilities.

8. If Techland can produce more of both grain and computers than Grainsville, Techland has a(n) _____ advantage in both products.

9. The difference between the most a consumer would be willing to pay for a quantity of a good and what a consumer actually has to pay is called _____ surplus.

10. We can better analyze the impact of trade with the tools of _____ and _____ surplus.

11. Once the equilibrium output is reached at the equilibrium price, the sum of _____ and _____ is maximized.

12. When the domestic economy has a comparative advantage in a good because it can produce it at a lower relative price than the rest of the world can, international trade _____ the domestic market price to the world price, benefiting domestic _____ but harming domestic _____.

13. When the domestic economy has a comparative advantage in a good, allowing international trade redistributes income from domestic _____ to domestic _____, but _____ surplus increases more than _____ surplus decreases.

14. When a country does not produce a good relatively as well as other countries do, international trade will _____ the domestic price to the world price, with the difference between what is domestically

supplied and what is domestically demanded supplied by _____.

15. When a country does not produce a good relatively as well as other countries do, international trade redistributes income from domestic _____ to domestic _____ and causes a net _____ in domestic wealth.

16. A(n) _____ is a tax on imported goods.

17. Tariffs bring about _____ prices and revenues to domestic producers, _____ sales and revenues to foreign producers, and _____ prices to domestic consumers.

18. With import tariffs, the domestic price of goods is _____ than the world price.

19. If import tariffs are imposed, at the new price the domestic quantity demanded is _____, and the quantity supplied domestically is _____, _____ the quantity of imported goods.

20. Import tariffs benefit domestic _____ and _____ but harm domestic _____.

21. One argument for tariffs is that tariff protection is necessary _____ to allow a new industry to more quickly reach a scale of operation at which economies of scale and production efficiencies can be realized.

22. Tariffs lead to _____ output and employment and reduced unemployment in domestic industries where tariffs are imposed.

23. If new tariffs lead to restrictions on imports, _____ dollars will be flowing overseas in payment for imports, which means that foreigners will have _____ dollars available to buy U.S. exports.

24. If a nation's own resources are depletable, tariff-imposed reliance on domestic supplies will _____ depletion of domestic reserves.

25. An import _____ gives producers from another country a maximum number of units of the good in question that can be imported within any given time span.

26. The case for import quotas is _____ than the case for import tariffs.

27. Tariffs and import quotas are rather suspect and exist because of producers' lobbying efforts to gain profits from government protection, which is called _____.

28. Dumping occurs when a foreign country sells its products at prices _____ their costs or _____ the prices they are sold at in the domestic market.

29. If a foreign country is found guilty of dumping, the United States can impose _____ tariffs.

30. Governments sometimes try to encourage exports by _____ producers.

31. With subsidies, a nation's taxpayers end up subsidizing the output of producers who, relative to producers in other countries, are _____.

32. Gains from trade in terms of world output are _____ by export subsidies.

Answers: 1. 15 2. imports 3. Voluntary 4. comparative 5. opportunity cost 6. comparative; absolute 7. different; different 8. absolute 9. consumer 10. consumer; producer 11. consumer surplus; producer surplus 12. raises; producers; consumers 13. consumers; producers; producer; consumer 14. lower; imports 15. producers; consumers; increase 16. tariff 17. higher; lower; higher 18. greater 19. lower; greater; reducing 20. producers; the government; consumers 21. temporarily 22. increased 23. fewer; fewer 24. hasten 25. quota 26. weaker 27. rent seeking 28. below; below 29. antidumping 30. subsidizing 31. inefficient 32. reduced

Key Terms and Concepts

comparative advantage 566   producer surplus 574   import quota 580
consumer surplus 574   tariff 577   rent seeking 580

Section Check Answers

20.1 The Growth in World Trade

1. Why is it important to understand the effects of international trade?

All countries are importantly affected by international trade, although the magnitude of the international trade sector varies substantially by country. International connections mean that any of a large number of disturbances that originate elsewhere may have important consequences for the domestic economy.

2. Why would U.S. producers and consumers be more concerned about Canadian trade restrictions than Swedish trade restrictions?

The United States and Canada are the two largest trading partners in the world. This means that the effects of trade restrictions imposed by Canada would have a far larger effect on the United States than similar restrictions imposed by Sweden. (For certain items, however, the magnitude of our trade with Sweden is greater than it is with Canada, so for these items Swedish restrictions would be of more concern.)

20.2 Comparative Advantage and Gains from Trade

1. Why do people voluntarily choose to specialize and trade?

Voluntary specialization and trade among self-interested parties only takes place because all the parties involved expect that their benefits from this specialization (according to comparative advantage) and exchange will exceed their costs.

2. How could a country have an absolute advantage in producing one good or service without also having a comparative advantage in its production?

If one country was absolutely more productive at everything than another country but wasn't equally more productive at everything, there would still be some things in which it had a comparative disadvantage. For instance, if country A was three times as productive in making X and two times as productive in making Y as country B, it would have a comparative advantage in making X (it gives up less Y for each X produced) and a comparative disadvantage in making Y (it gives up more X for each Y produced), relative to country B.

3. Why do you think the introduction of the railroad reduced self-sufficiency in the United States?

Prior to the introduction of the railroad, the high cost of transportation overwhelmed the gains from specializing according to comparative advantage in much of the United States (production cost differences were smaller than the costs of transportation). The railroads reduced transportation costs enough that specialization and exchange became beneficial for more goods and services, and self-sufficiency due to high transportation costs declined.

4. If you can wash the dishes in two-thirds the time it takes your younger sister to wash them, do you have a comparative advantage in washing the dishes with respect to her?

We can't know the answer to this question without more information. It is not the time taken to wash the dishes that matters in determining comparative advantage but the opportunity cost of the time in terms of forgone value elsewhere. If your younger sister is less than two-thirds as good at other chores than you, she is relatively better at washing the dishes and so would have a comparative advantage in washing the dishes. If she is more than two-thirds as good at other chores, she is relatively better at these chores and so would have a comparative disadvantage in washing the dishes.

20.3 Supply and Demand in International Trade

1. How does voluntary trade generate both consumer and producer surplus?

Voluntary trade generates consumer surplus because a rational consumer would not purchase if he did not value the benefits of purchase at greater than its cost, and consumer surplus is the difference between that value and the cost he is forced to pay. Voluntary trade generates producer surplus because a rational producer would not sell additional units unless the price he received was greater than his marginal cost, and producer surplus is the difference between the revenues received and the costs producers must bear to produce the goods that generate those revenues.

2. If the world price of a good is greater than the domestic price prior to trade, why does it imply that the domestic economy has a comparative advantage in producing that good?

If the world price of a good is greater than the domestic price prior to trade, this implies that the domestic marginal opportunity cost of production is less than the world marginal opportunity cost of production. But this means that the domestic economy has a comparative advantage in that good.

3. If the world price of a good is less than the domestic price prior to trade, why does it imply that the domestic economy has a comparative disadvantage in producing that good?

If the world price of a good is less than the domestic price prior to trade, this implies that the domestic marginal opportunity cost of production is greater than the world marginal opportunity cost of production. But this means that the domestic economy has a comparative disadvantage in that good.

4. When a country has a comparative advantage in the production of a good, why do domestic producers gain more than domestic consumers lose from free international trade?

When a country has a comparative advantage in producing a good, the marginal benefit from exporting is the world price, which is greater than the forgone value domestically (along the domestic demand curve) for those units of domestic consumption "crowded out"

and greater than the marginal cost of the expanded output. Therefore, there are net domestic gains to international trade (the gains to domestic producers exceed the losses to domestic consumers).

5. When a country has a comparative disadvantage in a good, why do domestic consumers gain more than domestic producers lose from free international trade?

When a country has a comparative disadvantage in producing a good, the marginal cost of importing is the world price, which is less than the additional value (along the domestic demand curve) for those units of expanded domestic consumption and less than the marginal cost of the domestic production "crowded out." Therefore, there are net domestic gains to international trade (the gains to domestic consumers exceed the losses to domestic producers).

6. Why do U.S. exporters, such as farmers, favor free trade more than U.S. producers of domestic products who face competition from foreign imports, such as the automobile industry?

Exporters favor free trade over restrictions on what they sell in other countries because it increases the demand and therefore the price for their products, which raises their profits. Those who must compete with importers want those imports restricted rather than freely traded because it increases the demand and therefore the price for their domestically produced products, which raises their profits.

20.4 Tariffs, Import Quotas, and Subsidies

1. Why do tariffs increase domestic producer surplus but decrease domestic consumer surplus?

Tariffs raise the price of imported goods to domestic consumers, resulting in higher prices received by domestic producers as well. Thus, the higher price reduces domestic consumer surplus but increases domestic producer surplus.

2. How do import tariffs increase employment in "protected" industries but at the expense of a likely decrease in employment overall?

Import tariffs increase employment in "protected" industries because the barriers to lower-price imports increase the demand faced by domestic producers, increasing their demand for workers. However, imports are the means by which foreigners get the dollars to buy our exports, so restricted imports will mean restricted exports (even more so if other countries retaliate with import restrictions of their own). In addition, by raising the prices domestic consumers pay for the protected products (remember that domestic consumers lose more than domestic producers gain from protectionism), consumers are made poorer in real terms, which will reduce demand for goods, and therefore the labor to make them, throughout the economy.

3. Why is the national security argument for tariffs questionable?

The national security argument for tariffs is questionable because tariffs increase current reliance on domestic supplies, which depletes the future stockpile of available reserves. With fewer domestic reserves, the country will be even more dependent on foreign supplies in the future. Buying foreign supplies and stockpiling them makes more sense as a way of reducing reliance on foreign supplies in wartime.

4. Why is the domestic argument for import quotas weaker than the case for tariffs?

Tariffs at least use the price system as the basis of trade. Tariff revenues end up in a country's treasury, where they can be used to produce benefits for the country's citizens or to reduce the domestic tax burden. Import quotas, however, transfer most of those benefits to foreign producers as the higher prices they receive.

5. Why would foreign producers prefer import quotas to tariffs, even if they resulted in the same reduced level of imports?

Restricting imports reduces supply, which increases the price that foreign producers receive on the units they sell, thus benefiting them. Tariffs, on the other hand, reduce the after-tariff price that foreign producers receive. If both reduce foreign sales by the same amount, foreign producers would clearly prefer import restrictions over tariffs.

6. Why does subsidizing exports by industries without a comparative advantage tend to harm the domestic economy, on net?

Subsidizing industries in which a country has a comparative disadvantage (higher costs) must, by definition, require shifting resources from where it has a comparative advantage (lower costs) to where it has a comparative disadvantage. The value of the output produced from those resources (indirectly in the case of specialization and exchange) is lower as a result.

True or False:

1. Although the importance of the international sector varies enormously from place to place, the volume of international trade increased substantially.

2. U.S. imports are considered a credit item in the balance of payment because the dollars sold to buy the necessary foreign currency add to foreign claims against U.S. buyers.

3. Our imports provide the means by which foreigners can buy our exports.

4. Nations' imports and exports of services are the largest component of the balance of payments.

5. When the United States runs a trade deficit in goods and services with the rest of the world, the rest of the world must be running a trade surplus in goods and services with the United States.

6. When the United States runs a trade deficit in goods, it must run a trade surplus in services.

7. In the global economy, imports equal exports because one country's exports are another country's imports.

8. In voluntary trade, both participants in an exchange anticipate an improvement in their economic welfare.

9. An area should specialize in producing and selling those items in which it has an absolute advantage.

10. Differences in opportunity costs provide an incentive to gain from specialization and trade.

11. The principle of comparative advantage can be applied to regional markets.

12. A trading area may be a locality, a region, or a nation.

13. If two nations with different opportunity costs of production specialize, total output of both products may be higher as a result.

14. By specializing in products in which it has a comparative advantage, an area can have more goods and services if it trades the added output for other goods and services that others can produce at a lower opportunity cost.

15. By specialization according to comparative advantage and trade, two parties can each achieve consumption possibilities that would be impossible for them without trade.

16. The difference between the least amount for which a supplier is willing to supply a quantity of a good or service and the revenues a supplier actually receives for selling it is called consumer surplus.

17. Trading at the market equilibrium price generates both consumer surplus and producer surplus.

18. Once the equilibrium output is reached at the equilibrium price, all of the mutually beneficial opportunities from trade between suppliers and demanders will have taken place.

19. The total gain to the economy from trade is the sum of consumer and producer surpluses.

20. When the domestic economy has a comparative advantage in a good, allowing international trade benefits domestic consumers but harms domestic producers.

21. When the domestic economy has a comparative advantage in a good, exporting that good increases domestic wealth because, while domestic consumers lose from the free trade, these negative effects are more than offset by the positive gains captured by producers.

22. When a country does not produce a good relatively as well as other countries do, international trade benefits domestic consumers but harms domestic producers.

23. When a country does not produce a good relatively as well as other countries do, allowing international trade will increase consumer surplus less than producer surplus decreases.

24. Tariffs are usually relatively large revenue producers for governments.

25. Tariffs result in gains to domestic producers that are more than offset by losses to domestic consumers.

26. The history of infant-industry tariffs suggests that the tariffs often linger long after the industry is mature and no longer in need of protection.

27. When foreign countries are dumping, they are trying to gain a greater share of the world market for their products.

28. What may seem like dumping may in fact be comparative advantage.

29. The overall domestic employment effects of a tariff imposition are likely to be positive.

30. If the imposition of a tariff leads to retaliatory tariffs by other countries, domestic employment outside the industry gaining the tariff protection will likely suffer.

31. Exporters in a country would generally be supportive of their country's imposing import tariffs.

32. From a national defense standpoint, rather than imposing import tariffs, it makes more sense to use foreign supplies in peacetime and perhaps stockpile "insurance" supplies so that large domestic supplies would be available during wars.

33. Like tariffs, quotas directly restrict imports; but the U.S. government does not collect any revenue as the result of an import quota, as it does with tariffs.

34. Nations have sometimes used product standards ostensibly designed to protect consumers against inferior, unsafe, dangerous, or polluting merchandise as a means of restricting foreign competition.

35. Because resources being spent on lobbying efforts could have produced something instead, the measured deadweight loss from tariffs and quotas will likely understate the true deadweight loss to society.

36. Unlike import tariffs and quotas, export subsidies tend to increase efficiency.

37. With subsidies, producers export goods not because their costs are lower than those of a foreign competitor but because their costs have been artificially reduced by government action transferring income from taxpayers to the exporter.

38. Export subsidies lead nations to export products in which they do not have a comparative advantage.

Multiple Choice:

1. Assume that the opportunity cost of producing a pair of pants in the United States is 2 pounds of rice, while in China, it is 5 pounds of rice. As a result,
   a. the United States has a comparative advantage over China in the production of pants.
   b. China has a comparative advantage over the United States in the production of rice.
   c. mutual gains from trade can be realized by both countries if the United States exports rice to China in exchange for shoes.
   d. mutual gains from trade can be realized by both countries if the United States exports pants to China in exchange for rice.
   e. all of the above except c are true.

2. In Samoa the opportunity cost of producing one coconut is four pineapples, while in Guam the opportunity cost of producing one coconut is five pineapples. In this situation,
   a. if trade occurs, both countries will be able to consume beyond the frontiers of their original production possibilities.
   b. Guam will be better off if it exports coconuts and imports pineapples.
   c. both Samoa and Guam will be better off if Samoa produces both coconuts and pineapples.
   d. mutually beneficial trade cannot occur.

3. Mutually beneficial trade will occur whenever the exchange rate between the goods involved is set at a level where
   a. each country can export a good at a price above the opportunity cost of producing the good in the domestic market.
   b. each country can import a good at a price above the opportunity cost of producing the good in the domestic market.
   c. the exchange ratio is exactly equal to the opportunity cost of producing the good in each country.
   d. each country will specialize in the production of those goods in which it has an absolute advantage.
   e. either b or d is true.

Questions 4–6 refer to the following data: Alpha can produce either 18 tons of oranges or 9 tons of apples in a year, while Omega can produce either 16 tons of oranges or 4 tons of apples in a year.

4. The opportunity costs of producing 1 ton of apples for Alpha and Omega, respectively, are
   a. 0.25 ton of oranges and 0.5 ton of oranges.
   b. 9 tons of oranges and 4 tons of oranges.
   c. 2 tons of oranges and 4 tons of oranges.
   d. 4 tons of oranges and 2 tons of oranges.
   e. 0.5 ton of oranges and 0.25 ton of oranges.

5. Which of the following statements is true?
   a. Alpha should export to Omega, but Omega should not export to Alpha.
   b. Because Alpha has an absolute advantage in both goods, no mutual gains from trade are possible.
   c. If Alpha specializes in growing apples and Omega specializes in growing oranges, they could both gain by specialization and trade.
   d. If Alpha specializes in growing oranges and Omega specializes in growing apples, they could both gain by specialization and trade.
   e. Because Alpha has a comparative advantage in producing both goods, no mutual gains from trade are possible.

6. Which of the following exchange rates between apples and oranges would allow both Alpha and Omega to gain by specialization and exchange?
   a. 1 ton of apples for 3 tons of oranges
   b. 3 tons of apples for 3 tons of oranges
   c. 2 tons of apples for 3 tons of oranges
   d. 1 ton of oranges for 0.2 ton of apples
   e. 1 ton of oranges for 0.8 ton of apples

7. After the United States introduces a tariff in the market for steel, the price of steel in the United States will
   a. decrease.
   b. increase.
   c. remain the same.
   d. change in an indeterminate manner.

8. If Japan does not have a comparative advantage in producing rice, the consequences of adopting a policy of reducing or eliminating imports of rice into Japan would include the following:
   a. Japan will be able to consume a combination of rice and other goods beyond their domestic production possibilities curve.
   b. The real incomes of Japanese rice producers would rise, but the real incomes of Japanese rice consumers would fall.
   c. The real incomes of Japanese rice consumers would rise, but the real incomes of Japanese rice producers would fall.
   d. The price of rice in Japan would fall.

9. The infant-industry argument for protectionism claims that an industry must be protected in the early stages of its development so that
   a. firms will be protected from subsidized foreign competition.
   b. domestic producers can attain the economies of scale to allow them to compete in world markets.
   c. adequate supplies of crucial resources will be available if needed for national defense.
   d. None of the above reflect the infant-industry argument.

10. Protectionist legislation is often passed because
    a. employers in the affected industry lobby more effectively than the workers in that industry.
    b. both employers and workers in the affected industry lobby for protectionist policies.
    c. trade restrictions often benefit domestic consumers in the long run, even though they must pay more in the short run.
    d. none of the above

11. Introducing a tariff on vitamin E would
    a. reduce imports of vitamin E.
    b. increase U.S. consumption of domestically produced vitamin E.
    c. decrease total U.S. consumption of vitamin E.
    d. do all of the above.
    e. do none of the above.

12. A new U.S. import quota on imported steel would be likely to
    a. raise the cost of production for steel-using American firms.
    b. generate tax revenue to the government.
    c. decrease U.S. production of steel.
    d. increase the production of steel-using American firms.
    e. do all of the above.

13. An import quota does which of the following?
    a. decreases the price of the imported goods to consumers
    b. increases the price of the domestic goods to consumers
    c. redistributes income away from domestic producers of those products toward domestic producers of exports
    d. a and c
    e. b and c

14. A crucial difference between the impacts of import quotas and of tariffs is that
    a. import quotas generate revenue to the domestic government, but tariffs do not.
    b. import quotas generate no revenue to the domestic government, but tariffs do.
    c. tariffs increase the prices paid by domestic consumers, but quotas do not.
    d. a and c
    e. b and c

15. If the United States could produce 0.5 ton of potatoes or 1 ton of wheat per worker per year, while Ireland could produce 3 tons of potatoes or 2 tons of wheat per worker per year, the country with the comparative advantage in producing wheat is _____ and the country with the absolute advantage in producing potatoes is _____.
    a. the United States; the United States
    b. the United States; Ireland
    c. Ireland; the United States
    d. Ireland; Ireland

16. According to international trade theory, a country should
    a. import goods in which it has an absolute advantage.
    b. export goods in which it has an absolute advantage.
    c. import goods in which it has a comparative disadvantage.
    d. import goods in which it has an absolute disadvantage.
    e. import goods when it has either a comparative or absolute disadvantage in producing them.

17. Relative to a no-international-trade initial situation, if the United States imported wine, the U.S. domestic price of wine
    a. would rise, but domestic output would fall.
    b. would fall, but domestic output would rise.
    c. would rise, and domestic output would rise.
    d. would fall, and domestic output would fall.

18. Relative to a no-international-trade initial situation, if the United States exported wine, the U.S. domestic price of wine
    a. would rise, but domestic output would fall.
    b. would fall, but domestic output would rise.
    c. would rise, and domestic output would rise.
    d. would fall, and domestic output would fall.

Problems:

1. Bud and Larry have been shipwrecked on a deserted island. Their economic activity consists of either gathering berries or fishing. We know that Bud can catch four fish in one hour or harvest two buckets of berries. In the same time Larry can catch two fish or harvest two buckets of berries.
    a. Fill in the following table assuming that they *each* spend four hours a day fishing and four hours a day harvesting berries.

	Fish per Day	Buckets of Berries per Day
Bud	_____	_____
Larry	_____	_____
Total	_____	_____

    b. If Bud and Larry don't trade with each other, who is better off? Why?

c. Assume that Larry and Bud operate on straight-line production possibilities curves. Fill in the following table:

	Opportunity Cost of a Bucket of Berries	Opportunity Cost of a Fish
Bud	_____	_____
Larry	_____	_____

d. If they traded, who has the comparative advantage in fish? In berries?

e. If Larry and Bud specialize in and trade the good in which they have a comparative advantage, how much of each good will be produced in an eight-hour day? What are the gains from trade?

2. The following table represents the production possibilities in two countries:

Country A		Country B	
Good X	Good Y	Good X	Good Y
0	32	0	24
4	24	4	18
8	16	8	12
12	8	12	6
16	0	16	0

Which country has a comparative advantage at producing Good X? How can you tell?
Which country has a comparative advantage at producing Good Y?

3. Suppose the United States can produce cars at an opportunity cost of two computers for each car it produces. Suppose Mexico can produce cars at an opportunity cost of eight computers for each car it produces. Indicate how both countries can gain from free trade.

4. Evaluate the following statement: "Small developing economies must first become self-sufficient before benefiting from international trade."

5. Evaluate the following statement: "The United States has an absolute advantage in growing wheat. Therefore, it must have a comparative advantage in growing wheat."

6. NAFTA (North American Free Trade Agreement) is an agreement among the United States, Canada, and Mexico to reduce trade barriers and promote the free flow of goods and services across borders. Many U.S. labor groups were opposed to NAFTA.
    Can you explain why? Can you predict how NAFTA might alter the goods and services produced in the participating countries?

7. If country A is the lowest opportunity cost producer of X and country B is the lowest opportunity cost producer of Y, what happens to their absolute and comparative advantages if country A suddenly becomes three times more productive at producing both X and Y than it was before?

8. Assume that Freeland could produce 8 units of X and no Y, 16 units of Y and no X, or any linear combination in between, and Braveburg could produce 32 units of X and no Y, 48 units of Y and no X, or any linear combination in between.
   a. What is the opportunity cost of producing X in Freeland? In Braveburg?
   b. If Freeland and Braveburg specialize according to comparative advantage, which directions will goods flow in trade?
   c. If trade occurs, what will the terms of trade between X and Y be?
   d. How large would transactions costs, transportation costs, or tariffs have to be to eliminate trade between Freeland and Braveburg?

9. To protect its domestic apple industry, Botswana has for many years prevented international trade in apples. The following graph represents the Botswana domestic market for apples. P_{BT} is the current price, and P_{AT} is the world price.

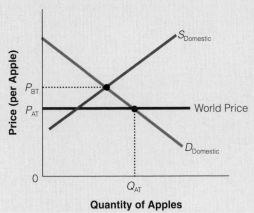

a. If the government allows world trade in apples, what will happen to the price of apples in Botswana? Why?
b. Indicate the amount of apples domestic producers produce after there is trade in apples as Q_{DT}. How many apples are imported?
c. Trade in imports causes producer surplus to be reduced by the amount b. Show b on the graph.
d. The gains from trade equal the amount increased consumer surplus exceeds the loss in producer surplus. Show this gain, g, on the graph.
e. Explain why consumers in Botswana would still be better off if they were required to compensate producers for their lost producer surplus.

10. Use the accompanying graphs to illustrate the effects of imposing a tariff on imports on the domestic price, the domestic quantity purchased, the domestic quantity produced, the level of imports, consumer surplus, producer surplus, the tariff revenue generated, and the total welfare effect from the tariff.

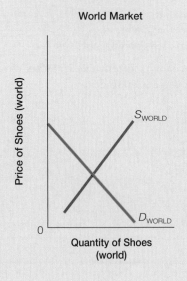

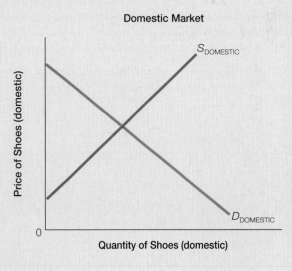

11. Using the accompanying graphs, illustrate the effects of opening up the domestic market to international trade on the domestic price, the domestic quantity purchased, the domestic quantity produced, imports or exports, consumer surplus, producer surplus, and the total welfare gain from trade.

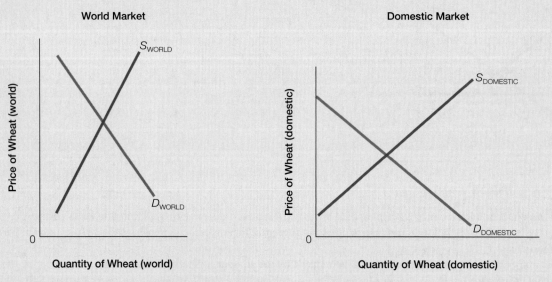

12. Explain why imposing a tariff causes a net welfare loss to the domestic economy.

13. If imposing tariffs and quotas harms consumers, why don't consumers vigorously oppose the implementation of these protectionist policies?

14. Why does rent seeking imply that the traditional measure of deadweight loss from tariffs and quotas will likely understate the true deadweight loss to society?

15. Would you be in favor of freer trade or against it in the following circumstances?
    a. The move to freer trade is in another country and you are an exporter to that country.
    b. The move to freer trade is in your country and you compete with imports from other countries.
    c. The move to freer trade is in your country and you import parts for products you sell domestically.

16. Go through your local newspaper and locate four news items regarding the global economy. Identify the significance of each of these news items to the U.S. economy and whether they are likely to affect international trade.

International Finance

21

When people travel to foreign countries, they pay for their goods and services in foreign currencies. For example, if we were in Italy and were buying Italian shoes, we would have to pay in euros—and we might want to know how much that will cost us in U.S. currency. In this chapter, we will learn how nations pay each other in world trade and how we measure how much buying and selling is going on. We will also learn about exchange rates. ■

SECTION
21.1

The Balance of Payments

* What is the balance of payments?
* What are the three main components of the balance of payments?
* What is the balance of trade?

Balance of Payments

The record of all of the international financial transactions of a nation over a year is called the balance of payments. The **balance of payments** is a statement that records all the exchanges requiring an outflow of funds to foreign nations or an inflow of funds from other nations. Just as an examination of gross domestic product accounts gives us some idea of the economic health and vitality of a nation, the balance of payments provides information about a nation's world trade position. The balance of payments is divided into three main sections: the current account, the capital account, and an "error term" called the statistical discrepancy. These are highlighted in Exhibit 1. Let's look at each of these components, beginning with the current account, which is made up of imports and exports of goods and services.

> **balance of payments**
> the record of international transactions in which a nation has engaged over a year

> **current account**
> a record of a country's imports and exports of goods and services, net investment income, and net transfers

The Current Account

Export Goods and the Current Account

A **current account** is a record of a country's imports and exports of goods and services, net investment income, and net transfers. Any time a foreign buyer purchases a good from a U.S. producer, the foreign buyer must pay the U.S. producer for the good. Usually, the foreign buyer must pay for the good in U.S. dollars, because the producer wants to pay his workers' wages and other input costs with dollars. Making this payment requires the foreign buyer to exchange units of her currency at a foreign exchange dealer for U.S. dollars. Because the United States gains claims for foreign goods by obtaining foreign currency in exchange for the dollars needed to buy exports, all exports of U.S. goods abroad are considered a credit, or plus (+), item in the U.S. balance of payments. Those foreign currencies are

---

section 21.1 exhibit 1   U.S. Balance of Payments, 2008 (billions of dollars)

Type of Transaction

Current Account			Capital Account		
1.	Exports of goods	$ 1,291	10.	U.S.-owned assets abroad	$ −54
2.	Imports of goods	−2,112	11.	Foreign-owned assets in the United States	599
3.	Balance of trade (lines 1 + 2)	−821	12.	Capital account balance (lines 10 + 11)	545
4.	Service exports	544	13.	Statistical discrepancy	128
5.	Service imports	−405	14.	Net Balance (lines 9 − 12 + 13)	$0
6.	Balance on goods and services (lines 3 + 4 + 5)	−682			
7.	Unilateral transfers (net)	−120			
8.	Investment income (net)	129			
9.	Current account balance (lines 6 + 7 + 8)	−673			

SOURCE: Bureau of Economic Analysis, Table 1.

later exchangeable for goods and services made in the country that purchased the U.S. exports.

Import Goods and the Current Account

When a U.S. consumer buys an imported good, however, the reverse is true: The U.S. importer must pay the foreign producer, usually in that nation's currency. Typically, the U.S. buyer will go to a foreign exchange dealer and exchange dollars for units of that foreign currency. Imports are thus a debit ($-$) item in the balance of payments, because the dollars sold to buy the foreign currency add to foreign claims for foreign goods, which are later exchangeable for U.S. goods and services. U.S. imports, then, provide the means by which foreigners can buy U.S. exports.

Services and the Current Account

Even though imports and exports of goods are the largest components of the balance of payments, they are not the only ones. Nations import and export services as well. A particularly important service is tourism. When U.S. tourists go abroad, they are buying foreign-produced services in addition to those purchased by citizens there. Those services include the use of hotels, sightseeing tours, restaurants, and so forth. In the current account, these services are included in imports. On the other hand, foreign tourism in the United States provides us with foreign currencies and claims against foreigners, so they are included in exports. Airline and shipping services also affect the balance of payments. When someone from Italy flies American Airlines, that person is making a payment to a U.S. company. Because the flow of international financial claims is the same, this payment is treated just like a U.S. export in the balance of payments. If an American flies on Alitalia, however, Italians acquire claims against the United States; and so it is included as a debit (import) item in the U.S. balance-of-payments accounts.

Net Transfer Payments and Net Investment Income

Other items that affect the current account are private and government grants and gifts to and from other countries. When the U.S. gives foreign aid to another country, a debit occurs in the U.S. balance of payments

Nations import and export services like tourism.

COURTESY OF ROBERT L SEXTON

because the aid gives foreigners added claims against the United States in the form of dollars. Private gifts, such as individuals sending money to relatives or friends in foreign countries, show up in the current account as debit items as well. Because the United States usually sends more humanitarian and military aid to foreigners than it receives, net transfers are usually in deficit.

Net investment income is also included in the current account (line 8)—U.S. investors hold foreign assets and foreign investors hold U.S. assets. Payments received by U.S. residents are added to the current account and payments made by U.S. residents are subtracted from the current account. In 2008, a net flow of $2 billion came into the United States.

The Current Account Balance

The balance on the current account is the net amount of credits or debits after adding up all transactions of goods (merchandise imports and exports), services, and transfer payments (e.g., foreign aid and gifts). If the sum of credits exceeds the sum of debits, the nation is said to run a balance-of-payments surplus on the current account. If debits exceed credits, however, the nation is running a balance-of-payments deficit on the current account.

The Balance of Trade and the Balance of the Current Account

The balance of payments of the United States for 2008 is presented in Exhibit 1. Notice that exports and imports of goods and services are by far the largest credits and debits. Notice also that U.S. exports of goods were $821 billion less than imports of goods. The import/export goods relationship is often called the **balance of trade.** The United States, therefore, experienced a balance-of-trade deficit that year of $821 billion.

> **balance of trade**
> the net surplus or deficit resulting from the level of exportation and importation of merchandise

However, some of the $821 billion trade deficit is offset by credits from a $139 billion surplus in services. This difference leads to a $682 billion deficit in the balance of goods and services. When $120 billion of net unilateral transfers (gifts and grants between the United States and foreigners) and $129 billion of investment income (net) from the United States are added (the foreigners gave more to the United States than the United States gave to the foreigners), the total deficit on the current account is $673 billion. Exhibit 2 shows the balance on the current account since 1975.

section 21.1
exhibit 2   U.S. Balance of Trade on Goods, 1975–2007

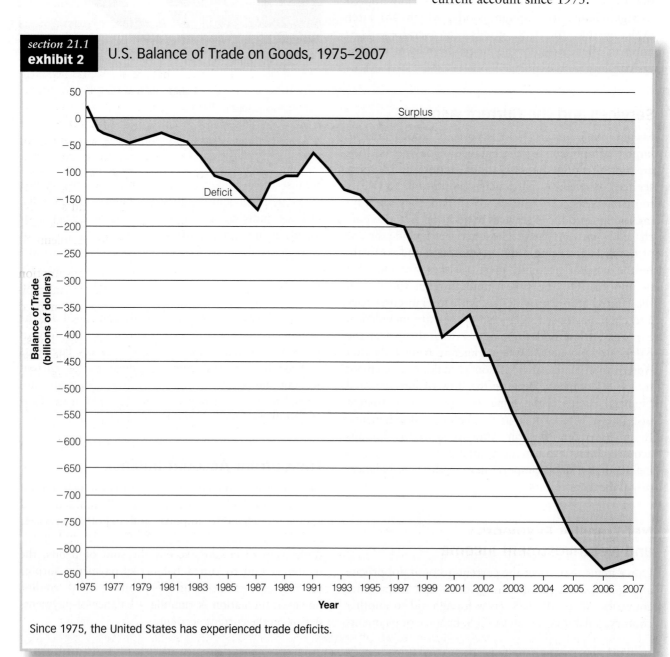

Since 1975, the United States has experienced trade deficits.

SOURCE: Bureau of Economic Analysis, 2009.

The Capital Account

How was this deficit on the current account financed? Remember that U.S. credits give us the financial means to buy foreign goods and that our credits were $545 billion less than our debits from imports and net unilateral transfers to foreign countries. This deficit on the current account balance is settled by movements of financial, or capital, assets. These transactions are recorded in the *capital account*, so that a current account deficit is financed by a capital account surplus. In short, the capital account records the foreign purchases or assets in the United States (a monetary inflow) and U.S. purchases of assets abroad (a monetary outflow).

> **capital account**
> records the foreign purchases or assets in the domestic economy (a monetary inflow) and domestic purchases of assets abroad (a monetary outflow)

What Does the Capital Account Record?

Capital account transactions include such items as international bank loans, purchases of corporate securities, government bond purchases, and direct investments in foreign subsidiary companies. In 2008, the United States purchased foreign assets of $54 billion, which was a further debit because it provided foreigners with U.S. dollars. On the other hand, foreign investments in U.S. bonds, stocks, and other items totaled more than $599 billion. In addition, the United States and other governments buy and sell dollars. On net in 2008, foreign-owned assets in the United States made about $545 billion more than did U.S. assets abroad. On balance, then, a surplus (positive credit) in the capital account from capital movements amounted to $545 billion, offsetting the $673 billion deficit on current account.

The Statistical Discrepancy

In the final analysis, it is true that the balance-of-payments account (current account minus capital account) must balance so that credits and debits are equal. Why? Due to the reciprocal aspect of trade, every credit eventually creates a debit of equal magnitude. These errors are sometimes large and are entered into the balance of payments as the *statistical discrepancy*. Including the errors and omissions recorded as the statistical discrepancy, the balance of payments does balance. That is, the number of U.S. dollars demanded equals the number of U.S. dollars supplied when the balance of payments is zero.

Balance of Payments: A Useful Analogy

In concept, the international balance of payments is similar to the personal financial transactions of an individual. Each individual has a personal "balance of payments," reflecting that person's trading with other economic units: other individuals, corporations, and governments. People earn income or credits by "exporting" their labor service to other economic units or by receiving investment income (a return on capital services). Against that, they "import" goods from other economic units; we call these imports consumption. This debit item is sometimes augmented by payments made to outsiders (e.g., banks) on loans and so forth. Fund transfers, such as gifts to children or charities, are other debit items (or credit items for recipients of the assistance).

As individuals, if our spending on consumption exceeds our income from exporting our labor and capital services, we have a "deficit" that must be financed by borrowing or selling assets. If we "export" more than we "import," however, we can make new investments and/or increase our "reserves" (savings and investment holdings). Like nations, an individual who runs a deficit in daily transactions must make up for it through accommodating transactions (e.g., borrowing or reducing personal savings or investment holdings) to bring about an ultimate balance of credits and debits in his or her personal account.

SECTION CHECK

1. The balance of payments is the record of all the international financial transactions of a nation for any given year.

2. The balance of payments is made up of the current account and the capital account, as well as an "error term" called the statistical discrepancy.

3. The balance of trade refers strictly to the import and export of goods (merchandise) from/to other nations. If our imports of foreign goods are greater than our exports, we are said to have a balance-of-trade deficit.

(continued)

1. What is the balance of payments?

2. Why must British purchasers of U.S. goods and services first exchange pounds for dollars?

3. How is it that our imports provide foreigners with the means to buy U.S. exports?

4. What would have to be true for the United States to have a balance-of-trade deficit and a balance-of-payments surplus?

5. What would have to be true for the United States to have a balance-of-trade surplus and a current account deficit?

6. With no errors or omissions in the recorded balance-of-payments accounts, what should the statistical discrepancy equal?

7. A Nigerian family visiting Chicago enjoys a Chicago Cubs baseball game at Wrigley Field. How would this expense be recorded in the balance-of-payments accounts? Why?

SECTION 21.2 Exchange Rates

* What are exchange rates?
* How are exchange rates determined?
* How do exchange rates affect the demand for foreign goods?

The Need for Foreign Currencies

When a U.S. consumer buys goods from a seller in another country—who naturally wants to be paid in her own domestic currency—the U.S. consumer must first exchange U.S. dollars for the seller's currency in order to pay for those goods. American importers must, therefore, constantly buy yen, euros, pesos, and other currencies in order to finance their purchases. Similarly, someone in another country buying U.S. goods must sell his domestic currency to obtain U.S. dollars to pay for those goods.

The Exchange Rate

The price of a unit of one foreign currency in terms of another is called the exchange rate. If a U.S. importer has agreed to pay euros (the currency of the European Union) to buy a cuckoo clock made in the Black Forest in Germany, she would then have to exchange U.S. dollars for euros. If it takes $1 to buy 1 euro, then the exchange rate is $1 per euro. From the German perspective, the exchange rate is 1 euro per U.S. dollar.

exchange rate
the price of one unit of a country's currency in terms of another country's currency

derived demand
the demand for an input derived from consumers' demand for the good or service produced with that input

Changes in Exchange Rates Affect the Domestic Demand for Foreign Goods

Prices of goods in their currencies combine with exchange rates to determine the domestic price of foreign goods. Suppose the cuckoo clock sells for 100 euros in Germany. What is the price to U.S. consumers? Let's assume that tariffs and other transaction costs are zero. If the exchange rate is $1 = 1 euro, then the equivalent U.S. dollar price of the cuckoo clock is 100 euros times $1 per euro, or $100. If the exchange rate were to change to $2 = 1 euro, fewer clocks would be demanded in the United States, because the effective U.S. dollar price of the clocks would rise to $200 (100 euros × $2 per euro). The higher relative value of a euro compared to the dollar (or, equivalently, the lower relative value of a dollar compared to the euro) would lead to a reduction in U.S. demand for German-made clocks.

The Demand for a Foreign Currency

The demand for foreign currencies is known as a **derived demand,** because the demand for a foreign

Q Why is a strong dollar (i.e., exchange rate for foreign currencies is low) a mixed blessing?

A A strong dollar will lower the price of imports and make trips to foreign countries less expensive. Lower prices on foreign goods also help keep inflation in check and make investments in foreign financial markets (foreign stocks and bonds) relatively cheaper. However, it makes U.S. exports more expensive. Consequently, foreigners will buy fewer U.S. goods and services. The net effect is a fall in exports and a rise in imports—net exports fall. Note that some Americans are helped (vacationers going to foreign countries and those preferring foreign goods), while others are harmed (producers of U.S. exports, operators of hotels dependent on foreign visitors in the United States). A stronger dollar also makes it more difficult for foreign investors to invest in the United States.

currency derives directly from the demand for foreign goods and services or for foreign investment. The more that goods from a foreign country are demanded, the more of that country's currency is needed to pay for those goods. This increased demand for the currency will push up the exchange value of that currency relative to other currencies.

The Supply of a Foreign Currency

Similarly, the supply of foreign currency is provided by foreigners who want to buy the exports of a particular nation. For example, the more that foreigners demand U.S. products, the more of their currencies they will supply in exchange for U.S. dollars, which they use to buy our products.

Determining Exchange Rates

We know that the demand for foreign currencies is derived from the demand for foreign goods, but how does that affect the exchange rate? Just as in the product market, the answer lies with the forces of supply and demand. In this case, it is the supply of and demand for a foreign currency that determine the equilibrium price (exchange rate) of that currency.

The Demand Curve for a Foreign Currency

As Exhibit 1 shows, the demand curve for a foreign currency—the euro, for example—is downward sloping, just as it is in product markets. In this case,

section 21.2
exhibit 1   Equilibrium in the Foreign Exchange Market

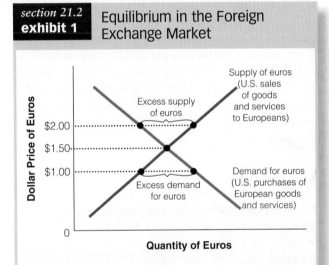

Suppose the foreign exchange market is in equilibrium at 1 euro = $1.50. At any price higher than $1.50, a surplus of euros will result. At any price lower than $1.50, a shortage of euros will result.

however, the demand curve has a negative slope because as the price of the euro falls relative to the dollar, European products become relatively more inexpensive to U.S. consumers, who therefore buy more European goods. To do so, the quantity of euros demanded by U.S. consumers will increase to buy more European goods as the price of the euro falls. For this reason, the demand for foreign currencies is considered to be a derived demand.

The Supply Curve for Foreign Currency

The supply curve for a foreign currency is upward sloping, just as it is in product markets. In this case, as the price, or value, of the euro increases relative to the dollar, U.S. products will become relatively less expensive to European buyers, who will thus increase the quantity of dollars they demand. Europeans will, therefore, increase the quantity of euros supplied to the United States by buying more U.S. products.

Hence, the supply curve is upward sloping.

Equilibrium in the Foreign Exchange Market

Equilibrium is reached where the demand and supply curves for a given currency intersect. In Exhibit 1, the equilibrium price of a euro is $1.50. As in the product market, if the dollar price of euros is higher than the equilibrium price, an excess quantity of euros will be supplied at that price; that is, a surplus of euros will exist. Competition among euro sellers will push the price of euros down toward equilibrium.

Likewise, if the dollar price of euros is lower than the equilibrium price, an excess quantity of euros will be demanded at that price; that is, a shortage of euros will occur. Competition among euro buyers will push the price of euros up toward equilibrium.

On January 1, 1999, the euro became the currency in 11 countries: Belgium, Germany, Spain, France, Ireland, Italy, Luxembourg, the Netherlands, Austria, Portugal, and Finland. If the euro becomes relatively less expensive in terms of dollars (it now costs less to buy a euro), what will happen to the U.S. demand for European goods? If the price of the euro falls relative to the dollar, European products become relatively less expensive to U.S. consumers, who will tend to buy more European goods.

AP IMAGES

SECTION / CHECK

1. The price of a unit of one foreign currency in terms of another is called the exchange rate.
2. The exchange rate for a currency is determined by the supply of and demand for that currency in the foreign exchange market.
3. If the dollar appreciates in value relative to foreign currencies, foreign goods become more inexpensive to U.S. consumers, increasing U.S. demand for foreign goods.

1. What is an exchange rate?
2. When a U.S. dollar buys relatively more British pounds, why does the cost of imports from England fall in the United States?
3. When a U.S. dollar buys relatively fewer yen, why does the cost of U.S. exports fall in Japan?
4. How does an increase in domestic demand for foreign goods and services increase the demand for those foreign currencies?
5. As euros get cheaper relative to U.S. dollars, why does the quantity of euros demanded by Americans increase? Why doesn't the demand for euros increase as a result?
6. Who brings exchange rates down when they are above their equilibrium value? Who brings exchange rates up when they are below their equilibrium value?

Equilibrium Changes in the Foreign Exchange Market

✳ What factors cause the demand curve for a currency to shift?

✳ What factors cause the supply curve for a currency to shift?

Determinants in the Foreign Exchange Market

The equilibrium exchange rate of a currency changes many times daily. Sometimes, these changes can be quite significant. Any force that shifts either the demand for or supply of a currency will shift the equilibrium in the foreign exchange market, leading to a new exchange rate. Among such factors are changes in consumer tastes for goods, income levels, relative real interest rates, and relative inflation rates, as well as speculation.

Increased Tastes for Foreign Goods

Because the demand for foreign currencies is derived from the demand for foreign goods, any change in the U.S. demand for foreign goods will shift the demand

schedule for foreign currency in the same direction. For example, if a cuckoo clock revolution sweeps through the United States, German producers will have reason to celebrate, knowing that many U.S. buyers will turn to Germany for their cuckoo clocks. However, because Germans will only accept payment in the form of euros, U.S. consumers and retailers must convert their dollars into euros before they can purchase their clocks. The increased taste for European goods in the United States will, therefore, lead to an increased demand for euros. As shown in Exhibit 1, this increased demand for euros shifts the demand curve to the right, resulting in a new, higher equilibrium dollar price of euros.

Relative Income Increases or Reductions in U.S. Tariffs

Any change in the average income of U.S. consumers will also change the equilibrium exchange rate, *ceteris paribus*. If on the whole incomes were to increase

section 21.3
exhibit 1 Impact on the Foreign Exchange Market of a U.S. Change in Taste, Income Increase, or Tariff Decrease

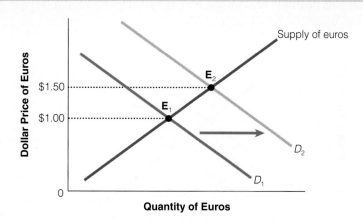

An increase in the taste for European goods, an increase in U.S. incomes, or a decrease in U.S. tariffs can cause an increase in the demand for euros, shifting the demand for euros to the right from D_1 to D_2 and leading to a higher equilibrium exchange rate.

What impact will an increase in travel to Paris by U.S. consumers have on the dollar price of euros? For a consumer to buy souvenirs at the Eiffel Tower, she will need to exchange dollars for euros. It will increase the demand for euros and result in a new, higher dollar price of euros.

in the United States, Americans would buy more goods, including imported goods, hence more European goods would be bought. This increased demand for European goods would lead to an increased demand for euros, resulting in a higher exchange rate for the euro. A decrease in U.S. tariffs on European goods would tend to have the same effect as an increase in incomes, by making European goods more affordable. Exhibit 1 shows that it would again lead to an increased demand for European goods and a higher short-run equilibrium exchange rate for the euro.

European Incomes Increase, Reductions in European Tariffs, or Changes in European Tastes

If European incomes rose, European tariffs on U.S. goods fell, or European tastes for American goods increased, the supply of euros in the euro foreign exchange market would increase. Any of these changes would cause Europeans to demand more U.S. goods and therefore more U.S. dollars to purchase those goods. To obtain these added dollars, Europeans would have to exchange more of their euros, increasing the supply of euros on the euro foreign exchange market. As Exhibit 2 demonstrates, the result would be a rightward shift in the euro supply curve, leading to a new equilibrium at a lower exchange rate for the euro.

---

section 21.3
exhibit 2   Impact on the Foreign Exchange Market of a European Change in Taste, Income Increase, or Tariff Decrease

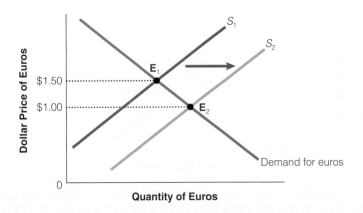

If European incomes increase, European tariffs on U.S. goods fall, or European tastes for American goods increase, the supply of euros increases. The increase in demand for dollars causes an increase in the supply of euros, shifting it to the right, from S_1 to S_2.

How Do Changes in Relative Real Interest Rates Affect Exchange Rates?

If interest rates in the United States were to increase relative to, say, European interest rates, other things being equal, the rate of return on U.S. investments would increase relative to that on European investments. European investors would then increase their demand for U.S. investments and therefore offer euros for sale in order to buy dollars to buy U.S. investments, shifting the supply curve for euros to the right, from S_1 to S_2 in Exhibit 3.

In this scenario, U.S. investors would also shift their investments away from Europe by decreasing their demand for euros relative to their demand for dollars, from D_1 to D_2 in Exhibit 3. A subsequent, lower equilibrium price ($1.50) would result for the euro as a result of the increase in U.S. interest rates. That is, the euro would depreciate, because euros could now buy fewer units of dollars than before. In short, the higher U.S. interest rates would attract more investment to the United States, leading to a relative appreciation of the dollar and a relative depreciation of the euro.

Changes in the Relative Inflation Rate

If Europe experienced an inflation rate greater than that experienced in the United States, other things being equal, what would happen to the exchange rate? In this case, European products would become more expensive to U.S. consumers. Americans would then decrease the quantity of European goods demanded and thus decrease their demand for euros. The result would be a leftward shift of the demand curve for euros.

On the other side of the Atlantic, U.S. goods would become relatively cheaper to Europeans, leading Europeans to increase the quantity of U.S. goods demanded and thus to demand more U.S. dollars. This increased demand for dollars would translate into an increased supply of euros, shifting the supply curve for euros outward. Exhibit 4 shows the shifts of the supply and demand curves and the new lower equilibrium price for the euro resulting from the higher European rate.

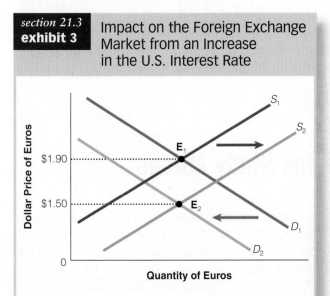

section 21.3
exhibit 3
Impact on the Foreign Exchange Market from an Increase in the U.S. Interest Rate

When U.S. interest rates increase, European investors increase their supply of euros to buy dollars—the supply curve of euros increases from S_1 to S_2. In addition, U.S. investors shift their investments away from Europe, decreasing their demand for euros and shifting the demand curve from D_1 to D_2. This shift leads to a depreciation of the euro; that is, euros can now buy fewer units of dollars.

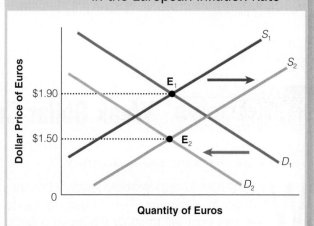

section 21.3
exhibit 4
Impact on the Foreign Exchange Market from an Increase in the European Inflation Rate

If Europe experiences a higher inflation rate than does the United States, European products become more expensive to U.S. consumers. As a result, those consumers demand fewer euros, shifting the demand for euros to the left, from D_1 to D_2. At the same time, U.S. goods become relatively cheaper to Europeans, who then buy more dollars by supplying euros, shifting the euro supply curve to the right, from S_1 to S_2. The result: a new, lower equilibrium price for the euro.

Expectations and Speculation

Every trading day, roughly a trillion dollars in currency trades hands in the foreign exchange markets. Suppose currency traders believe that in the future, the United States will experience more rapid inflation than will Japan. If currency speculators believe that the value of the dollar will soon be falling because of the anticipated rise in the U.S. inflation rate, those who are holding dollars will convert them to yen. This move will lead to an increase in the demand for yen—the yen appreciates and the dollar depreciates relative to the yen, *ceteris paribus*. In short, if speculators believe that the price of a country's currency is going to rise, they will buy more of that currency, pushing up the price and causing the country's currency to appreciate.

Use what you've LEARNED — DETERMINANTS OF EXCHANGE RATES

Q How will each of the following events affect the foreign exchange market?

a. American travel to Europe increases.

b. Japanese investors purchase U.S. stock.

c. U.S. real interest rates abruptly increase relative to world interest rates.

d. Other countries become less politically and economically stable relative to the United States.

A a. The demand for euros increases (demand shifts right in the euro market), the dollar will depreciate, and the euro will appreciate, *ceteris paribus*.

b. The demand for dollars increases (demand shifts right in the dollar market), the dollar will appreciate, and the yen will depreciate, *ceteris paribus*. Alternatively, you could think of it as an increase in supply in the yen market.

c. International investors will increase their demand for dollars in the dollar market to take advantage of the higher interest rates. The dollar will appreciate relative to other foreign currencies, *ceteris paribus*.

d. More foreign investors will want to buy U.S. assets, resulting in an increase in demand for dollars.

in the news — Weak Dollar Crimps Study Abroad

—KELLY EVANS AND SARA MURRAY

Wilmer Gutierrez, a 21-year-old junior at Goucher College in Baltimore, had hoped to go to Denmark next fall to study European politics. But the weak dollar has prompted a change of plan: Now, he will head to Argentina to study the Latin American political system.

With the greenback down 20% against the Danish krone and up 4% against the Argentine peso in the past two years, Mr. Gutierrez says he has little choice but to head south. "It's very frustrating," he says.

Many other college students, hit by sticker shock, also are steering clear of Western Europe, especially the United Kingdom, and opting for study-abroad programs in Asia, Africa and Latin America. Many of those destinations are cheaper to begin with and have currencies that haven't been as rough on the dollar.

Over the past two years, the dollar, while up a bit from recent lows, has lost more than 20% of its value against the euro and about 6% against the pound. The result: While programs in places like Rome, Paris, Barcelona and London are still at the

in the news   Weak Dollar Crimps Study Abroad (cont.)

top of students' lists, enrollment there is slowing. And interest in alternative destinations is surging.

Nearly a quarter of a million students from the U.S. studied abroad for academic credit during the 2005–06 school year, according to the most recent data from the Institute of International Education, a New York-based nonprofit organization that administers study-abroad programs. Each college handles study-abroad programs differently—some directly host programs in other countries so students pay the same tuition as they would for a semester at home in the U.S. Others allow students to enroll in programs offered by other colleges or by third-party study-abroad providers that enroll them directly in foreign institutions.

Language students often choose their location to become fluent speakers and learn about the culture of a chosen region; others, such as business students, may choose a program that enhances their resume (like China, India, or the Middle East).

Geoffrey Bannister, president and chief academic officer of Cultural Experiences Abroad, a company based in Tempe, Ariz., that runs study-abroad programs, says enrollment in the company's Western Europe programs grew just 8% for next fall, much less than the usual increase of 20% to 25%. Buenos Aires, meanwhile, is getting a lot of interest, he says.

Nathan Bullock, a University of Richmond sophomore who is majoring in history and international studies, considered expenses carefully when deciding between Hong Kong and France for the current semester.

The university was going to charge him the same tuition regardless of where he went, so his decision came down to room and board—and he knew his dollars would go further in Hong Kong, where the currency is pegged to the dollar.

"Just getting an apartment or living with a family would be so expensive in France," he says. In Hong Kong, his room and board costs about HK$3,000, or about US$385 a semester. In addition, it's an easy jumping-off point for other parts of Asia, where traveling can be a bargain.

Even in Shanghai, the most expensive place he has visited, Mr. Bullock spent only 55 yuan a

night—less than $8—for a room in a hostel. By comparison, in Paris, the cheapest hostels run 12 to 16 euros, or about $18 to $24.

American students in Europe understand the need to scale back. "Just to lead a normal student life here is so expensive," says Sarah Ott, a junior at Ohio's Kenyon College who is studying in Paris.

To save money, Ms. Ott says, she and other students avoid cozy cafes, which can easily charge $7 or $8 for a glass of soda. Instead, they get takeout sandwiches and carry around six-packs of Coca-Cola. They patronize bars offering cheap beer rather than nightclubs. And they pinch pennies during sightseeing jaunts to nearby cities.

"I went into it thinking traveling would be a cheap little weekend away," Ms. Ott says. "Not so much."

Daeya Malboeuf, a spokeswoman for Syracuse University's study-abroad programs, says the school urges students in its London program to save money by staying in the city on weekends. And it serves free coffee, so students "don't have to go to Starbucks," where a medium-size latte runs about 2.40 pounds, or about $4.75.

"We used to be able to say the cost of a semester abroad was the same as a semester here," Ms. Malboeuf says, because a strong dollar made traveling overseas relatively cheap. "We don't say that anymore."

While London, Florence and Madrid continue to be top destinations for Syracuse students, she says, Hong Kong, Beijing and Santiago are growing quickly in popularity.

consider this:

In March of 2009 it would cost you $125 to get 100 euros; a year earlier it would have cost you a $160. That is, the price of travel to nations using the euro is now less expensive. However since March the dollar has weakened against the Euro and in October of 2009 it cost $1.50 to get 100 Euros.

SECTION 21.4

Flexible Exchange Rates

* How are exchange rates determined today?
* How are exchange rate changes different under a flexible-rate system than in a fixed system?

* What major problems exist in a fixed-rate system?
* What are the major arguments against flexible rates?

The Flexible Exchange Rate System

Since 1973, the world has essentially operated on a system of flexible exchange rates. Flexible exchange rates mean that currency prices are allowed to fluctuate with changes in supply and demand, without governments stepping in to prevent those changes. Before that, governments operated under what was called the *Bretton Woods fixed exchange rate system*, in which they would maintain a stable exchange rate by buying or selling currencies or reserves to bring demand and supply for their currencies together at the fixed exchange rate. The present system evolved out of the Bretton Woods fixed-rate system and occurred by accident, not design. Governments were unable to agree on an alternative fixed-rate approach when the Bretton Woods system collapsed, so nations simply let market forces determine currency values.

Are Exchange Rates Managed at All?

To be sure, governments sensitive to sharp changes in the exchange value of their currencies do still intervene from time to time to prop up their currency's exchange rate if it is considered to be too low or falling too rapidly, or to depress its exchange rate if it is considered to be too high or rising too rapidly. Such was the case when the U.S. dollar declined in value in the late 1970s, but the U.S. government intervention appeared to have little if any effect in preventing the dollar's decline. However, present-day fluctuations in exchange rates are not determined solely by market forces. Economists sometimes say that the current exchange rate system is a **dirty float system,** meaning that fluctuations in currency values are partly determined by market forces and partly influenced by government intervention. Over the years, however, such governmental support attempts have been insufficient to dramatically alter exchange rates for long, and currency exchange rates have changed dramatically.

The exchange rate is the rate at which one country's currency can be traded for another country's currency. Under a flexible-rate system, the government allows the forces of supply and demand to determine the exchange rate. Changes in exchange rates occur daily or even hourly.

When Exchange Rates Change

When exchange rates change, they affect not only the currency market but the product markets as well. For example, if U.S. consumers were to receive fewer and fewer British pounds and Japanese yen per U.S. dollar, the effect would be an increasing price for foreign imports, *ceteris paribus.* It would now take a greater number of dollars to buy a given number of yen or pounds, which U.S. consumers use to purchase those foreign products. It would, however, lower the cost of U.S. exports to foreigners. If, however, the dollar increased in value relative to other currencies, then the relative price of foreign goods would decrease, *ceteris paribus.* But foreigners would find that U.S. goods were more expensive in terms of their own currency prices, and, as a result, would import fewer U.S. products.

> **dirty float system**
> a description of the exchange rate system that means that fluctuations in currency values are partly determined by government intervention

rampages and major currency revaluations under the fixed Bretton Woods system have significantly diminished. Under the fixed-rate system, price changes in currencies came infrequently, but when they came, they were of a large magnitude: 20 percent or 30 percent changes overnight were fairly common. Today, price changes occur daily or even hourly, but each change is much smaller in magnitude, with major changes in exchange rates typically occurring only over periods of months or years.

The Advantages of Flexible Rates

As mentioned earlier, the present system of flexible exchange rates was not planned. Indeed, most central bankers thought that a system where rates were not fixed would lead to chaos. What in fact has happened? Since the advent of flexible exchange rates, world trade has not only continued but expanded. Over a one-year period, the world economy adjusted to the shock of a four-fold increase in the price of its most important internationally traded commodity, oil. Although the OPEC oil cartel's price increase certainly had adverse economic effects, it did so without paralyzing the economy of any one nation.

The most important advantage of the flexible-rate system is that the recurrent crises that led to speculative

Fixed Exchange Rates Can Result in Currency Shortages

Perhaps the most significant problem with the fixed-rate system is that it can result in currency shortages, just as domestic price and wage controls lead to shortages. Suppose we had a fixed-rate system with the price of one euro set at $1.00, as shown in Exhibit 1. In this example, the original quantity of euros demanded and supplied is indicated by curves D_1 and S, so $1.00 is the equilibrium price. That is, at a price of $1.00, the quantity of euros demanded (by U.S. importers of European products and others wanting euros) equals the quantity supplied (by European importers of U.S. products and others).

Suppose that some event happens to increase U.S. demand for Dutch goods. For this example, let us

How Flexible Exchange
Rates Work

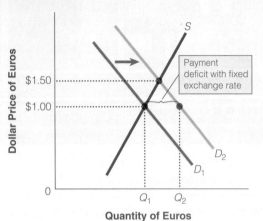

An increase in demand for euros shifts the demand curve to the right, from D_1 to D_2. Under a fixed-rate system, this increase in demand results in a shortage of euros at the equilibrium price of $1, because the quantity demanded at this price, Q_2, is greater than the quantity supplied, Q_1. If the exchange rate is flexible, however, no shortage develops. Instead, the increase in demand forces the exchange rate higher, to $1.50. At this higher exchange rate, the quantity of euros demanded doesn't increase as much, and the quantity of euros supplied increases as a result of the now relatively lower cost of imports from the United States.

assume that Royal Dutch Shell discovers new oil reserves in the North Sea and thus has a new product to export. As U.S. consumers begin to demand Royal Dutch Shell oil, the demand for euros increases. That is, at any given dollar price of euros, U.S. consumers want more euros, shifting the demand curve to the right, to D_2. Under a fixed exchange rate system, the dollar price of euros must remain at $1, where the quantity of euros demanded (Q_2) now exceeds the quantity supplied, Q_1. The result is a shortage of euros—a shortage that must be corrected in some way. As a solution to the shortage, the United States may borrow euros from the Netherlands, or perhaps ship the Netherlands some of its reserves of gold. The ability to continually make up the shortage (deficit) in this manner, however, is limited, particularly if the deficit persists for a substantial time.

Flexible Rates Solve the Currency Shortage Problem

Under flexible exchange rates, a change in the supply or demand for euros does not pose a problem. Because rates are allowed to change, the rising

U.S. demand for European goods (and thus for euros) would lead to a new equilibrium price for euros, say at $1.50. At this higher price, European goods are more costly to U.S. buyers. Some of the increase in demand for European imports, then, is offset by a decrease in quantity demanded resulting from higher import prices. Similarly, the change in the exchange rate will make U.S. goods cheaper to Europeans, thus increasing U.S. exports and, with that, the quantity of euros supplied. For example, a $40 software program that cost Europeans 40 euros when the exchange rate was $1 per euro costs less than 27 euros when the exchange rate increases to $1.50 per euro ($40 divided by $1.50).

Flexible Rates Affect Macroeconomic Policies

With flexible exchange rates, the imbalance between debits and credits arising from shifts in currency demand and/or supply is accommodated by changes in currency prices, rather than through the special financial borrowings or reserve movements necessary with fixed rates. In a pure flexible exchange rate system, deficits and surpluses in the balance of payments tend to disappear automatically. The market mechanism itself is able to address world trade imbalances, dispensing with the need for bureaucrats attempting to achieve some administratively determined price. Moreover, the need to use restrictive monetary and/or fiscal policy to end such an imbalance while maintaining a fixed exchange rate is alleviated. Nations are thus able to feel less constraint in carrying out internal macroeconomic policies under flexible exchange rates. For these reasons, many economists welcomed the collapse of the Bretton Woods system and the failure to arrive at a new system of fixed or quasi-fixed exchange rates.

The Disadvantages of Flexible Rates

Despite the fact that world trade has grown and dealing with balance-of-payments problems has become less difficult, flexible exchange rates have not been universally endorsed by everyone. Several disadvantages of this system have been cited.

Flexible Rates and World Trade

Traditionally, the major objection to flexible rates was that they introduce considerable uncertainty into international trade. For example, if you order some perfume

BIG MAC INDEX

The **Big Mac Index** is published by *The Economist* as an informal way of measuring the purchasing power parity (PPP) between two currencies and provides a test of the extent to which market exchange rates result in goods costing the same in different countries. It "seeks to make exchange-rate theory a bit more digestible."

The index takes its name from the Big Mac, a hamburger sold at McDonald's restaurants.

McDonald's Big Mac Purchased in Australia
The Big Mac Index was introduced in *The Economist* in September 1986 by Pam Woodall as a semi-humorous illustration and has been published by that paper annually since then. The index also gave rise to the word *burgernomics.*

UBS Wealth Management Research has expanded the idea of the Big Mac Index to include the amount of time that an average worker in a given country must work to earn enough to buy a Big Mac. The working-time based Big Mac Index might give a more realistic view of the purchasing power of the average worker, as it takes into account more factors, such as local wages.

One suggested method of predicting exchange rate movements is that the rate between two currencies should naturally adjust so that a sample basket of goods and services should cost the same in both currencies (PPP). In the Big Mac Index, the "basket" in question is considered to be a single Big Mac burger as sold by the McDonald's fast food restaurant chain. The Big Mac was chosen because it is available to a common specification in many countries around the world, with local McDonald's franchisees having significant responsibility for negotiating input prices. For these reasons, the index enables a comparison between many countries' currencies.

The Big Mac PPP exchange rate between two countries is obtained by dividing the price of a Big Mac in one country (in its currency) by the price of a Big Mac in another country (in its currency). This value is then compared with the actual exchange rate; if it is lower, then the first currency

© TERRI MILLER/E-VISUAL COMMUNICATIONS INC.

is under-valued (according to PPP theory) compared with the second, and conversely, if it is higher, then the first currency is over-valued.

For example, using figures in July 2008:

✽ the price of a Big Mac was $3.57 in the United States
✽ the price of a Big Mac was £2.09 in the United Kingdom (Britain) (Varies by region)
✽ the implied purchasing power parity was $1.56 to £1, that is $3.57/£2.29 = 1.56
✽ this compares with an actual exchange rate of $2.00 to £1 at the time
✽ the pound was thus overvalued against the dollar by 28%
  ✽ i.e. the actual exchange rate divided by implied purchasing parity → 2 divided by 1.56 = 1.28

The Euro-zone is mixed, as prices differ widely in the EU area. As of April 2009, the Big Mac is trading in

(continued)

Germany at 2,99EUR, which translates into 3,96 US$, which would imply that the Euro is slightly trading above the PPP, with the difference being 10.9%.

The Economist sometimes produces variants on the theme. For example in January 2004, it showed a *Tall Latte index* with the Big Mac replaced by a cup of Starbucks coffee. In a similar vein, in 1997, the newspaper drew up a "Coca-Cola map" that showed inverse proportionality between the amount of Cola consumed per capita in a country and that country's health.

In 2007, an Australian bank, Commonwealth Securities, adapted the idea behind the Big Mac Index to create an "iPod index." The bank's theory is that since the iPod is manufactured at a single place, the value of iPods should be more consistent globally. However, this theory can be criticized for ignoring shipping costs, which will vary depending on how far the product is delivered from its "single place" of manufacture.

The burger methodology has limitations in its estimates of the PPP. In many countries, eating at international fast-food chain restaurants such as McDonald's is relatively expensive in comparison to eating at a local restaurant, and the demand for Big Macs is not as large in countries like India as in the United States. Social status of eating at fast food restaurants like McDonald's, local taxes, levels of competition, and import duties on selected items may not be representative of the country's economy as a whole. In addition, there is no theoretical reason why non-tradable goods and services such as property costs should be equal in different countries: this is the theoretical reason for PPPs being different from market exchange rates over time. Nevertheless, economists widely cite the Big Mac Index as a real world measurement of purchasing power parity. McDonald's is also using different commercial[s] which can result in huge differences for a product, whereas there is a smaller price difference between both countries. For example, a Hamburger sandwich costs only 1 € in France, and 1,50 € in Belgium, but overall, McDonald's restaurants are cheaper in Belgium. In Estonia, the price difference between a Big Mac burger and the whole meal is sometimes as small as 3 EEK (0,20 USD), or 5% of the price of the burger alone.

from France with a commitment to pay 1,000 euros in three months, you are not certain what the dollar price of euros, and therefore of the perfume, will be three months from now, because the exchange rate is constantly fluctuating. Because people prefer certainty to uncertainty and are generally risk averse, this uncertainty raises the costs of international transactions. As a result, flexible exchange rates can reduce the volume of trade, thus reducing the potential gains from international specialization.

Proponents of flexible rates have three answers to this argument. First, the empirical evidence shows that international trade has, in fact, grown in volume faster since the introduction of flexible rates. The exchange rate risk of trade has not had any major adverse effect. Second, it is possible to, in effect, buy insurance against the proposed adverse effect of currency fluctuations. Rather than buying currencies for immediate use in what is called the "spot" market for foreign currencies, one can contract today to buy foreign currencies in the future at a set exchange rate in the "forward" or "futures" market. By using this market, a perfume importer can buy euros now for delivery to her in three months; in doing so, she can be certain of the dollar price she is paying for the perfume. Since floating exchange rates began, booming futures markets in foreign currencies have opened in Chicago, New York, and in foreign financial centers. The third argument is that the alleged certainty of currency prices under the old Bretton Woods system was fictitious, because the possibility existed that nations might, at their whim, drastically revalue their currencies to deal with their own fundamental balance-of-payments problems. Proponents of flexible rates, then, argue that they are therefore no less disruptive to trade than fixed rates.

Flexible Rates and Inflation

A second, more valid criticism of flexible exchange rates is that they can contribute to inflationary pressures. Under fixed rates, domestic monetary and fiscal authorities have an incentive to constrain their domestic prices, because lower domestic prices increase the attractiveness of exported goods. This discipline is not present to the same extent with flexible rates. The consequence of a sharp monetary or fiscal expansion under flexible rates would be a decline in the value of one's currency relative to those of other countries. Yet even that may not seem to be as serious a political consequence as the Bretton Woods solution of an abrupt devaluation of the currency in the face of a severe balance-of-payments problem.

Advocates of flexible rates would argue that inflation need not occur under flexible rates. Flexible rates do not cause inflation; rather, it is caused by the expansionary macroeconomic policies of governments and central banks. Actually, flexible rates give government decision makers greater freedom of action than fixed rates; whether they act responsibly is determined not by exchange rates but by domestic policies.

global WATCH   CHINA'S CURRENCY

From 1994 until July 2005, China maintained a policy of pegging its currency, the renminbi or yuan, to the U.S. dollar at an exchange rate of roughly 8.28 yuan to the dollar. The Chinese central bank maintained this peg by buying (or selling) as many dollar-denominated assets in exchange for newly printed yuan as needed to eliminate excess demand (supply) for the yuan. As a result, the exchange rate between the yuan and the dollar basically stayed the same, despite changing economic factors which could have otherwise caused the yuan to either appreciate or depreciate relative to the dollar. Under a floating exchange rate system, the relative demand for the two countries' goods and assets would determine the exchange rate of the yuan to the dollar. Many economists contend that for the first several years of the peg, the fixed value was likely close to the market value. But in the past few years, economic conditions have changed such that the yuan would likely have appreciated if it had been floating. The sharp increase in China's foreign exchange reserves (which grew from $403 billion in 2003 to $1.95 trillion as of March 2009) and China's large trade surplus with the world ($297 billion in 2008) are often viewed by critics of China's currency policy as proof that the yuan is significantly undervalued.

The Chinese government modified its currency policy on July 21, 2005. It announced that the yuan's exchange rate would become "adjustable, based on market supply and demand with reference to exchange rate movements of currencies in a basket" (it was later announced that the composition of the basket includes the dollar, the yen, the euro, and a few other currencies) and that the exchange rate of the U.S. dollar against the yuan was adjusted from 8.28 to 8.11, an appreciation of 2.1%. Unlike a true floating exchange rate, the yuan would be allowed to fluctuate by up to 0.3% (later changed to 0.5%) on a daily basis against the basket.

Since July 2005, China has allowed the yuan to appreciate steadily, but very slowly. It has continued to accumulate foreign reserves at a rapid pace, which suggests that if the yuan were allowed to freely float it would appreciate much more rapidly. The current situation might be best described as a "managed float"—market forces are determining the general direction of the yuan's movement, but the government is retarding its rate of appreciation through market intervention. From July 21, 2005 to April 13, 2009, the dollar-yuan exchange rate went from 8.11 to 6.83, an appreciation of 18.7%. The effects of the yuan's appreciation are unclear. The price index for U.S. imports from China in 2008, rose by 3.0% (compared to a 0.9% rise in import prices for total U.S. imports of non-petroleum products). In 2008, U.S. imports from China rose by 5.1% over the previous year, compared to import growth of 11.7% in 2007; however, U.S. exports over this period were up 9.5% compared with an 18.1% rise in 2007.

Many Members of Congress charge that China's policy of accumulating foreign reserves (especially U.S. dollars) to influence the value of its currency constitutes a form of currency manipulation intended to make its exports cheaper and imports into China more expensive than they would be under free market conditions. They further contend that this policy has caused a surge in the U.S. trade deficit

(continued)

CHINA'S CURRENCY (cont.)

with China and has been a major factor in the loss of U.S. manufacturing jobs. Although China made modest reforms to its currency policy in 2005, resulting in a gradual appreciation of its currency (about 19% through mid-April 2009), many Members contend the reforms have not gone far enough and have warned of potential punitive legislative action.

Although an undervalued Chinese currency has likely hurt some sectors of the U.S. economy, it has also benefited others. For example, consumers have gained from the supply of low-cost Chinese goods (which helps to control inflation), as well as U.S. firms using Chinese-made parts and materials (which helps such firms become more globally competitive). In addition, China has used its abundant foreign exchange reserves to buy U.S. securities, including U.S. Treasury securities, which are used to fund the Federal budget deficit. Such purchases help keep U.S. interest rates relatively low.

The current global economic crisis has further complicated the currency issue for both the United States and China. Although China is under pressure from the United States to appreciate its currency, it is reluctant to do so because it could cause further damage to export sector and lead to more layoffs. China has halted its gradual appreciation of its currency, the renminbi (RMB) or yuan to the dollar in 2009; keeping it at about 6.83 yuan per dollar (from January 1 through April 13, 2009). The federal budget deficit has increased rapidly since FY2008, causing a sharp increase in the amount of Treasury securities that must be sold. The Obama Administration has encouraged China to continue purchasing U.S. debt. However, if China were induced to further appreciate its currency against the dollar, it could slow China's

accumulation of foreign exchange reserves, thus reducing the need to invest in dollar assets, such as Treasury securities.

China's currency policy appears to have created a policy dilemma for the Chinese government. A strong and stable U.S. economy is in China's national interest since the United States is China's largest export market. Thus, some analysts contend that China will feel compelled to keep funding the growing U.S. debt. However, Chinese officials have expressed concern that the growing U.S. debt will eventually spark inflation in the United States and a depreciation of the dollar, which would negatively impact the value of China's holdings of U.S. securities. But if China stopped buying U.S. debt or tried to sell off a large portion of those holdings, it could also cause the dollar to depreciate and thus reduce the value of its remaining holdings, and such a move could further destabilize the U.S. economy. Chinese concerns over its large dollar holdings appear to have been reflected in a paper issued by the governor of the People's Bank of China, Zhou Xiaochuan on March 24, 2009, which called for the replacing the U.S. dollar as the international reserve currency with a new global system controlled by the International Monetary Fund. China has also signed currency swap agreements with six of its trading partners, which would allow those partners to settle accounts with China using the yuan rather than the dollar.

CRS Report RL32165, *China's Currency: Economic Issues and Options for U.S. Trade Policy,* by Wayne M. Morrison and Marc Labonte.

SOURCE: *Congressional Research Service,* April 2009.

SECTION CHECK

1. Today, rates are free to fluctuate based on market transactions, but governments occasionally intervene to increase or depress the price of their currencies.

2. Changes in exchange rates occur more often under a flexible-rate system, but the changes are much smaller than the drastic, overnight revaluations of currencies that occurred under the fixed-rate system.

3. Under a fixed-rate system, the supply and demand for currencies shift, but currency prices are not allowed to shift to the new equilibrium, leading to surpluses and shortages of currencies.

4. The main arguments presented against flexible exchange rates are that international trade levels will be diminished due to uncertainty of future currency prices and that the flexible rates would lead to inflation. Proponents of flexible exchange rates have strong counter-arguments to those views.

1. What are the arguments for and against flexible exchange rates?

2. When the U.S. dollar starts to exchange for fewer Japanese yen, other things equal, what happens to U.S. and Japanese imports and exports as a result?

3. Why is the system of flexible exchange rates sometimes called a dirty float system?

4. Were exchange rates under the Bretton Woods system really stable? How could you argue that exchange rates were more uncertain under the fixed-rate system than with floating exchange rates?

5. What is the uncertainty argument against flexible exchange rates? What evidence do proponents of flexible exchange rates cite in response?

6. Do flexible exchange rates cause higher rates of inflation? Why or why not?

Interactive Chapter Summary

Fill in the blanks:

1. A current account is a record of a country's current _____ and _____ of goods and services.

2. Because the United States gains claims over foreign buyers by obtaining foreign currency in exchange for the dollars needed to buy U.S. exports, all exports of U.S. goods abroad are considered a(n) _____ or _____ item in the U.S. balance of payments.

3. Nations import and export _____, such as tourism, as well as _____ (goods).

4. The merchandise import/export relationship is often called the balance of _____.

5. Foreigners buying U.S. goods must _____ their currencies to obtain _____ in order to pay for exported goods.

6. The price of a unit of one foreign currency in terms of another is called the _____.

7. A change in the euro-dollar exchange rate from $1 per euro to $2 per euro would _____ the U.S. price of German goods, thereby _____ the number of German goods that would be demanded in the United States.

8. The demand for foreign currencies is a derived demand because it derives directly from the demand for foreign _____ or for foreign _____.

9. The more foreigners demand U.S. products, the _____ of their currencies they will supply in exchange for U.S. dollars.

10. The supply of and demand for a foreign currency determine the equilibrium _____ of that currency.

11. The quantity of euros demanded by U.S. consumers will increase to buy more European goods as the price of the euro _____.

12. As the price, or value, of the euro increases relative to the dollar, American products become relatively _____ expensive to European buyers, which will _____ the quantity of dollars they will demand.

13. The supply curve of a foreign currency is _____ sloping.

14. If the dollar price of euros is higher than the equilibrium price, an excess quantity of euros will be _____ at that price, and competition among euro _____ will push the price of euros _____ toward equilibrium.

15. An increased demand for euros will result in a(n) _____ equilibrium price (exchange value) for euros, while a decreased demand for euros will result in a(n) _____ equilibrium price (exchange value) for euros.

16. Changes in a currency's exchange rate can be caused by changes in _____ for goods, changes in _____, changes in relative _____ rates, changes in relative _____ rates, and _____.

17. An increase in tastes for European goods in the United States would _____ the demand for euros, thereby _____ the equilibrium price (exchange value) of euros.

18. A decrease in incomes in the United States would _____ the amount of European imports purchased by Americans, which would _____ the demand for euros, resulting in a(n) _____ exchange rate for euros.

19. If European incomes _____, European tariffs on U.S. goods _____, or European tastes for U.S. goods _____, Europeans would demand more U.S. goods, leading them to increase their supply of euros to obtain the added dollars necessary to make those purchases.

20. If interest rates in the United States were to increase relative to European interest rates, other things being equal, the rate of return on U.S. investments would

_____ relative to that on European investments, thereby _____ Europeans' demand for U.S. investments.

21. If Europe experienced a higher inflation rate than the United States, European products would become _____ expensive to U.S. consumers, thereby _____ the quantity of European goods demanded by Americans, and thus _____ the demand for euros.

Answers: 1. imports; exports 2. credit; plus 3. services; merchandise 4. trade 5. sell; U.S. dollars 6. exchange rate 7. increase; reducing 8. goods and services; capital 9. more 10. exchange rate 11. falls 12. less; increase 13. upward 14. supplied; sellers; down 15. higher; lower 16. tastes; income; real interest; inflation; speculation 17. increase; increasing 18. decrease; decrease; lower 19. rose; increased; increased 20. increase; increasing 21. more; decreasing; decreasing

Key Terms and Concepts

balance of payments 598
current account 598
balance of trade 600

capital account 601
exchange rate 602

derived demand 602
dirty float system 611

Section Check Answers

21.1 The Balance of Payments

1. **What is the balance of payments?**
   The balance of payments is the record of all the international financial transactions of a nation—both those involving inflows of funds and those involving outflows of funds—over a year.

2. **Why must British purchasers of U.S. goods and services first exchange pounds for dollars?**
   Since U.S. goods and services are priced in dollars, a British consumer who wants to buy U.S. goods must first buy dollars in exchange for British pounds before he can buy the U.S. goods and services with dollars.

3. **How is it that our imports provide foreigners with the means to buy U.S. exports?**
   The domestic currency Americans supply in exchange for the foreign currencies to buy imports also supplies the dollars with which foreigners can buy American exports.

4. **What would have to be true for the United States to have a balance-of-trade deficit and a balance-of-payments surplus?**
   A balance-of-trade deficit means that we imported more merchandise (goods) than we exported. A balance-of-payments surplus means that the sum of our goods and services exports exceeded the sum of our goods and services imports, plus funds transfers from the United States. For both to be true would require a larger surplus of services (including net investment

income) and/or net fund transfer inflows than our trade deficit in merchandise (goods).

5. **What would have to be true for the United States to have a balance-of-trade surplus and a current account deficit?**
   A balance-of-trade surplus means that we exported more merchandise (goods) than we imported. A current account deficit means that our exports of goods and services (including net investment income) were less than the sum of our imports of goods and services, plus net fund transfers. For both to happen would require that the sum of our deficit in services plus net transfers must be greater than our surplus in merchandise (goods) trading.

6. **With no errors or omissions in the recorded balance-of-payments accounts, what should the statistical discrepancy equal?**
   If there were no errors or omissions in the recorded balance-of-payments accounts, the statistical discrepancy should equal zero, since when properly recorded, credits and debits must be equal because every credit creates a debit of equal value.

7. **A Nigerian family visiting Chicago enjoys a Chicago Cubs baseball game at Wrigley Field. How would this expense be recorded in the balance-of-payments accounts? Why?**
   This would be counted as an export of services, because it would provide Americans with foreign currency (a claim against Nigeria) in exchange for those services.

21.2 Exchange Rates

1. **What is an exchange rate?**

   An exchange rate is the price in one country's currency of one unit of another country's currency.

2. **When a U.S. dollar buys relatively more British pounds, why does the cost of imports from England fall in the United States?**

   When a U.S. dollar buys relatively more British pounds, the cost of imports from England falls in the United States because it takes fewer U.S. dollars to buy a given number of British pounds in order to pay English producers. In other words, the price in U.S. dollars of English goods and services has fallen.

3. **When a U.S. dollar buys relatively fewer yen, why does the cost of U.S. exports fall in Japan?**

   When a U.S. dollar buys relatively fewer yen, the cost of U.S. exports falls in Japan because it takes fewer yen to buy a given number of U.S. dollars in order to pay American producers. In other words, the price in yen of U.S. goods and services has fallen.

4. **How does an increase in domestic demand for foreign goods and services increase the demand for those foreign currencies?**

   An increase in domestic demand for foreign goods and services increases the demand for those foreign currencies because the demand for foreign currencies is derived from the demand for foreign goods and services and foreign capital. The more foreign goods and services are demanded, the more of that foreign currency that will be needed to pay for those goods and services.

5. **As euros get cheaper relative to U.S. dollars, why does the quantity of euros demanded by Americans increase? Why doesn't the demand for euros increase as a result?**

   As euros get cheaper relative to U.S. dollars, European products become relatively more inexpensive to Americans, who therefore buy more European goods and services. To do so, the quantity of euros demanded by U.S. consumers will rise to buy them, as the price (exchange rate) for euros falls. The demand (as opposed to quantity demanded) of euros doesn't increase because this represents a movement along the demand curve for euros caused by a change in exchange rates, rather than a change in demand for euros caused by some other factor.

6. **Who brings exchange rates down when they are above their equilibrium value? Who brings exchange rates up when they are below their equilibrium value?**

   When exchange rates are greater than their equilibrium value, there will be a surplus of the currency, and frustrated sellers of that currency will bring its price (exchange rate) down. When exchange rates are less than their equilibrium value, there will be a shortage of the currency, and frustrated buyers of that currency will bring its price (exchange rate) up.

21.3 Equilibrium Changes in the Foreign Exchange Market

1. **Why will the exchange rates of foreign currencies relative to U.S. dollars decline when U.S. domestic tastes change, reducing the demand for foreign-produced goods?**

   When U.S. domestic tastes change, reducing the demand for foreign-produced goods, the reduced demand for foreign-produced goods will also reduce the demand for the foreign currencies to buy them. This reduced demand for those foreign currencies will reduce their exchange rates relative to U.S. dollars.

2. **Why does the demand for foreign currencies shift in the same direction as domestic income? What happens to the exchange value of those foreign currencies in terms of U.S. dollars?**

   An increase in domestic income increases the demand for goods and services, including imported goods and services. This increases the demand for foreign currencies with which to buy those additional imports, which increases their exchange rates (the exchange value of those currencies) relative to U.S. dollars.

3. **How would increased U.S. tariffs on imported European goods affect the exchange value of euros in terms of dollars?**

   Increased U.S. tariffs on imported European goods would make them less affordable in the United States. This would lead to a reduced demand for European goods in the United States, and therefore a reduced demand for euros. And this would reduce the exchange value of euros in terms of dollars.

4. **Why do changes in U.S. tastes, income levels, or tariffs change the demand for euros, while similar changes in Europe change the supply of euros?**

   Changes in U.S. tastes, income levels, or tariffs change the demand for euros because they change the American demand for European goods and services, thereby changing the demand for euros with which to buy them. Similar changes in Europe change the supply of euros because they change the European demand for U.S. goods and services, thus changing their demand for dollars with which to buy those goods and services. This requires them to change their supply of euros in order to get those dollars.

5. **What would happen to the exchange value of euros in terms of U.S. dollars if incomes rose in both Europe and the United States?**

   These changes would increase both the demand (higher incomes in the United States) and supply (higher incomes in Europe) of euros. The effect on the exchange value of euros would be determined by whether the supply or demand for euros shifted more (rising if demand shifted relatively more and falling if supply shifted relatively more).

6. Why does an increase in interest rates in Germany relative to U.S. interest rates increase the demand for euros but decrease their supply?

An increase in interest rates in Germany relative to U.S. interest rates increases the rates of return on German investments relative to U.S. investments. U.S. investors therefore increase their demand for German investments, increasing the demand for euros with which to make these investments. This would also reduce the demand by German investors for U.S. investments, decreasing the supply of euros with which to buy the dollars to make the investments.

7. What would an increase in U.S. inflation relative to Europe do to the supply and demand for euros and to the equilibrium exchange value (price) of euros in terms of U.S. dollars?

An increase in U.S. inflation relative to Europe would make U.S. products relatively more expensive to European customers, decreasing the amount of U.S. goods and services demanded by European customers and thus decreasing the supply of euros with which to buy the dollars necessary for those purchases. It would also make European products relatively cheaper to American customers, increasing the amount of European goods and services demanded by Americans and thus increasing the demand for euros needed for those purchases. The decreased supply of and increased demand for euros results in an increasing exchange value of euros in terms of U.S. dollars.

21.4 Flexible Exchange Rates

1. What are the arguments for and against flexible exchange rates?

The arguments for flexible exchange rates include: the large expansion of world trade under flexible exchange rates; the fact that they allowed the economy to adjust to a quadrupling in the price of the world's most important internationally traded commodity—oil; and especially that it diminished the recurring crises that caused speculative rampages and currency revaluations, allowing the market mechanism to address currency shortages and world trade imbalances. The arguments against flexible exchange rates are that it increases exchange rate uncertainty in international trade, and can contribute to inflationary pressures, due to the lack of the fixed-rate system's incentives to constrain domestic policies which would erode net exports.

2. When the U.S. dollar starts to exchange for fewer Japanese yen, other things equal, what happens to U.S. and Japanese imports and exports as a result?

When the U.S. dollar starts to exchange for fewer Japanese yen, other things equal, the U.S. cost of Japanese imports rises, decreasing the value of Japanese exports to the United States. It also decreases the cost to the Japanese of buying U.S. goods, increasing the value of U.S. exports to Japan.

3. Why is the system of flexible exchange rates sometimes called a dirty float system?

The system of flexible exchange rates is sometimes called a dirty float system because governments do intervene at times in foreign currency markets to alter their currencies' exchange rates, so that exchange rates are partly determined by market forces and partly by government intervention.

4. Were exchange rates under the Bretton Woods system really stable? How could you argue that exchange rates were more uncertain under the fixed-rate system than with floating exchange rates?

Exchange rates under the Bretton Woods system were not really stable. While exchange rate changes were infrequent, they were large, with large effects. It could be argued that the cost of the uncertainty about the less frequent but larger exchange rate changes that resulted was actually greater as a result than for the more frequent but smaller exchange rate changes under the fixed-rate system.

5. What is the uncertainty argument against flexible exchange rates? What evidence do proponents of flexible exchange rates cite in response?

The uncertainty argument against flexible exchange rates is that flexible exchange rates add another source of uncertainty to world trade, which would increase the cost of international transactions, reducing the magnitude of international trade. Proponents of flexible exchange rates cite the faster growth of international trade since the introduction of flexible exchange rates, the fact that markets exist on which to hedge exchange rate risks (through forward, or futures, markets), and that the alleged exchange rate certainty was fictitious, since large changes could take place at a nations' whim, in response.

6. Do flexible exchange rates cause higher rates of inflation? Why or why not?

Flexible exchange rates do not cause higher rates of inflation. However, they do reduce the incentives to constrain domestic inflation for fear of reducing net exports under the fixed exchange rate system. Inflation, though, is ultimately caused by expansionary macroeconomic policies adopted by governments and their central banks.

True or False:

1. U.S. consumers must first exchange U.S. dollars for a foreign seller's currency in order to pay for imported goods.

2. The exchange rate can be expressed either as the number of units of currency A per unit of currency B or as its reciprocal, the number of units of currency B per unit of currency A.

3. The more foreign goods that are demanded, the more of that foreign currency will be needed to pay for those goods, which will tend to push down the exchange value of that currency relative to other currencies.

4. The supply of foreign currency is provided by foreigners who want to buy the exports of a particular nation.

5. As the price of the euro falls relative to the dollar, European products become relatively more inexpensive to U.S. consumers, who therefore buy more European goods.

6. As the value of the euro increases relative to the dollar, American products become relatively more inexpensive to European buyers and increase the quantity of dollars they will demand. Europeans will, therefore, increase the quantity of euros supplied to the United States by buying more U.S. products.

7. If the dollar price of euros is lower than the equilibrium price, a surplus of euros will result, and competition among euro sellers will push the price of euros down toward equilibrium.

8. Any force that shifts either the demand for or supply of a currency will shift the equilibrium in the foreign exchange market, leading to a new exchange rate.

9. Any change in the demand for foreign goods will shift the demand curve for foreign currency in the opposite direction.

10. A decrease in tastes for European goods in the United States would decrease the demand for euros, hence decreasing the equilibrium price (exchange value) of euros.

11. An increase in incomes in the United States would increase the amount of European imports purchased by Americans, which would increase the demand for euros, resulting in a higher exchange rate for euros.

12. If European incomes rose, European tariffs on U.S. goods increased, or European tastes for U.S. goods increased, the exchange rate for euros would tend to increase.

13. A decrease in U.S. tariffs on European goods would tend to have the same effect on the exchange rate for euros as an increase in U.S. incomes.

14. If interest rates in the United States were to increase relative to European interest rates, the result would be a new, lower exchange rate for euros, other things being equal.

15. If Europe experienced a higher inflation rate than the United States, the supply of euros would tend to increase and the demand for euros would tend to decrease, leading to a new, lower exchange rate for euros.

16. If currency speculators believe that the United States is going to experience more rapid inflation than Japan in the future, they believe that the value of the dollar will soon be falling, which will increase the demand for the yen, and so the yen will appreciate relative to the dollar.

Multiple Choice:

1. Which of the following would be recorded as a credit in the U.S. balance-of-payments accounts?
   a. the purchase of a German business by a U.S. investor
   b. the import of Honda trucks by a U.S. automobile distributor
   c. European travel expenditures of an American college student
   d. the purchase of a U.S. Treasury bond by a French investment company

2. What is the difference between the balance of merchandise trade and the balance of payments?
   a. Only the value of goods imported and exported is included in the balance of merchandise trade, while the balance of payments includes the value of all payments to and from foreigners.
   b. The value of goods imported and exported is included in the balance of merchandise trade, while the balance of payments includes only capital account transactions.
   c. The value of all goods, services, and unilateral transfers is included in the balance of merchandise trade, while the balance of payments includes both current account and capital account transactions.
   d. Balance of merchandise trade and balance of payments both describe the same international exchange transactions.

3. If consumers in Europe and Asia develop strong preferences for U.S. goods, the U.S. current account will
   a. not be affected, because purchases of U.S. goods by foreigners are recorded in the capital account.
   b. not be affected, because purchases of U.S. goods based on mere preferences are recorded under statistical discrepancy.
   c. move toward surplus, because purchases of U.S. goods are recorded as credits on our current account.
   d. move toward deficit, because purchases of U.S. goods by foreigners are counted as debits in our current account.

4. Which of the following would supply dollars to the foreign exchange market?
   a. the sale of a U.S. automobile to a Mexican consumer
   b. spending by British tourists in the United States
   c. the purchase of Canadian oil by a U.S. consumer
   d. the sale of a U.S. corporation to a Saudi Arabian investor

5. Which of the following will enter as a credit in the U.S. balance-of-payments capital account?
   a. the purchase of a Japanese automobile by a U.S. consumer
   b. the sale of Japanese electronics to an American
   c. the sale of an American baseball team to a Japanese industrialist
   d. the purchase of a Japanese electronic plant by an American industrialist

6. If the value of a nation's merchandise exports exceeds merchandise imports, then the nation is running a
   a. balance-of-payments deficit.
   b. balance-of-payments surplus.
   c. merchandise trade deficit.
   d. merchandise trade surplus.

7. When goods or services cross international borders,
   a. money must generally move in the opposite direction.
   b. payment must be made in another good, using barter.
   c. a future shipment must be made to offset the current sale/purchase.
   d. countries must ship gold to make payment.

8. The balance-of-payments accounts for and records information about
   a. purchases of U.S. financial assets by foreigners.
   b. purchases of foreign financial assets by Americans.
   c. the levels of imports and exports of goods and services for a country.
   d. all of the above.

9. Suppose the United States imposed a high tariff on a major imported item. Under a system of flexible rates of exchange, this tariff would tend to
   a. cause the dollar to appreciate in value.
   b. cause the dollar to depreciate in value.
   c. increase the U.S. balance-of-trade deficit.
   d. increase the U.S. balance-of-payments deficit.
   e. do b, c, and d.

10. Under a system of flexible exchange rates, a deficit in a country's balance of payments will be corrected by
    a. depreciation in the nation's currency.
    b. appreciation in the nation's currency.
    c. a decline in the nation's domestic price level.
    d. an increase in the nation's inflation rate.

11. If high-yield investment opportunities attract capital from abroad and lead to a capital account surplus, then the
    a. nation's currency must appreciate.
    b. nation's currency must depreciate.
    c. nation must run a current account deficit under a flexible exchange rate system.
    d. nation must run a current account surplus under a flexible exchange rate system.
    e. Both a and c are true.

12. If the dollar *depreciates,* it can be said that
    a. foreign countries no longer respect the United States.
    b. other currencies appreciate.
    c. it falls in value just as it does during inflation.
    d. it takes fewer dollars to buy units of other currencies.
    e. all of the above are correct.

13. On May 16, 1999, it cost $0.667 to buy one Canadian dollar. How many Canadian dollars would $1 U.S. buy?
    a. $1.50
    b. $1.30
    c. $1.00
    d. $0.67

14. If the exchange rate between the dollar and the euro changes from $1 = 1 euro to $2 = 1 euro, then
    a. European goods will become less expensive for Americans, and imports of European goods to the United States will rise.
    b. European goods will become less expensive for Americans, and imports of European goods to the United States will fall.
    c. European goods will become more expensive for Americans, and imports of European goods to the United States will rise.
    d. European goods will become more expensive for Americans, and imports of European goods to the United States will fall.

15. If the price in dollars of Mexican pesos changes from $0.10 per peso to $0.14 per peso, the peso has
    a. appreciated.
    b. depreciated.
    c. devalued.
    d. stayed at the same exchange rate.

16. Which of the following is most likely to favor the appreciation of the American dollar?
    a. a German professor on vacation in Iowa
    b. an American professor on extended vacation in Paris
    c. an American farmer who relies on exports
    d. Disney World

17. If the dollar appreciates relative to other currencies, which of the following is true?
    a. It takes more of the other currency to buy a dollar.
    b. It takes less of the other currency to buy a dollar.
    c. No change occurs in the currency needed to buy a dollar.
    d. Not enough information is available to make a determination.

18. If the United States experiences a sharp increase in exports, what will happen to demand for the U.S. dollar?
    a. It will decrease.
    b. It will increase.
    c. It will be unchanged.
    d. It will change at the same rate as the supply of dollars will change.
    e. There is not enough information to make a determination.

19. If fewer British tourists visit the Grand Canyon, what is the effect in the exchange market?
    a. It will increase the supply of British pounds.
    b. It will decrease the supply of British pounds.
    c. It will increase the demand for British pounds.
    d. It will decrease the demand for British pounds.

20. Suppose that the dollar rises from 100 to 125 yen. As a result,
    a. exports to Japan will likely increase.
    b. Japanese tourists will be more likely to visit the United States.
    c. U.S. businesses will be less likely to use Japanese shipping lines to transport their products.
    d. U.S. consumers will be more likely to buy Japanese-made automobiles.

21. Other things being constant, which of the following will most likely cause the dollar to appreciate on the exchange rate market?
    a. higher domestic interest rates
    b. higher interest rates abroad
    c. expansionary domestic monetary policy
    d. reduced inflation abroad

22. A depreciation in the U.S. dollar would
    a. discourage foreigners from making investments in the United States.
    b. discourage foreign consumers from buying U.S. goods.
    c. reduce the number of dollars it would take to buy a Swiss franc.
    d. encourage foreigners to buy more U.S. goods.

23. If the exchange rate between euros and dollars were 2 euros per dollar, when an American purchased a good valued at 80 euros, its cost in dollars would be
    a. $160.
    b. $80.
    c. $40.
    d. none of the above.

24. Suppose that the exchange rate between Mexican pesos and dollars is 8 pesos per dollar. If the exchange rate goes to 10 pesos per dollar, it would tend to
    a. increase U.S. exports to Mexico.
    b. decrease U.S. exports to Mexico.
    c. increase Mexican exports to the United States.
    d. decrease Mexican exports to the United States.
    e. do both b and c.

25. If a dollar is cheaper in terms of a foreign currency than the equilibrium exchange rate, a _____ exists at the current exchange rate that will put _____ pressure on the exchange value of a dollar.
    a. surplus of dollars; downward
    b. surplus of dollars; upward
    c. shortage of dollars; downward
    d. shortage of dollars; upward

26. In foreign exchange markets, the supply of dollars is determined
    a. by the level of U.S. imports and the demand for foreign assets by U.S. citizens and the U.S. government.
    b. solely by the level of U.S. merchandise exports.
    c. solely by the level of U.S. merchandise imports.
    d. solely by the levels of U.S. merchandise exports and merchandise imports.
    e. by the level of U.S. exports and the demand for U.S. assets by foreigners.

27. In foreign exchange markets, the effect of an increase in the demand for dollars on the value of the dollar is the same as that of
    a. an increase in the supply of foreign currencies.
    b. a decrease in the supply of foreign currencies.
    c. a decrease in the demand for dollars.
    d. none of the above.

28. If the demand by foreigners for U.S. government securities increased, other things being equal, it would tend to
    a. increase the exchange value of the dollar and increase U.S. merchandise exports.
    b. increase the exchange value of the dollar and decrease U.S. merchandise exports.
    c. decrease the exchange value of the dollar and increase U.S. merchandise exports.
    d. decrease the exchange value of the dollar and decrease U.S. merchandise exports.

29. If the rate of inflation in the United States falls relative to the rate of inflation in foreign nations, U.S. net exports will tend to _____, causing the exchange value of the U.S. dollar to _____.
   a. rise; rise
   b. rise; fall
   c. fall; rise
   d. fall; fall

30. If real incomes in foreign nations were growing more rapidly than U.S. real incomes, one would expect that, as a result,
   a. the exchange value of the dollar would decline relative to other currencies.
   b. the exchange value of the dollar would increase relative to other currencies.
   c. the exchange value of the dollar relative to other currencies would not change.
   d. the effect on the exchange value of the dollar relative to other currencies would be undeterminable.

31. If real interest rates in the United States fell relative to real interest rates in other countries, other things being equal,
   a. the exchange value of the dollar would decline relative to other currencies.
   b. the exchange value of the dollar would increase relative to other currencies.
   c. the exchange value of the dollar relative to other currencies would not change.
   d. the effect on the exchange value of the dollar relative to other currencies would be undeterminable.

32. Sweden's currency will tend to appreciate if
   a. the demand for Sweden's exports increases.
   b. the demand for imports by Swedes increases.
   c. real interest rates in Sweden decrease relative to those of the rest of the world.
   d. Sweden's inflation rate rises relative to inflation in the rest of the world.

33. A country will tend to experience currency depreciation relative to that of other countries if
   a. the profitability of investments in other countries increases relative to the profitability in that country.
   b. people in the foreign currency markets expect the value of the currency to fall in the near future.
   c. the foreign demand for its exports decreases.
   d. any of the above occur.
   e. any of the above except c occur.

34. If the dollar depreciates relative to the yen, we would expect
   a. that the Japanese trade surplus with the United States would increase.
   b. that Japanese imports from the United States would decrease.
   c. that Japanese exports to the United States would decrease.
   d. that a and b would occur.

35. As the number of British pounds that exchange for a dollar falls on foreign currency markets,
   a. the British will have an incentive to import fewer U.S. goods.
   b. the British will find it easier to export goods to the United States.
   c. the British will find U.S. goods to be more expensive in their stores.
   d. all of the above will be true.
   e. none of the above will be true.

36. If real interest rates in the United States rose and real interest rates in England fell, we would expect people to
   a. increase their demand for British pounds.
   b. borrow more from U.S. sources.
   c. buy relatively more U.S. assets.
   d. buy relatively more British assets.
   e. do both b and c.

37. If the Federal Reserve were to sell U.S. dollars on the foreign exchange market, a likely result would be
   a. a rightward shift in the dollar supply curve.
   b. at least a temporary decline in the exchange value of the U.S. dollar.
   c. at least a temporary increase in the exchange value of the U.S. dollar.
   d. a and b.
   e. a and c.

Problems:

1. Indicate whether each of the following represents a credit or debit on the U.S. current account.
    a. an American imports a BMW from Germany
    b. a Japanese company purchases software from an American company
    c. the United States gives $100 million in financial aid to Israel
    d. a U.S. company in Florida sells oranges to Great Britain

2. Indicate whether each of the following represents a credit or debit on the U.S. capital account.
    a. a French bank purchases $100,000 worth of U.S. Treasury notes
    b. the central bank in the United States purchases 1 million euros in the currency market
    c. a U.S. resident buys stock on the Japanese stock market
    d. a Japanese company purchases a movie studio in California

3. How are each of the following events likely to affect the U.S. trade balance?
    a. the European price level increases relative to the U.S. price level
    b. the dollar appreciates in value relative to the currencies of its trading partners
    c. the U.S. government offers subsidies to firms that export goods
    d. the U.S. government imposes tariffs on imported goods
    e. Europe experiences a severe recession

4. How are each of the following events likely to affect the value of the dollar relative to the euro?
    a. interest rates in the European Union increase relative to the United States
    b. the European Union price level rises relative to the U.S. price level
    c. the European central bank intervenes by selling dollars on currency markets
    d. the price level in the United States falls relative to the price level in Europe

5. If the demand for a domestic currency decreases in a country using a fixed exchange rate system, what must the central bank do to keep the currency value steady?

6. What happens to the supply curve for dollars in the currency market under the following conditions?
    a. Americans wish to buy more Japanese consumer electronics
    b. the United States wishes to prop up the value of the yen

7. Evaluate the following statement: "The balance of payments equals −$200 million and the statistical discrepancy equals zero."

8. Assume that a product sells for $100 in the United States.
    a. If the exchange rate between British pounds and U.S. dollars is $2 per pound, what would the price of the product be in the United Kingdom?
    b. If the exchange rate between Mexican pesos and U.S. dollars is 125 pesos per dollar, what would the price of the product be in Mexico?
    c. In which direction would the price of the $100 U.S. product change in a foreign country if Americans' tastes for foreign products increased?
    d. In which direction would the price of the $100 U.S. product change in a foreign country if incomes in the foreign country fell?
    e. In which direction would the price of the $100 U.S. product change in a foreign country if interest rates in the United States fell relative to interest rates in other countries?

9. How would each of the following affect the supply of euros, the demand for euros, and the dollar price of euros?

Change	Supply of Euros	Demand for Euros	Dollar Price of Euros
Reduced U.S. tastes for European goods	_____	_____	_____
Increased incomes in the United States	_____	_____	_____
Increased U.S. interest rates	_____	_____	_____
Decreased inflation in Europe	_____	_____	_____
Reduced U.S. tariffs on imports	_____	_____	_____
Increased European tastes for U.S. goods	_____	_____	_____

10. How are each of the following classified, as debits or credits, in the U.S. balance-of-payments accounts?

	Credit	Debit
a. Americans buy autos from Japan.	_____	_____
b. American tourists travel to Japan.	_____	_____
c. Japanese consumers buy rice grown in the United States.	_____	_____
d. United States gives foreign aid to Rwanda.	_____	_____
e. General Motors, a U.S. company, earns profits in France.	_____	_____
f. Royal Dutch Shell earns profits from its U.S. operations.	_____	_____
g. General Motors builds a new plant in Vietnam.	_____	_____
h. Japanese investors purchase U.S. government bonds.	_____	_____

11. What will happen to the supply of dollars, the demand for dollars, and the equilibrium exchange rate of the dollar in each of the following cases?

	Supply of Dollars	Demand for Dollars	Equilibrium Exchange Rates
a. Americans buy more European goods.	_____	_____	_____
b. Europeans invest in U.S. stock market.	_____	_____	_____
c. European tourists flock to the United States.	_____	_____	_____
d. Europeans buy U.S. government bonds.	_____	_____	_____
e. American tourists flock to Europe.	_____	_____	_____

ability to pay principle belief that those with the greatest ability to pay taxes should pay more than those with less ability to pay

accounting profits total revenues minus total explicit costs

adverse selection a situation where an informed party benefits in an exchange by taking advantage of knowing more than the other party

aggregate the total amount—such as the *aggregate level of output*

allocative efficiency where $P = MC$ and production will be allocated to reflect consumer preferences

asymmetric information occurs when the available information is initially distributed in favor of one party relative to another in an exchange

average cost pricing setting price equal to average total cost

average fixed cost (AFC) a per-unit measure of fixed costs; fixed costs divided by output

average revenue (AR) total revenue divided by the number of units sold

average total cost (ATC) a per-unit cost of operation; total cost divided by output

average variable cost (AVC) a per-unit measure of variable costs; variable costs divided by output

backward-bending labor supply curve above a certain wage rate, a worker may prefer to enjoy more leisure and less work to meet his or her own personal preferences (the income effect dominates the substitution effect)

bads items that we do not desire or want, where less is preferred to more, like terrorism, smog, or poison oak.

balance of payments the record of international transactions in which a nation has engaged over a year

balance of trade the net surplus or deficit resulting from the level

of exportation and importation of merchandise

bandwagon effect a positive network externality in which a consumer's demand for a product increases because other consumers own it

bar graph visual display showing the comparison of quantities

capital the equipment and structures used to produce goods and services

capital account records the foreign purchases or assets in the domestic economy (a monetary inflow) and domestic purchases of assets abroad (a monetary outflow)

capital intensive production that uses a large amount of capital

cartel a collection of firms that agree on sales, pricing, and other decisions

cash transfers direct cash payments like welfare, Social Security, and unemployment compensation

causation when one event brings about another event

ceteris paribus holding all other things constant

change in demand the prices of related goods, income, number of buyers, tastes, and expectations can change the demand for a good; that is, a change in one of these factors shifts the entire demand curve

change in quantity demanded a change in a good's own price leads to a change in quantity demanded, a move along a given demand curve

Coase theorem states that where property rights are defined in a clear-cut fashion, externalities are internalized

collective bargaining negotiations between representatives of employers and unions

collude when firms act together to restrict competition

command economy economy in which the government uses central planning to coordinate most economic activities

common resource a rival good that is nonexcludable

comparative advantage occurs when a person or country can produce a good or service at a lower opportunity cost than others

competitive market a market where the many buyers and sellers have little market power—each buyer's or seller's effect on market price is negligible

complements an increase (decrease) in the price of one good shifts the demand curve for another good to the left (right)

constant-cost industry an industry where input prices (and cost curves) do not change as industry output changes

constant returns to scale occur in an output range where LRATC does not change as output varies

consumer equilibrium allocation of consumer income that balances the ratio of marginal utility to the price of goods purchased

consumer sovereignty consumers vote with their dollars in a market economy; this accounts for what is produced

consumer surplus the difference between the price a consumer is willing and able to pay for an additional unit of a good and the price the consumer actually pays; for the whole market, it is the sum of all the individual consumer surpluses

consumption tax tax collected based on a taxpayer's spending

cooperative game collusion by two firms in order to improve their profit maximizations

correlation when two events occur together

cross-price elasticity of demand the measure of the impact that a price change of one good will have on the demand of another good.

current account a record of a country's imports and exports of goods and services, net investment income, and net transfers

deadweight loss net loss of total surplus that results from an action that alters a market equilibrium

derived demand the demand for an input derived from consumers' demand for the good or service produced with that input

diminishing marginal product as a variable input increases, with other inputs fixed, a point will be reached where the additions to output will eventually decline

diminishing marginal utility a good's ability to provide less satisfaction with each successive unit consumed; the concept that states that as an individual consumes more and more of a good, each successive unit generates less and less utility (or satisfaction)

dirty float system a description of the exchange rate system that means that fluctuations in currency values are partly determined by government intervention

diseconomies of scale occur in an output range where LRATC rises as output expands

dominant strategy strategy that will be optimal regardless of opponents' actions

Earned Income Tax Credit (EITC) a welfare program that allows the working poor to receive income refunds that can be greater than the taxes they paid during the last year

economic goods scarce goods created from scarce resources—goods that are desirable but limited in supply

the economic problem scarcity forces us to choose, and choices are costly because we must give up other opportunities that we value

economic profits total revenues minus explicit and implicit costs

economic rent the payment for the use of any resource above its opportunity cost

economics the study of choices we make among our many wants and desires given our limited resources

economies of scale occur in an output range where *LRATC* falls as output increases

efficiency when an economy gets the most out of its scarce resources

elastic when the quantity demanded is greater than the percentage change in price ($E_D > 1$)

empirical analysis the use of data to test a hypothesis

entrepreneurship the process of combining labor, land, and capital to produce goods and services

equilibrium price the price at the intersection of the market supply and demand curves; at this price, the quantity demanded equals the quantity supplied

equilibrium quantity the quantity at the intersection of the market supply and demand curves; at the equilibrium quantity, the quantity demanded equals the quantity supplied

excess capacity occurs when the firm produces below the level where average total cost is minimized

exchange rate the price of one unit of a country's currency in terms of another country's currency

excise tax a sales tax on individual products such as alcohol, tobacco, and gasoline

expansion path shows the least-cost input solutions for providing a given output

explicit costs the opportunity costs of production that require a monetary payment

externality a benefit or cost from consumption or production that spills over onto those who are not consuming or producing the good

factor (or input) markets markets where households sell the use of their inputs (capital, land, labor, and entrepreneurship) to firms

fallacy of composition the incorrect view that what is true for the individual is always true for the group

featherbedding practice of hiring workers who may not be necessary

fixed costs costs that do not vary with the level of output

fixed-proportions production function when it is impossible to substitute one input for another so inputs must be used in fixed proportions

flat tax a tax that charges all income earners the same percentage of their income

free rider deriving benefits from something not paid for

game theory firms attempt to maximize profits by acting in ways that minimize damage from competitors

goods items we value or desire

health maintenance organization (HMO) an organization that contracts with physicians, medical facilities, employers, and individuals to provide medical care to a group of individuals. Health care services are usually provided at a fixed price per patient. The cost of providing care is contained through the rationing of health care resources.

human capital the productive knowledge and skill people receive from education, on-the-job training, health, and other factors that increase productivity

hypothesis a testable proposition

implicit costs the opportunity costs of production that do not require a monetary payment

import quota a legal limit on the imported quantity of a good that is produced abroad and can be sold in domestic markets

income effect reduction in quantity demanded of a good when its price increases because of a consumer's decreased purchasing power

income elasticity of demand the percentage change in demand divided by the percentage change in consumer's income

increasing-cost industry an industry where input prices rise (and cost curves rise) as industry output rises

increasing opportunity cost the opportunity cost of producing additional units of a good rises as society produces more of that good

indemnity coverage compensation toward the cost of medical services in the event of illness or injury

individual demand curve a graphical representation that shows the inverse relationship between price and quantity demanded

individual demand schedule a schedule that shows the relationship between price and quantity demanded

individual supply curve a graphical representation that shows the positive relationship between the price and quantity supplied

inelastic when the quantity demanded is less than the percentage change in price ($E_D < 1$)

inferior good if income increases, the demand for a good decreases; if income decreases, the demand for a good increases

in-kind transfers in-kind transfers are transfers in the form of goods and services instead of money. In-kind transfers include food stamps, school lunch programs, housing subsidies, and Medicaid, among others.

intangible goods goods that we cannot reach out and touch, such as friendship and knowledge

interest the cost of borrowed funds

internalized externalities when an industry is forced to compensate those enduring some negative externality caused by its production

isocost (equal cost) lines graphical display of the various possible quantities of the two factors that can be purchased with a given outlay of money

isoquant curve showing the various factor combinations that can produce a given level of output

job-entry discrimination a worker is denied employment on the basis of some biological feature, such as sex or race, without any regard to productivity

joint profit maximization determination of price based on the marginal revenue derived from the market demand schedule and marginal cost schedule of the firms in the industry

kinked demand curve indicates the price rigidity in oligopoly when competitors show a greater tendency to follow price reductions than price increases

labor the physical and human effort used in the production of goods and services

labor intensive production that uses a large amount of labor

land the natural resources used in the production of goods and services

law of demand the quantity of a good or service demanded varies inversely (negatively) with its price, *ceteris paribus*

law of supply the higher (lower) the price of the good, the greater (smaller) the quantity supplied

long run a period over which all production inputs are variable

macroeconomics the study of the whole economy, including the topics of inflation, unemployment, and economic growth

marginal cost (MC) the change in total costs resulting from a one-unit change in output; the cost of producing one more unit of a good

marginal product (MP) the change in total output of a good that results from a one-unit change in input

marginal productivity theory of income distribution income is distributed according to marginal revenue product of the factors of production individuals own

marginal rate of technical substitution of labor for capital (MRTS) the quantity of capital that can be given up by using one additional unit of labor while producing the same level of output

marginal resource cost (MRC) the amount that an extra input adds to the firm's total cost

marginal revenue (MR) the increase in total revenue resulting from a one-unit increase in sales

marginal revenue product (MRP) marginal product times the price of the product

marginal thinking focusing on the additional, or marginal, choices; marginal choices involve the effects of adding or subtracting, from the current situation, the small (or large) incremental changes to a plan of action

marginal utility extra satisfaction generated by consumption of an additional good or service during a specific time period

market the process of buyers and sellers exchanging goods and services

market demand curve the horizontal summation of individual demand curves

market economy an economy that allocates goods and services through the private decisions of consumers, input suppliers, and firms

market equilibrium the point at which the market supply and market demand curves intersect

market failure when the economy fails to allocate resources efficiently on its own

market supply curve a graphical representation of the amount of goods and services that suppliers are willing and able to supply at various prices

means-tested income transfer program program in which eligibility is dependent on low income; food stamps, Medicaid, and housing subsidies are examples of means-tested income transfer programs

median voter model a model that predicts candidates will choose a position in the middle of the distribution

microeconomics the study of household and firm behavior and how they interact in the marketplace

minimum efficient scale the output level where economies of scale are exhausted and constant returns to scale begin

mixed economy an economy where government and the private sector determine the allocation of resources

monopolistic competition a market structure with many firms selling differentiated products

monopoly the single supplier of a product that has no close substitute

monopsony a market with a single buyer

moral hazard taking additional risks because you are insured

mutual interdependence when a firm shapes its policy with an eye to the policies of competing firms

natural monopoly a firm that can produce at a lower cost than a number of smaller firms can

negative externality occurs when costs spill over to an outside party who is not involved in producing or consuming the good

negative incentive an incentive that either increases costs or reduces benefits, resulting in a decrease in the activity or behavior

negative network externality increase in a consumer's demand for a good because fewer consumers are purchasing the same good

negative relationship when two variables change in opposite directions

net benefit the difference between the expected marginal benefits and the expected marginal costs

network externality when the number of other people purchasing the good influences quantity demanded

noncooperative game each firm sets its own price without consulting other firms

normal good if income increases, the demand for a good increases; if income decreases, the demand for a good decreases

normative statement a subjective, contestable statement that attempts to describe what should be done

opportunity cost the value of the best forgone alternative that was not chosen

optimum factor combination a point of tangency between the given isoquant and the lowest possible isocost line

payoff matrix a summary of the possible outcomes of various strategies

peak load pricing when producers charge different prices during different periods because the demand and the

cost of producing a product vary over time

permanent income hypothesis the hypothesis that consumption is more closely related to permanent income than current income

pie chart visual display showing the relative size of various quantities that add up to 100 percent

pollution tax tax levied by government on a firm for environmental pollution

positive externality occurs when benefits spill over to an outside party who is not involved in producing or consuming the good

positive incentive an incentive that either reduces costs or increases benefits, resulting in an increase in an activity or behavior

positive network externality increase in a consumer's quantity demanded for a good because a greater number of other consumers are purchasing the good

positive relationship when two variables change in the same direction

positive statement an objective, testable statement that describes what happens and why it happens

poverty line a set of money income thresholds, established by the federal government, that vary by family size and are used to detect who is poor; if a family's total income is less than the established family threshold, then that family, and every individual in it, is considered poor

poverty rate the percentage of the population who fall below the poverty line

predatory pricing setting a price deliberately low in order to drive out competitors

preferred provider organization (PPO) a network of doctors who agree to provide services to a health plan's enrollees at discounted fees

price ceiling a legally established maximum price

price controls government-mandated minimum or maximum prices

price discrimination the practice of charging different consumers different prices for the same good or service

price elasticity of demand the measure of the responsiveness of quantity demanded to a change in price

price elasticity of supply the measure of the sensitivity of the quantity supplied to changes in price of a good

price floor a legally established minimum price

price follower a competitor in an oligopoly that goes along with the pricing decision of the price leader

price leader a large firm in an oligopoly that unilaterally makes changes in its product prices that competitors tend to follow

price leadership when a dominant firm that produces a large portion of the industry's output sets a price that maximizes its profits, and other firms follow

price takers a perfectly competitive firm that takes the price it is given by the intersection of the market demand and market supply curves

prisoners' dilemma the basic problem facing noncolluding oligopolists in maximizing their own profit

private good a good with rivalrous consumption and excludability

private property rights consumers' right to use their property as they see fit

producer surplus the difference between what a producer is paid for a good and the cost of producing that unit of the good; for the market, it is the sum of all the individual sellers' producer surpluses—the area above the market supply curve and below the market price

product differentiation goods or services that are slightly different, or perceived to be different, from one another

product markets markets where households are buyers and firms are sellers of goods and services

production function the relationship between the quantity of inputs and the quantity of outputs

production possibilities curve the potential total output combinations of any two goods for an economy

productive efficiency where a good or service is produced at the lowest possible cost

profits the difference between total revenues and total costs

profit-maximizing level of output a firm should always produce at the output where $MR = MC$

progressive tax system tax system that imposes higher marginal tax rates on higher incomes; the federal income tax is designed to be a progressive tax system

progressive tax tax designed so that those with higher incomes pay a greater proportion of their income in taxes

public good a good that is nonrivalrous in consumption and nonexcludable

rational behavior people do the best they can, based on their values and information, under current and anticipated future circumstances

rational ignorance lack of incentive to be informed

regressive tax as a person's income rises, the amount his or her tax as a proportion of income falls

rent seeking efforts by producers to gain profits from government protections such as tariffs and import quotas

reservation price the maximum amount a customer would be willing to pay for a unit of output

resources inputs used to produce goods and services

rule of rational choice individuals will pursue an activity if the expected marginal benefits are greater than the expected marginal costs

scarcity exists when human wants (material and nonmaterial) exceed available resources

scatter diagram a graph showing the relationship of one variable to another

services intangible items of value provided to consumers, such as education

shortage a situation where quantity demanded exceeds quantity supplied

short run a period too brief for some production inputs to be varied

short-run market supply curve the horizontal summation of the individual firms' supply curves in the market

short-run supply curve the portion of the MC curve above the AVC curve

simple circular flow model an illustration of the continuous flow of goods, services, inputs, and payments between firms and households

slope the ratio of rise (change in the Y variable) over run (change in the X variable)

special interest groups groups with an intense interest in particular voting issues that may be different from that of the general public

specializing concentrating in the production of one, or a few, goods

substitutes an increase (decrease) in the price of one good causes the demand curve for another good to shift to the right (left)

substitution effect a consumer's switch to another similar good when the price of the preferred good increases

sunk costs costs that have been incurred and cannot be recovered

Supplemental Security Income (SSI) a welfare program designed for the most needy, elderly, disabled, and blind

surplus a situation where quantity supplied exceeds quantity demanded

switching costs the costs involved in changing from one product to another brand or in changing suppliers

Taft-Hartley Act legislation enacted in 1947 to somewhat restrict the power of unions granted by the Wagner Act

tangible goods items we value or desire that we can reach out and touch

tariff a tax on imports

Temporary Assistance for Needy Families (TANF) a welfare program designed to help families that have few financial resources

theory statement or proposition used to explain and predict behavior in the real world

time-series graph visual tool to show changes in a variable's value over time

tit-for-tat strategy strategy used in repeated games where one player follows the othe player's move in the previous round; leads to greater cooperation

total cost (TC) the sum of the firm's total fixed costs and total variable costs

total fixed cost (TFC) the sum of the firm's fixed costs

total product (TP) the total output of a good produced by the firm

total revenue (TR) the amount sellers receive for a good or service, calculated as the product price times the quantity sold

total utility total amount of satisfaction derived from the consumption of a certain number of goods or services

total variable cost (TVC) the sum of the firm's variable costs

total welfare gains the sum of consumer and producer surpluses

transferable pollution rights a right given to a firm to discharge a specified amount of pollution; its transferable nature creates incentive to lower pollution levels

unintended consequences the secondary effects of an action that may occur after the initial effects

unit elastic demand demand with a price elasticity of 1; the percentage change in quantity demanded is equal to the percentage change in price

util one unit of satisfaction

utility a measure of the relative levels of satisfaction consumers get from consumption of goods and services

variable something that is measured by a number, such as your height

variable costs costs that vary with the level of output

vertical equity different treatment based on level of income and the ability to pay principle

wage discrimination when a worker is given employment at a wage lower than that of other workers, based on something other than productivity

Wagner Act legislation enacted in 1935 that protected workers' rights to organize and bargain collectively

welfare effects the gains and losses associated with government intervention in markets

winner's curse a situation that arises in certain auctions where the winner is

worse off than the loser because of an overly optimistic value placed on the good

X-axis the horizontal axis on a graph

Y-axis the vertical axis on a grap